# THE NATIONAL ROAD

THE ROAD AND AMERICAN CULTURE

Drake Hokanson, *Series Editor*
George F. Thompson, *Series Director*


*Published in cooperation with the*
*Center for American Places, Harrisonburg, Virginia*

# The National Road

EDITED BY KARL RAITZ

Project Director and Director of Photography

George F. Thompson

CARTOGRAPHY BY GYULA PAUER

THE JOHNS HOPKINS UNIVERSITY PRESS

BALTIMORE AND LONDON

This book has been brought to publication with the
generous assistance of the Pioneer America Society
and the National Endowment for the Humanities.

The Johns Hopkins University Press
2715 North Charles Street
Baltimore, Maryland 21218-4319
The Johns Hopkins Press Ltd., London

Photo credits will be found at the end of this book.

LIBRARY OF CONGRESS CATALOGING-IN-PUBLICATION DATA

The National Road / edited by Karl Raitz ; George F. Thompson, project
    director and director of photography ; cartography by Gyula Pauer.
        p.     cm. — (The Road and American Culture)
    Includes bibliographical references and index.
    ISBN 0-8018-5155-6 (alk. paper : v. 1)
    1. Cumberland Road—History.   2. United States Highway 40—
History.   I. Raitz, Karl B.   II. Douglas, Henry W., 1906–1989.   III. Series.
HE356.C8N378   1996
388.1′0977—dc20                                                    95-40321

A catalog record of this book is available from the British Library.

In Memoriam

HENRY W. DOUGLAS

1906–1989

and for the American people

# Contents

# Preface

THE NATIONAL ROAD IS AMERICA'S FIRST FEDERALLY PLANNED AND funded highway. The idea for the Road was conceived by Albert Gallatin, and it was constructed in the context of nation-building. The purpose was to provide an overland link between East Coast cities and the old Northwest Territory and emerging Middle West, the vast and fertile country that lay west of the rugged Appalachian Mountains and north of the Ohio River. Road construction began at Cumberland, Maryland (the road was also then known as the Cumberland Road), in 1808 and reached Wheeling, West Virginia, a decade later. By fits and starts engineers and laborers brought the Road further west to Zanesville and Columbus, Ohio, to Indianapolis, and, finally, to its end at Vandalia, the Illinois state capital, in 1850. A few years later the Road was pushed to the Mississippi River at East St. Louis, while an alternate spur linked the Road to the river about 25 statute miles north of St. Louis at Alton, Illinois.

During the railroad era, travelers and freight moved by rail, and the Road, for want of both engineering innovation and financial support, dissolved into a mud track, more barrier to travel than routeway. The automobile and truck brought a new demand for improved roads by 1910, and in the 1920s the federal government instituted a series of policies that would designate important highways as part of a federal road network. Construction and maintenance would be financed, in large measure, by the federal treasury and engineering and signage would conform to federal standards. Nearly two centuries after its completion, the National Road was incorporated into US 40, the federal transcontinental highway that linked Atlantic City, New Jersey, to San Francisco, California. From the 1930s through the 1950s, engineers widened the highway and often redirected its bed to bypass small towns. Interstate 70 was built parallel to US 40 in the late 1960s and early 1970s, and more recently Interstate 68 opened along a Maryland section of the old highway.

This book is the first of a two-volume set on the National Road. Volume 1 is a historical and geographical appraisal of the Road from conception to its evolution as America's foremost highway. The Road's development provides a context for a larger examination of the nation's economic and cultural development. American culture is predicated in movement and to know America one has to understand its roads and highways and recognize that people build their lives around the access that roads provide and the activities they stimulate. The National Road is an archetypal road that has played a formative role in American life; a road that best illustrates how America's peoples have embraced the highway and the landscapes attendant to its route. More than a path through the frontier, the Road was a thoroughfare for the exchange of ideas and artifacts, a communications link between otherwise disparate and distance places, and a trial ground for practical application of transportation and travel technologies.

Volume 1 is organized into four parts encompassing twelve chapters. Part 1 places the American highway within a broad historical and cultural context. Chapter 1 examines the evolution of the American attitude toward transportation—movement equals freedom—and the landscapes that grew up as a product of our affinity for access to places near and far. Chapter 2 places the National Road in the context of the physical environment across which engineers had to direct its route, and a portfolio of paintings and prints introduces visual images of how the highway came to play a central role in American life. Part 2, "Building the National Road," includes four chapters, on planning and funding, surveying and construction, and evolving construction and transport technologies. Part 3, "Image and Landscape," comprises four chapters that examine historic travelers' impressions and experiences of the National Road; how the Road became a corridor for the movement of ideas as well as commodities and people; the merger of the Road into the national highway network as US 40 and how a new auto-oriented roadside landscape evolved; and an examination of the interstate and how its presence represents a standardizing federal presence across a varied countryside. Part 4, "The National Road as American Landscape Heritage," contains two chapters. Chapter 11 examines the role of accessibility in American culture. The concluding chapter examines the place of the Road, its attendant landscape, and all that they symbolize in the context of historic preservation.

Volume 2 is a companion guide to the National Road. Written for travelers and including nearly 300 original maps and photographs, the book offers a key to understanding present and past landscapes along the highway from Baltimore, Maryland, the Road's functional starting point, to East St. Louis and Alton, Illinois.

# Acknowledgments

THE AUTHORS AND I ARE INDEBTED TO A LONG LIST OF INDIVIDUALS AND institutions who contributed impetus, knowledge, records, and ideas, or who critically reviewed our interpretations of roadside historic events and geography. This project began in the mind of Mr. Henry H. Douglas, founder of the Pioneer America Society and National Road devotee. In 1981, Mr. Douglas and photographer Wm. Edmund Barrett of Shepherdstown, West Virginia, conceived a project that would yield a collection of photographs commemorating the National Road's existing structures. When Mr. Douglas died, he left a substantial bequest to the Pioneer America Society to carry the project forward.

Under the leadership of Society director Charles Calkins of Carroll College, the Society appointed a steering committee to establish a direction for the National Road project. The committee—Wm. Edmund Barrett, Glenn

Harper, John Jakle, Peirce Lewis, Keith Sculle, and Allen Noble—contacted me and requested that I outline and edit a book that would not only record the National Road in photographs, but also capture the essence of the role that this road, and roads more generally, plays in American life. The outline grew to two volumes, prepared by eighteen contributing authors and four professional photographers. To augment Mr. Douglas's bequest, I applied to the National Endowment for the Humanities for a grant to underwrite the project's field work, archival research, photography, and other publication expenses. It is with a great deal of pleasure that acknowledgment can be given to the National Endowment for the Humanities, an independent federal agency, which supported this project with a significant grant. Everyone affiliated with this project has done everything in her or his power to ensure that these books are enduring legacies for the American people.

Special thanks to George F. Thompson, president of the Center for American Places, whose inspired insights into the management of a project of this scope were invaluable. "Saint George," as he came to be known, directed the project's photography and editorial development. Not only is he a gifted editor and keen observer of landscape, but he is probably without peer in his zeal to encourage original writing, research, and photography about the American scene. In addition, I am grateful to Wolfgang Natter, of the German Department at the University of Kentucky, who contributed ideas and criticisms to the initial proposal and manuscript; and to Thomas J. Schlereth of the Department of American Studies at the University of Notre Dame, who carefully and critically reviewed the manuscript of both volumes and made numerous suggestions for corrections and improvements. Professor Schlereth was later engaged to prepare the two portfolios, for which I am most grateful.

We wish to acknowledge the following for their permission to publish maps and photographs: the Houghton Mifflin Company for illustrations from *U.S. 40* by George R. Stewart. Copyright © 1953 by George R. Stewart, © renewed 1981 by Theodosia B. Stewart, all rights reserved; the Historical Society of Western Pennsylvania for a photograph of the Endsley House from the Forrest Collection; Vernon Will of the Ohio Historical Society in Columbus for permission to print "National Road Marker," "National Road at Gratiot, 1914," and "National Road at Gratiot, 1915," and the "Broad Street Bridge under construction in Columbus"; the Lagonda Chapter of the Daughters of the American Revolution, Springfield, Ohio, for two photographs of the Pennsylvania House in Springfield; to Macmillan Press for permission to reprint illustrations of the old National Road; to Jean Yeshilian of Raisz Landform Maps for permission to reprint portions of Erwin Raisz, *Map of the Landforms of the United States,* 6th ed., 1956; to Random House Inc., and Alfred A. Knopf, Inc., for permission to quote from *Or Else: Poems 1968–1973* by Robert Penn Warren, © 1971 by Robert Penn Warren; to the Washington University Gallery of Art for George Caleb Bingham's *Daniel Boone Escorting Settlers through the Cumberland Gap;* to the New York State Historical Association for Thomas Waterman Wood's *Village Post Office;* to the Toledo Museum of Art for John Lewis Krimmel's *Village Tavern;* to Colonial Williamsburg Foundation for Joseph Henry Hidley's *Postenkill, New York;* to the Munson-Williams-Proctor Institute for Mary Keys's *Lockport on the Erie Canal;* to the Metropolitan Museum of Art for Edward Lamson Henry's *The 9:45 Accommodation, Stratford, Connecticut;* to the Nelson-Atkins Museum of Art for Thomas Proudly Otter's *On the Road;* to the Museum of Modern Art for Charles Sheeler's *American Landscape;* to the Founders Society Detroit Institute of Arts for Diego Rivera's *Detroit Industry: Production of Automobile Exterior and Final Assembly;* to Yale University Art Gallery for Edward Hopper's *Rooms for Tourists,* and Edward Hopper's *Western Motel;* to James Maroney for Grant Wood's *Arbor Day;* to Williams College Museum of Art for Grant Wood's *Death on Ridge Road;* to the National Gallery of Canada for George Segal's *The Gas Station;* to the Chicago Historical Society for Jay Wolke's *The Running Horse—Dan Ryan Expressway;* to National Museum of American Art for Mike Wilkins's *Preamble;* to the Oldsmobile Division of General Motors Corporation for "Work While You Work, Play While You Play"; to the Library of Congress for "Jackson's Inaugural Procession"; and to the Indiana State Library and Macmillan Publishing Company for permission to print "Stage Coach Barn," from *The National Road* by Philip D. Jordan, Copyright 1948 by The Bobbs-Merrill Company, renewed 1976 by Philip D. Jordan.

Thanks also to Carol Mishler at the Center for American Places, to Sonya Simms for valuable research assistance and also the expert staffs of the Geography and Map Division at the Library of Congress, the Newberry Library, the Mercantile Library, the Ohio Historical Library, the Indiana State Library, the Hagley Museum and Library, the University of Kentucky Library and Special Collections, and the Illinois State Historical Library; to the Miami Conservancy Office in Dayton, Ohio, and the Dunbar Library Special Collections and Archives at Wright State University in Dayton; to James R. Bertsch of Cambridge City, Indiana; to Mary Burtschi of Vandalia, Illinois; to Tom Thomas, National Park Service at the Denver Service Center; to Frederick C. K. Babb, National Park Service, Denver, Colorado; to William F. Edwards, Engineer at the Ohio Department of Transportation who provided historical data on US 40, and I-70 and I-75 traffic counts from 1956 to the present; to Daniel Reedy, dean of the Graduate School, University of Kentucky, who contributed an extended interview with his father, Ralph Reedy. The Reedy family lived beside the Road in Livingston, Illinois, and Mr. Reedy worked as a brick carrier when the road was resurfaced in the early 1930s; to Arthur Krim who contributed invaluable information on Interstate 70 to chapter 9; to Chris Robinson of London, Ohio, for piloting an aerial photography flight; and to Glenn Harper of the Ohio Historic Preservation Office at Wright State University for his contributions to project research.

I also wish to make a special acknowledgment to Gyula Pauer, director of the University of Kentucky Cartography Laboratory, who designed the maps and diagrams, and directed the cartographic work; and to Derran Broyles and Phillip Stiefel for their cartographic production work. Both volume 1 and volume 2 contain numerous original photographs by Charles Walters of Colorado Springs, Gregory Conniff of Madison, Wisconsin, Bob Thall of Chicago, and Michael Putnam of New York City. These photographers worked within the parameters of the project—to provide informative illustrations—but they went well beyond the call of duty in making works of art. In so many ways does their vision and effort hearken back to the photographers of the Farm Security Administration, like the National Road another federally funded project.

PART ONE     # Introduction

# The Landscapes of Mobility

PEIRCE LEWIS

*A road which for some reason has become established along an artificial line, a line not directly dictated by the formula of minimum effort, will "canalize" traffic, so that, even when an alternative and better way has been provided, institutions and towns and all that goes for human activity will have taken root along the old way and all history will be deflected by the deflection of the Road.*

HILAIRE BELLOC
*The Road* (1923)

THE WORLD'S PEOPLE ARE OF TWO KINDS: THOSE WHO ARE IN THE HABIT of moving, and those who are not. Much of human history is the story of nonmovers—sedentary peasants, rooted in the land they farmed and ruled by gentry whose wealth and power came from ownership of that land. That feudal system, which dominated much of the world's most densely populated regions until very recent time, was based on the unquestioned assumption that people should "know their place"—and stay there. But the story of America was different entirely—a whole nation of migrants from far-off places who, once they had arrived in America, continued ceaselessly to move. No proper understanding of American history can fail to note that fact and to recognize habitual mobility as a defining element of American nationhood. The propensity to move is not just one of several American habits. Mobility is an enduring, driving passion that has defined the whole American experience, and continues to do so.

**Thomas Hovenden,**
*Breaking Home Ties* (1890)

This hugely popular painting struck a deep and responsive chord with late nineteenth-century Americans, most of whom had experienced the pain of such inevitable partings. Mobility may be the key to success in America, but it often exacts a fearful price.

It has been so for as long as people have inhabited the North American continent. Native Americans trace their lineage from Asian peoples who drifted across the land bridge from Siberia to Alaska 30,000 years ago, and their descendants continued those migratory habits until they came to land's end in Tierra del Fuego. And from 1607 onward, new breeds of Americans would arrive from continents to the east. Franklin Roosevelt, that high-born patroon from one of America's "oldest" families, had it right when he addressed an audience of East Coast bluebloods as "my fellow immigrants."

The ability to move has always been the key to success in American society. In vernacular speech, Americans talk of "moving up in life," by which they usually mean moving up economically or socially, often both at the same time. But the key to that economic and social mobility has always been geographic mobility—the ability to move physically from one location to another in search of a better life. If a young person found small-town life stultifying, what was more reasonable than to leave for the gold camps of California or the bright lights of some far-off metropolis? If long-tilled farms of the East grew eroded and sterile, what was more reasonable than for a farmer to pack up his family and move to rich new land somewhere in the West—the Kansas prairies or the green valley of Oregon? If a person or group was persecuted for political or religious heresies, what was more reasonable than to hitch up wagons and drive to a new home—in Utah, or some other far-off place?

The old British aphorism that one should "know one's place" meant, of course, that one should know one's place in society and stay there. But "place" was geographical as well. An English peasant, bound to some ancestral patch of soil, was confined within an intractable structure of economics and society which guaranteed that tomorrow would be the same as today—not much better, and with luck not much worse. The easiest way—for many the only way—to escape that tyranny of place was to pull up roots and move, which is precisely what the ancient feudal system would not and could not permit. To most Americans, being told that they should know their place makes them see a bright shade of red: the injunction denies the most basic of American rights—the right to leave a bad place and move to a good one. The most evil institution in American history was human slavery, not only because slaves were ill-treated by their masters but also because slaves were denied the elemental American right to move from one place and go to another.

That unquestioning belief in the inherent virtue of mobility is a powerful part of America's collective mythology, a transcendent theme in popular American art and literature. Thomas Hovenden's hugely popular painting, *Breaking Home Ties*,[1] typifies a whole genre: an awkward young farm boy, about to leave home and seek his fortune, his grieving family gathered to bid him farewell. The painting, in dark somber colors, strikes a painful chord in American hearts because the viewer knows, just as the boy's family knows, that the youngster has no choice but to leave, that breaking home ties is inevitable if the boy is to make anything of himself in life. Thomas Hart Benton's *The Boy* carries the same message—a gawky farm lad trudging down the lane of a broken-down Ozark farm, suitcase in hand, while his aging parents wave goodbye. All three know that the boy will never return to farm that worn-out patch, that the parents will grow old alone. But all three share the unquestioned belief that pulling up roots, no matter how painful, is a necessary part of growing up in America.

The greatest of American novels tells the same story, of people seeking freedom through mobility. Huckleberry Finn and Jim on their Mississippi raft are each escaping their own brand of slavery as they drift down the river in search of freedom. It is a paradox, but no mystery, that Huck and Jim are most free while they are in the act of moving, on the raft in mid-river. John Steinbeck says much the same thing in *The Grapes of Wrath*. The story of the Joads fleeing dust-choked Oklahoma for the honeyed fields of California is blackest tragedy, for the Joads learn too late that they have moved in vain. Even today *The Grapes of Wrath* makes dismaying reading because Steinbeck is telling us that the age-old American hope of freedom through mobility is a lie, that a major tenet of the American dream is fraudulent.

But most Americans do not believe that, and never have. The Statue of Liberty, one of America's most cherished symbols, derives much of its

Thomas Hart Benton, *The Boy* (1950)

Benton's message is the same as Hovenden's. For the boy to succeed in life, he *must* leave home.

© 1994 T. H. Benton and Rita P. Benton Testamentary Trusts/VAGA, New York, NY.

Edward Moran, *The Unveiling of the Statue of Liberty Enlightening the World* (1886)

The statue might plausibly have been erected somewhere in mid-continent, but it was not. Facing the steamships entering New York harbor, the Statue of Liberty assures immigrants that their journey was not in vain—liberty is not won by people who stay at home.

symbolic power from its location. Liberty is not standing atop some great pedestal in middle America (as she might well have been) but triumphantly at the entrance of New York Harbor. The Statue of Liberty has a different message for two separate audiences. For immigrants arriving in New York City, the statue is a symbol of welcome—her lamp lifted beside the golden door at the end of one journey and the beginning of another. But the statue's second and equally powerful message is for Americans themselves, that the promise of American life can truly be realized by people who have the energy and courage to pull up roots and move. The Statue of Liberty is a permanent and unsubtle reminder that mobility is the key to success in America.

For all its benefits, that habit of ceaseless mobility has extracted ferocious costs from Americans and from their land. The emotional pain that comes from pulling up roots is well known to anyone who has ever left home; that, of course, is the message of Hovenden's and Benton's paintings. In the Old World, the tightly knit nucleated family was a secure and comfortable haven from a hostile world, but in America such families are much less common, simply because it is hard for American parents to stay in touch with footloose offspring. Many American family chronicles contain some hazy gossip about the vaguely disreputable Uncle Jake or Cousin Vaclav who got into some kind of trouble and went off to California, never to be heard from again. (There is often wistful speculation that Cousin Vaclav, under a changed name, has become a millionaire and may someday return home to share his riches with his stay-at-home relatives.)

Then, too, when people habitually move from one place to another, they are not always good caretakers of those places. America is full of abused, discarded places—worn-out farms, depopulated rural villages, ruined factory towns—used for a time and then thrown away when they ceased to be of use, while their inhabitants moved on to use and abuse yet other places. Broken homes and damaged places are prices Americans pay for their footloose habits.

Yet over most of their history, Americans have been more than willing to pay that price. The alternative—to be frozen in place or to be a stick-in-the-mud (American vernacular is full of such phrases)—is simply intolerable to most Americans. And because the benefits of mobility are so obvious and alluring, Americans have repeatedly invested huge energy in an effort to de-

vise new ways to make the act of travel as cheap and fast and easy as possible.

## ICONS OF AMERICAN MOBILITY

Just as Americans are in love with mobility as an abstract idea, they are enraptured with the people and things that make mobility possible. Some of America's great mythic figures are heroes of transportation, conquerors of geographic space, masters of the fastest vehicles of their time, fearlessly courting danger in order to go farther faster. Examples are legion: the Pony Express rider risking his life to ensure that the mail would go through; captains of clipper ships, lashing themselves to the mast to bring their storm-ravaged vessels to safe harbor; death-defying steamboat races between the *Natchez* and the *Robert E. Lee*. If heroes perish in the act, their heroism is so much the greater: Casey Jones immortalized with his hand at the throttle, astronauts immolated in a ball of fire as they set forth to explore the black vastnesses of space. America's popular mythology is alive with songs about

**Marathon, New York**

The depopulation of American's farms, combined with the building of a high-speed national road system helped seal the fates of small market towns like Marathon. Shortly before this photo was taken in the mid-1970s, Marathon's old main street, US 11, was bypassed by Interstate 81, crossing on the overpass in the middle distance. Both roads lead to Syracuse, 50 miles north, but no one drives to Syracuse on US 11 anymore.

***Through the Bayou by
Torchlight*** (1875)

The celebrated New York
firm of Currier and Ives
was the biggest and most
successful of numerous
firms that sold cheap illustrations of popular subjects
to a mass audience. Among
the most popular subjects
were fire-breathing
machines that defined danger and destroyed space.
Here, a torchlit steamboat
carves a flaming swath
through the gloom of a
Louisiana bayou.

***The Fast Mail*** (1876)

Gleaming with Masonic
symbols and polished brass,
the Lake Shore and Michi-
gan Southern's locomotive
number 317 bears news
from the outside world as
it tears through rural hamlets, spewing steam, smoke,
and romance. The resolute
engineer is plainly a hero,
and there is little doubt
what the little boy wants
to be when he grows up.

PEIRCE LEWIS

*As the Centuries Pass in the Night* (1924)

The New York Central Railroad commissioned this painting for its promotional calendar for 1924. Bad weather and long distances are of no concern to those who master the machines that devour space. (Courtesy of the New York Central Railroad.)

boats on the Erie Canal, trains like the City of New Orleans speeding through the night, truck drivers telling stories of freedom and tragedy on the open road.

Popular art is the same. In the mid-nineteenth century, Currier and Ives made their fortunes by finding popular subjects and making colored pictures of them. Some of the best sellers showed steamboats blazing new channels through the Mississippi swamps or the "Fast Mail" conquering space. Some of America's most successful popular advertising has seized the same theme, linking mobility with heroism, romance, and defiance of the elements. A striking and opulent example of this genre was a painting commissioned by the New York Central Railroad for its 1924 promotional calendar. *As the Centuries Pass in the Night* depicts the eastbound and westbound sections of the railroad's crack train, the Twentieth Century Limited, one headed for Chicago, the other for New York, passing at high speed in the moonlight. In the foreground snow and grit are roiled by the trains as they tear along the gleaming tracks, but the windows of the passenger cars glow with warmth and light, ignoring harsh nature, denying the frozen night. A good deal of auto advertising rests on the same theme, where cars become not mere vehicles, but instruments for the conquest of nature. Some of the least subtle ads are for motorcycles, shown not merely as fast two-wheeled

**"Cancel Distance and Conquer Weather," Ford advertisement (February 1925)**

The God-like claim that a Model-T Ford could "cancel distance and conquer weather" was only a slight exaggeration. Here, *mirabile dictu*, women could join in the adventure.

**Harley-Davidson advertisement (1970s)**

Like any machine of fast transportation, the Harley-Davidson FX-1200 is more than just a convenient vehicle: it is the "Great American Freedom Machine," "an ego-trip dedicated to freedom and good-time cycling."

vehicles but as "great American freedom machines." In the most extreme instances, the machine is itself a grinning anthropomorphic hero, rolling its raffish headlight eyes as it lunges across impossible terrain. Some of America's most popular video games appeal to the same impulse, putting children behind the wheel of speeding cars, tearing across electronic landscapes at impossible, death-defying speeds.

## NEW TECHNOLOGY, NEW GEOGRAPHY

Romantic mythology aside, America's preoccupation with transportation has a very practical foundation. America, after all, is a big country, and connecting the far reaches of the national territory has traditionally been seen as necessary, not just for economic well-being, but to ensure political cohesion. Paradoxically, in a country where the public is constantly warned against the dangers of oppressive government, and especially about the pernicious consequences of government interfering with private enterprise, political parties of left and right alike have repeatedly joined to support government financing of canals, railroads, roads, bridges, and airports. Throughout American history the attitude has remained the same: fast cheap transportation is good; slow expensive transportation is bad. The result is inevitable: whenever a new technology of transportation is found to

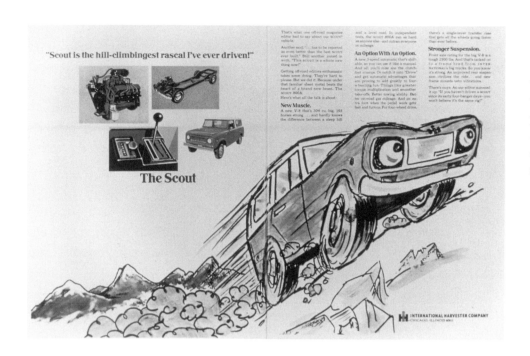

be better than an existing one, old forms are thrown aside and the new one embraced.

But transportation is not just movement. For as long as history records, there has been an intimate connection between transportation and the whole fabric of human geography. The way people live, and the way they arrange their lives, is hugely determined by the way they travel. In America one form of dominant national transportation has replaced an older one three times. Each time that happened, the whole fabric of America's human geography was shredded and then rewoven in patterns determined by the particular way the new transport technology operated, often in ways that seemed unpredictable at the time. Large chunks of those older geographies are still with us, however, even if the technology that originally produced them has long since been cast aside.

## FROM UNIMPROVED WATERWAYS TO CANALS AND TURNPIKES

The first major shift in transportation technology occurred during the last decades of the eighteenth century and the opening decades of the nineteenth. The revolution (for it was nothing less) was accompanied and provoked by the first great enlargement of America's national territory. Until the end of the eighteenth century, the bulk of settlement in the new United States was confined to a narrow coastal strip between the Savannah River in Georgia and Penobscot Bay on the coast of mid-Maine. Rarely was that settlement very far removed from tidewater or from navigable rivers, linked to a transportation technology that had not much changed since Roman times. Travel on land was by foot, oxcart, or horseback—slow, uncomfortable, inherently small-scale, and very expensive. And, with sparse population, there was rarely surplus labor available to build anything resembling a road network or canal system. Comfortable cheap transportation was necessarily by water, which meant sailing ships, and shallow-draft coastal craft and riverboats, powered by wind or human muscle, using whatever waterways that God had provided. The open ocean was the main highway that connected the northern and southern colonies, and coastal rivers and bays were tributaries to that highway. As long as population was concentrated along a narrow strip of Atlantic coastline, there was no serious impulse to change. To be sure, a few short canals and turnpikes had been built, chiefly in thickly settled parts of eastern New England and Pennsylvania, but they were minor details in a system of transportation that depended overwhelmingly on unimproved waterways.

Given these geographic circumstances, patterns of colonial settlement were entirely predictable. When America's first census was taken in 1790, the nation's population was about four million. Nearly everyone lived on farms, and most were necessarily located close to tidewater or at least near a sparse scattering of navigable streams. The only towns of consequence were places like Philadelphia and Boston, located at the heads of bays or navigable rivers, or like New York and Charleston, at the mouths of rivers that gave deep-water access to interior lands. Big inland towns simply did not exist, because the transport did not exist to support them.

But unimproved waterways were totally inadequate to meet the demands of a nation whose rambunctious population was pressing rapidly inland. Although America's Atlantic shoreline is richly endowed with bays and estuaries, few navigable rivers extend any distance into the interior. The deepest penetration is Chesapeake Bay, which helps explain why Virginia, with its skein of navigable tidewater estuaries, was the most populous of the thirteen original colonies, and why tiny Maryland was not far behind. In glaciated New England, there was only one important navigable river, the Connecticut, and most inland farmers necessarily depended on wretched

PEIRCE LEWIS

roads and a few badly maintained turnpikes. In the middle colonies, only the Hudson penetrated any significant distance inland, a fact that helped account for the early ascendancy of New York City. Falls or rapids blocked the other big rivers: the Delaware at Trenton, the Potomac just above Georgetown, and the Susquehanna near its mouth at Havre de Grace, Maryland. Although a few big Southern rivers, such as the James and Santee and Savannah, could be navigated by seagoing vessels as far inland as the Fall Line, the distance was seldom very far from the ocean.

What was needed was a wholly new *form* of transportation, capable of serving a hugely enlarged nation, with a growing population that was pressing uncontrollably into the interior. With independence recognized by England in 1783, the infant American nation had suddenly gained title to nearly all the land between the Atlantic and the Mississippi River. Then, just twenty years later, the new United States acquired the Louisiana Purchase, so that the total national domain totaled about two million square miles—all up for grabs for those who had the energy and ambition to pull up stakes and move. Trans-Appalachian America, furthermore, was magnificently equipped with two of the biggest inland waterway systems on the face of the earth: the Great Lakes, and the Ohio-Mississippi-Missouri River system with its myriad of tributaries, many of which were navigable. Plainly, the new American West was destined for great things, but it was equally plain that the West would go its own way, economically and perhaps politically as well, unless its economy and society could be tied with reliable transportation to that of the original thirteen coastal states. Good trans-Appalachian connections, then, were more than a luxury. They were essential if the United States was to remain united.

Given contemporary technology, there were only two feasible ways to make those connections. One was to build one or more roads across the Appalachians. The second was to build a system of canals. Both were attempted, with wildly different results. All else being equal, canals were overwhelmingly the better solution. Given the alternative of hauling wagons over rough, rutted frontier roads, canal boats could carry large heavy cargoes of freight and passengers smoothly, efficiently, and at surprisingly high speeds. But it was immediately apparent that all else was not equal, especially when it came to crossing rough terrain.

Any good map of the eastern United States reveals a simple but fundamental fact: the highest and most formidable country in the Appalachian

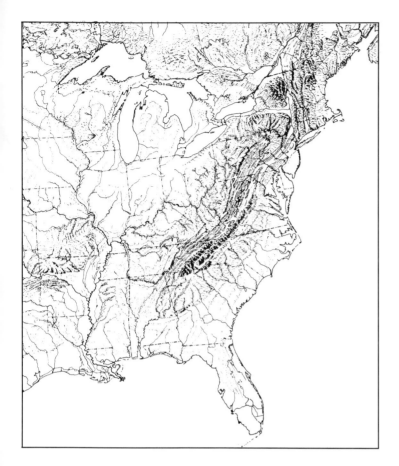

**The landforms of the eastern United States, by Erwin Raisz (1956)**

The Appalachians are highest and most formidable at their northern and southern ends. The easiest crossings are in the middle—in New York and Pennsylvania.

chain lies at its southern and northern extremities—not in the middle. At the southern end, along the border between North Carolina and Tennessee, the Blue Ridge forms a rampart more than a mile high, a forbidding barrier to east-west movement. In New England, the Green and White Mountains of Vermont and New Hampshire are almost as formidable. The middle Appalachians are considerably lower, however, and in New York and Pennsylvania there are several significant gaps. The lowest and most useful of those gaps is the valley of the Mohawk River, which snakes its way between the Catskills and Adirondacks to form a corridor from the middle Hudson Valley into the plains of Lake Ontario and Lake Erie. That was the route of the Erie Canal, which succeeded for the devastatingly simple reason that it connected the Atlantic Ocean and the interior of North America. That route was overwhelmingly the easiest of trans-Appalachian routeways and has subsequently been used as the corridor for transcontinental railroads and arterial interstate highways. It is no accident that the corridor is lined with towns that boomed mightily as America rose to industrial eminence in the late nineteenth and early twentieth centuries. Nor is it any accident that New York City, commanding the Atlantic entryway to that portentous corridor, rose to become the largest and most important city in the country.

The Erie Canal was wildly successful and provoked instant imitators. Some of the imitations succeeded, but most did not. A short branch of the main-line canal to Lake Ontario was easy to dig and paid off quickly, enriching both stockholders and the city of Syracuse. Other feeders, such as those to the Finger Lakes, proved to be deadends and were soon allowed to atrophy. The most spectacular of the Erie Canal's imitators, however, was engineered by the Commonwealth of Pennsylvania, which correctly saw the success of the New York canal as a threat to the fortunes of both Philadelphia and Pittsburgh. Rising to the challenge, Pennsylvania patched together a picturesque but Byzantine trans-Appalachian route that com-

PEIRCE LEWIS

bined a variety of technologies in a stunning display of technological bravado. The system's main spine was a "main-line canal" along the Susquehanna and Juniata Rivers, a piece of overland railroad to connect the Susquehanna with Philadelphia, and, most marvelous of all, a series of inclined planes that put canal boats atop huge railroad cars and hauled them bodily up the great escarpment of the Allegheny Front some 1,500 vertical feet through the forests of central Pennsylvania. From atop the Front, another series of planes lowered the still-amphibious boats to a place on the Conemaugh River near Johnstown, whence they floated downstream by way of twisting mountain rivers to the forks of the Ohio at Pittsburgh. That such a venture was contemplated and actually built is testimony to the importance of canals during those fevered years of national expansion between the 1830s and 1850s. Even though the Pennsylvania Main Line Canal (as it was called) never paid off, it was sufficiently important on political and symbolic grounds that the Commonwealth kept it in operation despite chronic financial woes.

**The U.S. Canal System, c. 1840–50**

The system is shown here at its peak, just before it was overtaken by railroads.

Efforts to build trans-Appalachian canals farther south failed utterly. The most ambitious scheme was a Chesapeake & Ohio Canal, designed to connect the headwaters of the Potomac with those of the Ohio—a project, which, if completed, would have duplicated the feat of the Pennsylvania Canal. The C&O Canal got as far as Cumberland, Maryland, but there construction stalled, frustrated by the extravagant cost of building a canal over an Appalachian ridge more than 3,000 feet high. It took the C&O Canal to prove what had long seemed obvious—that canals and mountains did not make good companions.

Thus, when all was said and done, there were only two genuine trans-Appalachian canal systems, and only one—the Erie—really fulfilled expectations. West of the Appalachians, however, it was a different story, and the boom in canal-building quickly reached the level of frenzy. The most obvious canals were built quickly, abetted by the fact that digging ditches through the Middle West's glacial flatlands (and often carved from old glacial river courses) was much cheaper than hacking channels across the Appalachians. Furthermore, the payoff was large and immediate in wide flat country with rich soil and no roads worth mentioning. Before the middle of the nineteenth century, the Great Lakes had been linked with the Ohio and Mississippi in half a dozen locations. Lake Erie alone was tied to the Ohio River by three systems, each with a number of branches. The Ohio & Erie Canal led south from Cleveland via the Cuyahoga and Tuscarawas, then leaped cross-country to the Scioto, south of Columbus, and on to the Ohio River at Portsmouth. The Miami & Erie connected Toledo with Cincinnati by way of the Maumee and Great Miami. The third and longest was the Wabash & Erie, which followed the Maumee from Toledo to a portage at Fort Wayne and then down the Wabash to the Ohio in southern Indiana. Perhaps the most important of all was the Illinois & Michigan Canal, which connected the southern end of Lake Michigan at Chicago with Mississippi near St. Louis, by way of the Illinois River. Farther west, and less successfully, canals were built from the end of Green Bay to the Mississippi, via Lake Winnebago and the Wisconsin River.

To glance at a map of those canals, two things become obvious immediately. First, the canals played a powerful role in shaping the urban geography of the American Middle West. Second, the new canal system greatly benefited the North but hardly touched the South.

The canals' effects on the settlement of the Midwest were dramatic. In a huge region, which had only recently been farmless and townless, settlers poured into some of the richest farmland on earth and founded towns to carry on the business of the exploding farm economy. Not surprisingly, the most successful of those new towns were those that commanded route junctions: places such as Pittsburgh and St. Louis where rivers joined, and places where the newly built canals made connection with a major river or one of the Great Lakes: Cincinnati, Cleveland, Toledo, and the greatest of all, Chicago. Furthermore, the impact of this growing canal system was not limited to the Middle West. Cities that commanded water routes between the Middle West and Atlantic slope were destined for unprecedented economic growth. Buffalo and New York City were the main beneficiaries of the new trans-Appalachian linkages, as were such intermediate places as Rochester, Syracuse, Albany, and various lesser places. And while the Pennsylvania Canal never matched the Erie in traffic or profits, Philadelphia,

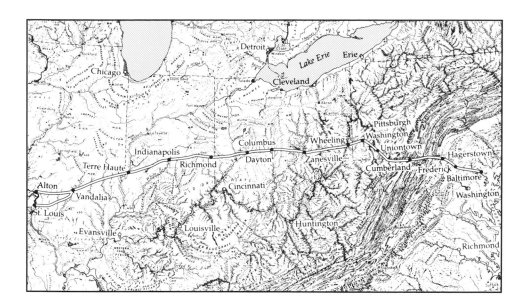

**The Route of the National Road**

The route of the National Road avoided the roughest Appalachian topography by veering into Northern territory, and thereby ceased to be a truly "National" road.

Pittsburgh, and intermediate places such as Harrisburg and Johnstown benefited considerably from the new trans-Appalachian traffic.

But the South, as a region, gained nothing at all from the new canals: the Appalachians south of the Mason-Dixon line were simply too high and rugged to cross—at least by canal. It was for that reason more than any other that Southern politicians supported the federal financing of a "National" Road, which would find an overland route to cross the Appalachians in the middle of the country—roughly along the boundary between North and South. It was the best trans-Appalachian route the South could hope for.

Despite its high-flown name, the National Road was a disappointment. In the first place, the route had converted it quickly into a Northern—not a Southern—road. Theoretically, the road was destined to connect the Chesapeake Bay and St. Louis, running along the borderland between North and South.[2] It headed west from Baltimore, that quintessential border city, cutting across the Piedmont of Maryland through Frederick and on to Cumberland, where it wormed its way through several Potomac River watergaps before ascending the Allegheny Front, the crest of the Appalachians. At that point things started going wrong, at least from the Southern standpoint. Instead of hewing to its border location, the Road veered northwestward through a corner of Pennsylvania, then crossed the Ohio at Wheeling, and finally headed due west through Ohio and Indiana—not just the corner of Ohio but squarely across the middle of the state. To South-

**Stone Bridge over Conococheague Creek**

The National Road near Frederick, Maryland, c. 1975. Structures like these were considerably more elegant and expensive than they needed to be.

erners, this was not a "national" road at all, but merely an expensive project that had been hijacked for the benefit of Northerners but was of no benefit to the South.

So the Road never got to St. Louis. Partly it was a victim of pre–Civil War regional politics and increasing hostility between slave and free states. But the other problem was simply the exorbitant cost of roads when compared with canals. It was already obvious that the burgeoning canal system provided a much cheaper and more efficient way to haul goods and people over long distances than could even the best of roads. Thus, while bits of the National Road proved locally useful, especially in its Appalachian sections, where a series of beautifully engineered stone arch bridges carried traffic across a number of difficult river crossings, it never came close to fulfilling its promise of providing reliable long-distance land transportation across the Appalachians.

There was nothing wrong with the road except its timing; it was a century ahead of its time. Increasingly disenchanted with the project, Congress starved its appropriations, and the National Road of the early nineteenth century finally whimpered to an ignominious end in the small southern Illinois town of Vandalia, seventy embarrassing miles short of its supposed destination in St. Louis. It would be almost a century before the National Road was resurrected as US 40 and converted into what it was intended to be, a genuinely national highway.

## THE AGE OF THE RAILROAD

The reign of canals was about to end. What killed them was the railroad, one of the most formidable instruments of change ever to be unleashed on the face of the earth, a juggernaut with a life of its own, sweeping all else before it. During its period of dominance, the railroad transformed much of the world, including much of the emerging United States. The reason was simple and powerful: it was the period when some of America's most aggressive territorial expansion took place, when a good share of America's human geography was first being shaped. It so happened that the railroad was on hand to do the shaping.[3]

To understand why the railroad, as an instrument of technology, so quickly dominated the making of America's landscape, it is helpful to put oneself in the context of America in the 1830s, when the first sign of a railroad system was beginning to emerge in the northeastern and middlewestern United States. Waves of settlers were surging westward into the continental interior. Although water transportation had opened the interior to very rapid development, most of the nation's territory still lay at an impossible distance from navigable water—territory that included much of the best agricultural land in the Midwest, and nearly all of the semi-arid country of the Louisiana Purchase, where waterways were virtually useless for transportation. It had seemed only natural, for example, that the main artery of transportation into the Louisiana Territory would be the Missouri River and its vast system of tributaries. After all, the Missouri is among the longest rivers in the world, and much of the Louisiana Territory was defined by the limits of the Missouri watershed. For serious navigation, however, the Missouri was at best a disappointment, at worst a trap. Upstream from Kansas City the ill-tempered river had an unpleasant habit of rising, falling, and shifting course without warning, and its broad, shallow bed came to be strewn with the carcasses of abandoned steamboats that had paddled hopefully upstream and suddenly found themselves out of water and stranded indefinitely on some isolated sandbar. Most other western rivers, even the biggest ones, such as the Columbia and the Colorado, were impossible to navigate, as their channels were often entrenched in deep canyons and interrupted with waterfalls and rapids. The rivers also fluctuated violently between flood and drought. To make matters worse, the whole northern system of water transportation, whether by canal or river or lake, froze solid during winter. Even the Great Lakes were impassable for several months of the year, as ice floes jammed the narrow passages between the lakes and piled up along shores and harbor entrances. But the problem with canals and river transportation was more basic than waterfalls and winter freezing. Even in the eastern Middle West, where the canal system was best developed, large chunks of productive territory still lay frustratingly distant from the nearest canal or navigable stream.

Yet the land was there, beckoning land-hungry migrants, who swarmed westward in spite of all difficulties, demanding transportation for themselves and their goods. Rivers and canals were simply not up to the job. What was needed, quite clearly, was a close-knit system of cheap land transportation. Nothing like that had existed on the face of the earth before. Indeed, for as long as history recorded, land transportation had always been grossly difficult, which is the reason why transport by water had always seemed so wonderfully alluring—always cheaper, faster, more comfortable and efficient than transportation by land—and why so much of the world's land area, even with the most fertile soil, was permanently exiled, in a state of backward isolation.

The railroads changed all that—as, indeed, they changed the whole basis of human settlement. No longer would people be bound by the tyranny of navigable water. Now they could go anywhere that rails could profitably be laid. And, in the fevered days of mid-nineteenth-century America, that seemed to be almost everywhere.[4]

Serious rail systems emerged in northwestern Europe almost fifty years before they did in America. But the American system was different simply because the scale was different. In Great Britain, the first important rail lines were laid during the late eighteenth century, built to carry coal from mines in Wales and the Midlands to seaports, never very far away, and they stayed in business as handmaidens to oceanic shipping. Even in its heyday, when a dense network of lines had been laid all over the United Kingdom, the British rail system was never really very big: for example, the longest main-line stretch, the famous run of the Royal Scot from London to Edinburgh, was only about the distance from Boston to Washington.

But it was not just size that made the American rail system different. In Britain, France, and Germany—the first parts of Europe to build anything like *national* rail systems—railroads were built to service an existing dense network of cities, towns, and villages, and that network had been in place for a very long time. In much of rural America, however, the rails were laid to serve a population that was relatively sparse, and west of the Mississippi the rails preceded settlement and town-building almost everywhere. To a much larger degree than in Europe, America's railroads played an active role in *shaping* the basic urban geography of much of the country. The nation's biggest cities grew big if, and only if, they were major rail terminals. New York City flourished as the Atlantic terminal of the New York Central, which used the old route of the Erie Canal, advertising itself as "the water-level route" to the Middle West. Philadelphia was the terminus of the Pennsylvania Railroad that cut across the Appalachians to Pittsburgh and thence west to Columbus, Chicago, and St. Louis. Baltimore was terminus for the Baltimore and Ohio, which roughly paralleled the route of the aborted C&O Canal and the National Road. Norfolk was the ocean port for the Norfolk & Western and the bituminous coal fields that the N&W was built to serve.

It was in the continental interior, however, with its vast areas of land-locked territory, where the railroads really blossomed and immediately began to create a whole new human geography. Strewn across the Middle West and West, a network of robust new cities emerged, all of them, without exception, rail junctions. Chicago, of course, was overwhelmingly the biggest, strategically located where the navigable water of Lake Michigan projects most deeply into the fertile black farmland of the Middle West—the place where railroads from all over the continental interior came to meet the head of navigation on the Great Lakes and a skein of railroads from the East that joined together as they rounded the end of the lake.[5] For a long while, Chicago possessed the biggest and busiest railyards in the world, and the city's character was shaped by those railroads, which brought raw materials to its voracious steel mills and stockyards and then carried Chicago's products away to markets all over the country. Like Chicago, a good many other towns that had been lake, or canal, or river ports also became rail junctions and flourished thereby: Pittsburgh, Cincinnati, Louisville, Nashville, Memphis, St. Louis, and many smaller places. Indeed, if a city failed to plug into that new rail network, it was automatically banished to economic limbo. Important Atlantic coastal towns such as Williamsburg, Charleston, and Savannah stagnated as unwitting museums of their past glories, while wealth went inland to the new upstart railroad towns—Richmond, Columbia, Chattanooga, Atlanta. Even a thriving commercial city like New Orleans, which had surged to fourth place among American cities during the steamboat frenzy of the 1830s, suffered badly as railroads in the upper Mississippi Valley reached westward to snatch the cargoes that previously had been offloaded at New Orleans. Only by becoming a rail terminal itself did New Orleans belatedly manage to retain some vestige of its former prosperity.[6]

While eastern railroads brought steroidal prosperity wherever they were built, their impact on the basic *patterns* of towns and cities was relatively modest. In the West, however, there were very few towns before the railroads arrived and, except for San Francisco, no genuine large-scale cities at all. Thus, when the western railroads arrived on the scene, they literally brought towns and cities with them. Dusty cowtowns such as Denver, Los Angeles, and Albuquerque, decreed as rail junctions or termini, promptly exploded into instant cities. Between those cities, a vast number of smaller towns were laid out by the all-powerful railroad companies, which had discovered that there was more money to be made in developing real estate than in selling railroad tickets. The most important of these lesser railroad towns were the so-called division points—towns 100 or so miles apart where train crews were changed on long-distance hauls. (In sparsely populated regions like eastern Montana, the division points were the only towns of consequence for miles in any direction and a good many—Billings, Miles City, and Livingstone—became the marketplaces that dominated large regions.) From the standpoint of the railroad companies there were huge profits to be made by converting raw land into "town lots"—especially when the company promised buyers quick and immediate profit as the paper towns grew into reality. Far more towns were laid out than actually came into being, and little effort was spent to design these railroad towns individually. Instead, the railroads devised standard plans, with streets predictably laid out in a grid—always with one or two main streets parallel to the railroad line, another at right angles to the tracks.[7] In all of these new settlements, towns and cities alike, the most valuable property was located near the railroad station, the gateway to the town and often the most imposing building. Indeed, everything in town was sited with reference to the railroad tracks. Alongside the railroad tracks were strung whatever industry the town had—in small towns a grain elevator, in larger places a string of factories and warehouses. Poor people lived on the "wrong side of the tracks," while the more affluent lived on the "right side." In a period of about thirty years—between 1870 and 1900—six transcontinental lines were built in the United States and each laid out a host of towns—on paper, if not on the ground. Along each line, at intervals of half a dozen miles or so, the towns were strung like beads on a string—and all looked very much alike. Small wonder, for they were all created at the same time, by the same forces, for the same reasons. Inevitably, the West ended up with vastly more towns than anyone needed. Many putative towns never got farther than the planners' drawing boards—or a few surveyors' stakes pounded into the grass alongside the tracks. Others, in spite of grandiose plans, produced a few dusty streets and a scattering of woebegone buildings. Still others flourished for a while, and then lapsed into oblivion. Only a few survived and became substantial places.[8]

The orgy of railroad building yielded a variety of other unintended and far-reaching consequences. Not the least was to drag a reluctant federal government into the business of financing and then regulating the railroads. During the early days of the railroad boom, private companies did all the building, and government supervision had seemed unnecessary. Eastern railroads, after all, had been built through settled regions with the reason-

PEIRCE LEWIS

**Union Station, Kansas City, Missouri (early 1930s postcard)**

More than just a railroad station, this imperial building was the ceremonial gateway to the city. In many fledgling American cities, the railroad station was overwhelmingly and deliberately the most impressive building in town. But the glory would not last; parked in front are the instruments of the railroad's destruction.

able expectation that local populations would provide enough freight and passenger revenue to make them self sustaining. That was not true in the empty West where, if rail lines were built, some outside agency would have to pay for them. That agency, of course, was the national government, which saw rail building as essential ties for hitching the East and West together. In those days before the income tax, however, it was utterly beyond the financial capacity of the federal government to pay for anything as costly as a transcontinental railroad—much less six of them.[9] Thus the federal government paid private companies to build railroads not with cash, but with land—and the government possessed land in abundance. Correspondingly, the railroad land grants were extremely generous and enriched the railroads far beyond anything that revenues from freight or passenger traffic could yield. Large portions of those grants survive to the present day, with the result that several of today's railroad companies are rich in land holdings, even after rail traffic has atrophied. In California today, for example, the largest private landowner, and one of its richest corporations, is the Southern Pacific Railroad Company.

By 1900, the American rail system was virtually complete. It bound the continent together, totally dominating not just the American transportation system but permeating American life. Railroads drove competing forms of transportation out of business or relegated them to inferior roles. Canals and waterways, for example, stayed in business mainly to haul heavy non-perishable bulk cargo like coal, iron ore, oil, and gravel cheaply over long distances. There was nothing resembling a national road system, nor did anyone see a need for one. As the nineteenth century wore on, and railroads increasingly monopolized long-distance transportation, the American road system degenerated until, at the century's end, the road system was worse than at any time in the history of the country. In rural areas, only local roads were maintained at all, and those badly. Thus, if a city street was paved (and outside big cities it was not likely to be), pavement usually came to an abrupt end as soon as it reached the edge of town. Most rural roads served only one function: to get farmers from their farms to the nearest railroad station—a formula that guaranteed that rural roads would be maintained at the most marginal levels and often were impassable except to the most determined traveler. Long-distance roads, designed to carry goods and people between cities or regions, simply did not exist. Seldom in the history of the world can one find any area of comparable size and wealth so totally dominated by a single technology as was turn-of-the-twentieth-century America dominated by the railroads.

It was only natural that nineteenth-century Americans told stories and sang ballads about trains and trainmen. Train wrecks and train robberies were routine stuff in early movies and boys' adventure stories. Popular novels hinged on dastardly plots hatched in railroad drawing rooms or tycoons' private cars. And in more than a few American cities and towns, rivaling courthouse or cathedral, the most imposing building was likely to be the railroad station—the ceremonial gateway to the town or the region, and the symbol of its wealth and self-esteem. In America of the early 1900s, there was simply nothing like the railroads for romance and sheer power over the ordinary lives of everyday Americans, and even the government itself. Individuals were at their mercy, which was not always tender. Even governments quailed before the might of railroad companies.[10]

## THE AGE OF THE AUTOMOBILE AND THE REVIVAL OF THE ROAD

In 1900 the United States was a country that in just three-quarters of a century had built a network of rails that spread across the face of a continent—that had tied the nation together economically and socially, had unlocked the riches of a continent. In no small measure, that mighty rail system helped lift the United States to the status of a world power. More than incidentally, it also helped ordinary Americans gain a measure of individual mobility which most people in the world could only dream of. An American in 1900, beholding the nation's railroad system and looking into the future, could scarcely have believed that much of this glittering structure would soon be demolished and thrown away like junk. But that was precisely what happened. Half a century later, the automobile had done to the railroads what railroads had earlier done to the canal system.

No one planned it that way. Certainly no one planned to set in motion a sequence of events that would totally redraw the human geography of the United States. But the automobile did that, and in company with a newly built system of all-weather roads would yield a variety of consequences that no one in America, no one on earth, could have foreseen. Once more, however, Americans were about to learn a basic lesson, that the fastest way to change a nation's geography is to change its basic mode of transportation and the technology that goes with it.

The history of the automobile, for all its devastating impact on twentieth-century America, from the beginning was a strangely hit-and-miss affair.[11] To begin with, no one person invented the automobile. During the last two decades of the nineteenth century, cars had evolved as mechanical curiosities, put together by mechanics on both sides of the Atlantic as diversions for themselves or for self-indulgent rich people who had nothing better to do with their time and money. It hardly made any difference that the automobiles of those days were temperamental, delicate, and outlandishly expensive. They were too fragile to operate on America's rutted rural roads, far too expensive for anyone but the rich to afford. They were, in short, irrelevant in the nation's day-to-day life.

All that changed abruptly in 1908 when Henry Ford's first Model-T rolled off the assembly line at his new factory in Highland Park, Michigan, outside Detroit. Overnight, the Model-T converted the automobile from a toy of the rich into an everyday instrument of personal transportation. Ford's genius was to see that the automobile, if it could be made cheap, sturdy, and reliable, could enable Americans to realize the age-old dream where ordinary individuals could go anywhere—to fulfill the dream of free personal automobility.[12]

The idea was nothing new, but the technology and corporate organization were. The automobile essentially finished what the railroad had

**Paved roads in America, 1926 and 1943**

In 1920, America was stuck in the mud. By World War II, most parts of the country were within easy reach of paved roads.

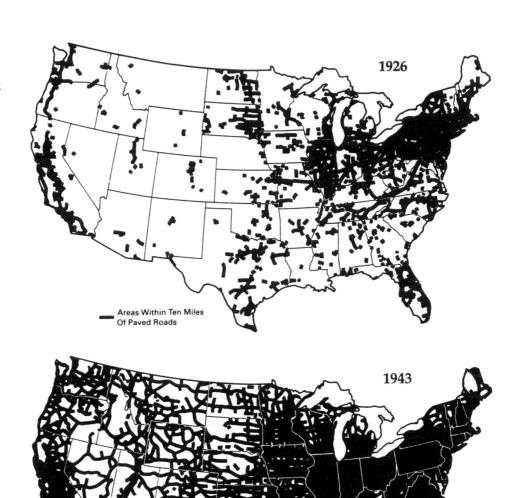

1926

— Areas Within Ten Miles Of Paved Roads

1943

started. Railroads, for the first time in history, had allowed ordinary people to travel rapidly and cheaply across land, independent of canals and navigable waterways, largely immune to the vagaries of weather and terrain. What Ford did with his cheap little Model-T was to make it possible for ordinary people to command their own personal travel machines, free of the tyranny of railroad stations and foreordained timetables.

But that could not happen without all-weather roads, connected into a nationwide system—and the United States had nothing resembling such a thing when the democratized automobile arrived on the scene in 1908. The only thing approaching an all-weather road system existed in a few large cities, and the majority of Americas still lived in rural areas, mostly on farms.[13] Although the Model-T was sturdy enough to withstand the battering of bad rural roads, there was no plausible way to travel long distances in it—partly because it was slow, partly because it was open to the weather, but mainly because most rural roads went nowhere, except to the nearest railroad station. Travel between cities or regions was still the monopoly of the railroads, and would remain so until cars were redesigned and roads rebuilt.

But that was about to happen, and the changes reinforced each other. As cars got better, there was rising clamor for better roads. And as roads got better, there was increasing opportunity for Americans to use the improved cars. And so it went, each improvement provoking louder demands for more. There was no grand plan, certainly no conspiracy—just a series of incremental changes, each of which seemed obvious and necessary at the time, but which in combination developed a self-generating momentum as time went on. It was not long before the process began to yield wholly unexpected consequences.

For example, it was not obvious at first that cars were suitable for long-distance travel. Indeed, the early Model-T was designed on the implicit and reasonable assumption that auto travel was inherently limited to short distances—a nice drive in the country—a Sunday visit to grandmother's house—perhaps a short daily trip from suburban dwelling to city office. Sturdy as they were, no one claimed that travel in a Model-T was comfortable. Although folding canvas tops were standard equipment, they were poor protection against bad weather. In a rainstorm or blizzard on a rutted country road, travel in a Model-T could be an elaborate form of purgatory. So the canvas tops gradually gave way to enclosed sedans, available as early as 1910 in high-priced models, then speedily invading the mass market. By 1927 competition from a host of competitors (notably Chevrolet) forced Ford to retire the Model-T and introduce his new Model-A, with a weatherproof body and improved engineering. The Model-A and its competitors made it possible for middle-class Americans to imagine traveling over distances that had previously seemed fantastic.

Meantime, of course, political pressure was building all over the country for the building of better roads, to accommodate these faster, more comfortable, long-distance automobiles. By the time the Model-T was rolling off the assembly line, there was emerging a kind of ad hoc lobby calling itself "the better roads movement." At first, the idea of "better roads" simply meant the improvement of road surfaces and the use of public money to improve them. In pre-automobile days, many of the rural roads that led from farms to village railroad stations were maintained by the farmers who actually used the roads—and such roads were kept up no better than they had to be. There was no mystery about how a permanent all-weather road should be built. The technology dated to the time of the Romans, and improvements on that technology took form through the innovative work of engineers such as John L. McAdam, the Scot whose name was given to the technique of building a coarse-textured road base, cambered upward to allow water to drain into roadside ditches, then adding packed layers of finer and finer crushed rocks until a reasonably smooth surface was achieved. But building and maintaining such roads was expensive business, even after it was discovered that pouring tar on McAdam roads would bind the aggregate together and produce a fairly good low-maintenance surface.

In 1920, road technology became even more expensive when the Wayne County Highway Department in Michigan discovered how to build paved roads that would stand up under the pounding of heavy truck traffic. The secret, it turned out, was to build a proper macadam base, then pour on eight inches of cement, reinforced with a mesh of steel bars, specially treated to resist corrosion. If the concrete was divided with expansion joints to prevent random cracking, a smooth-surfaced road could be expected to last for a long time with very little maintenance.

But all this was very expensive and required know-how far beyond the ability of local farmers or local governments to build and maintain. The solution, obviously, was to pass the job up to the state or federal government, and that was evident well before Wayne County began its experiments with reinforced concrete. By the 1920s a formidable economic and political coalition, a full-blown "highway lobby," had taken form. The members of that lobby were varied, but enthusiastic—and in concert they comprised a powerful political force, dedicated to the building of an elaborate all-weather road system, paid for by state and federal governments.

To list the membership in that lobby is an instructive exercise in applied political science—not to mention the law of unintended consequences. First were the automobile manufacturers themselves, who knew from experience that more and better roads would encourage the public to buy not only more cars, but also better and more profitable cars.[14] Then there was the petroleum industry, which had seen its profits dwindle as electricity replaced kerosene for domestic lighting and correctly perceived the new market for autos as a guarantee of eternal and growing profits. (It was no accident that oil companies began to hand out "free" road maps at their gasoline stations to help perplexed drivers find their way through a maze of uncharted rural roads.) There were lobbyists from the cement and steel industries, who saw that the promotion of smooth cement roads would create a large and permanent demand for their products. (Making steel for "rebars"—reinforcing rods—turned out to be a mammoth undertaking.) There were hosts of small-town boosters, who believed that better roads would connect them with larger markets and thus energize Main Street economies. (If one town did it, neighboring towns commonly did it also, lest they be "stuck in the mud.") There were farmers, of course, who welcomed with enthusiasm the idea of using public money to build "farm-to-market" roads—and by the turn of the twentieth century farmers had become very skillful at the art of lobbying at every level of government. Then there was government itself, which saw large-scale road-building as a universally popular enterprise, especially as more and more ordinary people acquired cars and insisted on their God-given right to drive on smooth roads. During the Depression, large-scale road-building became a way to make jobs for a large and varied workforce. Finally, there was the public at large, in possession of automobiles and eager to use them—a public increasingly impatient with being mired in mud or seeing their shiny new autos pummeled into junk by potholes.

Although motorists were politically influential for their numbers alone, their political power was greatly magnified through the creation of "auto clubs," ostensibly created as voluntary associations of motorists, but in fact highly profitable commercial ventures that charged membership fees, sold auto insurance (a newly invented and highly profitable institution), and extracted fees from roadside enterprises recommended by the auto clubs. As a part of their services, auto clubs distributed to their members "free" guidebooks and maps to make it easier for drivers to venture into unfamiliar territory. Meantime, a host of roadside entrepreneurs—managers of gas stations, restaurants, and motels (a term evidently coined in 1927)—joined the chorus demanding improvement of America's roads.

Just as no one person invented the automobile itself, no one person invented the highway lobby. It was an unplanned accumulation of individual elements that in combination proved to be far more than the sum of its parts. The key to its success was the general agreement that good roads were good things. There never was any plausible opposition to massive national road-building programs, any more than there had previously been opposition to public spending for railroad building, or the building of canals, or the improvement of waterways.

But "better roads" meant more than just better road surfaces. For an ambitious small-town motorist newly in possession of a shiny Model-A Ford, even the smoothest concrete highway did little good if it ended in a mudhole at the county line. If long-distance travel was to become a reality (and by the 1920s, people were demanding it stridently), there had to be long stretches of good roads, connected in some kind of coherent system.

Like most other institutions associated with the automobile, that nationwide highway system did not spring full-born from the head of Zeus, but instead as an accumulation of things and institutions put together, bit by bit. Seen in retrospect, however, the evolution of the system was inexorable.

The first sign of a genuinely national road system was the Lincoln Highway, the brainchild of Carl Graham Fisher of Indianapolis, an auto enthusiast, amateur dirt-track racer, and founder of the Indianapolis Speedway.[15] The Lincoln Highway Association was launched amid great fanfare in 1911 to promote the building of a paved transcontinental road, free of tolls, and paid for by states and local communities, and by contributions from private and corporate contributors. Despite its pretentious name, over most of its alignment the Lincoln Highway was a patchwork of existing roads, dodging erratically from one town to another, its location often determined by which of several towns was willing to put up the largest sum. Nevertheless, by the 1920s, drivers with enough patience and endurance could make their way across the continent, following the directional signs that bore the association's trademarked logo. Few motorists actually made that trip; in its western stretches particularly, the Lincoln Highway was more symbolic than real. But the symbol was important. A good many Americans, for the first time, could imagine driving a private automobile for a distance that had recently seemed unimaginable.

Inevitably, the federal government was drawn into the campaign to build a genuine national highway system—just as in an earlier epoch it had helped

PEIRCE LEWIS

design and underwrite a national rail system. As early as 1910, California voters approved a statewide bond issue for building public highways. But California, as always, was precocious in matters dealing with automobiles. To be sure, certain states had created state highway departments, but the most effective were mainly located in areas of high income and, therefore, of high per-capita auto ownership: the Northeast, the Middle West, and California. Elsewhere, in the sparsely populated interior West and in the South, there was neither the money nor the will to build long-distance roads at public expense. But in 1912, for the first time, Congress appropriated money for national highways. The appropriation was small, $500,000 to improve rural postal routes. It was a minuscule sum compared with the Babylonian treasures that would be spent on roads during the decades that followed—but it was a beginning. In 1916 and 1921, the first comprehensive federal highway acts were passed, offering matching grants for road-building to states that would establish highway departments.[16] These laws established the precedent of leaving highway building ostensibly in the hands of the states, while using the enticement of federal money to persuade states to build roads according to national standards.

Other landmark events followed quickly. In 1927, a system of national road numbering was put into effect, aiming to systematize the growing chaos of the growing road network. It was also designed to discourage the colorful but bewildering practice of naming long-distance roads. The black-and-white federal shields were highly visible symbols that a road system of continental scale was under construction—that these would not be merely local roads hitched together with tar, willpower, and a scattering of ad hoc directional signs, but were now truly national highways.

Transcontinental highways were assigned numbers divisible by ten; north-south highways from border to border were given numbers divisible by ten-plus-one.[17] US 10 from Seattle to Detroit was not quite transcontinental, nor was US 90 from Jacksonville to El Paso, but most of the others were—from US 20 in the north (Boston to Newport, Oregon) to US 80 in the south (Savannah to San Diego). The most famous transcontinental roads were absorbed by the new system and given the new egalitarian numbers. Thus, US 30 from Atlantic City to Astoria, Oregon, approximated the alignment of the Lincoln Highway over much of its length. And the National Road, resurrected from ignominious demise a century before, became the eastern half of the new transcontinental US 40. But unlike its ancestor, abandoned before

**San Joaquin billboard**
(1977)

This famous billboard was photographed by Dorotha Lange in the San Joaquin Valley of California in 1937.

it was finished, this reincarnation of the National Road truly ran from coast to coast, from Atlantic City to San Francisco. And in short order, it could be and would be used by long-distance drivers. By 1940, US 40, along with half a dozen other transcontinental highways, was paved from coast to coast.

To a prescient observer, it was rapidly becoming evident that the automobile was about to shoulder aside the railroad as the dominant mode of transportation. It was also becoming obvious that Americans greatly preferred cars over railroads—and, indeed, that the automobile had merely stimulated the fundamental appetite of Americans for mobility. The advantages of cars were obvious. One could go wherever there was a paved road—and, by the eve of World War II, that was almost anywhere in the populated parts of the United States. One could travel in privacy, without scrutiny from fellow passengers in a day coach or Pullman car. One could, in the course of time, back one's car up to the door of a motor-court or motel and unload one's baggage directly into the room without tipping an insolent bellboy, or running the gauntlet of loafers who commonly frequented small-town hotel lobbies—an experience that was especially har-

PEIRCE LEWIS

rowing for women traveling alone.[18] There was no need to wait on windswept platforms to change trains, no need to adhere to seemingly arbitrary timetables. Automobiles, it seemed, came very close to fulfilling the age-old American dream of perfect geographic mobility. Sociologists and others were increasingly writing about "the American love affair with the automobile," and advertisers sang praises to that romance.

But the American road system was choking on its own success. As early as the 1920s, drivers in urbanized parts of the East were lamenting chronic traffic jams in cities and towns, and intercity drivers were complaining about the growing clutter of roadside commerce and intersecting roads that was converting intercity driving into an exasperating and increasingly dangerous enterprise. The advantage of the automobile, supposedly, was the ability to go wherever one wanted, whenever, and at high speed—but that was becoming more and more difficult, especially if one contemplated a long-distance trip. And as automobiles became more reliable and comfortable, long-distance trips were very much on the minds of many Americans. For increasing numbers of motorists, it was outrageously frustrating to pay large sums to possess an automobile that would theoretically go 60 or 70 miles an hour, but realistically was confined to much less, and often stood motionless in traffic jams. It was the equivalent of acquiring a long-awaited gift and then being denied the use of it.

There was a solution, of course: to limit by law the number of access points to trunk highways and to forbid building along the roadside. To many, however, such a solution seemed un-American: free access to public roads, after all, seemed the key to mobility, the very key to being American. To limit that access seemed dictatorial. Indeed, the world's best example of a limited-access highway system was in Germany, where Hitler had built his system of *autobahnen* so that his Nazi armies could move quickly from one theater of war to another. But the main objection was less political philosophy than staggering cost. There was no way to convert existing free-access roads into limited-access roads without violating the property rights of those who fronted on the road—or, alternatively, to buy them out at a price so high that no one could imagine paying it. Clearly, if access to arterial roads was to be limited, it was much better to build a road from scratch—or, even better, an entire new road system. In Germany, with an all-powerful dictator, that might be possible. But not in America. It was very frustrating to be denied something that was so obviously desirable and so keenly desired.

The Pennsylvania Turnpike postcard (c. 1940)

Aerial view of the Pennsylvania Turnpike, America's "Dream Highway." This postcard, c. 1940, was one of many, depicting the joys of driving America's first long-distance limited-access highway. Cutting and filling on an heroic scale have produced a smoothly flowing artery, which contrasts invidiously with the narrow congested country roads that the Turnpike crosses and effectively ignores. Note the delicious absence of traffic.

Several events conspired to change America's collective mind on the subject of limited-access highways. The first was the example of the Pennsylvania Turnpike—a quite accidental product of seemingly unrelated things. During the 1930s, the creators of the New Deal discovered that building roads was a popular and effective way to put jobless men to work producing useful things. As a part of a massive program of public works, and under personal prodding from President Roosevelt himself, Pennsylvania's government was helped to acquire the roadbed of the long-abandoned South Pennsylvania Railroad (begun 1883, abandoned 1885), for purposes of building a four-lane divided toll road from the vicinity of Harrisburg to a point near Pittsburgh. Workers from the WPA (Works Progress Administration) would do most of the work. The project received high priority on grounds that the route cut squarely across the Appalachians, that ancient barrier to movement between the Middle West and the Atlantic seaboard. With some of the tunnels already built, and a low-gradient railbed already surveyed and partly finished, the Pennsylvania Turnpike was a relatively inexpensive project and was finished quickly, opening under a glare of national publicity in 1940. The public reaction was ecstatic. On opening day, motorists came from great distances for the chance to experience this marvel of engineering, one of the few instances in history where a road served not merely as a route for tourists but itself became a tourist attraction. The turnpike was immediately dubbed "America's Dream Highway," and it was. Not only was it America's first long-distance limited-access highway, it proved that Americans were more than willing to pay for the pleasure and convenience of driving long distances in safety and comfort—and, as drivers noted joyfully, legally at very high speed.[19]

Across the continent in Southern California, another epochal highway was also finished in 1940. The road was called the Arroyo Seco Parkway, a four-lane limited-access highway routed along a desiccated river course (*arroyo seco* means "dry gulch" in Spanish) to connect downtown Los Angeles with downtown Pasadena. On city streets in rush-hour traffic, the trip might take an hour or more. On the parkway, the eight-mile trip could be driven safely in eight minutes, or even less if safety was not a priority. Although the Arroyo Seco Parkway (later renamed the Pasadena Freeway) was much shorter and less sensational than the Pennsylvania Turnpike, it was epochal because it was funded not by tolls but out of general tax revenues. It was a "free way"—and Californians made it clear in election after election that

PEIRCE LEWIS

they were eager to spend public money if they could get more roads like this splendid highway to Pasadena. Tolls would be unnecessary. Roads, nearly everyone agreed, were a public good, and the public in concert should pay for them.

The third event occurred at the New York World's Fair of 1939–40. Coinciding with the outbreak of war in Europe, it was unfortunate timing for a world's fair, but Americans came nonetheless. Overwhelmingly the most popular exhibition at the fair was the General Motors Corporation's "Futurama," a scale-model that showed the public what the "city of tomorrow" might look like if it were properly built and money was no object. General Motors' notion of an ideal future, it turned out, was richly equipped with multilaned limited-access roads, on which tiny model cars spun and looped unimpeded through a gleaming white city without traffic jams and undimmed by human tears. The Futurama was rather like a large and elegant model train set left by Santa Claus under the Christmas tree—but equipped with highways and cars, not rails and trains. Throngs of American tourists beheld its wonders and came away enchanted with the General Motors vision of America's future.

Most large-scale highway projects were put on hold during the war and they stayed that way for several years thereafter, while the country converted back to peacetime life. But it was immediately obvious that something drastic would be needed to fix the nation's transportation system. Passenger and freight trains were still running at full capacity, but even so, the roads were impossible—badly deteriorated during the war, and now clogged with traffic. By 1948, the automobile industry was back in business making automobiles, and Americans, free from war and depression, were enjoying the most exuberant economic boom in living memory. With new money jingling in their pockets and a grateful government helping veterans to build and buy new houses, Americans bought cars in unprecedented numbers and promptly went driving—only to be trapped in traffic. It was very frustrating. The nation's highway system obviously had to be fixed, and Americans made it clear that they were impatient with waiting.

Pressures to improve the national highway system came from another direction as well. In the five years after World War II, the Cold War had grown steadily more frigid. When, in 1948, the Soviet Union exploded its first atomic bomb, it dawned on many Americans that the United States was militarily vulnerable as never before in its history. In previous time, two huge oceans had protected America from attack or invasion. Now, it seemed, an overseas enemy could visit atomic destruction on any place in America. One did not need to be a military analyst to realize that nuclear bombs falling on half a dozen major railyards could paralyze the entire country. So it was that the military joined with the chorus of frustrated civilians, demanding not just an improvement of the existing highway system, but a brand-new alternative network, *in addition to* the existing road system—essentially laid on top of it.

## INTERSTATE HIGHWAYS AND THE LAW
## OF UNINTENDED CONSEQUENCES

So it was, after a long season of intensive lobbying from all quarters of the country, Congress passed the Federal Aid Highway Act of 1956, establishing what was called the National System of Interstate and Defense Highways.[20] Over the full span of American history, one is hard-put to find a single legislative act that so profoundly altered the face of the American landscape, did it so quickly, and yielded so many unexpected and unintended results. In effect, the interstates were as revolutionary as the railroad had been when it arrived on the scene a century before. To be sure, the interstates used the same technology as free-access highways had done. Automobiles were still automobiles, and the techniques of paving roads and building bridges remained much as they had in previous time. But in several basic ways the interstate system of limited-access highways differed so radically from the existing network of free-access roads, and their effect was so profoundly different, that they must be seen as a brand-new *kind* of transportation.

In its details, the act was very complicated, but in broad outline it accomplished several basic things that had never been done before. It was, to begin with, a nationally planned *system* of limited-access roads. The scale of the project was prodigious: before it was finished, the United States would build 42,500 miles of interstate highways. Awed reporters vied with one another to discover new superlatives to describe the proposed system: the volume of concrete to be laid would be *X* times the volume of the Great Pyramids; more bridges would be built than in all of the Roman empire; it was the largest public works project in the history of the world, and so on. It was very heady stuff.

Furthermore, there would be no time lost in building the system. To avoid unseemly delays due to lack of money, Congress devised an ingenious

**The Interstate Highway System**

The Interstate Highway System was authorized by act of Congress in 1956. The system's 41,700-mile grid was designed to make all of America equally accessible to all other parts.

scheme whereby a special tax was imposed on motor fuels, tires, and certain kinds of heavy vehicles—and the money from those taxes was automatically funneled into a Federal Highway Trust Fund, to be used *exclusively* for building interstate highways.[21] The trust fund soon bulged with money, and even in lean times it continued to grow. Then, to preserve the fiction (invented in 1916) that states were in control of their highway budgets, for every dollar spent for interstates within a given state the trust fund would pay ninety cents; the state would pay only ten. For the states and their highway departments it was a bonanza—as it was for legions of contractors, engineers, surveyors, and lobbyists for innumerable industries that supplied the awesome volume of sand and cement and reinforcing steel needed to build thousands of miles of high-quality highways, not to mention a host of lesser things such as grass seed, workers' hardhats, and reflecting prisms for highway signs. The list of interested parties seemed to have no end, all unified in support of building the new interstate highways as quickly as possible.

Aside from a few querulous designers and injured property-owners along the right-of-ways, no one of consequence opposed this Babylonian project.[22] No one of consequence suggested that a project of this size would inevitably produce unforeseen byproducts that the nation might live to regret—and that it might be reasonable to go slowly and try to discover what those byproducts might be.

One of the byproducts became visible almost immediately. All over the country, interstates were built to federal standards: the trust fund arrangement made sure of that. Those standards were generous from the beginning, so that interstates were built *big*, and they were designed to endure very heavy loads of civilian trucks and military ordnance. Because part of their job was to haul troops and weapons in case of war, they were also built to move traffic in a hurry. Traffic lanes were a standard twelve feet wide; bridges had a minimum clearance of fourteen feet, and were designed to carry very heavy loads. Gradients were kept very low, and radii of curvature were designed to permit constant speeds far in excess of many states' speed limits. The main beneficiary of these standards was not the military for whose guns and tanks the heavy-weight standards were supposed to accommodate, but the exploding civilian trucking industry. Now, for the first time, a trucker could drive from coast to coast, confident in the knowledge that there would be no more unpleasant surprises in the form of bridges with low clearance or inadequate weight limits. Very quickly, trucks began to appear with standard-size length, height, and weight, and much larger than they had ever been before. The railroad companies protested (with some justice) that the trucking industry was getting a free subsidy, since, unlike a railroad company, it had no obligation to maintain the roadbed it used. The truckers replied that they paid for the road in higher taxes, but no one really believed it—least of all the railroads, whose freight revenues declined at precisely the same time that their passenger traffic was rapidly disappearing.

By the mid-1960s, the American railroad system was plainly coming apart. Despite panicked financial maneuvers and last-ditch mergers, railroad company after railroad company went bankrupt—the most spectacular being the bankruptcy of the Penn Central, itself a desperate merger of the once-mighty New York Central and Pennsylvania Railroads. Investigators charged the railroads' officers with corporate sabotage and accused them of looting the railroads' assets during their final days, and that is probably true. It is also possible that the U.S. railroad system would have collapsed anyway in head-to-head competition with cars and trucks. But there is no doubt of the effect that the interstate highway system would have upon the nation's railroad system—it was akin to giving poison to a elderly person with a terminal disease.[23]

A second unintended effect of the interstate system resulted from the geographic pattern of the new roads. The system's military purpose was to enable the rapid deployment of troops and ordnance in a nuclear war, and it made sense that the freeway system should make all parts of the country more or less equally accessible—irrespective of population density. That made political sense, too, since even states with the sparsest population have two senators, whose support the highway builders devoutly wished to earn and keep. The national system, therefore, was laid out in a crude grid—with east-west roads given even numbers while north-south were odd. The main roads north-south had numbers ending in five, while the east-west arterials (as in the old system) were divisible by ten.[24]

Theoretically, in a nuclear war cities would be primary targets. Given that assumption, it made sense for the interstates to give big cities a wide berth, certainly not to go through them. Financially, that policy made sense, too, since the cutting of interstate-scale swathes of land through urban areas was inevitably very expensive and often provoked fierce opposition from people whose homes and neighborhoods the new roads would inevitably destroy. But it was immediately obvious that this new system was not *really* a "defense" highway system, but in fact a network to serve the wants of private citizens and private firms, especially those affiliated with trucking.[25] When all the debate and horsetrading was over, most of the main interstates were built alongside existing arterial highways and essentially duplicated them. The reason was obvious and straightforward: the old highways connected cities; the interstates were designed to do the same thing. Cities, after all, were where the people were—and people voted. Hell had no fury like a big city spurned by the freeway planners, and consequently none were.

Building intercity roads in rural territory turned out to be relatively easy, and long rural stretches were finished almost immediately. The old National Road, which had become US 40 between Baltimore and St. Louis, now became I-70, parallel to old 40, and, in parts of Ohio and Indiana, literally on top of it.[26] Getting through big cities was something else again. A common tactic was to build a circumferential loop to bypass the city itself—and then attach the intercity roads to the loop. Subsequently, spur roads were hacked into and often through the vitals of the city, often at great cost—whether measured in money or in damage to low-income neighborhoods where inner-city freeways were usually built. (Planners avoided laying roads through affluent areas to avoid political heat.) The best known of these bypass loops were the Washington Beltway (numbered I-295 and I-495) and the Boston bypass (for a long time called Massachusetts Route 128 and more recently renumbered I-95).

Long before the new system of highways was finished, it was obvious that the combination of democratic roads and democratic automobiles would make major changes in the ways that Americans lived. To most Americans, the apparent changes were very welcome—increased mobility, increased freedom, increased access to a wide variety of goods, services, and people. What went unnoticed (except by a few prescient folk) was that the automobile was the deadly enemy of America's nineteenth-century system of towns and cities. The overwhelming majority of those urban places had grown up with the railroads, and the railroads had determined their shape—collecting and concentrating their vital forces as close as possible to the railroad station: the necessary entry to all nineteenth-century cities and towns. Roads and cars did just the opposite.

The wise old diplomat George Kennan, looking back from the vantage of a long life, recalls a lecture in the 1920s when he was an undergraduate at Princeton. The foresighted lecturer advanced an argument that is now obvious, but then was not:

> The railway and the automobile exerted diametrically opposite and conflicting disciplines on the development of the urban community—and . . . to the extent that one form of transportation was allowed to exclude or replace the other, was bound to have profound effects on American life.
>
> The railway . . . was capable of accepting and disgorging its loads, whether of passengers or freight, only at fixed points. This being the case, it tended to gather together, and to concentrate around its urban terminus and railhead, all activity that was in any way related to movements of freight or passengers into or out of the city. It was in this quality that it had made major and in some ways decisive contributions to the development . . . of the great railway metropolises of the Victorian age. . . .
>
> The automobile, on the other hand, had precisely the opposite qualities. Incapable, in view of its own cumbersomeness and requirements for space, of accepting or releasing large loads at many concentrated points anywhere, but peculiarly capable of accepting and releasing them at multitudes of unconcentrated points anywhere else, the automobile tended to disintegrate and explode all that the railroad had brought together. It was, in fact, the enemy of the concentrated city. Thus it was destined to destroy the great densely populated urban centers of the nineteenth century, with all the glories of economic and cultural life that had flowed from their very unity and compactness.[27]

In the 1920s, such forebodings might reasonably be dismissed as alarmism; after all, the road system was still primitive, the automobile still in its awkward adolescence, and the railroad system was still operating under full steam. By 1970, far too late to do anything about it, the predictions had come true, as Americans used their new cars and their efficient new road system to disperse themselves in an urban pattern that had never before been known. Residential building exploded first into suburbs and then far beyond the suburbs, into the heretofore rural countryside until the boundaries between urban and rural space were so blurred as to be invisible in most places. In city after city across America, great glittering downtown department stores shut their doors and, along with most other commercial businesses, moved en masse to shopping centers, located conveniently near freeway interchanges. Manufacturing did the same thing, moving from congested inner-city locations to low sprawling horizontal buildings with huge parking lots, whose only locational mandate was proximity to a freeway interchange providing access to labor, markets, and raw materials at the same time.

American cities, quite clearly, were coming apart, and so were thousands of small towns all across the country. Railroads had created and nourished most of those towns, which had prospered for two basic reasons: a dense concentration of farmers and a very bad road system that made it very difficult for those farmers to travel long distances. As late as the 1950s, main streets were crowded with farmers' Model-Ts, and sidewalks were crowded with town residents who came to buy their groceries or engage in daily business. By the 1990s, shop windows were boarded up and the sidewalks empty.

America's new Main Street, it turned out, was the limited-access highway. That was especially conspicuous around the fringes of big cities where the interstate loops had been built to bypass the cities but were rapidly attracting all the urban functions that once had been concentrated so tightly around nineteenth-century railroad stations. In combination a wholly new urban form was emerging, a "galactic city" that performed the same economic functions that the old nucleated city had done, but now adapted to the automobile and the road, not to trains and railroad stations. Now commercial, residential, and industrial functions floated in geographic space "like stars and planets in a galaxy, held together by mutual gravitational attraction, but with large empty spaces between them."[28]

Many thoughtful Americans were dismayed at what was happening to

**Main Street, Saturday morning, Gallipolis, Ohio, November 1956**

This photograph was taken the year Congress passed the legislation that enabled the Interstate Highway System. Within a few years, downtown Gallipolis would be a shell of its former self.

PEIRCE LEWIS

the nation's cities. George Kennan was among them—a person whose youth was illuminated by the glories of Victorian railroad cities both in Europe and America—and to whom the galactic city was no city at all, but an amorphous growth that neither looked nor behaved like a proper city. Kennan correctly names the automobile as the proximate cause of the new geographic arrangement, and he indicts the nation at large for letting it become the driving force behind America's daily affairs:

> The automobile . . . has turned out to be, by virtue of its innate and inalterable qualities, the enemy of community generally. Wherever it advances, neighborliness and the sense of community are impaired.
>
> One might have thought that this alone, much of what was surely becoming evident in the 1920s and 1930s, would have sufficed to cause Americans of that day to pause and to ask themselves whether they really wished to junk 99 percent of the great railway system that then existed and to confer upon the automobile and the truck the sort of near monopoly on transportation which . . . they have now achieved.

Kennan then draws a bill of indictment against the automobile, charging that the automobile destroys community and promotes antisocial behavior; that it is wasteful, polluting, and unhealthy; that it encourages forms of criminal activity that are very hard to contain; and that it isolates all those who cannot drive—"the very young, the very old, the sick, the poor, and the handicapped."[29] Kennan, of course, is not alone in his opinions. A good many Americans have come to believe that America's marriage to the automobile is a devil's contract.[30]

## THE NATIONAL ROAD AND THE ROMANCE WITH MOBILITY

Even the briefest history of transportation in America makes it obvious that the nation's romance with the automobile is more than a fixation with a particular mode of transportation. It is a fixation with mobility itself—the passport to freedom that most Americans would be very reluctant to surrender. Even if Americans in 1900 had possessed full knowledge of what the automobile would do to the American landscape before the century had ended, would they have chosen another course? We cannot know, of course, but one can be pardoned for doubting it. Never in American history have Americans abated their enthusiasm for seeking the fastest, cheapest, most comfortable mode of transportation that current technology made available. Never have they shown the slightest reluctance to cast aside older forms of transportation and the technological trappings that went along with them.

The National Road in its several incarnations stands as a tangible monument to that passion for mobility. As originally conceived, it represented a desperate effort by the federal government to forge a link between East and the frontier West, at a time when there seemed no other way to do it. But the very idea that the United States would have *a* single national road speaks volumes about the roads of the time. Paradoxically, it was obsolete because roads themselves were obsolete in a century that would be dominated first by canals and then by railroads. It was premature because it could not do what it was intended to do until the democratic automobile arrived on the scene a century later. By the end of the nineteenth century, dominated in turn by canals and railroads, the National Road had become one of innumerable displays in America's ever-expanding outdoor museum of discarded geographic artifacts. When the Road was reincarnated in the 1920s and assigned the democratic number US 40, it signaled the arrival of a truly national highway system for the first time. US 40 was a transcontinental highway, but only one of half a dozen others—*a* national road, but not *the* National Road.

Like so many other things in America's national landscape, the National Road, alias US 40, alias I-70, may be less interesting because it is unique than because it is typical. Today, the latest incarnation of the National Road is very much like a thousand other democratically numbered roads in America, unglamorously doing the job it was designed to do, but also producing quite unexpected byproducts, quite unintended landscapes.

But that is what transportation systems have always done in America. And until Americans abandon their belief in a God-given right to perfect mobility, that is what they will continue to do.

# The Face of the Country

KARL RAITZ

*Good roads have an influence over physical impossibilities. By diminishing the natural impediments, they bring places and their inhabitants nearer to each other.*

A. J. DALLAS
*Cumberland Road* (1816)

THE TREATY OF PARIS BROUGHT THE AMERICAN REVOLUTION TO AN official end in September 1783. And, as if the creation of a new nation of independent states was not sufficiently impressive, the treaty also doubled the United States' territory by declaring jurisdiction over the vast lands that extended west from the Appalachian Mountains to the Mississippi River. Rivers were the transport corridors of choice for moving things in volume, whether people and their belongings, or the commodities they produced. Therefore, the perspective of eastern mercantile interests and politicians was potamic, and one of their principal concerns was access to what they called the "western rivers." The Ohio River was the main trunk stream that drained this western country.

Tributaries from the south—the Kanawha, Sandy, Licking, and Kentucky—drained Virginia and the soon-to-be state of Kentucky. On the

Ohio's north side lay the Northwest Territory, still largely unsettled and, with the exception of a tract not yet ceded by Connecticut, held by the federal government. The Territory drained south into the Ohio via the Muskingum, Scioto, the Little and Great Miami Rivers; the Whitewater, the Big Blue, the White, the Eel, and the Wabash; the Embarras, and the Little Wabash. Beyond the Little Wabash in the Illinois country lay a drainage divide and beyond that the Kaskaskia flowed southwest into the Mississippi. And each major stream had several tributaries.

Thomas Hutchins, Geographer of the United States, estimated that this well-watered Northwest Territory contained some 220 million acres belonging to the government which could be sold to discharge the national debt.[1] And it was known as an immensely rich country. In 1796, Constantin Volney saw maize that was fourteen feet high growing on the Scioto River flood plain in Ohio. He concluded that the region's fertility was such that it would "be favourable to commerce and agriculture, and popular opinion has already manifested a preference for this district over Kentucky. It will, doubtless, prove hereafter the Flanders of America, and bear away the prize equally for pasture and tillage." To the west, the land's potential did not diminish. Volney found that "the forest ends just before you reach the Wabash, and from thence to the Mississippi . . . all is prairie or meadow. Here commences the American Tartary, bearing, in all respects, a strong resemblance to the Asiatic."[2]

But the Northwest Territory had one great disadvantage, at least as viewed through the eyes of Philadelphia and Baltimore merchants and their bankers; it was remote, accessible only by way of primitive trails across the rugged country of central and western Pennsylvania and Maryland. Politicians called for the construction of overland routes that would link the "navigable waters emptying into the Atlantic to the Ohio, to the said state and through the same."[3] Unfortunately, the Ohio flowed south and west, carrying regional commodities away from East Coast cities toward New Orleans via the Mississippi. Arguing this point in a report to Congress in 1808, Treasury Secretary Albert Gallatin pointed out that as early as 1793 a schooner had been built on the Monongahela River between Brownsville and Pittsburgh, loaded with local cargo, and successfully navigated to New Orleans via the Ohio and Mississippi, finally reaching Philadelphia. Subsequently, "numerous vessels, one hundred to three hundred and fifty tons burden, are now annually built at several shipyards on the Ohio . . . and bringing down to New Orleans the produce of the upper country."[4] To reduce the cost of overland transportation so as to redirect the flow of commodities directly to eastern ports and to "shorten distances, facilitate commercial and personal intercourse, and unite . . . the most remote quarters of the United States," Gallatin, supported by Henry Clay, Thomas Jefferson, and others, proposed a broad program of canal and road construction of which the National Road would be a key part.

In 1803, Pres. Thomas Jefferson's successful purchase of the Louisiana Territory from the French added urgency to the National Road project, for if the road were extended generally west from its Ohio crossing at Wheeling it would lead to St. Louis, the capital of Upper Louisiana. As Jefferson suggested in 1808, the road would "accomplish a continued and advantageous line of communication from the seat of General Government to St. Louis."[5] During the next decade, as steamboats began to carry Louisiana sugar and cotton to Pittsburgh against the Mississippi and Ohio current, the East Coast merchants' concern that they would be entirely cut out of trade with the Northwest Territory neared panic levels. In 1816, Treasury Secretary A. J. Dallas again reported to the president on road construction and argued that "with the great advantages of steam navigation, unless the roads across the mountains be much improved, the merchants of the western country will cease to purchase goods from the importers at New York, Philadelphia, Baltimore, &c., and New Orleans will soon become the sole emporium of their trade."[6]

The route the National Road would follow was chosen for geographical expediency but in topographic ignorance. The government's transportation concerns were generally stated in terms of linking the eastern rivers with the Ohio, meaning that the road could have originated in any of several port cities on the eastern seaboard, from Philadelphia south to Richmond. The route chosen would begin in Cumberland and link back, by way of older toll roads, to Baltimore. One had but to look at a rudimentary map of the day to understand why—the Baltimore harbor was closer to the Ohio River in direct overland distance than was Philadelphia or Richmond. But Congress also wished to ensure that the states through which the road would pass would have both sufficient wealth to supplement construction and maintenance costs and a productive hinterland that would generate a flow of commodities eastward. A route along the James River west from Richmond would have to engage the rugged and inaccessible Appalachian lands that lay beyond the Shenandoah Valley, a country that was thought to have limited mercantile potential.

The National Road alignment, then, would not be dictated by the position of major river valleys, the usual routes along which eastern city merchants had extended their trading, but would be forced more or less directly across the dividing uplands that lay between the Atlantic coast and the Ohio River Valley. The road would be an acknowledgment that politicians, not engineers, had chosen the route as an expediency to reduce travel costs and to direct western commodities into eastern port cities.

To approximate a direct route, the road would have to cross some of the most rugged terrain in the east. From New England south to Savannah, there was no "natural route" into the interior equivalent to the St. Lawrence–Great Lakes waterways, or the Mississippi, which drained directly south to New Orleans. Instead the Hudson, Delaware, and Susquehanna Rivers flowed north to south and only a western Susquehanna tributary, the Juniata, approached the Allegheny crest that roughly marked the drainage divide between the "eastern and western waters." Furthermore, the Susquehanna was a shallow stream with dangerous rapids near its junction with the Chesapeake Bay. The Middle Atlantic region's other major river, the Potomac, led southwest into steep-sided mountain valleys.

Unable to follow easy river-valley grades, the men commissioned by President Jefferson to select a routeway encountered a country whose general character was known but whose local topographic variation was only poorly understood. In their initial report to Jefferson, the men complained that "at a very early period it was conceived that the maps of the country were not sufficiently accurate to afford a minute knowledge of the true courses between the extreme points on the rivers." Further, the commissioners reported:

> The face of the country within the limits prescribed is generally very uneven, and in many places broken by a succession of high mountains and deep hollows, too formidable to be reduced within five degrees of the horizon, but by crossing them obliquely, a mode which, although it imposes a heavy task of hill-side digging, obviates generally the necessity of reducing hills and filling hollows, which, on these grounds, would be an attempt truly Quixotic. This inequality of the surface is not confined to the Allegany mountain; the country between the Monongahela and the Ohio rivers, although less elevated, is not better adapted for the bed of the road,

being filled with impediments of hills and hollows which present considerable difficulties, and wants that superabundance and convenience of stone, which is found in the mountain.[7]

Surveyors would have to route the road across a series of northeast-southwest trending mountain ranges. To comply with a requirement that the road not exceed a 5 percent gradient the preferred alignment would be a minimum energy route following creek valleys when possible, and gentle grades around hills and ridges instead of a more taxing route requiring cuts and fills.

About fifteen miles west and 2,000 feet above Cumberland stands Savage Mountain at the Allegheny Plateau crest. To gain that height, National Road surveyors had to make the best of any gradient advantages. Therefore, in the ridged country of western Maryland and Pennsylvania small creeks assumed an importance out of proportion to their flow volume because they had excavated low gradient valleys along the direction surveyors wished to go. One of these was Braddock Run, named for British general Edward Braddock who led an expeditionary force against the French Fort Duquesne at the Allegheny and Monongahela River confluence in 1755. Cumberland stands on the east side of The Narrows, a water gap cut through Wills Mountain by the combined flow of Wills Creek, Jennings Creek, and Braddock Run. The first National Road passed over Wills Mountain, just south of The Narrows, to reach Braddock Run, which provided a low-angle grade west toward Frostburg. Teamsters found Wills Mountain's grade too steep and engineers relocated the road through The Narrows and around the mountain to Braddock Run in 1834. Although Cumberland sat on the Potomac's north bank, no advantage lay with following this larger stream for its headwaters led off into rugged mountains to the southwest, well away from the Ohio River Valley.

## CONTENTIOUS TOPOGRAPHY

Access by sailing ships to East Coast cities, especially those from the Hudson River harbor south, was relatively simple. Arriving at Philadelphia or Baltimore, ships would not have to thread their way through shallow river delta channels as they would to land at New Orleans, but could proceed on deep water inland by way of broad drowned estuaries to sheltered harbors. During the Pleistocene glacial period when great continental ice sheets incorporated vast quantities of the earth's water, sea levels dropped and eastern rivers responded to the increased gradient by deepening and broadening their channels. Rivers easily eroded the soft sandstone bedrock along the coast, but downcutting into the more resistant metamorphic rocks further inland was a much slower process. As the glacial ice packs melted, thereby restoring sea level, the broadened river channels cut into the coastal rocks were flooded, creating the Delaware and Chesapeake Bays.

The soft rock zone parallel to the coastline corresponds to the Coastal Plain region, whose major topographic features are the low swells of old beach lines. The north-to-south band of more resistant rocks further inland underlie the Piedmont. The Fall Line marks the joint between Piedmont and Coastal Plain. Here streams tumble across rapids or falls. Settlements grew up at each point where a major stream crossed the Fall Line. Baltimore stands where several streams, the Patapsco, Gwynns Falls, and Jones Falls among them, drop off the Piedmont onto the Coastal Plain for a short reach before flowing into Patapsco Sound, one of Chesapeake Bay's large western arms.[8]

Early nineteenth-century wagon travelers on the Frederick Turnpike west of Baltimore—an early road that would later connect the National Road at Cumberland with Baltimore—crossed the rolling Piedmont by following the divide between the Patapsco River's south branch and the Patuxent River. Road construction here was not difficult. But ahead lay a disturbingly complex sequence of mountains and valleys that would frustrate road builders and tax teams and teamsters for decades. The Blue Ridge formed the first barrier. Fortunately, the ridge is relatively low where the pike crosses it west of Frederick. It divides into two arms of resistant metamorphic quartzites, Catoctin Mountain on the east, South Mountain on the west. Each mountain crests over 1,500 feet, but the pike was routed through lower gaps.

Beyond and 1,000 feet below South Mountain lies the Great Valley, which is thirty miles wide at this point. While not level, its gradients are so low along its 1,000-mile length—from the St. Lawrence Valley in Quebec to Al-

Geologic Cross-section—Coastal Plain to Savage Mountain

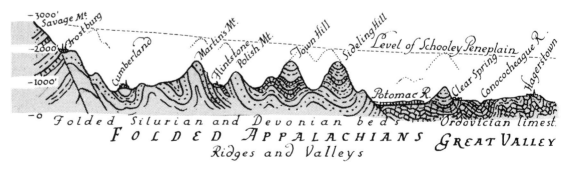

KARL RAITZ

abama—that it has long been a major north-south transport corridor. Against the valley's west side stands a vast suite of strongly folded sedimentary rocks collectively called the Ridge and Valley, which presented road builders with the most complex surface they would have to cross to reach the Ohio Valley. Ancient continental collision accounts for the deformation that folded the 40,000-foot-thick stack of Paleozoic dolomites, limestones, shales, sandstones, and conglomerate into a Cyclopean washboard of steeply pitching anticlines and synclines. Subsequently, streams cut the soft shales and limestones into valleys, and the more resistant sandstones and conglomerate emerged as flanking ridges.

The Great Valley is floored with limestones that spelled prosperity for farmers and road builders. These particular Ordovician-age limestones degrade into superb soils. When quarried and broken into four-ounce cubes by the turnpikers' round-headed hammers, the limestones made a resilient, long-lasting road-surfacing material. The valley pike surface was said to permit nineteenth-century coaches to negotiate the twenty-six miles from Frederick to Hagerstown in two hours, an average of three miles per hour faster than possible on other road sections.[9] Road quality held into the twentieth century when geographer J. Russell Smith observed that the valley had "several times as much good stone road as equally rich districts occupied by the same kind of people in the Piedmont but a few miles away."[10]

From the South Mountain crossing point, the old pike angled northwest toward Hagerstown, which stands near the valley's center on a low divide between Antietam and Conococheague Creeks. A few miles south, the creeks join the Potomac. Beyond the Great Valley, northeast-southwest trending ridges stand transverse to the route. Road surveyors avoided several ridges by working upstream along the Potomac following water gaps cut by the river. But after some fifteen miles the river route turned from a direct westerly course toward the southwest in long meandering loops that

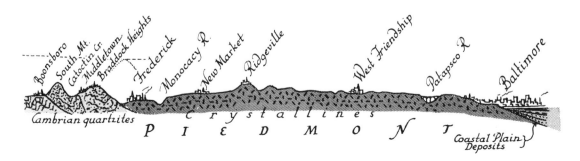

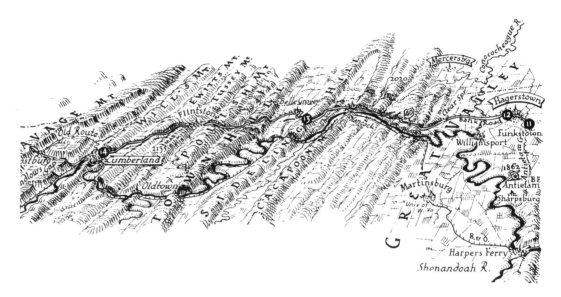

would later be followed by the Chesapeake & Ohio Canal and the Baltimore & Ohio Railroad to Cumberland. Congressional mandate required that the National Road follow the most direct route, and that lay straight west across ridges 1,000 feet high: Tonoloway Ridge, Sideling Hill, Town Hill, Green Hill, Polish Mountain, Warrior Mountain, Martin Mountain.

Finally, at Cumberland, surveyors encountered the splice between the Ridge and Valley and the Allegheny Plateau at the 2,400-foot Allegheny Front. The plateau is primarily underlain by Pennsylvanian-aged sedimentary rock, which dips gently to the west in low-amplitude synclines and anticlines. Compared to the Ridge and Valley, the plateau's sedimentary rocks seem to lie almost flat, although three broad anticlines provide rather spectacular elevation changes: Negro Mountain, Laurel Ridge, and Chestnut Ridge. All three exceed 2,700 feet at their highest points. The latter two incorporate resistant Mississippian-age sandstones.

Eastward-draining streams such as Braddock Run and Wills Creek cut into the front, giving it a beetle-browed appearance and low gradient routes past the crest. A few miles beyond the front, two Ohio River tributaries, the Youghiogheny and Monongahela Rivers, capture the plateau's drainage and carry it west. The plateau's relatively high elevation in relation to the low point of about 760 feet at Pittsburgh, where the Allegheny and Monongahela meet to form the Ohio, yields a steep gradient enabling the region's streams—especially the Youghiogheny—to saw the country into low but steep-sloped hills. This topography prompted road commissioners Elie

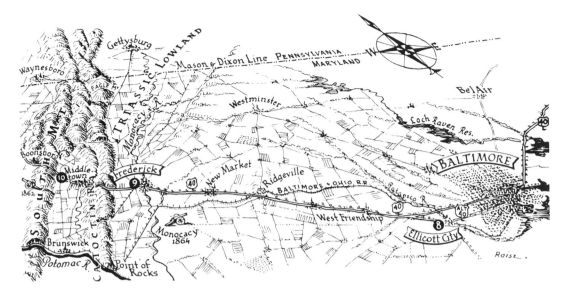

Williams and Thomas Moore to complain to Jefferson that, while survey-ing "through a country so irregularly broken, and crowded with very thick underwood in many places, the work has been found so incalculably te-dious, that without an adequate idea of the difficulty it is not easy to rec-oncile the delay."[11]

Bounteous bituminous coal beds underlay the Allegheny Plateau to the north in Pennsylvania and extended south and east into western Maryland. A few Maryland beds were thick and high quality and would spawn a local mining industry, but others were thin, spotty, and of relatively low value. West of Frostburg, Maryland, surveyors took the National Road northwest across the Youghiogheny defile and the three great anticlinal ridges toward Uniontown, Pennsylvania, where the road emerged onto the Pittsburgh coal seam, a huge, rich bituminous deposit that extended southwest toward West Virginia and Ohio. Beyond Uniontown surveyors routed the road along low ridges above the coal that would be converted into coke for Pitts-burgh-region iron furnaces.

Traffic to Pittsburgh had favored a route north from Brownsville, Penn-sylvania, along the Monongahela. But the Road was to run west through Washington, Pennsylvania, on a more-or-less direct route to the Ohio. Brownsville stood in the bottom of a steep-sided valley that required engi-neers to plunge the Road abruptly down the bank to reach a crossing point on the river. Beyond Brownsville, the first great objective, the Ohio River at Wheeling, lay across a few miles of choppy hills. An approach to the Ohio is

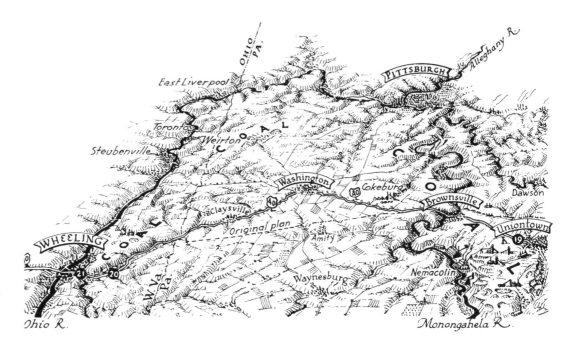

offered by the Wheeling River, which cuts a 500-foot-deep channel into the Ohio's east bluff, providing a relatively easy ramp into the valley, where stood Wheeling, the village at river's edge founded by Ebenezer Zane. The next objective was the Mississippi's east bank at St. Louis. To reach it involved moving off the Allegheny Plateau and onto a radically different surface that would further try the resourcefulness of engineers and construction crews.

Topography was not the only obstacle along the Road's eastern sections. Engineers found the summer vegetation so dense in the uplands that they had to postpone their exploration and surveying until the leaves fell in the autumn.[12] The woodland that still stood uncleared in 1808 was part of the great north Appalachian mixed forest that extended from the Fall Line west to central Ohio, and the Road law required that trees be cleared across a broad right-of-way, sixty-six feet along some sections, eighty feet along others. On the Piedmont, the white oak, hickory, and tulip-tree woodland was being cleared and the land developed into farms well before the pike construction period. The stony slopes astride Catoctin and South Mountains in western Maryland were not inviting to farmers and stood covered in a forest that included chestnuts, white and red oaks, hickories and ash. In Middle Town Valley, west of Frederick, Maryland, farmers had had to clear beech, hemlock, and tulip tree to make their fields. To the west, they largely cleared the Great Valley floor of its white, black, red, and scarlet oaks. The

KARL RAITZ

association of oak and chestnut woodland on the ridges, and beech and tulip tree in low, well-watered valleys, continued west across the Ridge and Valley. There timber cutters joined the quarrymen and digging crews building the roadbed.[13]

Beginning with an abrupt transition at the Allegheny Front, the plateau forest quickly graded into a richly diversified woodland with beech and basswood, sugar maple and buckeye, red and white oak, chestnut and hemlock as dominant species. This forest would greatly encumber road construction but would also provide building timbers and billets for charcoal burners.

## THE DECEPTION OF LEVEL LAND

Two happy topographic accidents made Wheeling a logical place to cross the Ohio. The twisting Wheeling River grade on the east side was the first. The second lay to the west across the Ohio, where Wheeling Creek cut down into the plateau to join the Ohio almost directly opposite the Wheeling River's mouth. Beyond the Ohio, the Allegheny Plateau continued west. To regain the plateau surface, surveyors staked the Road's route along Wheeling Creek, following an old Indian trail and the beginning of Zane's Trace, arriving back on the plateau surface near St. Clairsville, Ohio. From there the Road followed low ridges across the plateau to Zanesville along a line surveyed by Road commissioner Jonathan Knight. Between Wheeling

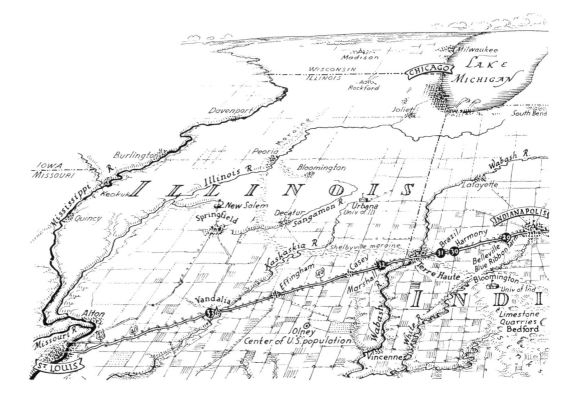

and Zanesville lay "hilly country," with "good materials . . . convenient and abundant for the mason work. . . . There is plenty of sandstone; but this . . . should only be used where limestone, or freestone of hard quality, cannot be procured at a reasonable expense."[14]

The hills grade into "level country" west of Zanesville, some of it with impassable swamps, and stone for macadamizing the road and building bridges and culverts was hard to find or nonexistent. To reduce costs, Knight recommended that stone not be hauled from distant quarries but that local gravels, which could be found in streambanks or in pockets below the clay soil, be used to surface the Road. The level country between Zanesville and Columbus would not, then, make for easy road construction. A shortage of building and surfacing materials would greatly increase costs. The route passed through dense forest that required clearing. The ground was flat and unexpectedly "wet," and frequent south-flowing streams had broad flood plains that would have to be bridged above flood level. Small streams on the plateau or Ridge and Valley could be bridged by relatively short spans using local stone. The "level country" streams had lower gradients and much broader flood plains, which would require longer bridges and considerable

KARL RAITZ

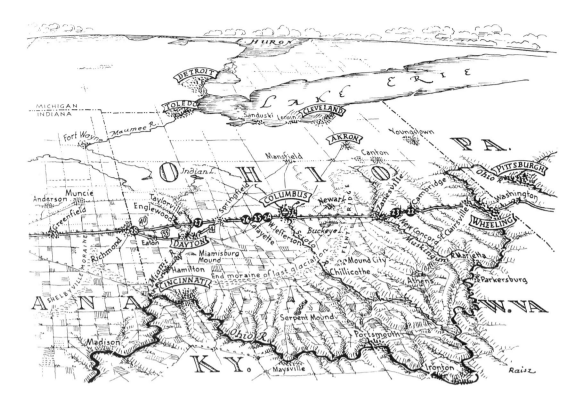

earth fill in some places to raise the road above flood level. And because building stone was so rare in the flat country between the streams east of Columbus, Knight suggested that the most economical bridges would have a wood superstructure and be "weatherboarded and roofed for preservation from decay."[15]

Engineers eventually moved stone by way of the Ohio Canal, which the Road crossed at Hebron, about halfway between Zanesville and Columbus, to those sections remote from bedrock ledges. The unfamiliar topographic circumstances prompted one construction engineer to complain to chief engineer Charles Gratiot in Washington about the "peculiar nature of the country through which the road passes."[16] Jonathan Knight did not record a name for this new level surface, but what he encountered when he moved off the Allegheny Plateau west of Zanesville was the glaciated Central Lowland.

During the Pleistocene period, the most recent million years or so of geologic history, several ice ages brought great glaciers south from Canada to inundate much of what would later become the Middle West. The two most recent glacial advances left behind landforms that would influence Road construction, and in a larger sense created a gently rolling surface that proved fertile and productive; eastern and immigrant farmers found it irresistible. The earlier ice sheet, called the Illinoian, crossed this country between 130,000 and 300,000 years ago and extended east to about the present-day boundary between Muskingum and Licking Counties in Ohio. Near the village of Gratiot, the Road passed from the Allegheny Plateau onto the Illinoian surface. Forty thousand years is sufficient time for streams to roughen this till plain—a mixture of sand and gravel, clay and silt, and assorted rocks carried in from distant ledges, some as far as central Canada—into scattered hills. A few miles further west, near Brownsville, the Road crosses a line of low hills, a terminal moraine, onto the 18,000-year-old Wisconsin-age glacial surface. The Road does not touch the Illinoian surface again until Putnam County, Indiana, east of Terre Haute, but remains on it from there almost all the way to the Mississippi River.[17] At that transition back onto the older Illinoian surface, Jonathan Knight had to cross ten to fifteen miles of hilly ground and find a route that would avoid knobs and ravines so that he could maintain the Road at a desired three-degree grade.[18]

Thick, slow-moving ice sheets essentially obliterate hills and fill in valleys on the surface they move across, and leave behind new landforms and a surface into which streams will gradually etch a new drainage network. The "level country" that Jonathan Knight surveyed was till laid down under the ice and exposed when the ice melted back. The hills he encountered were Wisconsin-age terminal or recessional moraines, great linear loops of clay, silt, sand, and gravel in huge heaps—some ten miles or more across—left standing where the ice had bulldozed them. The Road crosses a moraine east of Springfield, Ohio, another east of Richmond, Indiana. Bedrock was buried below yards of till or moraine and those few ledges quarrymen found were exposed primarily along stream bluffs. Sand and gravel, products of ice abrading local or distant bedrock, were sorted and deposited in pockets and lenses within the till by glacial meltwater steams. Gravel was rare in the Ridge and Valley or plateau, but was so common in the Central Lowlands that it could be used to surface the Road.

Across western Ohio and Indiana, road surveyors also found broad swamps and wet meadows, some miles across. Since glacial till buried existing drainage networks, the new streams that emerged from beneath the ice would require time to cut new channels linking low places. Marshes or "swamps" are common on new till plains. Road engineers tried to find routes around them.[19] Farmers dug ditches and lay tile underground to drain them.[20]

Road engineers were also confounded by the stream valleys they had to cross. The valleys were different from those further east. The region's level plains often ended abruptly at the edge of a steep-sided riverbank. And flood plains were much broader than the small streams flowing across them would seem to warrant. Jonathan Knight measured the Wabash at Terre Haute to be 180 yards wide, but its flood plain, the "breadth of the bottom subject to overflow," was 1,931 yards.[21] He had to decide whether to lay the road on fill of sufficient thickness to raise its bed above flood level, or build across the flood-plain surface. Either choice would require him to construct large earth ramps for each end of the bridge. The bluffs above the Great Miami and Stillwater Rivers west of Springfield, Ohio, were even deeper than the Wabash, and the two trench-like channels lay only eleven miles apart where the Road would cross them.[22]

These deep and broad stream valleys were spillways cut by glacial melt-water. As the ice pack melted, producing water in prodigious quantity, streams formed at the ice front and flowed downgrade toward the nearest river with sufficient force to cut quickly new channels into the unconsolidated till. Each major stream in southwestern Ohio, and southern Indiana and Illinois—and many smaller tributaries—flowed in such a spillway. Most drained more or less directly south, away from the ice, toward the Ohio River. For the engineers, this topography made for a series of awkward channel crossings, but not nearly as difficult as it would have been just a few miles south, where the spillways were often deeper and broader, as on the Whitewater, Flatrock, and Big Blue Rivers between Richmond, Indiana, and Indianapolis.

Topographic reality, legal specifications, and political expediency stood in agreement on the Central Lowland as they had not on the Ridge and Valley. Road surveyors were charged to establish the most direct route and not necessarily deviate to include established towns a few miles north or south—as they were tempted to do at Newark, Ohio, or Greencastle, Indiana.[23] The route most amenable to road construction—and the cheapest—would lay two to three miles north of a direct line west from Wheeling, a route that coincidentally would also link the two state capitals, Columbus and Indianapolis.[24]

While the transition from the Allegheny Plateau onto the Central Lowland was accompanied by a spectacular change in topography, the eastern woodland that impeded road construction seemed to continue unbroken. Along the route from Wheeling to Columbus, Jonathan Knight recorded a woodland that was "thick and heavy. The prevailing timber, beech, sugar-tree, hickory, elm, ash, walnut, buckeye, poplar, white-oak, sycamore, &c." Across Indiana, the country was "heavily timbered the whole way, except for the two prairies at the Wabash," and those places west of Richmond that were being cleared by settlers. Costs to clear an eighty-foot right-of-way varied from $730 per mile for a section east of Richmond to $3,400 per mile in the dense woods near Terre Haute.[25]

The beech and maple forest that Knight described extended across the Wisconsin-age till plain from central Ohio to western Indiana, where it gave way to a forest-to-prairie transition on the Illinoian-age "flats." American beech and yellow popular or tulip tree tended to dominate in broadly varied hardwood stands—including ash, oaks, and hickories—on rolling, stream-dissected uplands. These two were joined by sugar maple and bass-wood on north-facing slopes, with red and white oaks, and hickory on droughty south- and west-facing slopes. White elm, walnut, and especially sycamore covered the flood plains. West of the Wabash, on the Illinoian till plain, the beech and maple forest gradually opened to a wet grassy prairie where post and blackjack oaks occupied some "islands" on the drier up-lands, and pin oaks, river birch, and honey locust stood in groves around the low, swampy grasslands.[26]

Whether hardwood forest or prairie grass, vegetation was contingent upon soils. Beyond the Great Valley, road surveyors found little reason to comment favorably on the soils they found. That changed at the Wisconsin till boundary. In eastern Indiana, the chief surveyor judged soil quality "good, mostly very rich, principally clay of a dark color, frequently inter-mixed with sand in various proportions, and occasionally with sand and gravel . . . [but] rich with vegetable decomposition, and susceptible of sup-porting a dense population."[27] The soils west of Indianapolis contained more sand but, nevertheless, farmers would deem them very fertile.

The Road passed over a thin skin of Illinoian till to first emerge on the Wisconsin-age surface in Licking County, Ohio, between Jacksontown and Kirkersville.[28] This topographic boundary coincides with a transition from one major soil family to another. Inceptisols—young soils on weathered bedrock, generally with distinct mineralized layers—prevailed across the

Ridge and Valley and the Allegheny Plateau. Alfisols—moist, mineral-rich soils with a relatively high alkaline or base content, and relatively high fertility—developed on the glacial till. They continue across Indiana and Illinois and are interrupted by two narrow zones of mollisols—one along the Wabash River Valley, the other near the Mississippi. Soft grassland soils high in organic material and base content, mollisols are among the world's most productive soils. The largest extent of mollisols east of the Mississippi lies on Wisconsin-age till in Illinois north of the Shelbyville terminal moraine.

Had the congressional mandate to build the National Road set as its target the most fertile prairie land in the Northwest Territory, surveyors undoubtedly would have turned the road toward the northwest at Terre Haute, toward the Grand Prairie and what early settlers called "the beautiful land on the Sangamon" River north of the moraine.[29] Instead, the Road turns southwest across the older Illinoian till, toward the Illinois state capital at Vandalia; from there the road continues to East St. Louis and, alternatively, via a spur to Alton, Illinois, both on the Mississippi River. The soils that developed on the Illinoian surface are poorly drained, and often have a high sodium content. They do benefit from a deep layer of wind-borne silt, or loess, material picked up along the glacial spillways to the west—especially the Mississippi and Illinois River Valleys—and deposited to depths of two feet or more across this surface.[30] But their productivity proved relatively low when settlers began to plow and plant.

## TRANSREGIONAL ENTREPÔT

In 1816 a steam-powered boat successfully navigated up the Mississippi and Ohio Rivers to the falls at Louisville. A steamboat plowed across Lake Erie for the first time the same year. Engineers and Irish construction crews completed the National Road—with a surface capable of entertaining Conestoga wagon traffic—to the Ohio River at Wheeling by 1818. Seven years later, in 1825, the same year that the Erie Canal linked Albany and Buffalo across New York, Congress authorized funds to extend the National Road from Wheeling to Zanesville, Ohio, and survey a route across Indiana and Illinois to the Mississippi. Altogether, the fifteen-year period from 1815 to 1830 produced a flurry of road- and canal-building intended in large part to connect Ohio, Indiana, and Illinois to East Coast markets.

But Ohio Valley products, especially farm commodities, were already being delivered to East Coast cities in substantial volume. Flour, salt pork, and tobacco moved by way of flatboat to New Orleans, then were loaded onto ships to complete the trip. Drovers moved cattle directly from feed lots and pasture lands along the Scioto and Miami Valleys to eastern markets. They could choose from several routes, depending upon the destination. In southern Ohio the preferred route was via Gallipolis and the Kanawha and New River Valleys to Richmond, Virginia. In the northeast, the routes of choice were the Buffalo-Syracuse-Albany Post Road or the Great Western Turnpike to upstate New York. Along the National Road corridor, route choice also depended upon destination. Drovers might follow the North-western Turnpike (now US 50) to Parkersburg, West Virginia, and across the mountains to Winchester, Virginia, in the Great Valley. The Old Glade Road (now Pennsylvania 31) and Forbes Trace (now US 30) led east from Pittsburgh to Philadelphia and New York City.[31] Therefore, whereas Baltimore was the National Road's formal entrepôt, the traffic flowing along the route in either direction was not simply point-to-point but had a much broader regional constituency. Nor was the traffic exclusively commodities. Migrants and immigrants in substantial numbers—many directed by guide-books to disembark in Baltimore so they might follow the "less difficult" road—moved west along the Road, and with them came ideas and institutions that they would employ to fashion a new human geography on the trans-Appalachian landscape.[32]

The main East Coast reservoir or hearth for people and ideas that aligned with the National Road corridor was the Middle Atlantic or Midland cultural area.[33] There, residents of William Penn's colony contributed material artifacts, religious and agricultural practices, attitudes toward government, and the like to a distinctive cultural amalgam. Included were Quakers and others from the British Isles, Scots-Irish Protestants from Northern Ireland, and German-speaking pietists from the Upper Rhine Valley. During the eighteenth century, the Midland hearth expanded west across the Pennsylvania Piedmont and Ridge and Valley to the Allegheny Front, southwest across the Maryland Piedmont, and beyond the Potomac into Virginia's Shenandoah Valley.[34]

Migrants from the Midland hearth headed west along the National Road and other westward routes across southern and western Pennsylvania. Upon reaching the Ohio River they could continue west along the corridor the Road would eventually take or follow the Ohio River south to Cincinnati, where they turned north into the Miami Valley; others moved northwest to north-central Ohio. Scots-Irish tended to favor the Virginia Military lands between the Scioto and Little Miami Rivers, as well as the Miami Valley proper.[35] Pennsylvania Germans— among them Anabaptists (Amish, Brethren, Hutterites, and Mennonites), Moravians, Lutherans, Catholics, and Calvinists—tended to favor the low plateau lands northwest of Pittsburgh, although many moved to southeast Ohio and Miami Valley destinations.[36] Quakers moved west along the corridor and initiated settlements along its length. A Quaker founded Uniontown, Pennsylvania, for example, and Quakers established thirty-nine Friends meetinghouses along the road or in adjacent counties in Indiana, and the Quaker Earlham College in Richmond, Indiana.[37] These groups, together with migrants from New England and New York across the north, and migrants from Virginia, the Piedmont of North Carolina, and Kentucky, contributed to a distinctive Middle West culture and economy.

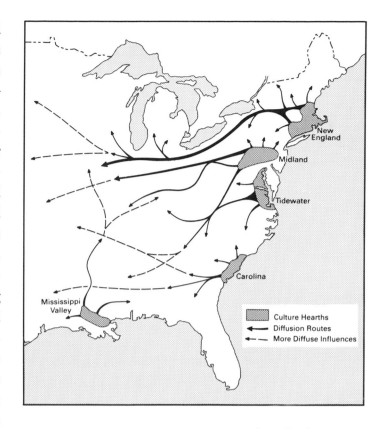

Eastern seaboard culture hearths

The early settlers who moved from the Midland hearth onto the Allegheny Plateau, and then into the Middle West, were a diverse lot who carried a blend of English, Scots-Irish, German, and American Indian traits that allowed them to fare well in the thick woodland that they would encounter all the way to the Wabash River. They were adept with wood-working tools, practiced a slash-and-burn agricultural system, lived in dispersed farmsteads, kept open-range livestock, and erected simple, efficient, interchangeable log buildings.[38] These pioneers would be followed by later migrants who established market towns, upgraded farms with blooded stock and careful crop husbandry, and initiated the economic and political institutions that would sustain the region. The National Road would follow the earliest settlers, not provide their avenue of entré. The advantage of traveling the finished Road would fall to later migrants. The route would parallel the backbone of Midland culture into the Middle West and so provide a cross-section along which we might trace the settlement sequence and landscape-creation process.

From the Maryland Piedmont to the Ohio River, settlers obtained their land through military land grants or bought it from a frontier family who had bought it from a speculator. Land parcels were often surveyed after settlement according to metes and bounds marked by occasional formal corner monuments, prominent trees, streams, roads, and other physical landmarks. The result was a patchwork of odd-sized farms and frequent disagreement between neighbors as to correct boundary lines. Beyond the Ohio both the method for obtaining land and the mechanism for delimiting property boundaries changed. There the federal government was the principal land-holder, and surveyors platted land according to directives in the Land Ordinance of 1785, which followed the ideas of Thomas Jefferson and others in Congress.[39] By following a clever yet simple system of standard baselines and principal meridians, surveyors laid out a grid of thirty-six-square-mile townships, marking each mile intersection. This became known as the Township and Range system. The survey had the salutary effect of identifying each square mile or section by a standardized number, and further subdividing each section into uniquely identifiable half (320-acre), quarter (160-acre), and quarter-quarter (40-acre) parcels. Congress designed the system to allow federal land-office employees to identify parcels quickly and accurately so that titles would be secure and land sales would not be compromised by litigation or delayed by repeatedly surveying individual parcels.

The Land Ordinance, and the Township and Range survey ordained by it, provided the guidelines for an unprecedented American landscape. Surveyors were to precede settlement rather than accompany it, as had been the case in the East. This meant that settlers could expect to visit a land sales office and for a small price obtain a land parcel that had known boundaries and a clear title. Thirty-six-square-mile townships were often also civil divisions and the first level of local government. Residents would erect a town hall, sometimes in town, often in the country, and use the structure as a polling center and a meetingplace for township trustees to decide on road maintenance and other issues within their jurisdiction.

Except on those areas where the topography was sharply dissected and rough, the survey lines ran across the countryside in north-south, east-west lines. The ordinance did not make allowance for road construction and property owners along the section lines were expected to donate the right-of-way required to build the roads that would run along most section lines. Of course, not every section line became a road, but many did and the resulting network became an organizational grid along which nineteenth-century settlers aligned their farmsteads. Settlers did not attempt to create rural community centers by placing their farmsteads at section road intersections but seemed more concerned that their buildings stand on a well-drained point central to their holdings, rather than off to one corner. This meant that farmsteads were largely isolated one from another. Given the dense forest covering most of Ohio and Indiana, and the exceedingly poor or nonexistent section roads, isolation would have been pronounced until well past mid-century.

Forest clearance—cutting trees and grubbing stumps—was grueling work, but farmers needed relatively few acres of rich land to produce crops sufficient to feed themselves and their stock. Consequently, farms in eastern and southern Ohio tended to be small, forty to eighty acres. Prairie land increased to the west, and that land was settled later, allowing farmers to utilize new inventions such as the reaper and steel plow to cultivate larger acreages. Along the National Road corridor, this transition in farm size is still present, small farms in the east, larger ones in the west.

Farmers gradually enlarged their forest clearings and rectangular fields emerged from the woodland, but they invariably left a woodlot of several acres standing on a back, hard-to-reach corner. Since their neighbors used a similar strategy, the result was blocks or bands of trees along a common property line. Woodland farmers might retain a few trees on the building site to shade the house and yard, and plant an apple orchard nearby. On the prairies, especially along the Wabash and in southern Illinois, section roads led off across rolling grassland, and farmers, recognizing their dependence upon trees for building materials, fuel, and fencing, placed their farm buildings at the woodland's edge or along a stream where gallery forest intruded into the prairie. Latecomers settled on the open prairies and soon found that a shelter-belt of quick-growing box elders, silver (water) maples, and cottonwoods would give some relief from cold winter winds and provide wood fuel. Today, many second- or third-growth woodlots still stand on the backsides of Ohio and Indiana farms, seen in the distance as a dense and sometimes unbroken tree line. Very little original forest remains, but careful observation will suggest where the original forest-prairie boundaries lay.

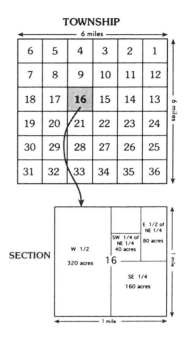

Township and Range survey

Farmsteads that have L-shaped groves on their northwest sides stood on the grassland. Those with few trees near the buildings and a woodlot a half-mile or more away likely were chopped from the primeval woodland.[40]

## RURAL EXEMPLARS

The farmers on the mid-eighteenth-century Pennsylvania and Maryland Piedmont had been among the best in Europe when religious persecution drove them to accept William Penn's invitation to migrate to his colony. They planted crops in rotation, fed hay and corn to cattle and hogs, and used manure to enrich the soil. Their huge barns served to shelter stock, to store grain and provide a sheltered threshing floor, and to store hay. Migrants from the Piedmont began to arrive in the Miami Valley of southwestern Ohio early in the nineteenth century where they transplanted their farming methods.

Although some Miami Valley farmers grew Indian maize for sale to distilleries, most fed it to their livestock and so marketed their corn as beef or pork. By 1839, Miami Valley farmers led Ohio in corn production. Hogs became an early speciality on Miami Valley farms. Farmers brought their swine to market weight by grazing them on clover, allowing them to "hog down" corn fields, and by penning them and feeding them pumpkins and ear corn.[41] This area became, as John Fraser Hart has termed it, the "second seed bed," the source for the crops and husbandry practices that would spread west through what would become known as the Corn Belt.[42]

The National Road and its successors, US 40 and I-70, crossed the Corn Belt's southern reach, from Columbus, Ohio, into southeastern Illinois. On each traditional farmstead the farmer built the structures required to make the farm work and by the early twentieth century many farms across the region contained a similar collection of buildings. The largest building was usually a barn for draft animals and implements. Some farms may have also had a second barn for dairy or feeder cattle. A wooden or cement silo for chopped corn storage usually stood beside the cattle barn. Most had a slatted crib for corn, a granary to store oats or wheat, a chicken coop, often with clerestory windows on the south side, and perhaps a shed for tools. The buildings stood in a cluster amid nearly equal-sized fields.[43]

Among the farm structure plans carried west by Midland hearth migrants, the barn is most noticeable. Migrants of English tradition brought a small and easily built side-entry barn. Germans preferred the huge Sweitzer—or

KARL RAITZ

Swiss—barn found in various forms across south-eastern Pennsylvania and the Maryland Piedmont and Great Valley. Derived from prototypes in the Prätigau region of eastern Switzerland and the Vorarlberg of western Austria, the Sweitzer barn possessed several characteristics that made it a particularly successful adaptation in Pennsylvania.[44] The barn was often very large, sixty feet or more wide and seventy feet long, although some were even larger. It had two or three separate levels. Stables and stalls for dairy cows and draft horses occupied the ground floor and opened directly onto a feed lot. A second level gave space for a granary and general storage. Above this was a third level, which included a threshing floor and bents for grain and hay storage. Carpenters tried to position the barn against a low hill so the farmer could drive grain and hay wagons, by way of a short ramp, directly onto the threshing floor. If the building site was more or less level, a large earth and stone ramp would be built. The ramp and third-level access door were always opposite the feed lot. Another distinctive Sweitzer barn characteristic was the forebay or second-floor extension out over the stable doors. Some forebays were cantilevered to extend ten feet or more beyond the first-floor wall, others were supported by posts. Complex mortise and tenon joints locked together the heavy timber post-and-beam frame. Some barns had stone foundations and end walls, others were covered by planking.

Migrants, especially Mennonites and Brethren, built the Sweitzer barn all along the Midland corridor. The largest concentrations still extant stand in east-central, southern, and southwest Ohio, although a few can be found as far west as Terre Haute.[45] Of course, the barn can be found across a much broader area—Wisconsin south to Missouri—but Terre Haute marks the approximate western extent along the National Road corridor. Converting a farm from general production to specialize in hog and corn production, for example, or changing technology did not favor continued use of this large structure in Indiana and Illinois. New implements invented to handle hay mechanically—the track-and-pulley lift system installed under the barn's ridge beam, for example—could not be readily adapted to the Sweitzer barn's heavy frame, and so by the early twentieth century farmers were building a simpler structure with an open haymow.

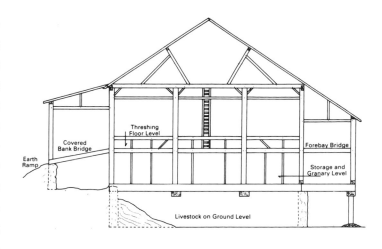

Cross-section of a large Pennsylvania barn

After World War II, Corn Belt farming became increasingly specialized. By employing modern large-capacity equipment and chemicals, some farmers were able to increase yields dramatically and so preferred to raise crops for cash sale instead of feeding them to livestock. On these farms, soybeans often replaced oats, wheat, and the hay crops. Other farmers increased the number of hogs or beef cattle they raised so that they fed most of their grain and might have to purchase more at their local grain elevator.

The contemporary farm landscape along the National Road corridor reflects this increasing specialization. The farmer converts the traditional farmstead to cash grain production by tearing down the corncrib, granary, and other small sheds. Erected in their place is a large sheet-metal pole barn—so called because it is simply constructed on a frame of telephone pole–sized timbers and rafter trusses engineered to span twenty-four feet or more—for machinery storage. Nearby is one or more 10,000- or 20,000-bushel-capacity round steel bins in which the corn or beans will be dried and stored until the market price is favorable for sale. The old barn may stand as a storage for small implements and farmstead oddments but its haymow is empty. Farms specializing in hog or beef cattle feeding may expand the old barn by adding lean-to sheds and increasing the feed-lot size. The old granary may still be used but will be supplemented with round steel grain bins and a mill used to grind corn into feed. The old silo may be the smallest of a set that often includes one or more tall blue Harvestores, which are sealed like a thermos bottle and contain self-unloading machinery. Farm families tend to be smaller, and children often leave the farm after high school to seek work in the city or attend college. For many farmers, this loss of helping hands means that tasks must be mechanized or abandoned. To compensate, the livestock farmer may convert the hay storage system from small rectangular bales, which are very labor-intensive, to large round bales. The round bales can be produced by one person running a tractor and baler, and although each bale weights more than 1,000 pounds, one person with a properly equipped tractor can move the bales from alfalfa field to farmstead. A line of round hay bales turning golden in the sun should signal to passersby that farming continues despite a labor shortage.

On both the cash grain and the livestock farms the old Victorian farmhouse has either been remodeled or replaced by a simple "ranch style" single-story structure. The new house is often built not by local carpenters using materials from the nearby lumberyard—very few traditional lumberyards can be found in middlewestern small towns any longer—but by large construction firms that specialize in building houses according to designs chosen from a catalog. Because farms have grown progressively larger over the past four decades, some farmsteads now stand vacant or are occupied by people who commute to work in a nearby town.[46]

## ALTERNATIVE ADAPTATIONS

Nineteenth-century settlers moving west along the Road from the Piedmont into the Ridge and Valley and the Allegheny Plateau beyond adapted to the resources they found, which often changed radically from one valley to the next. Rich roan limestone soils might cover the floor of one valley, while stiff, sickly ocher shale-derived clay lay beyond the next ridge. Iron deposits could be found along some ridges and became the basis for local iron furnace and charcoal-burning operations. Timber cutters fed the furnaces and supplied local sawmills. Coal outcropped near Frostburg, Maryland, and small mines supplied local smithies along the Road. By 1810, four-horse wagons made coal shipments to Cumberland, Maryland, where the coal was reloaded onto Potomac River flat boats for delivery at Georgetown in Washington, D.C., and other riverside markets.[47]

Beyond Chestnut Ridge, near Uniontown in southwestern Pennsylvania, bituminous coal seams reached commercial quality and thickness and, by the 1850s, provided the fuel for the iron and steel mills that stretched south from Pittsburgh along the Monongahela River. About seven miles east of Brownsville, near T. B. Searight's toll house, the National Road crosses the old Connellsville coke manufacturing district. Coke was produced by burning coal in brick beehive ovens to drive off impurities, thereby yielding high-carbon coke for the region's steel furnaces. In the hands of Pittsburgh-based entrepreneur Henry Clay Frick this became the state's most important coke-manufacturing district and production boomed from the mid-nineteenth century through World War I. Dozens of small company towns—among them Allison, Buffington, Continental No. 2, Fairbank, Filbert, Footedale, Herbert, Shamrock, and Tower Hill No. 1—dot the district. Some housed miners, others the families who tended the 40,000 ovens that once spread across these hills. Coal seams continued west under eastern Ohio, though with higher sulfur content. East of Cambridge, Ohio, the coal was shallow enough to be mined at the surface by huge draglines that left large overburden piles in their wake.

## URBAN PROTOTYPES

Towns and villages along the National Road corridor also carry the mark of Midland culture hearth origins. Larger towns at important road and river junction points usually incorporated a rectilinear street grid patterned after Philadelphia. Smaller settlements often followed a simple linear plan in which all buildings faced the road. Being only one lot deep on either side of the road, the linear town was just that, a narrow, tightly packed cluster of buildings with no cross streets or alleys. Somewhat larger settlements might have expanded the linear plan by incorporating regularly spaced cross streets that ran as far as the rear of the road-facing lots. The cross streets were then connected by a street or lane paralleling the main road. Typically, the village would incorporate two such rear streets and so this street form has been termed the linear-r plan.[48] Examples of linear or linear-r villages along the Road can be found in southwestern Pennsylvania at Addison, and in Ohio at Old Washington, Gratiot, and Etna.

House forms in towns and on farms along the Road corridor are quite varied and often difficult to attribute to a Midland hearth source. Narrow one-room-deep, two-story red-brick houses dominate farms and villages in the Maryland Piedmont west of Baltimore, but are also common in Virginia's Chesapeake country. Those found across southwestern Pennsylvania and along the Road across the Middle West states may represent contributions from both of these source areas.[49] Fred Kniffen termed this form an I-house, ostensibly because so many were built in Indiana, Illinois, and Iowa.[50] James Whitcomb Riley's boyhood home in Cambridge City, Indiana, is an example. The broader two-room-deep, two-story stone or brick house (and its variants in Georgian symmetry and styling detail) is found across the Pennsylvania Piedmont and Ridge and Valley, and along the Road west. This house appears in full four-rooms over four-rooms facade, and as a one-half width, or two-over-two rowhouse along the Road west into Ohio. This plan was a favorite with tavern builders across western Maryland and southwest Pennsylvania, and is the model for such well-known landmarks as the Mount Washington Tavern at Fort Necessity, Pennsylvania, and the Red Brick Tavern at Lafayette, Ohio.

## IDENTITY

Farther west, the Midland culture hearth's influence would be diluted by ideas and artifacts carried into the region by Yankees and New Yorkers who followed the Erie Canal westward, crossed northern Ohio's Yankee gangplank—Connecticut's Western Reserve—and moved into Indiana and Illinois; and by Upland South folk from Virginia, Kentucky, North Carolina, and Tennessee. The means by which national-scale industrial and commercial influences would flavor the National Road's hinterland became articulated by new transportation mediums, the steamboat and the steam railroad locomotive. Railroad companies such as the Illinois Central built dozens of towns along their tracks, each town plan the same square grid, the streets in each identically named, each with a depot demarcating the business district's edge. Both boat and train would provide local merchants with goods—everything from clothing and hardware to furniture and musical instruments—designed and produced in distant factories. Cleveland, Cincinnati, Chicago, and St. Louis grew up around the rim of the National Road's hinterland at points on rivers or lakes that provided access to the interior. Entrepreneurs in these places then exploited those advantages by knitting a network of linking roads and railroads across the countryside, and urban influences of many kinds began to flow back and forth across the land once known as the Northwest Territory, or more simply, the West. It was no accident that the Cincinnati, Indianapolis, St. Louis & Chicago Railway Company became known across the region as the Big Four Railroad. People in Effingham, Illinois, looked to Chicago for commodities and culture, not to Baltimore. When business people chose to erect great buildings in Richmond or Terre Haute, Indiana, they would as likely choose Chicago architects such as Daniel Burnham as someone from an eastern seaboard design firm. Small town and farm-home builders adopted Frank Lloyd Wright's Prairie style to replace the Georgian, Gothic, and Victorian forms contributed by early settlers imbued with eastern fashion.

Such cultural cross flow yields historical ambivalence. Where do one's heritage, identity, and allegiances reside? If tradition and rootedness matter, in which direction do people living along the National Road corridor look for their lineage? Although the Road's business and political advocates intended that it provide an overland link between eastern entrepreneurs and the Northwest Territory's fertile federal lands, they could not foresee how their efforts would introduce eastern ideas and ideals into the western country. But the transition from Piedmont to Blue Ridge, Ridge and Valley, and Allegheny Plateau topographies, in turn, would not offer uniform opportunity, or permit migrants along the route to employ narrow, time-tested adaptational strategies with the same success that they had experienced elsewhere. Economic success might depend as much on recognizing any advantage that lay embedded in local environments as attempting to replicate farming, manufacturing, or business schemes learned in the East, or in Europe. The glaciated interior lowlands offered greater potential for continuity, and quicker recovery from failed experimentation. Indeed, Pennsylvania and Maryland farmers who introduced their livestock and grain farming habits into Ohio were so successful prior to the Civil War that they soon filled Cincinnati's (Porkopolis's) abattoirs with corn-fed hogs and so founded the region's Corn Belt economy.

Although the National Road became the nation's first great East-West link, it could not so tie the disparate sections along the corridor into a single cultural milieu that it would adopt a singular identity. By 1900, people beyond the Ohio began to recognize their regional distinctiveness and soon the term "Middle West" became common to describe their region. But since middlewestern ways and attributes faded near the region's edges, internal transitions based on old migration patterns played out across the landscape. Ohio had been a state a century before it adopted the Middle West appellation, and east of Columbus that allegiance thinned perceptively, almost in proportion, it seems, to the increasing number of linear villages and Pennsylvania barns one finds from there eastward along the Road corridor. And across Indiana and Illinois, the National Road itself is recognized as a transition line. To the south, residents contend, culture becomes Southern, as though the road were the Mason-Dixon Line's westward extension.[51] The National Road was built to tie East to West, but in doing that it also cut across the national grain, exposing both topographic variation and the historical settlement sequence.

KARL RAITZ

# The American Highway in Art

THOMAS J. SCHLERETH

*To know the universe itself as a road, as many roads, as roads for traveling souls.*

WALT WHITMAN
*Leaves of Grass*

THE METAPHOR OF THE ROAD AS A MEANS FOR GAINING SELF-KNOWLEDGE and knowledge of one's universe has a long history in the American literary imagination, including, for example, Whitman's "Song of the Open Road" and Jack Kerouac's *On the Road*.

The American road and roadside have also inspired American artists. Assembled here are well-known painters (Edward Hopper, Grant Wood), plus others less familiar (Mary Keys, Joseph Hidley), who share a vision of the road that extends from New England to the American West. Included are rural pastorals where Arbor Day rituals are enacted and urban factory sites—where Charles Sheeler's precisionist River Rouge exterior and Diego Rivera's animated interior of Detroit industry—are depicted.

In addition to celebrating visions, American artists have depicted the highway's dark side: the loneliness of night travel, the banality of standardized service facilities, the possibilities of sudden death on a ridge road.

**George Caleb Bingham**
(1811–79)
*Daniel Boone Escorting Settlers Through the Cumberland Gap* or *The Emigration of Daniel Boone*
(1851–52)
Oil on canvas 36½″ × 50¼″
Washington University Gallery of Art, St. Louis
Gift of Nathaniel Phillips
(1890– )

ONE GENERATION'S TRIBUTE TO AN EARLIER ONE, BINGHAM'S HISTORical version of Boone's journey became a national icon for mobile fellow citizens. The artist, raised in Franklin, Missouri, along the Lewis and Clark Trail, converted Boone's trek through the trans-Allegheny wilderness into a powerful political and religious tableau. The expedition, traversing rocky terrain strewn with blasted trees, recalled the biblical journeys of Moses and the Holy family for many nineteenth-century Americans. Equipped with firearms, forest-clearing axes, and domestic animals, the resolute entourage advances on the viewer as if destiny guided its course to the Promised Land.

THOMAS J. SCHLERETH

Local establishments such as depicted here outside Philadelphia provided residents and transients with various services: lodging for travelers; refreshment for stage riders and their animals; places for business transactions (note desk and stool at right); gaming (checkers and cards); political, economic, and social news; and taproom libations. Communications abounded: posted notices, wall prints, almanacs (taproom door frame right), and newspapers available in wooden holders hanging on nails for patron use. A masculine enclave—the imploring mother and child here may be a temperance reference—roadside taverns were plain and practical spaces for reading and rhetoric, coming and going.

**John Lewis Krimmel**
(1786–1821)
*Village Tavern* or *Interior of an American Inn* (1913–14)
Oil on canvas  16⅞″ × 22½″
Toledo Museum of Art, Toledo, Ohio
Florence Scott Libbey bequest in memory of Maurice A. Scott

Thomas Waterman
Wood (1823–1903)
*The Village Post Office*
(1873)
Oil on canvas  30″ × 47″
New York State Histori-
cal Association, Coopers-
town, N.Y.

A PLACE OF BUYING (DRY GOODS, LEFT COUNTER; GENERAL MERCHAN-dise, right; flour, kerosene, molasses, rear wall) and barter (farm eggs exchanged for fancy calico), a crossroads store like this Vermont road institution frequently doubled as a local postal station where, before Rural Free Delivery in 1896, country people came to send and collect mail. With the exception of the male "village philosophers" circle (often focused around a stove or crackerbarrel), the post office/store was also a democratic social center frequented by young and old, women and children, commercial drummers and farmhands.

THOMAS J. SCHLERETH

RECORDED FROM AN IMAGINARY AERIAL VIEW IN ORDER TO CONVEY THE linear sweep of a nineteenth-century "string town" east of Troy, New York, this folk landscape includes figures at work and play, assorted vehicles, and the community's hotels, livery stable, and churches. Hidley, a local artisan who painted three other views of Poestenkill (two Dutch words meaning "tuffing or foaming creek") depicted the town's house types (including outbuildings) with care. Each facade on the main road was given a separate perspective in order to detail door and window treatments accurately.

Joseph Henry Hidley, Attribution (1830–72)
*Poestenkill, New York: Summer* (1865–72)
Oil on wood panel
20″ × 29¾″
Abby Aldrich Rockefeller Folk Art Center, Williamsburg, Va.

**Mary Keys (active 1830s)**
*Lockport on the Erie Canal*
(1832)

Watercolor on paper
15¼″ × 20¼″

Munson-Williams-Proctor
Institute, Utica, N.Y.

BEGUN IN 1817 AT ROME, NEW YORK, COMPLETED IN 1825 AT BUF-falo, the Erie Canal set off a canal-building fever producing 3,326 miles of waterways by 1840. Here folk artist Keys portrays a civil-engineering marvel at Lockport. A three-horse team (towpath right) pulls a canal packet with fashionable passengers aboard toward the city's famous "Double Flight" of five locks where three boats wait to ascend. Major canals spawned by Erie's example and crossing or paralleling the National Road include the Chesapeake & Ohio; Erie & Ohio; Miami & Ohio; and Wabash & Erie.

THOMAS J. SCHLERETH

Steamships, trains, oxcarts, bicycles, and automobiles intrigued Henry, a prolific (over 1,200 works) genre painter of late nineteenth-century America. Here, in addition to the meticulously rendered locomotive and cars, assorted vehicles (for example, stagecoaches, carriages, buckboards) expedite travelers. Fifty people—some watching, loitering, reading; others rushing, expecting, gossiping—crowd the morning scene. Three artifacts—a steam passenger train, the Gothic Revival station, a row of Federal-style homes—form a triptych with the station's platform serving as center stage for a local daily drama as well as separating social and economic classes on the two sides of its tracks.

Edward Lamson Henry
(1841–1919)
*The 9:45 Accommodation, Stratford, Connecticut*
(1867)
Oil on canvas  16″ × 30⅝″
Metropolitan Museum of Art, New York, N.Y.
Bequest of Moses Tanenbaum (1937)

**Thomas Proudly Otter**
**(1832–90)**
*On the Road* (1860)
Oil on canvas  22″ × 45⅜″
Nelson-Atkins Museum
of Art, Kansas City, Mo.
Nelson Fund

A SPEEDING TRAIN BESTS A LUMBERING CONESTOGA WAGON ON SEV-
eral counts in this panorama: size (weight and number of passengers
hauled), scale, speed, and directness of route. The wagon group, where humans are visible and in control, follows a natural but meandering route
along an arid riverbed and needs a milestone (whereon Otter carved his ini-
tials) to mark its slow progress. The train, charging along a graded track bed
and across a bridge, bisects the painting and its landscape. Indifferent to traditional surface travel (which it literally rolls over), it moves westward on an
engineered vector, oblivious of topography.

THOMAS J. SCHLERETH

SHEELER'S EPIC PANORAMA OF THE FORD PLANT AT RIVER ROUGE, Michigan, reinterpreted the term landscape for the industrial age. The painter's precisionist presentation of a segment of the 1,400-acre site—including a canal-like watercourse and boat slip; railroad tracks extending left and right; mountains of ore, limestone, and slag; the uniform silos of the cement plant (*left*) and the irregular outline of the slag screen house (*center*)—appears as if taken through a wide-angle camera lens. Here artifacts of the roadway (cement) and the road (Fords) are manufactured in a totally manmade environment.

Charles Sheeler
(1883–1965)
*American Landscape* (1930)
Oil on canvas  24″ × 31″
Museum of Modern Art,
New York, N.Y.
A gift of Abby Aldrich
Rockefeller (1934)

**Diego Rivera (1886–1957)**
*Detroit Industry: Production of Automobile Exterior and Final Assembly (South Wall, 1932–33)*

True fresco
5.40 × 13.72 meters
The Detroit Institute of Arts, Detroit
Founders Society Purchase Edsel B. Ford and gift of Edsel B. Ford

UNLIKE SHEELER'S TRANQUIL, LARGELY UNPEOPLED, EXTERIOR LANDscape dedicated to industrial progress, Rivera's depiction of a plant interior teems with men and machines. Simultaneous operations are compressed within the mural: a huge fender stamping press (*right* and *mid-foreground*) begins a process that conveyor belts expedite; a foreman (hat and glasses) oversees body part finishing (*top center*); a welding buck operates while below a V8 engine is lowered on a final assembly line. Edsel Ford and the Detroit Institute of Arts' director—the only men not working—appear in the pose of Renaissance patrons (*lower right*) while Henry Ford teaches a trade school class in one of six predella panels depicting daily worker life at the Rouge.

THOMAS J. SCHLERETH

TRAINS AND AUTOMOBILES MADE NIGHT TRAVEL EXPEDITIOUS AND lonely. Hopper, as fascinated with twentieth-century travel as Edward Lamson Henry had been with that of an earlier age, continuously explored the unsettling aspects of being on the road, in hotels, on trains, or searching for a night's roadside lodging. Facing the darkened street, with houses and flats to the rear, this Provincetown, Massachusetts, boardinghouse, a tidy temple-front building updated with Italianate details, is awash with light: its advertising sign noting vacancy; its white porch and facade proclaiming propriety; its incandescent hall and parlor suggesting a transient domesticity.

**Edward Hopper**
**(1882–1967)**
*Rooms for Tourists* (1945)
Oil on canvas  30″ × 40″
Yale University Art Gallery, New Haven
Bequest of Stephen Carlton Clark, B.A. (1903)

**Edward Hopper**
**(1882–1967)**
*Western Motel* (1957)
Oil on canvas  30¼″ × 50⅛″
Yale University Art Gallery,
New Haven
Bequest of Stephen
Carlton Clark, B.A. (1903)

A SOLITARY FIGURE AT A WINDOW, A SYMBOL OF MANY HOPPER INTER-pretations of modern life, sits pensively awaiting another travel day. The stark geometry of the unadorned room, window, and screen door suggest the impersonality and austerity of commercial lodging. A clock, two packed bags, and a green Buick outside evoke a sense of rootlessness. Yet the sunlit horizon, evident through the expansive picture window, beckons in a painting layered with horizontal elements—floor, bed, window, roadway, hills, sky, and the motel itself, still a single-story building type in the 1950s.

THOMAS J. SCHLERETH

ONE-ROOM, SINGLE-TEACHER SCHOOLS PUNCTUATED NUMEROUS AMERican county section-line intersections. Commissioned by the Cedar Rapids, Iowa, school board, Wood's April scene evokes Arbor Day—an annual rite of spring begun in the 1870s—while also providing a visual comment on local history: the past represented by a veteran farmer plowing fields first turned by his pioneer counterparts; the present symbolized by a pristine white (not red) district school building, a community institution with schoolmarm and woodshed; the future, the next generation planting a young sapling on a verdant, sunlit stage elevated above the rutted dirt road that follows a section line to a distant town.

**Grant Wood** (1892–1942)
*Arbor Day* (1932)
Oil on masonite panel
24″ × 30″
Private collection
Courtesy James Maroney,
New York, N.Y.

**Grant Wood** (1892–1942)
*Death on the Ridge Road*
(1932)

Oil on masonite
39″ × 46¹⁄₁₆″

Williams College Museum
of Art, Williamstown,
Mass.

Gift of Cole Porter

STARK ANGULAR SYMBOLS OF MODERNITY—UTILITY POLES, TELEPHONE and electric wires, a trio of combating motor vehicles—contest the rural roadway and roadside. In contrast to a later (1939) Wood painting titled *New Road* (an idyllic rural intersection including a turning lane but totally devoid of cars or people), this melodrama climaxes on a torturous "ridge road" first laid out by wagoners. Now paved and fenced for high-speed auto travel, it has become a two-way racetrack. Here an arrogant, aerodynamic towncar illegally passes a farmer's Ford only to encounter an oncoming red truck, causing a probable three-way collision.

THOMAS J. SCHLERETH

As with actual historical and contemporary experience of the roadscape, Segal's art environments are three-dimensional—architectural, sculptural, and artifactual settings composed with mundane objects such as vending machines, rubber tires, electric clocks. Minimalist and modern in architectural fabrication (concrete block, plate glass) and advertising display (oil cans in Pop Art repetition), the space seems empty and devoid of human purpose. The isolation of the eerie white plaster men adds to this feeling. One routinely services a car, the other consumes a Coke; each is indifferent to the other. Their abstract anonymity exhibits no personal identity.

George Segal (1924–   )
*The Gas Station* (1963–64)
Plaster, metal, concrete, and rubber  96″ × 164″ × 60″
National Gallery of Canada, Ottawa, Ontario

OUTLINED AGAINST A DARKENING SOUTHWESTERN SKY, TWO ROAD
icons—the entrance ramp and the billboard—dominate Wolke's color pho-
tographic interpretation of a Chicago expressway. Massive directional signage announcing local (a nineteenth-century canal town site) and national
(red-white-blue interstate corridors) routes frames an advertiser's genre ren-
dition of a cowboy longeing his stallion. Anonymous motorists, represented in ribbons of time-lapse imagery, speed along a suspended sculpture
of reinforced concrete into a night illuminated by halogen and flood light.

THOMAS J. SCHLERETH

DESIGNED FOR THE U.S. CONSTITUTION BICENTENNIAL, THIS CONCEPtual art project sequences fifty-one vanity license plates (an American motorist's form of self-expression) to spell out phonetically the document's fifty-two-word preamble. A multicolored collage democratically (alphabetized) mounted on green vinyl upholstery reminiscent of an automobile interior, the work signs and symbolizes the complexities of the national road system: state-licensing in a national union; uniformity (a common 4″ × 12″ size) versus diverse regional iconography on various plates; mass-produced yet personalized identities; the commemoration of a major national document partially sponsored by a foreign automobile manufacturer.

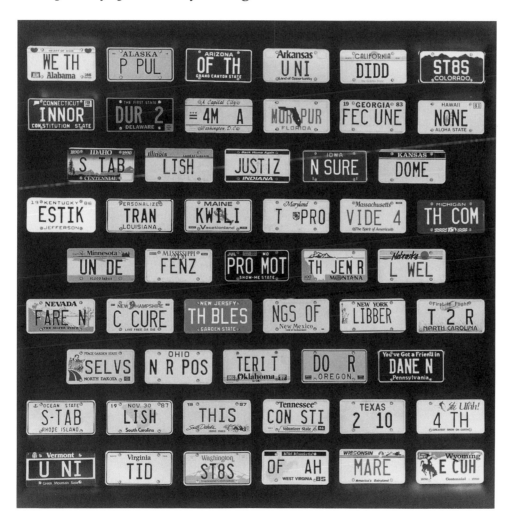

**Mike Wilkins (1960–  )**
*Preamble* (1987)
Painted metal on vinyl and wood  96″ × 96″
National Museum of American Art, Washington, D.C.
Gift of Nissan Motor Corporation in U.S.A.

PART TWO

# Building the National Road

# The Idea of a National Road

JOSEPH S. WOOD

*Good roads and canals will shorten the distances, facilitate commercial and personal intercourse, and unite, by a still more intimate community of interests, the most remote quarters of the United States. No other single operation, within the power of the Government, can more effectively tend to strengthen and perpetuate that Union which secures external independence, domestic peace, and internal liberty.*

ALBERT GALLATIN
(1808)

THE MODERN-DAY VERSION OF A NETWORK OF ROADS AND CANALS EN-visioned by Pres. Thomas Jefferson and his secretary of the treasury Albert Gallatin early in the nineteenth century is a "national information super-highway," as advocated by Vice-President Albert Gore Jr. This massive, national, multichanneled, fiber-optic network connected to personal comput-ers, telephones, and televisions will interlink every corner of the United States and penetrate every facet of our lives. It will reshape our geography in ways we can hardly imagine. To Americans of 1800, in a country viewed in vastly larger perceptual terms than what it has grown to be today, a na-tional network of roads and canals had the potential for reshaping Ameri-cans' perceptual geography in ways as grand and yet unimaginable as does an information superhighway today.

What came of Gallatin's vision of a network of roads and canals? In large measure, much of it was built in antebellum America, although little was coordinated, designed, funded, or constructed by the federal government. The federal government did, however, design, fund, and construct one road, variously called the Cumberland Road, Ohio's Road, the Great Western Road, Uncle Sam's Road, Gallatin's Road, America's Appian Way, the National Road, or simply the Road. The Road's eastern portion, the Cumberland Road, crossed the Appalachian Highlands between Cumberland, Maryland, and Springfield, Ohio, linking the Atlantic-flowing Potomac River drainage system with the Ohio Valley system flowing to the Mississippi River and Gulf of Mexico. In so doing, the Road provided a portage, in many ways more symbolic than functional. Functionally, the Road was an integral part of a social and economic landscape. Once the odyssey of American life, it carried heavy traffic in immigrants westward and in farm goods eastward in the antebellum period, before canals and railroads tapped its traffic. Symbolically, it interconnected a national state. "National Road" formally meant the portion built west of Wheeling on the Ohio River after 1820, which connected state capitals at Columbus, Indianapolis, and Vandalia, but the term came commonly to refer to the whole length of road from Cumberland to the Mississippi River. Although the Road was never fully constructed to Jefferson City, Missouri, and all of its links were never fully operational at one time, its very existence on maps gave it authority. Expressed cartographically, the National Road was an embedded social vision of spatial relationships among subnational regions.

In interregional terms, the idea of a national road highlighted concerns of a generation and more of Americans confronting a new environment, which they hoped to shape into a new human geography. It was one thing to survey and construct the Road, lay out adjacent and interconnected settlements, and generate a system of circulation of people, ideas, goods, and capital. It was another thing to conceptualize and define the West and to work out conflicts among competing visions of America's role there: how best to conquer, settle, develop, and exploit the West? The process led to debate over centralized or decentralized control of land and of transportation for economic development and for territorial management.

Agreement to build the Road did not come easily, for the Road thus carried heavy political baggage. Now largely a relict of a bygone era of transportation and political organization of geographical space, it is difficult to imagine why building such a road to bind together the nation was so polit-

JOSEPH S. WOOD

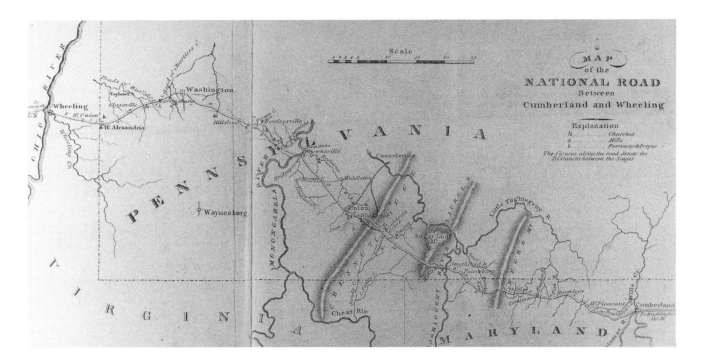

ically charged. However, the Road was one of the great porkbarrel projects in American history, with proponents and opponents often unable to place national interests above regional interests. State congressional delegations fought over the route to be followed, because they knew the impact on certain places would be significant, as it was at least while the Road was alive with traffic. Moreover, debates on siting and funding the Road were fraught with constitutional politics that played themselves out in regional conflicts, the most inflammatory of which was the Civil War.

This chapter deals with these interregional issues that established the context for the idea of a national road. Subsequent chapters delve much more deeply into the physical process of designing, funding, and constructing segments of that road, and thus into the social, economic, and technological processes of conceptualizing, defining, and controlling the land that lay beyond the Appalachian Mountains.

**The National Road between Cumberland and Wheeling as constructed 1811–18**

The National Road formed a functional and symbolic portage linking settled areas of the antebellum United States that drained eastward to the Atlantic and westward to the Mississippi River and the Gulf of Mexico.

## THE NATIONAL ROAD AND THE IDEA OF THE WEST

The West has always been, even in this century, open-ended, a realm of possibilities. Since 1492, "to the West" meant to Asia; cosmographical significance of that idea is with us still today, as many look to the potential of the Pacific Rim. Indeed, two centuries had to pass from Columbus's encounter with the West for Europeans to begin to think in terms of an America separate from Asia.[1] Even then, explorers sought an assumed south sea beyond the Appalachian Mountains; explicit in Lewis and Clark's 1803–5 Expedition was an expectation, finally, of finding the elusive Northwest Passage to Asia. Only with the American Revolution did Europeans both in Europe and in America begin to experience a cosmographical shift in perception: America was transformed perceptually from a western outpost of Europe on the eastern margin of a great new world to an incipient national core from which might spread westward across a continental frontier an empire of liberty.

Speaking for his generation, Jedidiah Morse noted in his 1789 *American Geography* the singular significance of the recently enacted Ordinance of 1787, the purpose of which was to establish national political control over territory north and west of the Ohio River.

> In the ordinance of congress, for the government of this territory, it is provided, that, after the said territory acquires a certain degree of population, it shall be divided into states. The eastern state, that is thus provided to be made, is bounded on the Great Miami [River] on the west, and by the Pennsylvania line on the east. The center of this state will fall between the Scioto and Hockhocking. At the mouth of one of these rivers will probably be the seat of government for this state: And, if we may indulge the sublime contemplation of beholding the whole territory of the United States settled by an enlightened people, and continued under one extended government—on the river Ohio, and not far from this spot, will be the seat of empire for the whole dominion. This is central to the whole; it will best accommodate every part; it is most pleasant, and probably the most healthful.[2]

Morse's geographical prediction was largely off in its particulars, but not in its sentiment. The Ohio River Valley would become an important political and economic force in the antebellum period.

The idea for such an "Ohio Country" in the West for European settlement derived from as early as the 1740s. Indigenous nations, by definition, saw it as home. The French, in contrast, saw the Ohio Country as a connecting link between their realms of exploitation in Canada and the Great Lakes drainage basin and in Louisiana and the Mississippi drainage basin. It was the English who first recognized the Ohio Country as an inevitable western settlement frontier, after several decades of phenomenal population and economic growth in coastal settlements. Writing of population

JOSEPH S. WOOD

growth in 1751, Benjamin Franklin argued that plentiful land would produce a society of large, independent farm families free to manage their own affairs. Land, to be had in the West, would free Americans from laboring for others and living in urban squalor. Land would make Americans morally superior to Europeans.[3] English interest in the West led inevitably to conflict with its indigenous nations and the French. The 1763 conclusion of the French and Indian War, during which the earliest pieces of what would become the National Road were blazed, cleared, and improved, placed the Ohio Country in English political hands, but did not remove it from effective control by indigenous nations. The American Revolution, which passed the Ohio Country from English to American political hands, did not settle territorial control either.

Effective trans-Appalachian settlement south of the Ohio River dates to the 1760s, but not until the 1790s did Americans come to think of the West as a fully habitable abode requiring interconnection to the East. By 1800, settlement east of the Appalachian Highlands stretched from the District of Maine south to beyond the Savannah River into Georgia. To the west, a wedge-shaped protrusion of trans-Appalachian settlement had its apex in the Nashville Basin with an outlier in the Bluegrass Country, and was dissected by the Ohio River and scores of its tributaries that drained the vast interior lowland into the Gulf of Mexico. Here settlers staked fortunes. They transferred portions of an older society with its sectional differences and regional distinctions, and they undertook to invent a new society on that foundation. While some sought solitude, the bulk of immigrants sought a stable world in which to build individual family competence and necessary social, political, and economic institutions from frontier disorder. Statehood provided the vehicle. Kentucky and Tennessee were admitted as the fifteenth and sixteenth states, in 1792 and 1796, respectively. Although most lands north and west of the Ohio River were legally open for settlement only after the Treaty of

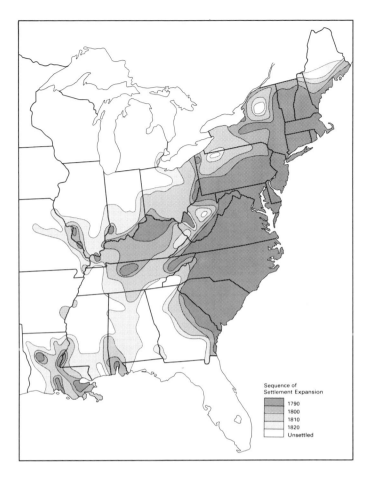

Sequence of
Settlement Expansion

1790
1800
1810
1820
Unsettled

**Settlement extends West**

By 1800 settlement was continuous from Maine to Georgia and inland to the upper reaches of the Ohio River. Over the next several decades, during which the Road was built, pioneers filled in much of the interstitial area not settled in 1800 and extended the wedge of continuously settled area beyond the Mississippi River.

Greenville in 1795, in 1800 45,000 Ohio Territory settlers were calling for statehood.

Still, nowhere in 1800 were eastern and western settlement regions contiguous. American expansion and development in 1800 were stymied by the difficulty of penetrating the Appalachians. Mountain crossing and river travel were hazardous undertakings, and before many Americans had seen the Rocky Mountains or the Sierra Nevada, they were enthralled by the Appalachians. As contemporaries understood, close overland communication alone could hold the geographical divisions of East and West together "either in interest or in fear." Yet, "no civilized country had yet been required to deal with physical difficulties so serious, nor did experience warrant conviction that such difficulties could be overcome."[4]

## CROSSING THE APPALACHIANS

When the West was Ohio, before the purchase of Louisiana and before accurate reports of far western mountains beyond Louisiana, the Appalachians, which some contemporaries called the Endless Mountains, were the "backbone" of the United States. This physical landscape, over and through which the Road was to be built, divided watersheds of rivers flowing through the settled eastern seaboard to the Atlantic Ocean from those flowing northward into the Great Lakes and St. Lawrence and westward into the Mississippi River and Gulf of Mexico.

An east-west transect reveals a number of physiographic provinces between the Atlantic and the Mississippi: The Atlantic Coastal Plain, the Piedmont beyond the Fall Line, the narrow Blue Ridge, the Ridge and Valley, including the Great Valley, and the Appalachian Plateau. The Piedmont is effectively an eroded surface of low hills, today less tree-covered than in the period of the early republic and more tree-covered than in the years when connection to the Road from the East was an important economic stimulant. The Blue Ridge runs southward from Carlisle, Pennsylvania, marking the entrance to the eastern highlands and widening as it goes. The Potomac River crosses the Blue Ridge near Harper's Ferry, where the Potomac's tributary, the Shenandoah River, drains northward from the Great Valley of Virginia. Summer makes the Ridge and Valley appear a sea of green waves, ridges densely treed with chestnut, oak, and poplar in lower elevations and beech, birch, and maple in higher sections. Summits offer an immense prospect, ridge after ridge cut by occasional narrow water gaps or shallow

JOSEPH S. WOOD

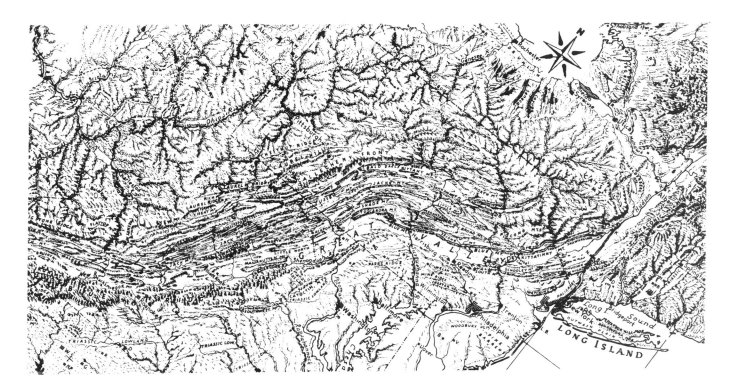

saddle-like wind gaps and interstitial gorges filled with blue and purple haze.

The Ridge and Valley's western margin is the Appalachian Plateau's eastern edge, often called the Allegheny Front. In contrast to orderly waves of ridges and valleys, the plateau is a wide and choppy sea of considerable local relief. Evergreens cloak its highest elevations. Its eastern and western edges are deeply incised. Numerous Ohio River tributaries, whose valleys and alluvial bottomlands attracted settlement in the late eighteenth century, drain the plateau to the north or west. The Allegheny and Monongahela Rivers drain the portion called the Allegheny Plateau; the Kanawha, Kentucky, Cumberland, and Tennessee Rivers drain the portion called the Cumberland Plateau. Stretching far beyond the plateau is a vast central lowland drained by the Mississippi River and its tributaries.[5]

To get around or over the Appalachian Highlands, New Englanders followed the Mohawk Valley across New York and the ridge road along the southern shore of Lake Erie into northern Ohio. Tidewater Southerners moved hesitantly around the Cumberland Plateau's southern end in Georgia. But settlers had long interpenetrated the Appalachian Highlands themselves, learning paths into and across it. Most western settlers moved west through Pennsylvania by the Forbes Road or from the Southern backcoun-

**The Appalachian Highlands, "backbone" of the early republic**

For pioneers in 1800, the Appalachians were a formidable barrier—they slowed the movement of goods and symbolized a division between the settled East and the to-be-settled West. Still, contemporary commentators recognized that the future of the United States lay west of the mountains, and referred to them as the new nation's "backbone."

**Principal routes westward, c. 1800**

Most movement westward in 1800 followed the Mohawk Valley and shores of Lakes Ontario and Erie, Pennsylvania's Forbes Road, or the Great Valley Road in Virginia and its Wilderness Road extension.

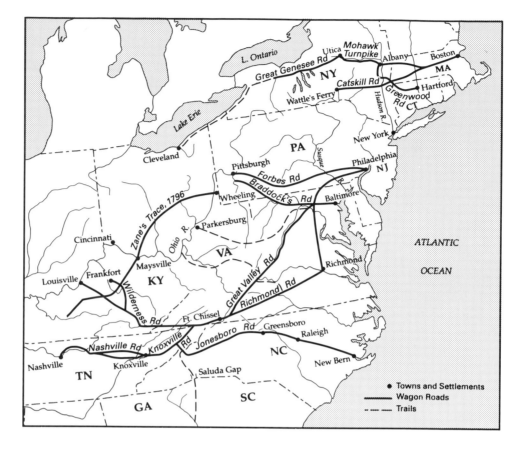

try via the Wilderness Road through Cumberland Gap, into the valleys and alluvial bottomlands of Ohio River tributaries draining the plateau.

Pennsylvania's Forbes Road, first opened in 1758 and otherwise unimproved in 1800, crossed the Ridge and Valley and climbed onto the Allegheny Plateau to reach Pittsburgh, at the confluence of the Monongahela and Allegheny Rivers where they form the Ohio. From Philadelphia, one could travel to Carlisle either via Reading, Lebanon, and Harrisburg, or via Lancaster, Wright's Ferry, and York. From there one proceeded to Shippensburg, Bedford, and over the Allegheny Front—the escarpment dividing Ridge and Valley from plateau—to Greensburg, Pittsburgh, and West Liberty, before reaching the Ohio River at Wheeling. The trip of 389 miles taking eight or nine days in 1800 led to settlements in western Pennsylvania and Virginia and was the most direct route to the Ohio Country.

Daniel Boone's Wilderness Road connected the Great Valley Road in the Shenandoah Valley, via Hagerstown (Maryland), Winchester, Staunton, and Abingdon (Virginia), with the trans-Appalachian West. It ran west through the Cumberland and Pine Mountain Gaps to Boonesboro on the Kentucky River and on to Louisville at the Falls of the Ohio. The objective was the Kentucky Bluegrass Country or Tennessee's Nashville Basin. The route's mountain section was little more than a pack trail in 1800.

A third road was no more than an overgrown path from Fort Cumberland on the Potomac River at the foot of the Allegheny Front to Pittsburgh—a relict road constructed during the French and Indian War and in 1800 barely passable for horses, let alone wagons. This path westward across the watershed divide, effectively a portage, connected feeder routes from the Piedmont through the Ridge and Valley section—from Frederick and Hagerstown in Maryland, or from Alexandria and Winchester in Virginia—before climbing the Allegheny Front at Cumberland, Maryland. When Congress approved a national road to connect east and west in 1806, it designated this path from Cumberland westward as the route to follow.[6]

The colonial system of commerce had been trans-Atlantic; each of the thirteen colonies was more closely connected to London than to one another. Roads were for local intercourse or channeled flows of traffic eastward to coastal ports. They did not interlink colonies generally. After 1783, however, Americans quickly recognized the need for land-based interstate and interregional access among the newly independent states and to the trans-

The "Endless Mountains" (date unknown)

To settlers crossing the Appalachians, the mountains seemed endless, both in the north to south extent, and in their breadth from east to west. The Ridge and Valley was separated from the Allegheny Plateau by the Allegheny Front. By the early decades of the twentieth century, the mighty ridges still impeded travel.

Appalachian interior, where, Jedidiah Morse had noted, would come to be "the seat of empire for the whole dominion."[7] Still, this West was filled with menace, and the potential for disunion from factors both internal and external was exceedingly great. European settlers streaming west in the 1780s had no necessarily vested interest in union with the East. Trade depended upon the Ohio River, flowing into the Mississippi and on to then Spanish-controlled New Orleans to move goods to markets in the East or overseas.

## COBBLING TOGETHER EAST AND WEST

Leaders recognized the need to construct roads and canals to integrate the fledgling nation. By 1800, one great north-south mail route from Portland, Maine, to Louisville, Georgia, connected North and South. Some 20,000 miles of post roads, however, "proved the vastness of the country and the smallness of the result." For east-west travel, the "Great Highway of Pennsylvania," the Forbes Road from Philadelphia to Pittsburgh, "was a more important artery of national life than was controlled by any other state."[8] The idea of a national road, however, was to link East to West where the trans-Appalachian wedge of settlement in 1800 was deepest and widest, and where the eastern terminus could connect to the Potomac, and thereby to the Chesapeake Bay, to Baltimore, and to the new federal capital at Washington. Moreover, need was for a "constructed" or "artificial" road, one ditched and surfaced with gravel or pounded stones to form a solid bed able to support wagon traffic.[9] Such a road was a costly enterprise that could not adequately be supported by local taxes or local citizens working off taxes. Nor could it be adequately funded by private interests intending to collect tolls. Only the federal government could provide the capital and equipment needed to build a broad, stone-paved highway across the mountains.

Thomas Jefferson, elected president in 1800, was responsible for assimilating the West politically and economically into the conceptual geography of Americans. He acquired Louisiana and sent Lewis and Clark to explore the West, seeking secure access to the fur trade, fertile land for occupation, and easy passage to Asia. Jefferson's treasury secretary, Swiss-born Albert Gallatin, who came to the United States in 1780, then set about to plan the economic and settlement geography of this West with a network of roads and canals. The consequent cobbling together of East and West in antebellum America created the foundation for a national economy and a political union. Newly independent Americans turned from looking eastward toward Europe to looking increasingly westward toward what they came to believe was their manifest destiny. The exotic and imagined became the material. America's romantic West was for large numbers a truly open-ended realm of possibilities that had before been available to only a few. Into this new geography Americans could introduce a modern conception of western civilization's proudest achievements. In this context, the Road, formally approved in 1806, would symbolize the search for union and economic stability and continued expansion of the trans-Appalachian West in antebellum America. Along the Road waves of immigrants would flow westward as the land's resources and the goods settlers produced flowed eastward.

For some time into the nineteenth century, the West was actually as much a problem as an asset. Three decades passed after the Louisiana Purchase before American military control over indigenous nations east of the Mississippi River was assured. Still, during this period, as the Road was designed, funded, and constructed, occurred one of the great migrations in history, far exceeding anything before it in numbers of people, land occupation, and national impact. By 1850, settlement had spread over a third of the continent—well beyond the Mississippi River. This antebellum trans-Appalachian migration conveyed a sense of energy that separated it from earlier frontier experience. Settlers were no longer disconnected from the current of national life, as had been their late-eighteenth-century predecessors. They carried westward American political, economic, and social ideals as much as sectional differences and regional distinctions, with all their virtues and prejudices, their strengths and weaknesses.[10]

## THE ELUSIVE REPUBLICAN VISION

Orchestrating such economic development and political union was the primary challenge facing government in post-Revolutionary America, and followers of Alexander Hamilton and Thomas Jefferson contested the means. Hamiltonians conceived of America as an economically advanced modern state equal to Great Britain. They accepted commercialization of society and development of industry at the expense of agriculture as not only inevitable but also fundamentally beneficial. Economic development modeled after Europe meant strong union. Jeffersonianism, in contrast, reflected an attempt to cling to traditional agrarian notions without disregarding imperatives of modern commercial society. Such republicanism, premised on free exchange and complementary interest, was meant to manage national territory and foster economic development for all while minimizing sectional rivalries. Mutually beneficial trade would produce a durable bond of union, encouraging Easterners to anticipate prosperous returns from new western markets and western farmers to cultivate strong ties to the East.[11] Hamiltonians and Jeffersonians played out this contest for America's future in the decades following the Revolutionary War. Each saw the Constitution as a vehicle to advance its vision of political economy, and each, when in power, found daunting the task of implementing its vision.

## THE AGRARIAN REPUBLIC

Jeffersonian republicanism connoted a specific configuration of assumptions, ideas, beliefs, and values that shaped a vision of expansion across America as a necessary alternative to the development through time of a society that was generally thought to bring with it both political corruption and social decay.[12] Jefferson was hard put to accept as a basic political premise that a state had a monopoly of legitimate control over a prescribed territory, and he treated the United States as a loosely bound confederation, even after adoption of the Constitution. His vision of an expanding empire of liberty over a huge continent posed no problems for his relaxed idea of a state. As long as Americans continued to believe certain things, they remained Americans. Jefferson's extraordinary belief in the "natural sociability" of people substituted for traditional force of government and made Hamiltonians dismiss him as a hopeless dreamer. Jefferson, indeed, had to overcome his constitutional scruples to buy Louisiana. Only because he understood a national road as geographically fostering "natural sociability" of a people to manifest itself could he be convinced to support it.[13]

Jefferson's republican conception of political economy was for America to sustain itself as a young and virtuous agrarian nation that offered opportunity for Europe's landless poor and a market for manufactured goods Europe was forced by population growth to produce. Agriculture, it was generally agreed, was inherently virtuous, the most natural of economic pursuits—an agrarian myth pervasive of political ideology today.[14] As long as Americans could balance open lands for settlement with adequate foreign markets for their produce, the United States would remain a nation of industrious farmers marketing surpluses abroad in exchange for necessary manufactured goods. The critical variable was access to market. On the one hand, if frontier farmers had no way to market what they produced, they

JOSEPH S. WOOD

had little incentive to emigrate to the West and, Jefferson feared, would develop industry and forever alter the familiar agrarianism that rooted Americans to the land. Lack of market would turn those industrious farmers who did settle the frontier lethargic, or worse. It was exactly this commonly held concern that justified appeals for internal improvements. On the other hand, in order to remain predominantly agricultural, America needed also to expand its export market, without which it would be required, like Europe, to increase manufacturing. Jeffersonians did not oppose the new Constitution, for to create an agrarian republic required a central government strong enough to shape a republican political economy in which Americans might industriously engage in virtue-sustaining occupations. Government needed to encourage westward expansion while opening foreign markets to American produce to ensure that Americans could sustain population growth in an agricultural and republican nation.[15]

Hamiltonians also supported the Constitution, in order to provide a central government strong enough to shape the necessary political economy to produce a powerful commercial state. With Federalists in control of government under George Washington and his successor John Adams during the 1790s, Treasury Secretary Hamilton maneuvered to advance his vision that America should move to achieve its fullest social and economic development. He wanted to raise public funds to produce growth-inducing capital to develop manufactures. To do so, he believed, required that he restrain western settlement and concentrate capital, as he did with a 1791 excise tax, to develop American industry. For many Americans, Hamilton's plan was turning the revolution upside down—it was "anglicization"—and opposition became emotional as well as ideological. Hamilton's plan threatened both the fundamental principles of a virtuous agrarian republic and democratic land ownership on which it depended. Antifederalists, as Jeffersonians came to call themselves, did not oppose household manufactures, but they did oppose what they called "artificial" forms of manufacturing that could not survive without government subsidy and special privilege. The matter came to focus on the "general welfare" clause of the Constitution, which Antifederalists feared Hamilton would employ to fashion a distinctly unrepublican society.[16]

While Hamiltonians carried the day politically throughout the 1790s, high European demand for American produce actually stymied Hamilton's plans, for capital generated was reinvested in trade, not manufacturing.

Prosperity enjoyed in the East encouraged commercial expansion and western settlement alike (161–65). Still, Antifederalists were not happy, arguing in 1799 that agriculture and commerce were naturally connected only when commerce directly encouraged agriculture. Since the bulk of America's foreign commerce at the time was in the carrying trade, involving little export of domestic goods or import of European manufactured goods, the commerce was "unnatural," "a sort of extraneous staple" (175–77).

In the 1800 election, Jefferson and his supporters engaged in a crusade to halt what they saw as a political economy undermining productivity and moral integrity of a republican citizenry. By winning election, Jeffersonians could implement alternative policies that would postpone for as long as possible that tragic day when the American republic would cease to be virtuously agrarian. This "Revolution of 1800" was a return to first principles and restoration of republican values and ideals—development of an agricultural empire extended across space—that had been repudiated under the Federalists (185–87). Still, tools required to carry out the vision challenged the integrity of Jefferson's philosophy itself, as constitutional issues and sectional rivalries conspired to undermine the vision.[17]

The Louisiana Purchase was the geographical complement of the Revolution of 1800. It provided the effective economic base to allow Jefferson to perpetuate his vision. Since the 1780s Americans had considered free navigation on the Mississippi to New Orleans essential to national interest. Pinckney's Treaty of 1795 with Spain granted rights to trade through New Orleans, and by 1800 the Mississippi provided primary access to market for produce of more than half a million Americans living in the trans-Appalachian West. But after Spain transferred Louisiana back to France in 1800, Napoleonic ambitions in the Mississippi River Valley posed a serious threat to the American republic's westward expansion. Jefferson contained frenzy over the threat and proceeded to purchase the whole of Louisiana, permanently solving the problem of market access via the Mississippi and New Orleans, and thereby of prosperity for western farmers. The very character of western society itself, fundamental republican insistence on interdependence of economic life and moral integrity of the individual personality, had been at stake. The Louisiana Purchase made possible existence of a republican civilization in the American West by permitting Westerners both to secure land and to engage in foreign commerce.[18] Federalists viewed the Louisiana Purchase as a "frivolous" enterprise, beyond gaining

JOSEPH S. WOOD

control of New Orleans, arguing that it dispersed population over too great a distance and thus led to decentralization of power. But for Jeffersonians, Louisiana promised a fundamentally agricultural American society for centuries to come. It was a bold geographical solution to a problem of sustaining a revolution to preserve republican character (200–201).

Louisiana also exposed contradictions within the republican vision. It was not enough to provide land and access to New Orleans. Settlement and trade required an interventionist foreign policy to expand export markets to absorb surpluses of active, industrious, republican farmers who would settle the newly acquired lands. Settlement and trade also required territorial aggression against native peoples and their removal from the newly acquired lands. Managing the pillars of republicanism engaged republicans in conflict over land within the West and over trade on the high seas (204–8). The resulting embargo and war footing limited the Jeffersonian vision and fostered concern that the domestic market was hindered by too dispersed a pattern of settlement. Roads became necessary to muster troops and defend frontiers from both indigenous nations and European powers and to permit greater productivity from an integrated domestic commerce in an elusive world of free trade (242).

## THE NATIONAL ROAD IN SHAPING THE NATION

On the pragmatic side in the Hamilton-Jefferson contest was the need for government to raise revenue and exercise authority. The imperative for cash resulted from federal assumption of state Revolutionary War debts in exchange for relinquishing ownership of western lands. If the union could achieve military primacy along its frontier arc and protect western trade, settlers might be inclined to accept federal control of western lands. More settlers would buy land, generating revenue to pay off federally assumed debts. In preparation for sale and settlement of land, Congress enacted the Ordinance of 1785 to reserve for the federal government land north and west of the Ohio and to provide for its survey into townships and sections. The Northwest Ordinance of 1787 further provided a framework of government and ultimate creation of three to five new states.

Treaties of Fort Stanwix in 1768 and 1784 defined the frontier arc north and west of the Ohio River which separated western nations of indigenous peoples from European settlers. Defense of their position by western nations held up sales of land north and west of the Ohio River, although the census of 1790 counted some 7,800 settlers there. As Jedidiah Morse cautioned in 1793, "The settlement of this country has been checked for several years past, by the unhappy Indian war, an amicable termination of which it is ardently wished, might speedily take place."[19] The mid-1790s presented a turning point. In the 1795 Treaty of Greenville following the 1794 Battle of Fallen Timbers, western nations abandoned 25,000 square miles of land north and west of the Ohio for immediate settlement. Jay's 1794 treaty led to British withdrawal from territory south of the Great Lakes as well. And Pinckney's 1795 treaty with the Spanish opened the Mississippi River to American trade. Land sales jumped after 1795.[20]

With slowness of land sales before 1795, Hamilton had imposed an excise tax. Westerners' response—the Whiskey Rebellion in western Pennsylvania in 1791–94—kept the Federalist government leery of Westerners and of increased sale of lands that would accelerate settlement. Selling land, as opposed to giving it away, of course, was a mechanism of screening for industrious, moral, and orderly settlement—only those with cash could afford to buy, presumed the Federalists, who wanted only loyal citizens to move west. So how could government regulate and restrain western settlement while generating enough income from land sales to provide defense against native peoples and control against secession? These matters put the federal government in a quandary. Both war with native peoples and rebellion and secession in the West would mean loss of revenue and higher military expenditures.[21]

Even with apparent settlement of conflict with the western nations in 1795, concern with disunion did not dissipate; indeed it was heightened. Albert Gallatin had himself been caught up in the Whiskey Rebellion. He had attempted to articulate demands of his neighbors in western Fayette County, Pennsylvania, and thereby preempt Hamilton's dispatch of federal troops to quell those refusing to pay excise tax on their only cheaply exportable good, which Hamilton needed to settle federal debt. The consequence was immediate enmity of Gallatin and Hamilton, and memory of Hamilton's treatment of the West weighed heavily on Gallatin when he replaced Hamilton as treasury secretary in 1801. Under his direction, the Jefferson administration relaxed land sales requirements imposed by Federalists, encouraging sales in smaller units and for easier credit than before, and thereby encouraging greater settlement in accord with Jeffersonian principles and belief in "natural sociability."[22]

JOSEPH S. WOOD

At the same time, the Aaron Burr affair became a fresh reminder of need to strengthen union. Burr, perhaps best known for killing Hamilton in a duel in 1804, was Jefferson's first-term vice-president. Jefferson and Burr were hardly political allies, and Burr was unceremoniously dropped from the Democratic-Republican ticket in 1804 in favor of fellow New Yorker George Clinton. By 1805, Burr was reported in the Mississippi Valley plotting a western confederation, and a year later was reported leading a band of armed conspirators in a filibustering expedition against the Spanish in Vera Cruz. Jefferson called for arrest of any conspirator, and troops captured Burr in 1807. Acquitted for lack of conclusive evidence, he retreated to Europe.[23] With such goings-on, it was no political impossibility, many in the period of the early republic believed, for the Mississippi Valley to separate eventually from the eastern seaboard. The situation was simple enough. The West sought political acceptance, and the East was concerned the West would become too independent. The contest of wills shaped subsequent politics.

In the context, then, of Jeffersonian republicanism and the economic and political tensions of the Jeffersonian era, the National Road must be viewed as a device for western development—potentially a generator of profits as well as a tool for managing and defending territory beyond the Appalachians. A road would enable land sales and settlement, and it would enable troops to move west to quell any uprising that might occur there. A road, in short, would extend the reach of central authority at the same time it pointed the direction that settlement, and possible disunion, might follow. Although Washington and Hamilton were early supporters of a federal role in internal improvements, chiefly roads and canals, it was left to their antifederalist successors, Jefferson and Gallatin, to take the first tentative steps to implement a plan. By 1800, many Americans recognized that links between the Atlantic coast and the interior were essential for both economic and political reasons. Jeffersonians could justify a federal transportation plan as necessary for shaping a rational and orderly republican geography.

## BUILDING THE NATIONAL ROAD

Important questions remaining were how and where to build the road. More common in the late eighteenth and early nineteenth centuries than today was the practice of setting up private corporations to develop internal improvements. Such corporations usually held monopolies and operated under local franchise and regulation of public agencies, although the dividend was often in trade generated, not tolls collected. The practice worked where profitable complementarity existed between places of some proximity, hardly the case here. Thus, private developers in conjunction with merchants in eastern cities were keen on federal support for internal improvements.[24] Adam Smith in his 1776 *Wealth of Nations* had noted that "functions of government should be limited to providing for external defense, affording legal protection, and undertaking indispensable public works," the latter of which "can never be for the interest of any individual, or small number of individuals, though it may frequently do much more than repay it to a great society." Following this logic, Westerners argued that the federal government owned the land and was obligated therefore to build the roads. Roads would attract settlers who would buy land that would pay a dividend to the treasury. Eastern cities anticipating competition with one another over western access, however, feared that one particular government-built road might give one city advantage. As a consequence, rancorous debate in 1806 over passage of enabling legislation for a national road exposed bitter rivalries and jealousies. Proponents of federal involvement in road-building asserted that authority to build roads was implied under the Constitution's "general welfare" clause. Strict constructionists, on the other hand, denied that government had authority to undertake internal improvements, except possibly in territories under direct federal jurisdiction. In the end, those who felt strongly about land sales to generate income for the federal treasury and western settlement to strengthen union decided the issue—at least for the National Road.[25]

The Potomac River was an obvious entry point to the Ohio Country. Here watersheds flowing to the Atlantic Ocean and to the Gulf of Mexico lie in especially close proximity. Geographer Jedidiah Morse, assessing prospects for trade from the Cuyahoga River at present-day Cleveland, Ohio, saw the matter clearly. Lake Erie, he argued, was closer to Alexandria, Virginia, via the Big Beaver, Ohio, and Potomac than to New York City via the Niagara, Mohawk, and Hudson by some 400 miles and by fewer and shorter portages. The Potomac rarely froze and was secure from threat of Indian tribes and the British in Canada. While the New York route was better known, extending navigation on the Potomac with a bypass of Great Falls was not difficult. Morse's only qualification was whether Philadelphia might succeed in establishing linkage via the Susquehanna River, in which

JOSEPH S. WOOD

case he predicted that Philadelphia "in all probability will become, in some future period, the largest city that has ever yet existed."[26]

Understanding this perceptual geography is important. George Washington quite purposefully sited the new federal capital district upon the Potomac in 1790, and Morse noted its geographical centrality:

> The situation of this metropolis [of Washington] is upon the great post road, equidistant from the northern and southern extremities of the Union, and nearly so from the Atlantic and Pittsburg[h], upon the best navigation, and in the midst of a commercial territory, probably the richest, and commanding the most extensive internal resources of any in America.[27]

Washington and the Potomac commanded access to the interior as no other place within reach of the Atlantic could. Functionally as well as symbolically, it made sense for a federal road to run west from the seat of power. Given concern for defense of frontier boundaries, the logic was doubly sound.

From the Potomac west, it made sense as well to begin at Cumberland, Maryland, effective head of navigation for small craft, if Great Falls above Georgetown, in the District of Columbia, was bypassed. As early as 1748, Wills Creek, later Fort Cumberland, was the jumping-off point for the Ohio Country. Previous paths west had begun there, passing westward through one of two low saddles or gaps in the Allegheny Front, either to the Youghiogheny River, a Monongahela tributary, or directly to the Monongahela, a portage variously of thirty-five to forty miles. Delaware Chief Nemacolin's Path, cut and cleared during early posturing of English with French, was a 1751–52 pack trail to the mouth of Redstone Creek on the Monongahela near Brownsville in Pennsylvania. As a pack trail, it required footing for animals carrying loads. In 1753–54, surveyor George Washington widened Nemacolin's Path for wagons to the Great Meadows stockade, which we have come to know as Fort Necessity. English General Braddock further widened and relocated the road as necessary for troops and wagons in 1755. Braddock's Road, chopped to a twelve-foot width, allowed 150 Conestoga wagons to pass single file for 115 miles from Fort Cumberland to the Monongahela at Turtle Creek in the vicinity of present-day Pittsburgh. After carrying Braddock's body and his defeated troops in retreat, the road reverted to an overgrown trace. Traders then used it only sporadically as a pack-horse trail, while the Forbes Road carried most overland traffic to and from Pittsburgh and settlements in western Pennsylvania and on down the Ohio River.[28]

The Northwest Ordinance specified 5 percent of the proceeds from public land sales be used to build a road to and within the first new state north of the Ohio River. Treasury Secretary Gallatin inserted in the 1802 Ohio statehood bill a provision for a road from the eastern seaboard across the breadth of the new state, and of the set-aside 3 percent was for construction of roads within Ohio and 2 percent to provide access both to the east and elsewhere in the Northwest Territory.[29] Following a report on the matter, Congress formally established a "2 percent fund" derived from sale of public lands to be used under Congress's direction for constructing roads to and through Ohio. With this action as precedent, Louisiana, Indiana, Mississippi, Illinois, Alabama, and Missouri, on their admission to statehood, received 3 percent grants for roads, canals, levees, river improvements, and schools. Congress later granted an additional 2 percent to these states, except Indiana and Illinois, which, with Ohio, had already received equivalency in expenditures for the National Road. The remaining twenty-four states admitted to the Union between 1820 and 1910 received 5 percent grants, except Texas and West Virginia, which at the time of statehood had no federal lands.[30]

People talked a lot about a road after Ohio statehood in 1803, but several years passed before enabling legislation in 1806 and funding for surveys in 1808. Construction began in 1811. Its chronology reveals much about the Road's history for succeeding decades. Sen. Thomas Worthington of Ohio introduced in 1805 a bill to appropriate the 5 percent of land revenues already collected, although it failed to pass. Still the 1805 Senate committee report on the bill was important. It rejected a northern route from Philadelphia and a southern route from Richmond in favor of a central route from Cumberland.[31] Both the Pennsylvania and Virginia congressional delegations opposed the bill, because of the disadvantage they saw to their respective states. Over their continued opposition, however, Congress passed an act in 1806 directing the president to appoint three commissioners to lay out and build the "Cumberland Road" from the head of navigation on the Potomac River at Cumberland, Maryland, to a point on the Ohio River. The act set certain minimum standards for the proposed road and called for an appropriation of $30,000 from proceeds of Ohio land sales to finance road location and to start construction.[32] Jefferson and the Democratic-Republicans favored the bill, of course. The Federalists' successors, the Whigs, led by former Northwest Territory governor Gen. Arthur St. Clair, opposed it, their concern being the West's too rapidly increasing importance with respect to the East's political power.

The Cumberland Road, so designated by the 1806 enabling act, was a national project effectively paralleling the Mason-Dixon Line dividing Maryland from Pennsylvania. Starting at Cumberland it was quickly to pass into Pennsylvania and then cross a small neck of Virginia on its way to Ohio and the Northwest Territory, while allowing Maryland to make the local connection eastward. Maryland had acted in 1792 to open a turnpike west from Frederick to Cumberland, and a plan for linking Baltimore to Cumberland dates from 1797. Maryland state banks financed the road, portions variously called the Bank Road, the Baltimore Pike, or the National Pike—not to be confused with the National Road. The connection to Cumberland from the east for George Washington and General Braddock had been via Winchester, Virginia, in the Shenandoah Valley. The National Pike offered a link from Baltimore across both the Piedmont and the Ridge and Valley to the beginning of Braddock's Road at Cumberland. Traffic from Washington, in the new District of Columbia, used this linkage as well, as it was more direct than the former Virginia path from Alexandria through Winchester. Following Braddock's Road, the new road was to proceed west and cross the Monongahela River at Brownsville, Pennsylvania, then a flatboat launching site, to complete the portage. Pennsylvania's representatives blocked construction until they could reroute the Road within Gallatin's western Pennsylvania. Consequently it swerved south of its westerly arc into Pennsylvania to pass through Uniontown and then north to pass through the town of Washington before heading for the Ohio River where it would connect to Zane's Trace in Ohio.[33]

Construction to Wheeling on the Ohio River was completed in 1818, but not until 1820 did Congress appropriate the funds to survey west of there, with instructions that the Road was to run as straight as possible toward St. Louis. In Ohio, the Road picked up Ebenezer Zane's blazed trail from Wheeling as far as the Muskingum River. It continued on eventually with little interruption in its westward trajectory through Indiana and Illinois toward the Mississippi. In subsequent years, Congress made occasional and minimal appropriations for extending and maintaining the Road, but they were inadequate to preserve it under ever-increasing traffic by wagoners and drovers with great herds of cows and pigs. In 1820, for example, Congress agreed to extend the National Road to the Mississippi River, but it only appropriated the necessary $4 million for construction in 1825. At that time, Congress modified the plan to connect new state capitals at Columbus, Ohio, Indianapolis, Indiana, and Vandalia, Illinois, and to extend the Road to Jefferson City, Missouri. Shortly thereafter, retreating from a direct national role in transportation, Congress returned the Road's eastern section to its respective states. Westernmost sections in Indiana and Illinois were unfinished when Congress refused to provide more money in 1838. The Road reached Vandalia, Illinois, 591 miles from Cumberland, Maryland, and 750 miles from Baltimore, only in 1850. By 1856 all rights connected with the entire road had been ceded to the states.[34]

As the Road crept westward, it increased local property values, much like the Interstate Highway System has done in the twentieth century. It was, likewise, a significant source of local construction profit and it generated local intercourse and reoriented local traffic. It served central Ohio and central Indiana well for those desiring to travel to Wheeling, but most traffic west of Wheeling remained local. East of Wheeling the story was different. Heavy traffic in goods and people, including slaves, moved into and out of the Ohio Country along the Road. It even allowed Baltimore momentarily to surpass Philadelphia as the second most populous city behind New York City in the 1820s.[35] Still, no economic transformational boom equivalent to the Erie Canal's opening accompanied the Road's construction.

In 1840, Ohio, a state for fewer than four decades, achieved third ranking nationally in population, as geographer Jedidiah Morse had expected it might. A string of Ohio Valley presidents in the latter nineteenth century attested to its political might. The Road, of course, guided settlement across the state from Wheeling, and it interconnected the capital, Columbus, with places both east and west of Ohio. The Road also linked places whose relative importance was much greater then than it is now: Cumberland and Frostburg in Maryland; Uniontown, Brownsville, and Washington in Pennsylvania; Wheeling in (West) Virginia; Cambridge, Zanesville, and Springfield in Ohio; Richmond, Greenfield, and Terre Haute in Indiana; and Vandalia in Illinois. Along the Road, moreover, developed the earliest trans-Appalachian industrial region before the focus shifted from western Pennsylvania to the Great Lakes after the Civil War. Still, by 1840, as the Road crossed Ohio into eastern Indiana, the railroad was proving its utility east of

JOSEPH S. WOOD

the Appalachians, and its potential as a threat to road-oriented business was apparent. The Baltimore & Ohio reached Wheeling in 1852, and within two years the Chicago & Rock Island reached the Mississippi. By the 1870s, the Road was little more than an underused lane over much of its length.

## THE ROAD AND INTERNAL IMPROVEMENTS

The Road was only a small portion of a geographical vision for the nation. Treasury Secretary Gallatin produced in 1808 a monumental report for the Senate on internal improvements that, if ever built, would shape a modern, orderly American geography. His *Report on Roads and Canals* was a comprehensive scheme for a federally funded system of transportation to extend across the nation and link eastern rivers with the Mississippi Basin. The scheme included an intercoastal waterway, a canal linking the Hudson River with the Great Lakes, and another canal around Niagara Falls. A great turnpike would connect the Atlantic states from Maine to Georgia. Four principal highways would cross the Appalachian Highlands, linking by means of heavy-duty turnpikes the Susquehanna River with the Allegheny, the Potomac River with the Monongahela, the James River with the Kanawha, and the Santee or the Savannah River with the Tennessee. Military roads would lead to New Orleans, Detroit, and St. Louis, defense as always a justification for building highways. Gallatin was convinced that only the central government could marshal the necessary resources, some $20 million over ten years, or one-seventh of the government's annual revenues. Even more than a network of highways and canals, however, Gallatin's report envisioned the economic underpinnings of Jefferson's agrarian republic. The report assumed the economic interdependence of several regions and pointed to a larger strategy, in Jeffersonian terms, of a single national market with regional specializations.[36]

### Albert Gallatin

Of all the actors in the National Road drama, Albert Gallatin may be the most important. Born into the old aristocracy of Geneva, Switzerland, in 1761, he was a student of Rousseau. Perceiving his future in Geneva limited by the very aristocratic conditions that allowed his liberal education, he departed in 1780 for America, where he became a land speculator in the backwoods of Virginia and Pennsylvania.

Gallatin gained effective locational control of goods that flowed through

**Albert Gallatin**

One of the handful of most influential people in the early republic and antebellum periods, Gallatin served as congressman, treasury secretary, and diplomat. Only the fact of his foreign birth seems to have kept him from the presidency.

the intersection of overland and river routes at the Monongahela, while simultaneously promoting western development. He joined the Philadelphia Society for Promoting Improvements of Roads and Inland Navigation, aware as he was of the economic geography that pitted Philadelphia and Baltimore against one another for control of western trade. But he hedged his bets. He supported the Lancaster Turnpike in 1794, the first privately franchised turnpike in the United States. He also saw his own Fayette County benefiting more from connections to Baltimore than to Philadelphia, and ultimately he staked his fortune on Baltimore.

As a congressman from 1795 to 1801, he voiced concerns that Westerners be protected against raids by native peoples and against unfavorable balance of trade with eastern merchants, and that they get transportation to and within the West. He encouraged land sales to further empower the West politically in the new nation. He opposed too strong a central government and was recognized as an articulate spokesperson for the antifederalist cause, which won Jefferson the presidency in 1800.[37]

In 1801, Jefferson appointed Gallatin treasury secretary and James Madison secretary of state, thus making Gallatin one of the two most powerful people in the new Democratic-Republican administration. Gallatin controlled finances, and his goals were to reduce federal debt, reduce taxes, and bring efficient administration to the treasury, something he had accused Hamilton of not doing. He encouraged the Louisiana Purchase, all the while bemoaning the cost, and he arranged finances for the deal. In this strange mix of European nobleman and American nationalist and frontiersman, he was both an Antifederalist and a strong unionist. He favored western development, he shared Jefferson's vision of an agrarian republic, and he dreamed of a Rousseau-like Eden in the Kanawha Valley, today an industrial wasteland. He worked to achieve these ends—the first Jeffersonian pillar of political economy—by favoring defense against European imperialism, accession of new territories to the union, democratic and systematic opening of national domain to settlement, and construction of roads and canals to unite all sections.

In this respect, his National Road support was part of a large scheme, not only for ensuring internal improvements, but also for formulating a complete national plan. A comprehensive system of land sales would produce a sinking fund to retire federal debt, while a coastal survey and construction of a network of roads and canals would enhance commerce. Gallatin had

JOSEPH S. WOOD

always supported land sales at reasonable prices, and he worked to encourage access to frontier land for the less affluent. Believing that land makes people wealthy, he opposed Federalist concerns for screening by high prices. It was Gallatin, moreover, who in the Ohio statehood bill in 1802 earmarked federal land proceeds in Ohio to construct roads from the Atlantic seaboard and across the breadth of the state. His support for the Cumberland Road was politically important, and his reports on roads and canals in 1808 and on manufactures in 1810 were significant documents in shaping an American geographical consciousness in the early republic.

Constitutionality

Foreign affairs and impending war with Britain kept the attention of Jefferson's and Madison's administrations, and delayed Gallatin's projects. Still it is questionable if Congress would ever have adequately funded them, given the National Road's history. War heightened the issue of defense of western lands, especially during and after the War of 1812, which made communication with the West and with outposts on the Great Lakes and the Gulf of Mexico more imperative than ever before. After the War of 1812, government leaders felt almost unanimous enthusiasm for improved roads to the old Northwest frontier with Canada and the old Southwest frontier—Arkansas Territory—with Mexico. The British blockade of the eastern coast had stimulated land carriage and emphasized highway inadequacies. And there was precedent for federal spending on postal and military roads. What is surprising, then, is the long and inconclusive constitutional debate over internal improvements that followed. In 1817, Rep. John C. Calhoun of South Carolina and Speaker of the House Henry Clay of Kentucky proposed their "American System" of higher tariffs to protect domestic manufacturers and underwrite a modest national transportation network. They noted, hopefully, that in the wake of war nationalism would take precedence over party and sectional feelings, Calhoun declaring, "Let us bind the republic together with a perfect system of roads and canals."[38] Jefferson, no longer in office, opposed the American System, based as it was on a national bank, a protective tariff for manufactures, and a program of federally sponsored internal improvements. To Jefferson, this system was thinly disguised Hamiltonianism. That Clay and other Republicans conceived of and defended the American System as the logical fulfillment of mature Jeffersonian principles, which sought creation of a balanced, independent, and self-sufficient economy, did nothing to appease him. The plan occasioned bitter wrangling, and when it finally passed Congress, Pres. James Madison, in one of his last presidential acts, vetoed it on constitutional grounds.[39]

Madison's was not the only veto of internal-improvements legislation, nor were he and his successors always consistent by supporting some and not other internal improvements. Pres. James Monroe vetoed an act authorizing collection of tolls on the National Road as an unwarranted extension of power vested in Congress to make appropriations. Toll collection implied to Monroe a power of sovereignty that was not granted the federal government by the Constitution and could not be unilaterally conveyed to any state without a constitutional amendment. It was one thing, in other words, to make appropriations for public improvements, and another to assume jurisdiction where improvements were made. Monroe's veto established the federal position on state highway grants, which endured until the mid-twentieth century.[40]

Finally, Pres. Andrew Jackson's veto of a bill in 1830 funding the Maysville Turnpike in Kentucky profoundly influenced national policy with respect to internal improvements of purely local character. Jackson was not personally hostile to internal improvements; in fact, this first western president recommended to Congress distributing among the states an embarrassing yearly surplus of federal revenue from land sales to be used for internal improvements.[41] But veto of the Maysville Turnpike bill, which would have allowed the federal government to purchase stock in a sixty-mile Kentucky turnpike, brought most discussion of direct federal involvement in internal improvements to a close. Jackson later boasted in his farewell address that he had "finally overthrown . . . this plan of unconstitutional expenditure for the purpose of corrupt influence."[42] States continued to fund state-owned turnpikes, such as one in Virginia from Winchester to the Ohio River at Parkersburg completed in 1838.[43] And the federal government continued to build highways within territories; for instance, the Little Rock to Memphis Road that opened in 1828 was the generous product of Congress.[44] Successive Congresses and presidents did approve grants-in-aid to specific highways and annually increase appropriations for internal improvements from Jefferson's administration to Jackson's.[45] Still, expenditures were easy targets for belt-tightening Congresses, especially when regional interests mitigated any national interest. Constitutional issues over how to fund such a plan defeated implementation of Gallatin's scheme for national intercon-

JOSEPH S. WOOD

nection. Even to those who held a national view, it was unconstitutional for the federal government to support internal improvements that were of local importance.

## SECTIONALISM

The Constitution was not the only obstacle to federal participation in internal improvements. Underlying the issue was centralization of power in federal hands, or, said another way, sectionalism and state jealousies. Because every specific project benefited some sections and not others, internal improvements became an exercise in geographical discrimination. Advocates for certain projects knew fully well the benefits of flows of people, goods, capital, and ideas, and those not served raised objections.[46] Especially after 1820, sectional politics made any kind of consensus difficult. A most obvious example was the fierce struggle in the 1850s between North and South over location of the eastern terminus of a transcontinental railroad, a conflict that prevented construction before the Civil War.[47]

The National Road, in effect, had manifest a new set of spatial relationships in the antebellum period. The road divided North from South literally and figuratively, even as it connected East and West literally and figuratively. It paralleled effectively the Mason-Dixon Line between Maryland and Pennsylvania, at least to the Ohio River. From there westward it served to interconnect the capitals of the southern tier of states carved out of the Old Northwest, Ohio, Indiana, and Illinois, before reaching the Mississippi River. Down the Road in 1829 came Andrew Jackson's inaugural procession, marking in many ways vindication of Jefferson's geographical vision of a road for an agrarian class of Americans bound by "natural sociability" to a union. Still, at the Road's intended western end was Jefferson City, Missouri, capital of the state whose admission to the union was a consequence of temporary arrangements employed to delay an inevitable sectional conflict. The Missouri Compromise of 1820 allowed admission of the District of Maine and Missouri as states perpetuating a balance of power between slave and nonslave states in the U.S. Senate.

Sectional issues unresolved by the American Revolution and adoption of the federal Constitution included disposition of public land, funding of internal improvements, chartering of a national bank, imposition of tariffs, and states' rights. On these issues, politics made strange bedfellows. The South wanted a low tariff to allow overseas purchases, while the Northeast

**Jackson's Inaugural Procession (*Harpers Weekly*, March 12, 1881)**

Andrew Jackson's election as president in 1828 marks in a way the rise of the West to equal stature with the East and the South. The Tennessean's 1829 inaugural procession carried him eastward along the Road to represent effectively the people's will in the nation's western reaches.

required a high tariff to stimulate development of manufacturing, which the West saw to its advantage as well. Both the Northeast and the South supported high prices on federal land sales to generate federal income, while the West wanted low prices to generate settlement. On internal improvements, both Northeast and West saw benefit in encouraging greater trade, while the South, Clay and Calhoun's American System notwithstanding, opposed federal funding for fear that such programs would strengthen central government at regional expense and create precedent for federal intervention in other state matters.[48] The essential issue was states' rights, including the property rights involving slavery. Sectionalism, thereby, was a stranglehold. It is remarkable, indeed, that the union held, for no matter the political issue, during the antebellum period one could not remold the nation's human geography to equalize the proportionate advantage of some cities, states, or regions.[49] The political balance of sectional rivalries kept the issues unresolved until the Civil War, which effectively marked the ascendancy of the Hamiltonian vision over the Jeffersonian vision for an American political economy.

Although never constructed in a systematic fashion, by 1850 much of Gallatin's larger design for internal improvements had been built in some form by various combinations of private, local, state, and federal sources.[50] Ultimately, providing land directly in exchange for private development of transportation supplanted earlier attempts to sell land to provide public funding of transportation. Of all the various proposals for federal funding beyond construction of military roads, the only project to survive was the National Road, the first acknowledgment of its responsibilities with respect to internal improvements by the federal government.[51] Never at one time was a good road complete and in good repair from Cumberland to Vandalia, but road completion was never the point. In the antebellum period, the Road represented the central government's power to shape geography, to open wide the Middle West, even as the geographical imbalance between North and South and East and West underlay much of the difficulty and division over the Road's construction and the larger issue of internal improvements.

JOSEPH S. WOOD

## CONCLUSION: THE IDEA OF A NATIONAL ROAD

The National Road was a symbolic highway of America, which both literally and figuratively divided North from South and connected East with the West that became America. The idea for a Road came to fruition during the period 1790–1840, when American society transformed itself from a rural to an urban orientation, from an agrarian to an industrial way of life, and from an artisanal to a mechanical mode of production. This period, the decades when Americans designed, funded, and constructed the National Road, witnessed an extraordinary expansion of settled territory. For the first time in European movement westward a plan of massive scale for settlement and for social order, political authority, and economic enterprise had preceded settlement. A huge expanse of good-quality land had been available at a modest price. Its proximity, geographical familiarity, essential emptiness, and readiness for domestication by established methods of pioneering had been inviting. Prevailing principles of private initiative within an effective framework of government control had encouraged its taking. Ordinances of 1785 and 1787 had seen to it that space was arranged for ordering society, and a concurrent revolution in transportation had opened this land to settlement.[52] The Road reflected the ideal of a rural, agrarian, and artisanal society seeking to extend itself over geographical space. By 1850 the center of population in the United States was in the Ohio Valley, not far from the mouth of the Scioto, where Jedidiah Morse had predicted a new empire would flourish. And it was here, in the Middle West, the territory north and west of the Ohio, the region for which the National Road performed as Main Street, that many contemporary issues—land, internal improvements, tariffs, and states' rights—came to be played out.

Little wonder that the Road never became functionally all its supporters intended or claimed. The Road became an anachronism, thwarted by constitutional issues and sectional rivalries, and overtaken by technology before Americans completed it. True, wagoners and drovers maintained critical trunk connection between East and West, and volume of traffic over the road was considerable. But new, more sophisticated, and technologically complex modes of transportation than a road, favoring especially New York and Philadelphia, quickly overshadowed any commercial advantage that had accrued to Baltimore from the Road's opening. Even more than as a functional trunk link, however, the Road marked symbolically an important historical and geographical period in which Americans defined themselves, identified themselves with a continent, and proceeded to resolve significant ideological and sectional differences. It is axiomatic that landscapes people produce reflect their basic values and conflicts. The landscape of the National Road, as we will come to understand in subsequent chapters, reflects the basic values and conflicts of antebellum America. The National Road was truly an odyssey of American life.

JOSEPH S. WOOD

# Surveying and Building the Road

BILLY JOE PEYTON

*As I said before, the road traverses seven different States of the Union, and in its whole extent will cover a distance of near 800 miles. Who, then, can doubt its nationality? Who can question the allegation that it is an immensely important national work? Who can reconcile it to his conscience and his constituents to let it go to destruction?*

HON. T. M. T. MC KENNAN
speech to Congress, June 6, 1832

AMERICA'S HISTORY AND PROSPERITY HAVE BEEN GREATLY IMPACTED BY its transportation systems. Early political leaders recognized the importance of internal improvements and the development of a national transportation network. In addition to navigable waterways, an integrated improvements program logically included a trans-Appalachian land route to connect the eastern seaboard with the "western waters." Indeed, several viable geographic alternatives for breaching the mountains were considered, but none offered the natural advantages of the Potomac River Valley.

Cumberland, Maryland, nestles at the base of the Appalachian Mountains' eastern slope, near the continental divide that separates eastward and westward flowing waters. Here the Potomac River slices a deep water gap called The Narrows into Wills Mountain, creating one of the few convenient passages through the mountains between New York and Alabama.

This happy erosional accident made the site an attractive place to begin the first leg of a "national road" to the Ohio River. No other transportation corridor has played a larger role in this nation's history than our first interstate highway—known alternately as the Cumberland Road, National Road, Uncle Sam's Road, Great Western Road, or simply the Road.[1]

## EARLY TRANSPORTATION IN THE UNITED STATES

Travel was difficult, at best, in eighteenth-century America. Travelers had two alternatives—over land or over water. By and large, journeying overland was extremely slow, uncomfortable, and dangerous; navigable waterways, on the other hand, generally proved more efficient, reliable, relatively comfortable, and comparatively cheap. Long voyages usually required a combination of travel on both land and water.

Few roads led to the American interior at the close of the French and Indian War. Settlement for the most part clung to within 150 miles of the coastline for the first two centuries of European colonization, in part due to the geographical barrier presented by the Appalachian Mountains. Few dared challenge the formidable obstacle until the defeat of the French and Indians in 1763, but when settlers finally came they did not stop until they reached the rich lands beyond the Appalachians, west of the Ohio River.

They cleared roads as they went. Among the handful of early long-distance routes that breached the Appalachians was the Wilderness Road, blazed by Daniel Boone in his quest for land in present-day Kentucky; the Pennsylvania Road, also known as Forbes Road, widened by British general John Forbes during the French and Indian War as an alternative route to the Forks of the Ohio; and Braddock's Road, so named for the ill-fated Maj. Gen. Edward Braddock, sent to the colonies by the English crown as generalissimo of all royal troops on the continent in 1755.

Braddock's mission to seize Fort Duquesne and liberate the Ohio Valley from the French ended in disaster in western Pennsylvania. Before it did, however, his troops cut a swath through the wilderness, improving on what was then known as Nemacolin's Path for the well-known Delaware Indian scout who blazed it. For a short time it became Washington's Road, after his troops improved it en route to Great Meadows and their famous encounter with the French at Fort Necessity. In all its various incarnations, the National Road can trace its origins to this trail.

British troops hacked a twelve-foot-wide clearing out of the mountain

BILLY JOE PEYTON

wilderness—an extremely difficult task for soldiers using only hand-held axes, mattocks, and other simple digging, felling, and grubbing tools. Coldstream Guards captain Robert Orme traveled on temporary duty with General Braddock in June of 1755 and provides this brief description of the ruggedness of the Monongahela country through which they toiled: "we marched about nine miles to Bear Camp [on the Maryland-Pennsylvania border] over a chain of very rocky mountains and cliff passes. We could not reach our ground 'till about seven of the clock . . . as there was no water, nor even earth enough to fix a tent, between the Mountain and this place."[2]

Braddock's Road became widely recognized for its association with Washington and the French and Indian War. Popular taverns and wagon stops sprang up beside such well-known sites as Fort Necessity and Jumonville Glen, and travelers wrote of seeing them as they passed. The road's reputation grew over time, not so much as a reliable transportation corridor as for the historic events that occurred along it. Historical context notwithstanding, most travelers in the 1780s opted against taking Braddock's Road, or any other overland route to the country's interior.

Responsibility for road construction and maintenance often fell to local governments with little money or interest, and usually resulted in feeble or token efforts at maintenance. As expanding national business and trade brought a corresponding increase in country-to-city traffic, especially near America's largest cities, the concern for quality roads grew. Only after the new nation sorted out its post-Revolutionary economic problems could it begin to deal with the matter of internal improvements. When that time came, citizens turned to their respective states for help. In 1791, the Society for Promoting the Improvement of Roads and Inland Navigation submitted to the Pennsylvania legislature the first statewide transportation plan in the nation.[3] Private turnpike companies chartered under this model built roads and charged tolls. One of the first turnpikes was the Philadelphia to Lancaster Road, opened in 1796.

Even with growing national interest in developing a safe and reliable overland transportation nexus, existing roads were little more than cleared dirt paths that deteriorated with each passing season. By 1800, most states had not yet begun to build stone-paved and finished roads, nor carried out repairs to existing ones in any systematic fashion. Even the most important of the westward passages were being reclaimed by nature from want of maintenance. Indicative of the situation nationwide, Braddock's Road devolved to a mere thread comparable to the original Nemacolin's Path from which it originated.

## A NEED FOR INTERNAL IMPROVEMENTS

Despite the deplorable road conditions that existed before 1800, the number of Easterners moving west soared after defeat of the Native Americans at the Battle of Fallen Timbers in 1794. The nation's population nearly doubled (from 3.9 million to 7.2 million) between 1790 and 1810, as did territorial possessions after the acquisition of the Louisiana Territory. With such rapid physical expansion came opportunities to extend commercial markets and increased pressure to settle and develop lands west of the Ohio River.

As outlined in chapter 3, Albert Gallatin presented his landmark *Report on the Subject of Public Roads and Canals* in 1808 in response to growing interest for internal improvements.[4] His report presented internal improvements in the context of a boon to transportation, communication, and the economy, and received praise for being far-reaching and national in scope. Rapid population growth in the Northwest Territory and imminent statehood for Ohio presented irresistible opportunities for the federal government to become actively involved in the internal improvements movement. An act creating a "2 percent fund" for building roads "to and through" Ohio made it possible for a federally funded road to be built.[5]

The Appalachians presented a most ominous and daunting geographical barrier. Constructing a substantial roadway over them would be a difficult task, but one that made sense to political leaders and business interests. But where would such a road be built? The Senate Committee on Internal Improvements debated this point, finally settling on a preferred corridor by process of elimination. The committee declined to consider routes north of Philadelphia and south of Richmond because the law specified that roads must strike the Ohio River at some point contiguous to the state of Ohio. And an all-Virginia route up the James River and down the Kanawha was inappropriate because such a road would enter Ohio in the sparsely populated extreme southern part of the state.[6] Citizens of Ohio had the most commercial intercourse with Baltimore and Philadelphia, which helped narrow the choices. Pennsylvania already had the "spirit and perseverance" to build a road from Philadelphia to the western waters, while Maryland was engaged in road-building westward from Baltimore. Thus the committee felt any intervention in either state's efforts would "produce mischief instead of benefit."

BILLY JOE PEYTON

Since Maryland had no vested interest in building a road beyond the mountains, the committee

> thought it expedient to recommend the laying out and making a road from Cumberland, on the northerly bank of the Potomac . . . to the Ohio river, at the most convenient place on the easterly bank of said river, opposite to Steubenville, and the mouth of Grave Creek, which empties into said river, Ohio, a little below Wheeling in Virginia. This route . . . will cross the Monongahela at or near Brownsville, sometimes called Redstone, where the advantage of boating can be taken.

With this blueprint for the road's location, Congress passed an act to regulate layout and construction. The act set very broad parameters that left "the manner of making said road, in every other particular" up to the president. It authorized President Jefferson to determine the exact route by appointment of "three discreet and disinterested citizens of the United States to lay out a road from Cumberland . . . to the State of Ohio," and to spend the sum of $30,000 which was "hereby appropriated, to defray the expenses of laying out and making said road."

## A ROAD FROM CUMBERLAND TO WHEELING

From the beginning of federal involvement with the Cumberland Road, the president of the United States held ultimate jurisdiction over its construction. His authority included the right to appoint a board of road commissioners and accept or reject their recommendations, adopt measures to secure the consent of states through which the Road passed, and exercise judgment and control over actual construction, administration, and finances. Later authority granted the president the right to appoint superintendents to oversee construction and repairs.

The president chose three commissioners—Joseph Kerr, Thomas Moore, and Elie Williams—to lay out the Road. Joseph Kerr, who hailed from Ohio, was deputy surveyor of the Virginia Military District, and a U.S. senator. Thomas Moore, from Maryland, later served as second chief engineer of the Virginia Board of Public Works and eventually became involved in the planning of the Chesapeake & Ohio Canal. Elie Williams, head of the commission, lived much of his life in Hagerstown in his native Maryland, served as a colonel in the Revolutionary War and commissary to Gen. "Light Horse Harry" Lee during the Whiskey Rebellion of 1794. His involvement with the internal improvements movement in this country dates to 1797, when he served on a planning committee for the Baltimore Turnpike. (After completing work on the National Road, Congress appointed Williams a surveyor on a proposed Potomac River canal, which finally became a reality in 1828 as the C&O Canal.)[7] It is doubtful if any of the commissioners or other team members had formal training in engineering or surveying; rather, they learned their skills in apprenticeship under practicing professionals. Joseph Kerr gained valuable experience as deputy surveyor in the Virginia Military district, which ably prepared him for the arduous job of surveying a road through some of the most rugged mountain wilderness in the eastern United States. In the final analysis, the commissioners and their entire team received very high marks for their outstanding work of laying out the Road.

As specified in the March 29, 1806, "Act to Regulate the Laying Out and Making a Road From Cumberland, in the State of Maryland, to the State of Ohio," the Cumberland Road expedition consisted of the three commissioners, one surveyor, two chainmen, and one marker. A vaneman and a pack-horse man (with horse) were added to expedite matters.[8] The surveyor's wages totaled three dollars per day plus expenses, while the chainman and marker each earned one dollar per day plus expenses. Their mission was to lay out a road from Cumberland to the east bank of the Ohio River opposite the northern boundary of Steubenville and adjacent to the mouth of Grave Creek (near Wheeling). As soon as the commissioners laid out the Road, they presented their findings to the president in a plan detailing total distance, elevations, markers and monuments, topography, and estimated expense of the proposed route.

The surveying team set out on their assignment while the commissioners met in Cumberland on September 3, 1806, to begin their work. This put the team in the woods about a month before foliage came down for the season, which undoubtedly made the going extremely difficult at the outset. But an early September start also meant that the hottest summer weather was over and they had ten to twelve weeks before the first measurable sign of winter.

The commissioners made daily forays into the countryside to cover the ground between Cumberland and Wheeling, ever vigilant in their search for the best route for the Western Road. They stayed in hostelries or with residents living along the way, often accompanied in their explorations by knowledgeable locals who knew the area and offered suggestions on the best ground. It soon became apparent that professional surveyor Josias Thompson would require help to carry out his mission. Arthur Rider, originally hired as vaneman on the expedition, assumed the role of second surveyor from September 22 until December 1, when he became an assistant to the principal surveyor.[9] His employment from then until the end of the season involved copying field notes and helping complete a draft report.

Surveying work required the skillful use of standard tools of the trade and involved the charting of meridians with geometry and trigonometry using a table of logarithms. The surveyors had to keep their eyes fixed on the magnetic needle of their compass and remember to go around with the sun, keeping the land under survey to the right. Gunter's scales and dividers solved problems of angles and degrees, and the surveyors set six-foot stakes and iron pins adorned with flags of red flannel as markers. A chain signified the length of measurement. The standard chain was 66 feet, and four rods of 162 feet formed a chain.

Actual surveying work proceeded something like the following oversimplified description. After a designated axman cleared away underbrush and obstructions, Thompson drove a sharp-ended compass stake into the ground. Into a top socket of the stake he inserted the circumferentor, a compass with its face divided into degrees and adjusted to a horizontal position. He slowly and methodically turned the instrument around so that its south end faced the struck stake at the far end of the line. Reading from one side, he sighted the compass until he lined up the stake through the fine slits in both sides. After the needle settled on the circumferentor he read off the degrees and entered his reckonings in his field notes, which were later transferred in final form to maps. Thompson recorded his final calculations and then set stakes, notched trees, or noted natural features like boulders, springs, or waterfalls as markers. This process repeated itself over and over again the whole length of the proposed Road.

By the first week of October the commissioners had reached Fayette County, Pennsylvania, in the vicinity of Washington and Brownsville. Much of the first two weeks of November were spent in and around the Wheeling area in search of the best route to the Ohio River, and by the third week winter arrived in the form of snow. The team ultimately suspended its efforts for the season on December 6 after an early snow made it impossible to continue surveying and marking the route. On agreement, the commissioners retired to Cumberland intent on resuming their work in the spring. They also agreed to submit an interim report to the president. After instructing Josias Thompson "to prepare with all convenient dispatch a compleat & comprehensive map of all their work," the commissioners left Cumberland with plans to "meet in Washington as soon as their journal & report could be made up to be presented with their plat to the President of the United States."[10]

An interim report submitted on December 30, 1806, contained details of findings from the previous summer's work and revealed the commissioners' insight on related topics like the inaccurate maps at their disposal, and the amusing and somewhat vexing problem of inhabitants in the surveyed area who "conceived their grounds entitled to a preference" in selection of an exact route for the Road. They also admitted that "the duties imposed by the law became a work of greater magnitude, and a task much more arduous than was conceived before entering upon it."[11]

Cumberland ultimately became the eastern terminus of the National Road without controversy, partly out of propriety and partly out of geographic necessity resulting from its location at the eastern slope of the Appalachians, which confined the Potomac River so that access from the east was considered impossible at any other point without great expense. After a careful study of the ground west of Cumberland the commissioners fixed their attention on a most desirable route. Four objectives directed their decision:

1. The shortest distance between navigable points on the eastern and western waters;
2. A point on the Monongahela River that maximized the potential of portage to the country within reach of it;
3. A point on the Ohio River most capable of combining river navigation with road transportation, and which considered the potential growth of the lands north and south of that point; and
4. The shortest road with the most benefits.

The route as selected originated at lot No. 1 in Cumberland and extended westward over the gap in a hill where Braddock's Road passed, crossed the Youghiogheny River near the mouth of Roger's Run, passed over Laurel Hill near the forks of Dunbar's Run and close to Isaac Meeson's house, through Brownsville, and across the Monongahela to Bridgeport (West Brownsville). From there it took "as straight a course as the country will admit to the Ohio, at a point between the mouth of Wheeling creek and the lower point of Wheeling Island" (31–32).

BILLY JOE PEYTON

The commissioners believed that the formidable topography would not allow traditional cut-and-fill techniques to reduce the Road to an acceptable five-degree grade. Their report included a table of heights above Cumberland where the Road crossed. (The heights as calculated by the expedition are not exactly correct, but close in most instances.) A partial list of these elevations rounded to the nearest foot above Cumberland (which represents zero) plainly illustrates the difficulty encountered between Cumberland and Uniontown, the most mountainous part of the route (38–39):

| | | | |
|---|---|---|---|
| Summit of Savage Mountain | 2,022 | Little Youghiogheny River | 1,323 |
| Savage River | 1,742 | Summit of Negro Mountain, | |
| Summit Little Savage | | highest point | 2,328 |
| Mountain | 1,900 | Big Youghiogheny | 646 |
| Branch Pine Run, | | Summit of Laurel Hill | 1,550 |
| first western water | 1,700 | Courthouse at Uniontown | 275 |
| Summit Little Meadow | | | |
| Mountain | 2,026 | | |

The commissioners suggested crossing the mountains and hollows obliquely, which would require a great deal of hillside digging but preclude the need for costly cuts and fills. As far as utilizing the existing Braddock's Road, its indirect course and frequent elevations and depressions exceeded the limits of the law and "forbid the use of it, in any one part for more than half a mile, or more than two or three miles in the whole" (34). Thus, the commissioners recommended an entirely new road, which cost more than one incorporating parts of the old route.

Methods and materials employed in building the Road were important factors for consideration. To the commissioners, "nothing short of a firm, substantial, well-formed, stone-capped road can remove the causes which led to the measure of improvement" (34). Such a national road with a fine and durable surface could be expensive to build, but very much worth the effort.

After submitting their interim report, the commissioners and survey crew had to wait until the Pennsylvania legislature granted permission for the Road to pass through its borders before resuming their work. Permission came too late to start field work in advance of emerging vegetation in the spring of 1807, so the teams waited until autumn. When again they ceased for the winter, they submitted a second report to the president on January 15, 1808.

The third and final season of field work began in the spring of 1808 and culminated in a final report prepared by Thomas Moore and Elie Williams, which they submitted to the president on August 30 of that year without the assistance of Joseph Kerr, who left the expedition at the end of 1807 to attend to domestic concerns and did not return. By this time, the surveyors had finished locating, grading, and marking the route from Cumberland to the Ohio River. Later that year most contracts for clearing a portion of the right-of-way had also been let.

In the final analysis, Elie Williams, Thomas Moore, Joseph Kerr, Josias Thompson, Arthur Rider, and the other expedition members whose identities will never be known should be remembered for their collective contribution to this country's history and development. They carried out their respective duties with vigor, a high degree of professionalism, and meticulous attention to detail, no small accomplishment considering their meager compensation and rather imprecise orders. Between 1806 and 1808 the group ran an exhaustive survey over 131 miles of mountain wilderness, carried out extensive field explorations, met with local residents and community leaders, spent countless hours in careful deliberations, and submitted to the president three carefully studied and insightful reports. With the exception of the proposed route in Pennsylvania, which did not originally include Washington or Uniontown, they generally received few complaints or criticisms from the president, Congress, or the American people. Indeed, their dedication to purpose formed the very foundation upon which our first interstate highway, the "Road from Cumberland, in the State of Maryland, to the State of Ohio," was built.

In their reports the commissioners called for the new road to be built through Maryland, Pennsylvania, and (West) Virginia "in the style of a stone-covered turnpike." Owing to the ruggedness of the landscape and requirement by law for a sixty-six-foot right-of-way, the Road would be "nothing short of well constructed" with "completely finished conduits" to render it passable at every change of seasons, after rainstorms and snowfalls. Cost was estimated at $6,000 per mile, excluding bridges over principal streams (39).

The route as selected took in some of the most rugged and beautiful country in the eastern United States. In the east it connected with the Baltimore Pike at Cumberland, from where it snaked its way in a more or less northwesterly direction over Big and Little Savage, Little Meadow, and Negro Mountains. In Pennsylvania it climbed over Chestnut Ridge and Laurel Hill on the general alignment of Braddock's Road to the point where the

BILLY JOE PEYTON

former veered toward Pittsburgh (at the summit of Laurel Hill) just east of Uniontown. Continuing west, the Road passed over less rugged terrain between Brownsville and Washington before reaching its western terminus at Wheeling. From Wheeling the Road connected with Zane's Trace, an important existing post road running from the west bank of the Ohio River through Zanesville, Ohio, to Limestone (Maysville), Kentucky. A portion of this key route later became incorporated into the western segment of the National Road.

The commissioners wasted no time getting started; contracts let under the superintendence of Thomas Moore for partial clearing of timber and brush were already underway and scheduled for completion by March of 1808 (40). Progress slowed after this initial activity, and it ultimately took three more years to begin building the Road.

Funds to build the Road were not plentiful at first, a factor that contributed to the slow rate of progress. Aside from an initial $30,000 from Congress, the National Road project received on average only $48,000 each year between 1810 and 1812 (total appropriations during that time equaled $143,786) (100, 101). If one assumes the commissioners' construction estimate of $6,000 per mile is close to accurate, this equals about twenty-four miles of completed road by 1813. This is probably close to accurate, because a labor shortage and sluggish economy slowed progress during the War of 1812.

General management of finances and contracts associated with the National Road rested with the Treasury Department under Secretary of the Treasury Albert Gallatin. Although general oversight responsibilities origi-

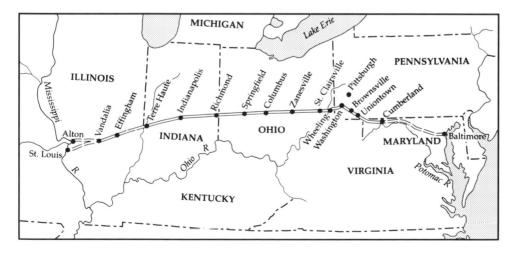

Original route of the National Road, Cumberland to Vandalia (with extensions to St. Louis and Alton)

nated with the Treasury Department and its secretary, civilian construction superintendents let the contracts, disbursed funds for construction, and provided on-site supervision of work. The superintendent also corresponded regularly with the secretary of the treasury regarding Road matters.

Contrary to popular belief, the U.S. Army Corps of Engineers had no involvement whatsoever with laying out or building the National Road from Cumberland to Wheeling. It may seem odd for the nation's engineering agency not to be involved in the largest public works project undertaken to date in the United States, but the Corps of Engineers had no authority to get involved in civil works projects of any kind until congressional passage of the General Survey Act on April 30, 1824. This act authorized the president to use Army engineers to survey road and canal routes "of national importance, in a commercial or military point of view," and to employ any engineers "in the public service which he deemed proper." As a result, in 1825 the Corps became actively involved in National Road construction west of the Ohio River and in making repairs to the existing Road east of that point.

Prospective contractors submitted bids for work as advertised in the local papers and on posters displayed in public places. They included samples of materials they planned to use (e.g., stone and mortar) and stated the total price of their work in their bid. Specifications were to be adhered to and all work completed by the date specified in the contract.[12]

David L. Shriver Jr. of Cumberland served as first superintendent of the National Road. Shriver is an unheralded figure who is scarcely mentioned in Thomas Searight's or Archer Hulbert's classic works on the subject, but deserves to be recognized for his dedication to the job. Indeed, Shriver merits a rightful place in the annals of the National Road alongside such well-known names as Henry Clay and Albert Gallatin, men who are generally given credit for getting the Road built.

Shriver began his professional career in partnership with his brother in the improvement of their family property before serving in the Maryland House of Delegates from Frederick County. He eventually gave up his political aspirations to become superintendent in charge of laying out and building the Reistertown Turnpike. After Shriver successfully completed this work, the federal government named him superintendent of the National Road, a post he held until being selected as one of three commissioners in charge of surveying the Road west of the Ohio River in 1820.

Shriver served as the lone superintendent until 1816, when it became necessary for the government to divide the Road administratively into an eastern and western division, with the boundary line near the Monongahela River just east of Brownsville, Pennsylvania.[13] Josias Thompson, a Virginian and surveyor on the original expedition to lay out the route, became Shriver's counterpart in the west.[14]

The superintendent's duties included letting contracts, supervising construction, and insuring contractual obligations were successfully carried out. His job was not without travails, however. Keeping supplied with proper tools and materials presented a constant problem, as did the quest to find competent labor. Moreover, the superintendent stood by as workers grumbled about their pay, spring freshets made rivers of creeks and swept away survey markers, and contractors swore their work was too difficult to complete.

Construction commenced on the initial contracts for the first ten miles of road west of Cumberland in the spring of 1811, with most work reportedly done by the late fall of 1812. Progress slowed somewhat after that, as work on the next eleven miles began in the summer of 1812 and did not finish until early 1815; the following eighteen miles took from late summer of 1813 to 1817 to complete. By the fall of 1815, contracts were let on the first forty-five miles of the Road to a distance six miles west of Smithfield, Pennsylvania (319–20).

The first of the monumental stone bridges on the National Road was constructed between 1814 and 1817. Built by the firm of Abraham Kerns and John Bryson under the supervision of Superintendent Shriver, it is known as the Little Crossings Bridge spanning the Casselman (or Little Youghiogheny) River in Maryland. Its arch cleared 80 feet and was the nation's largest ever constructed up to that time; the entire bridge measures over 300 feet long and 50 feet high.[15] It still stands just east of Grantsville.

To the west of the Little Crossings Bridge is the second monumental bridge on the Road, spanning the Great Crossing of the Youghiogheny River. Great (or Big) Crossings Bridge is a triple-span stone arch structure erected between 1815 and 1818 by the contracting firm of Kinkead, Beck and Evans. The longest bridge on the National Road when built by James Kinkead, James Beck, and Evan Evans, it now lies submerged under the deep waters of Youghiogheny Lake at the former site of the old pike town of Somerfield, Pennsylvania. Both this and the Little Crossings Bridge used locally quarried sandstone in their construction.

Traveler Uria Brown, a surveyor and conveyancer from Baltimore, took notice of these two magnificent structures in 1816, writing that "the Bridges & Culverts actually do Credit to the Executors of the same, the Bridge over the Little Crossings of the Little Youghegany river is positively a Superb Bridge." At the Great Crossings he observed that "they have Commenced the erection of the Bridge over this River, [and] no doubt from the specimen of the work already on the road, but this Bridge will be a superb & Magnificent Building."[16]

Contractors built other important sandstone bridges too, like the triple-arched span that still stands over Wheeling Creek at Monument Place in Elm Grove, or the strange (by modern standards) arched "S-bridge" that once stood nearby. The S-bridge is so named for its curved approaches that meet the arch at opposite angles resembling the tails of the letter S and thus allow the stream itself to be crossed with a straight arch, an easy alternative to the more technologically complicated skewed arch. A rare surviving S-bridge stands (in part) near Taylorstown, Pennsylvania. In addition to the notable S-bridges and multispanned structures, numerous smaller single-span arch bridges and culverts helped carry the National Road from Cumberland to Wheeling.

Road construction continued swiftly after 1816. All contracts in Pennsylvania to the (West) Virginia state line were let by the spring of 1817, with the exception of a segment from Washington to Brownsville. U.S. mail service began running between Wheeling and Washington, D.C., in 1818, although some Road sections around Wheeling still lacked a finished top coat

Great Crossings Bridge during low water (November 1991)

of stone, referred to as "metal." The final contract for work in (West) Virginia was let in 1820, with all construction to the Ohio River subsequently completed the following year.[17]

Construction did not always proceed smoothly. Private contractors bid on construction contracts, and competition for work proved great. Once awarded a job, contractors had their own way of carrying out a contract, which sometimes led to quarrels with surveyors over angles and grades. Most contractors were builders, not engineers, who cared little for the consequence of a one- or two-degree difference in grade to a horse pulling a heavy load over the mountains. Moreover, many contractors sublet work to subcontractors or even sub-subcontractors, which could further exacerbate potential problems. Fortunately, contractors came from the area, including such well-known local individuals as John Hagen, Thompson McKean, Thomas and Matthew Blakely, Parker Campbell, and Col. Moses Shepherd.[18]

Burly axmen began the construction process by felling all trees along a clearing sixty-six-feet wide through the forest. They were followed by choppers, grubbers, and burners, whose work might take weeks to complete in heavily timbered sections. Roots were grubbed out by hand, stumps were pulled by oxen and horses straining against heavy chains. After grubbing, the road had to be leveled by pick-and-shovel wielding laborers. This earth-moving army cut into hillsides, flung tracks of fill across hollows, and hauled away excess earth and rock.[19] Finally, the graders, stone crushers, and pavers laid the roadbed.

Laborers broke stones with round-headed, long-handled hammers, and

Road worker using a hammer to break stones by hand

sized them to fit through rings measuring seven and three inches. One Pennsylvania farmer observed workers descending "a thousand strong, with their carts, wheel-barrows, picks, shovels, and blasting tools, grading those commons, and climbing the mountainside, leaving behind them a roadway good enough for an emperor to travel over."[20] Indeed, construction activity dominated the local landscape, and area residents turned out in large numbers to view the work for themselves. It must have been an incredible sight to witness the large crews of men plowing, grubbing, and breaking stones for Uncle Sam's Road.

Work probably seemed to proceed haphazardly to the casual observer, but contracts were let systematically for specific "sections" of road averaging a couple of miles in length. Contractors submitted bids based on a "per perch" construction rate, with one perch equal to 16½ feet (the same distance as a rod). Because a number of contracts were simultaneously in progress, it is difficult to determine exact completion dates for separate sections of roadway.

Superintendent Shriver found fault with the contract system, citing inadequate pay to laborers and the potential ruin of the road as reasons to abandon it in favor of paying a daily rate. An 1813 labor shortage even brought about the idea of using slaves, which did not come to pass.[21] Labor crews consisted almost entirely of Irish and English immigrants, many of whom settled in the northern panhandle of (West) Virginia and western Pennsylvania. Construction camps made up of shacks and tents along the Road echoed at night with the sounds of traditional British ballads. One observer near Wheeling noted that all immigrant workers seemed "well fed, well clothed and comfortable," adding that "the Irish here have not lost in our esteem; two or three times we have been beholden to individuals of that nation for good-natured little services. . . . I heartily return them the good wishes they so frequently expressed as we passed them."[22]

In its authorizing language for the National Road, Congress specified a roadway of raised stone, earth, or gravel and sand that measured four rods (sixty-six feet) cleared width, with a maximum grade of five degrees (8.75 percent). An 1811 contract specified that stumps be grubbed and the roadbed leveled to thirty feet. Fill, where needed, would include proper allowance for settling—no stumps, logs, or wood could be used. Ditches or "water courses" were to be made, if not already present.[23]

The sixty-six-foot roadway set a standard that is surprisingly close to mod-

BILLY JOE PEYTON

ern specifications of seventy-two feet for an urban, four-lane, controlled access freeway. Also, the 8.75 percent maximum grade is amazingly stringent through such steep grades and narrow valleys, especially since modern construction standards allow for maximum grades of 8 percent on rural primary routes in hilly or mountainous terrain with one-way traffic counts of 250 vehicles an hour and a speed limit of 40 miles per hour.[24] An 1818 survey disclosed only one location that failed to meet the standard, that being the most mountainous stretch between Cumberland and Uniontown, measuring 9.2 percent (5.25 degrees).[25]

While the surveyors, engineers, and laborers who laid out and built the Road certainly deserve much credit, construction did not exactly embody cutting-edge technology. Caspar Wever, a National Road superintendent west of the Ohio River, describes the original roadway in the east as being a prepared "bed, or channel" of the prescribed width and about one foot deep, inside which was placed a base of stone about one foot in height. Another layer of stone laid above the first formed as even a surface as possible. The large base stones were set edgewise; according to Wever, they appear to have been laid "promiscuously" with attention paid only to balancing the thickness of the pavement and the firmness of the surface. Over this substrata was placed a six-inch layer of stone, broken and sized to pass through a three-inch ring.[26] This construction method is also mentioned by Albert Gallatin, who describes a road "covered with a stratum of stones twelve inches thick, all the stones to pass through a three-inch ring."[27] While this system looked acceptable from the surface, it proved little more than a ditch filled with rocks of varying sizes that wore out quickly under heavy traffic.

## NINETEENTH-CENTURY CONSTRUCTION METHODS

Two commonly accepted road-building technologies could have been employed to build the Road. The first is the Tresaguet method, developed in the 1770s by master French engineer Pierre Tresaguet. He believed good drainage and proper selection of materials to be essential. His road had a crowned subsurface and stone pavement of a uniform depth throughout, with a bottom layer of stone seven inches thick laid on end and hammered in place. On top of this he placed a layer of hammered-in smaller stones; the surface, which in profile had a central crest with each side sloping down to the edge, consisted of small hard stones. Finally, he separated the substrata from the wearing surface, as opposed to forming one uniform foundation. French road builders generally accepted Tresaguet's system, which spread to central Europe, Switzerland, and Sweden after 1760.[28]

The second system in common use at the time was named for English engineer Thomas Telford, a former stonemason who developed his method around 1802. He advocated a level subsurface set edgewise and fit tightly by hand, with irregularities broken off by a hammer and interstices filled with stone chips. Smaller stones were added on top to a depth of seven inches at center, sloping to three inches at the sides. Horses compacted the small stones placed at the center. One and one-half inches of clean gravel covered the whole road.[29]

Tresaguet influenced Telford's work to a great extent, but their systems differed considerably in cost. Telford's roads carried a much higher price tag because of their heavy foundation, extra expense of laying down the various stone layers, and the fact that the top layers of pavement quickly wore out if not maintained in good order. His system became popular in Britain but was not conducive to economical road-building in America where construction materials had to be hauled over greater distances, and money and labor were scarce.

Tresaguet and Telford notwithstanding, the most influential and well-known of the nineteenth-century road builders was John Loudoun McAdam, a Scottish engineer and road surveyor. McAdam, inspired by Tresaguet, first improved on the Telford system by using small broken granite pebbles as his primary material. According to McAdam, a stone surface did not function to support vehicular weight but rather to form a covering over the natural soil to support the road's weight. He deemed a heavy metal (broken rock) course as unnecessary, and the porosity of large stones proved unacceptable. The same principle applied to road crowns, considered unnecessary because they concentrated traffic toward the center of the roadway and hindered drainage by causing ruts to form.[30] He explained that "no artificial road can ever be made so good, and so useful as the natural soil in a dry state, [therefore] it is only necessary to procure and preserve this state." McAdam felt thickness of such a road to be of no consequence, but "if water passes through a road and fills the native soil, the road, whatever its thickness, loses its support and goes to pieces."[31]

Macadamization gained recognition as a durable and inexpensive road surface in Britain shortly after publication in 1816 of McAdam's seminal work entitled *Remarks on the Present System of Road-Making* (which proved so popular that it went through nine printings by 1827). McAdam's contributions to road-building cannot be overstated. They were such that near the end of his life he was offered a knighthood for his achievements, but declined because of age and infirmity.[32]

His principles, so revolutionary that Parliament ordered an investigation to determine the validity of his claims, deviated from Tresaguet's and Telford's in several important ways. First, he advocated a flat foundation, which contrasted with Tresaguet's crowned surface. Because he did not have rigid rules for construction, the number of necessary layers varied by road. An imperviousness to water was paramount, inasmuch as moisture destroyed a road's weight-carrying capability if allowed to penetrate to the natural soil beneath the road.[33]

McAdam enforced the use of a two-inch ring for sizing stones that he claimed should not exceed six ounces in weight. To him, every stone over an inch in size was "mischievous" because it increased permeability and might be easily dislodged by wheels. He did not roll his roads, but preferred applying stones in thin layers and allowing traffic to compact each successive application. He also sought to keep the road as level as possible to avoid sharp ascents and descents detrimental to proper drainage.

His theories met with some resistance among contemporaries, who feared doing away with the tradition of a hand-laid foundation. His watertight pavement proved sound, however, and the system proved its worth. As his influence spread across the globe, McAdam's name became synonymous with a style of road-building known as "water-bound macadam" that dominated in the late 1800s and is still used today.

French and English variations of the McAdam and Telford systems eventually spread over Europe in the nineteenth century, when many older roads were resurfaced using the newer technologies. More important, American engineers who studied these methods in Europe put their experience to work in this country. By mid-century, people like W. M. Gillespie and Q. A. Gillmore developed their own improved methods of road-building based on the principles they learned abroad.[34]

## A REGIONAL VARIATION ON TRESAGUET'S SYSTEM

A commonly held myth about the National Road is that it originally had a macadamized surface. This is not the case. In truth, McAdam's principles had not yet spread to North America by 1821, date of the Road's completion to Wheeling. (It did eventually get a macadam surface, but not until the government funded repairs in the late 1820s and '30s.) The roadway as *originally* constructed to Wheeling appears to be something of a regional variation on the Tresaguet system, with some exceptions in places that had only a single layer of broken stone pavement.[35]

Contractors were expected to follow specifications, but the quality of work varied from contract to contract. Lax supervision and no existing federal standards for road-building gave contractors a fair amount of freedom in the execution of contracts. Contractors had no formal training in road-building, and so they relied on written specifications to complete their work. Many had outstanding reputations and performed admirably, while others took shortcuts, scrimped on materials, or showed little pride in workmanship. Potential problems might be attributed to any number of things, such as inexperience, mismanagement, shortage of funds, or an overriding desire to open the Road at all costs.

Actual cost of construction to Wheeling averaged $13,000 per mile, more than double the commissioners' original $6,000-per-mile estimate.[36] From Cumberland to Uniontown the Road cost $9,745 per mile, a fair price considering the rugged terrain; from Uniontown to Wheeling it shot up to around $16,000 per mile, an exorbitant figure attributed to reckless extravagance and too-liberal contracts.[37] Following an investigation into this discrepancy, Josias Thompson was investigated and relieved of his duties as superintendent of the western section.[38] Thompson had no formal affiliation with the Road after this time, but went on to help found, settle, and serve as first mayor of the National Road town of Triadelphia, (West) Virginia.[39]

National Road construction successfully overcame the daunting Appalachian Mountain topography. But in so doing, it embodied no new or significant road-building technology, nor spawned any great innovations in road engineering. It generally followed basic and commonly held practices of the day for creating metal-surfaced roads. Although the Road cut transit time considerably, travelers still suffered through a long and bumpy ride in springless wagons.

Considering the Road's status as national exemplar, it is ironic that the metaled roadway was neither innovative nor necessarily well-constructed, yet the engineered structures were extraordinary. While existing roads meandered around or through streams, the stone bridges and culverts carried the Road up and over the water courses that crossed the right-of-way in a

STONE BROKEN TO PASS THROUGH A 3" RING

STONE BROKEN TO PASS THROUGH A 7" RING

After John T. Hriblan (IHTIA)

manner that defied local geography and allowed the Road to follow a surprisingly straight path to the Ohio Valley. It also marked one of the first
mergers in this country of vernacular road-building with finely engineered
structures.

*Original National Road construction, a variation of the Tresaguet method*

## CONSTRUCTION IN THE WEST

Settlers heading west sought the Ohio River, where flatboats and reliable
steamers plied the waters from the time the Cumberland Road first opened.
The Road's completion to the Ohio realized the national government's
primary objective of providing a portage over the Appalachians and connecting to this western riverine thoroughfare. But another, more ambitious,
goal remained. Business and government supporters of internal improvements wanted to extend the eastern coast link into the Northwest Territory
and the new states of Ohio, Indiana, and Illinois by bridging the Ohio River
and extending the Cumberland Road to the Mississippi Valley.

In 1820, Congress appropriated $10,000 to survey the Road between
Wheeling and the Mississippi River's east bank. Three commissioners directed the surveys, David Shriver, William McRee, and Alexander LaCock.
As in the East, several years passed before they completed their work and
Congress found the words and the will to fund construction in the West. Finally, that body appropriated $150,000 in 1825 for "opening and making a
road from the town of Canton [Bridgeport], in the State of Ohio, opposite
Wheeling, to Zanesville, and for the completion of the surveys of the road"
through Ohio, Indiana, and Illinois, to the permanent seat of government
in Missouri.[40]

A great groundbreaking ceremony took place on July 4, 1825, commemorating the start of construction in Ohio, complete with toasts to Andrew
Jackson and an oration declaring the Rocky Mountains as the Road's ultimate destination.[41] Next came Superintendent Caspar W. Wever, who
opened an office in St. Clairsville, advertised for bids, and carried out the orders of Maj. Gen. Alexander Macomb, chief of engineers of the U.S. Army

and who had overall responsibility for construction. The axmen, choppers, grubbers, and burners arrived to build a road over the hilly and broken ground, tangled with brush and strewn with exposed slate, and, in some cases, a soft lime substrata.[42]

Construction progressed through 1826 on the first Ohio segment between Bridgeport, on the west bank of the Ohio, and Zanesville.[43] In 1827, Congress appropriated $170,000 to finish the work. When completed in 1830, this initial seventy-three-mile stretch became the country's first *new* road to be built in the macadam style.[44]

Jonathan Knight headed a U.S. commission to locate the next section of Road between Zanesville and Columbus.[45] Knight, a Pennsylvania Quaker, civil engineer, and surveyor, selected a location over ground with a comparatively easy grade where travelers and animals could get plenty of water and building materials were easily obtained. The alignment that Knight chose shortened the existing Road's length by eight or nine miles.

The entire segment from Wheeling to Columbus opened in 1833, entering the latter on Friend Street (now Main Street). It immediately improved travel to the state capital, and saved five hours in the delivery of mail between Zanesville and Columbus.[46] Clearing and grubbing had started west of Columbus by this time, subsequently reaching Springfield, forty-eight miles west of Columbus, by 1834. Eventually, Madison, Clark, Montgomery, and Preble were added to the growing list of Ohio counties spanned by the Road. By the time it reached the Indiana border, the National Road passed through nine counties and stretched over 200 miles in Ohio alone. Construction through Ohio averaged about $3,400 per mile, as contrasted to $13,000 per mile east of the Ohio River.[47] Relatively gentle terrain and incorporation of existing roads helped keep costs low.

Starting in 1831, the federal government began transferring just-completed sections of road to the state of Ohio for operation as a turnpike. By the end of 1835, the entire Road east of the Indiana border was no longer national, but state-owned. This was followed by the elimination of all congressional appropriations for road construction after 1838. Fortunately for Ohio, completion of its segment had come a few years before.

The situation was different in Indiana, where surveying and construction progressed through the 1820s and '30s through heavily wooded countryside, with the exception of the two prairies of the Wabash and areas of prior improvement.[48] The Road spanned Wayne County on the Ohio border by

BILLY JOE PEYTON

1827. Steady progress continued for the next ten years, so that by 1838 more than four-fifths of the grade on the whole line was completed. Contractors encountered problems with light and porous soils, in places too thin to support the Road, resulting in the grade being cut to pieces "in an almost ruinous condition."[49]

Grading, draining, and bridging from Richmond to Centerville, Indiana, was nearly completed when federal appropriations finally ran out in 1838. A macadamized surface had also been laid in both Richmond and Centerville. By the time the government gave the Road over to the state of Indiana in 1849, over $1.1 million had been expended on its construction.[50] Still, in many places it remained little more than a cleared and graded dirt track.

Road-building activity in Indiana centered around Indianapolis, with work radiating east and west from that point. Problems held up progress on the middle section around the settlement in 1838. At no time had "the contractor employed a sufficient force; nor had he complied with his contract as to the time of laying on the first coat of metal."[51] With at least part of the blame given to "domestic afflictions" plaguing the contractor and an "almost unparalleled sickness" that decimated the workforce, officials still believed the contractor had not done all in his power to complete work as scheduled.[52] In this situation, where a contractor failed to meet his contractual obligations, the option of declaring the contract in forfeit lay with the superintendent. It is not known whether a forfeiture occurred in this particular case.

Construction began in Illinois following the completion of surveys in 1830. Work in Illinois is not well documented, and exact details of progress remain somewhat sketchy. By the time congressional funding ended in 1838, $746,000 had been spent there, considerably less than any of the other five states on the Road.[53] The state received less because the roadway remained unimproved its whole length, with only clearing and grading done so the right-of-way might be used for a future railroad, if desired.[54] The Road held little importance in Illinois from the start, and so it passed quietly into obscurity after an 1856 act ceded all interest in the Road to the state.

Work orders on the western segment emanated from division offices under the direction of a superintendent, aided by as many as three assistants, one inspector and assistant, a superintendent of masonry, and four principal overseers. Two office clerks handling paperwork stayed busy filling out a battery of forms and requisitions.[55] Contractors and laborers received payment at their respective places of employment at the end of each month, with records of hours worked by laborers and owners of teams kept by overseers, countersigned by the section superintendent or superintendent of masonry or carpentry, and endorsed by the assistant before being submitted for payroll.[56] Payments for purchases were reimbursed upon presentation of a bill of sale. Reconciliation of accounts and abstracts of disbursements were prepared monthly, insofar as an accurate accounting of appropriated funds minimized the potential for fraud or embezzlement. Meticulous records of expenditures also had to be kept for inclusion in the superintendent's annual report to Congress.

The western segment proved easier for engineers to build than the eastern one, owing to the overall gentler terrain and incorporation of pre-existing roads into the alignment. Maintenance problems did not exist on the same level as in the East, either, since the western section reportedly had less traffic. Thomas Searight contends that about two-fifths of all business and travel on the National Road originated between Brownsville and Cumberland with the intention of exiting the Road at Brownsville and continuing via steamer down the Monongahela River; he claims another two-fifths came to Brownsville from the Wheeling end to make the same river connection, thus leaving only about one-fifth of all Road traffic on the western portion of the Road, most of which originated locally.[57] Road chronicler Archer Hulbert takes issue with this assumption, however, comparing toll receipts in 1840 for Pennsylvania ($18,429) and Ohio ($51,365) to suggest that the Ohio Road section did the greater business.[58] Hulbert does admit that travel west of the Ohio "may have been chiefly of a local nature."[59] Unfortunately, accurate traffic counts do not exist for either section.

A straight alignment and broad eighty-foot right-of-way characterized the Road's western section. Except in eastern Ohio, construction standards did not equal the quality of repairs undertaken between Cumberland and Wheeling in the 1830s. The scarcity of good building stone in the Middle West's glaciated till areas and diminishing national interest in road-building were principal reasons for the lower roadbed quality.

By the time the Road opened its entire length in the West, the nation was consumed by canal fever and railroad mania, and roads were increasingly regarded as obsolete. Many states had already developed ambitious plans to build canals and railways. Eventually, the great federal experiment in road-building unraveled as expenditures were diverted elsewhere. Original plans

BILLY JOE PEYTON

called for the Road to terminate on the Mississippi River at St. Louis, but the westward push stalled about seventy miles east of there at Vandalia, Illinois. The government spent just over $4 million to build the western section from the Ohio River to there, where today a "Madonna of the Trail" statue marks the Road's original terminal point along Gallatin Street in the old Illinois state capital's center.[60]

The nineteenth-century dream of a National Road to the Rockies ended when the Road petered out on the south Illinois plain. Ironically, the dream would be realized, then bettered, after the route became incorporated into the transcontinental National Old Trails Road in the 1910s.

## A ROAD IN DISREPAIR

Great crowds poured onto the National Road almost as soon as it opened east of the Ohio River. A long and steady stream of dollars would be necessary to maintain this first-class highway, lest it deteriorate into just another "shake gut" passage. By 1822, although just over four years old in places, the Road was wearing out from overuse and deferred maintenance. R. J. Meigs Jr. reported to Congress while on an inspection trip in western Pennsylvania:

> The western (being the newest) part of the Road is in ruinous state, and becoming rapidly impaired. In some places the bed of the road is cut through by wheels, making cavities which continually increase and retain water, which, by softening the rock, contribute to the enlargement of the cavities. In other, the road is much impaired by the sliding down of the earth and rocks from the elevated hills; and by the falling off of parts of the road down steep and precipitous declivities of several hundred feet; so much abridging the width of the road that two carriages cannot pass each other.[61]

Overuse, coupled with the harmful effects of wagoners locking their brakes on the steep mountain terrain, caused rapid deterioration of the original roadbed. Contractors and civilian construction superintendents contributed to the problem insofar as their general lack of knowledge and skill in the science of road-building left an inferior roadbed in places.

Original construction east of the Ohio consisted of little more than a trench dug into the ground and filled with large stones, over which was placed a layer of smaller stones. Since the bed was lower than the ground, drainage ditches could hardly be sunk deep enough to keep water from

A "detour" on the National Road east of Gratiot, Ohio (1914)

seeping into the roadbed. Water ran under the road and kept the foundation wet, which forced the bottom stones down in summer and heaved them up in winter, thus causing the top layer of pavement to break up and disintegrate under the weight of traffic. Narrow-tired wagons exacerbated the situation by cutting thin ruts into the roadbed, thereby scattering the top stone layer and exposing the large bottom stones to traffic, rain, and frost. Slow-moving, heavy wagons compounded the problem by pushing surface stones down and causing deep ruts.

While construction progressed west of the Ohio, badly needed repairs were deferred in the East as Congress wrestled with the constitutionality issue. A logical solution to the problem was to turn the route into a toll road, but President Monroe vetoed a measure for the establishment of a turnpike system on the grounds that it represented an unwarranted extension of the

BILLY JOE PEYTON

powers of Congress.[62] Resolution of the crisis finally came when Monroe authorized an act for direct appropriations to pay for repairs. This 1823 act appropriated a paltry $25,000 for repairs and authorized the president to appoint a superintendent to "make all contracts, receive and disburse all moneys, etc." at a salary of $3.00 per day.[63] As it turned out, this small amount barely began the long process of returning the shine to America's tarnished crown jewel.

Meanwhile, the Road's condition steadily worsened. Congress received impassioned pleas from local government officials and others, including the superintendent of the National Road in the West:

> The attention of the Department was called, in my last annual report, to the dilapidated condition of the United States' road east of the river Ohio. I do not deem it necessary to add what was then said, except remark that its progress towards complete and irretrievable ruin has been, since that time, much more rapid than I expected it would be. Is there not a saving power somewhere, and a disposition too?[64]

Writer Charles Fenno Hoffman, traveling on the Road between Washington, Pennsylvania, and Wheeling, commented sarcastically that "the ruts are worn so broad and deep by heavy travel, that an army of pigmies might march into the bosom of the country under the cover they would afford."[65] Drivers of mail stages even resorted to taking detours through neighboring farms or into surrounding woods to avoid obstructions.

A road in ruin presented serious problems for travelers, not to mention embarrassment to the federal government, which had invested a large sum of public money in its construction only to see the roadbed disintegrate for lack of maintenance. One traveler stated the problem succinctly: "The Cumberland Road, so interesting to the nation, will (in my opinion, formed by observation when upon it) cease to be useful unless repaired."[66]

Appropriations for repairs totaled only $55,000 between 1823 and 1827, an average of just $88 per mile—barely enough to keep ditches maintained. It was not until after 1829, when Congress appropriated the sum of $100,000 "for repairing bridges &c., on the road east of Wheeling," that serious maintenance work actually began. Between 1829 and 1835, appropriations for the Cumberland Road east of the Ohio River exceeded $1 million.[67] Repairs carried out under this arrangement were tantamount to a complete overhaul of the Road. Upon completion of each section, the fed-

Toll house at LaVale, Maryland, built in 1835

eral government turned jurisdiction and maintenance over to the respective states for operation as a turnpike. Toll houses were erected along the route for the purpose of collecting fares.

Repairs undertaken in the East between 1831 and 1835 were carrried out by civilian contractors under direct supervision of U.S. Army engineers who served as superintendents under the chief of engineers. This differed markedly from the original construction carried out by civilian contractors working under civilian superintendents, who in turn answered to the Department of the Treasury. This level of direct Army involvement and supervision over the work added a measure of consistency and professional engineering expertise not present in original construction.

Repairs in the East differed from original construction in another very important way. They were done on the macadam plan, noted for its superior qualities in repairing and reconstructing existing roads. A macadam surface applied over an existing system offered a cheap alternative to new construction, which is precisely how the first application of the macadam system came about in the United States. Repairs completed in 1823 on the "Boonsborough Turnpike Road," a privately built route that ran from Hagerstown to Boonsboro, Maryland, and fed into the National Road east of Cumberland, are generally considered the first application of the macadam principle on an American road.[68]

First use of the macadam system to build the National Road from the west bank of the Ohio River opposite Wheeling to the east bank of the Muskingum River at Zanesville, Ohio, is credited to the U.S. Army Corps of Engineers, who carried out the plan under the aegis of Secretary of War James Barbour and Maj. Gen. Alexander Macomb, chief of engineers.[69] Credit for the first application of the macadam plan for Road repairs also goes to the U.S. Army engineers, who received extensive training in road-building and bridge construction as part of their civil engineering curriculum at the U.S. Military Academy. Specific instruction at West Point on the elements of road-building included reconnaissance of lines for roads, surveying, mapping, excavation, grading, drainage, road coverings, repairs, and materials.[70] Correspondence between the chief of engineers and officers assigned to carry out repairs on the Road repeatedly mention the macadam plan as being the most desirable for repairs. Capt. Richard Delafield, superintendent of the Cumberland Road, even includes excerpted quotes from the classic *McAdam on Roads* in a letter of justification to Chief of Engineers Gen. Charles Gratiot.[71]

Great competition existed for awarding repair contracts. "For some sections as many as thirty-six offers were made by different persons, and for no one section less than six. The most advantageous offer was accepted for each section, and an agreement entered into with the individual to execute the work by the time specified." Successful execution of contracts east of Ohio required close supervision, and so the Army divided the Road into seven divisions with an engineering officer assigned to help the chief of engineers oversee work in each one. His duties included carrying out the general law of Congress and seeing to it that specific contracts made under that law went into effect. Eleven superintendents were employed to assist the officers in the daily inspection and examination of work. Each division also had a clerk who handled the records and books as required by the War Department.[72]

Lt. Joseph K. F. Mansfield, on a temporary three-month stint in 1832, served as first military superintendent of repairs east of the Ohio.[73] An 1822

Laborers laying the first section of macadam in the United States on the Boonsboro Pike

graduate of the U.S. Military Academy, Mansfield later became chief engineer with Gen. Zachary Taylor's army in the Mexican War and eventually died at Antietam in the Civil War.[74]

Undoubtedly, the best-known superintendent was Richard Delafield, who served a long and distinguished career with the U.S. Army Engineers. Delafield graduated as a second lieutenant from West Point in 1818. After serving as a draftsman on the northern boundary survey of the United States, an assistant engineer building Forts Monroe and Calhoun, and engineer on improvement projects on the Mississippi River, he assumed the position of superintendent of repairs on the Cumberland Road's eastern section in 1832. He spent six years in that capacity. A captain when he started, Major Delafield left his post on the National Road in 1838 to assume the superintendency of the U.S. Military Academy. After being relieved from the academy in 1845, he went back to the business of engineering internal improvements. Delafield returned to the superintendency of West Point from 1856 until 1861, became chief of engineers of the Army in 1864, brevetted major general in 1865, and retired in 1866.[75]

Many lesser-known graduates of West Point served with distinction on the Cumberland Road. Each one brought his own special expertise and skill to the job. Army engineers who served as project superintendents knew of John McAdam's work, and they expected contractors to carry out repairs as per his specifications. Civilian contractors and construction supervisors, however, did not share the same knowledge or understanding of McAdam's principles. Occasionally, this caused friction for failure to follow mandated specifications. Superintendent Delafield wrote of "the headstrong obstinacy of some of the contractors" in carrying out orders. He also felt "compelled to have printed a manual or primer, with a few lithographic sections, that the sight may aid the mind in a proper understanding of the business."[76]

Some civilians questioned the validity of calling the Road repairs "macadamized." One such skeptic was writer Charles Fenno Hoffman, who first encountered the National Road about thirty miles from Wheeling and observed:

> It appears to have been originally constructed of large round stones, thrown without much arrangement on the surface of the soil, after the road was first levelled. These are now being plowed up, and a thin layer of broken stones is in many places spread over the renovated surface. I hope

2" LAYER OF 1" BROKEN STONE

4" LAYER OF 2"-2 1/2" BROKEN STONE
(6 OZ. STONES)

4" LAYER OF 2'-2 1/2" BROKEN STONE
(6 OZ. STONES)

SUBSOIL

*After John T. Hriblan (IHTIA)*

the roadmakers have not the conscience to call this Macadamizing. It yields like snow-drift to the heavy wheels which traverse it, and the very best parts of the road that I saw are not to be compared with a Long Island turnpike.[77]

Although Hoffman's comments may have originated from witnessing an early phase of work before compacting of the roadbed, the quality of macadam proved only as good as the contractor laying it down.

Repairs were usually begun by breaking up and removing the original paving stones, followed by raking and flattening of the bed. This left a rise in the flat base of no more than three inches from the thirty-foot roadway's side to its center. Ditches on each side, and drains leading from them, insured that water would remain eighteen inches below the lowest part of the road's surface, keeping the foundation dry.

Ditches were cleaned, drains adjusted, and culverts cleared and altered to allow water to pass away from the road, an extremely important measure to insure a consistently dry roadbed. Workers then used shovels and rakes to spread and smooth a new layer of stone reduced to four ounces or less in weight to form a cover ranging between six and nine inches in thickness, which was compacted and left to thoroughly dry. In no case was it considered necessary to put on a covering of more than nine inches. Original road material was used only when it was of sufficient hardness; no clay or sand could be mixed as a binder for the stone.[78] After opening the Road in segments to allow passing traffic to compact it, workers stood by to rake smooth any ruts or uneven spots caused by moving carriage wheels.

Owing to the importance of a thoroughly dry and compacted natural earth base under the stones, paved drains or catch-basins were placed diagonally across the road to channel water away before it could penetrate the foundation. Such appurtenances were built with gradual curvature so as not to upset carriages traveling over them.[79] Engineers preferred limestone, flint, or granite for roadmaking, because of their inherent strength. An abundance of limestone quarries east of Ohio made it the material of choice for repairs on that part of the Road. Quarrying and hauling the limestone proved somewhat costly, however, because the beds lay in the lowest valleys and creekbeds underneath several feet of earth, and because it sometimes had to be transported several miles to the construction site.[80] Contracts for quarrying and hauling rock generally were let so the work took place during winter months, thus insuring an adequate stockpile for the construction season.

In addition to upgrading the roadway, workmen repaired and repointed bridge, culvert, and sidewall masonry. It was considered very important that all masonry foundations be well pointed with hydraulic mortar to a depth of eighteen inches below the ground, and no pointing was allowed after the middle of October in order to protect against frost.[81] A fine quality hydraulic cement for use on surfaces that came into contact with water could be supplied by several natural cement mills operating along the Potomac River in Maryland and (West) Virginia at the time. These mills also supplied mortar for structures on the C&O Canal as well as many federal government buildings in Washington, D.C.[82]

One of the National Road's landmark bridges was erected over Dunlap's Creek in Brownsville, Pennsylvania, during the repair period. The "Old Iron Bridge," completed in 1838, is the first all-metal bridge built in the United States.[83] Capt. Richard Delafield drew plans for its construction during his tenure as superintendent. Delafield believed that a wooden bridge was vulnerable to rot and fire, and that the rock needed for a stone bridge was too costly to ship to Brownsville. He argued successfully for the all-iron bridge, which still stands, albeit in a considerably altered state.

America's first iron bridge, Dunlap's Creek Bridge in Brownsville, Pennsylvania

In 1835, Congress appropriated a final amount of $346,186 to finish repairs in the three eastern states, thus completing a massive overhaul of the Road that took about as long as the original construction itself.[84] Passage of this act also put the United States permanently out of the business of maintaining a national road east of the Ohio River.

Throughout its long and storied history the National Pike never did pay for itself, even after it became a toll road. One scholar estimates "that the yearly expense of repairing the Ohio division of the road was $100,000.00 while the greatest amount of tolls collected in its most prosperous year [1839] was hardly half that amount [$62,496.10]." Hence, the governor of Ohio borrowed money for repairs as early as 1832, a plight shared by other states grappling to maintain their Road sections.[85]

Transportation by rail eventually supplanted travel on the old Road. When the burden of repairs became too great on the states, they transferred management responsibility to individual counties. The counties, in turn, either deferred maintenance or shifted responsibility over to local governments.

By the close of the Civil War, the National Road had reached a sorry state, its traffic gone, grass growing up through its pavement. *Harper's Weekly* reported in 1879 that "the old iron gates have been despoiled, but the uniform toll-houses, the splendid bridges, and the iron distance posts show how ample the equipment was."[86]

Many remnants of Uncle Sam's Road still remain in place 125 years later. Charles Ellet's great suspension bridge at Wheeling, built in 1849 and unequaled as an international civil engineering landmark, is restored and still carries US 40 over the Ohio River. While its future is safe, the fate of dozens of lesser structures that stand derelict in woods and fields from Cumberland to Vandalia is not so assured.

## REDISCOVERING THE ROAD

American roads in the late nineteenth century deteriorated into deplorable condition all across the country, escorted into their Dark Ages by the railroads. The National Road sank into oblivion, too, where it languished in relative obscurity for years. The first call to repair the nation's roads came in the 1880s through the efforts of such grassroots groups as the League of American Wheelmen, allied with farmers who needed decent roads to bring their produce from farm to market. A national Good Roads Movement eventually formed with a mission "to pull America out of the mud." The movement helped galvanized popular support in the cities, primarily through civic leaders who realized good roads were only possible with adequate funds raised through taxation of urban and rural property.[87]

Given America's blossoming love affair with the automobile, interest in a series of transcontinental highways developed quickly. First came the Lincoln Highway (now US 30) in 1913, followed shortly by the founding of several other "national trail" associations that incorporated parts of historic trails into their routes. Among those promoted or in existence by 1920 were the Dixie Highway, Pikes Peak Ocean-to-Ocean Highway, Yellowstone Trail, Midland Trail, and the National Old Trails Road—which included the National Road.[88]

In 1911, Congressman Albert Douglas decided to drive his automobile from Washington, D.C., to his home in Chillicothe, Ohio. What he encountered was an excruciatingly slow journey on the National Road in a Ford that sputtered up and down the mountains of Maryland, Pennsylvania, and West Virginia. Four days later he crossed the Wheeling Suspension Bridge and entered "the promised land." According to Douglas, the Road's condition ranged from good to bad.[89] His voyage brought increased attention to the need for uniform and reliable long-distance roads in the United States, and demonstrated the growing preference among Americans for driving an automobile instead of taking a train on long trips.

Closely reminiscent of the events that led to the building of the National Road 100 years earlier, the public began to demand federal aid for better roads. A Post Office Appropriation Bill of 1912 made it possible for federal funding to be used for "post-road" improvements (an intangible benefit came with the excellent training this gave highway engineers employed by the Office of Public Roads).[90] The act supported only 455 miles of road construction nationwide, but one of the first grants reportedly went to rebuild a 50-mile portion of the National Road between Zanesville and Columbus, Ohio.[91]

After the end of World War I, highway travel in the United States increased rapidly and the government found it necessary to adopt a national transportation policy. The result was passage of the Federal Highway Act of 1921, intended to encourage states to build connector highways "interstate in character." National Road revitalization became a reality under this legislation.

A National Old Trails Association had already formed by then, and Indiana Congressman Henry A. Barnhart introduced a bill to continue the transcontinental highway through Ohio, Indiana, Illinois, and Missouri. Reminiscent of the original 1806 act to lay out the Cumberland Road, the

Highway workers erect
the first uniform signs
on US 40 in the 1920s

Highway workers erect the first uniform signs on US 40 in the 1920s

bill also authorized three national highway commissioners appointed by the president.[92]

In 1922 and '23 the National Road was overhauled. The old macadam pavement began to disappear, replaced from Cumberland to Indianapolis by a concrete ribbon nine inches thick and eighteen feet wide. Eventually, this new surface covered the Road to St. Louis. Brick paving became popular for a time and replaced the concrete or old macadam surface in places.[93]

Meanwhile, in the 1920s Congress authorized continuation of the National Old Trails Road to the Pacific coast in California. A uniform highway numbering system ultimately led to the Road's designation as US Route 40. Erection of standardized road signs made it official—the old National Road had come full circle as part of a new national highway.

# Extending the Road West

GREGORY S. ROSE

*The travel west of Wheeling was chiefly local, and the road presented scarcely a tithe of the thrift, push, whirl, and excitement which characterized it, east of that point; and there was a corresponding lack of incident, accident, and anecdote on the extreme western division.*

THOMAS B. SEARIGHT
*The Old Pike: A History of the National Road . . .* (1894)

IN HIS DIARY OF A SURVEYING TRIP ACROSS THE APPALACHIANS IN 1784, taken at the behest of fellow Virginian Thomas Jefferson, George Washington recommended that the new nation "open a wide door, and make a smooth way for the Produce of that Country to pass to our Markets before the trade may get into another channel." That New York might develop superior connections with the trans-Appalachian West and divert the region's trade from Virginia's markets concerned Washington, but an additional worry carried far greater geopolitical implications. Another entry in his diary expressed concern that "the Western settlers . . . stand as it were on a pivet" which might tip them toward economic or political alliances with "the Spaniards on their right or Great Britain on their left."[1]

The idea that roads were needed to connect the transportation systems and settlements on the eastern and western sides of the Appalachian Mountains was not new. Since at least 1752, as an investor and as part of his military service during the French and Indian War, Washington had recognized the need for such roads and had traveled their precursors; other leading lights during that extraordinary period in American history shared his view.[2] Transmontane connections slashed through the forest had existed by the end of the War of Independence but these unimproved paths, such as Braddock's Road and Forbes Road, were absolutely insufficient to service the newly acquired and rapidly peopling territory west of the Appalachian crest.[3] Canals, portage roads, or both were needed to join eastern-flowing rivers with the Ohio, the key westward-flowing river. Private financiers, including Washington, had attempted with little success the former solution along the upper Potomac River; the latter solution, since "no one state could afford to construct such an enterprise alone and the individual states were too jealous of each other to cooperate," would require support from the new national government.[4]

## DEVELOPING THE NATIONAL ROAD PROGRAM

A funding mechanism to finance such a national road-building project from the proceeds of federal land sales in newly admitted states had been proposed by Secretary of the Treasury Albert Gallatin and was written into the 1802 statehood enabling act for Ohio. Not until 1806, however, following a few years of pleas from the West for Congress to authorize a road or at least advance each state the funds necessary for the state to begin road-building, was "An Act to Regulate the Laying Out and Making a Road from Cumberland, in the State of Maryland, to the State of Ohio" approved by Congress.[5] As required by the act, three commissioners were appointed by President Jefferson to plan the Road's path. Congress also requested that Secretary Gallatin prepare a comprehensive review of the new nation's transportation needs. His report, submitted in 1808, recommended among other projects the development of a national road to connect the new cities in the trans-Appalachian region with the East Coast, with funding to come from the federal treasury since private investors likely would consider settlement levels in the West to be too low to justify the risk.[6] Besides, as pro–National Road senators argued later in response to attempts to end federal funding for the Road, it was an interstate project through territory still mostly owned by the United States (although located within individual states), placing both constitutional and commonsense responsibility on the federal government for its construction; furthermore, the federal government benefited from the

Road because "it brought emigrants, emigrants purchased land and proceeds from land sales went into the Federal treasury."[7]

The first two of the three earliest questions facing the Road's promoters—how to pay for the Road and who would control its construction—were settled even before the National Road project officially began. The statehood enabling acts for Ohio, Indiana, and Illinois pledged that each state would receive 5 percent of the receipts from the sales of federally owned lands in each respective state for use in a variety of internal advancements.[8] In Ohio the internal advancements listed in the enabling act were roads, in Indiana they were roads and canals, and in Illinois they were roads, canals, and education. In each case, 60 percent of the reserved fund was to be spent on improvements within the state and controlled by the state legislature, while 40 percent was to pay for a road or roads to or to and through each state, the construction of which would be under the control of Congress. Ohio's statehood act included a phrase giving the state the right of approval for congressional location decisions, but the acts for Indiana and Illinois did not include such a phrase. The notion that consent of the state was necessary would encourage proponents of routes alternative to those selected by Congress, upon recommendation by the Road commissioners and the president, for the states west of the Ohio. Ultimately, however, congressional decisions about the western route stood, despite local or state protests, breaking the precedent set east of the Ohio River.

Answering the third question—where to locate the Road—was more difficult. Selecting the route to be followed by the early, eastern phases of the Road required that Congress weigh recommendations, petitions, and pleas by the Road commissioners, the president, state legislators and governors, townspeople along potential routes, and congressional colleagues during the debates over funding and placement. These discussions presaged others to come as the western course of the Road was determined. Perhaps in an effort to avoid repeating for the western route the wrangling accompanying establishment of the eastern route, congressional decisions about the path west of the Ohio River were made earlier and generally adhered to, despite pressures applied by state and local interests.

### East of the Ohio River

The act of March 29, 1806, the first legislation actually appropriating funds to begin planning the National Road, empowered the president to appoint three commissioners, whose responsibility was to make recommendations (which could be accepted or rejected) concerning placement and construction of the Road. The commissioners were "to lay out in such a direction as they judge, under all circumstances the most proper, a road from [Cumberland] to the river Ohio."[9] Their first report to Congress, dated December 30, 1806, proposed a route between Cumberland and Wheeling developed according to the following "governing objects": "Shortness of distance between navigable points on the eastern and western waters," finding the best portage point on the Monongahela River, identifying "a point on the Ohio river most capable of combining certainty of navigation with road accommodations" and taking into account where Ohio's population was and was expected to be, and applying the "best mode of diffusing benefits with least distance of road." Their report reflected extensive field work done by the commissioners. Obviously, since having the National Road pass through your town or across your farm practically guaranteed an economic windfall, the public was very much interested in the commissioners' reconnaissances. The commissioners noted, for example, "the solicitude and importunities of the inhabitants of every part of the district, who severally conceived their grounds entitled to a preference," providing an early hint of the pressures to be applied to Congress by states, counties, towns, and individuals.[10]

The route recommended by the commissioners ignited the first major location controversy, primarily focused on the proposal to cross southwestern Pennsylvania through Brownsville and Connellsville.[11] Although this brouhaha occurred outside of the region covered in this chapter, it provided a model for battles waged west of the Ohio River. Pennsylvanians determined that this route was unsatisfactory, for it would bypass Uniontown and therefore bypass Pittsburgh's commercial sphere, causing traffic and commerce to be linked more directly with Baltimore than with Pittsburgh and Philadelphia. Pennsylvania was unwilling to grant the necessary permission for the Road to traverse the state until it was diverted to Uniontown; further efforts resulted in the Road being diverted to Washington, Pennsylvania. The commissioners had considered a route through Uniontown and "were not insensible of the disadvantage which Uniontown must feel from the want of that accommodation" (that is, of being located on the Road), but they felt the need to provide the shortest path across the mountains took precedence: "Considerations of public benefit could not yield to feelings of minor import."[12] Under pressure from Pennsylvania, however, President Jefferson unwillingly approved in 1808 a plan to place the Road through

GREGORY S. ROSE

Uniontown and in 1811 Congress permitted further deviation of the Road to Washington, Pennsylvania, by passing an act giving the president the power to alter the route between the principal points of Cumberland and Wheeling, but not to alter the principal points themselves.

The controversy over the path through Pennsylvania served as a precursor for subsequent but less successful attempts to change the Road's route. And the controversy over where to locate the Ohio River terminus of the Road's eastern leg indirectly affected Ohio, since the point across the river in Ohio would begin the Road's westward continuation and would help determine its path across the Old Northwest. The 1806 legislation establishing the Cumberland Road outlined the general location for the Ohio River terminus, proposing to meet the river "at the most convenient place, between a point on its eastern bank, opposite to the northern boundary of Steubenville . . . and the mouth of Grave Creek . . . a little below Wheeling, in Virginia."[13]

Whenever the precise location of the Road was not fixed in the initial legislation but remained for later decision, as was true for much of the Road's eastern leg but especially for its Ohio River terminus (and later its Mississippi River terminus), at least some controversy seemed guaranteed. Steubenville, Ohio, hoped to capitalize on the traffic generated by the Road to continue its expansion and growth; it already had obtained a federal land office. Proponents made fervent pleas urging that the terminus be located at a point across the river in Charlestown, Virginia (now Wellsburg, West Virginia). The recommended Ohio River terminus downriver at Wheeling bypassed Steubenville, however, and made St. Clairsville the first major stop on the Ohio River's west bank. The commissioners chose Wheeling to avoid rapids and seasonally low water, thereby providing a better jumping-off point for subsequent navigation down the Ohio River or for crossing the river. In their words, "obstructions on the Ohio . . . lay principally above the town and mouth of Wheeling," while Wheeling was a common "place of embarkation and port of departure in dry seasons"; furthermore, "a safe crossing is afforded at the lower point of the island by a ferry at high water, and a good ford at low water."[14] In addition, Wheeling had a historical advantage, since many local trails converged on the town from the east and since Zane's Trace, Ohio's first road, began across from Wheeling on the Ohio River's west bank. Wheeling fell within the recommended range of locations, met the commissioners' "governing objects" of shortness of distance and intersection of the best navigation points, and was reinforced as the terminus by the legislation of 1811 confirming that the Road's end points were not to be moved.[15]

### West of the Ohio River

As the statehood enabling acts and first legislation authorizing funds to pay for survey of the Road were prepared in Congress, Ohio and the other western states abided for the most part by the locational decisions of Congress and the president. The National Road would pass through all three states; at first it appeared to be up to local interests to make whatever pleas they felt necessary to locate the Road in a particular place. In Jefferson's note of 1808 communicating the latest report of the National Road commissioners to Congress, he wrote of his approval of the route "as far as Brownsville," Pennsylvania, noting that west of the Ohio River the route "is still to be decided," promising to "pay material regard to the interests and wishes of the populous parts of the State of Ohio," and directing that the Road connect with another leading "from the Indian boundary near Cincinnati by Vincennes to the Mississippi at St. Louis."[16] To accomplish this, the first western section of the route was to pass "through Chillicothe, Lebanon, and Hamilton in Ohio" before connecting "with the military road leading through Vincennes to St. Louis," but Jefferson's initial path became obsolete with the opening of more westerly and northerly parts of the Old Northwest.[17]

To avoid experiencing in the West the same locational controversies that erupted from rivalries between places in the East, Congress set some guidelines. Two laws passed in the 1820s essentially determined the Road's final location.[18] The act of May 15, 1820, provided in part for planning a straight-line Road west of Wheeling to meet the Mississippi River somewhere between the mouth of the Illinois River and St. Louis. This lack of specificity showed that not all lessons from the East had been learned: the resulting controversy never was resolved and probably helped speed the demise of the National Road west of Vandalia, Illinois. The act of March 3, 1825, required in part that the Road pass through the state capitals of Ohio, Indiana, and Illinois. Two of the three state capitals had attained their permanent sites by the time the 1825 bill was passed: Ohio's moved to Columbus in 1812 and Indiana's just had relocated to Indianapolis (the site was selected in 1821, but government activity did not begin there until January 1825), while Illinois' capital was still at Vandalia. As a result, the Illinois portion of

GREGORY S. ROSE

the Road was surveyed to pass through Vandalia rather than through the future capital of Springfield, which was not selected until 1837. The Road was moved north from Jefferson's originally proposed path because "the southern parts of Ohio, Indiana, and Illinois were being fairly well accommodated by steamboat navigation on the Ohio" and "the tide of immigration [had shifted] to the northern sections" of Ohio, Indiana, and Illinois.[19]

Passage of these two acts did not eliminate every controversy surrounding the exact location of the National Road through Ohio, Indiana, and Illinois. In Indiana, the Road's location did not elicit much discussion "as the country was thinly settled," permitting the route from Richmond to Terre Haute to be established in 1828.[20] But one minor locational controversy in Ohio and two major ones in Ohio and Illinois generated heated debates, beseeching testimonials, and formal resolutions from towns, counties, and state legislatures reminiscent of those generated during the debates over locating the Road in western Pennsylvania and determining its terminus on the Ohio River.

A minor controversy erupted in Ohio over the bypassing of Newark and Granville by the Road's Zanesville-to-Columbus leg. Between St. Clairsville and Zanesville, the path of the old Zane's Trace was largely followed, but the surveyors cut directly westward of Zanesville to Columbus rather than bending northward to continue along Zane's Trace as it intersected Newark and Granville. Although citizens of those towns gave spirited efforts to relocate the Road for their benefit, they were unsuccessful. The reasons cited for their failure, that "Ohio had not, like Pennsylvania, demanded that the road should pass through certain towns," and that the Road was to follow a straight line through the state capitals, would frustrate future combatants in far larger controversies.[21]

In the first of the Old Northwest's two major locational struggles, supporters of Dayton and Eaton, Ohio, attempted to bring the National Road through their cities rather than have it follow the surveyed route westward from Springfield, Ohio, to Richmond, Indiana. The strength of argument and the involvement of the state legislature made the efforts of Dayton and Eaton's supporters to change the Road's path reminiscent of those of western Pennsylvanians but with one major difference: they failed. Springfield, intersected by the direct line between Columbus and Indianapolis, had been reached by the "completed" Road in 1837. The next leg would carry the Road directly westward to Richmond, but Dayton and Eaton backers proposed a southward diversion through their cities. Convincing arguments claiming that a host of benefits would be gained at a cost of merely four additional miles were prepared to support the Dayton-Eaton argument.[22] The southern route through Dayton, a well-established town soon to be on the Mad River & Erie Railroad line, gave access to the Mad River Valley's burgeoning mills and industries and provided direct contact with the daily mail stage between Columbus and Cincinnati. In stark contrast, they argued, a route directly westward from Springfield would cut through a sparsely settled region, much of which was flat and wet. Of equal if not greater importance, however, Ohio's statehood-enabling act gave the state control over the course of the National Road, and the petitioners looked upon Pennsylvania's success in moving the Road as a precedent.

The Ohio legislature supported the Dayton-to-Eaton boosters. A resolution passed in 1830 noted that the southern route would be superior for the transportation of the mail and would promote "public interest." In response, Congress passed an act in 1835 requiring reexamination of the Springfield-to-Richmond route and a survey of the Dayton-Eaton route to be certain that whichever one became final would "best promote the public convenience and interest." President Jackson, using authority granted by the first National Road appropriation bill in 1806, reaffirmed the Springfield-to-Richmond route originally selected since it met all the legal criteria.[23] Unwilling to accept Jackson's decision, the backers of the Dayton-Eaton route and the Ohio legislature again brought the issue before Congress. A House of Representatives committee heard the arguments and reported in favor of the petitioners, but the entire House refused to challenge Jackson's decision and the Springfield-to-Richmond route remained. Ironically, in some ways the backers of Dayton-Eaton and Springfield-Richmond both lost this struggle. The diversion was never approved but neither did the federal government build the National Road along either proposed route: contracts were let in 1838 for a private turnpike company to construct, manage, and collect tolls on the section between Springfield and Richmond.[24]

In vehemence and content of argument, the debates about the Dayton-to-Eaton and the Vandalia-to-Mississippi-River route proposals were similar. They differed, however, in three significant ways: the latter debate was not about shifting an already determined portion of the Road, it did not affect a centrally located section of the Road, and it remained unresolved for so long that it became entangled in the larger constitutional and sec-

GREGORY S. ROSE

tional questions that halted the Road's federal sponsorship. In 1825, by virtue of being the states' capitals, Vandalia in Illinois and Jefferson City in Missouri were identified as towns through which the Road would pass, but neither the exact route from Vandalia to Jefferson City nor, most important, the point at which the Road would cross the Mississippi River was determined. According to the 1820 law, which was still in effect, the commissioners were to select for the crossing "a point on the left bank of the Mississippi river, between St. Louis and the mouth of the Illinois river." They examined a possible southern route from Vandalia to St. Louis in 1828, and then continued on to Jefferson City and scouted a northern route from Jefferson City to Vandalia along the north side of the Missouri River in 1829. Although the northern route was considered less expensive to build, they recommended the southern route since it crossed the Mississippi River at the commercially and militarily important city of St. Louis, a city which, the commissioners' report noted, promises "from its peculiar situation to become one of the most important cities of the West."[25]

The commissioners' report touched off a lengthy and heated debate between the backers of the two different crossing points: those supporting Alton, Illinois, located south of the junction of the Illinois and Mississippi Rivers but just north of the intersection of the Missouri and Mississippi Rivers, and those supporting St. Louis. The Illinois legislature argued that not only was Alton superior but St. Louis really did not qualify—the 1820 law called for a crossing *between* St. Louis and the Illinois River, not *at* St. Louis—while the Missouri legislature supported the commissioners' recommendation and warned that the Alton crossing would necessitate establishing an overland mail route to connect Alton and St. Louis which would follow the difficult-to-traverse Mississippi River floodplain. Resurrecting the argument used by Pennsylvania and Ohio—that the act of 1806 required the federal government to obtain state consent for any proposed route—the Illinois legislature in 1834 gave its consent "to extend the National Road through . . . the state so as to cross the Mississippi river at the town of Alton . . . and at no other point."[26]

At this stalemate—for a decade—sat the question of route location. Meanwhile, the entire National Road project hung in the balance, buffeted by winds from the constitutional, sectional, and financial debates swirling about in Congress. Finally, in 1844 the Senate Committee on Roads and Canals proposed accepting the Vandalia-to-Alton route since, in the committee's view, approval by Illinois was needed and the state had consented to this route. Congress failed to act on the recommendation in 1844, in 1845 when the proposal was floated again, or in 1847 when a revised recommendation simply to settle on the Vandalia-to-Alton path without appropriating any survey or construction funds was forwarded. Since by that time the federal government was basically out of the road construction business, "the question was never decided by Congress, and the road was not located west of Vandalia, Ill.," where its westward lengthening stopped in front of the Old Statehouse, falling far short of the Mississippi River and calling into question the appropriateness of the term "National" in its name.[27]

### Attempts to Change the Road's Course in the West

For those requesting route deviations, achieving success in changing the path of the Road meant (if the rhetoric can be believed) the difference between an economic boom for an established town and its slow slide into obscurity, or the difference between life for a paper town and its total failure to develop. A contemporary observer traveling through Greenville, Illinois, found that "since the National Road will bypass this little town, the inhabitants fear that it will be doomed. . . . The town already is deteriorating." West of the Ohio River, requests for rerouting generally were as unsuccessful as the ones submitted for the route east of the Ohio River in Pennsylvania had been successful, with the memory of squabbles over location, especially in Pennsylvania, apparently discouraging Congress and the president from approving major route alterations. Denied were requests that would violate the two basic principles in the legislation of 1820 and 1825: that the straightest path be followed by the Road (the "shortest distance" concept initially appeared in the commissioners' first report in 1806) and that the state capitals be intersected.[28] Indeed, the most dramatic deviation from the second principle appears in the failure to reroute the National Road to the new Illinois capital of Springfield when the government moved from the old capital of Vandalia in the late 1830s.

A number of reasons that reflect not only the specifics of the Illinois situation but also the general public and political climate facing the National Road by the 1830s may explain why the National Road's route in Illinois was not changed.[29] The decision to intersect the state capitals had been made in 1825 and the actual survey to Vandalia was completed in 1828, nearly a decade before the capital was moved. Rerouting the Road in Illinois not only

GREGORY S. ROSE

would have lengthened it but also could have reopened many recently settled debates over alternative routes, especially as proposed by the residents of Dayton and Eaton, Ohio. To deviate from surveyed or partially completed portions of the Road, since construction west and east of Indianapolis began in 1830 and by 1835 the Road was passable but unfinished to Terre Haute, would be costly. New surveys and new construction for the detours would be required while possible abandonment of already constructed sections might be necessary, surely eliciting howls of protest from towns once on the main line of the Road but now relegated to a spur or less by the rerouting. Springfield is at approximately the same latitude as Indianapolis and Columbus, but west of Indianapolis the Road bent southwestward through Terre Haute, permitting it to intersect Vandalia and to meet the planned Mississippi River terminus to be located somewhere between the mouth of the Illinois River (near Alton) and St. Louis. A straight-line connection between Indianapolis and Springfield would have bypassed Terre Haute, caused the Road from Springfield to Alton or St. Louis to turn sharply southward, and considerably lengthened the total mileage between Indianapolis and the Mississippi River.

In addition to the perils of rerouting, popular fascination with canals and railroads seemed to be turning interest away from roads, reducing both the possibility of funding roads and the political attractiveness of doing so.[30] As constitutional and sectional issues heated up, the political winds in Congress and the presidency also seemed to be turning interest away from federal financial support for internal improvements.[31] As funding requests for the National Road met with increasing resistance after the mid-1820s, the Road's supporters in Congress may have been loath to propose abandonment of a completed survey, a completed roadway, or even a partially completed roadway while requesting appropriation of funds for new ones. Such a request could have endangered what little remained of federal funding for internal improvements.

Perhaps some local popular enthusiasm for the National Road in the West was sapped because it seemed impossible, despite strenuous efforts to do so, to alter the route of this interstate corridor after the federal government had selected it. In contrast, the paths followed by intrastate canals and railroads, financed by private capital, land donations, or state assistance, were more flexible. Siting decisions by canal or railroad companies could more readily be influenced by local groups promoting one place over another or by canal or railroad commissioners playing one locality against another to gain more commercial concessions, greater local financing, or larger land grants. In an effort to gain the benefits of location on the canal or railroad, intense rivalries between towns and even between neighborhoods within towns erupted. Relying on private, local, or state financing meant that "most of the projected western railroads were designed at first to serve primarily local needs and objectives," and much the same could be said for the canals although more state aid typically supported them.[32] From the West's perspective, however, the National Road, being directed by the federal government, seemed to reflect national rather than local priorities in a number of respects, including its immovable location and its susceptibility to national political and sectional conflicts.

### THE ROAD AS SETTLEMENT CORRIDOR

The National Road, wrote Archer B. Hulbert in his groundbreaking study, "was not to Indiana and Illinois what it was to Ohio . . . for the further west it was built the older the century grew." Hulbert's context attributed this diminished importance to innovations in transportation technology, but his statement also holds true for the Road's role in the settlement of the western states it crossed. Especially in Ohio and Indiana, but even in much of Illinois, settlement occurred before the Road's construction. "By 1830 pioneers had penetrated far into the interior of the Old Northwest and settled on lands distant from water transportation. The establishment of state capitals at Indianapolis and Springfield, both inland from the Ohio river, increased the necessity of overland routes."[33] Many routes existed long before the National Road arrived and, in response to intense local pressures, were improved and upgraded by expenditures from the "3 percent fund," each state's portion of the revenue from the sale of federally owned land within it.[34] Although some migrants used the Road as a route westward, most probably veered off it to search for open lands northward in the lesser-settled portions of Ohio, Indiana, and Illinois. Other overland transportation routes, and the important water routes of the Ohio River and the Great Lakes, brought settlers to the Old Northwest before the National Road appeared and continued to do so afterward.

The National Road mainly followed settlement rather than preceding it because, essentially, the Road came too late to dramatically influence settlement in Ohio or to significantly influence settlement in Indiana and Illinois. Although the benefits of building a road to the West were described by George Washington and others during the latter half of the 1700s, such a road was not approved by Congress until 1806. By then, Ohio had achieved statehood (1803), and the southern portions of Indiana Territory (including Illinois) most accessible to the Ohio River were attracting settlers. A litany of problems caused further delays—Pennsylvania's refusal to approve the route until it had been altered to state specifications, slower and more expensive than anticipated construction east of the Ohio River, the War of 1812, presidential vetoes of construction bills in 1817 and 1822, financial chaos resulting from the Panic of 1819, and constitutional and sectional struggles in Congress—preventing road construction west of the Ohio River from beginning before 1825. Westerners rejoiced at the apparent resumption of the project: "The act of 1825, authorizing the extension of the great road into the state of Ohio, was greeted with intense enthusiasm by the people of the West. The fear that the road would not be continued beyond the Ohio River was generally entertained, and for good reasons." But when the groundbreaking ceremony on July 4, 1825, in St. Clairsville, Ohio, celebrated the start of work on the Road's westward continuation, the Road as legislation and the Road as reality already were separated by twenty years; the Road as idea and the Road as reality were separated by many more. And the gap between legislation and reality was greater still for residents of territory west of St. Clairsville. During the years between idea, legislation, and reality, Indiana (1816) and Illinois (1818) achieved statehood, Ohio became the fourth largest state in the Union with 937,903 residents in 1830, and heavy immigration rapidly spread at least pioneer-level settlement throughout most of Indiana (147,178 people in 1820 and 343,031 in 1830) and much of Illinois (55,211 people in 1820 and 157,445 in 1830). In many respects, by 1830, the true frontier in the region was in the northern Old Northwest and even beyond the Mississippi River.[35]

The northward and westward shift of the settlement frontier in the Old Northwest resulted in just one major (and early) relocation for the National Road. As proposed by Jefferson in 1808, the Road was to cross the southern Old Northwest, passing through Chillicothe, Hamilton, and Vincennes. By 1825, the shifting focus of initial settlement "to the northern sections" of the three states was one factor that "induced Congress to designate by law the capitals of Ohio, Indiana, and Illinois as points on the road."[36] But given the time necessary for survey and construction, and that by the mid-1830s federal funding had dried up although the Road was far from finished, the 1825 decision to move the Road northward still came too late to assist the frontier settlement already occurring farther north and west. Rather than implying that the Road was unimportant to populating the Old Northwest or to its economy, this assertion merely indicates that initial settlement across the Old Northwest did not wait for, or solely depend upon, the National Road.

### Timing of Construction and Intensity of Settlement

One way to measure the relationship between the intensity of settlement by immigrants and the stages of construction for the Road is to compare the completion dates for various Road segments as it crossed the Old Northwest with the population density achieved in the counties it had reached and the date each county was formed. If the National Road provided the first migration path used by settlers to reach a particular area, then one would expect that area's population density to be quite low, and probably insufficient to justify formation of a new county, until the Road arrived. Once the Road was available, a sudden influx of settlers should have occurred. If the National Road reached the area after settlement had begun, then one would expect the area's population density to have been at least at frontier level and that a county should have been formed by the time the Road appeared.[37]

Identifying exactly when a Road segment was complete is difficult because different levels of completeness were achieved at various times during the construction process.[38] All along its course, specifications required that the Road be cleared to a width of sixty-six feet, graded to slopes no more than 5 percent, drained, and macadamized, but the requirements and the reality often did not match, especially in the West: as one author put it, "that part of the National road between Cumberland and Wheeling was much more substantially built than those portions of it lying between the Ohio River and its western terminus."[39] One level of completion was achieved when the Road's path was cleared (although stumps sheared off just above ground might remain), another level when the roadbed was graded and the base prepared (at that point the Road typically began to be used), and still another level when the Road was macadamized. Yet some parts of the Road never achieved the third level and the Road was never truly completed, not only because its westward reach halted at Vandalia but also because some of it was never fully built. For example, a guidebook author

GREGORY S. ROSE

wrote in 1837 about the section between the Indiana line and Vandalia that "little has been done on this road during the last two years," although a Senate report noted that in 1835 an eighteen-mile stretch had been worked on: "some finished, some partly finished, and the sod only removed from the other."[40] Some Road segments were built much later than surrounding segments, such as between Springfield, Ohio, and Richmond, Indiana.

The Road's push westward from Cumberland, Maryland, had seemed slow enough, with construction beginning there in 1808 and concluding nine years later in Wheeling, but the trans–Ohio River section developed even more slowly.[41] In 1825, eight years after the Road reached Wheeling and a time when many wondered if the project ever would be resumed, construction west of the Ohio River began at St. Clairsville, Ohio. By 1828 the completed Road was open to Zanesville; by 1833 it had arrived in Columbus. Construction marched westward from Columbus to Springfield, reached by the Road in 1838, but controversy over the path beyond Springfield interrupted further progress through Ohio. To speed the Road's extension across the Old Northwest (Westerners "complained that, at the slow rate of construction, they were enjoying no immediate benefits"), contracts were let for road-building east and west of Indianapolis in 1830.[42] The eastern leg arrived in Richmond, Indiana, sometime between 1835 and 1841 (the sources vary); the western leg was open to Terre Haute by 1835 and completed by 1838. Completion, however, did not mean macadamizing: only the stretch through Indianapolis had received that degree of finish by then. Also in 1838, Congress appropriated the last funds for the National Road, drawing to a close the era of federally directed road-building.[43] Although the Road was open to Vandalia, Illinois, by 1839, it was incomplete, surfaced only with clay, and never macadamized. Not until after 1850 was construction finished to Vandalia, but that work was funded not from the federal treasury but by the state. One contemporary observer, writing of his "Wanderings in the West in 1839," noted,

> The road is macadamized and finished in the most desirable manner as far as Columbus in Ohio. About four miles at Richmond, Ind., a short piece at Centerville, about six miles at Indianapolis, and three miles at Terre Haute, together with a few bridges are completed in the same substantial manner; the remainder of the way the road has been graded, that is, the road bed has been formed with earth, some of the hills have been excavated, and valleys embanked, and in that situation has been open to public travel.[44]

Census data (when population density in a county reached two to six persons per square mile) and date of National Road "completion"

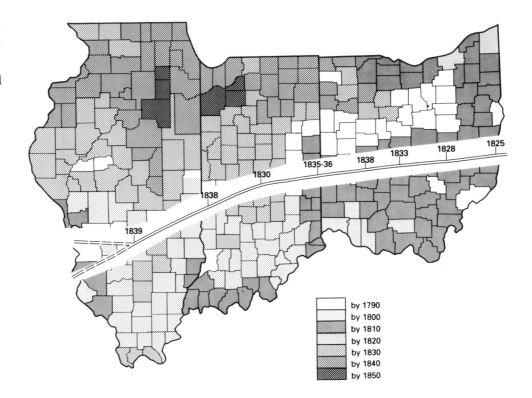

Decade of county formation and date of National Road "completion"

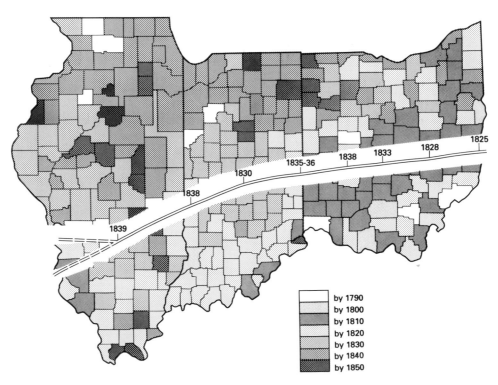

GREGORY S. ROSE

The population density from St. Clairsville (Belmont County) to Columbus (Franklin County), along the first trans–Ohio River segment of the National Road, was two to six persons per square mile by 1810, fifteen years before Road construction began.[45] The same density level was achieved by 1820 between Franklin County and the Indiana line. In eastern Indiana, some counties had as many as six persons per square mile by 1810, while others did not reach that density until 1820; it took until 1830 for central Indiana to be populated that densely and for work on the National Road to begin. Western Indiana and eastern Illinois counties had two to six persons per square mile by 1820, while in the Vandalia area of south-central Illinois that density was reached by 1830. The differences in settlement dates largely reflect differences in accessibility. Eastern Ohio was accessible early on via Zane's Trace, eastern Indiana via the Whitewater River valley, western Indiana and eastern Illinois via the Wabash River valley.[46] The central portions of Indiana and south-central Illinois were somewhat less accessible, although the White River brought some contact to central Indiana, and their settlement was delayed as a result.

The formation of new counties in Old Northwest states typically occurred when population growth in a portion of the initially huge county caused the settlers to demand more accessible services and greater autonomy.[47] New counties were organized by lopping off territory from larger counties, territory they did not always readily relinquish, or in areas recently ceded by Native Americans such as central Indiana's "New Purchase" of 1818. By 1850, barring a few minor adjustments, most southern Old Northwest counties were nearly in their present form. Most Ohio counties crossed by the National Road existed by 1810, with only a few in the west not being formed until 1820. Eastern Indiana counties and some in western Indiana existed by 1820 with the balance across the central region appearing by 1830, just as Road construction began. In Illinois, Fayette County, including Vandalia, and counties closer to the Indiana line had been established by 1820, fifteen years before work on the Road started, while other counties just east of Vandalia were organized by 1830.

Not only were most counties crossed by the National Road settled to a density of at least two to six persons per square mile by the time the Road reached them, but many had been settled well above the frontier level for years. Not only were most counties crossed by the National Road formed by the time the Road reached them, but many had been established for as much as two decades previously. In the initial, more southerly position planned for southern Ohio, Indiana, and Illinois, the Road would have traversed already settled areas. Even after 1820, when its position was pushed northward into central Ohio, Indiana, and Illinois nearer to more northerly portions of those states recently opened for non-Indian settlement, the Road appears not to have been responsible for the initial settlement of those areas. Compounding the delayed construction, repositioning of the Road came too late and was not sufficiently far north to permit it to serve as a funnel for frontier settlers. Although the Road did make accessible the central portions of Ohio, Indiana, and Illinois not served by the Ohio River or the Great Lakes or their tributaries, this accessibility benefited more the processes of economic maturation and commercial development than the establishment of initial settlement. As an observer in Columbus in 1830s remembered, the Road was full of emigrants' wagons going "to establish homes in the western states," presumably meaning Indiana and Illinois as well as states farther west and north.[48]

## TRAFFIC ON THE ROAD

Can it be determined, with the passage of over a century and a half, how much traffic on the Road consisted of settlers and how much consisted of freight, farmers' produce in wagons or on-the-hoof, and passenger traffic? Contemporary observers of and travelers on the Road left valuable descriptions of all types of traffic, and historians have combed these records for information. One of the most famous wheeled vehicles in American history regularly traversed the Road: the great Conestoga wagon. Most looked alike, with deep wooden beds curved upward at each end to stabilize loads while bumping across rough roads, canvas tops, wide iron-banded wheels, and typically drawn by six-horse teams pulling perhaps 10,000 pounds of freight along rutted roads and up and down the mountains. They "hauled flour, wool, hemp, and tobacco from the western frontier to eastern markets and on the return trip carried calico, sugar, and coffee to fill the shelves of merchants."[49] Not all produce from pioneer farms was carted by professional freighters, for farmers carried their own goods by wagon or cart. Nor was all their produce literally hauled: some of it walked its way to market along the National Road, which served, until the railroads diverted most of the traffic, as "the arterial livestock route for all of central and western Ohio and the states beyond."[50]

GREGORY S. ROSE

Reminiscing many years later about his boyhood along the Road in eastern Indiana, Benjamin Parker remembered that "the greatest wonder and delight of all was the stage-coach, radiant in new paint and drawn by its four matched horses in their showy harness, and filled inside and on top with well-dressed people."[51] The stagecoaches ran on established schedules and carried a variety of passengers: "Ordinary citizens riding in coaches on the National Road literally rubbed elbows with" notables of all kinds—former presidents or presidents-to-be, senators, congressmen, frontier heroes, entertainers, and tourists. While stagecoaches may have been the most memorable of the vehicles, the "freighters made more profit than stagecoaches on the National Road."[52]

Newly arriving settlers also traversed the National Road. As Benjamin Parker recalled,

> Many families occupied two or more of the big road wagons then in use, with household goods and their implements. . . . Single families, occupying only a single one- or two-horse wagon or cart, frequently passed along . . . while even the resolute family, the members of which carried their worldly possessions on their backs or pushed them forward in hand wagons, was not an unfamiliar spectacle.[53]

Writing early this century, Seymour Dunbar described "emigrant families crawling slowly to the West in their smaller canvas-covered wagons" (smaller, that is, than the Conestoga freighters) and a more recent author identified "movers," emigrants hauling their worldly goods westward in covered wagons, as the "largest single class of travelers" on the Road.[54]

One of the first National Road historians, Thomas B. Searight, noted that at Uniontown, Pennsylvania,

> As many as twenty four-horse carriages have been counted in line at one time on the road, and large, broad-wheeled wagons . . . laden with merchandise and drawn by six Conestoga horses, were visible all the day long at every point, and many times until late in the evening, besides innumerable caravans of horses, mules, hogs, and sheep.

Although the particular cargo in each vehicle cannot be discerned today, passengers and freight seem to have dominated but emigrants were not specifically mentioned. Furthermore, he suggests that "two-fifths of the trade and travel of the road were diverted at Brownsville [Pennsylvania, onto the Monongahela River] . . . and a like proportion descended the Ohio from Wheeling." This left only one-fifth of the traffic choking the Road east of the Ohio River still traversing it in Ohio, Indiana, and Illinois. Another author has disputed Searight's conclusions using Searight's own figures for tolls collected at various points along the Road.[55] Given the far better condition of the eastern section of the Road and its more discontinuous character as distance westward increased, plus the obvious attraction of the Ohio River's superior freight-handling capacity, the assertion that the National Road carried more traffic on sections east of the Ohio River than west of it is not hard to accept.

Historians have described the movement of emigrants along the National Road. In a popular account of the Road, the author wrote that "the horde of emigrants hurrying westward . . . had been forming an endless procession ever since the Cumberland Road was opened." They followed the National Road, he continued, filling in succession Pennsylvania, Ohio, and Indiana while they "clung to the National Road like a mosquito to a denizen of the American Bottoms. It was the people's highway, and the people crowded it from rim to edge until their carts, wagons, stages and carriages challenged one another for the right of way." After the National Road arrived in Ohio, wrote another historian, "thousands now began pouring into and through the state by wagon from the more thickly populated districts of the east. Many settled in the more remote sections of the state and many more passed through to the fertile prairies beyond." A third historian provided some general, unsubstantiated, and most likely highly inflated statistics measuring that movement: "Indiana and Ohio received more than ninety thousand inhabitants a year for a generation and at least ninety per cent of them came by way of the Pike . . . the average number traversing the Cumberland Road every year was close to two hundred thousand."[56]

The importance assigned by these historians to the National Road as an immigrant highway seems exaggerated for at least two reasons. First, as we have seen, settlement largely preceded the Road's arrival. Second, an isolated and inconclusive piece of information suggests that the Road mostly served other transportation needs. Seth Adams, the tollkeeper at Zanesville, Ohio, counted and categorized the traffic passing through his tollgate in 1832.[57] These data provide a traffic count of sorts, as long as one recognizes that they are a limited sample, being from only one year and at one location, that the direction of travel was not specified, and that one cannot tell exactly what type of vehicle was used for what purpose, although contemporary

GREGORY S. ROSE

descriptions provide some guidelines. Numerically, most traffic consisted of livestock: driven cattle (just over half the total number of 190,328 livestock), hogs (more than one-quarter of the livestock), sheep, and horses and mules. The large number of livestock suggests that the Road was being used by established (not pioneer) farmers and drovers to walk their produce to market. Another 35,310 horses, with passengers aboard, passed his toll station in 1832. The remainder of the traffic consisted of 14,907 one-horse carriages, 11,603 two-horse carriages and wagons, and 2,357 three-horse wagons.

If Parker's description of immigrant traffic is accurate, then settlers moving westward might have used any of the wheeled vehicles as well as their feet. However, their conveyances seem more likely to have been wagons, if substantial amounts of personal effects were hauled, than carriages. If it is assumed that all three-horse wagons and half of the two-horse wagons carried immigrants and their possessions (probably an unrealistic assumption given that farmers also used wagons to move produce overland), and that all of the wagons were headed west, then at most 8,159 wagonloads of settlers on the National Road passed through Zanesville toward new lands in 1832. An "unofficial" count of traffic through Richmond, Indiana, a few years later found more activity on the Road. According to a local newspaper, in May 1837 "40 wagons a day moved through town; by September of that year . . . the number [was] over 100 a day."[58] At the Zanesville rate, even with ten persons per wagon, the Old Northwest would have filled with white settlers very slowly (an average of just over twenty-two wagonloads passed through that tollgate per day); the numbers for Richmond would yield a higher settlement rate, with the caveat that the warmer months of May and September probably showed greater activity than did the colder months. Considering the traffic counts for either town and remembering that settlers did not comprise the sole traffic on the Road, pathways other than the National Road must have carried far more immigrants for the Old Northwest to have grown as it did.

Yet the Road was not an unimportant pathway for immigrants. Press reports and private letters mention the many migrants on the Road or gathering at particular locations, waiting for ferry crossings to resume or for the Road to become passable. Along it in Franklin County, Ohio, in the 1830s, reminisced a contemporary observer, "in the spring and fall of the year this highway was literally white with moving wagons covered with white canvass, going to establish homes in the western states. There were also numerous persons both on foot and on horseback traveling along this highway."[59] But J. Gould, traveling from Richmond, Indiana, through eastern Illinois in 1839, rarely mentioned encountering other wagons on his way (near the National Road in eastern Illinois he "found six wagons and as many families of emigrants from the east"), although he did not avoid mentioning the terrible road conditions he experienced. Another traveler found that although much of the Road east of Vandalia was "nothing more than a track . . . there was a good deal of passage on it." Furthermore, the Road was cited by local boosters as a means of encouraging emigration, and early geographies and emigrants' guidebooks included it as one of the ways to the West and discussed the conditions and experiences likely to be encountered while traversing it.[60]

## THE ROAD AS REGIONAL FOCUS

Various immigrant groups appear to have used the Road in their westward migration but since Pennsylvania, Virginia, and Maryland were crossed by the Road their emigrants found it to be the most accessible route.[61] Other roads, such as Forbes and Braddock's, were available to these Middle States pioneers, and many followed them or the National Road as far west as the Ohio River upon which they completed their journeys. Some settlers from other regions used the National Road, but more Kentuckians or Carolinians migrated northward along local roads, major paths such as the Wilderness Road or the Warrior's Path, or the rivers flowing to the Ohio. Settlers from New York and New England more typically followed the Genesee Road or Mohawk Trail through upstate New York, the "Great Trail" along the south shore of Lake Erie, and the Chicago Road across southern Michigan or the Erie Canal and the Great Lakes.

Generally, migration into Ohio, Indiana, and Illinois was both westward and latitudinal, although southern Indiana and Illinois received many Kentucky and Tennessee natives especially early in the white-settlement period.[62] The westward and latitudinal pattern developed partly because the earliest means of travel, the Ohio River, flowed in that direction and westward movement along the Great Lakes was possible, partly because constructed additions to the transportation network (like the Erie Canal and the National Road) responded to the demands of pioneers and reinforced the westward flow, and partly because of the economic advantages of settling in environmentally similar regions that extended roughly east-west.

GREGORY S. ROSE

The distribution of Northern and Southern immigrants living in Ohio, Indiana, and Illinois in 1850 reveals some of the potential impact the National Road had on the nativity pattern. Northerners, the settlers native to states from Pennsylvania and New Jersey northward, accounted for 57.1 percent of the immigrants born in the United States, while Southerners, natives of Virginia, Maryland, Delaware, and states southward, accounted for 42.9 percent.[63] Except for a cluster of counties north and west of Cincinnati and a few counties scattered through southern Illinois, above-average percentages of Northerners concentrated in counties within the northern halves of Ohio, Indiana, and Illinois. Southerners tended to dominate in counties within the southern half of each state, pushing toward the northwestern corner of Ohio, fairly far north in Indiana, and northwestward in west-central Illinois. The clustering of counties influenced by Northerners and by Southerners supports the idea that the National Road served as a boundary separating Northern from Southern influences in the Old Northwest, and as the westward extension of the Mason-Dixon Line which traditionally marked that boundary in the East.[64] In addition to the nativity pattern, cultural evidence supports this division as boundaries between Northern and Southern dialects, religion, and architecture roughly fall parallel to the National Road. Having nativity and cultural boundaries drawn close to the

Counties having percentages of Northern or Southern immigrants above the Ohio-Indiana-Illinois average, 1850

Note: Northerners averaged 57.1% of the U.S.–born immigrants, and Southerners averaged 42.9%.

Northerners
Southerners

National Road is odd if both groups traversed the Road on their way west: why would immigrants from the South for the most part turn southward when selecting land to settle upon (especially since land to the south was already more heavily populated) and Northerners turn northward?

The distribution of immigrants native to particular states within the North or the South and populating Ohio, Indiana, and Illinois in 1850 reveals a greater degree of complexity in the nativity pattern, making generalizations about the importance of the National Road with respect to settlement patterns even more difficult to support. Pennsylvania and Virginia provided the largest average percentages of immigrants from eastern states in Ohio, Indiana, and Illinois, respectively accounting for between 16.4 and 8.8 percent of the total immigrant population (inhabitants not born in Ohio, Indiana, or Illinois) in the three states. Above-average percentages of immigrants from Pennsylvania appeared in nearly every Ohio county but in only a few northern Indiana and northern Illinois counties. If Pennsylvanians relied exclusively on the National Road as a means of reaching Ohio, then they must have traveled far north and south along connecting roads to become distributed as they ultimately did. Yet proportionally fewer continued westward into Indiana and Illinois, and those who did settled well north of the Road. A similarly confusing pattern occurs for the Virginian natives. The southern two-thirds of Ohio and Indiana contained most of the counties with above-average percentages of Virginia natives, while a swath of counties across central Illinois accounted for most of that state's concentration. If Virginians relied exclusively on the National Road to reach Ohio, then they must have traveled somewhat north but particularly south along connecting roads to become distributed as they ultimately did. For natives of both eastern states, using routes of entrance to Ohio, Indiana, and Illinois other than, or in addition to, the National Road, such as the Ohio River or the Great Lakes and the maze of connecting or side roads, would have resulted in the distribution pattern shown for 1850.

The National Road also could have been used by pioneers leaving one of the western states through which it passed and migrating still farther west. Such a step-wise pattern commonly characterized migration across the Old Northwest.[65] Examining the distribution of above-average concentrations of Ohio natives in Indiana and Illinois and of Indiana natives in Illinois, one sees the impact of latitudinal migration but not necessarily the impact of the National Road in directing that migration. Ohioans accounted for 19.8

GREGORY S. ROSE

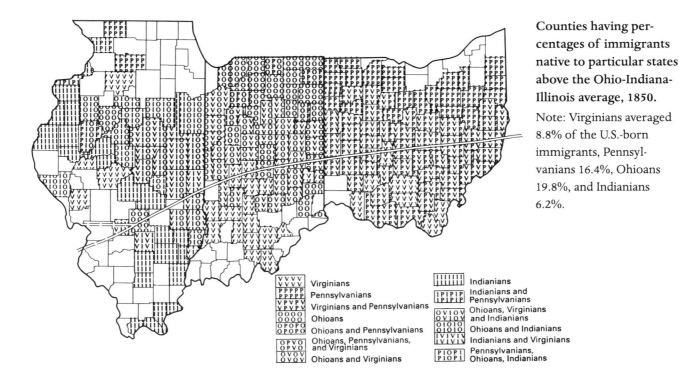

**Counties having percentages of immigrants native to particular states above the Ohio-Indiana-Illinois average, 1850.**

Note: Virginians averaged 8.8% of the U.S.-born immigrants, Pennsylvanians 16.4%, Ohioans 19.8%, and Indianians 6.2%.

| | |
|---|---|
| V V V V / V V V V | Virginians |
| P P P P P / P P P P P | Pennsylvanians |
| V P V P V / V P V P V | Virginians and Pennsylvanians |
| O O O O / O O O O | Ohioans |
| O P O P O / O P O P O | Ohioans and Pennsylvanians |
| O P V O / O P V O / O V O V / O V O V | Ohioans, Pennsylvanians, and Virginians / Ohioans and Virginians |

| | |
|---|---|
| I I I I I I | Indianians |
| I P I P I P / I P I P I P | Indianians and Pennsylvanians |
| O V I O V / O V I O V / O I O I O / O I O I O / I V I V I / I V I V I | Ohioans, Virginians and Indianians / Ohioans and Indianians / Indianians and Virginians |
| P I O P I / P I O P I | Pennsylvanians, Ohioans, Indianians |

percent of all immigrants in Indiana and Illinois, settling heavily in the northern two-thirds of Indiana and the more easterly areas of central Illinois, in each case nearly directly westward from Ohio but not obviously along the National Road. Indiana supplied 6.2 percent of all immigrants in Illinois; most counties with above-average percentages of Hoosier natives were in the eastern and west-central portions of the state, a distribution again not obviously affected by the position of the Road.

Did the Road induce settlement patterns by encouraging Northern settlers to turn northward from the Road and Southern settlers to turn southward? This seems unlikely for a number of reasons, one being the determinist ability this attributes to an inanimate object (the Road) and another, more significant, being that the Road largely was built after settlement, especially in Ohio and much of Indiana, meaning that the initial or basic patterns of nativity already were mostly in place. A third reason is that so many immigrants arrived in Ohio, Indiana, and Illinois using routes other than the National Road, filling the states from the south via the Ohio River and from the north via Lake Erie or Lake Michigan and the shoreline roads. Perhaps the nativity distribution pattern is primarily coincidental to other factors, such as the alignment of the transportation network, the accessibility of land and the timing of its availability, and environmental similarities between the old home and the new.

## LINKAGES TO THE ROAD

The road network in place in the southern Old Northwest during the first half of the nineteenth century features the National Road as a great east-west thoroughfare but also includes numerous north-south roads crossing the National Road without appearing actually to emanate from it. Many roads and turnpikes later funded or encouraged by the states enhanced existing traces and trails, some in use since Indian times. From St. Clairsville to Zanesville in Ohio, the National Road itself followed the earlier Zane's Trace. Native Americans or pioneers established many north-south trails and roads connecting the Great Lakes with the Ohio River years before the National Road's belated arrival. The importance of roads was clear to early settlers who had struggled into the Old Northwest along primitive pathways and then sought ways to communicate and trade with the outside world. After the War of 1812 as before, "the necessity for roads was so pressing and obvious that the subject was, with politics, the most discussed."[66]

It may have been unnecessary to encourage road-building efforts, but Ohio governor Allen Trimble did so in his 1827 message to the legislature. Noting that the paths of the National Road, other roads, and canals to and across the state had been established, he "urged" the people "to lay out a greater number of roads in order to make the most of the through east-and-west route (the National Road) and the through north-and-south routes (the canals and rivers)."[67] The need was such that action followed talk. After the War of 1812, Ohio, Indiana, and Illinois embarked upon great road-building projects that were supplemented and eventually supplanted by canal- and railroad-building projects, many tying into the National Road; as an example of the importance of internal improvements, 44 percent of Ohio's legislative acts in 1825 concerned transportation, while in 1826 55 percent did ("the greater number of these acts had reference to roads").[68]

As it slowly crept westward, the National Road was added to the existing road system. Following the Road's 1833 arrival in Columbus, Ohio, reminisced a witness, "side roads were demanded as feeders to the canals and highways, with the result that road construction was in full swing during this decade," while another description of Ohio identified a transportation system in which from the National Road "radiated scores of lesser roads and private lanes, [leading] eventually into practically every corner of the state."[69] From Indianapolis, where "the National Road passed through, other roads radiated to the corners of the state" and, according to the *Wheeling Times and Advertiser* in 1845 (allowing for some journalistic hyperbole), the National Road "is of importance itself as the trunk of the tree is to its branches, but there never was a trunk from which more numerous branches projected than from this. Scarce a mile of the National Road is found in [Ohio] from which does not diverge a road leading to important towns, villages, and farms."[70]

## SETTLEMENTS AND THE ROAD

In some cases, settlers chose land near the Road, or its projected course, to take advantage of its potential as a means of moving products to market. In Madison County, Illinois, just across the Mississippi River east of St. Louis, a settler wrote in December 1831 explaining his choice of land. Among the reasons was that "the great national highway . . . is now already advanced to Vandalia and next year will be finished to St. Louis. This important highway will then run within one or two miles above our property."[71] As it turned out, neither the timetable nor the construction goal was achieved, but the fact that he included the National Road among his reasons indicates that he expected to benefit from its proximity. Even in longer settled areas, opportunities to be reaped by locating along the Road encouraged commercial ventures ranging from taverns and inns to stagecoach companies and vehicle-repair shops.

Some towns were established specifically to take advantage of the projected or actual route of the Road. Beginning perhaps as a wheelwright's shop, a blacksmith's shop, a general store, or a tavern or inn, small centers sprang up along the Road. In Indiana, the list includes East Germantown (1825), Stilesville (1828), Belleville and Manhattan (both in 1829), and Knightstown (1827, named for Jonathan Knight, National Road commissioner, engineer, and surveyor in Indiana); in Illinois, Cumberland County and the towns of Effingham, Marshall, and Greenup (named for the superintendent of the Road in Illinois) were established because of the National Road. Some towns, discovering that the Road would bypass them, either abandoned their sites to relocate on the Road or faced decline: in Indiana, "the National Road was south of the small town of Vandalia and within five years, the residents relocated one half mile south on the east bank of the

Whitewater River as East Cambridge. It also appears that the location of the National Road to the north of Salisbury was the final blow for the town."[72]

As a result of the delay in constructing the National Road in the Old Northwest, many places through which the Road would pass already existed. Larger towns, such as St. Clairsville, Zanesville, Richmond, and Terre Haute, were well established prior to the Road; three others, the state capitals of Columbus, Indianapolis, and Vandalia, were intentionally intersected by it.[73] Since the National Road was required to cut through the capitals anyway, the surveyors marked it directly in front of the state capitol buildings, causing it to pass through Columbus on Broad Street, Indianapolis on Washington Street, and Vandalia on Gallatin Street. The Road's arrival caused some reorientation of economic activities in established towns. In Richmond before the Road arrived, the primary commercial avenue had been the north-south Front Street but "with the survey of the National Road, commercial development spread to the east and west along Main Street," and in Centerville, Indiana, the price of and demand for lots along the Road's path through the town caused "the original 100 foot Main [Street to be] reduced to 60 feet and the additional ground used to construct new buildings in front of the older ones" with an "arch" being "used in this construction to allow access to the older portions of the building."[74]

## FEDERAL WITHDRAWAL FROM THE ROAD

As the nationally directed transportation system envisioned by Washington and Jefferson, proposed by Albert Gallatin, and supported by such Easterners as John Quincy Adams and Westerners like Henry Clay crumbled under the pressure of constitutional questions, funding constrictions, sectional conflicts, changing popular interests, and increased private entrepreneurship, so crumbled the National Road project. Especially eastward of the Ohio River, the Road had been well built (although at first not necessarily well maintained) with substantial bridges, graded, drained, and graveled roadbeds, only moderately steep grades, and service facilities at regular intervals.[75] Beyond the Ohio River, the gradual westward deterioration and increasing discontinuities of the Road project mirrored the gradual removal of federal funding and the increased diversion of popular interest toward other modes of transportation. Ultimately, the National Road project collapsed after coming to a halt in Vandalia, Illinois, never even reaching the interim goal of the Mississippi River.

GREGORY S. ROSE

From the federal government's perspective, the National Road project essentially was over by the late 1830s. Federal funding for construction west of Vandalia and for finishing the many incomplete sections in Ohio, Indiana, and Illinois dried up, and funds for maintenance of the completed portions became scarce. During the 1830s responsibility for the Road began to be transferred to the states, giving them the authority to charge tolls to complete and maintain the Road or to contract with private corporations for those services.[76] From the perspective of local need, benefit, and interest, by the 1830s the National Road project also essentially was over. Not only did distance from popular frontier destinations due to lateness of construction and competition from other immigrants' routes limit the Road's role in regional settlement, but it had been largely supplanted, especially in public enthusiasm and interest, by other transport systems. "The road was never so important to Indiana and Illinois as to Pennsylvania and Ohio, for much of the through traffic was diverted by the Ohio River, and other means of transportation were competing strongly by the time the western stretches were completed," wrote R. Carlyle Buley.[77] A similar observation by Hulbert, noted above in the discussion of the Road's value as a settlement artery, makes the same point.

Changes in Transportation Technology

As early as 1836, following many annual committee reports comparing the advantages and costs of road, rail, and canal transportation, it was proposed in Congress that the funds needed to complete the National Road west of Columbus, Ohio, be expended instead to construct a railroad along the same route.[78] Mirroring the financial analyses in the annual reports, this proposal admitted that constructing a railroad would be more costly than constructing a road but predicted that maintenance costs for the railroad would be considerably less. Furthermore, and probably most attractive, the benefits of speed and ease of transportation offered by a railroad would far outweigh the initially greater costs. The proposal failed, but that such a proposal bolstered by facts and figures was introduced at all reveals how far new transportation technologies were advancing and that interest in benefiting from them was growing. In the same way that the National Road seemed revolutionary when first approved so now, thirty years later, the railroad seemed to be on the "cutting edge" of the transportation revolution.

Popular enthusiasm for new transportation technologies, coupled with the National Road's reduced importance as an immigrant pathway and debates about the constitutionality of federal involvement in roadmaking, had a direct effect on its ability to command congressional interest and funding.[79] An author early this century wrote:

> Long before the road reached the town of Terre Haute . . . it was realized by the people that the highway . . . [was] not destined to be the chief means and method for all future communication with the East. Canals had come, only to be threatened by the westward creeping iron rails, and desire turned from the old ways to seek the new.

Another writer at approximately the same time explained that the Road "could get no further" than Vandalia: "It had dragged its slow length along for nearly half a century. It was, however, finally overtaken by the steam railway and then ceased to exist as an object of national attention." A more vivid description of the superior attraction of a railroad appeared in an 1846 speech by "the celebrated Georgian, Mr. Yancey" (presumed to be William L. Yancey of Alabama), who conceded that "when first conceived" the National Road "was needed as a great highway for the trade and produce of the fertile west" but noted that on the roads of the era a traveler had made good time "when jolted over them at the rate of sixty miles a day." "How different now!" Yancey claimed, since steam navigation on the Ohio River and railroads across the land had appeared. "Why, sir, men are behind the times with this old road. The spirit of the age is onward. Thirty miles an hour on land . . . is deemed ordinary speed."[80]

The advances attracting most enthusiasm and facilitation from the public, the press, and legislatures throughout the United States involved either the application in new places of existing transportation technologies such as canals or the utilization of newly developed transportation technologies such as the railroad.[81] Canals and railroads, as "modern" modes of transport, captured the popular mind with promises of speed, ease, and low cost. But even as canals and railroads appeared to be the wave of the future, the federal government was reducing its role in financing internal improvements, especially but not only the National Road, and was passing responsibility for maintenance and further construction to the states through which it ran. Ironically, the federal government initially had involved itself in the National Road project because "it was felt that settlement at the time was not sufficient to attract private capital; and this being the case, the pro-

GREGORY S. ROSE

ject should be subsidized by the Federal Government."[82] The federal treasury never could cover all the proposed projects and federal support was in any case too tenuous to be relied upon, as the struggles over National Road funding had shown. Private capital was tapped but also was insufficient; many of these financing arrangements were best described as "schemes," given the plans for raising capital outlined by their early proponents. Public pressure mounted for state governments to encourage internal improvements directly by supplying funds, issuing bonds, chartering companies or projects, and by making special arrangements with private investors for turnpikes, canals, and railroads.

Canal projects linking the East Coast to the West began with the unsuccessful Washington & Potomac Canal, but whatever cautionary advice that project provided for future investors was totally erased by the Erie Canal's success.[83] It opened in 1825, the same year that federal funding for construction of the National Road west of the Ohio River again began to flow. Also in 1825, Ohio approved an extensive canal-building program of its own, breaking ground for the Ohio & Erie Canal and the Miami & Erie Canal, and in 1830, Ohio issued its first charter for a railroad company, followed by many more in subsequent years.[84] At about the same time Congress was debating whether to substitute a railroad for the National Road west of Columbus, Indiana embarked on a massive program of internal improvements, including the Wabash & Erie Canal running diagonally across the state, and a railroad from Madison on the Ohio River to Indianapolis. Illinois supported the construction of railroads, including the Illinois Central from the state's southern tip to its northwest corner, and the Illinois & Michigan Canal to join Lake Michigan with the Mississippi River. Funded directly by the state or with state backing, the internal improvement schemes of the 1830s were so ambitious that they, with the assistance of the Panic of 1837, bankrupted Indiana and deeply indebted Illinois and Ohio.[85]

### Opposition to Continuing the Road

Given the economic benefits created by the National Road, it is not surprising that great disappointment arose in the West as appropriation bills were slowed by the debate over constitutional powers and the beginnings of sectional discord, ultimately dooming federal support for the National Road.[86] Western legislators in Congress, of course, recognized the Road's importance to the region. But Southern representatives generally opposed the Road, arguing against it on constitutional and sectional grounds. From the constitutional point of view, they opined that the federal government did not have the right to expend taxpayers' dollars for internal improvements generally, and for the National Road specifically, in the absence of such authority being clearly spelled out in the Constitution. From a sectional point of view, they argued that since the Road supported settlement and economic development in the Old Northwest but the South did not enjoy any similar federal road project, the National Road obviously did not benefit the entire country. The vehemence of Southern opposition to the Road indicates that it was at least perceived as an economic value to its region and presaged the increased sectional discord that ultimately erupted in the Civil War.

## THE ROAD AS ECONOMIC ENGINE

The National Road provided an economic engine not only for towns along the way but also for the states it traversed and for the entire region. The Road's economic impact is revealed in two ways: by the efforts of citizens and communities who were not on the proposed route to alter the Road's course, and by the efforts of citizens along the route to take advantage of commercial opportunities appearing with the Road's arrival or to cash in on the increased land values the Road brought. Hopes of future economic gain drove these efforts, for the federal government did not directly compensate owners of land taken to build the Road. Legal right-of-way was not obtained, either by the owners voluntarily ceding the land or by the government applying the principle of eminent domain: "Because the road brought 'nothing but benefits and blessings in its train' . . . owners of land along the route gladly donated a strip sixty-six feet wide through their farms."[87] Actually, this statement may be an exaggeration. In Wayne County, Indiana, where four owners "had not relinquished claims to the right of way . . . bidders [for work contracts] were cautioned not to touch a tree on those sections to avoid claims for damages against the government." In another instance, the Road's survey ran directly through the house of Thomas Croft, who refused to accept the $500 offered in exchange for his residence. "The road was then of necessity made around his house, and so near it as to loosen its foundations, and it toppled and fell down, causing him to lose his house, and the sum offered him as damages besides."[88]

Planning and constructing the Road provided plenty of employment and commercial opportunities for surveyors and their assistants, laborers (many of whom were recent immigrants, often from Ireland), farmers who provided food for the workers and rented their labor and teams, and local purveyors of lumber, building stone, and gravel. Farmers working on the Road typically received wages of 62½ cents per day, "higher than the going rate for labor," and "gangs of laborers, mostly Irishmen, were paid $6 a month to break limestone with round-headed hammers into pieces" for macadamizing the Road's surface. Traffic on the Road demanded a level of services far beyond what was required by the local rural population. Entrepreneurs established inns, taverns, liveries and stables, repair shops, and stores; jobs for mail-carriers, stage-drivers, wagonmasters, laborers, and other workers appeared. These sorts of people along the Road in Columbus "said the National Road was responsible for most of their prosperity"; in Indianapolis traffic along the Road during the 1840s "brought life to Indiana's capital, swelling its population and dropping profits into merchants' pockets." Farmers within reach of the National Road could use it to get their products to market, generating opportunities for sale or exchange which farmers with poorer access to the Road, and through it to distant markets, did not have. Immigrants following the Road westward contributed to the local economy along the way by purchasing goods and services and by settling in the states traversed by the Road. After the Road was ceded to the states, it also became both a source of state revenue from tolls charged or contracts let to private companies for operation and maintenance and an expense for the states, most significantly because of the continuous need for maintenance.[89]

## THE NATIONAL ROAD AS ARTERY TO THE OLD NORTHWEST

Why was the pressure to extend the National Road not as great, and the support in Congress not as strong, once the Road reached the Ohio River? Why did the federal government allow the National Road project to grind to a halt during the 1830s? A variety of issues facing the federal government contributed to the National Road project's demise: Constitutional, sectional, financial, technological (due to alternative and newer transportation), and chronological.

Perhaps as important as anything was that the National Road's original objective had been achieved in 1818 when it reached the Ohio River at Wheeling. From the beginning, the driving concern had been to provide access to the trans-Appalachian West, to establish a means of crossing the mountains separating the East Coast and the Northwest and specifically, as the project developed, to link Cumberland, Maryland, on the east-flowing Potomac River with Wheeling on the west-flowing Ohio River. When the National Road was completed to Wheeling in 1818, "Washington's dream had been realized—the eastern and western waters were joined," and the first seers of this vision and architects of its realization—Washington, Jefferson, Gallatin—were deceased or out of powerful positions in the government; in addition, the country's attention was no longer solely focused on nation-building.[90] When constructed west of the Ohio River after 1825, the Road became an important means of moving products and people, but certainly not the only means or, arguably, the most important one. Even east of the Ohio River, one author claimed, the Road's "greatest utility was . . . in the transmission of the mails," an activity requiring a means of transport able to carry items with some dispatch but not items of great bulk. Furthermore, in the southern Old Northwest the Road's significance was reduced from what it had been in the East: essentially, it now "served the central parts of Ohio and Indiana, rather than the nation as a whole."[91] How important to migration and initial settlement could the National Road in Ohio, Indiana, and Illinois have been, given its discontinuities, incompleteness, often very poor condition, and lateness of construction? In many ways, the National Road was a transportation artery to, not through, the Old Northwest, an artery constructed to serve, not to settle, Ohio, Indiana, and Illinois.

GREGORY S. ROSE

# Adapting the Road to New Transport Technology

CRAIG E. COLTEN

*A road in principle is simply an inclined plane, one of the most elementary inventions of man. However, the application of the principle of the earth's wrinkled surface is a highly developed and difficult art in which proficiency can be attained only by study and long practice.*

F. W. CRON
"The Art of Fitting the Highway to the Landscape"

WHEN INVENTIONS OR IMPROVED TECHNOLOGY AFFECT TRANSPORTA-tion, routeways and the country that they pass through will reflect the change, sometimes subtly, often in spectacular fashion. The National Road corridor can be cited as an exemplar of how the application of new technologies comes to change entire landscapes. John Borchert observes that "the metropolitan physical plant has accumulated through various historical epochs, and clearly those epochs were distinguished from one another by different ideas and technologies."[1] Several successive transportation epochs produced tremendous and seemingly permanent change to the towns and countryside along the National Road's route between Baltimore and St. Louis. Yet, as the advantages of each new technology captured a greater share of travelers and shippers, the new transport medium replaced its predecessor as the dominant influence in shaping the roadside.

What had seemed revolutionary and permanent became quickly obsolete. The initial phase of transportation modifications along the National Road solidified the domination of existing land and water routeways and was largely in place by 1835. During this initial period, the National Road was a route of national significance and had a tremendous impact on the pace and scale of travel across the Alleghenies. A second phase, dominated by the railroad, reached its apex by 1890. The railroad produced a major re-orientation of interregional trade patterns and left the National Road as a series of locally controlled farm-to-market roadway segments. During the early twentieth century, federal and state funds injected new life into the highways and led to an integrated national highway system of which US 40 was a part. By 1950, paved highways carried a significant portion of inter-state cargo and stimulated significant reworking of urban form to accom-modate the auto/truck traveler. Although the railroad remained dominant at this juncture, it was on the verge of decline. By 1990, the highway had largely reversed the railroad's nineteenth-century dominance. Federally funded, limited-access, four-lane highways, like Interstate 70, supplemented the old highway and allowed individual motorists and corporate truckers to reshape the roadway traffic, renewing the highway's dominance. This chap-ter will examine the series of shifts in preference for certain transport sys-tems and their impacts along the National Road corridor.

## IMPROVEMENTS IN PACE AND SCALE TO 1835

Initial transportation modifications centered on improving existing route-ways—both water and land—thereby increasing the pace of travel and also the capacity of cargo-carrying equipment. By the mid-1830s, an integrated system of engineered roadway, cleared river channel, steam navigation ca-pabilities, and feeder canals was in place linking the Middle Atlantic states to the Ohio River Valley. Nevertheless, the optimal journey from Baltimore to St. Louis in 1800 required five to six weeks. The routeway west to the Ohio River was a narrow track through the forest with minimal improvements. Indians, militia men, and adventurers had packed the path, although horses tended to macerate the roadway, particularly where soggy conditions ex-isted. Wagons could make the journey although their wheels chewed at the loose soils and bedrock, contributing to the road's poor condition. At the outset of the nineteenth century, a person anticipating a journey from Wash-ington westward to the Mississippi River had limited options for traversing the thousand-mile route. Most likely one would travel by land to Pittsburgh

CRAIG E. COLTEN

or Wheeling and by water from there. The initial leg might include wagon or eventually stage travel, but in 1800 locomotion by foot or horseback was most common, limiting the volume of cargo that could be moved.

Before 1810, cumbersome wagons could transport manufactured goods from Baltimore to the Ohio River in six to eight weeks, while a horseman carrying the mail could travel the distance in only a week. Canoe passage from Wheeling to the mouth of the Ohio took approximately twenty-five days. A canoe, moving with the current, provided greater capacity for cargo, but not much more than a few hundred pounds. Flatboats served as a valuable vernacular boat form that had much greater capacity than a canoe and at high-river stage could complete the trip from Pittsburgh to the mouth of the Ohio in fifteen days, although at low water it was not uncommon to require two weeks simply to reach Louisville.[2] Neither boat provided an efficient means for moving large cargoes upstream. Hence, the initial movement of agricultural produce—pork, corn, and whiskey—from the Ohio Valley was with the major river's current. Precious little cargo moved upstream, even after the keelboat became available about 1790.

The U.S. government officially opened the Northwest Territory in 1787 and purchased the Louisiana Territory in 1803, stimulating public and governmental demands for dependable access to the Ohio Valley. Congress initially questioned the constitutionality of federal expenditures on transportation linkages with the interior. Congressmen who favored national roads believed that adequate transportation connections would help preserve the Union, stimulate economic development, provide for the efficient movement of the mail, and enable effective military operations. Ultimately, they won the debate. Legislation creating the National Road (1806) included guidelines calling for a roadway to accommodate existing transportation technologies and an engineered road that would offer tremendous advantages over the worn and unreliable route that was in use at the time. To accommodate traffic in both directions, road-building crews followed Congress's direction in clearing a route and finishing the surface. These guidelines reflected contemporary road-building technologies for animal-drawn and pedestrian traffic and the resulting roadway favorably impressed some travelers. Thomas Hulme may have exaggerated somewhat in 1819, reporting that "this road is made for ever; not like the flint roads in England, rough, nor soft or dirty, like the gravels; but, smooth and hard. When a road is made in America it is well made."[3]

**Major commercial thoroughfares, 1835 and 1890**

The National Road was an important land route to the upper reaches of the Ohio River during the early nineteenth century. Canals reinforced the "southerly" flow of midwestern agricultural produce.

By the end of the century, however, railroad networks largely supplanted the long-distance transportation function of roads and waterways.

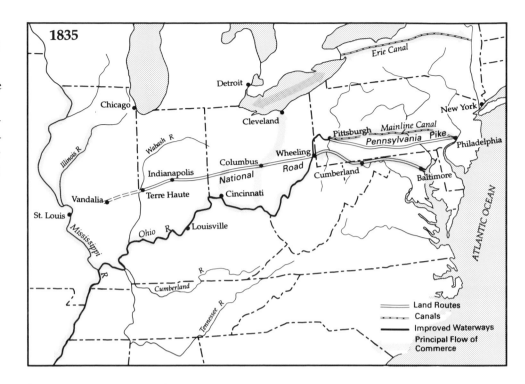

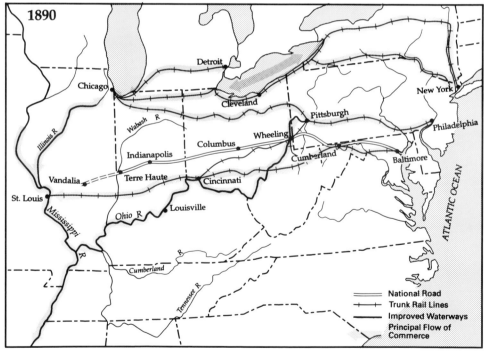

CRAIG E. COLTEN

The initial road segment from Cumberland to Wheeling, built at federal expense, opened in 1818 even though work continued after that date; and it offered tremendous advantages in the pace and scale of travel. Mail made the journey from Washington to Wheeling via stagecoach in only two days. John Woods reported traveling from Cumberland to Wheeling with two wagons in eight days. The new road allowed ox-drawn wagons, with cargoes averaging about 10,000 pounds, to negotiate that distance in three to four weeks, or half their previous time. Traveling on horseback, Aaron Miller noted in his diary that he covered the approximately 120 miles from Cumberland to Wheeling in four days, while foot travelers boasted of traversing as much as 40 miles in a day along the improved route.[4]

By expediting travel, the road quickly became the principal artery for westbound commercial traffic. James Flint reported that some 4,000 wagons were engaged in the trade between Pittsburgh and the two seaboard cities of Philadelphia and Baltimore in 1818. In 1822, 5,000 wagons reached Wheeling, and many more unloaded their supplies at Pittsburgh or other towns along the way. In large measure, travelers were settlers seeking new homes in the West or teamsters transporting some of the 10 million pounds of cargo shipped annually to Wheeling and other Ohio Valley communities. One estimate placed the volume of traffic at 200,000 individuals a year along the initial stretch of completed road.[5] Overall, initial road construction merely provided a more efficient means of moving goods and people to the Ohio River's upper reaches by allowing the traditional route to serve as an improved feeder to that waterway.

Although designed and constructed to provide a durable surface, the crushed stone roadway prescribed by Congress proved to be inadequate to the demands made by the tremendous volume of traffic along the Road's eastern stretch, and by 1820 its condition had already deteriorated. Congress considered appeals to provide resources for repair and maintenance and eventually authorized funds for this purpose and to extend the road west of the Ohio River in 1824. The federal construction project pushed across Ohio and Indiana and the road was opened to the banks of the Wabash River in 1834. Traffic along this section consisted mainly of livestock drivers and some pioneer settlers from the Kentucky country. Aaron Miller noted passing three droves of eastbound cattle in his 1832 diary. Although the Road was initially planned to extend to St. Louis, high costs diminished federal enthusiasm for continuing National Road expenditures.

Construction stopped on the Illinois portion in 1840, even though the work was far from complete and only a partially finished route reached Vandalia.[6]

As work on new Road sections progressed in the western states, repairs commenced in the East. The Road also passed from federal to state control. Maryland's governor insisted that federal repairs include a complete roadway resurfacing in his state. The Army engineers inspected the route and found that it needed extensive repairs and recommended a macadamized surface. They oversaw the laying of a thirty-foot-wide macadamized surface between Cumberland and Wheeling by 1837. Upon completion of these and other improvements, the federal government turned the Road over to Maryland and Pennsylvania. The transfer enabled Congress to avoid a prickly constitutional issue while providing a means for the states to collect revenue for ongoing maintenance. Maryland took possession of its segment of the Road in 1835 and set up two tollbooths thereafter. Pennsylvania followed suit and gathered significant revenues from the toll system over the next few decades. The toll system encouraged the use of wide wheel rims by charging higher fees on the more destructive narrow wheels, while permitting vehicles with rims over six inches to pass for free because they effectively packed the roadbed. By mid-century, both Ohio and Indiana had taken over their road segments, but they opted to lease the road to private toll companies. What had begun as an integrated federal project now passed back into state hands, with greater authority held at the county level or by private leasers. Therefore, by the mid-1830s, the National Road had lost its continental complexion and tended to serve local traffic, particularly west of the Ohio River.[7]

Attendant with the rapid expansion of traffic along the National Road, there arose an extensive network of service facilities. They included wagon shops for repairs, relay stations for stage teams, and a variety of accommodations for travelers—including taverns, inns, and hotels. Obviously the most common form of roadside service was the inn or tavern. Given the atomistic nature of travel, there was no centralized clustering of these service facilities. Scattered along the Road, inns and taverns evolved from farmsteads and provided lodging and meals. East of the Ohio River, travelers reported inns spaced at approximately one-mile intervals, while Fortescue Cuming encountered inns in eastern Ohio about five miles apart in 1808. With increasing traffic volume the number of service facilities increased; at one time there were at least 294 inns between Baltimore and Wheeling.[8]

Tavern- and innkeepers generally selected rural sites or locations on the

CRAIG E. COLTEN

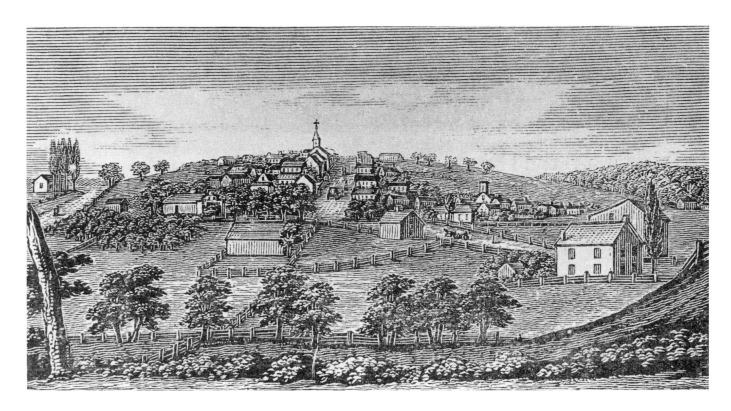

margin of communities where they would have space to corral draft animals and raise fodder and victuals. Henry Howe's drawing of St. Clairsville, Ohio, in 1846 shows the National Road passing through the center of the town and "Neiswanger's old tavern" on the extreme right. Likewise the Huddleston House (c. 1839) at the western edge of Cambridge City, Indiana, consisted of an inn, seventy-eight acres of land, a barn, and a stable (currently a historic site). Sizable pastures were necessary for horse and ox teams that pulled family wagons, stages, and the larger Conestoga wagons. If the inn hosted drovers herding livestock to market, still larger pastures were required.[9] In either case, locations at the margin of a town or in a rural area suited such land use.

Hotels represented a different type of accommodation for travelers. Generally more refined, they occupied sites near the town center and catered to those traveling by stage or private coach. Hotels lacked extensive wagon-yards or pasture areas, although before 1850 a barn and small pasture would not have been uncommon. Hotels, too, added a touch of urbanity to the string of frontier communities along the National Road and were highly desired amenities for fledgling communities. They often rose several stories above the street and were among the larger buildings in a community. Howe's 1846 sketches of Ohio towns frequently show a hotel facing the

**St. Clairsville, Ohio, on the National Road, 1846**

In this view of St. Clairsville from the west, Neiswanger's tavern appears in the foreground. The spire in the center is atop the courthouse and the tower on the right is on the Presbyterian church.

**Transportation and changing urban morphology, 1835–1990**

In 1835 taverns and inns were scattered along the National Road.

By 1890, railroads had drawn hotels and service industries to the side of the tracks.

Improved highways completed during the twentieth century introduced strip developments to the fringes of towns along US 40.

Interstate clusters have prompted still another re-orientation of commercial activity to the exchanges along the limited-access highways.

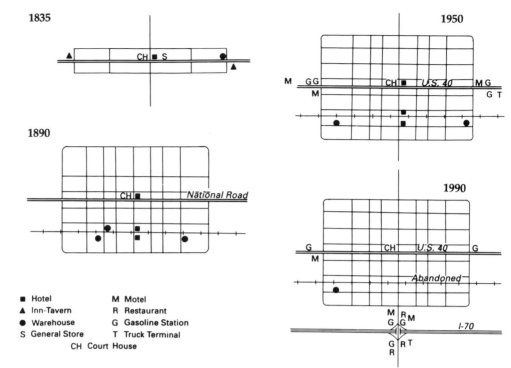

■ Hotel
▲ Inn-Tavern
● Warehouse
S General Store

M Motel
R Restaurant
G Gasoline Station
T Truck Terminal
CH Court House

market square or courthouse.[10] They were particularly important in county seats where they served those traveling with the circuit court and thereby provided accommodations to both long-distance and local travelers. Proximity to the center of town placed the hotel near both the court facilities and the principal road intersection.

In 1835, the National Road was facing competition from the Pittsburgh Pike and the Erie Canal for overland transport, but was still the only effective link between Baltimore and the Ohio River, although both a canal and rail system were in planning stages. Beyond its intersection with the Ohio, there was far less travel overland as people and goods shifted to the fluvial course. River flatboats were the transport of choice at the time the National Road reached Wheeling and remained a dominant form of water travel through the 1840s. In 1810–11, approximately 1,200 flatboats departed the upper Ohio River carrying tons of agricultural produce, most notably flour, bacon, and whiskey. The movement of bulky agricultural goods, which did not demand rapid delivery, followed the waterways to Cincinnati and New Orleans. In the 1830s, one traveler counted an average of twenty-five flatboats floating by daily, with a cargo of 500 to 600 barrels each.[11] During the 1820s, steamboats, which were able to move with equal ease against and

CRAIG E. COLTEN

with the current, quickly displaced the keelboats as effective cargo carriers, but were unable to wrest all traffic from the inexpensive downriver flatboats. Jointly, steamboats and flatboats solidified the Ohio River's position as chief mover of people and freight across the west.

Federal expenditures on "improvements" bolstered the rivers as the dominant cargo movers in the West after 1824. In response to lobbying by western states and following a series of low-water years, Congress appropriated funds to remove navigational obstructions such as sandbars and snags. The Army engineers constructed experimental wing dams that forced the river to scour a channel that would prevent sandbars from obstructing navigation. Private contractors removed snags from the low-water channel. By removing hazards to navigation, steamboat traffic in particular benefited greatly. Between 1827 and 1835, insurance rates on river cargo dropped substantially as navigation hazards became less of a risk and by 1830 steamboats claimed a share of downstream commerce equaling that of flatboats.[12]

Following termination of work on the route, the National Road fostered negligible change in the overall composition of commerce between the Chesapeake Bay and the Ohio River Valley. Manufactured goods from seaboard cities arrived at the headwaters of the Ohio for shipment to out-

**National Road passing through Zanesville, 1846**

The Eagle Hotel stands on the right and the county courthouse on the left.

lets throughout the interior, while agricultural produce moved with the river's current to the packing houses in Cincinnati and on to the port of New Orleans. Corn, whiskey, and pork constituted the dominant downstream export from Ohio River communities. Pork shipments passing Louisville increased from about 27,600 barrels in 1810–11 to 114,000 a decade later. Throughout the upper Ohio Valley, farmers could drive their hogs to riverfront markets and Cincinnati developed a particularly productive hinterland. In fact, this one river port accounted for some 100,000 hogs packed annually in the early 1830s. Other smaller urban centers prospered as entrepôts for pork shipments as well.[13] The orientation of this trade was strictly "south" and ran across the grain of the National Road. A limited number of livestock arrived at eastern cities on the hoof, but this was a small part of the region's overall production and was affected only minimally by the National Road's completion.

A spate of state-funded canal-building in the 1830s reinforced the position of the pork-packing centers in the regional economy. The shipment of agricultural products across the breadth of southern Ohio tended toward the Ohio River, while the Great Lakes–Erie Canal captured an emerging dairy-wool specialty to the north. Wheat production became an important crop in the north, while corn remained the staple grain in southern Ohio. The major east-west canals threatened but did not displace the preexisting dominance of downriver trade, fended off in part by steamboats on the river. The canals did make inroads and siphoned some trade toward the Great Lakes and the Erie Canal route.[14] Thus, the western canals provided an additional transportation option that ran across the grain of the National Road, further dissuading the Road's use for interregional trade and transportation.

Ultimately, the canal-river links had a marked effect on urbanization in the Midwest. Urban growth up to the mid-1830s depended upon two basic conditions: connection to other locations via transportation systems and size of the local hinterland. Waterways, as the main carriers of trade, proved to be the most important connectors from 1800 to 1830. Cincinnati, for example, occupied an important position on the Ohio River and drew on three rich hinterlands. Secondarily, intersections between land and water routes proved important to towns such as Chillicothe and Zanesville, Ohio, but they were on lesser rivers, which provided important water-power functions, and did not experience rapid growth as did Cincinnati.[15] West of Wheeling, the principal routes were waterways; location along the National Road did little to

CRAIG E. COLTEN

stimulate growth in towns across southwest Ohio and southeast Indiana.

By 1835 the National Road had slipped into a secondary transport role. Certainly stage travel from Washington to St. Louis in eleven days was a vast improvement over the three to four weeks required in 1800. Nonetheless, the Road's primary interstate function was to move mail.[16] In Maryland, Ohio, and Indiana, it remained a roadway superior to local roads, but it had only minor impact on shaping regional economies; rivers and canals had a more pronounced influence. Locally, the Road contributed to the emergence of pioneer urban places and roadside services, but this landscape was on the verge of wholesale alteration with the railroad's arrival.

## LAYING RAILS AND DECAYING ROAD, 1890

In their initial form, the American railroads were merely short lines serving waterfront cities with passenger service, and were no threat to the well-established land and water routes of the 1830s. By the early 1850s, however, railroads had made the first of several trans-Appalachian crossings and began to compete with their predecessors: the turnpikes, toll roads, and canals. Yet several decades elapsed before the rail lines provided an effective and integrated transportation system from the seaboard to the Mississippi River's western bank. In fact, principal waterway bridge crossings were not complete until the 1870s and corporate integration and gauge consistency required another score of years to finalize. Nonetheless, by 1890 the railroads had constructed an extensive track and support facilities network between seaboard cities and the emerging urban centers of the Midwest, and had captured the bulk of interstate commerce. With its rise to dominance, rail travel stimulated many changes in regional economic growth, urban form, and use of the National Road.

Commercial interests in Baltimore, with an eye to the successful Erie Canal in New York, sought a viable technology to capture their share of trade with the interior territories. Supporters of a waterway from Baltimore to the Ohio River resurrected the moribund Potomac River improvement project and won state assistance to press ahead with a canal in 1825. At the same time, businessmen considered Baltimore's position relative to the rich Ohio Valley and even the Southern cotton-producing regions, and noticed a geographic advantage that lacked only a viable routeway connecting the productive interior and the seaports. When they calculated the costs of moving freight by canal or railroad versus the inland rivers–coastal route, they discovered obvious savings. This convinced them to appeal to the legislature for support of a land-based transportation system to the interior and in 1827 the Maryland Assembly granted a charter to the Baltimore & Ohio Railroad (B&O). Stock was offered for sale to private investors and a portion was reserved for the state of Maryland and the city of Baltimore. At its outset, then, the B&O was conceived as a joint public-private venture. Public investment in a large-scale project was justified as a means of capturing a significant portion of the trans-Allegheny trade that would pay dividends through general prosperity for the city and state.[17]

Work began on the B&O line in 1828 and progressed much more rapidly than the canal. In spite of tremendous engineering difficulties, the line reached Wheeling on the banks of the Ohio River in 1853. While the achievement was worthy of celebration in Baltimore, the feat of reaching the Ohio produced few immediate economic impacts on the orientation of trade in the upper Ohio Valley. At the time, Cincinnati was the undisputed commercial center of the interior, and it was essential for the railroad to reach the Queen City. By 1857 the B&O had accomplished this objective via a series of related lines. From Cincinnati, passengers could travel to the banks of the Ohio across from Wheeling in thirteen hours and then arrive in Baltimore overnight after another seventeen hours of travel.[18]

The B&O completed a second extension, the Ohio & Mississippi line, in 1857 and it provided a critical shortcut across the southern portions of Indiana and Illinois, linking Baltimore with the banks of the Mississippi at East St. Louis. This line ran more or less parallel with the Ohio River, although following a much more direct path, and initiated an effective challenge to waterborne commerce. Both in terms of distance and speed, the railroad dramatically cut the travel time for passengers and freight in the late 1850s. A river steamer required approximately six days to navigate from Pittsburgh to St. Louis, while rail connections delivered passengers across the same distance in about thirty-one hours. Freight could be shipped via rail in about seventy-six hours or about half the time for packet service. For travelers, speed was a much greater concern and the trains quickly absorbed much of the region's passenger traffic. For shippers of bulky cargo, cost was a more critical issue than speed and rail freight fees remained significantly higher than steamboat charges during normal water.[19]

Rail service offered many advantages over water movement. Strictly in terms of dealing with natural elements, there was no shallow-water season

CRAIG E. COLTEN

and no winter-ice interruptions. Rail lines could extend directly to a customer's loading platform, thereby eliminating intraurban shipment and transfer to or from a watercraft. In response to the increasingly obvious advantages of rail, much of the grain cargo began to shift to rail carrier by 1860. This trend only increased following the Civil War—about one-third of all grain bound from the Middle West to the East Coast moved via rail before 1860, but by 1876 railroads carried three-quarters. The B&O transported 600,000 barrels of flour in 1852 and over 980,000 barrels in 1856.[20] In conjunction with the Pennsylvania Railroad, which also had lines running parallel to sections of the National Road, the B&O captured much of the grain trade and diverted it directly to the eastern seaboard, performing the function envisioned for the National Road half a century earlier. Unlike the road at its peak, however, the railroads by the late nineteenth century offered cost advantages over water transport to eastern markets.

Territory drained by the Ohio River contributed greatly to railroad traffic and, in turn, was greatly affected by the rail's impact. Before the Civil War, Cincinnati was the leading meat-packing city in the interior and its position was enhanced by its relative position on the river system. Rail service, however, achieved greater economies of scale when processing was concentrated in a few locations from which full trains could depart on long-distance hauls via trunk lines. This prompted a major reorientation of agricultural processing in the Middle West toward Chicago. The railroad also fostered growth in other well-placed cities such as Indianapolis. These fundamental economic shifts in the region's urban hierarchy led to a corresponding decline in formerly important packing towns along the Ohio, namely Cincinnati, and locations along the Illinois River.[21] Although the Ohio Valley pork-packing center hinterlands did not wither as agricultural counties, the major concentration of urban growth moved toward the most advantageous location on the new rail transport network.

Agricultural specialization in the Middle West evolved into a corn-hog complex that was well established by this time and also well suited to the region's climate. This earned the Middle West the designation as the Corn Belt. In addition, new agricultural specialties began to emerge, oriented to local urban markets. Dairy products, for instance, became increasingly important in northern Ohio.[22]

River passenger traffic faced increasing competition from the railroads in the last quarter of the nineteenth century. To compete more effectively, the steamboat companies consolidated, mimicking the railroads' corporate structure, thereby eliminating many of the small individual operators. Reflecting this change, regular packet service began on the Ohio and sought to capture travelers from the railroads. Some steamboats even coordinated arrival times with the railroad departures, reflecting a concession to the rail as the ascendant transport mode. Despite a relatively prosperous year in 1880, river freight traffic was on the wane.[23]

Any hopes that road advocates or shippers had of recapturing a dominant freight tonnage share was lost during the later decades of the nineteenth century as railroads completed their campaigns to integrate a regional rail web. Bridge-building over the Ohio River began in 1849 with legal wrangling between bridge companies and steamboat interests who argued that suspension spans obstructed their movement. The B&O finally completed bridges with high clearances over the Ohio River in 1871 at both Bellaire and Parkersburg and thereafter avoided the delays associated with breaking and ferrying trains over the river. Boosters in St. Louis oversaw the financing and construction of the Eads Bridge in St. Louis, which eliminated still another barrier in 1874. Over the next decade or so, companies such as the B&O and the Pennsylvania Railroad worked to eliminate the final barrier to fully integrated systems—gauge inconsistency. In 1861, for example, the B&O subsidiaries west of the Ohio ran on three different gauges. By 1890 these lines had adopted a single gauge which enabled trains to run uninterrupted between Baltimore and St. Louis. The Penn system and the B&O claimed to move some 26 million tons of cargo by the early 1890s, far eclipsing the roadways or the Ohio River.[24]

Both river and rail transportation systems during the mid-nineteenth century relied heavily on wood for power. Riparian forests provided wood for steamboats, but by the 1860s most of the serviceable trees near the major waterways had been cleared. And only when the wood supply was largely depleted did rivermen show much interest in coal. The transition in fuel was most pronounced on the upper Ohio Valley where woodland had been cleared to supply domestic, industrial, and transportation customers and coal was plentiful and cheap. Railroads relied on wood until after 1865, and as they converted fuels in the nineteenth century's last quarter they contributed to increased demand for coal.[25] Ironically, water transport was best suited to move the large quantities of coal now required, and coal shipping in part accounted for the struggling steamboat industry's survival.

CRAIG E. COLTEN

As New York and Chicago became the two most important nodes on the eastern rail network, the towns along the National Road's route between Baltimore and St. Louis became less significant way stations. Some towns retained certain local trade advantages and most eventually became linked to the rail net. Along with the large-scale reordering of regional economic patterns brought about by the railroads, the towns and cities along the National Road witnessed profound changes to their form. Both the Pennsylvania Railroad and the B&O ran along segments of the National Road corridor and thereby introduced several rail-oriented features to these communities.

By the mid-nineteenth century, people along the National Road realized that the new transportation system promised economic prosperity for those towns connected to a rail line. Competition for canals in the 1820s and the impacts of canal traffic had confirmed the need for national transportation linkages and communities now actively lobbied for rail service. The two principal rail lines across the Ohio Valley did not parallel the river, nor did they terminate in river towns as had the canals. Consequently, most river towns, excepting Cincinnati, experienced negligible growth after 1850. Interior towns that served as intersections for several rail routes, such as Richmond, Indiana, and Dayton, Ohio, increased the volume of trade and with it their populations. Edward Muller found that Ohio Valley towns that experienced increased "nodality" as rail junctions experienced greatest growth in nonagricultural manufacturing and saw significant population growth following 1850.[26]

**B&O Railroad bridge and trackside industries, Bellaire, Ohio, 1887**

As the B&O completed its bridges in the early 1870s, uninterrupted rail service between the eastern seaboard and the western Ohio Valley became a reality.

Although rail service tended to concentrate agricultural commodity processing and population growth in certain cities, some contend that it had a negative influence on small-town growth. Regional trade centers such as Chillicothe, Ohio, which provided initial processing, frequently found the arrival of rail service a disadvantage. Railroads could pick up grain at local elevators and transfer it to major processing centers like Richmond, Indiana. No longer was there a need for primary collection and initial processing at the regional centers. Consequently, local grain elevators appeared at five- to ten-mile intervals along most tracks. As part of an export-oriented farming economy, the elevators required only a small number of farmers to support them. This tended to stabilize small towns, while regional centers declined in relative importance. Mid-sized regional centers, such as Circleville, Ohio, withered as processing industries ceased operation and they came to resemble the smaller towns with a landscape dominated by a grain elevator and its business office set on a rail siding.[27]

Since railroads entered National Road towns long after they were initially platted, the rails were intruders. Railroads introduced what John Stilgoe has called a "metropolitan corridor"—a stretch of rail-oriented activity.[28] It was quite common for the tracks to parallel the main business thoroughfare, often the National Road, set a few blocks north or south of the commercial district. Unlike the towns built by western railroads, the railroad companies did not determine the location of all urban functions, but they certainly had a dramatic influence. Businesses serving rail customers discovered that they had to centralize operations near the station or along the town's sidings and railyards. Frequently, the commercial district was pulled toward the new railroad line. Industry and commercial businesses required large storage areas and rail shipment facilities tended to cluster along the tracks. In addition, large railroad hotels replaced or supplemented the scattered inns and taverns common in the early nineteenth century. These new hotels brought lodging and dining facilities under a single roof and catered to a rail-traveling clientele. They also stood as symbols of urbanity and introduced a level of comfort uncommon in the former taverns and inns.[29] Concentrated around the rail depot, the hotels were convenient for travelers and reflected the function of cities as way stations on a vast rail network rather than as destinations that individuals traveled to and experienced.

During the second half of the nineteenth century, the railroad landscape became associated with progress, urbanity, and prosperity. From the small-

CRAIG E. COLTEN

town grain elevator to the grand railroad hotel, the complex of features that characterized rail travel became the signatures of a society on the move. The old toll roads served local farmers while the moribund canals silted up. Steamboats declined in number and piloting a riverboat lost its glamour as a desirable profession. The dominance of the railroad seemed unchallengeable for decades, but the road was to return.

## PAVEMENTS PARALLEL THE RAILS, 1950

Roadway travel underwent a major resurgence between 1890 and 1950, which stimulated a reworking of the dilapidated thoroughfare, both in its physical condition and popular opinion. As the railway reached its peak in the 1890s, a series of postmortems on the National Road began to appear in print. As a group they reflected on the "lost" routeway that had served nineteenth-century pioneers. Thomas Searight lamented that "he saw it [the National Road] in the zenith of its glory, and with emotions of sadness witnessed its decline."[30] A. B. Hulbert could not wait for the road's centennial to publish his commentary (1901), so complete was its demise by the turn of the century.[31] The historians' theme was that the National Road was gone, overtaken and overrun by the powerful locomotives and rail transportation. Yet as these eulogies were in preparation, Congress was considering ways to reinvigorate government support for and involvement in highways. In fact, Congress created the Office of Road Inquiry in 1894 and in doing so reasserted federal recognition that roadways were important to the national interest.[32] During the next half century, state and federal agencies presented a convincing case that government support for highways was essential to an efficient economy and society. This resulted in a tremendous effort at all levels to modernize and improve the flow of traffic on highways. Stimulated in large measure by the new automobile and truck, public support for these improvements was unwavering and led to deterioration of the railroads as the principal mover of people and goods.

By the 1890s much of the National Road had been resurfaced in the eastern states and portions in the heavily traveled urban districts of the Midwest, while companies laid plank roads on other sections. But the states along the road now controlled construction and maintenance and the result was uneven access and surface quality. In Ohio, farmers had enclosed right-of-way within fences and interurban railroads occupied former roadbed segments. Other roadway sections had, through neglect and lack of maintenance,

**National Road leading into Zanesville, 1887**

By the 1880s, the National Road in most sections of Ohio was in poor condition and was ill-suited for long-distance cargo shipments.

become seasonal quagmires and virtually useless for long-distance travel.[33] Throughout its length, the road was managed by a variety of uncoordinated entities: state governments, county commissioners, and private companies.

Austin Byrne, in an 1893 treatise on highway construction, compared highways to railroads. He argued that railroads successfully handled hundreds of tons of freight and did so efficiently because they conducted scientific study of their systems and quickly replaced defective parts. By contrast, "pavements," he claimed, "once laid are left to batter the vehicles and the vehicles, in return, to pound the pavements: little or no attention being

CRAIG E. COLTEN

paid to them until they finally become unendurable and are entirely renewed." He then offered some scientific observations on the ability of draft animals to pull a load across different road surfaces and also the life expectancy of road construction materials. One horse, he noted, could pull a ton over asphalt; at least two were necessary to handle the same load across stone blocks in fair condition, while two and one-half to three horses could do the chore on good quality macadam. At least five horses would be needed for moving the same load across loose stones.[34] Highway advocates recognized that road improvements required the application of science and engineering and engineers began compiling and quantifying information that would revolutionize road construction and maintenance.

Effective government support for improved roads came at about this same time from the Office of Road Inquiry. This small branch of the U.S. Department of Agriculture collected information on road construction and promoted a national system of good roads that would link farmers to markets and other urban amenities. With support from influential bicyclists, and initially the railroads, the Office of Road Inquiry sent engineering teams across the country to perform road-building demonstrations and thereby disseminate the information they had gathered. By 1905 the office was reorganized into the Office of Public Roads and initiated a systematic program of field tests seeking optimal road surfaces and construction techniques. Based upon its experiments, the Office of Public Roads earned a reputation as the leading authority on road-building matters. Officials regularly published revised construction specifications, which gained widespread acceptance among state and local authorities.[35] Engineering texts took up the cause, touted the advantages of improved farm-to-market roads, and hailed the economic savings of good, all-season highways.[36]

Town and city residents also agitated for better roads; in fact, between 1880 and 1924 most urban streets were resurfaced, a reflection of changing expectations. In 1880, gravel or macadam served as the principal surface for most city streets, while cobblestones were laid on heavily trafficked routes. The public was increasingly concerned about sanitation and these traditional surface materials were not well suited for drainage or removal of animal wastes. Although urban rail systems had solved the problem of soggy roads, accumulations of manure, mud, and puddles still plagued city officials who argued for improved pavements. One early solution was creosote wood blocks. They drained well, were quiet and fairly durable—but they could also burn. New developments in cement and asphalt road-surface materials offered other viable options in the early twentieth century. Chosen primarily for their sanitation advantages, these surfaces also dramatically improved travel.[37] Municipal engineers used these materials extensively, providing highway and road-building officials with information on their desirable qualities.

Turn-of-the-century efforts to improve rural transportation focused on providing farmers using horse-drawn vehicles with roads to towns where their agricultural produce could be loaded on rail cars. And such programs initially met with support from the railways. In fact, the Pennsylvania Railroad and the Illinois Central supported Department of Agriculture programs by providing transportation for demonstration equipment and educational exhibits between 1908 and 1911. By 1912, Congress responded to increasing public interest in good roads and appropriated federal funds for road-building, under the auspices of improved postal roads.[38] In 1916, the Good Roads Act provided direct federal funding for farm-to-market and post roads.[39] By this time, however, the internal combustion engine-powered truck and automobile were available and would lead to a tremendous shift in road-building requirements and also ultimately undermine railroad support for rural roads.

The combination of technologies that brought mass-produced automobiles, trucks, and buses to the nation's roads is a story that has been told in many forums.[40] Among the technological breakthroughs were affordable automobiles, adequate supplies of gasoline, and new forms of highway construction. Prior to World War I, most roads and highways were designed and built to accommodate horse-drawn traffic and hence could not withstand heavy loads or motorized vehicle traffic necessitating substantial changes in highway engineering. When truck fleets drove over the old National Road during the war to coastal ports, they inflicted unprecedented damage.[41]

Following World War I, the government's first important step to restimulate local road improvements was to donate large quantities of war-surplus road-building equipment to the states. Several years later, the Highway Act of 1921 altered the direction of federal subsidies for highway construction. Rather than focusing on local roads, the new priority was to "expedite the completion of an adequate and connected system of highways, interstate in character."[42] An underlying objective of a national highway network was to provide for internal transportation in the event of another war.

To receive federal dollars, states had to form highway departments. These organizations, with advice from the federal Bureau of Public Roads, worked to create consistent standards for road construction and to begin an integrated network of highways that ostensibly would connect all major cities within ten years.[43]

As states assumed the responsibility for upgrading and maintaining highways, they quickly recognized the need for adequate funding. Tolls had served this function along the National Road, but twentieth-century highways required different solutions. Initially, registration fees assigned the burden of construction and maintenance to road users. Increased traffic and rising maintenance costs, however, stimulated the demand for additional revenue. A gasoline tax proved one of the most effective, equitable, and widely accepted forms of highway funding. Those who used the most fuel, and presumably caused the most wear on highways, bore the greatest cost. Through the 1920s state legislatures enthusiastically adopted this form of taxation for highway improvements.[44]

Once the combination of federal funds and new state revenues was in place, highway improvements began in earnest. States along the National Road assumed responsibility for the improvement and maintenance of the roadway within their boundaries. In 1922, state-maintained road mileage included: Maryland 1,852 miles, Illinois 4,800 miles, Indiana 3,600 miles, Ohio 3,000 miles, and Pennsylvania 3,900 miles. Over three-quarters of the federal- and state-funded miles were concrete, representing a vast improvement over the macadamized surfaces.[45] In each state, a new routeway (US 40) followed or paralleled the National Road and became part of an integrated federal highway system.[46]

Until the 1920s, the major engineering works of the country were canals and railroads, and many practicing engineers received their training on these projects. Converting roads from farm use to modern highways took several decades and progressed from a form that mimicked railroads to one that was thoroughly designed for motorists. Although extensive literature on road-building existed, the practical work of the Office of Road Inquiry and state highway departments was in its infancy.[47] A critical concern for road and right-of-way design and durability was saturation and drainage. Wet conditions weakened the roadbed and permitted rapid deterioration. Railroads overcame this problem by building raised beds with ditches. While this was a suitable solution where rails held the vehicles on the raised

**Major commercial surface thoroughfares, 1950 and 1990**

The U.S. highway system provided multiple routes between seaboard cities and the urban centers of the Midwest. Most followed trade routes established by railroads.

The Interstate Highway System provided efficient routes across the country's midsection for trucks and automobiles. Abandoned rail routes reflect the diversion of cargo shipments to highway carriers.

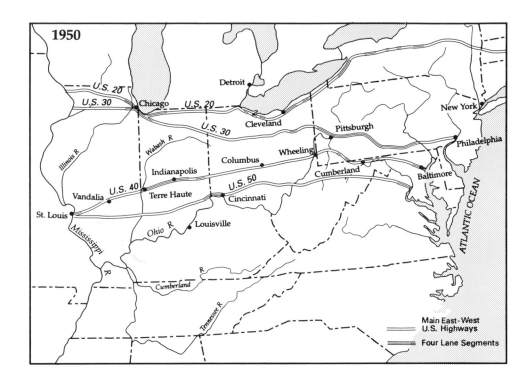

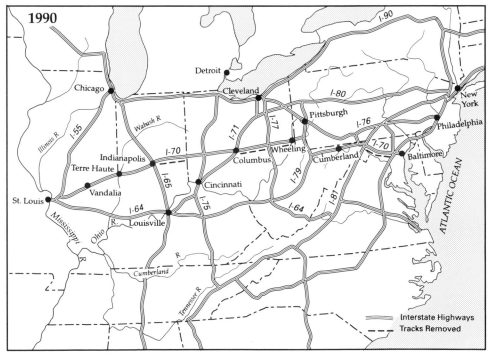

CRAIG E. COLTEN

surface, highway engineers had to consider the consequences of a car careening off the highway. Designers wished to create a roadway "such that an automobile traveling at the rate of fifty or sixty miles an hour may leave the pavement at a thirty-degree angle, cross the ditch, and crash through the right-of-way fence without capsizing."[48] To do this, road builders gradually reduced the height of the raised road, flattened the ditches, and called for fences to be set back a greater distance from the road. The gently sloping cross-section proved to be advantageous for those forced to make an unexpected detour off the road, and also adequately drained wet areas. In addition, these modifications expanded the width of roadside maintenance from about 50 to over 150 feet.[49]

A wide shoulder required acquisition of broader swathes of land from adjoining landowners. In rural areas, land acquisition brought the highway crews nearly to the doorsteps of some farm homes and reduced field size as well. Broad, unobstructed shoulders not only provided space for wayward automobiles, but gave the driver greater visibility: oncoming traffic could be seen at a greater distance, even around a curve, and traffic entering the highway from a side road would be more apparent. This was increasingly important as driving speeds increased. It also made mowing and snow removal simpler.[50]

With a broader right-of-way to maintain, and influenced by parkway design concepts, highway departments began adding amenities to the roadside. In 1935, the Indiana Highway Commission announced that tree and shrub planting would commence on US 40 between Cumberland and Greenfield. Federal money helped fund these roadside improvement programs that included grading highway shoulders and introducing locally adapted decorative plants. In addition to work carried out contractually, the Indiana Roadside Council, an independent organization that advocated scenic highways, mobilized local garden clubs to plant "memorial trees, to erect kiosks at rest areas, and plant vegetation to control erosion." Although some garden-club plantings proved costly to maintain, they reflect an attempt to involve the public in roadside improvements. Roadside parks or rest areas also consumed some of the broad shoulders at intervals along the highway. Illinois began building rest areas in 1916, including urban "comfort stations." Rest areas and parks were to be erected at ten- to fifteen-mile intervals along major highways, and they became a common feature along major thoroughfares such as US 40.[51]

**US 40 highway improvements in Muskingum County, Ohio, c. 1932**

The newer route followed a straighter course and actually overrode the old National Road in places. It also replaced the old S-bridge with a wider concrete structure.

Bridge technology was modernized during the first half of the twentieth century. Older highway bridges were commonly steel truss structures, but with improvements in concrete and composite steel and concrete design the massive truss structures began to disappear.[52] Concrete proved to be an adaptable material and was suitable in arched bridge designs or in post and beam construction over short spans. The American Association of State Highway Officials (AASHO) developed standards that introduced improved bridge construction guidelines to interstate highways and local roads as well. Bridges also required widening. Prior to 1920, most bridges accommodated only one lane of traffic. But motorists traveling at high speeds did not wish to stop and await other vehicles to clear a bridge. Consequently, as the old truss bridges were taken down, bridges that could accommodate two lanes of traffic took their place. Indiana undertook a vigorous campaign to widen its bridges from fourteen to sixteen feet during the later half of the 1930s. Likewise, Ohio eliminated numerous narrow bridges as it improved stretches of US 40. Highway departments also applied new bridge-building technology to the separation of road and railroad grade crossings. A portion of National Industrial Recovery Act funds were earmarked for grade separation work, and Indiana completed a total of sixty grade separations

CRAIG E. COLTEN

between 1933 and 1937.[53] Highway officials hailed both types of bridge modifications as major safety improvements.

Improved roads attracted increasing traffic and this engendered additional highway safety modifications. As early as 1928, highway designers proposed highway bypasses that would skirt congested communities and avoid delays for through traffic. In addition, subtle design features such as a gentle S-curve served to slow traffic where the roadway did not deviate around a rural community.[54] Such features are still visible along the full length of US 40.

Dual-lane highways were more important and effective in reducing traffic accidents. Among the US 40 states, Indiana pressed forward most aggressively with divided, four-lane highways. Divided highway advocates proclaimed that the safety benefits far outweighed added costs for dual pavements and additional right-of-way. Indiana began widening its major routes in 1936 and in 1937 had plans to expand sections of US 40 between Brazil and Cloverdale, Indianapolis and Cumberland, Dunreith and Knightstown, and Mt. Meridian and Stilesville. By 1950, most US 40 sections through the state were at least four-lane, and portions included a divided highway.[55] In Illinois, by contrast, only very short segments of US 40 provided the advantages of divided highway.

Through the 1930s, state highway departments straightened and converted the route to four lanes by following the existing corridor. Ohio engineers made some deviations from the old route, but only slight, and in some cases they laid the new surface directly over the older road. For example, the 1920s Broad Street bridge project in Columbus merely improved passage over the Scioto River, it did not reroute traffic away from the older commercial district.

As traffic increased along the newly resurfaced US 40, an array of auto-oriented businesses clustered along the roadways at the entrance to most towns and cities. Initially campgrounds served travelers, but local entrepreneurs upgraded lodgings by building cottage clusters. By the late 1940s, the twenty-unit motor courts or motels became the standard accommodation for highway wayfarers. Situated by the roadside, they offered an informality unavailable at the railroad hotels.[56]

Motel changes mirrored in many respects the successful corporate franchising pioneered by gasoline service stations. From curbside pumps located at hardware stores or livery stables, gas stations evolved into corporate symbols, complete with signature architecture and signs. By the early 1930s, most stations offered off-street service at multiple pumps, repair bays, and restrooms.[57] The proliferation of stations continued until gasoline rationing forced a substantial decline in the number of operating stations during World War II. During this period, many central city stations closed and newer stations contributed to the emerging commercial strip along major routes leading in and out of towns.[58] The county atlas for Springfield, Ohio, for example, shows a central city hotel near the rail depot in 1876. By 1950, travelers' services, in the form of gasoline stations and motels, had appeared along the former National Road east of the city center. The transformation of the roadside was a national phenomenon and took place along US 40 as elsewhere.

Railroads continued to play a significant role in long-distance transportation, but the competition of highway travel had become obvious by 1950. For short-distance shipping, trucks offered more flexible timetables, door-to-door service without the cost of constructing expensive sidings, and cost-effective service for small loads. In Indiana, truck competition led to the abandonment of 409 miles of track by 1927. In 1931, the Wheeling interurban dropped freight service, while the Western Penn continued its freight service until 1941. Ohio interurbans lost over 200 million passengers

CRAIG E. COLTEN

between 1919 and 1933. The inability of trains to meet an increasingly independent traveling public and community of shippers would only continue after 1950.[59]

## INTERSTATE HIGHWAYS DOMINATE THE NATIONAL ROAD ROUTE

Improved highways attracted ever-increasing traffic during the post–World War II years. As early as 1938 highway engineers had begun to consider premature highway obsolescence brought about by strip development and congestion. German autobahn studies and experiments with parkways provided evidence that highways with limited access and grade separations offered improved safety and efficiency.[60] Construction of the federal Interstate Highway System, in response to these concerns, brought about significant changes after 1950. The previous modifications along the National Road's route were limited in their aerial extent: the road and inns occupied a fairly compact right-of-way, and the railroad demanded only a narrow path and encouraged centralized services. Even the early twentieth-century roadways were accretionary. The changes associated with the Interstate Highway System, however, involved destruction of old features, or building a completely new replacement road across open land.

By 1951, the ability of highways to carry existing traffic was at a "near crisis."[61] The resumed manufacture of personal automobiles following World War II, the use of trucks to move freight, and ample fuel availability all contributed to this situation. These factors spawned increasing traffic on highways left in extremely poor condition by deferred maintenance and excessive use by overloaded vehicles during the war. In addition, rapidly increasing numbers of roadside services, such as motels, gas stations, and restaurants, contributed to congestion. As retail outlets moved to strip developments to capture motorists using major routes, conditions worsened. The initial response to highway congestion was to revive the toll-road program of limited-access, long-distance highways. By 1950 the Pennsylvania Turnpike was speeding traffic between Philadelphia and Pittsburgh. Its connection with turnpikes in New Jersey to the east and Ohio and Indiana in the west permitted vehicles to make the journey from New York to Chicago without encountering a stoplight by the mid-1950s. These routes relieved some pressure on the older federal highway system, but many groups, most notably the trucking industry, objected to tolls. After years of debate, Congress authorized funding for a 41,000-mile limited-access highway system (1956). The legislation provided for federal funding—raised through taxes on gasoline, commercial vehicles, and tires—of up to 90 percent.[62] Interstate 70 was the component of this system that followed the old National Road route.

Congress legislated the basic Interstate Highway System design, as it had done for the initial National Road design over a century earlier. Based on recommendations assembled by the AASHO and the Bureau of Public Roads, the basic guidelines called for two pairs of single-direction lanes separated by a median and enclosed within a right-of-way. Traffic would enter the highway via entrance ramps and there would be no highway or railroad crossings at grade. Highway geometry was to permit safe travel of at least 50 miles per hour in mountainous terrain and 70 miles per hour on flat country. These "uniform" interstate highway system guidelines, although subject to local modifications, prescribed that a broad swath of land be converted to high-speed highway traffic.[63] In some rural areas, entirely new highways caused subdivision and separation of farm fields. Along other segments, existing highway sections became one lane and a second lane, constructed alongside the existing road, converted it to interstate specifications. To serve cities, interstate highways required either demolition of blocks of residential and commercial property, or entirely new bypass routes.

Train travel from Washington, D.C., to St. Louis via the National Limited took only twenty hours in 1950—a far better pace than auto travel at the time. By 1990, interstate highways allowed motorists to cover the same course in about fifteen hours and on their own schedule. The freedom and convenience of automobile travel have contributed to an upsurge in traffic over the past four decades. In 1950 intercity passenger miles attributed to automobiles was about triple that of railroads; by 1990 cars accounted for over 1.5 trillion passenger miles annually, while railroads claimed an insignificant portion of the national total. Rail service has held a fairly constant volume of intercity freight movement, although trucks have expanded their share steadily. As early as 1950, trucks were hauling significant quantities of cattle, lumber, and fresh produce, commodities that were once the sole province of railroads. And as truck numbers and carrying capacity increased, so did damage to older roads designed to handle lighter loads.[64]

The most dramatic indication that highway transportation has displaced rail service is evident in the mileage of railroad tracks removed. Since 1920

CRAIG E. COLTEN

there has been a net loss of track each decennial period, although the pace has quickened since 1950, and during the 1970s there was a 30 percent loss of trackage across the country.[65] Pennsylvania Railroad tracks that ran through Cambridge City, Indiana, a National Road town, have been removed, leaving derelict overpasses that loom over the idle industrial buildings set behind the town's main street. The raised interstate sweeps above the former roundhouse and yards that terminated at the waterfront at East St. Louis. With this trackage decline has come an attendant displacement of railroad corridor industrial activity, particularly in small towns. As the railroad's ability to centralize function is lost and track is removed, depots and railroad hotels succumb to wrecking crews or find new uses as local museums, nostalgia-peddling restaurants, or senior-citizen housing.

Along the older city highway commercial strips, transformation has been underway as well. Congestion on major highway thoroughfares rendered them useless for interstate travel. The Illinois Department of Transportation advocated bypass highways, new routes that deviated around a community and directed through traffic away from the business district and the strip. They constructed a traffic loop around Vandalia in 1951–52. Local business people objected, fearing their economy would suffer. To combat this convincing argument, the Department of Transportation monitored local retail sales in communities with bypasses and reported an unexpected outcome. Retail sales in Vandalia grew by 20 percent in the five years following the completion of the bypass; this was attributed to the elimination of congestion, which attracted shoppers.[66] During the 1960s and 1970s the Interstate Highway System produced still another bypass set further away from the town center.

Interstate 70 brought about dramatic changes for local and long-distance travel along the National Road corridor. Through traffic shifted to the more expeditious routeway, leaving the commercial strips to local commerce. Several landscape changes ensued along the lesser-traveled routes. Motels, gasoline stations, and restaurants on the old highway strip gradually lost business. Many locally owned motels remained open by serving as temporary housing for transients or as retreats for clandestine trysts. Gasoline stations generally lingered until gas shortages during the 1970s forced many independent stations to close. Typically, the old full-service stations found adaptive reuse as auto-repair shops or other businesses. With increasingly stringent environmental laws regarding underground storage tank aban-

**Interstate 70 construction through East St. Louis, 1966**

The new interstate highway and bridge approach sliced through residential neighborhoods and overrode the old railyards.

donment, the stations closed during the 1970s have become frequent targets of tank removal and station obliteration in recent years.[67]

Interstate 70 seldom passed directly through smaller towns and cities; instead, slight adjustments in route alignment directed traffic around these communities. This prompted the creation of new service clusters at interstate interchanges, which offered an ideal setting for the new national franchise motels and restaurants. A typical cluster consists of a few gasoline stations, a motel or two, and one or more chain restaurants. The major franchises, such as Holiday Inn, provide a predictable room and meal and, by placing their familiar logos atop stilt signs, attract customers from the interstate. In Indianapolis and Columbus there has been a corresponding clustering of traveler services and commercial enterprises. Shopping malls, office

CRAIG E. COLTEN

parks, and truck-oriented manufacturing plants have selected sites near interstate interchanges.[68]

Springfield, Ohio, provides an example of this wholesale, small-city highway-oriented business conversion. By the mid-1960s, US 40 occupied the former interurban route and provided four lanes for travel through the city. Motels and restaurants lined US 40, particularly on the town's eastern edge. By 1981, I-70 had become the major east-west thoroughfare. The super highway fostered the growth of a typical interchange commercial cluster that includes two motels, four gas stations, and ten eateries. That interchange has pulled commercial activity out of its traditional east-west orientation along the former National Road toward the interstate on the town's south side. US 40 now serves local traffic.[69]

**Interstate interchange commercial cluster, Springfield, Ohio**

Highway-oriented businesses relocate from US 40 to the interstate, creating a new "village" at a key interchange.

The National Road, canals, railroads, and the improved highway have each had revolutionary impact on transportation routes linking Chesapeake Bay and the Mississippi River. Each transport mode has reoriented the pattern of national commerce. The Interstate Highway System provided a web of high-speed, high-capacity freeways similar in outline to the pattern of the rail net, which reinforced the nodality of existing urban centers. Today, trucks haul most of the high-value and time-sensitive freight. Rails continue to move bulky cargo and waterways are favored for shipping low-value, high-volume freight such as coal, ore, and grain. Interstate highways have been less influential in the sweep of interregional trade, but they did alter urban form. Interstate loops or beltways surround the major urban centers—Baltimore, Columbus, and Indianapolis—and draw urban activity toward the city peripheries. Limited access diverts traffic from the old national highways and forces commercial activity to cluster tightly around interchanges both in major cities and in smaller towns along the route. Truck transportation, subsidized by government spending on highways, has rendered spur railroad lines economically untenable and prompted the abandonment of many miles of track. Landscape dereliction has followed. Railroad facilities in urban centers no longer serve their original function and relict motels and gas stations stand along the shoulders of US 40. These patterns are not unique to the path of the National Road, but typify a broader national sequence of events associated with this most recent shift in transport technology.

# PART THREE

# Image and Landscape

# Travelers' Impressions of the National Road

JOHN A. JAKLE

*There is certainly not any nation that can boast of a greater disposition for travelling than Brother Jonathan.*

KARL POSTL [CHARLES SEALSFIELD]
*The Americans as They Are* (1828)

FOR OVER SEVEN GENERATIONS THE ROAD'S LANDSCAPES HAVE STIMU-lated travelers. Some observers have felt an intimate relationship to the Road, while others have engendered only passing, cursory association. Some have moved slowly on foot, by horse, or by stagecoach; others have moved rapidly by automobile. Some have detailed carefully things seen; others have painted only in broad strokes trying to generalize to whole regions, and even to an entire nation. The National Road has always seemed a cross-section of something vital needing description and explanation. It was, at first, an axis for the development of the trans-Appalachian frontier. Later, it was an axis for an emergent system of automobile highways. My association with the National Road has been long-term and, I would like to think, of the intimate kind. My earliest remembered trip by automobile was east out of my native Terre Haute on US 40 when I was barely four years old. Parents, grandparents, and great-grandparents lie buried in cemeteries literally within feet of today's highway at various locations between Brazil in Indiana and Effingham in Illinois. But it is not to residents along the Road, living or dead, that I turn. It is the stranger traveling as outsider through new places that claims my attention. What did they think of the National Road and the country it traversed? How can their impressions amplify our appreciation of the Road today?

Daniel Drake, the pioneer Cincinnati physician and early chronicler of the trans-Appalachian West, described what a traveler ought to do and be. "An acute and vigilant observer," he wrote, "finds improvement in the smallest object or humblest event, as well as in those impressive phenomena, which can only arouse the attention of the dull and heedless." The alert traveler suffered nothing to pass without inspection and from habit connected everything experienced with the memory of things previously experienced. One sought "new qualities, relations and functions" in the objects that lay along one's path in order to become "original and inventive." And the early American West that the National Road penetrated, Drake argued, was exactly the kind of region that would render observations acute.

> The extended limits of the West . . . exert on the mind that expanding influence, which comes from the contemplation of vast natural objects; while the distant visits and long migrations to which this condition invites . . . personally call its inhabitants from place to place, opening new sources of observation, and establishing fresh and profitable modes of intellectual communion.[1]

Few travelers who described the National Road in writing came close to Drake's ideal observer. But one senses tremendous effort in this regard, especially from European travelers who were engaged in understanding America as a foreign land.

There were organizing questions motivating the keepers of personal diaries and the publishers of formal travel books. For example, J. Gould, a New England farmer traveling east of Terre Haute in 1839, noted:

> According to my usual custom, I made particular inquiries about the country, and I learned that it is generally unhealthy in the latter part of summer and autumn, when bilious fevers and ague prevail. There are some public schools in which are taught orthography, reading, writing, and arithmetic, and the people seem to have no idea that any other branches are necessary except for doctors and lawyers. The farmers pay little attention to their cattle: they have good horses and abundance of hogs.[2]

JOHN A. JAKLE

Most travel diaries originated in such random jottings—field notes if you will—recording impressions as gathered. Elaboration was added at taverns or at other stops by way of summarizing segments of a trip. These notes, combined with other recollections, would inform finished manuscripts, again often written by stages as a trip progressed, an author delaying days or even weeks to accomplish a particular task. From uninformed first impressions to fully calculated final interpretations, the written records surviving provide great diversity of travel observation for the contemporary scholar of the National Road to sort and digest.

Journalists or diarists were obviously literate or their observations would not have been recorded. This means that most were well educated and, therefore, of the middle or upper classes. Observations reflected class and status biases. What they described in their journals reflects expectations substantially rooted in the experiences of their caste. And yet America of the early to mid-nineteenth century was a place where egalitarian ideals had come rapidly to the fore. Even the elite traveled as the "common man," making observations and judgments about people and things highly tolerant of the new democratic principles. We cannot say that travelers' recorded observations reflect a social mainstream. But, just as clearly, we cannot always establish that they do not. The National Road penetrated a new western frontier in which the commonplace was a principal attractor—the frontier as leveler of custom, if not of elite pretensions. Much of what was recorded did represent commonplace views that transcended class.

What travelers on the National Road experienced and what they chose to describe in written narratives reflected not only expectations brought to new locations but also the realities of those places. Thus when a traveler described a particular scene from the basis of past experience, today's interpreter can assume that something real in the landscape did, indeed, stimulate the report. And, as repeated travelers made the same reports, one can establish the outline of that reality. Significant were the beliefs and attitudes travelers brought to a place as well as their intentionalities—the behavioral predispositions that drove their traveling. What made a place similar to other places? What made a place distinctive? How might being in a place prove satisfying? Or bring dissatisfaction? Such was the game that travelers played. What they mention in their journals reflects anticipations validated or invalidated, the strengths of such understandings usually dictating inclusion or exclusion.

What a person recorded or elaborated also reflects what he or she had previously recorded, by way of reinforcing journal observations or avoiding redundancies. To evaluate a journal is to assess what its author included, but also to assess what he or she ignored or excluded. In using a diversity of diaries and journals to reconstruct the realities of past landscapes—specifically those of an evolving highway—one looks for the commonalities of inclusion and exclusion. One seeks the normative through the synthesis of agreement, and then measures the deviations implicit in diverging views expressed.

## NATURAL LANDSCAPES

Starting in the East and traveling west, which was the way the majority of National Road descriptions ran, scenes of mountain wilderness dominated initial observations. In departing Cumberland in 1822, one stagecoach passenger summarized as follows: "The road begins to ascend almost immediately and passes through a rough and mountainous country, thickly covered with forest, which is chiefly oak, here and there interspersed with pine and cedar." The understory of laurel was thick, he wrote. "It is only at considerable intervals, that even by the site of the roadside, a small spot of settled or cleared land can be seen, while at a distance from the road, the country is perfectly wild." Upon reflection, the greatest benefit of being in a wild country, he found, was the game served in the taverns along the route.[3]

James Dixon, a Methodist minister traveling in the early spring of 1848, was at once in the same world of wilder images and in his own world of calculated insight. He seemed always in search of a Sunday sermon. Leaving Cumberland, the coach "plunged" into the midst of rocks and precipices, the Road meandering among racing cataracts. "The impression was a very melancholy one," he wrote, "in exact agreement with the somber aspect of all things around: —the stillness, the indefinite and mystic character of the forest, as if forming a sort of infinite labyrinth; the stupendous rocks and precipices; the moaning of the waters, as they rolled down the gullies, or dashed among the stones." The forest trees taught a lesson. There was life and death all around for "the generation now in their prime stood towering over the prostrate and decaying; and the innumerable young . . . [trees] of every age and size, filled every atom of soil left betwixt the living and the dead." Here was vividly displayed the cycle of nature and the stages of life through which humans as well as trees passed invariably. And then there were frogs chirping, seemingly in the millions. "How good is God! All things serve him in their season," he concluded.[4]

Travelers relished the views obtained from the heights of various mountains traversed from Hagerstown to Uniontown. Vistas opened and closed with the turning of the Road. As the German traveler Frederick Von Raumer observed, "The parallel ridges of the Alleghanies running from northeast to southwest rise and fall so frequently and present so great a variety of mountain and valley, that the attention is continually excited and yet never wearied." Not all travelers could appreciate the panoramic vistas all the time, however. "We did get a transient view of the western country as we were upon the last ridge," wrote the Englishman Archibald Prentice in 1848, "but tired and sleepy, I grumbled out to Mr. Brooks that the view over Nottinghamshire from the high ground near Newark was worth half-dozen of it." Even in the early twentieth century, when automobilists were rediscovering the "Old Pike" as a routeway west, much of the country was still heavily wooded. "Fields and forests combine to make a series of landscapes that keep the traveler in an expectant attitude," wrote travel essayist John Faris; "he knows there must be something still better beyond, yet he wonders how there could be anything better." Generally speaking, the quality of the scenery was found by most travelers to fall off in the West with diminishing topographic relief.[5]

Appreciation of the picturesque was a cultivated affectation whereby the traveler deliberately sought out "views" and "scenes" composed like paintings, engravings, or photographs. Europeans were particularly attuned to landscape aesthetics and were quick to decry the general lack of such appreciation in Americans, especially those who were actively creating the new built environment of the West. James Silk Buckingham, the English essayist and public orator, wrote of the National Road west of Wheeling in 1842:

> The constant succession of hill and valley in our route was complained of as an evil by most of our companions, who had no perception of the beautiful in landscape; indeed, this absence of taste for the sublime and beautiful in Nature, appears to be a national characteristic, as visible in the more educated and opulent classes, as in the humbler and poorer.

This was a misfortune, he thought, as it was a privation of an important source of "exquisite and innocent enjoyment." He was chagrined by the total loss of forest trees in eastern Ohio and wished that at least a row of giant trees could be left standing on each side of the highway to afford shade if not beauty. In America, utilitarian and not picturesque values dominated. In

Ohio the forest had been vigorously stripped away in the creation of a transitional agrarian landscape of little beauty save, perhaps, when glimpsed from a far ridgetop. "At present, nothing can be more uninviting than the rude log-cabins, with the mass of fallen trunks of trees around them, and the total absence of all cleanliness, neatness, or taste, in the habitations of the people," Buckingham summarized.[6] Nature was unsentimentally regarded as commodity. Where wealth could be extracted, nature was appreciated. Where it could not be extracted, Americans were generally indifferent to it.

The flat, open prairies encountered in Ohio, and then again in Illinois, were very different landscapes to eyes attuned to hill and forest. There panoramas exposed the country's vastness. The prairies had resulted from centuries of seasonal burning and in as-yet-unsettled areas the forests and prairies abutted in full contrast. From a distance, forest boundaries appeared to many travelers like seashores across waves of grass. Groves rose up abruptly from the grass, "hemming it in as with a wall," wrote William Oliver in 1843. Elsewhere, where fires had been kept off for several seasons, trees were actively colonizing the prairie and forest margins were fringed by growths of young trees and bushes.[7] Travelers of more scientific bent, like Oliver, sought such evidence of cause and effect in landscape in addition to pictures.

## CULTURAL LANDSCAPES

Attention focused not only on nature but also on the evolving built environment in its various stages of transformation. Always immediate was the Road itself as a physical fixture directing the traveler's attention in movement. Then there were the highway margins, where people, farms, and towns could be inspected close at hand. Until the coming of modern limited-access freeways, with their extremely wide rights-of-way, travelers felt variously part of larger scenes for which immediate roadsides stood symbolic.

### The Road

In Maryland, Pennsylvania, (West) Virginia, and eastern Ohio, the National Road was generally constructed from east to west. In western Ohio, a competing turnpike diverted much traffic south through Dayton, keeping the National Road undeveloped. In Indiana, construction proceeded outward from Indianapolis. For Illinois, it is difficult to say that there was coordinated construction since the National Road was little more than an intention attached to sequences of marginally improved local connectors.

JOHN A. JAKLE

Road construction took time. At the end of the National Road's second decade, work crews were still toiling across eastern Ohio. Although the federal government acknowledged the need to create the highway, it did not always acknowledge the need to maintain it and, with heavy traffic, completed sections quickly fell into disrepair. To solve the maintenance problem, respective sections of the Road were turned over to the states and tollgates erected to generate sufficient revenues for repair. Not until the twentieth century was the Road, as an automobile highway, fully improved and well maintained everywhere all at the same time. Most travelers described the Road and its condition, each according to their own circumstances of time and place.

In 1819, John Woods, bound for the English Prairie of southern Illinois (where he would establish a farm), reported the first sixty-two miles of the National Road "just finishing with construction crews encountered at frequent intervals." "Many thousands of trees, that were cut for making the turnpike lay rotting by the side of it," he continued. "I believe I have seen more timber in their wasting state, than all the growing timber I ever saw in my life in England." In the same year another English traveler observed crews employed in plowing up the rights-of-way with "machines" drawn by eight oxen while others drew large wooden scoops or shovels to move and embank the dirt. Westward beyond Wheeling little work was evident early in the century's second decade. "The roads at present are altogether in a state of nature, the trees only just chopped off about a foot from the ground, and rocks, and stones, and gullies left to be got over as we can," he complained. Beyond Zanesville, John Wright had difficulty keeping to the main road. "If a tree happens to fall across the road, no one thinks of disturbing it; new paths are opened, and these, winding about to shun sloughs, underwood, hillocks, wind falls, and other obstructions, cross each other in all directions." The traveler faced, he said, "successive labyrinths."[8]

By the 1830s, older stretches of the Road in the East had fallen into substantial disrepair, offering very sharp contrast to newly opened sections farther west. Between Brownstown and Wheeling, for example, Charles Hoffman described the Road as originally "thrown without much arrangement" on a leveled surface. These surfaces were being freshly covered with a thin layer of broken stones, which yielded "like snow-drift" to the heavy wheels that transversed it. The ruts were worn so broadly and deeply, he concluded, that an army of pygmies could march into the country undetected. There were, however, massive stone bridges to admire. Hoffman wrote, "Their thick walls projecting above the road, the round stone buttresses and carved keystones, combine to give them an air of Roman solidity and strength. They are monuments of taste and power that speak well for the country."[9] Near Wheeling a monument had been erected to Henry Clay, the Road's principal champion in Congress.

In 1839, J. Gould found the highway macadamized and otherwise "finished in the most desirable manner" as far as Columbus, Ohio. Except for similar stretches outside Richmond, Indianapolis, and Terre Haute in Indiana, the remainder of the way through to St. Louis had only been graded, with the roadbed formed of earth, and the occasional hill excavated and depression embanked. The Road was deeply gullied across much of its length in Indiana. "I was twice thrown out of my wagon at these pitches," he confessed, "and many places were so bad that I dared not ride at all." There were few bridges and travelers constantly were forced to ford streams large and small.[10]

During the 1840s, travelers continued to commend hard-surfaced sections of the highway, especially in Ohio. James Silk Buckingham could write, "To us, indeed, who had been jolted and shaken, plunged and precipitated, over the rough roads and deep pits of other states . . . it was no ordinary luxury to travel on this smooth and equable National Road." It was as good, he said, as any public road in England. Buckingham also reported a visual effect that would intrigue travelers for generations. "The road is perfectly level; and as it is cut through the dense forest in a perfectly straight line, you can see sometimes eight or ten miles ahead, till all trace of the road is lost in the closing of its forest boundaries, thus reducing the white line to a thread by the diminishing effects of perspective." So also in Indiana did the highway run in a straight line, but there the country was not so hilly. William Oliver found the going monotonous save for the occasional views ahead. "Hemmed in by a wall of forest the traveller can sometimes see a distance of many miles before him the cleared roadway diminished to a thread-like tenuity."[11]

To Oliver the Road in Illinois was "nothing more than a track," although it had been surveyed and timber cut and removed, the stumps being left. At points, he encountered workmen excavating the earth from each side and throwing it into the Road's center. "On passing a house newly built," he wrote, "we had to avoid a deep hole dug right in the middle of the road . . . from which the clay for daubing the chimney had evidently been taken."

"One interferes when it suits his convenience," Oliver continued, "and there is nothing uncommon in coming up to a fence which has been thrown across the road, thereby causing the traveller to make a detour in order to regain the track." In Illinois, the 1843 Road seemed "flung about from farm to farm" and in a manner "perfectly vexatious and perplexing," he complained. Bridges consisted of two trees laid side by side and crossed by split logs laid "en corduroy," loosely pinned down by sleepers at both sides. Rails rolled and clattered as wagons passed, rendering passage "very insecure and unpleasant." The 1850s saw the National Road created to Vandalia, the former Illinois state capital, and connections finished to the Mississippi River both at St. Louis and at Alton.[12]

J. Richard Beste, an affluent Englishman, brought his family of twelve on an 1854 excursion to America's western states. From Cincinnati they rode the railroad to Indianapolis where Beste secured wagons to convey his troop westward. Beste found everywhere rights-of-way cleared to a similar width, the quality of the road surface varying according to the aspirations of the respective townships through which it passed. In low areas, corduroy had been laid which "rose and sank under us with the elasticity of the floor of a ballroom." Elsewhere the Road had been given a gravel surface, although much of it was found to be severely "furrowed" and "pitted." At intervals of four to five miles, wells had been provided for the watering of both animals and people. Worm fences of split-rails separated the Road from adjacent fields. But at Reelsville they lost the Road. He wrote,

> Not a track was to be seen on the smooth green turf beneath the tall, shady oak trees. Some citizens, driving wagons, pointed out the track to me. It led down to the side of a pretty stream, I believe some of the headwaters of the White River. They were rather deep; but we forded them, and clambered up on the other side. Here many scores of laborers were at work on cuttings and embankments for the railroad from Indianapolis to St. Louis.[13]

The railroad was not the only new innovation evident along the Road. Of the approach to Terre Haute Beste described the "eternal electric telegraph wire," which seemed to have accompanied their every step "striding along on its huge unhewn poles." Charles Weld, also traveling in 1854, described the telegraph between Wheeling and Zanesville. "Those accustomed to the trim and regular lines . . . will be astonished by the rough and simple mode in which the American telegraph is constructed. It consists of a single wire dangling between poles or trees—for the line is frequently carried through the forests." Through the remainder of the nineteenth and into the twentieth century utility lines strung on poles added substantially to the visual character to the Old Pike. In 1909, Albert Douglas observed three systems of poles and wires along the route. Douglas, a member of Congress, chose to drive home to his native Columbus during the congressional recess of 1909, becoming one of the first long-distance motorists to navigate the highway. Travel writer R. H. Johnson, publishing the year before in *Travel Magazine,* wrote, "The National Road possesses a distinctive individuality. From sixty to eighty feet wide, with two and sometimes three lines of telegraph and telephone poles there is not the least chance that the tourist will lose his way." Also reinforcing the Road were the century-old mileposts.[14]

Improvement of the National Road for automobile travel began after 1910. In Ohio the seventy-five-mile section west of Wheeling was given a brick pavement, the longest continuous brick-paved road in the nation when completed.[15] Brick proved popular wherever potteries and kilns abounded, as in West Virginia, eastern Ohio, and western Indiana. (US 40 was carried on a narrow brick pavement west of Martinsville in Illinois as late as 1950—a vivid memory that I carry from childhood travel.) Then came wider ribbon and then slab concrete pavements, regradings, and even realignments, which left sections of the old Road marooned and fossilized. Few travelers reported these changes. Save for an initial enthusiasm for promoting the Road for automobile travel, few descriptions of the National Road were made after 1900 and most of these were historical in orientation, concerned more with what the Road had been as opposed to what it was becoming. An exception, of course, was George R. Stewart's *U.S. 40: Cross-Section of the United States of America.* Stewart, a professor of English at the University of California at Berkeley, organized his essay around photographs taken along the whole of the highway coast to coast. Included is a photo taken east of Richmond, Indiana, showing a four-lane express highway with median separations dividing opposing traffic.[16] Here was the contemporary highway at its best, and Stewart gloried in it. US 40, as did the National Road in its day, symbolized the technological prowess that was modernity.

### Traffic

Nothing was more invigorating to travelers than to feel themselves part of a massive movement, to be on a major route of commerce and migration. As Joseph Gurney wrote in 1841, "Undoubtedly the most interesting and surprising circumstance which engaged my attention during the journey on the main route to the westward, was the unparalleled scene of movement . . . of which we were witness."[17] The stagecoaches painted in their vivid colors, the large freight wagons, the wagons of movers, travelers on horseback and on foot, and the drovers with their herds provided a colorful mix through the 1840s. Many travelers kept counts. In a day's travel west from Frostburg in Maryland, one traveler noted seven coal wagons, twenty regular "road wagons," and some 200 sheep and 500 hogs eastbound, and some fifty "movers wagons" westbound. The next day he noted droves of over 1,000 hogs, and another twenty freight wagons.[18] The penchant to count things was very much a utilitarian orientation to place. Some travelers counted taverns while others counted brick buildings or churches, statistics usually calculated to suggest the vigor or the progress of a place.

A trip by stagecoach was an adventure. In 1848, Walt Whitman arrived by railroad at Cumberland and transferred to the Good Intent Stage Company for the trip to Brownsville. He had an opportunity to see National Road stages in their highest state of perfection. A clerk stood by calling the passengers' names as inscribed on a roll; two or three blacks manned a patent weighing machine. "The clerk calls your name—your baggage is whipped on the machine, and if it weighs over fifty pounds, you have to pay extra. You are then put on the stage, (literally put in, like a package, unless you move quickly), your baggage is packed on behind—and the next name called off—baggage weighed—and so to the end of the chapter."[19] Each drawn by four horses, stages moved off into the night in a small caravan.

The stages of the Great Western line carried passengers inside on four benches set crosswise the coach, and five passengers outside up top near the driver. Canvas curtains rolled down to protect those inside from inclement weather. When the curtains were down, passengers saw nothing of the passing scenery and were forced to tend fully with one another as they jolted along. James Buckingham found his fellow passengers to be men of coarse appearance and manners, "being farmers, country-dealers, and speculators, passing from town to town." Nonetheless, there was a "spirit of mutual forbearance and good nature." The seventy-four-mile trip from Wheeling to Zanesville required twelve hours including stoppages for meals and the changing of horses.[20]

Accidents were frequent, and their anticipation amplified the sense of adventure. "The drivers drive down these hills, jehu like on a full run," Buckingham reported, "and now they are so fatigued with extra work that it's necessary for one of the passengers to ride outside to keep them awake." Lady Stuart-Woortly complained:

> One cannot wonder at accidents in crossing these mountains for the drivers appear to be frequently intoxicated, and are rough and reckless, cruel to their horses . . . and cruel to their passengers, driving often full gallop over the worst part of abominable roads, to the almost dislocation of their limbs and bumping and thumping of their unfortunate heads against the hard roof of the vehicle.[21]

Walt Whitman found Cumberland to be "the great rendezvous and landing place of those immense Pennsylvania wagons." "You may see Tartar looking at groups of these wagons, and their drivers, in the open grounds about,—the horses being loosed—the whole having not a little the appearance of a caravan of the Steppes."[22] To Whitman the wagons, with their arched roofs of white canvas, were enormous and, being built high at each end and scooped down in the waist, they looked to him somewhat like Chinese junks. Teams of four or six horses provided the motive power, the lead horses often ornamented with bells that alerted pedestrians of a wagon's approach. Emigrant or movers' wagons, pulled by two horses or two oxen (although frequently by one), were smaller. Most contained household furniture and trip provisions with the women and young children piled atop, the men and older boys walking along beside. In 1841, Joseph Gurney noted, "Occasionally we observed a wagonload of these migratory people returning eastward. The dejection and disappointment evidently marked on their countenances, formed a singular contrast to the comparatively careless and more hopeful aspect of those who were journeying towards the setting sun."[23] The Road's traffic funneled through toll stations at intervals—one gate every twenty miles or so. One station west of Cumberland had no gate, a large stone suspended by rope blocking the way. "Our wagoner, when we came up to this machine, bawled lustily to the tollkeeper who, after detaining us 'til he found it convenient, received his dues, a ten penny piece, and hauling the stone aside, permitted us to move on."[24]

The automobile promised new life to the Old Pike, a new kind of traffic moving at speeds unpredictable when the National Road was conceived. Congressman Douglas predicted in 1909, having negotiated the Road in a Ford: "Our children may see its glories revive, its way repaved with modern

JOHN A. JAKLE

metal, its broken and defaced old mile-posts repaired or replaced, its toll houses rebuilt or reoccupied." And, as a modern road, its margins would be lined with colossal advertising signs, "darkening the view."[25] Soon, much sooner than Douglas predicted, the Road filled with automobiles and trucks, the truck convoys of World War I literally tearing the Road apart. In the automobile age, traffic came to mean something very different than previously. If freight wagons had seemed large, the new tractor-trailer trucks that emerged in the 1930s were huge. Previously, commercial traffic had closed down at night, save for the stagecoaches that picked their way through the darkness by flickering lantern light. But now the trucks rolled night and day, slipping from gear to gear in ascending and descending grades. Two Russian humorists, Ilya Ilf and Eugene Petrov, toured the United States by car in 1935. The heavy trucks "frighten you to death" they wrote, especially at night when outlined by a chain of green and red lights. "It is frightful to race at night over an American highway. Darkness to right and to the left. But the face is struck by the lightning flashes of automobile headlights coming at you. They fly past, one after the other, like small hurricanes of light, with a curt and irate feline spit."[26]

## Taverns and Hotels

"Public houses of entertainment" formed the centers of the smaller towns, each competing stage company patronizing a different house in a given place. Most taverns contained a dining room (with a bar to one corner from which the proprietor or an employee ran the establishment), a reading room (where newspapers were available), and guest rooms (many of them dormitories) containing beds. A sign, hung from a post twenty or thirty feet tall and visible from a distance, announced each inn to passing travelers. Buckingham noted that in eastern Ohio Rising Sun was the most frequently used name for taverns. One tavern sign featured an Irish harp with a bald eagle perched atop and a ribbon with the word "Liberty." Most tavernkeepers were either Irish or Scots, it seemed. In western Indiana, William Oliver thought that George Washington dominated. "The patriot commonly stands, his eyes fixt on vacancy, with a cocked hat in one hand, whilst the other has . . . a tumbler, into which some liquor . . . is falling."[27]

In the mountainous East, the stage companies maintained small stations for the changing of horses. Many were combined with blacksmith shops and liveries and served limited tavern functions. Walt Whitman wrote of the Road between Cumberland and Brownsville:

The places at which we changed horses, (which was done every ten miles), were generally long, old, one-story houses, with stupendous fires of soft coal that is so plentiful and cheap here. In the night, with the mountains on all sides, the precipitous and turning road, the large, bare-armed trees looming up around us, the room half-filled with men curiously enwrapped in garments of a fashion till then never seen—and the flickering light from the mighty fire putting a red glow upon most objects, and casting others into a strong shadow—I can tell you these stoppages were not without interest.

It was the stuff from which romance derived, affording "first class scenes for an American painter—one who . . . seizes original and really picturesque occasions of this sort for his pieces."[28]

Crowded taverns usually required travelers, especially those outside the sheltering purview of a stage company, to share a bedroom (and often a bed) with strangers. Occasionally the only accommodation to be had was a pallet on the floor of a public room. Toilet facilities were privies located out back where washbasins and public combs and brushes were also provided. Some taverns catered specially to movers, others to wagoners. Many families living along the National Road took in transients as so-called private houses. Few families living along the Road could avoid the practice, so much demand was there for accommodations, especially in the summer. Farmhouses in less-developed country could fill to overflowing. In 1807, the Irish traveler Fortescue Cuming stopped for the night in a double cabin east of Cambridge, Ohio. He shared the floor of one room with a drover and his six assistants, two horsemen, the contents of two family wagons, and the contents of a stagecoach.[29]

Cities and larger towns sported hotels that were much like public taverns except larger. The Prairie House at Terre Haute was an example. It was there Richard Beste and his family spent several months in 1854 fighting and recuperating from cholera. The hotel was crowded with the families of construction foremen employed by the new railroad. Some of the town's leading families, including that of future president Benjamin Harrison, also boarded there. The day began at 6:30 A.M. with a boy walking through the hallways, floor by floor, ringing a bell and calling out "Breakfast ready." Breakfast eating ranged across hot and cold breads of different sorts including corn bread, pancakes and fritters smothered in butter, molasses or preserves, and steak, roast beef, and chicken. "As waiters, there were six or seven boys, the oldest from eight to twelve years old, who ran about the

JOHN A. JAKLE

room barefooted, but who were, otherwise, neatly drest in white jackets and aprons."[30] At 7 A.M. a second bell rang for the children and their attendants, and at 7:30 a third bell beckoned all the servants. "The negroes and negresses eat at a different table from the white people . . . each seemed to despise the other equally," Beste reported.[31] At noon, steaks, roast beef, veal, mutton cutlets, boiled ham, pigeons, and chicken and veal pies were served with peas, beans, hominy, potatoes, and, in the summer, corn and squash. Desert featured fruit pies. Those who had been guests at the hotel the longest sat nearest the head of the table and were served first. Supper was a simpler meal with mostly coldcuts. A single chambermaid, a German woman, went about the hotel cleaning and making beds. Other employees included a laundress, a pastry cook, a black chef, and an Irishman, "whose only work seemed to be sleeping in the bar and taking charge of the ice and answering with rudeness when spoken to."[32] A black steward kept a barbershop in his room.

As traffic on the National Road diverted to the Baltimore & Ohio and other railroads, the rural taverns languished, those surviving converted more to local boarding houses. At first, the automobile promised revival. "A hundred Cumberland Road taverns will be opened, and bustling landlords welcome, as of yore, the travel-stained visitor. Merry parties will again fill those tavern halls, now long silent, with their laughter," cheered the historian Archer Hulbert.[33] Some of the old country inns were revitalized as restaurants and tearooms, but in the large towns and cities hotels tended to adjust first to railroad- and then to automobile-travel markets. At Terre Haute in the 1880s the Prairie House gave way to the Terre Haute House, a rambling Victorian red-brick affair with turrets. In the 1920s the site was cleared and a new Terre Haute House was constructed with an automobile entrance and a large adjacent parking garage. Off the main lobby was located the office of the local automobile club. I have vivid memories of numerous stays at this hotel. Later, in visiting Terre Haute, my family would stay in the new motel east on US 40—the Woodridge—which would later give its name to one of the city's larger suburban residential developments. Motels, drive-ins, and gasoline stations came to line Terre Haute's Wabash Avenue after World War II.

### The Rural Scene

Travelers liked to think that they were seeing and thus experiencing regions through which they passed. In the nineteenth century they sought to witness the great frontier transformation sweeping west. In Ohio, Indiana, and Illinois, land from the public domain could be purchased relatively cheaply, and a farmer and his family could break and work it, buying it with the surplus of five or six crops. Such opportunity generated a massive migration from the East, much of it over the National Road as the numerous movers' wagons testified. Here was the essence of a new America aborning—the apparent great event of the nineteenth century. Travelers intending to publish their journals had a sense of obligation not only to describe this great event, but to appraise it. Many offered advice to prospective migrants. What was the new western agrarianism like? Who should come and who should stay at home? Travelers played at being reporters, questioning those knowledgeable when encountered on the stagecoaches, in the taverns, and on the farms themselves.

Through the 1880s the traveler's view was usually forward in time. Rural landscapes were described not only for what they were, but for what they were becoming. If travelers sought to witness anything, it was progress—a booming, boisterous, adolescent, and thus distinctly American sort of progress signified in the conversion of wild nature into a would-be pastoral garden. Later on, the matured agrarian landscapes along the National Road would become very commonplace and could be taken very much for granted.

In 1803, Thaddeus Harris reflected the prevailing attitude regarding agrarian progress. When one saw the land cleared of its enormous trees, one could not help championing the industry of yeoman farmers "who by dint of toil and perseverance changed the desert into a fruitful field." He continued:

> When the solitary waste is peopled, and convenient habitations arise amidst the former retreats of wild beasts; where the silence of nature is succeeded by the buzz of employment, the congratulations of society, and the voice of joy; in fine, when we behold competence and plenty springing from the bosom of dreary forests—what a lesson is afforded of the benevolent intentions of Providence.

So elegant a statement was this that other authors over the next twenty years, in fleshing out their own journals, copied it, sometimes nearly verbatim, for example, George Ogden in 1823.[34]

By 1860, the cash economy of a commercialized agriculture had been introduced along most of the National Road, although still evident were remnants of the old pioneering order of farmers clearing land and living substantially in self-sufficiency augmented by barter and trade. Edward Dicey, traveling across Ohio on the line of the Baltimore & Ohio Railroad, which closely paralleled the highway, could write:

> You seem to pass . . . through the successive strata of the emigration era. Sometimes there were long tracts of forest land, where the axe was yet unknown. Then you came to the half-reclaimed lands, where, amidst an undergrowth of brushwood, the great trees stood, dead and leafless, ready for felling. . . . Then followed the newly reclaimed fields, with black, charred stumps still standing . . . and marked out by snake-fences, with their unfastened rails, piled crosswise one upon the other; and then, from time to time, you came upon a tract of field-land, hemmed in by the tight post and cross-bar fences, with every stump and trunk rooted out, and with a surface . . . smooth, and rich, and green.[35]

Thus the traveler could mark every stage of the settlers' life in this new western America. The increased speed of travel on the new railroad enhanced the sense of juxtaposition, making the mosaic all the more vivid.

Farms coexisted with the forest even after generations of land clearing. It simply took time for landowners to clear fields out to the edges of their properties, and, even then, many farmers left woodlots standing. Land owned by speculators often remained uncleared for decades. As the nineteenth century waned, much of the less fertile land was abandoned to reforestation. In the more developed areas west of the Ohio River, especially on the prairies, rural landscapes began to "square up"—the geometry of the Township and Range Survey system playing out in roads and field lines.

Interest in the productive capacity of the land ran high. On the prairies near Springfield, Ohio, in 1828, one traveler calculated yields at sixty to eighty bushels of corn to the acre. Farmsteads tended to the edges of the timber, with farmers owning from 80 to 320 acres. Many farmers pastured large herds out on the prairie grasses with herds of upwards to 300 animals not uncommon.[36] In 1817, an earlier traveler near Springfield marveled, "Corn grows from ten to fifteen feet high; one ear on a stalk. I have seen ears so high that I could not hang my hat upon them while standing on the ground. Hogs will not waste the corn when turned into it. It troubles them so much to tear [it] down." To European eyes American farming appeared scruffy. As William Faux described in 1823: "Ploughing seems shamefully performed, not half the land is turned over or downwards. It seems . . . as though it was ploughed with a ram's horn, or the snout of a hog, hungry after grubs and roots." The idea behind farming in the West was to have "as many acres as possible cleared, ploughed, set, sown, planted, and managed by as few hands as possible." "Instead of five acres well-managed," he continued, "they must have twenty acres badly managed. It is not how much corn can be raised on an acre, but how much from one hand or man, the land being nothing in comparison with labour." The system bred success for many farmers. Morris Birkbeck, an immigrant himself to Illinois in 1817, learned at a tavern of one Ohio farmer's newly gained affluence. "Thus the poor man who entered his quarter section of 160 acres twelve years ago and had paid 320 dollars for it at the end of five, has supported his family during this time, and now finds himself worth from three to four thousand dollars, besides his movable property."[37]

## The Urban Scene

Towns anchored the National Road at intervals, some fully creatures of the Road itself, but all dependent upon it early on. Later, the railroads would reinforce only selected Road towns in creating new connectivity networks. The auto tourists found not only growing, congested courthouse and industrial towns, but stagnant, fossilized hamlets and villages little changed from coaching days. National Road travelers have at all times witnessed towns birthing, towns booming, towns languishing, and towns dying (if not dead).

"Gain! Gain! Gain! Gain!" Morris Birkbeck exclaimed, "is the beginning, the middle, and the end, the alpha and omega of the founders of American towns." A proprietor stakes out lots to sell at auction.

> The new town then assumes the name of its founder: —a storekeeper builds a little framed store, and sends for a few cases of goods; and then a tavern starts-up, which becomes the residence of a doctor and a lawyer. . . . [There] soon follow a blacksmith and other handicraftsmen . . . [and] a schoolmaster, who is also the minister of religion.[38]

In 1804, Fortescue Cuming described one new town in Ohio. A plat of land only recently had been surveyed into 100 one-third-acre lots, but already the town contained two taverns, three stores, a courthouse and jail, and some twenty houses. One house was frame and another of stone, with all of the others of log. Only a few towns blossomed, since there were simply too many created for all to thrive.[39] One traveler in western Indiana commented in 1839, "We passed several straggling villages which are dignified with names of towns, for in this part of the country a petty tavern and grocery makes a town, and if there be a blacksmith shop and two or three log cabins besides, it is a 'right smart town.'"[40]

Travelers sketched the growth of the larger places in their notes. In 1810, one visitor found Zanesville to contain an estimated 250 houses and 1,200 people. Many houses were already built of brick and a few of stone. A courthouse and several mills anchored the place architecturally. There were no churches.[41] In 1830, another visitor estimated 1,000 houses, principally of brick, and the town could claim five churches along with several large mills powered by steam. Crossing the Muskingum River was a bridge that forked near the middle to form a Y.[42] In 1840, James Buckingham offered the following:

> The plan of the town of Zanesville is very regular; the streets broad, placed
> at right angles, and with excellent side-pavements, bordered with trees,
> many of them fruit trees, now in full blossom. The stores are large and sub-
> stantial buildings of brick and stone . . . and many of the private dwellings
> are unusually pretty, with neat and well-trimmed gardens around them.

The town contained seven churches and, in addition to the courthouse, an Anthenaeam with a library and a museum and a sign that read "Gentlemen are requested not to spit on the floors or on the walls." Here was a cotton mill, three woolen mills, two rope walks, a brass factory, a glass works, several paper mills, several sawmills, and a large number of iron foundries. The population stood at about 7,000 people.[43]

Every diarist who reached Wheeling felt obligated to offer at least some cursory description. Wheeling was a principal destination for travelers who changed from land to water transport, the majority during the 1830s and 1840s taking steamboats to or from Cincinnati. The town was uniquely situated, clinging as it did to the side of a steep bluff and spreading in a narrow band of streets up and down the river's bank. In 1841, Eliza Steele wrote of the hill above the town: "We looked down upon as fair a scene as any we had seen in our travels. The town was strewn over the hill below us, while the beautiful Ohio lay like a circlet of silver around a pretty island covered with waving corn and dotted with farmhouses." Most visitors thought that the coal smoke and soot from foundries, potteries, and other industrial activities, as well as from domestic heating, gave the city a dark and dingy look. One traveler thought the town looked "indisputably old." It was "that half-spurious sort of antiquity which we sometimes see clinging to a family that is down in the world." To Edward Dicey the place looked English with its "broad herringbone-flagged High Street; the narrow-windowed red brick houses, with their black chimney pots; the shabby-looking shops, with the flies buzzing about dirty window panes."[44] Here a system of ferries operated to carry National Road traffic across the Ohio. The suspension bridge (one of the earliest in the United States) was completed in 1849, destroyed shortly thereafter by a tornado, and rebuilt. It still stands as a principal landmark of the place.

Towns were noted for their unusual situations and for their unusual fixtures, which served as landmarks. The extraordinary always served as a framework around which to develop memory. Robert Bruce, traveling by automobile in 1916, found Uniontown, Pennsylvania, exceptional for its tall buildings. Within the town the route of the National Road followed the best paved streets past the principal hotels and best garages. But, rising higher than any of the surrounding structures, was the First National Bank Building, "containing 500 rooms, and said to be the largest building in any town of its size in the country."[45]

The National Road touched few large cities. Excluding Baltimore and St. Louis, the de facto terminals east and west, only Columbus and Indianapolis counted as big cities. Wheeling in West Virginia, Springfield in Ohio, and Richmond and Terre Haute in Indiana were really overgrown towns. That indictment was frequently reserved for Columbus and Indianapolis as well, however. Urban places, large or small, tended to share many similarities. Edward Dicey could pronounce:

> There is one striking peculiarity . . . common to almost all American towns, and that is that they have no sights. When you have taken your first half-hour stroll about any town . . . you know as much about it externally as if you had lived there for a month. Every town is built on the same system, has the same large spacious stores, the same snug, unpicturesque rows of villas, detached or semi-detached as the case may be, the same somber churches . . . the same nomenclature of streets—the invariable Walnut, Chestnut, Front, and Main Streets—crossed by the same perpendicular streets, numbered First, Second, and so on to any number you like.[46]

The same economic engines and political governors were seen to operate everywhere, producing highly standardized urban landscapes. The nine-

JOHN A. JAKLE

teenth-century American city was a creature of laissez-faire capitalism and supportive local political cultures that operated primarily to boost economic development by providing basic public infrastructures and otherwise remaining unobtrusive. Of course, there was distinctive character place to place, but it was often very subtle—only slight variations on standard themes.

One traveler, visiting Columbus in 1832, entered the city from the west. He found the approach, notwithstanding the city's commanding site, far from pleasing since the best line of houses backed on the river, and the buildings on the immediate brow of the hill were "mean and irregular." When he reached High Street, however, he was struck with the flourishing appearance of the place. High Street was 100 feet wide with sidewalks paved of brick. The street presented a "busy scene" in a "constant and lively animation" with carts, wagons, horses, pedestrians all competing. "Casting the eye along the line of buildings to the right, a large Hotel and two Blocks of handsome well built stores (of three stories) form the principal features. They comprise two public houses, two bookstores, two or three medical stores, and no less than ten well stocked mercantile establishments." At the intersection with the National Road stood the statehouse. In sum, he concluded, "The general appearance of this infant Capital indicates greater age than it possesses, but you are soon reminded of its newness by the fresh look of the brick and mortar, and scattered groups of horses, sheep, and cattle from the woods clinking their copper bells thro' the streets."[47]

James Buckingham found the city's entrance from the east pleasing, there being large public buildings on each side of the Road (the asylum for the insane and the asylum for the blind) and numerous "well-built" private residences. The city appeared clean owing to the absence of coal smoke, wood being the only fuel used. The Scioto River was crossed by an impressive covered bridge, but the capitol he found to be a plain edifice without beauty. The various state-run institutions attracted attention, especially the attention of foreign visitors interested in characterizing American society. But visits to prisons and asylums usually produced little more than litanies of tabulation. Joseph Gurney was told that the state prison, visible from the National Road, contained 374 convicts, 16 of whom were black and 4 female. They worked at lace-weaving, tailoring, shoemaking, and the manufacture of saddle trees as well as stone quarrying. Another traveler was assured that crimes against property peopled the prison. "Perhaps the respect of American society for the 'Almighty Dollar,' which makes the acquisition of wealth the aim of every exertion, may account . . . for the thefts, larcenies, and forgeries." As for the asylum for the insane, another traveler wrote, "Among the prevailing causes of insanity in Ohio, may . . . be specified religious excitement, the abuse of ardent spirits, and the panics which sometimes arise in the money market."[48]

Indianapolis was, like Columbus and most American cities, organized on a grid of streets, except that from a circular public plaza one block north of the National Road (at the center of which originally stood the governor's house and where now rises the impressive Soldiers and Sailors Monument) avenues were surveyed outward as the spokes of a wheel cutting across the grid. This was the city's one great play for physical distinctiveness. Richard Beste explored the city on foot in 1854. As he moved outward from the center, more and more vacant lots appeared, dispersed houses dotting the lines of streets not yet established until the city gave way abruptly to either woods or cultivated land. The city seemed to grow as follows: "As the vacancies on each side of the street are filled up, side pavements are made, trees are planted to overshadow them, and the centre of the street is paved, and gas and waterpipes are laid down." Indianapolis, unlike Columbus, was oriented east-west along the axis of the National Road. Beste thought the city as yet "but one continuous street, with stems of other streets shooting off from it." The capitol, west of the circle, was of classical design, modified somewhat after the Parthenon at Athens. Finally, there were churches with domes and spires and towers that would not have done "discredit to any European capital." The principal retail street, Washington Avenue, was the National Road. "The merchants," observed one traveler, "have a custom which I never noticed elsewhere, of hanging a festoon of red cloth, generally flannel, over their doors to catch the eyes of a passenger at a distance and these are the first objects that attract the notice of a stranger coming into town."[49]

Automobile tourists saw much larger, much matured, and otherwise very different townscapes in entering and exiting Columbus and Indianapolis. Broad and Main Streets in Columbus and Washington Street in Indianapolis would become commercial strips initially formed by streetcar lines. The motorist of the 1920s and 1930s fought, especially at rush hour, the congestion of commercial and commuter traffic. Neighborhoods adjacent to US 40 were, for the most part, working-class or "blue-collar," the age of housing becoming progressively older as the motorists penetrated into the centers of each respective city. With major urban development oriented to the north in both places after the Civil War, the National Road's margins during the early automobile era were quite undistinguished and, therefore, unmemorable. Even the discerning George R. Stewart could write in 1953, "Columbus and Indianapolis . . . present little that is distinctive among American cities."[50]

Today's traveler can whip into, through, and out of Columbus and Indianapolis on I-70 and not bother with the cumbersome US 40. The densities of gasoline stations, fast-food restaurants, and other businesses increase with each interchange closer to the city. Subdivisions once scattered now seem to coalesce and crowd up to the freeway. A distant skyline of tall bank and insurance buildings begins to grow, the traveler still cutting across layers of time reflected in housing increasingly dated. In Columbus, I-70 slices close to the southern edge of the business district, tall buildings looming immediately above the freeway. The again-fashionable German Village—now a designated historic district immediately to the south—shows a lesser profile of church steeples and breweries, many of the latter recycled into shopping malls. In Indianapolis, I-70 keeps its distance from downtown, sweeping in graceful curves first on the east and then on the south for westbound motorists. Then it cuts southwest through an extensive industrial zone until the airport is reached and the city begins to thin out into open country. At high speeds, such cities are quickly reduced to sets of easy generalizations connecting things across space in patterns of loose association. The traveler no longer needs to contend with the fine texture of complex urban fabric.

## THE FUTURE VERSUS THE PAST

In the decades after the railroads arrived, relatively few descriptions of the National Road were published. Most travelers rode the trains. Once rediscovered by automobilists, the Road invited from essayists and journalists a very different orientation than previously. Whereas the Road had once invited anticipation as to what America would become, now it invited primarily retrospection as to what America had been. There was a shift from boisterous expectation to nostalgic reminiscence. Travel was no longer future-oriented to places becoming, but was past-oriented to places surviving, withering, and even dying. A kind of rearview-mirror contemplation set in, with the National Road a historical feature to be romanticized. Travelers were invited to drive the Road as a means of experiencing history first-hand.

*Harper's New Monthly Magazine* featured an essay in 1879 entitled "The

Old National Pike." A writer was sent to explore the Road between Baltimore and Cumberland (thus never really experiencing the true highway at all). Nonetheless, its author, a careful observer, communicated the personality of the once-vital thoroughfare lost in its sunset years. Beyond Hagerstown he found little of interest save for the capacious taverns, mostly in disuse, and the stables and smithies, relics of earlier times. The withdrawal of traffic had left the towns indigent. At Clear Spring the street drowsed under its chestnuts. At the tavern the proprietor dozed without any expectation of customers. There the author found one of the few residual stagecoaches once so prominent on the highway. It was "a massive vehicle in faded grandeur, with panelled landscapes and a super abundance of gilt ornamentation . . . and a commodious interior upholstered in crimson damask out of which all brilliancy has been extracted by time."[51]

William Hale wrote nostalgically of a childhood home located on the National Road at Centerville, Indiana. The Road ran past the gate where on long summer days he used to swing as a boy. The highway was central in his life then. "Its direction gave the road an indubitable connection with the eternal structure of the universe, for the very sun seemed to travel it, coming along every morning out of the east." The highway swept into town on a plane of its own, an embankment raised high above the tasseled corn. It passed out of town through a covered bridge. "I can see it now that bridge," he wrote, "the broad, white road descending and swinging into the shadows of its dark, double-barrelled passage, very dusty in summer, but sweet with hay (the toll of high-stacked wains that could just squeeze through) clinging to the rafters."[52] But in 1911 there was a "monstrous desecration!" An interurban trolley line paralleled the Road along one margin, curving to claim the Road's center in the towns.

In 1915, Robert Bruce drove the National Road to Wheeling, collecting impressions for a monograph he published a year later. Bruce's intention was to promote a marked highway across the continent following various historical roads or trails—the National Old Trails Ocean-to-Ocean Highway. Even though the Road had been largely forgotten and little used as a long-distance thoroughfare, it still represented a remarkably straight course across the rugged terrain of the Appalachians. Not only was it picturesque, he argued, but it was the very essence of history, a relic of an important historical event—the settling of the West. His narrative contains a litany of places historical. Beyond Frederick, Maryland, memories of the Civil War dominated. Here was the house where Rutherford B. Hayes was nursed after being wounded in the Battle of South Mountain. There was the place where William McKinley received his first battlefield promotion. All along the Road were cast-iron markers outlining the movement of troops. "Nowhere else in the entire country," Bruce concluded, "can the influence of topography upon the course of history be so clearly traced."[53]

Toward Cumberland, Bruce left behind Civil War scenes to encounter the region fought over during the French and Indian War. "It is part of the charm of this trip to feel one's self literally following in the footsteps of the 'Father of his Country,'" he wrote. Then there were the "Shades of Death" and other stretches of road that had been celebrated in the past for some distinctiveness. The "Shades," a once-luxuriant pine forest, was "cut down, sawed up and shipped to market," although many of the larger stumps were still in the ground with others built into stump fences. Near Somerfield, Pennsylvania, evidence of Braddock's Road could be seen in long, shallow trenches. At the Great Meadows, the site of George Washington's Fort Necessity had been marked as well as General Braddock's grave. Frequently encountered were the distinctive S-bridges. At intervals the old toll houses were passed.[54]

George R. Stewart's *U.S. 40* is also highly retrospective. His work stimulated a follow-up effort in 1983 by two geographers, Thomas and Geraldine Vale. Stewart looks back at the past, and the Vales look back at Stewart. Stewart organized his book around a set of photographs, each of which he carefully describes in short vignettes. At Mount Prospect, Maryland, he shows a grand house built on a hill by a local gentry family. Surrounded by a spacious lawn with mature shade trees, the house and its yard spoke of comfort, security, integrity. But the Vales found the home demolished, the trees gone, and, indeed, the hillside totally excavated. Their photograph shows a sun-baked municipal parking lot surrounded by concrete retaining walls, furnished with utilitarian light standards and power poles and a lone telephone booth at one corner. The parking lot spoke to them of desolation. "In general," the Vales wrote, "we found changes in the appearance of the landscape along U.S. 40 to be a source of enjoyable fascination, sometimes even when the changes were the sorts commonly decried. But at Mount Pleasant, more than at any other site, . . . we regret what has happened."[55] The backward view could be painful.

## LANDSCAPE IN MOTION

The old National Road had seemed a marvel to nineteenth-century travelers as it cut across the grain of the country to form a direct route to the

Ohio River. Even early automobilists recognized that this was no ordinary road that wandered aimlessly as rural byway. Nonetheless, with widening, grading, improved pavements, and, indeed, the bypassing of whole sections to flatter, straighter rights-of-way, the Road became increasingly an architectural expression capable of dominating travel experience in its own right. At higher speeds, neither drivers nor passengers had much time to study the passing scene. "A flat, widely open highway tends to be monotonous," wrote Christopher Tunnard and Boris Pushkarev in their 1963 classic *Man-made America: Chaos or Control?* The sense of enclosure that obtained from the up-and-down, twisting-and-turning old roads heightened traveler interest by enhancing, at slow speeds, anticipation.[56] Improved roads, on the other hand—for example, the four-lane divided pavements built across Indiana in the 1940s and 1950s—isolated the traveler substantially, a removal even more enhanced on I-70 and other limited-access freeways that came to parallel the National Road in later decades.

As modern highways evolved, most travelers welcomed them uncritically. High-speed driving on smooth white concrete pavements brought novel sensations. Jan and Cora Gordon, who traveled but a short distance on US 40 in 1928, wrote of the new highways generally. "They were frank, they had no subterfuge; they were architectured into the country and, holding their unrelenting way across the green, green land, emphasizing the bases of hills with their strict and positive curves, they gave a welcome contrast and brought a sense of order amongst the fluid shapes of river, field and wood." "And so in the end," they concluded, "we found them like poetry, like a strong serious rhythm holding down the rich riot of unhampered nature; so that what at first struck with a sense of distaste, from its mere unfamiliarity, became the basis of a new series of observations and contrasted qualities and a source of delight."[57]

George R. Stewart called the new roads "dominating highways." "A dominating highway is one from which, as you drive along it, you are more conscious of the highway than of the country through which you are passing." The landscape becomes in such high-speed travel a kaleidoscope of images too ephemeral to register vivid memories. The close-up view of natural and cultural landscapes tends to be replaced by sensations of auto travel itself. There were the visual sensations of different light conditions playing upon the Road. "The low sun behind, with the shadows long ahead. The low sun ahead with the shadows pointing the way, and the glare in the eyes. The sun

JOHN A. JAKLE

above, and the light full on the Road, with the shimmer of heat-waves rising from the asphalt. No sun at all and the darkness thick, with the beams of the headlights picking out the curves ahead." There were the sounds. "The whir of the tires on concrete. . . . The soft squish of wet tires on pavement running with rain. The continual whirl and hiss of air around the windows. The little click of windshield wipers. The quick zee-ip, zee-ip as you pass something close by." There were the smells. "The smell of the car . . . a subtle blending, of oil and upholstery, and cigarette smoke, and people." There were, finally, the kinesthetic sensations. "All the rivers of fresh air coursing over the face. The pressure backward with acceleration, and the pressure as the body swings forward when the brake goes on. And the continual jogging from the springs."[58]

As speed of highway travel increases, concentration fixes on the approaching ribbon of road more and more. The point of concentration recedes with acceleration, the eye focusing at 25 MPH some 600 feet ahead, at 45 MPH some 1,200 feet, and at 65 MPH some 2,000 feet.[59] Speed thrusts the human intellect ahead toward the destination as goal. There comes a blending of driver and machine in, according to James Flagg, an "unescapable impulse to keep going—to keep up the pace." "The continuous motion forward begets a habit of mind," he wrote, "and the mere thought of stopping, except from exhaustion is repugnant." Drivers pitted themselves and their machines against the Road in setting records of endurance—300 miles in a day, 350 miles, 400 miles. "The national bird," Flagg mused, "instead of being the eagle, is the squirrel in the cage."[60]

Whole new categories of things would be created to capture the motorist's eye—prime among them billboards. Even the lack of billboards could be arresting. "The scenery is curiously different from that further back east," James Flagg wrote in 1925 of eastern Ohio along US 40. "Then it burst upon me," he continued. "There were no billboards! Unless you have seen it you cannot imagine what a sordid dull thing landscape is minus billboards. Just plain sky and trees, brooks, valleys and hills." "The billboards ruin everything," Stewart complained of US 40 in Maryland. "The historical flavor, the old-time architecture, even the beauty of the wooded hillside—all are sacrificed." Power and telephone lines could be accepted since, like fences, they offered a sense of integration to landscape. "They do their work without striving to be conspicuous, and often their not-ungraceful curves add a touch of interest, an intricacy of pattern, even some beauty." Billboards were different. They deliberately clashed with their backgrounds, shouting commercial messages loudly.[61]

Travelers of all eras grappled variously with the National Road as a thing to be experienced. They sought to render it meaningful each in their own way. I, in turn, have sought to reduce a wide sample of recorded impressions into broad categories of understanding contrasted and compared place to place, one time to another. Are there any overarching lessons to be learned applicable in the modern scientific sense of applying to all people everywhere? The landscape of a highway (and the objects that they contain organized by highway travel as landscape) can be a source of endless stimulus and pleasure to travelers who work at "reading" the passing scene. Part and parcel of such endeavor is an empathizing with past travelers in trying to imagine what they might have experienced place to place. Sought is a mental reconstruction of the passing scene such that an understanding of landscape change accrues. What did those who came before know? What could/would they likely have known? It is the stimulus of juxtapositioning things in the linear array of Road geography. It is the stimulus of things variously juxtaposed in time, place to place. Perhaps this is a process of inquiry worth exciting universally even if universally applicable generalizations do not necessarily accrue. Let us not be scientific. Let us simply read the highway for its diverse cultural meanings.

The route of the National Road is an especially appropriate place to practice the art of landscape interpretation. Along nearly its entire length it has retained its integrity as a highway with the accretions of almost two centuries of building and rebuilding evident along original rights-of-way. There are relatively few highways in the United States where as well a developed "time-depth" is so evident over so long a distance. Here in linear array is a display awaiting the adventurous landscape interpreter. Could the excitement (indeed, the adventure) be any less rewarding today than in previous times? Today's traveler sees not the frontier, but residuals of the frontier juxtaposed in mosaics accumulated over subsequent times—everything from remnant taverns to ubiquitous billboards. Here history is thickly layered in surviving veneers of material culture along a highway trajectory of true historical importance.

What did earlier travelers see of the National Road, and think to record in writing? In gathering their impressions they responded to landscapes as

JOHN A. JAKLE

they found them according to the realities of place and according to social expectations brought. At first they traveled to validate an America becoming. Much later travelers turned to validating the past as captured in layers of historicity encountered. Perhaps today's traveler might redirect attention along the earlier line of inquiry—to use the National Road once again to assess an America becoming? The National Road offers a linear array of American successes and failures variously defined. Along with the sleepy villages and hamlets seemingly fossilized, one finds booming metropolises. What does it all mean? What does it imply we want our nation to be? What might we want wilder and rural places to become? What do we expect of our cities? Driving the Road provides an opportunity to contrast and compare—to think about what was supposed to have been, what might have been, but, more important, what future options might be. That was the challenge that the early keepers of diaries and the early writers of travel journals accepted.

# The Road as a Corridor for Ideas

HUBERT G. H. WILHELM

*It is firmly believed that the Cumberland Road, under construction from funds derived through the sale of public lands, will facilitate the intercourse of the people east and west of the Appalachians and "substantially unite them in interest which . . . is the most effective cement of union applicable to the human race."*

RALPH H. BROWN
*Mirror for Americans: Likeness of the Eastern Seaboard, 1810*

A COMMENT IN THE *COLUMBUS DISPATCH*, JANUARY 31, 1993, RAISED the issue of the National Road as an avenue for transfer of people, things, and ideas to the level of an exotic culinary detail—the availability of fresh oysters. The author pointed out that before the National Road, pickled oysters, eaten with bread or crackers, butter, and, at times, a side dish of pig's feet or tripe, were among the common fares offered in roadway taverns and wagoners' houses. After completion of the National Road to Zanesville, Ohio, in 1831, Col. Henry Orndorff, who operated the National Hotel in that city, began the fresh oyster trade into the interior. He apparently introduced them also to Columbus, Chillicothe, Lancaster, and Cambridge. The subsequent demand for these seaboard morsels was so great that the wagon line that rushed them from Baltimore was known as the Oyster Line.[1]

Any type of communication, whether the primitive, early woodland trail or today's sophisticated electronic gadgets, contributes to that very geographic of processes spatial diffusion. Communication breaks down isolation and furthers the spread of people, ideas, and things. Our concern is the Road as a carrier of peoples and their cultural baggage. The Road's trans-Appalachian location, between regions of very contrasting physical geography, settlement history, and development, assured it an honored position as an important factor in the country's westward progression. It was, and through its eventual successors US 40 and I-70, remains even today the embodiment of the new nation's idea of "manifest destiny." How it contributed specifically to diffusion, both west- and eastward, is the concern of this chapter. I will focus upon the built-up landscape, and the Road's a priori effects on that landscape.

## THE ROAD AS CAUSE OR CONSEQUENCE OF INTERIOR DEVELOPMENT

Answering whether the Road was the cause or the consequence of interior development may appear obvious, but involves a complex process. During the long years of its inception and final implementation, the Road was more consequence than cause. When Congress in 1806 authorized the construction of a road from Cumberland, Maryland, to the Ohio River, the state of Ohio was already three years old and Marietta, Zanesville, Chillicothe, and Cincinnati were thriving towns. Surveyors dragged their chains across Ohio into Indiana and Illinois, enforcing the government's pronouncements in the Ordinances of 1785 and 1787.[2] Ebenezer Zane finished the first interior road in 1797, and a 1810 Ohio map depicting the state's road network shows an extensive pattern of routes within the settled areas. National Road construction would greatly benefit from the presence of Zane's Trace, however primitive, and the segments of other earlier roads that it eventually followed.

The Road's function was to link the East with the rapidly growing West, which otherwise might decide to follow a path of development inconsistent with eastern notions of how the country should evolve. Paradoxically, the government, including the administrations of James Monroe and John Quincy Adams, recognized the extension of federal support to the West in the form of a highway as unconstitutional. The problem was, of course, federal incursion on states' rights. Road opponents argued repeatedly that the government could not become involved with internal improvements that gave advantage to some states at the expense of others.

Congressional approval of the Road finally came in a 66-to-50 vote with

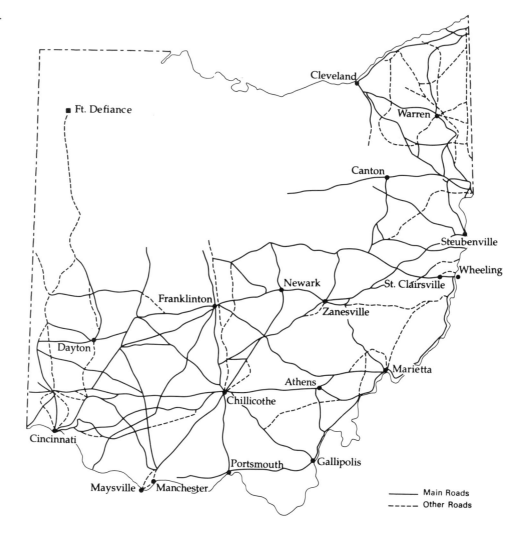

**Major roadways throughout Ohio, 1810**

Following Ohio River tributaries, migrants settled Ohio from the east and south. The early road network focused on frontier settlements.

Ft. Defiance

Cleveland

Warren

Canton

Steubenville

Wheeling

Newark

St. Clairsville

Franklinton

Zanesville

Dayton

Marietta

Athens

Chillicothe

Cincinnati

Portsmouth

Gallipolis

Maysville    Manchester

——— Main Roads
- - - - Other Roads

Pennsylvania, South Carolina, and Virginia voting against. Pennsylvania felt that too little of the Road was in its territory, nor was Philadelphia on it. Southerners generally opposed the Road because they feared that it would pull on their population and adversely affect development of the region. Both states' rights and sectionalism continued to be hurdles for the Road. When it came to the responsibility of its upkeep, the fervor for a "national" road disappeared. By 1835, it was no longer "national"; instead, individual states had taken charge of its upkeep and improvements.[3]

One of the Road's more ardent supporters was Andrew Jackson. He supposedly was responsible for the remark that "America begins at the Appalachians." As a "Westerner," he understood the importance of the Road

HUBERT G. H. WILHELM

for the far-flung regions beyond the Appalachians. During his campaign for the presidency, Jackson had used the Road frequently. It was not unusual for him to meet with local citizens when he stayed in one of the many inns along the National Pike. Because news travels fast along a highway, Jackson's ideas and plans for the presidency became well known. There was no better place to have one's ideas pronounced to the hinterland than the road tavern or inn. Closely spaced, taverns functioned as democratizing institutions where the humble and powerful mingled and from where an aspiring politician could expect to gain a measure of geographical influence not readily available in the early 1800s.

The ascendancy of Andrew Jackson to the presidency in 1829 represented the acceptance of Western or frontier ideas and practices. This heralded a new era for Washington, which had been dominated by seaboard interests. One can be certain that the National Road was a factor in the diffusion of "what was good for the West was good for the country." It was not only a spearhead from the East toward the West, but, as a true link between diverse regions, also carried ideas and things eastward.

Among some of these "Western" notions was one that until recent times has both marred and solidified the relationship between Washington and its interior outposts. As a Westerner, Jackson understood frontier politics and knew that frontier politicians, as politicians anywhere, expected to be rewarded for the help or support that they had provided. The new president did not disappoint them. His election "in the Autumn of 1828 brought the spoils system into national politics." During Jackson's presidency, federal offices in the West multiplied and appointments went to the frontier politician seeking "the greatest source of patronage in his region, the federal government."[4] Post offices, Indian agencies, land offices, surveyors' districts, and so on were filled with Westerners, including political friends, and created an important support base that would serve President Jackson well in future years. The National Road was the physical base on which that patronage and support flowed back and forth between the interior and Washington. Would it have happened without the Road? Most likely. The West was filling in and before long would make its im-

"Old Hickory at Barton House" (1879)

Roadside taverns functioned as community centers in addition to providing food and lodging for travelers. They were ideal locations for politicians to address a gathering of local voters.

print on the East and Washington. The Road, however, did exist and facilitated travel as never before. It became an avenue for diffusion.

In 1803, Ohio entered the Union as the seventeenth state. One year earlier, the territorial legislators had passed the Enabling Act, which would permit the new state to take some money from the sale of federal lands and use it for highway construction. The amount was set at 5 percent, but was later reduced to 3 percent. The "3 percent fund," as it is affectionately called in Ohio, was a significant factor in internal transportation improvements and helps to explain the number and density of roads in existence by 1810. It set a precedent in the relationship of an individual state and the federal government by allowing funds obtained from the sale of public lands to be used for state improvements. The congressional vote on Ohio statehood was conditioned on the inclusion of the Enabling Act. That historic fact was crucial to the eventual success of a "national" road project.

## THE ROADSIDE LANDSCAPE

As the Road crept westward, the demands for access generated spiraling land values. Everyone wanted access to the Road. It offered work and income and brought variety to the drudgery of frontier living. In the process, it became an artery of settlement and the country's first extensive roadside strip. Property owners placed their houses, fences, yards, and gardens right next to it and sometimes even altered the direction of the Road.[5] An old farmer, perhaps, said it best when he commented on the changes along the Road after it began to decline: "The loss of it isn't very bad. . . . When it was at its height all the people along here depended on it for a living, and now they are driven to farmin', which is much better for them."[6] Most likely, he did not directly benefit from the Road and expressed his satisfaction about the decline of a way of life where individual effort was, at least in his mind, too highly rewarded.

### The Linear Road Town

The National Road was built parallel to the east-west axis of national development and greatly encouraged linear growth of settlements. Although it began at Cumberland, Maryland, it connected culturally with the greater Middle Atlantic region, especially Pennsylvania. As Peirce Lewis has argued, "the Pennsylvania Culture Region may have set the tone for cultural life in much of the central United States."[7] Because of its location, the Road became the purveyor of Eastern, instead of Southern or New England settle-

HUBERT G. H. WILHELM

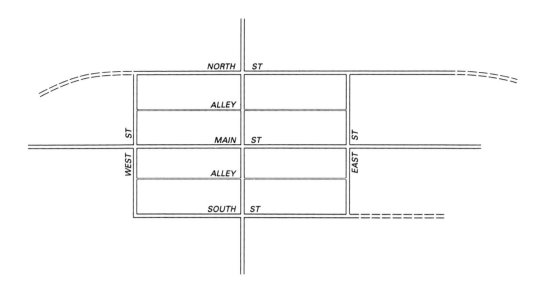

**Main Street and back street of Morristown and a road town model**

Teamsters and drovers were expected to divert their wagons and herds to the back streets to avoid causing traffic congestion on Main.

ment effects, including family and place names, religion, farm practices, house and barn forms, town plans, and language forms. To this day, "smear case" instead of "cottage cheese" can be heard from older residents of central Ohio's rural areas. The word, of course, comes out of the Pennsylvania-Dutch culture, whose members used the Road in large numbers as they spread into the rich farmlands of the interior. Beyond Ohio the Road contributed greatly to settlement convergence and, especially, Southern settlement forms vie with those from the East for landscape dominance.

Town development along the National Road was dominated by the Main Street model of settlement. While town location was dictated by a variety of factors, especially the presence of an intersecting road and the need for regularly spaced services such as inns or watering and feeding places for horses and other livestock, their plan was repetitive and consisted of a principal street and one or two parallel backstreets.

Main Street and backstreets were mutually interdependent, especially during the Road's peak years. Main Street attracted residences, businesses, and inns, while the back street continued to be used for the Road's heavy traffic. In Ohio, the back street was frequently a segment of the old Zane's Trace where wagoners and drovers sought respite from their long hauls and toil. Main Street became the residential and commercial center, accentuated, to be sure, by its linear form. There was neither space nor the proper ambiance for the various public structures such as churches and schools. These would eventually be built on the backstreets. The Pennsylvania town "was for trade, and the town center was a commercial, not a social or religious place."[8]

The National Road, because of its location and function, encouraged the Main Street town plan. The linear-road town was a response to cultural antecedents in the Middle Atlantic region of the country and the presence of a single major business thoroughfare. In time, both the place and idea of Main Street "became an enormously influential landscape symbol, widely assumed to represent the most 'typically American.'"[9] Walt Disney made it the centerpiece of his California theme park, and for most Americans Main Street remains meaningful in the place we call "downtown."

### Inns, Taverns, Wagoners' and Drovers' Houses

Nothing expressed the vitality of Main Street better than the taverns or inns. They marked the location of settlement and transportation advance and often were the first buildings to be constructed.[10] The attraction that brought many to the National Road was the offering of food, drink, and shelter in return for "hard cash." According to one traveler, "no matter how small the town, there are always from two to five or even eight taverns to choose among."[11] Of course, any person who lived on the Road could benefit from offering "board and room" and many did.

These "public houses," because of their names and appearance, gave character to Main Street. They were usually the largest buildings in town, two stories and frame- or brick-constructed. They functioned according to the "American Plan," which included meals taken at a common table, the sale of liquor, and lodging. Their interiors consisted of two rooms downstairs, one that functioned as lobby, meeting and drinking place, and the other for dining. Meals were taken together and cost the same for everyone. The upstairs consisted of a single large room for sleeping.[12] A few of these buildings survive today. Among the best preserved are the Smith House and Headley Inn, west of Zanesville in Muskingum County, Ohio.

Wagoners' and drovers' houses differed from taverns or inns because of their placement at the outskirts of towns, or along the back street. They also served a different clientele, including large numbers of horses and other livestock. Functionally, the wagoners' houses antedate the contemporary motel because they served all those whose livelihood was directly tied to the Road. The truckstop is the modern-day version of the wagoners' house.

Among the structures at the wagoners' places were barns for both the stabling of horses and the storage of hay and grain. An early artist left a sketch of a typical "stagecoach" barn.[13] It resembles an industrial-type building, a foundry or mill. Is it possible that this building might have influenced the development of the common middlewestern feeder barn that has also been identified as a "three portal" barn?[14] Form and functional resemblances make these two structures fraternal if not identical twins. Both are ground-level buildings with entrances on the gable side. The roof ridge runs parallel to the central alley or drive of the barns. Questions about the origins of the "three portal" barn remain. Did the National Road contribute to the diffusion of a traditional American barn type? The question remains unanswered.

**Stagecoach barn in Indianapolis**

Stage barns sheltered coaches and teams, and contained a supply of fresh hay and straw in the second-floor mow.

The National Road affected the distribution of inns, especially in areas west of the Ohio River, but also contributed to their demise. Any new road is built to improve the connectivity between places, to get from place to place faster and more efficiently. The National Road, by following a straighter course than earlier roads, would naturally bypass places. This was particularly true in its eastern segment between Cumberland and Wheeling. Here, the older road was Braddock's Road and tavernkeepers on it "were as earnestly opposed to the building of the National Road, as those on the latter were to the building of the railroad, and for like reasons."[15]

More significantly, however, the National Road probably influenced passage from the traditional American inn or tavern to the European hotel system. Because of its dual function as east-west link and main connector for tributary routes, the National Road influenced regional and urban growth. Cumberland, Wheeling, Zanesville, Columbus, Richmond, Indianapolis, Terre Haute, and other cities grew in size and functional diversity. Their populations were informed and anxious to compete with the sophisticated cities of the East. The inn with its complete fare of food, drink, and lodging no longer "filled the bill." The inns were literally "overpowered by the rise of a monied class capable of paying five dollars for a meal à la carte which would have cost 50 cents at the table d'hôte [common table]."[16]

These developments were accelerated with the coming of the railroads. A very early rail crossed part of the National Road's hinterland, linking the

Ohio River at Madison, Indiana, to Indianapolis. The date was 1836. By 1841, one could travel on rails from Sandusky to Dayton. From the 1850s on, the Road no longer could compete and sank into a long period of decline. Only local farm folk and the adventurous used it. Its eventual resurrection by the automobile meant changes in road-building technology and more bypassed places. The following verse speaks well about the inn's demise and is apropos for all places that lost their livelihood because of the "new" route and its more efficient location:

> . . . a day came at last when the stage brought no load
> To the gate, as it rolled up the long, dusty road.
> And lo! at the sunrise a shrill whistle blew
> O'er the hills—and the old yielded place to the new—
> And a merciless age with its discord and din
> Made wreck, as it passed, of the pioneer inn.[17]

## THE ROAD AND THE PROCESS OF SETTLING THE WEST

For a considerable time before the National Road, both the image of and the actual access to the West were controlled by the Ohio River and its valley. This all-important routeway into the interior contributed to the convergence of American migrants from the Northeast, East, and South. A preferred gathering point was at the Forks of the Ohio at Pittsburgh. From the East, two roads, those of Forbes and Braddock, the latter a predecessor to the Cumberland Road, offered access to the Ohio River. Northeasterners used the Allegheny River and its valley to get to Pittsburgh and the river. Other early roads, including several branches of the Wilderness Road, stopped at the Ohio River where settlers continued their downriver journey; some would travel as far as the Mississippi River, others to the Indiana or Illinois territories. The river functioned like the lower part of a funnel as it pulled together migrants from a vast eastern area and sent them off toward a common destination—the West.

John Jakle has written that the Ohio Valley prior to 1830 was the single most important routeway for Americans moving West because of persistent Spanish control over the South and continued British dominance of the Great Lakes region. The Ohio Valley, therefore, "became synonymous with the West."[18] The river was used as the dividing line for the two large territorial governments of the interior, the Territory North West of the Ohio (1787), and the Territory South West of the Ohio (1790). Because of its sig-

HUBERT G. H. WILHELM

nificance as a settlement and development artery, the Ohio Valley contributed greatly to the early economic orientation of the interior that was downriver, toward New Orleans.

The gradual settlement of middlewestern plains and prairie lands—north of the eroded interstream areas or interfluves next to the river—signaled a new identity with and economic orientation in the West. By the 1830s, the idea of an Ohio River region was diminishing in favor of "a Middle West emerging to the north of the Ohio River in contrast with the South."[19] Simultaneously, the Great Lakes and the Erie Canal became the region's principal outlet toward the East.

What was the National Road's impact upon these dramatic spatial readjustments that would so alter the nation's geography? *Images of the Ohio Valley* includes a series of decadal maps showing travelers' routes and destinations. The map for 1830–39 shows a dramatic increase in the use of overland routes north of the Ohio River, including the National Road. Travelers by the Road could go no farther than Terre Haute, Indiana. Vandalia, Illinois, the Road's planned terminus, is among travelers' destinations on the 1840–49 map, the result of the Road's late completion in Illinois. On the final map (1850–60), travelers have almost totally abandoned roads in favor of the railroads.[20]

From Wheeling west, the National Road functioned effectively for approximately twenty years, 1830 to 1850. That stretch never seriously rivaled the river for the movement of goods. The reason was simple economics. When the Madison-to-Indianapolis rail line opened in 1836, shipping costs on the river were 0.5 cents per ton-mile, on the canal 2.5 cents, on the railroad 6.5 cents, and for road-bound wagons 15 cents per ton-mile.[21] The Road's connection with the Ohio River, the Cumberland-to-Wheeling segment, was the most important. Yet the entire Road became an integral part of the regional realignment between the East, the Ohio Valley, and the Middle West. Because it was one of the first truly improved roads, it was the preferred route for migrants seeking land in the Ohio Country. The Road also provided a symbolic link between East and West. That symbolism, however intangible, contributed to the events and processes responsible for the evolution of an "American heartland."

## MIGRATION, CONVERGENCE, AND DIFFUSION

In 1800, the first two land offices opened in the Ohio Country, one at Marietta and the other up the river at Steubenville. The latter was to conduct sales for the first area to be surveyed, the Seven Ranges. Although the area has a narrow frontage on the Ohio River, land in the Seven Ranges is among the roughest in Ohio. As one might expect, business was slow during the early years and even an attempt by the land office to give land away to Hessian soldiers was unsuccessful.

Access to the region was poor at best. Zane's Trace, a path wide enough for a person on horseback, had been completed in 1797. It began at the site of the present town of Bridgeport just opposite Wheeling, and followed a course due west, through Belmont and Guernsey Counties, to Zanesville in Muskingum County. A short distance west of Zanesville, it angled off toward the southwest, reaching the Ohio River at Manchester opposite Maysville (formerly Limestone) in Kentucky. The National Road would eventually align itself with portions of the older trace usually called Zane Road in eastern Ohio.

West of the Seven Ranges, dominated by the well-eroded sandstone ridge called the Flushing Escarpment, the lay of the land improves greatly. This is the Muskingum River drainage basin and includes two principal tributaries, the Tuscarawas and Licking. Much of this land lay within the U.S. Military District that was flanked north and south by congressional lands. The combination of amenable terrain and congressional and military land districts proved an attraction for the legions of settlers moving west, including large numbers of Pennsylvania Dutch. Ohio's third land office opened for business in Zanesville in 1804, a response to increased settlement within the region. The eastern migrants brought into Ohio several traits that would spread westward along the principal avenue into the Middle West, the National Road.

The distribution of early settlers in the country between the Ohio River and the Great Lakes has received considerable attention from several scholars.[22] The region became the geographical foci for migrants from the Northeast, East, and South. Across Ohio, Indiana, and Illinois, migrants settled within three east-west belts that are linked to migrant source areas and the routes followed. Easterners moved along the National Road, for example, and Yankees and Yorkers followed the Erie Canal and over land roads across New York into northern Ohio. Southerners followed branches of the Wilderness Road to Ohio River crossings at Maysville, Covington (opposite Cincinnati), and Louisville, Kentucky. But this tripartite division of the Middle West into cultural subregions is not clear-cut. Settlers mingled and mixed and the middle belt especially became a "cultural hybrid."[23] People along the National Road adjusted to one another's cultures, an acculturation ideally expressed when tavern hosts offered travelers "johnnycake fragrant with pork drippings."[24] New England and South melted together in the stewpots proffered in the inns along the Road. Just as the Ohio River route attracted migrants who would settle across the southern belt, the Road became the arterial feeding the middle, thereby contributing to the cultural "hodgepodge" that became the Middle West.

### The "Old Wheat Belt"

Before the Road "travelers spoke of going into and out of the west as though it were the Mammoth Cave."[25] After the Road, the phrase became "going West." It represented a different mindset, one less encumbered by perceived obstacles and lack of familiarity. News traveled rapidly along the Road. In good weather and with fine sets of horses, stages could make over 100 miles a day.[26] Information about the interior flowed back east along the Road, encouraging those contemplating westward migration. Relatives who had already made the trip were an important, supportive incentive.

Settlers from Pennsylvania were significant, both for their numbers and their contributions. The phrase "the Pennsylvania beehive" originated because of the seemingly never-ending stream of migrants moving from the southeastern quarter of that state. In billowing canvas-covered Conestoga wagons they pushed into the interior. The Cumberland Road carried them to Wheeling where they ferried across the Ohio to pick up Zane's Trace. By the late 1820s, the National Road's extension into Ohio provided a corridor for Pennsylvanians to move deeper into the Middle West. By 1850, they were the principal out-of-state group in Ohio, 190,396, or over twice as many as the next largest group, the Virginians.[27]

Pennsylvanians came in search of fat country; "sweet lands" was their term for well-drained land with lime-rich soils. They found it along the Road—and to the north and south of it—in the congressional areas. They brought with them fine cattle and small grain culture, especially wheat. After the Ohio & Erie Canal (from Portsmouth to Cleveland) opened in 1832, Ohio wheat could be shipped to eastern markets and east-central Ohio became known as the Old Wheat Belt. The Belt centered along or near the National Road in Muskingum, Licking, Belmont, Harrison, Jefferson, Coshocton, and Knox Counties. It extended into several other counties, including Ashland, Holmes, Wayne, Stark, Tuscarawas, Columbiana, and Carroll. These counties lay astride Ohio's "Backbone" country, the divide from which rivers ran north toward Lake Erie or south toward the Ohio. The Backbone also coincides with the old Congress lands immediately south of the Connecticut Western Reserve and is Ohio's archetypal Pennsylvania-Dutch country. Facetiously, the "Dutch" called the Reserve "cheese country," obviously a comment recognizing the New Englanders' preoccupation with dairying, in contrast to "Dutch" wheat farming.

The National Road did not greatly contribute to the rise in wheat production. That was stimulated by the canals and, later, the railroads and lake ports. The Road was *the* factor in the relocation of Pennsylvania settlers. Robert Leslie Jones, in his comprehensive *History of Agriculture in Ohio to 1880,* gives credence to this generalization when he points out that the Old Wheat Belt of eastern Ohio "constituted in reality an extension of the wheat country of western Pennsylvania."[28]

As early as 1835, farmers in the Muskingum Valley applied "land plaster" or gypsum to their fields. The practice of liming fields, often related with Pennsylvania-Dutch farming methods, apparently spread from Pennsylvania into Ohio and helped progressive farmers with their land husbandry.[29] In 1839, when the National Road was almost completed, Ohio led the five principal wheat-producing states. A few decades later, however, the Wheat Belt had shifted westward, while Ohio farmers began to adjust their agricultural production to the growing urban centers in the northeastern and southwestern parts of the state (see table).

|  | *1839* |  |  | *1859* |  |
|---|---|---|---|---|---|
| Ohio | 16,572 |  | Illinois | 23,837 |  |
| Pennsylvania | 13,213 |  | Indiana | 16,848 |  |
| New York | 12,286 |  | Wisconsin | 15,657 |  |
| Virginia | 10,110 |  | Ohio | 15,119 |  |
| Kentucky | 4,803 |  | Virginia | 13,131 |  |

*Source:* Jones 1983, 58.

## PENNSYLVANIA SETTLEMENT LANDSCAPES
## IN THE MIDDLE WEST

The National Road passed through country almost ideal for agriculture, reinforcing the relationship between the Pennsylvanians and the replication of their favored vocations in the West. As a result, the middle section of Ohio, Indiana, and Illinois includes settlement forms, family and place names, religious denominations, town street patterns, and traditional architecture, whose roots are in the "Pennsylvania Culture Area."[30]

These Pennsylvania characteristics are best expressed in Ohio and diminish westward. The National Road lies across an important cultural contact line where traditional forms—houses and barns, for example—give way to popular forms. Because the completion of the National Road in Indiana and Illinois coincided with the rise of rail transportation, the Road's effectiveness as a line of interregional communication and transportation declined rapidly. The railroad, combined with increases in the number of post offices and telegraph communication (the first intercity message was sent in 1844) ushered in a new era. Reliance on tradition declined in favor of "modern-fashionable" products. Even the middlewestern farmer, because of the strong mutual interdependence of farm and town, learned about and accepted "new" things that led to the "metropolitanization" of the countryside.[31]

Nonetheless, one may follow the remaining segments of US 40 and appreciate the persistence of Pennsylvania cultural traits in the landscape—town forms and patterns, house types, and barns. Each is a part of the greater Middle Atlantic culture trait complex whose westward spread was greatly assisted by the Old Pike.

### The Pennsylvania Town

Many towns along or near the National Road were platted according to the Pennsylvania Town model, itself derived from William Penn's plan for Philadelphia. Streets intersected at right angles, creating square or rectangular blocks. An alley bisected each block forming a boundary between adjacent properties. The road town centered on Main Street, the focus of residential and business development. Similar to Pennsylvania, people built structures close to the street, leaving little space for sidewalks or frontyards. Main Street lots were in greatest demand and filled in rapidly, houses placed with their long axes facing the street. Many houses abutted each other, pro-

**The White Swan Inn, Uniontown, Pennsylvania**

The rowhouse roof ridge usually paralleled the street and buildings were set gable-to-gable on narrow lots. Here the White Swan Inn, a grouping of four or five buildings, some of them made of log, is being demolished in the early 1900s.

ducing a typical Pennsylvania Town characteristic, the rowhouse. The Main Street rowhouses gave these towns what Wilbur Zelinsky calls their most diagnostic characteristic: "Perhaps the most measurable peculiarity is sheer compactness and tightness."[32] Farther west, the rowhouse idea was adapted to the more open Middle West town, where the demand for lots facing the Road was less marked then on the densely populated Piedmont. When spaced apart, the houses often became distinguishable as belonging to somewhat different floor plans.

Following the Pennsylvania Town model, National Road Main Streets were a mix of shops, residences, and businesses. Private entrepreneurs often combined home and workplace in a single building. Two-story rowhouses functioned ideally for that purpose, family quarters on the second floor, shops and offices on the first and directly adjacent to the Road. Public places, other than the inns or taverns, came later and took space on the "back roads," which were the first parallel streets behind Main Street. Among these were churches, whose congregations shunned profane locations on Main Street.

Another Pennsylvania Town characteristic is its orientation to a central square. Many Ohio, Indiana, and Illinois town plats include a square that "must be added to the farm practices, rural and urban settlement patterns and house types, the Kentucky Rifle and the Conestoga wagon, that settlers carried with them from southeastern Pennsylvania."[33] The Philadelphia or Diamond square is distinctive, formed by taking corner lots from four central blocks. The resulting square or diamond often has a circular drive at the center of the four converging streets. Indianapolis, among the larger cities on the Road, was laid out in this pattern. The square is often an open park-like area faced by public buildings, such as the courthouse or city hall, which occupy one or another of the diamond's four corners.

Although the Diamond plan was repeated often across the eastern Middle West, not many Road towns exhibit the pattern. One reason may be that strip development on Main Street was all-controlling and negated town layout around a central square. Another influence was the federal rectangular survey that begins in Ohio. Since the survey encouraged "cross-roads" town

HUBERT G. H. WILHELM

plats, the central square pattern was primarily applied to future political sites, especially county seats. Road towns that eventually ascended to political centers placed their courthouses in any available space along Main Street, a logical solution when political power arrived long after the town had experienced its initial road-related strip development. Several Road towns in Ohio fit this category, including St. Clairsville, Cambridge, and Zanesville. On the other hand, the courthouse-square town plan, in which the courthouse stands in a central square block dedicated to that purpose, is but one of several Southern traits that settlers from Virginia and Kentucky carried northward into southern Ohio and Indiana.

**Rowhouses in Centerville, Indiana**

In plan, the house in the foreground is called a one-and-one-half (one first-floor room to the side of the door and hallway, two rooms on the second floor), and the house on the right is a small I-house. Houses like these, when stood gable to gable, often with a common end wall, became rowhouses in many eastern National Road towns.

### The I-house, a Pennsylvania Folk Building

Among America's traditional houses, the I-house occupies a special niche simply because it became one of the most widespread house forms in the central Middle West. Because it was largely a rural house, the I-house, probably more than any other structure, "became symbolic of economic attainment by agriculturalists."[34] The term *I-house,* now widely accepted, comes from Fred Kniffen's work on folk housing in Louisiana.[35] He used the term for houses he found in northern Louisiana that had been built by immigrants from the three "I" states, Indiana, Illinois, and Iowa. The house's geographical roots, however, are in the East, including Pennsylvania.

Although questions remain about the origins of the I-house, there is little argument that it came into the Middle West among the cultural baggage of two peoples, migrants from the Middle Atlantic and from the Upland South, especially the former. According to Kniffen, "the great contribution of the Middle Atlantic source area were the English 'I' house and German log construction and basic barn types."[36] To this Peirce Lewis has added, "If architecture is any guide, Middle America is an extension of Pennsylvania."[37] The I-house is by far the most prominent architectural feature in the towns along the National Road, and suggests the Road's importance in the diffusion of Pennsylvania ideas.

An I-house is two stories high, two rooms in length, but only one room deep or wide. It may have a single or two front doors. The number and location of windows varies. Some houses have a single central chimney, but more often two chimneys at or near the gable ends. Many middlewestern I-houses exhibit "classical" details with strong adherence to symmetry represented by the central door and hallway, the number and regular spacing of windows, and gable-end chimneys.

Eastern I-houses were built across Maryland and western Pennsylvania and coincided closely with areas of English and Scots-Irish settlement.[38] Thus, these houses stood along principal migration routes into the interior, primarily the National Road. Because the English and Scots-Irish were usually the first settlers into an area, they carried their bias for one-room deep housing westward. Others who followed, including the Pennsylvania Dutch, who usually preferred two-room-deep houses in Pennsylvania, joined the popular trend and the I-house became the house of choice among most settlers from the East. A survey of folk houses in Indiana confirms that the I-house survives as one of the dominant forms in central Indiana close to the National Road.[39]

The I-house was well adapted to Road towns. With a length of between 35 and 45 feet, it fit on an average-size 50-foot town lot. Its two-story facade and classical symmetry made for an impressive appearance along the street. Preference for a lengthwise orientation could be further adapted by stringing two or three I-houses together in rowhouse form so typical of Baltimore and other eastern cities. Brick was the preferred house construction material, especially in southwest Pennsylvania and eastern Ohio. Further west, timber-framed and clapboard-sided houses occurred more frequently. This transition indicates an increasing availability of dimensional timbers from sawmills. The "balloon frame" made its appearance in the 1830s in Chicago and greatly popularized building structures around light internal frames instead of the traditional practice of using thick, load-bearing brick or stone walls to support joists and roof beams.[40] The National Road probably affected an eastward diffusion of this middlewestern construction method that eventually replaced heavy hand-hewn timber and brick construction.

Both the Road and I- or rowhouses existed in a kind of symbiotic relationship. The Road encouraged strip development along a main street and these stretched-out houses offered the appropriate architectural response. The middlewestern town, then, consisted of a principal street with tightly packed, two-story houses, a town form that became an American standard.

The I-house remained popular over an extended period and is one of six house forms classified as a "national type."[41] Its demise toward the end of the nineteenth century came with changes in the social and technological character of the American home and with suburbanization.

### The Pennsylvania-German Barn

A cultural residual of early trans-Appalachian settlement in southeastern Ohio is Ohio University in Athens, Ohio. The university was founded in 1803 by a group of New Englanders and was the first institution of higher learning in the Northwest Territory. It is frequently confused with Ohio State University, which causes immediate and great consternation among students, faculties, and townfolk. Although Athens is an area that had been acquired by the Ohio Company of Associates in Boston, Massachusetts, most of the town and the surrounding area were eventually settled by Virginians and Pennsylvanians. The cultural contact line between Pennsylvania and Virginia settlement lies only a few miles north of Athens. That line

**Pennsylvania-German barn**

The Schroeder barn west of Englewood, Ohio, stands beside the National Road. It bears the distinguishing extended forebay, louvered ventilator windows, and ramp to the threshing floor (out of view on the left) that are common to the large barns built by Germans across southeastern Pennsylvania.

becomes visible in the landscape because of regionally varying settlement forms, among these the Pennsylvania-German barn.

Over a period of several years in the late 1960s, I located many of these barns in southern Ohio, thereby establishing regions of contrasting settlement influences between the East and the South. Although, the boundary has been modified by subsequent research by Robert Ensminger,[42] the distribution of the Pennsylvania-German barn coincides very well with the spread of settlers from Pennsylvania into central Ohio along the National Road, then diverging both north and south into preferred settlement areas.

Like the I-house, the Pennsylvania-German barn is illustrative of the diffusion of Middle Atlantic material traits into the central Middle West. The diffusion path was along the National Road and its network of tributary roads. Further west, in Indiana, these barns are less common but when they do occur "they stand isolated or in small widely scattered clusters north and south of the old National Road."[43]

The Pennsylvania-German barn, also known as a banked, forebay, or Sweitzer barn, originated in Switzerland and therefore is Germanic rather than German.[44] Its identification as Pennsylvania-German resulted when many "Dutch" folk, including new immigrants from Germany, adopted the barn. It is always a two-level barn, with the lower level "banked" or built into a slope. On flat terrain a ramp replaced the natural slope. The barn's most easily recognized diagnostic feature is the second-story overhang or forebay. It projects by several feet over the lower level or stabling area. The latter is adjacent to a walled or fenced cattleyard.

From its American source area in southeastern Pennsylvania, the barn spread southward along the Shenandoah Valley and westward across a broad area that reaches from southern Ohio, Indiana, and Illinois northward into Ontario, Michigan, and Wisconsin. Outside Pennsylvania, the greatest concentration of these barns is in Ohio where they flank the National Road both north and south. They diminish westward, but there are important outliers in Illinois, Iowa, and Wisconsin.[45]

The thinning of Pennsylvania cultural traits westward in no way detracts from the significance of the Old Pike as a route of diffusion. The Road's late completion in Indiana and, especially, in Illinois coincides with a period of changing fashions in America, particularly the decline of tradition in favor of modern, popular products. Among the major reasons for these cultural changes was the transition to fast and efficient railroad transportation that assured improved connectivity between places and the dissemination of goods and information.

Another important reason for landscape transition along the National Road beyond Ohio was that area's attraction to settlers from converging migration streams. In Ohio, the three principal American migrant groups, Southerners, Easterners, and New Englanders, were concentrated within specific settlement belts. New Englanders focused on the Connecticut Western Reserve, while Southerners settled Ohio's Virginia Military District. Both areas were the geographical legacy of colonial days and their survival helped channel regional migrants into predesignated areas. West of Ohio, specific settlement districts were less important. As a result, settlers were not as confined and could seek out lands wherever they preferred. This led to considerable mixing of peoples and subsequent acculturation. The National Road, because of its route through the center of Indiana and into Illinois, was a major catalyst in bringing settlers from different source areas together. The result was that "the part of the Middle West that had the most heterogeneous origins lies where one would expect it—in the middle."[46]

## THE NATIONAL ROAD AND SOUTHERN MIGRATION

Cross-river migration was assured by the Northwest Ordinance. Seven years before the ordinance, population numbers in Virginia and in its western appendage of Kentucky were estimated to be "538,000 or over 200,000 more than in Pennsylvania, the next largest state." Trans-Appalachian migration into the Kentucky territory increased rapidly after 1775 when Daniel Boone blazed the Wilderness Road from Cumberland Gap and Pine Mountain Gap into the Bluegrass Basin. By 1779, Louisville, a major outpost on the Ohio River, had been platted at the Falls of the Ohio. The Treaty of Greenville in 1795 opened the greater part of the Ohio Country to settlement by the "new" Americans. Land cessions from Indian tribes, completed between 1803 and 1819, opened more land in Indiana, Illinois, and the far western parts of Kentucky.[47] Both Marietta and Cincinnati, sited on the river's north side, were founded in 1788, one year after passage of the Northwest Ordinance. The stage was set for migration into the country north of the Ohio River.

Although the Ohio River is commonly perceived as the westward extension of the Mason-Dixon Line, culturally it has not been the case. Southern settlement north of the river assured the spread of Southern traits as well.

To this day, "pone" remains a well-known substitute word for cornbread in southern Ohio, and the landscape across the southern parts of Ohio, Indiana, and Illinois contain many Southern settlement characteristics. Gregory Rose has argued that the National Road was an all-important "pull factor" for cross-river migration of Southern settlers.[48] Naturally, these migrants wanted to cross the hilly terrain next to the river in order to acquire better land farther north. In Indiana and Illinois the Road was close to the dividing line between the flat lands and the stream-dissected interfluves to the south.

One indication of the effect of Southern settlement in the counties near the National Road was the issue of slavery. Lincoln and Douglas crossed the Pike into southern Illinois to argue the case. Opinion varied, but there was no topic in south-central Illinois that "provoked more heat and less light than slavery, unless it was the road itself."[49] One can be certain that news of the controversy traveled rapidly through the small towns and inns on the National Road. There had been race riots in Cincinnati in the 1830s and '40s. Especially in Ohio, the National Road was an integral part of the Underground Railroad, a system of routes and settlements that offered refuge to escaped slaves.[50] In the final analysis, the Road helped spread abolitionist sentiment in direct support of the "free soil" mandate of the Northwest Ordinance of 1787.

### Diffusion of Southern Corn-Livestock Agriculture

The National Road, particularly through Ohio and into Indiana, became synonymous with the spread of Middle Atlantic migrants and their traditions. The Pennsylvania-Germans or "Dutch" were known as grain and livestock farmers and they helped to establish the middlewestern wheat belt as they settled in the fertile, glaciated plains alongside the Old Pike. The idea of and the motivation for wheat farming were strongly related to the thousands of migrants from Pennsylvania and Maryland who followed the lure of new and better land west on the Cumberland and National Roads.

As wheat farming shifted westward, into the drier parts of the interior plains, agriculture in Ohio and elsewhere in the Middle West began to adjust to new influences and specializations. These included the rotation-based grain, grass, and livestock farming among Pennsylvania-German settlers in southwestern Ohio, especially the Miami Valley, and agricultural practices peculiar to Southerners, particularly Virginians.[51] They cultivated corn that they fed to beef cattle and hogs in "dry" or feed lots.

　　HUBERT G. H. WILHELM

Because of the likely pull exerted by the National Road on Southern immigrants into the middlewestern states, an agriculture foreign to settlers from both the Middle Atlantic and New England was transferred northward and diffused along the Old Pike. The area important to the introduction and subsequent spread of this new kind of agriculture extended from the Pickaway Plains in Ross and Pickaway Counties, just south of Columbus in Ohio, north into Madison County. The latter borders Franklin County on the west and was bisected by the National Road. Here, in this three-county area of Ohio near the National Road, a type of livestock farming first developed on the South Branch of the Potomac River in western Virginia was transplanted and matured.[52] It was carried westward by Southern pioneers into Kentucky, and from there north into Ohio's Virginia Military District. In all likelihood, Ohio's Scioto and Miami Valleys are the core area for a much greater American agricultural region, the Corn Belt, a place where farmers believed that to make money raising corn it had to be fed to cattle or hogs. Marketing grain-fed stock was greatly aided by improvements in transportation, the rise of cities, and changes in the American diet—the love of ground beef or hamburger. Its roots, however, are in Middle Atlantic and Southern rural traditions.

Pickaway and Madison Counties in Ohio are part of a larger physiographic region known as Ohio's till plain. The terrain is the product of glacial deposition and ranges from nearly level to rolling. The glacial debris or till that covers this area is calcareous, incorporating minerals derived from the underlying limestone or gypsum bedrock.[53] The soils that developed on the till were especially fertile.

Natural prairies occurred as discontinuous grasslands—or barrens, as they were also called—on the till plain. Most, like those in Madison and Clark Counties, had excellent soils. Their greater significance during the initial settlement period was that they attracted cattle graziers from Kentucky, probably as early as the late 1790s. The combination of cattle-raising and eventual "improvements in communication, notably the National Road, made it possible for the Ohio graziers to maintain and expand sales of stock cattle and even of grass-fattened beeves across the mountains."[54]

Yet, more significant to the rise of the Southern corn-livestock complex than the graziers of Madison and Clark Counties were developments on the Scioto Valley's Pickaway Plains. Here, in Ross and neighboring Pickaway Counties, Ohio's best-known dynasty of cattle barons, the Renicks, established cattle-producing methods brought into the area from the Potomac country. Brothers Felix and George Renick were both born on the South Branch of the Potomac in what is now Hardy County, West Virginia. Felix moved to the Ohio Country in 1801 after hearing glowing accounts about superb land in the Scioto Valley. George followed a year later and both became residents and large landowners in Ross County.[55]

The Renicks introduced the practice of feedlot fattening of beef cattle from the Southern Branch of the Potomac into Ohio where it became known as the Scioto Valley System.[56] The system was based on the availability of stock cattle and corn. George Renick proved the success of the system when he drove a herd of cattle to Baltimore in 1805 and sold them for a fine profit. From that date, this new agricultural enterprise began to spread rapidly and the National Road was part of that experience. The Renicks and others ranged through central and southern Ohio and surrounding states to purchase stock cattle. Most cattle in the Scioto Valley feedlots were "imported directly from Indiana, Illinois, and Missouri" and were driven eastward on the Old Pike and other roads.[57]

By the 1830s, the Renicks had begun to import breeding stock from Europe to upgrade the quality of local beef cattle. The first shipment of English Shorthorns arrived in Ross County in 1834. Some of these cattle were driven overland to the Scioto Valley, in all likelihood on the National Road. In 1836, farmers came together to bid on the new cattle and the Renicks' Shorthorns were sold to "cattlemen from Ross, Pickaway, Highland, Fayette, Madison, Pike, and Scioto counties."[58] It was hardly a coincidence that the spread of a new type of agriculture should occur after the completion of the National Road in Ohio and Indiana. The Road was at once the purveyor of stock cattle to feedlots in Ohio and elsewhere, of fattened beef driven to eastern markets, and of news about this new kind of farming.

### The Spread of Southern Building Practices

The preliminary construction tasks required to build the National Road through Indiana included "cutting timber, grubbing stumps, and digging ditches, . . . and [the task was] completed in 1834." By 1839, the Road's unfinished section from the Indiana state line to Vandalia opened for traffic.[59] These dates coincide with a great land boom in the Middle West. "The all-time record year for land sales was 1836; [when] more than twenty million acres, a chunk of real estate larger than the entire state of South Carolina,

HUBERT  G.  H.  WILHELM

were sold."[60] Intense land-office activity occurred in the Black Belt of Alabama and Mississippi (an area of black, prairie-like soils), southern Michigan, central Indiana, southern and central Illinois, and northern Missouri.

This was an era of massive settlement convergence in the Central Plains along the country's north-south and east-west axes. American migrants and European immigrants alike followed river and overland routes into the heartland, through thinning forests, ever-larger expanses of tall grasses, and deep, black, prairie soils. St. Louis and Chicago were dynamic urban outposts on the western frontier. By the late 1830s, two inventions, steel plows (i.e., John Deere and Oliver) and balloon framing, helped settlers successfully adapt to an increasingly treeless habitat and heavy prairie soils. Similarly, the shortage of wood for fencing, a ubiquitous problem in middlewestern settlement, was ameliorated somewhat by the introduction of the osage orange (*Maclura pomifera*) as a hedge plant from Texas in the 1840s.[61] In 1832, Congress set a minimum price of $1.25 per acre of federal land and a minimum purchase of 40 acres, for a "threshold price" of $50.[62] Small homesteaders from the South benefited especially from this policy.

As the physical and symbolic trans-Appalachian link, the National Road and its tributary system of state roads functioned as foci for settlement and the distribution of ideas and things. The peddler of osage orange seeds and the wagoner hauling milled timbers for a house or barn used the routes to deliver their products and spread innovations. Eventually, the railroads would speed this process and improve connectivity. But it all began with the Old Pike, whose destination in Vandalia in south-central Illinois placed the Road's final reach effectively within an area of Southern settlement.

### The Southern Town, House, and Barn

Many towns laid out by Southerners are different in form from the linear town that spread along the Road from the East. Southerners, both literally and symbolically, placed the courthouse on a central square surrounded by a regular grid of city streets and blocks. This town layout, representing a modification of the Philadelphia plan, has been identified as the Shelbyville plan because of the frequency of towns with central, block-type squares in southern Middle Tennessee, including the town of Shelbyville.[63] This plan diffused northward and became particularly common in southern and central Indiana and Illinois towns where Southerners settled. Both Danville and Greenfield, the county seats respectively of Hendricks and Hancock Counties in Indiana, are on the National Road. Both have block-type, central squares occupied by the courthouses.

Although courthouse styles are elaborate, often with Greek Revival or Italianate influences, many early middlewestern courthouses were simple cubic or four-square buildings with a pyramidal roof topped by a turret. The distribution of these courthouses shows a close relationship with counties either on or near the National Road, particularly in Ohio, but also in Indiana and Illinois.[64] The earliest state houses of Ohio, Indiana, and Illinois were all the four-square type. Another case of diffusion along the Old Road? Perhaps.

Southern building traditions included a greater variety of construction methods and house and barn types than was true for the migrants from the East. This variety resulted from a greater social and economic stratification in the South, and was conditioned by making a living in forested areas. For example, it was primarily the Southern settler who brought log building techniques and types of log structures north of the Ohio River. Many Americans are familiar with the log homes of the Lincoln family in Kentucky, Indiana, and, finally, in Illinois. One typical house form in southern Ohio, Indiana, and Illinois, a single-story, two-room or double-pen house, may have had its origin in the log architecture of the Upland South. This house form, and a one-story, pyramidal-roof type, represent part of the Southern settlement imprint that extends northward toward the National Road.

Southern settlers did share with their Eastern compatriots a common preference for the I-house. Convergence of Eastern and Southern settlers along the National Road, in all likelihood, gave additional support to the popularity of a house type already in use among the area's early residents.[65]

The Virginia or Southern I-house differs little from those carried westward from Pennsylvania, two rooms long, one room deep and two stories high. One can identify some regional contrasts. The Southern type may include a pediment-shaped dormer or full two-story portico. The latter protects two central doors, including one on the second story. Rarely will the Southern I-house have chimneys attached to the house's outside gable ends.

While I-houses with porticoes are common in southern Ohio, they are less frequent in southern Indiana and Illinois. The I-house with full portico flourished in central Kentucky between 1840 and 1890, and has been associated with the slave-holding planter culture of the region.[66] Large landowners from there carried it into Ohio's Virginia Military District. Conversely, settlement in southern Indiana and Illinois that did not offer similar, exclusive land options was much more democratic, and by that benefited the small homesteader.

The National Road, because it attracted migrants from different regions and diverse backgrounds, became the proving ground for all sorts of structures: houses, sheds, barns, fences, churches, bridges, and more.[67] The first *permanent* settlers to occupy an area usually set the tone for the built landscape. Their influence was powerful and has been called the "doctrine of first, effective settlement."[68] Permanent settlers' preferences explain why so much of the National Road landscape in Ohio is of Pennsylvania origin. Further west, Southerners used the Road as much as peoples from other regions, and their settlement forms, including the Southern or Virginia I-house and the Southern barn, are part of that landscape.

In central and western Ohio, the Pennsylvania-German barn is one of the best indicators of the spread of Middle Atlantic or Eastern traditions westward on the National Road. Westward the Dutch barn begins to diminish in numbers and shares the agricultural countryside with other types, especially modified New England or three-bay barns, and a barn whose origin may be in the South. The latter type, mentioned above as a "three portal" barn, is widespread throughout southern Ohio, Indiana, and Illinois and, as noted, may have a connection with wagoners' barns built in road towns.

Southern log-building traditions produced a variety of crib barns, including the "transverse crib barn."[69] When built in frame, this barn has a series of corncribs or boxstalls next to a drive or alley. A large gabled roof covers the cribs and stalls and the roof ridge is parallel with the drive or ground-level alley. There is usually a hay door to the sizable loft above the barn's gable-end entrance. The hay door or opening is often protected by a projecting hay hood or hay bonnet.[70] With the addition of side sheds and separate gable-side entrances, the barn assumes the form inherent in the term "three portal" barn. In contrast to the Dutch barn, it is never banked.

The connection between log and frame transverse barns remains unclear. The distribution of these barns appears to suggest a close relationship with Southern-type corn and livestock agriculture. It was a structure ideally suited to the type of agriculture that spread westward from the Scioto Valley of Ohio. A study of traditional barn types in two Ross County, Ohio, townships—one on the west side of the Scioto River in the Virginia settlement area, the other on the east side of the river where Pennsylvanians were dominant—demonstrated an overwhelming presence of regional types. To the east, Dutch banked barns predominated, while farms to the west featured "transverse frame" and "three portal" barns.[71]

Although these traditional building forms were eventually subdued by the universal acceptance of standardized, popular structures, sufficient numbers remain to allow generalization about original source areas of migration, diffusion, settlement convergence, and acculturation. These processes were greatly furthered by the presence of the country's principal interior road that provided an avenue for the spread of peoples, ideas, and products. Its location, through the middle of the new region, the Middle West, was most fortunate. This was the area where the dynamics of human presence and contact would create a national *heartland*.

## CONCLUSION

In 1950, this writer was in a group of some eighty German teenagers who had been invited to come to America for one year. Most of the young people were of a rural-farm background and were looking forward to spending the next twelve months with American farm families. Because the majority were to live in the Middle West, a three-bus caravan proceeded from dockside in New York into America's great interior. Somewhere in Pennsylvania the buses parted and headed toward their separate destinations. Ours, the Illinois bus, followed US 40 through Columbus and Indianapolis. What an experience! As I look back over forty-plus years, my memories are clouded, but the impressions that I shall never forget center on the land's vastness, its flatness, the corn- and wheatfields, little woodland, few towns, and the road's straightness. US 40, consisting mostly of four lanes, was similar to the Autobahn, but I will never forget how straight it was. Nor shall I forget the motels, the gas stations, and the colorful advertisements alongside the highway. Little did I realize then how important Route 40 was to the historical and geographical development of America's interior and what kind of earlier highway and traffic had preceded it. Nor had my eyes been trained to recognize the profusion of different settlement forms, the houses, churches, barns, cribs, and fences. That would come later. Back then, it all merged into a picture of a vast expanse of flat land crossed by a ribbon of straight road.

The automobile resurrected the Old Pike to its earlier significance. Archer Hulbert, writing in 1901, anticipated the Road's revival when he commented,

The old National Road will become, perhaps, the foremost of the great roadways of America. The bed is capable of being made substantial at a comparatively small cost, as the grading is quite perfect. Its course measures the shortest possible route practicable for a roadway from tide-water to the Mississippi River. As a trunk line its location cannot be surpassed.[72]

How true these words ring as I recall my first trip into the American land-scape.

Of course, it had been the "gangplank" for a young country, striving to assert its "God-given" right of western conquest. For almost a half century, the National Road was the single most important highway between the eastern seaboard and Illinois. This period coincided with the greatest set-tlement advance into the Middle West. Eastern settlers, especially the Penn-sylvania migrants in their Conestoga wagons, traveled across the rough Old Pike's macadam surface toward the glory lands of Ohio, Indiana, and Illi-nois. Similarly, Southerners were pulled northward toward the Road, and of course there were throngs of European immigrants. They all brought their traditional preferences or methods for land settlement, ideas about how to lay out towns and farms, build houses, barns, and fences.

Even such common practices as what side of the road to use were in-fluenced by the Old Pike. Conestoga-wagon drivers typically rode or walked on the left side of the six-horse team and wagon to have a clear view of the road ahead. In the East, the English tradition of driving on the left side had been popular for 200 years, but in 1813 New Jersey became the first state to make traffic holding to the right a law.[73] The teamsters, with their sixty-foot-long assembly of horse team and wagon, reinforced the custom.

The Road assured contact between people. If the inns, taverns, and wag-oners' houses did not provide sufficient social life, then roadshows with their singers, midgets, and Indians helped to break down frontier isolation. Conversely, the Road generated its own delinquent bands of highway-men.[74] Stagecoach travelers along some eastern stretches were advised to expect trouble and to carry pistols. Worse, during the cholera outbreaks of the first half of the nineteenth century, the Pike became a highway of death and "not a single community on the National Road, from Cumberland to Columbus, escaped, despite most valiant efforts to stem the disease."[75]

The National Road was much more than a mere transportation route or overland link between East and West. It was America's highway of the spread of ideas that contributed to a new geographical reality—the Middle West, a region where peoples and traditions came together to lay the foundation for the country's cultural core, the American heartland. Speaking for the Road, a poet summarizes the process:

> And I can tell how all this came to be,
> how all these paths were joined in me.
> From Cumberland to Wheeling first I trailed,
> across the Appalachian Mountains sailed,
> against the Allegheny uplands fought,
> into the valley travelers brought,
> turned in sweeping spirals west,
> joining paths that were thought best,
> steadily through the valleys swept,
> where silence and a wildness slept.[76]

# The US 40 Roadside

KARL RAITZ

*It would be interesting to find out why Americans do so much motoring. It can't be the love of speed, the joy of feeling the air rush by one's face. . . . It can't be the love of beautiful scenery, of getting close to nature. Every few hundred yards there is a petrol-filling station, half a dozen colored pumps before it. In connection with the stations and between them are huts carrying the sign "Hot Dogs." What is there in this motor mania?*

MARION BALDERSTON
*American Motor Mania* (1928)

THE INTERNAL COMBUSTION ENGINE IS THE FIRST OF A HOST OF CONtingent technical and social ideas that, taken together, comprise a cascade of revolutionary inventions, the product of which was no less than a radical transformation of American society. The engine's direct application to the truck and automobile stimulated widespread alterations along the old National Road corridor and produced a new composite landscape: the US 40 roadside. And although federal road construction standards would shape the Road itself, the landscape that grew up beside it was initially the product of local people, individuals guided by nothing more formal than what their imaginations or nearby examples might suggest. The US 40 roadside, then, begins as a largely vernacular landscape that is gradually formalized and structured by institutional additions—the general store with a gas pump is replaced by a Standard Oil station. As a motorized roadway, US 40 provided the context for such cultural change along its length with spectacular effect.

## PRECURSORS

During the four decades preceding World War I, the railroad dominated traffic along the National Road corridor. The long-haul freight wagons that had carried manufactured goods from the East into the Middle West had been replaced by the boxcar. Wagon freight warehouses were torn down, replaced by freight depots along rail sidings—like the one that still stands on the south end of Main Street in Washington, Pennsylvania. By 1915, the railroad was the primary supplier of both consumer goods to city and small-town merchants and building materials to the construction trades. The Road had been designated the National Trails Highway two years earlier but was no longer a key arterial of long-distance freight commerce or personal travel. The Federal Aid Road Act was still one year away and while the old Road was graded and stone-surfaced for much of its length, the countryside through which it passed was poorly served by rutted dirt tracks that rain turned into mud wallows. Ford's first Model-T debuted in 1908 and incorporated tall wheel rims that gave the frame sufficient clearance to negotiate abysmal country roads.

Travel and freight movement were sharply differentiated into two categories. One was the national system of high speed, high volume, and relatively efficient railroads, the other a slowly emerging network of local, poor quality roads that served wagons and carriages, themselves the products of technologies now centuries old. The limitations on movement imposed on farmers and small-town residents by poor roads produced a locally scaled culture and economy. Although one could shop Main Street stores in county seats along the road and find goods supplied by the railroad system, the produce farmers could market was restricted to what horses and wagons could haul over country roads to railroad sidings in town. And social networks were largely confined to neighborhood or church groups, with occasional visits to distant city relatives by train or interurban. Within cities served by the National Road, the streetcar moved people about much more readily.

This discontinuity in ease and cost of movement between national and regional rail networks and urban transit on the one hand, and the inconvenience of travel to road-bound small towns and farms on the other, was gradually remedied by adopting the truck and automobile and by extend-

ing hard-surfaced roads into the trunk highway's rural hinterland. The existing discontinuity between the rural/small-town locales and the city fostered political redress through a farm-to-market road improvement program in 1933, and a host of differences in how the roadside landscape would be put together, who used its different specialized niches, and who would be affected by that use.[1] For example, as road engineering improved and traffic increased, property values in towns and cities along the highway rapidly escalated as business people sought sites with direct access to drive-by traffic. Although roadside businesses enjoyed increasing sales advantage over the traditional Main Street merchants, the cost was increased traffic congestion. Many farmers, on the other hand, were indifferent to road-frontage strip development and willingly subdivided and sold highway-fronting farm fields as piano-keyed lots, allowing highway departments and drivers to worry about the ensuing congestion.

**The National Road east of Zanesville**

In the 1920s, before the National Road was paved with concrete, the surface was passable only in dry weather and even then monumental ruts made for wary travelers.

The 1916 Federal Aid Road Act provided monetary support toward construction of a hard-surfaced cross-country road network—"The Hard Road," as it became known. The act would provide national-scale access to local road-oriented places although actual construction would not be a straightforward task. As L. W. Page, Bureau of Public Roads director, wrote in his 1918 report to the secretary of agriculture, government-backed road and highway construction was controlled by an interlocking web of federal offices.[2] The Department of Agriculture controlled construction appropriations for the Office of Public Roads and Rural Engineering, for example, and the Fuel Administration held access to bituminous materials such as oil and asphalt. While the U.S. Highways Council, formed in 1918, brought some coordination and regulation to these conflicting interests, road improvement would not become either methodically linear along a given route or systematic in adding connections to regional networks. Priority for upgrading the old National Road that linked Marshall, Illinois, and St. Louis in 1922, for example, was no greater than for hundreds of other projects initiated that year.[3] And neither federal aid nor administrative bureaucracy would bring continuity to construction practices along the road. While federal road-construction specifications—width, grade, and general alignment—might be generally adhered to, local variation yielded highways that were as much the product of workmen's geomancy as engineer's geome-

**Kirkersville, Ohio, milestone**

The National Road was formally marked across Maryland and Pennsylvania with cast-iron mileposts and across much of Ohio with sandstone markers. This one stood at 190 Main Street in Kirkersville, Ohio.

KARL RAITZ

try. In Indiana, farmers worked out their taxes by hauling gravel on their roads but no regulations specified how or where to spread the material and so it was commonly dumped in piles, its spreading along the surface left to passing traffic.[4] Furthermore, states and localities employed their own methods of highway route markings and numbering designations, making long-distance travel a navigational challenge. Therefore, a tension remained between national road construction standards and local idiosyncrasy in applying those standards, not only along the National Road corridor, but across the entire country. Federal-level standardization would not easily overcome local vernacular habits or political and social institutions.

The upshot of these confounding interests was that the American road network developed erratically. If one had wished to travel by automobile from Pittsburgh to Chicago in 1923, the most direct route would have been to follow the Lincoln Highway by way of Canton, Lima, and Fort Wayne. But, because long sections of this road were in wretched condition, the favored route was to drive a short distance south from Pittsburgh, join the National Road at Washington, and then follow it to Marshall, Illinois, where a reliable link north to Chicago could be made.[5] But even along the National Road, the central Ohio section from the little village of Brandt, west of Springfield, to the Indiana state line was in such poor condition until 1926 that traffic diverted south into Dayton and then followed a road west to Eaton before rejoining the old highway east of Richmond. Nevertheless, the National Road corridor remained the route of choice for midcontinent travel.[6]

As the economic boom of the 1920s progressed, traffic and the demand for high-quality roads increased dramatically. In 1925, Congress adopted a national gasoline tax to help pay for new highway construction, and within a year or two, state governments along the National Road corridor had come to the conclusion that highway building and maintenance had become an "industry of the first rank."[7]

The Joint Board on Interstate Highways established highway sign standards in 1925. Now familiar danger and caution signs were to be black letters on a yellow background and displayed in four different shapes. Direction and route signs were black letters on a white background. Most distinctive of this second group was the sixteen-inch-high shield route marker. Its top third declared the state's name, while the letters US and large bold highway numerals filled the white space inside the shield. The colored strips that highway

**Brick-surfaced US 40 east of Marshall, Illinois**

The old concrete ribbon road was widened by concrete aprons on each side, now linear bare strips, and the surface was bricked over. Two bricklayers could cover the road's eighteen-foot width with special high-density seven-pound bricks along 800 linear feet in a ten-hour day in the early 1930s.

boosters painted on telephone poles to mark routes or hand-painted signs announcing a town's name would remain as examples of waning local idiosyncrasy as national values and standards began to assert themselves.[8]

In November 1926, the year that nationwide automobile registrations exceeded 20 million for the first time, the American Association of State Highway Officials adopted a system of uniform route number designations for the nation's roads, and the National Road became US 40. Within two years, amendments to federal-aid highway law allowed states to expend federal monies to erect standardized highway number markers and direction and danger signs.[9] Official route designations and continued federal aid for new construction and improvements encouraged increased highway usage. In eastern Ohio, for example, over 1,700 cars and trucks were passing over US 40 each day by the late 1920s.[10]

General traffic counts are misleading because during the earliest years of motorized travel highway use was marked by daily and monthly variation. Pennsylvania and Ohio passenger-car traffic in 1924, for example, reached a maximum in August, spurred by warm temperatures in a time when open touring cars encouraged a weather eye. Lowest traffic flows occurred in January. The Sunday driver was also a creature of the early automobile. Sunday's highway traffic might be as much as 85 percent greater than the

KARL RAITZ

US 40 crossing Cono-
cocheague River west of
Hagerstown, Maryland,
1933

By the 1930s, much of US
40 had been resurfaced
with brick or asphalt and
was an all-weather driving
surface. Some businesses
that had served carriage- or
coach-borne passengers
continued in business to
serve the auto trade.

weekly average. Truck traffic peaked in October, although seasonal flows in the counties along the National Road corridor were much more consistent than that of automobiles.[11] But the increased traffic had costs, one of them being damage to the new concrete ribbon that had been laid atop many sections of the Road during the 1920s. Much of the concrete was thin, nine inches or less, and was simply poured between edge forms with little reinforcing steel bar and few if any expansion joints. Expansion and contraction with changing temperatures cracked the solid ribbon and heavy traffic pounded the fractured road surface into large shards. In the early 1930s, many Road sections were widened with twenty-four-inch concrete aprons on each side and covered with heavy-duty 4 × 8½–inch brick, which provided a wider, resilient surface.

An auto- and truck-oriented roadside landscape began to emerge by the mid-1920s, built atop and amid relict vernacular artifacts from the earlier wagon-road era. The new concrete, or brick, or asphalt road, now with curves straightened and grades flattened, and trussed iron and steel structures replacing wooden covered bridges, inspired travelers to brave longer distances. And along the Old National Road's east-to-west length they would find accommodations and other travelers' services, even in small towns, at least adequate to their needs.

The physical layouts of business sections and residential areas in America's eastern cities, no less the structures built along the National Road, were strongly influenced by contemporary transportation technologies. Before the automobile, the omnibus and the trolley linked high-density residential neighborhoods with high-density central business districts. In Indianapolis, the National Road followed Washington Street and where it passed the city center near the Soldiers and Sailors Monument Circle fifty streetcar lines converged.

Business buildings along nineteenth-century Main Streets fronted the sidewalk and gave no ground to horse-drawn carriage or wagon. Whether in the linear road–oriented string villages in eastern Ohio or along the broader streets of western Indiana and Illinois towns, wagoners drew up at street's edge or parked in wagon lots on a side street. And the street contained many fewer wagons than the stores had customers because hitching a team to a wagon or carriage for a six-block ride to Main Street was sufficiently time-consuming and inconvenient that one would do it only once a week or so. Mostly people walked to downtown stores and carried their purchases back home or had merchants pack them on the delivery wagon.[12]

But the freedom and flexibility provided by the automobile would bury such commonsense beneath a layer of hedonistic self-indulgence that would only get deeper with time. Part of the auto's attraction was ease of movement. "A landscape in movement is in a sense [one's] own creation, . . ." it was said, "and [people] become wholly absorbed in changing its features by a process of rapid motion."[13] The automobile soon became the magic coach to everywhere, and critics compared the freedom it offered to an opiate.[14] Only the limitations imposed by gas and tire rationing during World War II would force people back into the streetcar for a brief time.

Ten years after the debut of Ford's Model-T, cars were not only shouldering carriages and wagons off Main Street, they were beginning to choke the central city during workday hours, and by the mid-1920s downtown congestion was held to be the single greatest problem in America's cities. Some congestion could be attributed to people who had in the past traveled by train but found that the automobile offered much greater scheduling flexibility. Before the automobile, for example, salespeople would arrive on the train, spend a few hours in town taking orders from Main Street merchants, road contractors, or farm supply stores, then catch a later train to the next town. In the early 1920s, salespeople found that a car would allow them to triple the calls made each day, reach small villages without hard-surface roads, and not be confined in a one-train-a-day town longer than necessary.

Additional congestion was caused by shoppers who wished to park at the department store's front door, as did the clerks who worked in the building. But merchants quickly realized that a street lined with parked cars only gave the appearance of business activity while the stores remained empty for the most part. Turn-of-the-century street use by wagons and carriages had been largely unregulated. City residents and merchants struggled to contain the automobile, resulting in increasing management and centralized political control of street space.

If one source of street congestion was a lack of off-street parking for workers and store patrons, a second was that the main business and shopping streets usually also carried cross-town or through traffic.[15] The oldest towns had narrow streets that were further restricted by angle parking, forcing some cities to insist upon parallel parking in the central city. A third source stemmed from the nature of the businesses along a downtown or gateway street—the gateway being the few blocks of trunk highway that pass through a town's oldest residential district next to the central business area, generally a place of mixed residential and business use. Old blacksmith shops might use the street's edge to park wagons or cars undergoing repair. Carriage dealers often evolved into automobile dealers who used the street to store newly arrived models for display and sale. Early garages sold gasoline from drums, and when the gas pump became available, dealers installed them at curbside, forcing cars to park in the street in order to have their tanks filled. Not until the first small shopping plazas were planned and built in the 1930s would buildings be systematically set back to allow space for off-street automobile parking.

*"Work while you work, play while you play"—the*

# OLDSMOBILE

is your best help in both. To the business man it has become a necessity—it doubles the value of time. To the pleasure seeker it has become indispensable—it doubles the joys of existence.

Our cars possess efficiency without complication. Are the most thoroughly tested cars on the market—are held to higher standards of quality. This explains why they were the only light cars awarded a Gold Medal at the St. Louis Exposition.

Standard Runabout, 7 h. p., $650   Light Tonneau Car, 10 h. p., $ 950
Touring Runabout, 7 h. p., $750   Touring Car, 20 h. p. (2 cyl.) $1400

All prices f. o. b. factory. Write us for detailed specifications and information. Send 10c for *six months' trial* subscription to Motor Talk, a monthly magazine devoted to automobile interests. Address Dept. F

## Olds Motor Works, Detroit, U. S. A.
*Member of Association of Licensed Automobile Manufacturers.*

Drawing Copyrighted 1905.
Brownell & Humphrey, Detroit.

**Oldsmobile advertisement, 1905**

This advertisement declares the 1905 Runabout a business and recreational necessity, pointing out its role in increasing efficiency in both theaters of activity.

The larger the city, the worse the congestion, for high land values in the central city prompted developers to build multistory buildings, perhaps even an early skyscraper, which itself might contain a worker population equivalent to a small town. In 1909, for example, the seventeen-story Merchants National Bank building at Washington (US 40) and Meridian Streets opened in Indianapolis, and in 1927 the forty-seven-story American Insurance Union Citadel opened at Broad (US 40) and Front Streets in Columbus. But resolving the responsibility for the resulting traffic congestion was not a straightforward task. Some architects argued that building size was not related to street traffic congestion, but that the skyscraper turned horizontal movement into vertical movement that reduced foot-traffic density at street level.[16] Others, including Thomas Edison, argued that pedestrian foot traffic near large building clusters would be so great that it would block streets and sidewalks and ultimately prove very costly in time lost.[17]

Clearly, curbside street parking could not begin to accommodate all those wishing to work or shop in the business district, and so other strategies were required. In 1920, Baltimore condemned a rundown residential section and converted the open lots to parking.[18] New office buildings began to incorporate parking basements. The multistory enclosed parking garage was invented, which provided some relief, and some US 40 cities built municipal garages. But the public associated these early parking garages with repair garages and their stink of oil, gas, and exhaust, and their undesirable hangers-on.[19] More pragmatically, concrete and steel parking ramps were expensive to build—$1,000 per car or more in the 1920s—and during the Depression 90 percent of ramp garages defaulted on their bonds. Thus, under the impetus of depression economics, cities often chose slum clearance as a strategy to provide cleared land leading to the predominance of the open, ground-level parking lot.[20]

By the mid-1920s, city retail businesses, especially grocery and drug stores, were beginning to decentralize into what were then called "subcenters." Merchants quickly recognized that these sites were gaining new business at the expense of traditional downtown stores. Subcenters were the first shopping plazas. They were usually placed at the intersection of through streets and designed to provide parking space in front of each store. Baltimore's west-side Edmonson Village Shopping Center along US 40 is a later example. "They go where they can park," downtown merchants complained.[21] For those downtown, the shopping decentralization process was an exercise in diverting trade. They may not have realized it at the time, but the automobile was also encouraging a parallel chain of trade diversion to operate at the bottom of the urban hierarchy. Rural folk could now drive into town for necessities in less time than it had taken to hitch a team to a wagon or carriage and head for the crossroads country store a few miles away. In turn, residents of small US 40 villages in eastern Indiana, like Dunreith and Ogden, could now drive the twenty miles into Greenfield in a few minutes and have a much broader range of stores in which to shop. Greenfield residents, on the other hand, could drive a similar distance into Indianapolis and shop at the Normandy-styled Irvington strip shopping center on East Washington Street, built before 1920 and one of the city's first such store clusters. Thus circumscribed, the country store's business withered and the owner soon locked the door and moved away. As roads improved, small-town merchants found themselves in the same predicament.

The *New Republic* declared in 1936 that the solution to Main Street's intolerable traffic congestion was at hand: the parking meter. Street space control tightened perceptibly as pavement was marked into twenty-foot parking spaces and a coin-operated meter installed to guard each one. The all-day parking hog was eliminated and merchants believed that traffic congestion would soon lessen and their stores would brim with customers.[22] When meters were successful in one town, merchants in nearby towns responded to the demonstration effect by demanding them, convinced that out-of-town shoppers were more attracted by the possibility of finding a parking place than offended by having to pay for the privilege.[23] But the meter added no additional parking area and so its salutary effect was largely limited to towns and small cities. And as businesses began relocating to a town's edge strip, the symbol declaring that the remaining shopping district merchants recognized their impending discomfort was a line of decapitated parking meters down both sides of Main Street.

## ROADSIDES

Business people quickly recognized that drivers were reluctant to contend with central city congestion and to explore an unknown town for meals or fuel; they preferred to patronize businesses with the foresight to build along the road at town's edge or at a highway crossroads. Financial success demonstrated the wisdom of roadside business locations and the highway rapidly became an accretion of small businesses in what town planners called "ribbon development." In 1934, *Fortune* magazine editors would term this new highway business strip the "Great American Roadside," which was "the most hugely extensive market the human race has ever set up to tease and tempt and take money from the human race."[24]

As American travelers adopted the auto and the highway they also began to extract themselves from the central city. Drivers would prefer to eat, sleep, and refuel along the roadside that consequently became a new kind of town. So successful were the merchants who catered to this clientele that Main Streets began to hemorrhage business as towns tried to turn themselves into roadsides. By 1949, one-seventh of U.S. businesses derived their sales from the highway and all U.S. business sold to that seventh.[25] Thus, the roadside strip began as the product of local people making independent decisions about highway access and business. Franchise chains with centrally designed structures and planned site development would not be sufficiently widespread to influence strongly the form the roadside would take until after World War II.

### Gas Stations

Many businesses are direct adaptations to the newly developing roadside, and the gasoline station is one of the most prominent. The American oil industry was born when the internal combustion engine was successfully mounted on wheels. Before national franchises, advertising, and brand loyalty, gas was sold at livery stables, auto dealers, garages, hardware and general stores. In towns where businesses had clustered around the courthouse square or central intersection for a century or more, successful entrepreneurs built new gas stations at what at the time must have seemed an odd location, the edge of town. This site had the happy advantage of providing the first assurance to traveling motorists that they could purchase fuel while avoiding the confusion and congestion of the town's central *terra incognita*. The need to stop frequently for fuel and crankcase oil, or to seek repair of seemingly perpetual tire blowouts, made the gas station with a "flats fixed" sign a beacon for the cross-country traveler. But the station also offered other services; geography lessons to the lost or bewildered, cultural information, or culinary, ethnographic, or meteorological advice. Stations often supported a coterie of local gossips and so the information exchange between local resident and travelers from every state and social strata was reminiscent of the democratic discussions in a nineteenth-century roadside inn.[26]

"The rise of the filling station is coincident with the conquest of America by Americans," observed one 1920s commentator.[27] By 1932, the nation sported over 250,000 filling stations. US 40 was lined with them. Besides independent dealers, one could purchase from regional franchisers: American Oil and Standard Oil of New Jersey in Maryland and Pennsylvania; Socony-Vacuum in Pennsylvania, West Virginia, and part of Ohio; Standard Oil of Ohio and the Ohio Oil Company in Ohio; Standard Oil of Indiana and Lubrite in Indiana and Illinois; and Sinclair and Shell along the entire route.[28]

But while company auditors complained that to turn a decent profit a station required at least 400 steady automobile-driving customers, only West Virginia along the US 40 corridor could approach 300. Indiana and Illinois stations struggled with fewer than 200 customers on average. The problem was twofold; population density declined to the west, and tinkering with automobiles was an increasingly popular male pastime—even obsession. How better to cultivate an obsession than to build one's own service station? The result was a station at most crossroads settlements. And a county-seat town of 1,500 people might have four or five clustered together on each end of Main Street. Competing managers tried to attract customers with gas wars and huge signs advertising prices. Often the station itself was made into a sign, all the better to create an identity that would set one's business out from the crowd and build a dependable clientele. Since gas stations were a new contrivance, entrepreneurs lacked a model to follow. Owners adopted old buildings or built what they could afford. The result was a roadside lined with stations characterized as "strange architecture," where entrepreneurs capitalized on "blatancy of color and design" to produce monuments to "bad taste."[29]

The earliest gas stations were hardly stations at all, but simply pumps and tanks placed at the front of a general store or auto repair shop, usually near the center of town. Free-standing sheds housing oils, grease, and equipment accompanied some pumps.[30] After 1920, oil companies began building stations on corner residential lots along the highway, and in a conscious attempt to make the stations blend with their neighborhoods designed them to resemble small houses. Some house-type stations added canopies that extended the roof over a driveway to two pumps perched on a concrete island about twelve feet from the station's front door. An exceptional example of the house-type station still stands at the corner of US 40 and State 48 in Englewood, Ohio, west of Dayton. Others can be found in Springfield, Ohio, and Richmond, Indiana. Stations also stocked convenience food and household items—candy, tobacco, canned goods, cold cream, soap, gloves, first-aid kits—to supplement gas sales income. A station near Wheeling on US 40 sold booklets about coal mining to travelers. Ironically, the gas station came to resemble the old country general store that the auto had put out of business.[31]

By the mid-1920s, the new house design station had acquired an attached service bay with an in-ground grease pit that allowed a mechanic easy access to the oil drain plugs on a car's engine, transmission, and differential. Such service built business and customer loyalty, while the bay made the station wider, requiring a larger lot.[32]

During the 1930s, the house motif was discontinued in favor of a simple, flat-roofed oblong box built of a prefabricated steel framework and covered with porcelain enamel metal panels or stucco or brick. The appearance was not only simple, clean, and neat, but "modern" and therefore sure to benefit by comparison with the new International-style architecture then beginning to appear. The box often included large plate-glass windows with displays intended to encourage motorists to purchase tires, batteries, and accessories. Franchise filling-station design was standardized through trademark colors and signs placed atop streetside posts as companies sought to encourage brand identification by making the station into a symbol, the meaning of which was fostered by increasing budgets for national advertising that portrayed gasolines as capable of adding power and reliability to auto engines.

After World War II, the box remained popular with independent gasoline retailers who favored small structures, some with extended canopy roofs, built of concrete block and faced with vinyl or plexiglas. These stations usually sold only petroleum products and so needed no service bay with grease pit or lift. Major gasoline companies again attempted to domesticate their station's exteriors. Some firms cultivated a Colonial look with subdued Greek Revival pediment roof lines; others looked to Las Vegas for styling ideas and created station fronts that resembled a 1960s motel or ranch house with rakish roof lines and even fake stone facade coverings.

Gas stations in a full range of ages and incarnations align US 40. Few remain the "bright siphons gleaming in the sunshine, . . . symbol[s] of speed, of regularity, of deep desire for adventure . . . , of the looseness of our attachment to the soil," as Charles Mertz saw them in 1925.[33] The design and placement of those that have failed provide a landscape Rosetta stone for

**Marathon gas station in Brazil, Indiana**

The flat-roofed, oblong box form gas station became popular with several gasoline companies. The Ohio Oil Company built many Marathon stations in the 1950s or early 1960s following 1930s International-style architectural percepts. White porcelain enamel panels and steel window and door frames create a clean, streamlined image.

interpreting how the roadside economy and culture evolved. Some stations failed because they were no doubt poorly located. Others were operated by independent retailers who were squeezed out when new franchise stations came to town. Small-town stations were often stranded when the highway was realigned to bypass the business district in the 1940s. And many US 40 stations foundered when Interstate 70 opened. Business failure meant that gasoline sales stopped. Nevertheless, the structure usually stood, sometimes abandoned but more often converted into another business, or even a residence. In Bridgeport, Ohio, a 1920s brick box-and-canopy station is now a used car lot—a very common conversion. An old station may have a grease rack or at least a service bay for minor repairs and washing, simplifying the change. The Bridgeport station conversion illustrates an important convention that operates all along US 40: the preferred sales location for any business continues to be the high-traffic route. When a bypass—be it simply the rerouting of the highway around a town or the construction of an entirely new routeway—siphons traffic from the old route, business sales usually fall. Relocation to the new route may follow. Considering that such decisions are unilateral and based upon eclectic influences, the result is unexpectedly uniform along the road's length. For example, few automobile dealerships now sell new cars on US 40. In Columbus, and some small or medium-sized cities like Cambridge, Ohio, or Uniontown, Pennsylvania, new car dealerships may still sell Buicks or Plymouths along the old highway in the central business district. In smaller towns, auto dealerships are often converted to used car lots in a parallel to the conversion of Main Street retail stores into antique shops.

### Auto Camps and Motels

When the National Road was designated US 40, auto travel, whether for business or recreation, was an established phenomenon supported by a growing assortment of roadside businesses. The centrally located city hotel had served stagecoach and railroad passengers but its close confines prevented easy access and parking by motorists. Travelers often packed camping gear and joined other auto campers in grounds provided by local citizenry. In 1924, the *Hobbs Guide* declared that if one wished to stop in Washington, Pennsylvania, for the night, the choices for accommodation were the George Washington Hotel at $5 to $8 for a double, or the William Henry Hotel at $3. One dollar got you a parking place in the George Washington Garage. Cheaper accommodations were available ten miles from the center of town at the Keystone Camp that featured "50c a car; tents for rent; a splendid camp; well managed and maintained; most every convenience; groceries; electric lights; lunch room."[34] All along the highway one could find camping accommodations on courthouse squares, churchyards and school grounds, fairgrounds, Grange hall lots, or in farmers' groves and pastures.

Campground operators might build rows of small cabins—squalid clapboard shacks, or chicken coops as some called them—to house those without camping equipment. Cabin camps offered additional convenience at low cost, a critical consideration during the Depression. By the mid-1930s the cabins were larger, more substantially built, and usually included a bathroom and an adjacent parking place. In part because the buildings were more house-like in building materials and comfort, and in part because of the way operators preferred to erect the buildings in clusters around an open parking lot, these businesses were called cottage courts. Some provided garages that proved popular, and by the 1940s operators attached the garages and cottages together in alternating pairs to form a continuous roof line.

The next adjustment in form was to make the cottages into large rooms placed side by side to share common walls, thereby reducing construction costs and increasing the number of units one could build on a land parcel.

This motor court, as it was initially called, shared a single continuous roof line and often separate accommodations for the owner. The larger courts might include a restaurant or coffeeshop. By the late 1940s, the term "motor court" had been replaced by "motel" and the facades, rather than continue as generic boxes, were often decorated to evoke images of exotic travel destinations, especially the West. The form was new; the idea was as old as the stagecoach stop along the National Road.

Motel franchises became popular after World War II, and some chain operators required standardized buildings and signs. Along US 40, franchisees built Howard Johnsons or Holiday Inn motels in the larger towns and cities. Small-town motels were often independently owned or part of a referral chain in which owners complied with furnishing standards and participated in a system for referrals and reservations.[35]

While the few early motel chains adopted standardized designs and colors to assure customer recognition, the independent motels were similar only in general plan and basic construction materials. Independent operators might build motels in an I, U, L, or open-L form. Motels in town often placed one end to the street with the backside along a property line, leaving the remaining lot space for parking. Since travelers usually made their motel choice from their car window, and this building position meant that the motel facade could not be seen from the street until one was directly in front of the property, a tall sign was essential to alert and attract potential customers. At the edge of town or in the country, where low land costs allowed much larger lots, owners built motels parallel to the highway. Here signs could be more subtle and the building facade could be fully developed as an advertisement. With brick veneers and a pedimented door arch or cupola, a motel could be made to look Georgian; stark white paint and rounded glass block windows on the same building would evoke the Moderne.

Motel placement, compared to other town businesses, often seems random instead of the result of a studied examination of traffic flow or consideration of a patron's need for easy access to a theater for an evening's entertainment or a restaurant for morning breakfast. Many prospective motel operators often sought farmland beyond the urban fringe where they could buy road frontage cheaply, or built near another motel instead of within the gateway where the highway entered town. Such oddly located motels frequent the US 40 roadside and many were in business for a short time before being converted to other uses or simply abandoned. Motels in towns and

**The 40 Motel, West Washington Street, Indianapolis**

The 1950s automobile strip along US 40 in west Indianapolis is similar to those in other American cities. The 40 Motel, the adjacent Sands Motel, and the Diner were all built about 1954. Of the three supplemental signs that have been added to the original 40 Motel sign, the faded hand-painted one invited truck parking.

cities were less casually sited. Along West Washington Street (US 40) in Indianapolis, for example, the motor courts accumulated in a linear strip amid new subdivisions in what Bernard DeVoto called a "motel town."[36] A motel town or cluster was rarely completed within a few years and consequently its appearance was not that of a set piece. Instead, it gradually accumulated over two or three decades, differences in design or form representing the fad current during construction. Building age, level of maintenance, and owner's entrepreneurial spirit differentiated motel towns into distinct classes. The very best motels were usually the newest and neatest. Fresh paint and carpet, a spacious room with tiled bath and porcelain tub, and an easy chair with reading lamp set the top class apart from the thirty-year-old cabins that were usually cramped, musty, and poorly ventilated.

Standardized concrete or cinderblock gained popularity among builders in the 1930s and soon became a favored construction gadget for box-shaped motels, garages, restaurants, and other roadside buildings. The blocks were relatively cheap, fireproof, and their standard sizes allowed quick construction. Also important, fledgling entrepreneurs did not need architects to design block buildings; a construction crew could follow a simple sketch and build a functional structure with block walls, standard door frames and window casements, and a flat or trussed-wood gable roof. The block-built lookalike structures became so pervasive by the end of World War II that a *Harper's* editor was prompted to describe their roadside collectivity as "cinder block culture."[37]

Designed to purvey commodities and services to mobile customers, the cinderblock landscape was narrowly delimited within the highway corridor, and though it might appear "urban," this was not simply a linear town. Socially it was a temporality, and spatially it was oddly two-dimensional. It was inhabited by transient consumers and the locals who arrived to offer up goods or services usually lived elsewhere. Like dots irregularly spaced on a line, it had length and width but its single-storied structures produced no urban skyline. Nor was it historically stable. The US 40 roadside, as with many other American highways, was a place of experiment and trial for vernacular notions of how to locate and conduct a business, and failure was frequent. One failed business made way for another experiment as cinderblock gas stations evolved into used car lots or garden supply stores.

Further, chronic locational instability was a characteristic of a roadside culture that was the product of a variety of constantly changing highway construction and automotive technologies and political priorities. When Interstate 70 opened in the 1960s, many remaining US 40 businesses without access to freeway interchanges failed, among them dozens of motels from Ohio west through Illinois. They, like the old gas stations, were converted to other uses. Their unit plumbing and electricity and internal connecting doors made for straightforward conversion into nursing or retirement homes or low-income housing. Others were used for storage or business offices. The converted residential motel can be distinguished from the traditional travelers' motel by signs that advertise weekly or monthly rates; by old automobiles, some on blocks in need of repair; children's toys; wash lines; plants and pets. The Silver Swan Motel, east of Springfield, Ohio, stands as an example that has completed this full site transition.

Some roadside businesses serve viable local industries and are little concerned with road-borne customers. Coal miners in Pennsylvania and eastern Ohio depend upon specialized service industries that have chosen to build along the highway, as have the steel-pipe and equipment suppliers to the oil drilling and pumping industry near Marshall, Illinois. The farming economy is most dynamic in western Ohio and Indiana and here business people in US 40 towns continue to operate feed, fertilizer, and grain stores, grain elevators, and diesel-fuel dealerships.

### The Drive-In Landscape

Attracted to the traveler's dollar, other businesses laid claim to a place at the highway's edge. In 1933, Richard Hollingshead built the first drive-in theater in Camden, New Jersey, and within fifteen years 400 dotted American roadsides.[38] Several remain along US 40, many more are now gone. East of Brazil, Indiana, all that remains of the US 40 Theater is the rusted marquee on the road's south side and the layer of crushed rock laid down across the sloped parking lot to keep down dust and provide a tractive surface after a heavy rain. East of Columbus, Ohio, far enough from the city limits so the owner could afford five acres of land with road frontage, stands the 40 East Drive-In Theater, still in operation and well maintained. The 40 East has two screens that stand some 300 feet apart facing one another across a large common lot. The entire site is surrounded by fence to keep out freeloaders.

**Melody Drive-In Theater, Springfield, Ohio**

After World War II, the drive-in theater became a popular family entertainment center and an important node on the young adult's courtship map. Since the screen backed up to the road (to discourage freeloaders), the chore of selling the theater as an attraction fell to the roadside sign. When television brought people back to their new ranch houses and family rooms by the 1960s, most outdoor theaters failed.

KARL RAITZ

Highway travelers require sustenance, which was initially supplied by roadside stands offering hot dogs and cold drinks. The early stands were little more than shacks, but gradually they incorporated the permanent structure and service techniques used by Main Street cafés. By the 1930s, town's edge drive-in restaurants, built on lots large enough to allow cars to park off the highway, begin to appear in the larger US 40 towns and cities. Some restaurants were drive-ins only in the sense that they catered to highway-borne traffic and offered a place to park. Before Howard Johnson's innovative coffeeshop franchise, which replicated menu and building design and decor in each new store, roadside restaurants were largely the idiosyncratic creations of their owners.[39] By the 1950s, drive-in restaurants exhibited some common forms: direct access to the highway, a canopy-covered parking area where customers could be served by "car hops" and eat in their cars, and a kitchen building that also might include indoor seating. Most county-seat towns had at least one small drive-in. Other drive-ins, like Al Green's on US 40 east of Indianapolis, might stand on lots of half an acre or more and

**Mr. G Drive-In, Baltimore**

The signs at the 1950s Mr. G Drive-In at Rolling Road and US 40 in west Baltimore employ both iconic symbols of ice cream cones and sandwiches, and words to describe the available fare.

provide parking space for forty cars. Early drive-in restaurants had catered to traveling salespeople, truckers, and vacationing families. With the 1950s came a new market: teenagers, driving the family sedan or their own cars, often prewar coupes or roadsters modified into hotrods for street or strip drag-racing. After school or work the drive-in became a social center where teenagers cruised in their highly polished cars looking for someone to race or someone to date. A generation before, the courtship ritual had centered on the front porch, the parlor, or the Main Street theater. Now it moved to the highway and the roadside.

Early restaurateurs found that to attract customers they needed to erect large signs visible from the road. "Eat" and "Café" signs soon sprouted from roadside and rooftop or covered the buildings' sides that faced the road. Some owners turned the entire building into a sign by building a structure that resembled an ice-cream container or coffeepot. Of course, roadside businesses employed signs and billboards to pitch everything from gasoline to hot dogs. Some erected billboards in a manner intended to obscure or draw attention from official directional and warning signs. Highway officials complained that the sign blizzard one encountered at town's edge was a blot on the countryside's natural beauty and a menace to the traveling public. Critics writing in the popular press thought the signs and attendant structures constituted an ugly roadside slum, for "wherever there is a hill or a quiet valley or a road running through the fields, or something pleasant for the eye to rest on, the advertisement man has been there first and left his mark."[40]

Where roadside businesses opened, accidents on the highway increased by as much as 50 percent over open country roads. Debates arose between billboard companies and governmental and automobile interest groups over roadside control. Planners and engineers advocated confining roadside commercial development to designated districts, requiring roadside buildings to be set back from the right-of-way, and controlling building appearance, especially the use of signs. In 1926, the U.S. Supreme Court ruled that cities had the right and the power to regulate building construction within their jurisdictions. The billboard industry, led by the Outdoor Advertising Association, countered by organizing property owners into a national Highway Property Owner's Association, which would assure that if roadside control legislation was proposed in any state, legislators would be blitzed by protest letters.[41]

By 1954, a major argument for a new four-lane, controlled-access interstate highway system was that long stretches of American highway had become walled by a rampart of garages, gas stations, restaurants, gift shops, motels, and other small businesses that survived from highway traffic. To push a four-lane highway through such areas would be a financial impossibility. The obvious solution was to build the new freeway system to one side of the existing right-of-way, leaving the old two-lane road for local traffic, but also forcing roadside business either to relocate, be satisfied to serve local clientele, or close.

### The Motor Truck's Landscape

Freight-carrying motor trucks did not generally share with autos the same specific destinations and so generally did not share common roadside facilities. This was not a new form of traffic segregation. Nineteenth-century teamsters sought shelter and sustenance at roadside wagon houses where they could find large yards to park their ten-ton wagons and feed their twelve-horse teams. Stagecoach and carriage passengers might stay at upscale brick or stone taverns or city hotels. As trucks replaced freight wagons they tended to reinforce established links between shippers and receivers while adding new ones, thereby gradually creating a truck-oriented landscape.

**The Red Brick Tavern, Lafayette, Ohio**

Drovers and wagoners may have preferred to overnight at modestly priced inns that provided large parking yards and water and feed for harness horses and livestock. The Red Brick Tavern (1837) probably catered to carriage and coach passengers.

The motor truck quickly proved to be exceptionally well adapted to providing the short-haul link between railroad or water-line terminals and local consumers, or in providing the producers of perishable farm produce a timely market delivery.[42] Early heavy trucks rolled on solid rubber tires that offered no spring action on irregular road surfaces and, consequently, the rough ride punished both drivers and cargo. Balloon tires for trucks became available in the early 1920s and had the revolutionary effect of allowing trucks to haul heavier loads longer distances at higher speeds.[43]

Properly equipped, the truck had several advantages over the railroad. Rail companies preferred to ship commodities by the railcar load, and anything less was a less-then-carload-lot or l.c.l. Freight consignments might be kept standing in a freight yard for days awaiting additional cargo so that l.c.l. cars could be filled and sent on their way. Such small loads were the truck's forte. Because railroads often built freight yards and depots close to the city center, as the business district expanded toward the tracks railroads found their yards and tracks occupying some of the city's most valuable land. By the early 1920s, a single freight car awaiting a load might occupy land worth $4,000 or more. Property taxes and land-value differentials put pressure on railroad companies to limit expansion in the business district. Trucking firms, on the other hand, chose to build terminals on cheaper land near industrial districts at the edge of the city with good highway access.[44]

Trucks also could use rail-oriented freight facilities. In Indianapolis, for example, trucks began delivering livestock to the track-side stockyards in 1912, and by 1923 90 percent of the hogs received from within a fifty-mile radius were delivered by truck. This meant that small-town stockyards along US 40 from as far east as Knightstown, Indiana, or as far west as Brazil became gathering points for hog shipments into the Indianapolis yards. Most haulers were farmers or independent operators with one truck. They could earn extra income by filling the truck with feeder stock, feed, or general merchandise for the return trip home. The Farm Bureau built its feed warehouse near the Indianapolis stockyards and so either stock or feed would be the easiest return load to assemble; merchandise would have to be picked up at different warehouses scattered across the city.[45] Should these farm- or small-town-based truckers eventually establish offices, they favored their hometowns instead of moving into the larger cities such as Columbus and Indianapolis. This meant that small towns, Knightstown, for example, might have a stockyard truck terminal near the highway.[46]

According to surveys taken by states along US 40, the largest traffic volumes occurred on those sections near large towns and cities. Trucks comprised only about 10 percent of highway traffic and most were small, 2½-ton capacity or less. Moving companies were vanning household goods in larger solid rubber–wheeled trucks up to 600 miles by the early 1920s. Most smaller trucks made trips of less than thirty miles, carrying manufactured goods, especially gasoline or groceries, the most important truck cargo if measured in volume. Coal, clay, gravel, and other mined materials for construction or industry were also common cargo.

As truck technology and road conditions improved, vehicle capacity increased and haul distances gradually lengthened so that by 1932 regularly scheduled truck trips commonly exceeded 500 miles along fixed routes and the average truck trip length had increased to 70 miles.[47]

Terminal buildings supporting truck commerce began to appear across the city—at sooty industrial district rail sidings or by an oily yard at the edge of town where two highways intersected, places not generally frequented by people who drove autos. Highway trailers—as the large intercity tractor-trailer trucks were termed in the 1930s—delivered processed food stuffs or manufactured consumer goods to a low frame or concrete-block building with good highway or rail access. A large terminal might have forty or more tractor-trailer parking bays. Across the 20,000-square-foot storage floor, on the opposite side of the building, was another line of docks occupied by smaller "pickup" trucks that received goods for delivery directly to city merchants or manufacturers. When the pickup-truck drivers had completed their deliveries, they then reloaded with outgoing freight at stops across the city and returned to the terminal, where that cargo would be sorted and reloaded on outgoing highway trailer trucks. The truck terminal became metaphorically, if not literally, the heart of the city.

City drivers worked regular daytime shifts generally, whereas the over-the-road driver might have to cover 300 miles to make a second-day delivery at another city terminal. The highway driver might have an apartment within walking distance of the terminal in one city and, at the route's other end, stay at a dollar-a-night hotel near the terminal. Should the load be destined for greater distance, relay drivers would await the truck near the trip's midpoint at a city hotel patronized by the trucking company. On the highway, trucks usually made no stops except for gas and oil, or meals at roadside diners. Selected gas stations—Socony-Vacuum contracted to supply

**Truckstop at Fairdale, Ohio**

The late 1940s truckstop on the west side of Fairdale, Ohio, stands beside US 40. The old National Road bed, brick-covered, ran behind the station through the pine trees. The two-story concrete-block buildings behind the station are dormitories for drivers.

fuel to some large trucking companies that served US 40 towns and cities—became "control points," where company rules required the driver to service the truck and record driving times.[48]

By the eve of World War II, most long-haul trucks were still gasoline-powered. As diesel engines were improved and adapted to truck use, gasoline stations added diesel-fuel pumps, but segregated them from the gas pumps to provide enough space for trucks to park without interfering with automobile access. The relay hotel and the control-point gas station of the 1930s and '40s were the precursors to the modern diesel truckstop. The nation's first large-scale truckstop opened in 1946 near Bakersfield, California.[49] During the 1950s, oversized gas stations catering to truckers began to appear along US 40—at Fairdale, Ohio, west of Cambridge, for example. Seventy-foot-long trucks required open space measured in acres for parking and maneuvering, and truckstop managers knew that truckers were loath to back their vehicles amid congested traffic. A truckstop's first requirement, then, was space, and since cheap land adjoining the highway could generally be found only in the countryside or, at best, on the edge of town, truckstops were generally found at such places. Fuel pumps were widely spaced and service bays for oil changes, lubrication, and minor repairs were oversized. Inside the service building, the driver could use a bank of pay telephones to contact the central dispatcher, get a hot shower or comfortable bed, or play cards in an air-conditioned clubroom.

But, ironically, cities did not welcome trucks into their centers, especially to Main Street. In the city business district, drivers followed "Deliveries in the rear" signs to back-door loading docks. The alley system, such as the one in Washington, Pennsylvania, was especially well adapted for pickup-truck access. But in many small towns and older cities, off-street access was rare and so trucks frequently tied up traffic. The designated truck route, which was intended to confine trucks to industrial corridors away from residential areas or the retail business district, became a popular way to maintain truck segregation, and offers a direct parallel to the back street nineteenth-century drovers were expected to follow in guiding their livestock through National Road towns in Ohio and Pennsylvania.[50]

By the end of World War II, the nation's 7 million commercial long-distance trucks had become the primary movers of many of the nation's commercial commodities. Trucks forced the railroads to abandon uneconomic

**1910 Pennsylvania Railroad bridge, Cambridge City, Indiana**

An emphatic statement about the competition between freight trains and trucks to carry American's material goods. The trucks won!

The Ridge and Valley country of western Maryland, here near Bellegrove between Town Hill and Sideling Hill, was difficult for cars and heavy long-haul trucks to negotiate. The completion of I-70/68 through these mountains drew most traffic off US 40 and gas stations and truck-stops began to cluster at interstate interchanges.

branch lines, leaving hundreds of small communities without rail service. The use of trucks in agriculture increased 60 percent during the 1940s and most farm products began their destination to market or processor by truck.[51]

Trucks and autos shared the same roadway, to the rapidly increasing consternation of drivers in both groups, and congestion points developed at railroad crossings and highway intersections, narrow bridges and the narrow streets of small towns and city business districts, and along steep grades. A heavily loaded truck might grind up a 3 percent grade at no more than 20 miles per hour, trailing a line of cars half a mile or more in length. A 10 percent grade on US 40 at Old Washington, Ohio, was regarded as one of the nation's two worst congestion points.[52]

## THE BYPASS

On small-scale maps the National Road appears as a series of nearly straight segments, especially the western half. But the road's surveyors closely followed local topography, choosing the easiest grades around hills and at stream crossings. In later years the same effect could be gained by employing large-scale earth-moving equipment to cut down slopes and fill valleys.

During the 1940s, major construction projects realigned and rebuilt sec-

**US 40 bypass around South Vienna, Ohio**

South Vienna is about halfway between Columbus and Springfield, a heavily traveled section of US 40 until completion of I-70 in the late 1960s. After World War II, US 40 was widened to four lanes, given a broad grass median, and realigned to sweep past small towns. The old National Road still functions as Main Street.

tions of US 40. Along the highway's western sections in Ohio and Indiana, the realignments were primarily at grade changes near streams and bypasses around small towns. The bypass remains curiously distinct from the older Road alignment. Long road sections had become corridors of buildings—farmsteads, businesses, and postwar commuters' homes. But the bypass often has buildings on only one side, the town side; on the other stand trees or open farmland as at South Vienna, Ohio. Most small towns were

**Empty billboard along US 40 near Bluff City, Illinois**

Road-oriented business declined with the construction of the US 40 bypasses and I-70. Those that closed or moved to another location often abandoned their billboards. The Art Deco frame suggests that this board may predate World War II.

rural service centers and so some businesses were more dependent upon local farming populations than upon highway travelers. The grain elevators along the railroad track, the truck and tractor dealers, and the veterinarian were not concerned with highway-borne customers.

Nevertheless, the bypassed town's merchants were reluctant to accept circumscription. The town's gas station relocated to the intersection of the old highway and the bypass—or the main cross street and the bypass—with a new motel and restaurant. Businesses with geographical inertia—large investments in buildings or special facilities—might not move to the bypass but will place signs there to inform passersby that they are still in business. Should a business on the old Road close, its sign along the highway will be converted or abandoned. And most bypassed villages erect identifying name signs along the new highway, often with a large arrow pointing toward the settlement's remains.

Open country highway in Maryland, Pennsylvania, and Ohio remained two lanes. Heavily traveled approaches to larger towns and cities were widened to four lanes, sometimes separated by a hard surface or grassed median that continued through the auto business strip. Near the larger city centers—Columbus, Springfield, and Indianapolis—traffic was fully separated and directed along one-way streets. For merchants dependent upon drive-in customers, the inconvenience of being tethered to a one-way street was another barrier to overcome and another rationale for closing shop and moving to the strip at the city's edge.

By the early 1950s, the pre-interstate reconstruction of US 40 had been completed. Realignments in the western sections were relatively few. In some eastern sections realignment was more substantive. In Pennsylvania, for example, as much as 50 percent of US 40 had been relocated away from the original National Road alignment.[53] Bypassed Road sections become "white highways." They no longer merit regular maintenance, and as the asphalt oxidizes and the aggregate bleaches in the sun the road turns gray, and then white. Expansion joints in the old concrete road that serve as the foundation for the asphalt surface continue to move and checker the asphalt cap with "reflective cracks." In some places grass erupts from the center-line crack in a thin green line that bisects the white surface like a lilliputian hedgerow. The white highway signals slower speeds are appropriate as rubber tires growl against checked asphalt; the grass center-line and unmown shoulders are reminders that unless you have reached your destination you should retrace your route and find the new highway, the bypass.

## AMERICA ANTIQUED

Highways built to bypass towns, or interstate freeways built to bypass highways, isolate places that to earlier generations had been growing, vibrant communities. Economic stagnation often follows; on the US 40 roadside, it became translated into urban lethargy. Some Road-oriented businesses closed, others converted from national franchise to local independent owners. People tore down fewer old buildings to make way for modern structures, and since facade remodeling and updating was unnecessary, Main Streets often remained intact. During the interstate highway era, large American cities, especially those along the Middle Atlantic seaboard, have added extensive residential suburbs. Businesses now prefer suburban locations in modern or postmodern office towers at major freeway interchanges. Such places attract shopping centers and all the services one would associate with a city business district. A galactic pattern of discontinuous suburban housing clusters now extends west from Washington, D.C., Baltimore, and Philadelphia onto the Piedmont and beyond the Blue Ridge into the Great Valley. Commuters are rediscovering old National Road villages bypassed by newer highways and coveting them for their "historical value." Venerable buildings that once housed banks, barbershops, hardware stores, and attorneys' offices are now being converted to antique shops. New Market, Maryland, just east of Frederick, has become the state's antique capital. But one cannot expect to sell expensive antiques, folk art, or other "collectibles" from a dowdy storefront, so people gut the interiors, paint the facades in "original" colors and other-

**A new billboard frame awaits its sign near Marshall, Illinois**

Freeway interchanges provide new linkages to potential road-borne customers. Inertia prevents many businesses from moving from Main Street to the interchange or the access road, but it is hoped that new signs will direct those that leave the interstate toward the services in town.

wise try to recreate Main Street according to how they think the ideal "olde shoppes" in the town's center should look. Within the commuting or weekend excursion ring around the Road's larger cities, in small towns like Greenup, Illinois, Centerville, Indiana, or Cambridge, Ohio, for example, the conversion to antique shops and tour-bus restaurants mimics that at New Market. Beyond that distance such conversions are a more problematic business investment, although almost every bypassed Main Street along the entire route from Ellicott City to East St. Louis will sport at least one or two such stores, and proceeds may surpass that of any business that formally occupied those buildings. The theme of conversion and re-creation along the National Road and US 40 corridor continues in many guises into the 1990s.

## CONCLUSION

The conversion of the National Road into US 40 was the result of a complex combination of technical inventions and contingent social, economic, and political processes. The buggy and wagon were mechanically transformed into automobile and truck; yet the new vehicles were required to travel upon old roads. Road technology advances did not lead the twentieth century's transportation revolution; mechanical contrivances did. Nor would road-building technique or funding and new construction catch up to the ever larger, faster products rolling from automotive assembly lines. And old or new, road configuration did not create a demand for a new roadside landscape, the new contrivances and their owners did.

Why was this the case? The automobile represented freedom and flexibility that few individuals had previously experienced, and, once adopted, they would be unwilling to relinquish unless it became too expensive or too immoral. Until the automobile, Americans "saw the sights" from the train's window or the steamboat's deck. But, excepting the traveling salesperson or the family with enough money to vacation via train or boat, most people related primarily to those landscapes that lay between home and factory, store, or church. More commonly, to become landscape consumers they would have to seek out static landscapes in art museums, or watch moving landscape images at a nineteenth-century "panorama" or early twentieth-century movie. The automobile altered this parochial perspective by moving the viewer through the landscape instead of moving the landscape image itself. Through the venue of this new mobility, Americans could link their identity to larger, modern places or broader regions while uncoupling from traditional identities with extended family and neighborhood, be it urban or countryside.

The escalating demand for automobiles drives a creative technology that will always compete to provide consumers with the most "attractive" personalized transportation mode, whether measured in body style, color, power, or amenities (termed "options" on the automobile order form). From its early days, the car also possessed many qualities of the home. It had walls that defined the interior as one's own space insulating those inside from the unusual, unacceptable, or unknown, and windows through which one could establish landscape context. Part of the car's attraction was its parlor-like fit and finish; the mirror of that special room in the home where the finest furnishings waited to be used only on special occasions. And at night the car's interior offered security against the unseen as would a kitchen where the family gathered in warm, cozy, dimly lit togetherness. So close became the linkage between the automobile and the home that by the mid-1920s, architects were experimenting with innovative ways to bring the two together by attaching a garage and moving the auto into the home as a family member.[54]

As the purveyor of freedom of access and conservator of time, the automobile provides the context for a powerful bonding of individuals with a broad new repertoire of places while retaining some comfortably familiar home-like qualities. Such bonding is overcome with great difficulty. We have invested national fortunes in vehicles, highways, and roadside landscapes and created a geographic and psychological inertia that may be too great to overcome. Even if the cost of fossil fuels should become prohibitive, the search for alternative fuels will likely be more exhaustive than the search for alternative modes of collective transportation.

Another product of personalized transportation has been an odd disjuncture between society's implementation of technology and the landscape upon which that technology is applied. On the one hand, America's attachment to the automobile has not only been stable, it has intensified over time. We expect to drive on good roads to reach almost any destination, and that effort is supported by a host of legal, economic, and political conditions especially designed to assure that this privilege will continue. On the other hand, the automobile roadside that people built to accommodate the new democratic mobility was inherently unstable. The very technological changes that provided the venue for a vernacular roadside culture to develop made it a place of chronic impermanence and perishability.

**Interstate 70 at South Vienna, Ohio**

The broad swathe of I-70 carries high-speed travelers through the Ohio landscape, ignoring the old parallel ribbon of US 40. The new roadway appears to be beckoning the town of South Vienna to leave the past behind.

# The Interstate 70 Landscape

RICHARD H. SCHEIN

> *The point is to drive. That way you learn more about this society than all academia could ever tell you. . . . This creates a new experience of space, and, at the same time, a new experience of the whole social system.*
>
> JEAN BAUDRILLARD
> *America* (1988)

CONTEMPORARY TRAVELERS ARE MOST LIKELY REMINDED OF THE National Road and US 40 from a vantage point on Interstate 68 and Interstate 70—often high above the old roads and always at speeds that reduce the past to a blur in the rearview mirror. Indeed, across the United States old routeways have given way to the 42,000-mile Interstate Highway System (IHS); and this 1 percent of America's road mileage now carries 20 percent of the nation's traffic.

This chapter is about Interstates 68 and 70 (I-68/70) as the successors to the National Road and US 40. I-68/70's concrete and asphalt ribbon parallels the old roads across six states—one or two miles away along some stretches, directly atop the old roads in others. The interstate is much more than a physical roadway. These multilane highways now carry the mantle of national transportation ideals; and like the old roads before them, the interstates have dramatic impact upon the American land and implications for American life. Explaining the interstate highway as a new theater of American life requires extending one's viewpoint beyond the road itself, both figuratively and literally. Figuratively, a view beyond the road takes in the interstate's political and economic context and its place as a symbol of modern American life. Literally, an extended view places the interstate highway at the center of new American landscapes, reconfigurations of the built environment altering the spatial and visual arrangements of an earlier America.

This chapter explores the I-68/70 landscape in its broader contexts: as three views beyond the highway, though the highway remains the story's central component. First, the interstate system's political economy is critically reviewed. In the 1950s, the Cold War was underway; the service sector first overtook manufacturing as America's economic mainstay; Congress passed the Interstate Highway Act; and engineers began building the first interstate highways across the countryside. Creating and constructing I-68/70 took place within the Interstate Highway System's national framework, a national spatial discipline that would guide the development of the nation's future. That national framework first and foremost was organized and implemented from "above" as a federal *strategy of national cohesion*. Second, the Interstate Highway System's resultant spatial discipline was *inhabited* by the people who live and travel along its routeways and was modified to suit their needs and desires. Where the federally imposed I-68/70 intersects with local people's lives along the Maryland-to-Illinois corridor the effects are manifest in the landscape. The third view depicts the interstate as a *symbol* of modern American life.

## THE VIEW BEYOND THE INTERSTATE
### Strategies of National Cohesion

The Interstate Highway System's intersecting roadways are a Euclidian framework that organizes the nation's daily circulation of people and commodities. The system's 42,000-plus miles are a gridlike network of linked roadways that rationally order and control American space. Federal policy originally "imposed" that order and control in a macro-scale public works program headquartered in Washington, D.C. The IHS was Pres. Dwight D. Eisenhower's pet project and legislation that finally implemented the program passed during his administration. As an American national strategy for joining the entire country in a single transportation system, the IHS is

RICHARD H. SCHEIN

an umbilicus of national cohesion, a lifeline serving at least two traditional concerns of the political state: defense and trade (or, today, commerce). The IHS is a huge project embodying the economic and political elements of America's "military-industrial complex." Eisenhower coined that phrase; thus it seems fitting that the IHS was created during his presidential tenure. A national-scale map reveals the system's spatial ordering and completeness. The map's empowering view-from-above makes it clear that the IHS blankets the country in an all-encompassing continental web (see p. 37).

One can trace the interstate's apocryphal origins to General Pershing's fifty-six-day transcontinental march immediately after World War I. The trip's difficulty made an indelible impression upon one of the caravan's members, young Lieutenant Colonel Eisenhower, who later cited that experience as seminal to the development of his highway policy. When he became president, Eisenhower acted to fill the perceived need for a nationally coordinated transportation system serving defense needs. But the story is not so simple. Mark Rose's exposition on express highway politics' labyrinthine workings demonstrates that the story has many twists and turns between World War I and 1956.[1] Additionally, automobile historian James Flink cast doubts upon the actual need for specifically defense highways, although not necessarily on the Cold War rationale for their federal funding.[2] Flink suggests that the IHS also must be viewed within a larger context in which the automobile is crucial to the nation's economic viability and the interstate is the key to the automobile's continued acceptance. Within this political-economic context—perceptions of Cold War defense needs and a burgeoning manufacturing economy—the IHS was conceived and ultimately orchestrated.

Although the benefits of increased military mobility promised by a coordinated national transportation system were articulated as early as World War I, it was the early 1950s Cold War political climate that served as the catalyst for a defense-justified IHS.[3] Americans remembered that Axis strength had a transportation base; Italy's 1920s Autostrade was the world's first limited-access roadway, and the German Autobahnen constituted the first limited-access highway system—by World War II its roadways totaled over 1,000 miles.[4] In 1954, President Eisenhower appointed Gen. Lucius Clay to head a committee assessing American transportation needs. The committee's final report in 1955 provided the basis for Eisenhower to present Congress with an argument for the IHS: "In the case of an atomic attack on our key cities, the road net must permit quick evacuation of target areas, mobilization of defense forces and maintenance of every essential economic function. But the present system in critical areas would be the breeder of deadly congestion within hours of an attack."[5]

Eisenhower's message also included the claim that "one out of every seven American gains his [sic] livelihood and supports his family" from "the Nation's highway system." By the 1950s, the United States had become a "fordist economy," dependent upon mass production and consumption, in which the automobile played a central role. And the construction industry boon promised by such a massive undertaking as the IHS also appealed to a nation well versed in the recent turn to Keynsian "pump priming" as a central government function.

The automobile's dramatic rise to prominence in American life has occurred within living memory. In 1895, only about 300 automobiles—all manufactured in Europe—rolled along America's streets and roads. Americans registered 23 million vehicles by 1930, and 60 million by 1960, when American companies manufactured almost 7 million units, over half the world's. Fewer than 2 percent of those vehicles were exported; by the early 1970s the United States could claim one automobile for every two persons. Between 1950 and 1970 automobile ownership was extended to the American working class, thus accounting, in part, for the doubling of vehicle registrations during that period. Seven of the ten largest American corporations in the 1950s produced either automobiles or oil. The auto industry—including manufacturing, sales, repair, and spin-off industries such as upholstery, insurance, glass, rubber tires, and electronics—accounted for one-sixth of the U.S. Gross National Product. People saw the automobile as a "public good" (as opposed to mass transit which they generally viewed, ironically enough, as "private enterprise"), and governments at all levels were willing to "subsidize" the industry through road construction. Between 1946 and 1950, local, state, and federal road-construction expenditures exceeded $8 billion (and this before investment in the IHS). In 1956, when Congress passed the IHS, Ford Motor Company offered its stock to the public for the first time, an appropriate gesture.[6]

The automobile's centrality in the American political economy ensured the proposed IHS a strong support base among postwar Washington, D.C., lobbyists. One very vocal and powerful lobbying group was the loosely formed Project Adequate Roads, comprising forty major organizations, in-

RICHARD  H.  SCHEIN

cluding commercial truck operators, motorists (the AAA, for example), auto and truck manufacturers, government officials, planners, union leaders (for fleet operators, commercial carriers, oil companies), chambers of commerce, highway engineers, and a national association of road construction contractors.[7] There were, of course, disagreements among the supporters as to the proposed system's exact details. Fierce debates during the decade prior to 1956 embroiled the Project Adequate Roads and other lobbying groups, Congress, and the president. Nevertheless, a consensus was building, at least in Washington, D.C., that the system should be built. That consensus was reached in 1956.

Among the voluminous federal legislation touching upon national transportation networks, bills passed in 1916, 1921, and 1944 generally are cited for initially proposing an interstate highway system, planning its routes and construction requirements, and providing required funding.[8] Public Law 87, enacted in 1921, first mentions a "connected system of highways, interstate in character"; while public laws in 1944 specifically called for "a national system of interstate highways." The key law is Public Law 627, enacted June 29, 1956. Title I, the Federal Aid Highway Act of 1956, includes Section 108, the "National System of Interstate and Defense Highways," which declared the system "to be essential to the national interest." Section 116 specifically suggested that the national interest largely was dictated by "the needs of local and interstate commerce, the national and civil defense."

Public Law 627 has two particular aspects that provided elements crucial for ensuring the IHS's success. The first was paragraph (e) of Section 108, which increased the federal share of interstate construction to 90 percent. The second was Title II, the Highway Revenue Act of 1956, which included Section 209 creating the Highway Trust Fund. The Highway Trust Fund became the transportation lobby's sacred cow, and was not successfully attacked and modified until the Nixon administration, after most of the IHS had been built. Highway user taxes fed the trust fund—taxes on gas, oil, tires, and excise taxes on buses and trucks—and that money was reserved exclusively for highway construction. The more miles Americans drove, the larger the trust fund; and the larger the trust fund, the more road mileage that could be built. The trust fund potentially was a "bottomless pocketbook" funding a perfect "self-perpetuating construction financing system."[9] It was and it did—at least until roads and bridges began to wear out twenty or thirty years after federal construction funding was not matched by local and state maintenance support. To transportation proponents in early July 1956, however, the future was rosy.

Although the IHS supposedly was the product of the American democratic process, that process was increasingly influenced, even dominated, by political action committees and industrial lobbyists whose focus was the federal legislature. When the legislature created the IHS, the system became a true *national* strategy of a continental empire. The strategy was dictated by the "national interests" of commerce and defense. Timing of interstate construction ensured that the project was implemented and facilitated by an army of experts, the bureaucrats and engineers overseeing the process.[10] Although the IHS was initiated by and for Americans, the program was beyond the control of most American people. Certainly the IHS benefited "common" people, but as a tangible roadway it generally "appeared" on the local scene—whether it was Columbus, St. Louis, New York, or Seattle—largely through political machinations well beyond the local citizenry's immediate control. This external control was apparent especially during early planning phases in the legal powers of seizure granted for acquiring IHS rights-of-way.

If the cultural landscape is "our unwitting autobiography," then the interstate road network provided by Public Law 627 contains a story about the American political economy of Modernity.[11] Interstate design, the system's continental scale, its general disregard for existing American spatial order, and the appearance of "sameness" or homogeneity along its routeways all speak to a central government policy imposed during a time when American federal power was close to its pinnacle.

The interstate landscape's hallmark is standardization stemming from centrally controlled design criteria. Public Law 627 mandated "the geometric and construction standards to be adopted for the Interstate System shall be those approved by the Secretary of Commerce in cooperation with the State highway departments. . . . The Secretary of Commerce shall apply such standards uniformly throughout the States." Those standards include restrictions and guidelines for speed, sight distance, curvature, gradient, access, number of lanes, width of lanes, shoulders, slopes, medians, curbs, exits and interchanges, bridge heights, structural capacity, and other details. The traveler on I-68/70 glides along a roadway at an optimum speed of 65 miles per hour, in a lane twelve feet wide, assured that in case of a flat tire the ten-foot shoulder will accommodate the disabled vehicle. Truckers

**Interstate reststop, Madison County, Ohio**

Standardization, order, and large-scale are hallmarks of the federal interstate highway. This reststop in Ohio might as well be anywhere on the vast, continental system—with standard infrastructural specifications and forced segregation of commercial and private traffic/trucks and cars.

know that all bridges clear the road surface by fourteen feet.[12] Federal standards produced roads with the same (or similar) guard rails, speed limit, yield, "wrong way," and exit signs, reststops, construction barrels, jersey barriers, light poles, and, of course, red, white, and blue shields of the IHS. One cannot doubt that this is the imprint of central authority.

Federal roadway control included the so-called Highway Beautification Act of 1965, which regulated outdoor advertising and junkyards adjacent to the interstates and provided construction funding for "landscape and roadside development," including rest areas. The act specifically restricted billboards from within 660 feet of the roadway. This directly increased the interstate corridor area under federal control and effectively promoted a "monster billboard" industry that would erect giant advertising signs along an isoline demarcating the restricted area's edge. By 1960, even the view from the interstate reflected federal strategy.

The monster billboards also illustrate that federal highway strategy has effects beyond the legally defined roadway. Human landscapes, perceptions of landscape and space, and even social life all have been altered by the system's national scope and scale, its concrete web, and the speed enabled by its individual roadways.

Landscape changes, even disruption, caused by the IHS federal strategy can be seen and experienced by traveler or local resident. Just west of

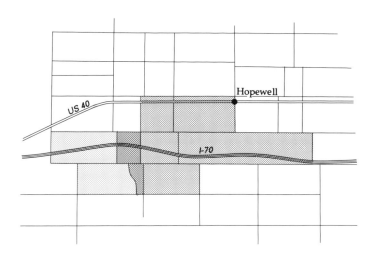

**Landholdings and the interstate**

The interstate appears indifferent to previous human settlement patterns. I-70 splits three Township and Range landholdings in Muskingum County, Ohio.

Zanesville, Ohio, for example, I-70 West traverses Muskingum County on its way to Columbus. A large-scale regional map depicts the interstate competing with the cardinal alignment of the Township and Range Survey system, itself a product of an earlier national cohesion strategy (or even empire) implemented in the late eighteenth century.[13] The Township and Range Survey, however, assumed an empty land. The survey's townships—made up of square-mile sections—were inscribed on the earth's surface after Native Americans had been dispossessed and before Euro-Americans settled. The survey's timing ensured that the subsequent farm landscape—including roads, fences, and field boundaries—would conform to federal policy–dictated right-angled lot lines, producing the characteristic "checkerboard" field pattern of the American Middle West.[14] The interstate, in contrast, was a strategy implemented after effective settlement of the territory, and thus had the effect of ramming through the settlement landscape, often splitting landholdings and individual farms. To be sure, turnpikes and highways often have run through farmsteads in the past and even have linked farms to outside social and economic contacts. But earlier rural roads were explicitly farm-to-market oriented at a time when most Americans still lived on farms. The interstate serves an American population that is overwhelmingly urban. The system's national strategy is to connect cities with over a 50,000 population in a national framework that seemingly ignores older, more locally oriented boundaries and networks of daily life. The interstate limits access and this functionally splits landholdings—sometimes leaving farm buildings on one side of the roadway and fields on the other. Not only has the farm lost its road access, it has become fragmented and parts are inconveniently isolated. The farmer becomes the victim of competing "spatial orders," losing free access to Interstate 70's imperial design.

The competing spatial orders are grounded in two different scales; one national, the other local. Each embodies different perceptions of distance, space, and landscape; and each is indicative of two different time periods of American landscape development. The farmstead's eighteenth-century scale was part of a local social life that was more "human" or even "humane" than

RICHARD H. SCHEIN

the reorganization of American space effected by the twentieth-century IHS, an organization that encompasses the vast territorial swathe of a continent. Speeding along unimpeded at 65 miles per hour, the I-68/70 traveler has a sense of viewing the landscape from the "backyard." The passing scene is not oriented to the interstate roadway, save for exit interchanges and billboards. Everything off the roadway seems slightly askew, seldom at right angles to the interstate. Houses display their "off sides," reserving the front view for more accessible local roads with their more leisurely traffic flow. The traveler may glimpse entire towns from a distance, as the interstate generally ignores the nineteenth-century spacing of eastern American places settled when horses and walking provided the way to "get into town." Small-town America is now out of sight, and can be conveniently "out of mind." One sees from above the central cities of Wheeling, Columbus, and Indianapolis as flashes of urban decay, obsolescence, or rejuvenation—the route often explicitly chosen to pass though inner-city neighborhoods in simultaneous pursuit of two often paradoxical goals: urban access and urban renewal. The central city *can* be reached, but more often the traveler's destination is somewhere else. Highway engineers might be excused for the I-68 traveler's view of Cumberland, Maryland, from a roadway raised upon concrete stilts, dozens of feet above the town. There are few water-gap options for breaching the folded Appalachians in western Maryland. But traveling though Columbus, Ohio, in 1994, one looks down upon a large abandoned and decayed school building, once the educational center for an active and thriving community. While I-70 might not have caused the school's abandonment or the central city's social state, there is little doubt from the vantage point high above the urban scene that I-70 was conceived and built without regard for that locality. The highway's raised revetments split city neighborhoods just as they separated farmsteads from farmland. The national-scale interstate has not always proven compatible with local-scale social institutions.

A recent crime investigation story illustrates the human consequences of scale shifts and competing spatial orders engendered, in part, by federal strategy. Ten separate murder investigation cases in Ohio, New York, and Pennsylvania had baffled independent law enforcement agencies for a number of years. Despite the amazing similarity among the cases, it took a fifteen-agency homicide task force to link the murders to the IHS web of Interstates 70, 71, 87, and 280, and to identify interstate truck drivers as the prime suspects.[15] Individual sheriffs' and police departments were constrained by jurisdictional boundaries conceived and implemented in the eighteenth and nineteenth centuries. Those boundaries were challenged, and beaten, by criminals operating within a national transportation system and able to routinely cross old political spatial orders with ease.

The (original) interstate travel speeds of up to 75 miles per hour are an integral part of the IHS federal strategy and its national scale. Faster speeds require roadside businesses to erect signs large enough and tall enough to be visible at a distance sufficient to allow recognition and decisionmaking. Roadside stilt signs in primary colors tower in thickets above exit interchanges, attempting to lure travelers off the interstate. Most signs announce food, fuel, and lodging; and they, too, display a national strategy, albeit one adopted by corporate America. The same Burger King, Hardees, Kentucky Fried Chicken, McDonald's, and Wendy's; BP, Exxon, Gulf, Mobil, and Shell; Comfort Inn, Day's Inn, Holiday Inn, Motel 6, and Travelodge stand at exits along I-68/70. They are interchangeable cogs in a national order of a different sort: the commercial domination of local culture by the same hamburger, tank of gas, or motel room available nationwide.[16]

Everything about the Interstate Highway System—from its lane widths to the coffee at its interchanges to the view it affords of the passing countryside—represents "outside forces" imposed upon local land and life, strategies designed to conquer space (and time) in the "national interest." Yet, intent and success in national strategy are not one and the same. Despite the magnitude of the interstate project, one can find evidence that the Eisenhower highways and the military-industrial complex have not completely eradicated the "local" from the American landscape.

The Centerville Rest Stop is just west of Richmond, Indiana, on I-70's north side. At first glance it seems just like every other government-designed and -built reststop on I-68/70. It even has a sign in front of the building indicating that I-70 is the Dwight D. Eisenhower Highway. Inside the restroom building, however, is a curious amateur exhibit chronicling the historical rise and fall of nearby Centerville, a town not only bypassed by the interstate highway, but by the twentieth century in general. Exhibits like this are common in historical societies across the country, but usually are considered to be interesting only to local residents, or tourists who specifically seek them out. This exhibit's presence on the interstate is a mystery. There is no tourist pitch to come and spend money in Centerville. No clues suggest who put the exhibit there, or why. The reststop on I-70—the federal interloper that by-

**Interstate interchange, Effingham, Illinois**

National commercial domination of local culture is reinforced through the sheer scale of roadside enterprise such as these gas stations, motels, restaurants, and truck terminals.

passed the town itself—has been coopted by local interests and incorporated into their sense of place about Centerville and its environs.

At first glance, the McDonald's restaurant at exit 60, where I-70, US 40, and Ohio 497 intersect, seems just like every other McDonald's, advertising Egg McMuffins and Big Macs for the hungry traveler. Inside the restaurant, however, framed prints adorn the walls. They are all of *local* scenes: along the National Road, of nearby Concord, "Home of Muskingum College," of Zanesville's famous Y-bridge and train station. The prints are not for sale.

No signs explain their presence. The prints express the specific locality and even civic pride, a dramatic contrast to the corporate facade and the standardized offerings of the restaurant itself.

These two examples suggest that although the interstate highway and its attendant corporate enterprises may represent imposed national strategies, American life still is lived in local places by local people. In short, the Interstate Highway System's federal strategy has been inhabited by specific people in specific places. These people have altered and adopted and adapted to the federal order of the I-68/70 landscape.

### Tactics of Inhabiting

Social individualism, political democracy, and laissez-faire capitalism are highly esteemed ideals in the American value system. They also provide the basis to challenge the national strategies embodied in the Interstate Highway System. The battle is as old as Hamiltonian federalism versus Jeffersonian democracy. The IHS represents a centrally imposed and controlled spatial discipline of the nation. Yet there are possibilities for manipulating, maneuvering, or even inventing ways within those disciplinary boundaries. Social interaction with and use of the interstate highway, as a roadway and a system, bends and alters the "rules of the game" to fit people's needs. In short, people institute *tactics* through their everyday activities that make the system's spatial discipline habitable.[17] For individuals, such tactics may be as simple as traveling with on-board radar detectors to circumvent OPEC-era speed limits. Such actions eventually may alter imposed disciplines. In this example, one can attribute some credit for the repeal of the Carter administration–imposed 55-MPH national speed limit to popular opposition, expressed through radar detector use.

Some people have successfully challenged the IHS national strategy. Helen Leavitt's book *Superhighway—Superhoax,* written when the IHS was barely half completed, is dedicated to "urban dwellers everywhere" and captures the spirit of many interstate opponents. Leavitt's book stands for a shift in interstate politics away from general American deference to the power and expertise of national politicians, corporate leaders, planners, and engineers. By the early 1960s, "advocates for environmentalism, and elimination of Interstate routings in cities" and "localism" were challenging the IHS national strategy.[18] Such opposition agrees with Flink's third stage of American automobile consciousness, "when Americans began to have crit-

RICHARD H. SCHEIN

ical second thoughts about the automobile industry and its product."[19] The Highway Beautification Act of 1965 is part of that shift, illustrating how the tactics of opposition can be incorporated into the system's original disciplinary strategy. Along I-68 in western Maryland, popular opposition to interstate construction in the mid-1980s caused engineers and planners to choose an alternative route. This final leg of the so-called National Freeway was delayed and eventually abandoned in favor of upgrading US 40 when local groups protested the original route through the Green Ridge State Forest. The substitute route was hailed in Maryland newspapers as a victory for a western Maryland group called the "Route 40 Advocates" and the Maryland Wildlife Federation.[20]

Despite such successful opposition to the interstate's route or appearance, tactics people employ to inhabit the IHS more commonly occur where local lives merge with the umbilicus of national cohesion: the IHS exit interchanges. Where the interstate highway has bypassed towns, the towns physically have "come out" to meet the highway. The regional or national scale of travel engendered by the interstate demands food, fuel, and lodging at locations previously unserved by commercial enterprise. As populations grow and cities spatially expand, they are molded to the contours of the IHS, prompting at least one observer to suggest that the interchange cloverleaf is a new American village green, the focus for national franchise culture.[21]

Individual and collective response to the interstate's presence contributes to new spatial arrangements in daily life and new forms in the American cultural landscape. While these new landscapes are the direct product of collective reaction to the interstate's presence, it would be wrong to credit the interstate highway as the sole "engine of change" in American life.[22] Instead, interstate highways serve as magnets for morphological changes in the American landscape that are part of a larger cultural context, just as the IHS itself is embedded in a larger political economic context. For example, American cities would have experienced a post–World War II suburban boom with or without the IHS congressional act in 1956. Increasing affluence, general American economic improvement, affordable automobiles, the GI Bill, American mortgage policy, the baby boom, inner-city infrastructural decay, changing urban ethnic composition, and other factors all played a role in creating the modern galactic city.[23] But the interstate's presence greatly influenced the direction and form suburbanization would follow. Therefore, tactics for inhabiting the IHS strategic design have created new landscapes that also must be seen within late twentieth-century American social, political, and economic contexts.

IHS habitation takes many landscape forms. Following are several examples of landscape change along I-68/70 which illustrate the interstate's role as magnet for spatial and visual landscape rearrangements. Examples include rural, small-town, and urban America, and "wholecloth" creations of new places as well as places modified in tactical response to the roadway's presence.

*Spiceland Exit*    Exit 123 on I-70 in central Indiana stands in the middle of open farmland. The Indiana state map shows that the nearest settlement is tiny Spiceland (population 757) two miles south, while the nearest towns of any note are Newcastle (17,753), a county seat seven miles north, and Rushville (5,533) seventeen miles south. I-70's Spiceland exit displays all the hallmarks of an "interstate dependent rural strip." Businesses at the interchange exclusively provide "food, fuel, and lodging," the central trinity in the interstate traveler's experience. Because interstate interchanges enjoy a "spatial monopoly" of access in a limited-access system, they have achieved importance out of proportion to the few gas stations, motels, and burger joints that grace their roadsides. The IHS interchanges are important enough to have their own literature documenting the patterns and regularities of such matters as which interchange form is preferred for commercial site location (diamonds win over cloverleafs), the amount of land a given business requires or uses, the corner favored as peak-value real estate (first on the right on the interstate side nearest a town), and the optimum traffic volumes, distances to urban centers, mix of services and their placement, and much more.[24] In 1950, the Spiceland exit site was the middle of a field bisected by a branch of the New York, Chicago, & St. Louis Railroad. By 1970, the interchange was in place, and I-70 appeared on Indiana maps, paralleling US 40 (four miles south), although the interstate would not be completed statewide for several more years.[25] The new Spiceland exit was exactly halfway between Richmond, on the state's eastern border, and Indianapolis. According to acknowledged site-selection principles, the exit's situation midway between two cities made it an ideal rural location for automobile-related commercial development. The 1990s interstate traveler could find eight business establishments here, all on the west side of Indiana 103: a truck parts dealership, a Shell gas station/convenience store (open 24 hours), a Marathon gas station/snack store, a Denny's restaurant, and the L and K motel on the interchange's north side; a Phillip's 66 gas station, a 76 "I-70 Pantry" and gas station, and a BP combination restaurant/travel store/gas station on the interchange's south side. Should one require car repair, that service must be sought elsewhere because these "gas stations" now depend more upon the sale of packaged junk food than radiator hoses, wheel bearings, or universal joints. It is a landscape familiar to all interstate travelers. This is a place to fill the tank, grab a bite to eat, use the restrooms, and get back on the road on the way to somewhere else.

No population centers nearby are large enough to support all these Spiceland exit establishments, and the area's rural population might support or demand one or two of them at best. Informal interviews with five business managers/owners here suggest that the exit as a whole is dependent upon the interstate, that it also serves local people, and that these businesses partly replaced establishments formerly located elsewhere in the county. Local people astutely capitalized on the interstate as a source of customers and it became a magnet encouraging relocation shortly after the interchange opened. Four of the five business people were firm in their claim that the majority of their clientele are interstate travelers (with estimates as high as 75%), although all said they also served local patrons. This pattern conforms with site-location studies that point to the need for interstate businesses to have some local customers to make ends meet.

Two examples summarize this brief account of one "wholecloth" I-70 landscape creation. The BP restaurant/travel store owner belongs to a family who previously owned a drive-in restaurant on US 40, and they opened the Spiceland exit business within a year of the interchange's completion. Another person, who draws the majority of his clientele from local, not interstate, traffic (although he also draws from the highway), is a strong booster of the local community. His store accepts food stamps, and he supports local activities such as a Little League baseball team. His "draw" was from the general Spiceland area, and his store served as a new type of "central place," albeit advantageously placed adjacent to I-70 rather than in tiny nearby Spiceland.

*Truckstops*    The Spiceland exit primarily serves automobile travelers. Similar kinds of food, fuel, and lodging stops exist for the truckers frequenting I-68/70. Since the first IHS sections opened, America's freight increasingly has moved by truck rather than by railroad. During the 1950s, freight carried by trucks on intercity routes alone almost doubled, reaching close to one-quarter the national total. During the same period, railroad freight traffic fell in both absolute and relative terms. The tractor-trailer truck became the long-haul vehicle of choice during the 1940s and 1950s, so that by 1960, four years after the Interstate Highway Act, over one million were on the road. Although the railroad still carries more "ton-miles" of freight than tractor-trailers on interstate highways, the figures reflect the railroads' efficiency as carriers of heavy, bulky material. In total U.S. freight haulage, the amount carried by all trucks combined exceeds any other transportation system.[26]

The trucker's food, fuel, and lodging stop often is an interstate-dependent rural strip, such as those found at exits 126 and 79 in central Ohio. Columbus is a major middlewestern truck terminal and these two exits flank the city's east and west sides, approximately twenty miles from the suburban fringe. Eighteen-wheel tractor-trailer sizes and broad turning radius, combined with the trucker's constant concern for time, make rural sites the most accessible and desirable for interstate truckstops. Close proximity to urban destinations also is advantageous. Exit 126 on I-70 is dominated by the Unocal 76 truckstop and Truck-O-Mat truck wash, and the combination Dairy Queen/Pilot truckstop. Both places have scales for the truck drivers to check load weights. Both have asphalt parking lots so large they do not seem full even with thirty or forty tractor-trailers parked in them. This truckstop is a response to the IHS on the part of long-haul truckers and the commercial enterprises that depend upon them. It represents the new spatial arrangement of cross-country freight movement and a realignment of the service sector to the new order.

Exit 126 enjoyed brief national notoriety as the focus of a segment on a Geraldo Rivera television program "exposing" the steamy nightlife in America's cross-country truckstops. Large interstate-scale truckstops boast a social life all their own, further evidence that such places serve as important quasi-urban centers in the national transportation grid. Additional confirmation comes from a shop selling and repairing citizen's band radios at exit 126. The proprietor chose to locate his shop not in a town-center, or even a shopping mall, as are most retail outlets. Rather, he selected the interchange as a place he could meet the needs of his long-haul truck-driving customers, many of them "regulars" who need interstate-accessible radio service. The trucker's late twentieth-century coast-to-coast mental map of central places does not include many old nineteenth-century town centers, but is based on a new service hierarchy adapted to interstate routes.

RICHARD H. SCHEIN

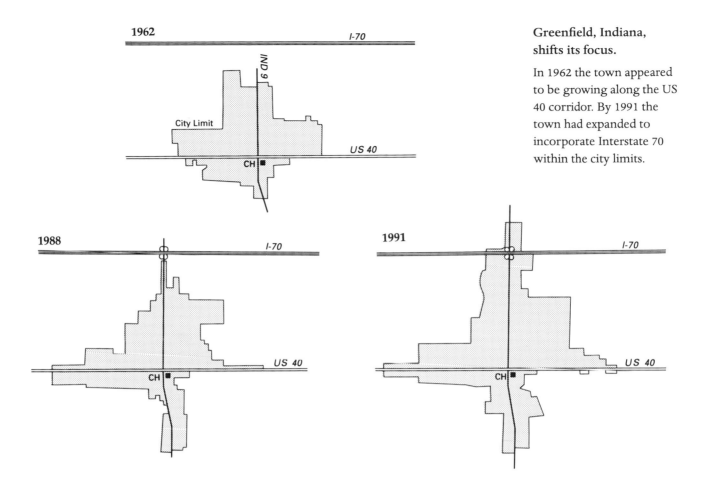

**Greenfield, Indiana, shifts its focus.**

In 1962 the town appeared to be growing along the US 40 corridor. By 1991 the town had expanded to incorporate Interstate 70 within the city limits.

*Greenfield Exit*   Greenfield, Indiana, is the Hancock county seat with 11,657 people.[27] In 1940, the town's population was 4,821. During the 1950s and '60s the town grew, largely as a response to industrial expansion at Indianapolis, twenty miles west. Thirty-six of the 111 new families in Greenfield in 1957 drew their support from the Ford and Western Electric plants on Indianapolis's eastern fringe. The main connection with the capital was US 40, and as Greenfield grew it expanded along US 40, its lifeline to the outside world. In 1951, for example, developers announced plans for a major new subdivision called Weston Village, to include a parochial school and a shopping district, with its main entrance on US 40 west of the town center. When a new bowling alley replaced the old downtown lanes in 1957, the logical place to build was along US 40 West. Some residential development occurred north and south of the town center along Indiana 9, the main north/south route through town. Indiana 9 intersects US 40 at the courthouse in the central business district. Commercial and industrial development, for the most part, however, clung to the US 40 routeway on its east/west transect through Greenfield, or centered on the Pennsylvania railroad tracks paralleling US 40 several hundred yards south.

In 1961, townspeople learned that the new I-70 roadway would bypass the town a little more than two miles north of the courthouse. Greenfield's annexation pattern over the next three decades shifted from its old east/west US 40 orientation in favor of northward expansion along Indiana 9 to "meet" the I-70 interchange. The town's commercial focus now is along Indiana 9 north of the courthouse. So much commercial development moved to this "strip" that the largely abandoned town center has been the focus of recent revitalization efforts.

Since Greenfield was demographically and spatially expanding long before I-70 was built, town development cannot be attributed solely to the interstate's presence. As the first county east of Indianapolis, Hancock County no doubt would have experienced that city's postwar expansion in some form. But as late as 1960, US 40 seemed a satisfactory avenue along which to expand. The interstate changed that. The city has "shifted directions" and "moved" north to capture the freeway. In the past five years the town political boundaries have been extended to take in the interstate interchange, and have continued north along Indiana 9.

The commercial strip that now links the Hancock County courthouse and I-70 is the town's new commercial lifeline. It contains more than just the food, fuel, and lodging stops required by interstate travelers. The strip is lined with banks, grocery stores, strip centers, department stores (including the ubiquitous small-town newcomer, Wal-Mart), realtors' offices, and insurance agencies. Even the town's newspaper has moved its plant and offices to a site near I-70, and a sign in front of the motel at the I-70 interchange indicates that Greenfield's civic organizations meet there in favor of the downtown hotel, such organizations' traditional meetingplace. Indiana 9 between the courthouse and I-70 is burgeoning with activity. US 40, on the other hand, is a relict landscape, home only to the Massey Ferguson and John Deere farm machinery dealerships and a feed mill, all residuals from an earlier era, an earlier transportation corridor, an earlier economy, and an earlier town morphology and landscape.

*Richmond's Exits*   Richmond, Indiana (38,705), also is a county seat, although it is much larger than Greenfield and more than the traditional ser-

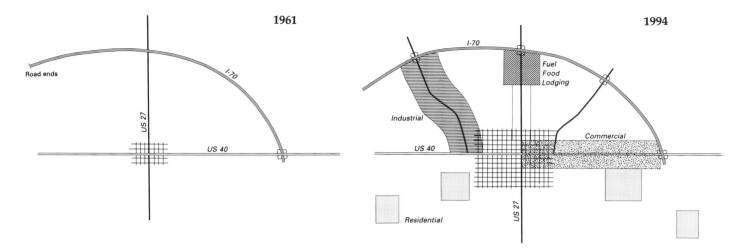

vice center of a surrounding agricultural hinterland.[28] Richmond has a larger twentieth-century industrial base than Greenfield, and lies further from the developmental shadow cast by Indianapolis. US 40 runs through Richmond's center, and I-70 bypasses the city center along an northeast-to-northwest arc. Richmond residents knew the interstate was coming in 1957. In fact, on March 22, 1957, shortly before bids opened on the I-70 Richmond bypass, the local newspaper announced plans for a proposed $1.5-million Richmond Plaza shopping center at the proposed US 27/I-70 intersection, where a real-estate developer had taken an option on twenty acres. The shopping center was never built, but the proposal suggests that from the start Richmond's post-1957 spatial expansion would be strongly affected by the interstate routeway.

Today, the I-70 bypass has four exits providing access to Richmond. One is undeveloped. The other three have different characters as the axes of Richmond's post-1960 urban growth. The first exit on the east is on the Ohio-Indiana state line, and intersects US 40 four miles from the courthouse. By 1962 plans were set for a new shopping center on US 40 at the city's then-eastern edge on the way to the interstate. Since then, US 40 between downtown and I-70 largely has replaced the central business district as the city's commercial focus. Although some commercial development aligns US 40 on Richmond's west side, it is modest compared to the eastside commercial strip. The second developed exit, at the intersection of I-70 and US 27, has food, fuel, and lodging for travelers and fewer retail establishments similar to those on US 40. The third important I-70 Richmond exit provides access to Richmond's industrial district, which was beginning to

Richmond, Indiana, has grown to meet the interstate.

Industrial, commercial, and tourist-oriented enterprises now align the axes leading from the city-center to Interstate 70. Residential development appears unaffected by the highway.

spread west along US 40 prior to interstate construction. It most recently has served a large ALCOA plant.

Since I-70 opened around Richmond, the city has spread toward the freeway along these three axes: one offering primarily traveler services, one industrial access, and one oriented to both commercial and traveling customers. The interstate's role in Richmond's urban form was proclaimed in a 1982 newspaper article with the headline, "I-70 May Be Lifeline for Area Commerce." Richmond's only post-1960 development that was not strongly influenced by I-70 is residential growth, which occurs throughout the city but especially south of US 40 on both sides of the central business district. Richmond is small enough that commuting distances are not long and residential access to the interstate is not critical. The I-70 corridor has proven an attractive industrial and commercial location, its transportation access promises convenience and "extra" customers from the interstate (I-70 around Richmond averaged over 20,000 vehicles a day in 1990).[29] Residential subdivisions find no such advantage in interstate access and follow patterns established before I-70 was proposed or built.

*Columbus Circumferential*  Columbus, Ohio (632,910), displays a "galactic city" form, and a cultural landscape typical of postwar American urban expansion.[30] Not only have retail, wholesale, and industrial activities moved outward from the central city, residential development also has followed in a city large enough to suffer daily commuter traffic snarls. Pre-interstate Columbus grew along radial axes connecting the city center with surrounding towns and villages, especially along US 40 East and West, US 33, Ohio 3, and Ohio 16 East. Central city traffic congestion reached such levels by the 1940s that planners proposed a beltway around the city. Interstate 270, the circumferential ring-road averaging eight miles distance from downtown, was proposed in the mid-1950s. I-270's first stretch opened in 1964 and the full urban loop was completed in 1975. Initially, land acquired for the road was largely agricultural. Recent urban growth has been immediately adjacent to or outside the beltway, a process foreshadowed in a 1970 Columbus annexation policy review that cited the I-270 routeway as a magnet or catalyst for suburban expansion.

Columbus's rapid growth means that formerly "independent" small towns and villages in the hinterland have been "swallowed" by urban expansion, and the entire urban area is served by "regional shopping centers."

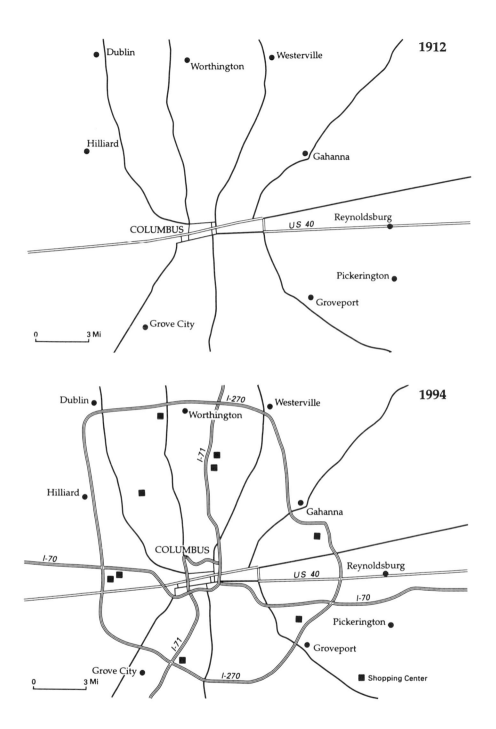

**1912**

**Columbus, Ohio, is a galactic city.**

Surrounding towns and villages have been incorporated into the greater Columbus metropolitan area and are linked by the I-270 beltway.

**1994**

■ Shopping Center

**Pickerington, Ohio, is now the edge of greater Columbus.**

This town has expanded to meet Interstate 70 three miles north of the old village center.

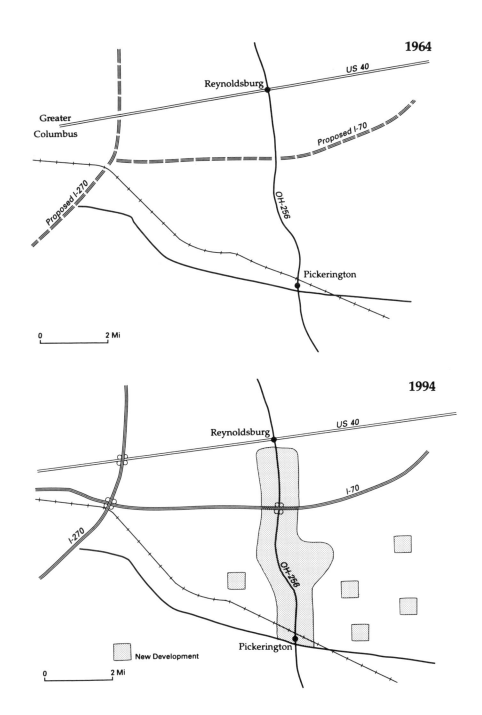

RICHARD H. SCHEIN

Towns once five to ten miles from city center—Hilliard, Reynoldsburg, Pickerington, Grove City, Groveport, Dublin, Westerville, Worthington, and Gahanna—are now Columbus suburban "neighborhoods" or, at the very least, are almost indistinguishable as separate urban places.

Pickerington is an example of a small town absorbed into the Columbus urban fabric, a process aided by the interstate highway's proximity. Pickerington is a once-small village just outside the I-270 beltway on Columbus's southeast side, which experienced over a 100 percent residential growth rate between 1970 and 1980. The town is connected to I-70 at exit 112, three miles north, along Ohio 256. In 1964, when I-70 was merely a line proposed on a map, the same map depicted Pickerington as a spatially compact village along a branch of the New York Central railroad. Suburban Columbus's easternmost edge still was over six miles away across farmers' fields. Today Pickerington is at the city's eastern edge, and Ohio 256 between the old town center and I-70 is solidly lined by brand-new residential and commercial developments. Two juxtapositions in the Pickerington landscape capture the scope and rapidity of change brought by the interstate.

First, at the first stoplight south of I-70 on Ohio 256 lies the Pisgah Cemetery, a once-isolated rural graveyard on the intersection's southeast corner. The site overlooks the roadway's west side, whose northwest corner includes an open field labeled "Winderly Place" with "For sale" signs surrounded by stacks of PVC pipe ready to go in the ground. At the southwest corner stand the Shoppes at Turnberry, a low-to the-ground cut-limestone suburban shopping center offering low-order goods and services. The second scene is just to the south. Here, on the road's west side, are the Residences at Turnberry, a luxury condominium complex, complete with golf course, whose rental office is the refurbished, late-Victorian mansion of the original farmstead. What is presumably the old farm's barn sits directly across the road, vacant and for sale. From this point on, into old Pickerington center, the road is either prominently marked by "For sale" signs, flanked by fields with houses being constructed, or lined with shopping centers, individual retail stores, and offices. Across the fields, to the east and west, according to what can be seen and read on a topographic map, are numerous examples of "guerrilla suburbia," subdivisions that have leapfrogged the continuous line of suburban expansion and sit in uneasy next-door relationship to farmsteads and farm fields.[31] Ohio 256 is an old, once little–traveled two-lane country road, now suffering under develop-

## West Columbus, Ohio

Intersecting interstates are attractive sites for wholesale and industrial enterprise just west of the Columbus central business district.

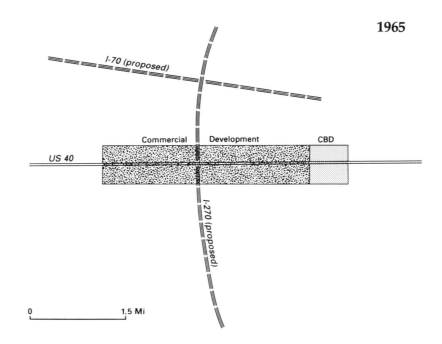

**1965**

I-70 (proposed)

Commercial    Development    CBD

US 40

I-270 (proposed)

0    1.5 Mi

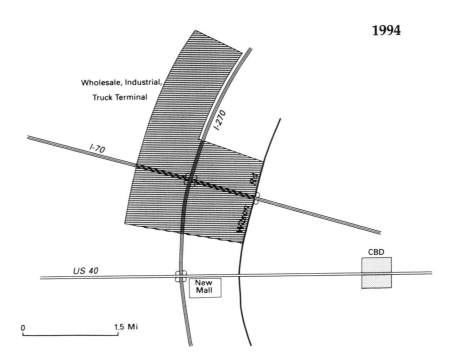

**1994**

Wholesale, Industrial, Truck Terminal

I-270

I-70

US 40

New Mall

CBD

0    1.5 Mi

RICHARD H. SCHEIN

ment impress. During rush hour this narrow road is inadequate to its new status as a suburban interstate connector. Small-town Pickerington is now firmly attached to greater Columbus through the I-70 umbilicus and the tactical responses of real estate developers, suburban homeowners, and entrepreneurial business people.

Columbus's west side also has been molded to the interstate's presence. A 1965 city map shows suburban expansion following the US 40 corridor, although the I-70 and I-270 roadways exist as "proposed" hints at the future. By 1973 both interstate roadways had been built, and residential and commercial developments (most notably in a large shopping mall) clustered around the US 40 and I-270 intersection, thereby amplifying earlier suburban patterns but focusing on the ring-road. Intersecting interstate roadways generally are not ideal sites for residential or commercial development. The transportation access promised by two national-scale roadways is appealing for industrial or wholesale-business development.[32] In 1993, the land surrounding this intersection still contained the agricultural remnants of chicken and truck farms, but was dominated by tractor-trailer terminal facilities, wholesale distribution warehouses, oil storage tanks, and industrial parks for several miles on either side of I-270 where it crosses I-70. The old country lanes are now urban "shortcuts" for commuters and shoppers attempting to bypass the bypass and avoid the interstate's main route in and out of the city. I-70's Wilson Road exit leads onto Interchange Road with access to Distribution Road. Driving through this landscape is like playing tag with the Columbus corporate limits, as the gerrymandered lines of newly annexed territory try to capture development within the city's boundaries, where tax incentives can be offered and taxes levied. The changing arrangement of Columbus's residential, commercial, and industrial components over the past several decades demonstrates the general pattern whereby "the average freeway interchange [has] collected its share of the galactic metropolitan tissue that [is] erupting all over the country."[33]

These examples of newly emerging landscapes along the I-68/70 corridor suggest that the Interstate Highway System in general, and these two parts of it in particular, have been instrumental in shaping new spatial forms in many American places. From interstate-dependent rural stops for food, fuel, and lodging, to small-town and small-city adjustments to an interstate bypass, to the galactic city's many components, the tactics employed by individual Americans, acting in many different contexts, have served to in-

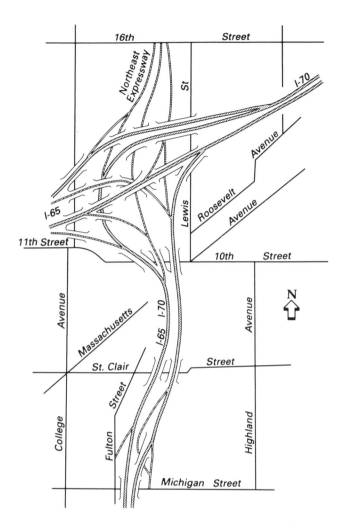

**Two interstate highways cross in central Indianapolis**

The Interstate Highway System is enormously space consuming. The I-65/70 interchange in Indianapolis includes eight miles of traffic lanes, covers seventy acres, involved over 900 separate land parcels, and is almost one mile long from north to south.

habit and modify the Interstate Highway System's national strategy. The IHS may have been a centrally imposed, regulated, and constructed transportation network, but Americans have overwhelmingly "voted" in favor of its existence by manipulating American life and landscape in response to its ubiquitous presence.

### Symbol of Modern America

The 1956 congressional Interstate Highway Act that established the system set the stage for Interstates 68 and 70 to parallel roughly the old National Road and US 40 from Maryland west through Illinois. Like their predecessors, the new interstate roadways represent American technological progress and a mobile society's desire and ability to tie itself more closely together. National Road remnants reflect a fledgling nation's first attempt to connect its rapidly developing hinterlands to East Coast control centers. US 40 is part of a national grid representing the automobile's role in radically reshaping American life and landscape. I-68/70 is one of the limited-access highways that finally removed all obstacles from almost-straight-line, nonstop, high-speed, transcontinental land connections.

Each successive transport mode involved changing technologies and shifts of scale. By the time the interstate was begun, the sheer size of the undertaking was staggering. The roadway and its interchanges now take up more space than any previous transport system. In the forty years before the interstate's inception, mule-drawn earth-moving equipment with the capacity to shift one-quarter cubic yard had been replaced by self-propelled scrapers, moving at 35 miles per hour and shifting thirty cubic yards of earth at a time.[34] The I-68/70 traveler keenly appreciates modern technological possibilities at the Sideling Hill road cut, about twenty miles east of Cumberland, in western Maryland. Here, engineers bored scores of ten-foot-deep holes, loaded them with high explosives, and blasted a 360-foot-deep road cut through this synclinal ridge, suggesting that not even 340 million years of ge-

RICHARD H. SCHEIN

**Sideling Hill, Hancock, Maryland**

Modern technological capabilities are clear in the cut made through Sideling Hill to level and straighten I-68 near Hancock, Maryland, pictured in this postcard.

ologic accumulation can match modern industrial prowess. The Sideling Hill road cut testifies to human capabilities to reduce distance to time. A stagecoach journey between Baltimore and Wheeling in the 1820s took over fifty hours. Today, the trip can be accomplished in less than one-tenth that time. Thus all three roadways—the National Road, US 40, I-68/70—incorporate technological improvements in national transportation ideals. All three roadways dramatically decreased the friction-of-distance in American life. All three roadways represent progress. They are (dirt, macadam, asphalt, and) concrete manifestations of time-space compression in the modern era.

It is important to see the interstate highways as technological successors to earlier transportation networks. At the very least, such a view emphasizes that the idea of weaving together the nation's political, economic, and social interests is long-standing. It is equally important to realize, however, that the interstate highways are more than simply an idea, and they are more than just a form of technological progress. Interstates like I-68/70 are modern landscape features with dramatic implications for modern American life. To uncover those implications we have looked, figuratively and literally, beyond the roadway simply as a four-lane, limited-access, high-speed pavement. Figuratively, the view beyond the road takes in I-68/70's cultural context, including its original political-economic justification and its role in reshaping American spatial perceptions as well as daily life. Literally,

I-68/70's concrete ribbon traverses a broader landscape to which it is intimately connected. The limited-access highway is central to American landscape reordering and extends far beyond the legally defined roadway right-of-way—incorporating exits and interchanges, access roads and farmsteads, and the cities and towns that it bypasses as well as those it bisects. To be sure, the broader view partly is enabled by technological progress, and so must recognize the advances in twentieth-century human ability to manipulate the material world. But it is the uses to which technologies are put (and how, and by whom) rather than the technology per se that are most interesting in any account of human activity.

A view beyond the highway also enables a perspective in which the interstate-in-context stands as a tangible metaphor for modern American cultural processes with their inherent tensions and contradictions.[35] Every traveler along the I-68/70 corridor knows those tensions viscerally. They are blindingly clear during that moment of the interstate experience when a sense of "where we are" is completely lost. The road design, exit signs, bridge overpasses, passing tractor-trailers, fast-food hamburgers, gasoline brands, and music on the radio combine to mask any sense of locality other than "somewhere in the United States of America." The interstate landscape is the product of a thousand assembly lines and is constructed from infinitely interchangeable parts. The world seems to have converged to a moment in the modern era when "place" has no meaning. National cultural values of mass consumption and mass mobility appear to have conquered the roadside and reduced it to anywhere or nowhere.

Suddenly the reverie of a-topia is shattered by passing cars mostly bearing Ohio license plates. Tobacco barns standing near vernacular I-houses in surrounding fields, and farmsteads with the animal husbandry necessities for producing hogs all come into focus. The letters on the last exit sign formed a familiar toponym brought by settlers 200 years ago from the next state east. In short, some visual diligence makes it clear that all is *not* the same. Surrounding artifacts suggest the perseverance of regional American subcultural practices, challenged but perhaps not overwhelmed by the homogeneity of national franchise strategies. Even the radio dial (or LED readout) might be twisted (or punched) to tune in a radio announcer whose voice emits not the Dan Rather–like tone of national broadcasting dictates, but a regional accent shared by multigenerational residents of the countryside so fleetingly glimpsed.

RICHARD H. SCHEIN

The modern tensions or contradictions between local/national, place/placelessness, somewhere/nowhere, cultural diversity/cultural convergence, and even between friend/stranger made clear through interstate travel are even more apparent at the interstate highway interchange: the meeting point of interstate-sameness/local-distinction. The exit/entrance to I-68/70 is a gateway, a splice, or a hinge of these seeming opposites, where local life meets federal strategies. The interstate interchange is the node joining national, regional, and local worlds in the country's daily circulation, all in a nation whose "restlessness is its most mercurial trope."[36]

The interstate also embodies contradictions in not-so-tangible ways. Creating, building, and maintaining the roadway is an enormous bureaucratic undertaking requiring massive coordination and organizational skills. Yet, the big-government project's most heralded aspect is the increased sense of personal freedom and personal mobility afforded by interstate highway access. The Interstate Highway System (and cheap gas) promotes individual movement made possible through tightly managed central control.

The modern interstate roadway thus is a continuation of American national transportation developments, incorporating myriad technological innovations, at the same time that it makes clear many of modernity's discontinuities or tensions. The Interstate Highway System's national framework is akin to Clifford Geertz's conception of culture as a "web."[37] Both are humanly made contrivances, social products of concerted effort. Both, however, transcend their social construction in day-to-day life and serve to guide, even discipline, individual activities or movement—whether that movement is, literally, from point A to point B or, more abstractly, the movement of political, social, and economic life.

# PART FOUR

# The National Road as American Landscape Heritage

# Never a Stationary Highway

## GRADY CLAY AND KARL RAITZ

*Deeply embedded within the highway scene lies a myriad*
*of access points, ramps, roads, routes, each providing*
*circulation, which is the essence of all exchange. Without*
*access, there are no arrivals, no departures, no movement,*
*no flow. Access, its rules and its locales, are key elements*
*in a common abstract system in which all places may be*
*observed, studied, quantified, and compared. Access keeps*
*geographic systems alive. Access generated "the hidden*
*network that determines the way they [i.e., places] confront*
*one another."[1] Access embodies the assumption—even*
*though it is widely violated—that it is a universal good,*
*not to be denied or restricted.*

GRADY CLAY
*Real Places* (1994)

A HEALTHY POLITICAL LANDSCAPE REQUIRES THAT ITS RESIDENTS HAVE access to a network of roads. Historically, European roads that avoided small communities and linked political capitals or industrial centers were accessible primarily to a small and powerful group of users. These are bad roads just as roads in poor repair are bad, for both will handicap an economy and doom countryside residents to immobility and political inaction. A bad road is also one that defeats sociability and provides no sense of rewarding destination.[2] Access to good roads allows movement of people and ideas as well as vehicles. On the good road, movement becomes a process that creates new places that provide the context within which social and economic transactions can take place. Access is the basic component of place-making; without access "there is no there." Limiting access is therefore a way of sustaining dominion over both social and material resources through enforcing the role that distance plays in limiting or curtailing the interaction people have with places. Unlimited access has the opposite effect; it allows people to create an axis of information and commodity flows whereby they stretch their social and cultural systems from one place to others.

Access to a good road creates a corridor along which change proceeds through a community. Innovations in access, such as road surfacing, bridges, grade reduction, proceed along the road, followed by changes in social behavior and landscape—a country church is abandoned in favor of one in the city. When access is truncated by alternatives such as canals, railroads, or interstate freeways, the corridor stagnates and conversion begins.

## THE GREAT FLOW

When human traffic shifts from old to new routes, from slower to faster speeds, it does so under compulsions that come mostly from a distance, that is, from production schedules and crowded calendars, from shipping deadlines, and international weather. In the process, power is transferred from local to distant hands that control schedules, deadlines, calendars. In the end, those controls extend to thousands of locations.

Deadlines and schedules are universal necessities for compressing time and space for profit and budget. They apply worldwide, wherever capital flows with its orders, contracts, and schedules. It is a global shift. When this land of the National Road was all "farming country," the great flow consisted of food and fiber—farm and forest products headed from farm and frontier to East Coast market cities. A counterflow brought wagonloads of manufactured and imported goods back from the East—glass panes for windows, brass hinges for doors—materials to build the interior's landscape. Today the flows continue, many orders of magnitude greater in volume. And content is different—the flow is now dominated by packaged consumer goods moving from towns and cities over the highway and settling alongside in the urbanizing countryside.

One hundred tons of merchandise arrived each day at the National Road's wagon terminals in Wheeling during the 1840s.[3] A century later US 40, the Road's successor, carried a continuous procession of trucks, some headed east, others west, but all loaded with goods destined to consumers. Although widened with additional lanes, the old highway proved inadequate for providing high-speed goods transfers. A wider, nonstop corridor was opened next to—even on top of—the old Road, Interstates 70 and 68.

Federal regulations that were written largely for the trucking industry created, as they now dominate, this landscape. In the process, the power over access and movement shifted abruptly from the old Road to the new.

The older the road, the better the fit between road surface and topography and the more direct access those living along its sections would have. The oldest surviving stretches of the National Road were carved from the landscape by hand tools—shovels, wheelbarrows, and mule-drawn scoops and graders—and a great amount of labor. Highway builders followed surface contours. But by the 1920s dirt-moving machines transformed the road-building task; cut-and-fill expanded in scale with deeper cuts, steeper fills. In the process, what once was a grassy swale alongside the old Road became a precisely angled machine-made cut that functions as a drainage ditch designed to speed the flow of rainwater away from the road's surface. Before cut-and-fill and directed drainage, the Road's surface more closely matched the surrounding land and farm driveways tended to join the old highway at the "topobreak," or the point at which the land's slope joined the grade of the road with no abrupt drop or rise. As an access point, it was a topographic bargain. Old National Road taverns had been built at *topobreaks* (our term) to facilitate access to horse-drawn wagons and coaches.

By the 1930s road builders had acquired the legal and engineering tools to plunge straightaway through the countryside. Improvements to US 40 straightened curves, the little swoops and rises in terrain were leveled out, and drivers could match their vehicles' power and speed to an appropriate surface. Those driving the highway to reach a distant destination no doubt appreciated the engineers' efforts to streamline the Road. Not everyone shared that elation:

> A concrete highway has no respect for the countryside. It cuts through
> the richest farmlands; it reduces the hills to a 4-percent grade; it marches
> through valleys on a level mound of earth; always it is designed for dis-
> tance and high speed. Belonging not to townships or counties, but to
> the nation, it is a long tentacle of the metropolis.[4]

This gradual process of recutting the highway bed could have continued indefinitely—but was diverted into construction of the giant interstate with uniform maximum 3 percent grades and wide-radius curves.

Those old highway sections that were not recut before the freeway diverted traffic are easy to identify. One section lies west of Springfield, Ohio, near Donnelsville. Here the road crosses a corduroy of Mad River tributaries and branches in alternating low-amplitude swells and swales sufficient to hide a car from view though only a quarter-mile away. Perhaps the main reason why this section, and others, did not undergo cut-and-fill leveling has to do with the comparative density of demand for access between city and country. City streets and residential lots all required direct access to the highway. Unless the roadway was leveled, some houses stood well above the road—as though on a podium—while others stood below in the swale. Cutting the road frontage back and down, using the excess dirt to bring low sections up to grade, equalized access angles. The "podium effect" can still be seen in the old eastern Ohio towns laid out before modern regulations and equipment where twentieth-century road widening has sliced into frontyards, leaving homes awkwardly perched several feet above the road. Elsewhere, the moment one leaves the "city" for the "country" the dirtbank level along the road changes, often abruptly. "Country" is where the land rises and falls alongside the road; "city" is where dirt becomes a commodity, to be sold, and its former site graded flat down to road or street level. Country dwellers have no scarcity of dirt; city residents find dirt is scarce and expensive. Consequently, the handling of dirt—its grading, transport, buying, and selling—has become a speciality business.

### Backwater

Let us consider this accessibility shift that is taking place along the US 40 and I-70/I-68 corridor. The corridor includes the original National Road, its many realignments, some as US 40, and the parallel interstate. The two concrete ribbons are linked by interchanges and connecting roads, a pattern resembling a ladder laid on its side, but the effect of these access points has been to siphon off the flow of commodities and, therefore, power from US 40. And the many connections between the two highways, 176 in 800 miles, assure that the hemorrhage is comprehensive. The old Road has become a "backwater" route: it serves more directly those local needs and interests that still depend upon access to the earlier pre-interstate alignments. The old Road had provided a long-distance arterial of unlimited access points which, in large measure, have been shunted off to the speedier freeway. Interstate accessibility is concentrated at federal-standard interchanges standing miles apart. A recurrent symbol of this process is the relocation of nationally franchised and advertised gas stations and motels off of US 40 to the interstate interchanges and connecting roads. Off-brands move in to sell gas in old Gulf, Standard, and Shell stations that once stood beside US 40.

### Hardening

The National Road was once known to folks living along it as "the Hard Road"—the first in many a county to be paved. Hardening the road dramatically increased traffic flow but also set in motion a process whereby the adjacent roadside would undergo conversion, growing "hard." To describe what is so clearly visible in the 250-mile stretch from the Ohio-Indiana border west to Effingham, Illinois, it is necessary to use the terms *conversion* and *hardening*. We are seeing the end product, the highly visible conversion of long stretches of highway frontage from open farming landscape to the chopped-up, subdivided and more densely populated roadscape of an auto-based commuting roadside culture. (Only by stretching the term can we call this a roadside "society.")

In the process, another sort of hardening goes on. Along most of the frontage, the original forest edge has disappeared. Today's frontage is mostly a human product. The roadside is physically hardened—developed—with curbs, entrances, driveways, mailboxes, utilities underground and above, drainage ditches or gutters, occasional sidewalks, and endless yard-tackle, not to mention such declarations of turf as vehicles standing in driveways or on hardstands; the street or route numbers, the owners' posted names and the occasional "Keep Out," "For Sale," or "Bookkeeping Services" sign, plus fences, corner markers, roadside plantings or hedges upfront or all around. Mailboxes still stand at the roadside, but we see clusters of the new rationality: steel, locked mailboxes ganged together on hardstands or in small shelters.

A similar hardening has swept up dinky tourist cabins and single-bay filling stations of the 1940s. Some owners simply enclosed the old cabins into larger roadside motels or apartments. East of Seeleyville, Indiana, an old 1941 motel has segued into a string of cheap apartments, a tanning sa-

**Brighton, Ohio**

Two lanes of US 40 bypass Brighton and continue east through open farmland. Dispersed farmsteads align the highway. Pastures and poorly drained land are wooded, and rows of hardwoods mark property boundaries or fence lines.

**Harmony, Ohio**

Only nine miles est of downtown Springfield, Harmony stands at the point where I-70 crosses US 40. The old highway necks down to pass through town and then splays to four lanes with a broad grass median. Campgrounds cluster together on both sides of US 40 just beyond the freeway interchange. Farmsteads still align the road but some farmland has been converted to residential lots.

lon, and small ventures: Matrix, Focus, and Sloppy Joe. Old filling stations—especially if anchored to now–illegally leaking underground tanks—serve out their time as cheap retail salesrooms or bars. East of Casey, Illinois, a nice old hip-roofed barn has been converted into the Casey Christian Church.

Before commuters, before the ranch houses, mini-farms, and campgrounds hardened the roadside strip, farm fields and farmsteads dominated the foreground and background of the roadside scene. By seeking direct access to the road, the commuters have built a linear suburb at roadside, establishing a stronger "presence" than the older farm scenes that now form the background, glimpsed only through the hardened foreground of inhabited roadside. In Ohio, Pennsylvania, and Maryland, the metaphor of a growing modern commuter roadside coming to the fore and displacing a declining agricultural presence into the background has merit. Here abounds the disconnected farmstead—the cluster of buildings that once served as the center of a working farm. The land is still cultivated by someone who may till thousands of acres using high-capacity machinery like that found on vast Great Plains wheat farms. But the farmstead is no longer a functioning part of a working farm and so it is disconnected from the land surrounding it. The farmhouse is now occupied by commuters who capitalize upon the site's access to nearby city jobs.[5] The signs of disconnectedness might be subtle—no livestock means no smells or muddy pens; neatly painted barns, granaries, and outbuildings; a uniformly mown grass yard devoid of tractor-worn bare spots; and the only machinery is often a garden tiller, riding lawnmower, or "antique" John Deere tractor that someone is restoring.

Farther west, across the Corn Belt counties of western Indiana and Illinois, the disconnected farmstead is present but harder to find. Here the traditional farmstead remains, surrounded by corn, soybeans, small grains, and alfalfa in forty-acre fields. Any driver over the National Road corridor's full length

GRADY CLAY AND KARL RAITZ

will see that the heartland still has a strong agricultural base. Hidden from view are the land transfers and rental agreements that have consolidated land-holdings to fewer farmers, increasing farm size and leaving some farm buildings empty or occupied by commuters. The viable farmsteads now feature new machine sheds, huge grain storage bins and driers, and those feeding livestock often have tall blue Harvestore silos. After a summer thunder-shower, trails of mud lead from small side roads onto the highway, which farmers now use to move equipment to their fields, some adjacent, some miles away. Conversion has altered the background as it has the foreground.

As a final element in the rural hardening process, the frequent proximity of old and relocated stretches of US 40 produced a number of double-frontage locations, where tracts of land ended up with the advantage of frontage on both old and new roadway. This encouraged many landowners to subdivide and develop the tracts. These recurring little clusters of drive-ins, service buildings, and contractors' hardstands can only be explained by the unplanned gift of double frontage.

In downtown Indianapolis, quite another form of urban "hardening" has taken place along Washington Street, the original US 40 alignment. Here modern developers have created a "superblock" convention center that co-erces all traffic into a few well-controlled entrances, in contrast to the old Victorian-era block with many doorways, owners, and choices of access. While designers have attempted to soften the superblock's monolithic im-pact by offering grassy pockets as visual amenities along one side, the struc-ture has extended the hardening process to its ultimate urban form: the deadening appearance of the downtown fortress. This structure also draws an analogy to the construction of the interstate atop US 40 and the result-ing change in access.

## THE OTHER-DIRECTED ROADSIDE
### Production to Consumption

Highway access has shifted from a consistent swathe of productive, sin-gle-ownership, full-time farms and farmers to a host of small-holders who are essentially consumers; that is, they use their road frontages chiefly to help them and their families act out their roles as commuters to distant work-places, and as consumers of road frontage, place, space, terrain, utilities, and goods brought from a distance. The "production" of export goods and ser-vices from these atomized roadside parcels is negligible, beyond that by the occasional home gardener, backyard mechanic, or rural service-provider.

Access to the highway helped alter social and economic relationships. Local neighborhood social linkages expanded to a regional scale. Consumption moved toward the larger towns and cities. Older, local forms of social organization faded, making way for mass society, mass culture, and a world of strangers.[6] Consumption has been abetted by business transformations that have enhanced access by compressing space. Forty—even twenty—years ago, most people shopped in Main Street stores for farm and household needs. A Saturday afternoon shopping trip could include the grocery store, the 5 & 10, the shoe store, the department store—often named for the owner—the bank, the lumberyard, and the hardware store. The lumberyard and hardware store have been compressed into Home Depot. Other main street stores are now compressed into K-Mart and Wal-Mart. Access to one large store now gives greater opportunity to consume from one source than was offered by an afternoon's walk along old Main Street with its multiple shops—and its stimulating shouts and murmurs between people in cars and people afoot.

What roadsiders also consume is now often presented to the public as furnishings in the frontyard, which functions as an extended room of the house—a fresh-air parlor. Implements once used for production are now consumed as "antiques." Grandpa's "plow that broke the plains" is no longer out back by the barn or under shelter. It stands out front, painted a bright reddish pink on a concrete pedestal, amid yard-tackle of other genre. A small plastic replica of a Mexican donkey-cart with sombrero-topped figure recalls or imagines someone's trip to Phoenix or Tijuana. Plastic deer and concrete Norwegian gnomes abound. Lawn furniture stands in prominent locations. Cars are offered for inspection, and sometimes for sale, on circular driveways.

One might expect a landscape to descend into decrepitude once its accessibility is transcended and its commodity and capital flows are siphoned away by new highways. *Not* on US 40, however, or on most of the short bypassed remnants of the old National Road. To find abandoned, ramshackle, falling-down structures—mostly anachronisms from the nineteenth century or those abandoned during the Great Depression—one must venture further into the back country. Today's national roadside, on the whole, is put to today's uses. Shunting traffic to the high-speed interstate has simply redirected US 40 movement into local zones. People's penchant for consumption remains and is manifest as a recycling of roadside structures into new forms and uses. In a sense, the roadside returns to the vernacular after decades of control by national chains, franchises, and capital. The result is an ambivalent landscape, an ensemble of places and cultural habits that are neither wholly new and sound nor old and relict. Functions and histories are mixed. Nonprofit places—an old roadside home—become profitmaking places, say, a bed-and-breakfast.[7] To find "historic" depth one must scout deeper into the deadends, cutoffs, and backwatered stretches.

It is especially important to recognize that the National Road's corridor landscape ensemble seemed acceptable to its residents, who created it, and its transients, who observed it through the windshield. The harshest criticisms of this new landscape came during the transitional years when horse-drawn carriages and wagons gave way to automobiles and trucks. The horse-drawn landscape had three major parts: towns or cities, isolated taverns and wagonyards, and open country dotted by farmsteads and fields or woodland. If read as a text, this was a tableau of American culture with a predictable order, and relationships between the three parts could be readily understood. Each discrete part had a function, and the ensemble had an easily recognized sequence or flow that repeated over and over as one traversed the road: town-country-tavern-country-town. The road and the life on it and along its edge, then, was like a play. The landscape became a theater that provided the context and the play was presented in a sequence or flow of discrete acts, one after the other.[8]

The familiar form and flow of landscape elements began to change when motorized vehicles were introduced, bringing competition for roadside access by entrepreneurs eager to capitalize on the rapidly increasing volume of travelers whom the roadsiders saw as passing consumers. Gas stations, restaurants and hotdog stands, cabin camps, and souvenir shops shouldered one another along the roadside, each announcing itself with large signs or billboards. The old sequence of standard cultural forms became a miscellany, a jumble, a jigsaw puzzle, initially indecipherable. The new corridor was a discomforting place to those familiar with the old roadside. By the early 1930s, the transport corridor had become a "scorching ugliness of badly planned and laid out concrete roads peppered with impudent billboards," scolded Benton Mackaye and Lewis Mumford; "there is a vast, spreading metropolitan slum of multiple gas stations and hot-dog stands; and . . . there is . . . conflict between speed, safety, and pleasure."[9]

Within a generation, however, the new roadside was no longer seen to be discordant by the ordinary motorist, although traffic engineers continued to fret over the dangers posed by myriad access points that required driver caution. Reading and interacting with the roadside was little different from reading and understanding a modern newspaper, or a radio or television broadcast. Like the media, the roadside had become a miscellany of often unrelated features. A newspaper, after all, was a composite of discrete but unrelated news events, editorials, photographs, announcements, advertisements, maps, reports, puzzles, and comics. Television and radio programming were a series of timed units: news, advertisements, music, different advertisements, weather, different music, still different advertisements, and so on. Yet people came to see, and to read, these discrete units as a sequential flow, as a planned program.[10] The motorized highway landscape gradually lost its image as an alien place; it came to be seen as part of mainstream culture and understood in the same manner as the most common communication venues with which it shared a common sequence or flow of seemingly unrelated parts or units.

**Visual Access**

Because the modern road is first and foremost a consumption corridor, the roadside has become a linear zone of competition within which businesses vie for access to road-borne customers. Obscurity is anathema to the commercial roadsider. American roadside businesses have rarely relied upon street addresses to mark their locations. Street signs and address numbers are incidental, for postal, FedEx, and UPS delivery but not for customer reference. Street numbers are still nonexistent in many places where local rules are lax or unenforced. Instead, roadside businesses rely upon visibility and position to differentiate one from the others. Since the foreground provides the most visible sites, purveyors prefer places with road frontage. Given the direction of travel, some sites are largely invisible because they lie "beyond the intersection." Those businesses that purvey directly to autoborne customers seek sites at roadside and signs proclaim their wares. Announcing their place through signs and symbols becomes a supporting industry. Other businesses use the road to move their product, ready-mix cement plants for example, and these transport-intensive industries also seek direct roadside access. Still other industries need not be seen from the road; dairies, bakeries, brick plants. They are satisfied with access to mate-

GRADY CLAY AND KARL RAITZ

rials, transportation, and broader markets. Their plants are bunkered anonymously in generic steel and concrete rectangles away from road frontage, announced by small signs that direct deliveries.

Eye-shot

Residential access is both motive and visual. Historically, when the National Road was the only surfaced road, home owners sought mud-free, road-frontage lots. They placed their houses parallel to the track so that traffic could be seen from the front porch. The frontyard became a public space. The backyard was a work place, with a garden, with livestock—chickens and wagon horses—and with a parking place for implements and carriages—not the things one would place in public view. Until the early twentieth century, travel was slow and very expensive. Most people led stationary lives, traveling very little, and only short distances when they did. The roadside offered a special vantage point from which to watch the traffic pass, in part because it provided interest and topics for conversation in a pre-electronic media world, and in part because it may have represented "progress." Placing their house beside the road made them part of that action. The alternative would have been to orient the house or porch to the side yard—as in the historic part of Charleston, South Carolina—overlooking a garden, or the backyard for the same reason. Houses were never situated to command a fine view across rough topography or across a river valley, although those sites abound, especially along the Road east of Uniontown, Pennsylvania.

Roadside merchants responded to motor traffic in fundamentally different ways from their relationship to wagons and carriages. Automobiles traveling at 15 or 20 miles per hour gave the passengers little time to identify a particular business and differentiate it from its neighbors. Main Street merchants capitalized on their frontage by erecting a store-front sign and opening their stores to the sidewalk and street by installing large windows for goods display. The key was a location within clear eye-shot of the street. Small 1940s and '50s strip shopping centers also adopted display windows and signs, visible from their parking lots, to entice customers. The modern shopping mall and suburban "super store"—Wal-Mart or K-Mart—have internalized Main Street under one roof. These entrepreneurs have no concern for outside window displays, their stores are fully enclosed by windowless walls. The only visual access required to signal the motorized consumer now is the roadside sign or the building itself.

### Day and Night

Visual access is tempered by light. During the early years of motorized travel the preferred travel milieu was daylight, whether one was a bread-truck driver or a hardware purveyor. Night-time touring was touted by some in the late 1920s as an adventure, where the open road at night provided the "tonic of darkness" for those bored with crowded streets and sick of traffic jams. Speeding at night could be "enchantment" for some, lending a "wonderful feeling of airiness, of outright freedom, of downright exhilaration."[11] But regular night driving might be expected only of truck drivers hauling mail, fresh farm products, or cargo in demand by industrial customers.

At dusk, as light receded, the highway for some became a narrow track through an alien place. Before the mercury vapor yard light illuminated middlewestern farmsteads, the night-time countryside was pitch black. The horizon closed in, the way illuminated only by two small ellipses of light in front of a car or truck that give minimal comfort against the surrounding world of darkness should a fanbelt break, a generator fail, or one simply run out of gas. Lighting country highways was folly, engineers argued during the 1920s; auto headlights were a better choice for night illumination than "pole lights" spaced at irregular intervals.[12] Only the faint glow of distant town lights against the black sky reminded one that a few miles ahead another town's restaurants, service stations, and motels stood waiting in welcome on a familiar horizon. The first lights on the edge of town seemed like daylight after fifteen miles of darkness. Houses lit from inside assured one that people lived here who, if asked, might provide help should one need it. During the summer, local baseball teams played "under the lights," steel towers surrounding the field, each with two or three banks of high-wattage bulbs. The glow from the ballfield could be seen for miles. Town lights became "navigational," directing the eye and thus imposing a geography of structure and order on the night-time countryside. By day, such concerns passed as daylight revealed that the world was really there at roadside and extended away to the horizon.

Drivers would discover and auto accident surveys would confirm that, although early automobiles had lights, night driving was dangerous, and often fatal.[13] Lighting engineers argued that intensively illuminating city streets at night made driving much safer and had the added benefit of deterring crime. And because enlightened city administration officials be-

GRADY CLAY AND KARL RAITZ

lieved this, street lighting became associated with the "progressiveness of its inhabitants," and the "surest indication . . . of municipal efficiency." "Good street lighting [would] create . . . a psychological impression of thrift and progress, advance . . . civic pride, attract . . . favorable publicity, and aid . . . in the promotion of other improvements."[14]

Of places served by the National Road, Baltimore was the first city to install fixed streetlights, oil lamps in 1784, with conversion to gas by 1818. The intensively lighted shopping district originated with merchants who erected lights in front of their stores to create a "white way" shopping zone, named after the Great White Way on Broadway in New York City, an area lit initially not by street lamps but by commercial electric signs and store windows.[15] Engineers saw these uncoordinated commercial lighting installations as undesirable advertising for one section when the "proper approach" would be a coordinated city-wide plan aimed at providing uniform safety and protection.

Columbus, Ohio, installed what was probably the nation's first city system of electric streetlights about 1887. Thirty-seven years later, Columbus became an outdoor laboratory for streetlight testing when the Chamber of Commerce arranged for lighting manufacturers to erect specially designed lighting systems across the city. Planners divided the city into five lighting districts, each with a specified wattage per lineal foot—residence, boulevard, business, central business, and intensive business or "White Way." Broad Street—the National Road—near the state capitol building was designated a White Way, and was awarded unlimited wattage.[16] Two years later in 1926, the same year that the National Road was designated a part of US 40, Indianapolis completed installation of a new streetlighting system. Like Columbus, engineers divided city streets into five classes with the most intense white way lighting reserved for the primary business district—including a mile of Washington Street or US 40.[17]

Nightlife in towns and cities drew its special atmosphere from the light that fell onto the pavements and streets from shop windows and restaurants. Business people found that light emitted through large store windows would advertise their wares and would attract evening customers, and night-time shopping fell to unacceptably low levels if streetlights were turned off.[18] Business lights, or "commercialized festive illumination," were fundamentally different from streetlights, the light of an engineered and policed order. Illuminated shop windows became miniature stages, the street

**The Paradise Inn Motel in Effingham, Illinois**

Few advertising techniques are as effective in capturing the attention of highway travelers as the neon sign set against a black night sky.

became a theater and the passersby the audience.[19] Planned street systems utilized lights of uniform brightness and systematic spacing. Commercial shop lights were different in color and brightness, usually much brighter than uniform street lights; turned off, they revealed the streetlights' geometry, a reminder that merchants' business buildings were still influenced by vernacular expression, although within the context of governmental facilitation.[20]

Business people and engineers found common interests in night lighting for not only could it be shown to increase automotive safety and reduce crime, it also dramatically increased the flow of potential shoppers. All of this mediated for higher property values along well-lit streets, which in turn allowed the city to assess higher taxes. For just as "shipping naturally gravitates to the cities with good harbors, so the populace of a community at night instinctively turns toward the well-lighted thoroughfare or to amusement places where the magnetic influence of attractive lighting has drawn it," engineers argued.[21] And all the better if a lighting system was designed with streetlamps that would cast sufficient light upward to illuminate the facades and upper cornices of business buildings.[22] Chicago's Columbian Exposition in 1893 was a stunning demonstration of how buildings, fountains and waterways, streets and walkways might be illuminated at night. The Panama Pacific International Exposition in San Francisco in 1915 featured night lights focused on buildings in what was called the "Architecture of the Night." Thereafter, commercial lighting was increasingly used to illuminate not just signs but the upper stories of hotels and business buildings, including the capitol in Columbus and the Soldiers and Sailors Monument in Indianapolis.[23]

Central business-district merchants embraced "light as a salesperson." For the post–World War II suburban strip business, night lighting was more akin to combining Barnum & Bailey with emerging Las Vegas. The successful strip business presumes understanding the geography of the night. The linkage between merchants and engineers is less obvious on the strip, although roadside merchants did seek to create "shopping magnetism," which would allow them to compete with downtown business districts by lobbying their cities to erect fluorescent streetlights on steel poles along the shopping strip.[24]

Borrowing lighting techniques pioneered in Las Vegas and California, motel owners erected signs lit by large incandescent bulbs hung from gooseneck reflectors. These were soon replaced by neon—which could be made to pulse "Vacancy" in red or pink—and sequentially blinking bulbs. No matter how vivid a sign might appear in the daytime, at night pulsing lights against a black night sky could make the winged horse atop the Mobil gas station appear to fly, or the neon palm trees outside the Paradise Inn motel appear to sway in a breeze. But electric signs were expensive, and a tacky greasy-spoon restaurant with a small blinking "Eat" or "Food" sign was not lifted to comparability with the nearby supperclub by night-time obscurity.

Designers conceived the backlit plastic sign that provided large lighted message panels announcing places that invited personal access.[25] Contemporary roadside businesses, especially furniture stores and video rental shops, open their interiors to the street through ground-to-ceiling glass walls so that a brightly lit interior casts light onto the parking lot and roadside, announcing to passersby that shoppers are welcome. New gas stations place their self-serve pumps under a canopy that protects patrons from rain, and at night its white underside serves as a giant reflector to spread a large pool of inviting light well beyond the immediate premises.

## NATURAL HISTORY

The original National Road track was never a stationary corridor but was adjusted periodically as construction techniques and materials changed and funding improved. Those adjustments disclose the road's natural history. Because the Road's construction proceeded in irregular stages in general succession from east to west, an evolutionary model must be seen as representing different places, especially during the early decades. For example, the first of seven stages represents eastern sections of the Road in 1806, which were little more then wilderness tracks, whether they followed General Braddock's trail across western Maryland or, a decade or more later, the trace hacked from the Ohio woods by Ebenezer Zane's crew.

Stage 1: Initially, travelers cross small rivers at convenient fords, and these crossings become logical places to establish work camps for masons and laborers that bridge the streams. Settlers following the Road chop roadside fields from the retreating woodland. Land claims between the stream and the river follow a metes and bounds survey like that in Ohio's Virginia Military District. Beginning at the river's west bank, land is surveyed into rectangular parcels based upon the Township and Range systematic survey.

Stage 2 (1825): Teamsters wind their wagons downgrade into the valley and cross the river on a stone bridge, the labor camp is gone, and a few buildings cluster in a linear village at the point where a north-south trail now crosses the Road. The forest retreats as farmers expand their open fields. A few rowhouses, one room deep and two rooms wide, line the Road, and a large four-over-four Georgian-style house opens as a roadside tavern. East of the village, a wagon and drover's tavern with space for stockpens and grazing and a stream for watering stands beside the Road.

Stage 3 (1835): Within the past decade, the Road, which had approached the river valley at an angle to avoid a direct descent downhill, has been realigned modestly by way of shallow cuts and fills to address the bridge straight on. A dump has been created on the old grade, probably on the town side or west side of the creek. The crossroads settlement is now a county seat with wood-frame courthouse and a small street grid. Large blocks of farmland open the woodland away from the Road, and some farmers are reserving woodlots on the back of their properties.

Stage 4 (1855): A small creek to the east now gets a large bridge, the old alignment here is abandoned. Merchants have established several Main Street businesses along the National Road and residential density has increased. A railroad parallels the Road and passes a short distance north of the town's crossroads where a depot now stands. Along the road one encounters more fields than woodland, although farm woodlots are ubiquitous.

Stage 5 (1900): A brick and stone courthouse stands on a square along the National Road. Residential streets have been added south of town, a line of Victorian business buildings front two or three blocks on Main Street, which is also the National Road. Several businesses have been built on streets paralleling the railroad track north of the National Road. Churches and schools stud the town's main residential streets; a county fairgrounds is relegated to the river flood plain east of town. The depot is enlarged with warehousing across the street and industrial buildings at sidings along the tracks. A small grain elevator and stockyard stand between the track and the National Road with access to both. The town has built a waterworks north of the road on the river. Woodland is found only in residual blocks at the back side of each farm, and since the countryside is covered by a grid of country roads each mile, following the Township and Range survey, the tree lots abut one another near the center of each section in uneven edges.

Stage 6 (1950): The National Road became US 40 in 1926 and after being bricked over in the early 1930s has been widened to four asphalt lanes and rerouted to bypass south of town. A large concrete grain elevator and livestock shipping terminal stand beside the railroad tracks. Several new residential streets have been added southeast and west of town, away from the railroad tracks. New motels have been built and gas stations have relocated to the new highway. A small strip with an early drive-in restaurant is under construction south of the bypass. East of the river a drive-in theater has been built on farmland along the widened US 40. Meanwhile, old motels on the edge of town will soon be closed or converted to offices (see Stage 7). Automobile and farm-implement dealers have moved their businesses to the bypass. The Chamber of Commerce has erected a sign on the bypass pointing to downtown.

Stage 7 (1990): Interstate 70 bypasses the town south of US 40. A cloverleaf interchange links the north-south crossroad with the interstate, and the crossroad now carries more traffic than old 40 or Main Street. North of the interchange, a "village" of highway services has developed, including a motel row, gas stations, and a truckstop. A fast-food strip links the old downtown and the interchange. Beyond the new motels at the end of the access road is a KOA campground. The 1949 US 40 bypass is engulfed with residential and business development. A new subdivision with curvilinear streets and large homes has been built on the river's high western bank. The river has been dammed just north of the freeway and a small "lake" created to enhance the view for the subdivision above. Main Street is lined with antique shops within refurbished storefronts that are on the National Register of Historic Places, as is the post office. At the edge of town along US 40, auto dealerships sell only used cars and gas stations offer independent brands. Local people have built a small railroad museum on a former industrial siding, and several old industrial buildings stand empty along the tracks. The grain elevator is enlarged with several round steel grain tanks standing next to the 1950s concrete bins. The stockyard has closed. To the east, an old leg of the original road that crossed the creek is now a shack town, and the old drover's tavern has been converted into a bed and breakfast establishment.[26]

**The natural history of the National Road**

This sequence of idealized roadside change diagrammatically model the evolution of a typical National Road segment from 1806 to 1990.

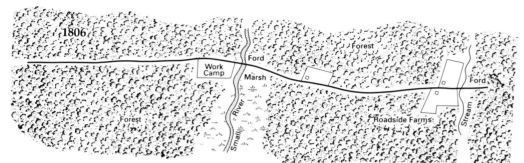

Stage 1

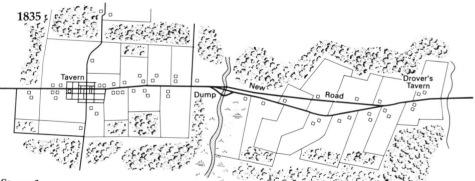

Stage 2

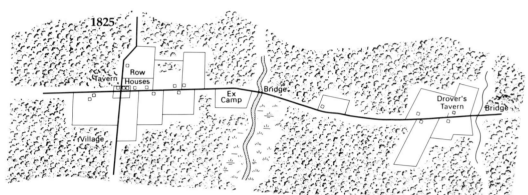

Stage 3

Stage 4

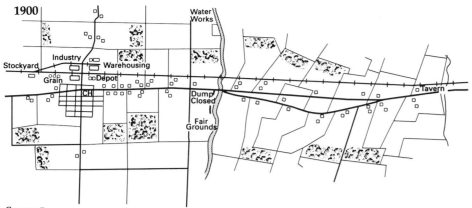

**Stage 5**

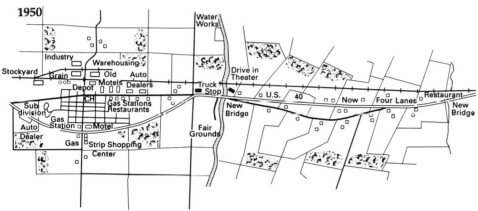

**Stage 6**

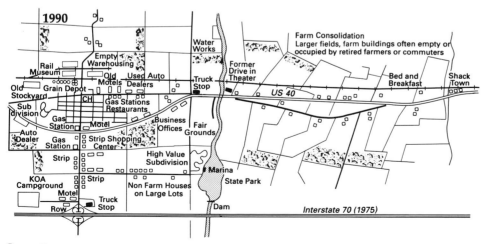

**Stage 7**

## THE BYPASS

With millions of automobiles on the nation's highways by the early 1930s, traffic congestion reached crisis levels. The problem was easy access, contended highway engineers, who attributed "a considerable share of present highway transport inadequacies to . . . the accessibility of a road or street to anybody who chooses to utilize it in a lawful manner."[27] Bypasses around towns and cities that avoided all previous road alignments, engineers argued, were required to make automobile travel safe, fast, and efficient. Federal studies recommended bypasses for small towns. But traffic surveys around large cities revealed that as much as 90 percent of main highway traffic at a city gateway was destined for points within the city, often the central business district. And officials from Columbus, Ohio, representative of attitudes toward congestion in larger cities, were concerned that through traffic was of value to city business only if the travelers stopped overnight in the city.[28] A 1939 motorist survey near Cumberland and Hagerstown, Maryland, moderate-sized US 40 cities, found that 88 percent were intent on shopping and conducting business in town.[29]

Large cities, in fact, were cross-country traffic destinations and so bypasses would have little effect upon their congestion problems. Bypasses would eliminate small towns as traffic choke points, and, the engineers claimed, allow the towns to retain their civil charm and attractiveness. Furthermore, local businesses would be aided because local people would have a fair chance to park their cars on Main Street.[30] But small-town merchants knew otherwise: highway congestion in front of their shops meant business to them, and despite the engineers' optimistic tone bypasses would have a stultifying effect upon the villages and small towns that began as minor service centers along the National Road.[31] Of course, business did decline on Main Street, in part because of the bypass, in part because the "merchant of death"—a large, mass-merchandizing chain store—was built on the bypass or in a nearby town. This alleviated the parking problem. As long as central business-district merchants enjoyed a monopoly on retail sales locations, parking on Main Street was at a premium, often controlled by meters, which had the effect of limiting the duration of access. With the bypass, or increased competition for edge-of-town merchants, downtown businesses tried to compete for a time. The first step was often to increase access by cutting off parking-meter heads to allow unlimited free parking.

Since the early Road followed local topography, the Road and the village buildings usually shared the same grade. For residents the Road was functionally no more than a street to be crossed. But a bypass would alter the road-village relationship. If the village stood on a rise of land, the new road would be cut into soil and rock to reduce the grade and lengthen sight lines for speeding drivers. Broad ditches and shoulders doubled or even tripled right-of-way width. A half-mile or more from the first village building the new road began a long sweeping curve to right or left passing a hundred feet or more behind the houses that had fronted the original track. Malcolm Cowley describes such a village bypassed about 1930 in southwestern Pennsylvania:

> The village had shrunk and weathered like an old man in the sun. The church, almost paintless, stood crazily at the edge of a deep cut. The houses seemed smaller; they had lost their lawns and most of their trees. The general store, which I remembered for its enchanted Barlow knives, its bolts of calico, its jury box (a polished plank supported by nail kegs, where you listened to tales of good crops and incredible fishing), but especially for its counter of stale delicious candy—the store, empty of clients and hangers-on, stood like a prisoner guarded by two red gasoline pumps.[32]

Older Road realignments, built in the 1930s, were usually short, and were intended to access new bridges or straighten a short stretch of road while bypassing several farmsteads or a small hamlet. The new US 40 bypasses—circa 1946 to 1949—were of grander scale. If a small village was to be bypassed, the new road usually held very close to original alignment, leaving a narrow sliver of land between the old Road and the new which now had access to both. Some bypasses were simply new lanes built beside the old concrete ribbon, which was closed off on either end but continued to function as "augmented access" by providing a convenient pull-off point, parking strip, or even a place for children to play away from the new highway's traffic. Thus, this form of bypass altered the relationship between the building and the highway. Roadside residents no longer had to depend on a tight, narrow driveway that opened directly onto the 55-MPH highway, but could now use the old right-of-way as a frontage road to "stage" themselves for entry onto the new road.

Along US 40, open country highway traffic was largely confined within two lanes. At the approach to larger towns and cities the highway widened to four separated lanes that continued through the auto business strip. Near the city center, traffic was fully separated and directed along one-way streets, as is the case in Columbus, Springfield, and Indianapolis. For merchants dependent upon drive-in customers, the inconvenience of being tethered to a one-way street was another barrier to overcome and another rationale for closing shop and moving to the strip on the city's edge.

### Interstate Interchanges

The grand bypass—the interstate highway—greatly altered access for farms and settlements along US 40 in the 1960s. The change in access brought by the limited-access interstate was not critical for farmers, but exacerbated the business lethargy experienced in small and medium-sized towns. The interstate paralleled US 40, often at a distance of a mile or less, usually within eye-shot. And in the summer semi–trailer truck convoys seemed to sail along on a sea of soybeans if you watched the interstate traffic from the old highway. Interchanges at major crossroads provided an access point whereby local traffic could join the national stream. Naturally, the road connecting the interchange to US 40 would be widened, quickly evolving into a strip of new or relocated businesses attracted by the obvious access this provided to the huge new stream of potential consumers.

Through-truck traffic along US 40 declined rapidly when Interstate 70 opened—by 90 percent or more along some stretches. Auto counts also declined, although less precipitously—by half to two-thirds depending upon the section.[33] But the interstate is more than a simple traffic siphon. Its influence upon accessibility spreads along a corridor well beyond its immediate right-of-way. Local US 40 traffic, for example, is subjugated by the new interstate even though the freeway is a mile or more away. Near Gem, east of Indianapolis, US 40 traffic must stop for a traffic light at an open country intersection where cornfields abut all four corners. This crossroad leads north to an I-70 interchange. And at Jacksontown, Ohio, State Highway 13 crosses US 40 and links to an I-70 interchange about two miles south. US 40 traffic must now acknowledge a four-way stop at the Jacksontown intersection.

### Cross Flows

Although few technical transportation studies have addressed large-scale changes in regional traffic flows, one senses that a wave of change has swept mid-America since the National Road opened the West, "carried the load" of commerce and expansion, and united a nation from the Atlantic to the Mississippi. The post–World War II growth of the South and other internal changes have brought on a shift in traffic patterns both along, and most notably across, the National Road's axis. North-south routes now assume much heavier auto traffic loads than before the turn of the twentieth century. There are few more significant directional shifts than this one. It was already apparent in the 1950s.

If, in 1956, we had stood at the crossing of US 40 and US 25 north of Dayton, Ohio (near the future interchange of Interstates 70 and 75), we would have counted more than 10,400 cars and 1,000 commercial trucks moving daily north-south on US 25. The east-west flow on US 40 was already less: 6,200 cars and 860 trucks. The arrival of the interstates reinforced the directional shift. By 1970, the east-west flow of cars on I-70 was only 55 percent of the north-south cross traffic on I-75 where the two highways intersected. The I-70 car count gained a few percentage points during the ensuing twenty years, but by 1990 could still not muster more traffic than about three-fifths that of I-75. But the volume of truck traffic moving north-south versus east-west remained fairly close together; in some years I-70 is 95 percent of I-75, in others it is 105 percent.[34]

The job of distribution performed by Interstates 70 and 75 is markedly different. Interstate 70 moves people and goods within the old Manufacturing Belt from Baltimore to St. Louis. West of the Appalachians, it soars along the Corn Belt's southern flank. For travelers, the most marked change along the I-70 corridor is topographic. Crossing the Appalachians on the modern interstate is a stunning visual experience, not the physical drudgery of traveling slowly over ridge and valley more than a century ago. The east-to-west topographic transition along the route is more striking than is the change in primary or secondary economy. On the other hand, "going South" (or North) offers a barrage of cultural and climatic shifts, and complementary markets. Interstate 75 links Florida vegetable growers with cold-country grocers; it ties together Frost Belt retirees with their Sun Belt trailer parks. It connects families in Lima or Toledo, Ohio, with the Deep South's tourist centers. Transplanted Appalachian workers move along the corridor from northern industrial towns to visit family on weekends. It also provides the new auto-assembly plants and parts-makers a modern form of strung-out production line along the "just-in-time" delivery routes through Ohio, Kentucky, and Tennessee. Somewhere along this route one crosses an intangible "anti-union line," along with a host of subtle cultural lines or "belts": Bible Belt, Cotton Belt, and the "Grits Line," among others.[35] In this process, the once-unique function of the National Road, and its successors US 40 and I-70, as *the* American interregional link has lost much of its distinction. There has come a shift. No longer does the "westward movement"—of population, freight, wealth, political power—retain its historic dominance. And future international trade agreements between the United States and its north-south neighbors will only reinforce this shift.

## THE ROAD AS LIFE'S STAGE

From start to finish, the National Road has served as a stage for American life, a setting where history can be spun out, landscape controversies resolved, and local folk learn business acumen through trial and error. This early transcontinental span, from Baltimore on the Chesapeake Bay to East St. Louis and Alton on the Mississippi, this bridging leap across the eastern third of the American grain, has unfolded like the progressive stage drama that the setting deserves.

The National Road has witnessed its own conversion from a place of work-and-production to a venue for consumption. But that is only part of the story. Along the National Road, generations of Americans have worked out their lives and fortunes or misfortunes across uneven ground; here on America's first federally funded highway, the cast of characters kept changing its ethnic and economic makeup.

When the roadside becomes a metaphorical stage, its inhabitants no longer just live or work there; they present themselves, their goods and chattel, in endless variations; they display their taste in house type, position, and decor, and in their choice of flora and fauna, of fence design. They move the house back from the road for greater visibility, its major length-and-mass parallel to the roadway. Within farmstead building clusters the house—not the barn or granary—is the most important building, and the farmer placed it along the Road. The farm driveway links the Road directly to the house; the barn and other outbuildings are more subservient.

In the transition from frontier wilderness to American road and culture, poisonous snakes and surveyors' stakes emerged and disappeared into the brush, and the brush became farms, towns, cities, and homes with lawns. Grubby tools, worn-out equipment, junk and leftovers were moved offstage, out back, and out of sight. New possessions—trim lawns, late-model cars, pets, toys, swings and other yard-tackle—are hauled onstage, upstage, and closer to the contemporary audience.

Meanwhile, the Road and those who use it become part of the act. Long before the term "information highway" came into vogue, folks who lived in a house by the side of the Road also lived out the message: "I'll tell the world!" Passersby, whether families in cars or over-the-road truckers in huge rigs, learned to flaunt themselves at the roadside spectators. Truck-trailers carry trademarks and ads, Stage 1 in their transition to night-lighted, mobile billboards of the future.

On both road and roadside, on the old Road as well as on US 40 and the new interstate, it is a question of scale, time, and economic manipulation. On the old highway, the interaction is fairly continuous; on the new interstates it concentrates around the interchanges. But one way or another, the public—both mobile as well as sedentary—practices on this national stage its own evolving forms of American life and culture.

# Preserving the National Road Landscape

GLENN A. HARPER

*We cannot crystallize or pickle the past, nor can we, where there is vigorous life in a community, turn back the clock as it was possible to do, through a combination of hardly-to-be-repeated circumstances, in Williamsburg. But we can and should, through imaginative adaptation, preserve, in large segments, not only isolated historic sites but whatever architectural and natural features will give continued grace and variety to our cities, towns, and countryside.*

WALTER MUIR WHITEHILL
in Charles B. Hosmer, *Presence of the Past* (1965)

WRITING FOR *HARPER'S NEW MONTHLY MAGAZINE* IN NOVEMBER 1879, freelance correspondent William Henry Rideing described the "national turnpike" as "a glory departed." Although he traveled from Frederick to Cumberland, Maryland (not part of the original National Road), in the summer of that year, the scenes Rideing described, including reminiscent "octogenarians" momentarily recalling the excitement of bygone days, sleepy villages, abandoned inns and taverns, and empty stables, could have been encountered anywhere along the National Road during the late nineteenth century.[1]

Despite its central role in the settlement of the young nation, by the 1870s the National Road had already experienced nearly three decades of decline and neglect, a victim of the nation's love affair with its rapidly expanding railroad network. The period of disuse and decay continued well into the

1900s, when the growing use of the automobile and an accompanying interest in the historic significance of the National Road jump-started slow but steady reconstruction and improvements.

Ironically, neglect and lack of use during the last 150 years has helped preserve many of the historic resources that now define the National Road corridor. Today, this remarkable linear landscape is once again receiving the local, regional, and national attention and recognition it deserves. Fueled by the possibilities of tourism and related economic development, while benefiting from the nation's growing interest in cultural landscapes and other large geographic areas that reflect our heritage, the National Road is now the focus of numerous protection and preservation plans and strategies.

This chapter reviews both the Road's decline and the efforts to preserve this historic corridor and the buildings, sites, structures, and objects that define its cultural landscape. It examines the institutions, organizations, and individuals who have contributed to the preservation of the Road and artifacts along the route, and the techniques preservationists have used to accomplish their goals. The chapter also explores the beliefs and values behind these efforts and how they have influenced the appearance of the National Road corridor today. Throughout, efforts to preserve the National Road are discussed within the context of the broader events of the period, including the national historic preservation movement of the nineteenth and early twentieth centuries, the coming of the automobile era and the so-called Good Roads Movement.

**Traveling the National Turnpike in 1879**

Freelance correspondent William Henry Rideing described scenes of sleepy villages, abandoned inns and taverns, and empty stables.

### EARLY PRESERVATION EFFORTS

The history of efforts to preserve the National Road or at least to recognize its historic significance began shortly after the Road was constructed and parallel the evolution of the historic preservation movement in the United States. Among the first to recognize and promote the heritage of the National Road was James Reeside, the owner of a leading stage company. During the Road's early years, Reeside (and probably others) advertised the historic sights that greeted his passengers along the route, printing posters that proclaimed: "Western Pennsylvania offers a panorama of the struggle for Independence. Our luxurious coaches follow the old road that Gen. Washington and Gen. Braddock made famous. Watch for the ruins of Fort Necessity and for the Braddock elm and grave."[2]

Of course, the automobile was the prime motivating factor behind the early twentieth-century resurrection of the Road and many associated buildings, sites, and structures. The philosophical and ideological underpinnings of the nation's historic preservation movement established in the mid-nineteenth century, however, help to explain the nature of much of the preservation activity along the National Road during the last 100 years.

The direction the historic preservation movement was to take was defined initially by Ann Pamela Cunningham's successful effort in 1853 to save Mount Vernon, George Washington's home.[3] Cunningham's rescue of Mount Vernon is important for several reasons. The Mount Vernon Ladies' Association, of which Cunningham was the leader, served as a successful administrative model and became both an inspiration and a source of information for other early preservation efforts around the country. It acknowledged and defined the role of patriotic, affluent women specifically, and private citizens in general, not governments, as the appropriate advocates for historic preservation. Also, from the Mount Vernon experience grew the belief that buildings and sites were worthy of preservation solely because of their historic, military, or political associative value rather than for any intrinsic, aesthetic, or architectural significance, and that such sites were to be revered as shrines or icons.[4]

Therefore, it is not surprising that initial preservation activity along the National Road or at least attempts to memorialize its history also were motivated by a patriotic desire to recognize historic military personages and events. Most of these early preservation efforts focused on people and events that predated the construction of the National Road and were in some respects incidental to the Road's location and subsequent importance. The existence of the Road, however, had long provided access to key historic sites when they might otherwise have vanished or been forgotten.

Apparently the first national figure to be so venerated was the long-deceased Gen. Edward Braddock, the English general killed during the French and Indian War. Road workers discovered what were believed to be his remains in 1804 about a mile from Fort Necessity and a short distance from the National Road. Despite the inability to identify the body, the discovery was given credence because it was believed that Braddock had been buried in the middle of the road in the hope that wagon tracks would conceal the grave, thus avoiding discovery and desecration by Indians.

The new grave, which was under a large tree adjacent to the National Road, was for many years identified by a handpainted sign that read: "Brad-

GLENN A. HARPER

dock's Grave." During much of the nineteenth century, it was a well-known landmark, but despite its significance, by 1871 it was marked only by an old stump. At this time, the grave gained the attention of Josiah King, editor of the *Pittsburgh Gazette,* who apparently improved the site by planting English elms and larches, Norway spruce, American shrubbery, and a weeping willow cutting from Napoleon's grave as multinational botanical memorials to the fallen general. King, who is credited with preserving the grave, also paid the landowner to build a board fence around the grave. Finally in 1913, Braddock's grave was formally recognized when the General Braddock Memorial Association raised $10,000 through private subscriptions and purchased twenty-three acres, including the grave, and erected a permanent monument. By the 1930s the grave was marked by a granite monument enclosed with an iron fence and landscaped with evergreens.[5]

**Braddock's grave in June 1984**

Initial preservation efforts along the National Road were motivated by a desire to recognize historic military personages and events. After what was believed to be Gen. Edward Braddock's grave was discovered in 1804, it became a well-known landmark. Now maintained by the National Park Service, interpretative plaques tell the story of the famous general and the military road he constructed.

Fort Necessity, the scene of Washington's first battle and only surrender, was the focus of the second major preservation effort along the National Road. The chronicle of efforts to commemorate and preserve the history and meaning of this site could be described as a microcosm of the historic preservation movement. Here, in 1754, at the site he called the Great Meadows, Washington built a stockade in an attempt to repel the advancing French and Indian forces. Although he was unsuccessful, the events involving Washington that transpired later in the eighteenth century, including the successful conclusion of the Revolutionary War and his election as the nation's first president, provided the old fort site with the shrine-like stature necessary for its preservation.

Baltimore merchant Timothy Collins, upon visiting the swampy meadow where Fort Necessity had stood in 1818, referred to the site as a "holy place," a judgment later given credence by the tradition of not disturbing the site by never allowing it to be plowed. By 1850, the Commonwealth of Pennsylvania had incorporated the Fort Necessity Washington Monument Association. W. H. N. Patrick, editor of a Pennsylvania newspaper, began a private effort to erect a monument at the site in 1854 (the battle's centennial), laying the monument's cornerstone during a public celebration on July Fourth of that year. But the project was never completed. Two acres of the site were later purchased privately and donated to the War Department, then the custodian of national battlefields. It was not until 1931, however, with automobile traffic bringing increasing numbers of tourists to the site, that Congress appropriated $25,000 for the purchase of additional land and designated Fort Necessity as a National Battlefield Park. A year later the national society Sons of the American Revolution erected a "tablet" at the site.[6]

To commemorate the bicentennial of George Washington's birth the following year, the federal government constructed "a large stockade with high pickets" on the Fort Necessity site. Although supposedly based on archaeological excavations, the reconstructed fort apparently bore little resemblance to its predecessor. Architectural integrity notwithstanding, the fort was dedicated with pomp and circumstance before a crowd of 20,000, including military representatives from England and France. In 1937, the park expanded when the Pennsylvania legislature approved the sale of surrounding state-owned land to the federal government. In 1952, Congress created a 312-acre National Battlefield Park and the following year the 1932 fort was demolished and a new, more historically accurate fort was constructed. The second reconstruction was dedicated in 1954 with a pageant entitled "Frontier of Freedom."[7]

### PRESERVATION IN THE TWENTIETH CENTURY

The patriotism that had always motivated the nation's historic preservation movement sustained itself into the early years of the twentieth century when "architecturally motivated" preservation and a growing interest in the educational value of historic sites began to take root. Chief among those holding this new preservation philosophy was William Sumner Appleton, whose Society for the Preservation of New England Antiquities (SPNEA) was among the first organizations to promote the aesthetics of architecture as a basic preservation criterion. John D. Rockefeller's restored and reconstructed Williamsburg and Henry Ford's collection of moved historic buildings known as Greenfield Village served as prototypes for museum-oriented preservation for public education purposes. The first significant government involvement in preservation occurred after the turn of the century

　　GLENN A. HARPER

with the passage of the Antiquities Act in 1906 and the establishment of the National Park Service in 1916. This legislation later directly affected the administration of Fort Necessity, discussed earlier.[8] It was the automobile, however, the source of much of the Rockefeller and Ford fortunes, that would have the greatest impact on National Road preservation efforts.[9]

## "DOING THE PIKE": NATIONAL ROAD PRESERVATION IN THE AGE OF THE AUTOMOBILE

In a 1910 article entitled "Building a Thousand Mile Boulevard," Rene Bache noted that a growing appreciation of the old Cumberland Road's historical value had encouraged the states through which it passes to begin making repairs. Bache predicted that if the federal government could be persuaded to join the states in reconstructing the Road from Cumberland to St. Louis, the old highway would again become a busy thoroughfare. Taverns would once again open their doors and it would become fashionable to "do the pike." Bache also informed readers that a trip on the Road might be made merely for "the extraordinarily picturesque and beautiful scenery."[10] Although it was the increasing number of "gasoline cars" on the National Road and not simply an appreciation of its history that encouraged repairs, travelers also were attracted to the Road because of its historic significance. And it was the automobile that got them there.

At the very dawn of the automobile age, Archer Butler Hulbert, author of *The Old National Road: A Chapter of American Expansion*, predicted the auto's impact on the National Road. Hulbert wrote his "monograph" in 1900 when the Road and its related buildings and structures were still in decline. He noted that a "few ponderous bridges and a long line of sorry looking mile-posts marked the famous highway" while "scores of proud towns . . . once thriving centers of a transcontinental trade have dwindled into comparative insignificance." Hulbert forecasted a "revolution in methods of locomotion" that would reverse the National Road's long downward spiral. "The bicycle and automobile presage an era of good roads, and of an unparalleled countryward movement of society. With this era is coming the revival of inn and tavern life, the rejuvenation of a thousand ancient highways. . . . The old National Road will become, perhaps, the foremost of the great roadways of America."[11]

The evolution of bicycle technology, including the invention of "cold rolled steel, accurately machined gears, ball and needle bearings, and pneumatic tires," were, of course, all necessary for the development of the automobile. Charles Duryea had introduced his "motor carriage" in 1896 and the first automobile show in America was held in January 1900 in the old Madison Square Garden. By 1903, the magazine *Outing* carried articles about the rediscovery of America by automobile. In 1908, Henry Ford introduced his moderately priced Model-T to thousands of eager owners and *Country Life* considered the automobile an absolute necessity of American country life. The public was ready to take to the highways but most highways were not ready for them. In fact many, including the National Road, were in deplorable condition.[12]

By 1900, most people would have agreed that the National Road was "dead and buried." Once a strategic highway connecting East and West, it was derisively referred to as a "farmer's highway" and "a bumpkin's thoroughfare, a place where hayseeds, in silly straw hats and blue overalls and barn-dirtied boots, hauled potatoes." Only old-timers in the villages and towns through which the Road passed still referred to their Main Street as the National Road. The Road suffered other indignities. "Wood choppers" in central Ohio had sharpened their axes on mileposts, knocking off large chips and mutilating them in the process. Some property owners had actually encroached on the right-of-way by fencing in as much as ten feet of the roadbed. Rural mailboxes, telephone poles (neither in existence when the Road was built), and even barns further impeded travel.[13]

Meanwhile, the roadbed itself was in deplorable condition. In some places it was too narrow to accommodate higher speed motoring traffic. Elsewhere, "it had been worn down to the large foundation stones, while on the hills it gullied into a very rough uneven roadway." Large rocks filled holes in the Road and refuse from side ditches piled up in the center of the highway.[14] A stretch of Road west of Zanesville, Ohio, locally referred to as the West Pike, was typical of the period. In some places "the original surfacing . . . had virtually disappeared. Chuck-holes and ruts marred its appearance and water stood in puddles in its low places, and in one spot at least, a small stream had washed away a part of the road." The Road's condition was evident from a sign posted where a county road joined the West Pike. It read, "Any Persons Traveling This Road, Do So At Their Own Risk."[15]

Public facilities and other buildings and structures along the Road fared little better. Although numerous original buildings and structures remained, by the 1900s many had been abandoned or received minimal maintenance.

Ohio Congressman Albert Douglas, traveling the Road by automobile in 1909, noticed "deserted taverns, moss-grown mile signs and sagging tollgate posts." Roadside inns had almost entirely disappeared. Author Rufus Rockwell Wilson, traveling the Road in 1902, noted the complete absence of taverns in a forty-mile stretch between Hancock and Cumberland. Dilapidated small-town hotels that had replaced the earlier inns often provided little more than uncomfortable beds and bad food. Although important landmarks were occasionally rescued by local groups and organizations, they were just as likely to suffer the indignities of inappropriate use and inconsiderate owners. A toll house a mile east of Braddock's grave was demolished about 1894. Another one near West Alexander, Pennsylvania, became a "notorious speakeasy" and was eventually demolished. The well-known Headley Inn, west of Zanesville, Ohio, became a sheep-shearing house.[16] Pike towns declined and, in a few cases, disappeared. Tadmore, a tiny crossroads village at the intersection of the National Road, the Great Miami River, and the Miami & Erie Canal, north of Dayton, Ohio, was abandoned to make way for a flood-control reservoir in 1916.[17] The old Pennsylvania village of Somerfield and the stone bridge that spanned the Youghiogheny River at this site suffered the same fate in 1942 with the construction of the Army Corps of Engineers' dam.[18]

The road was slowly improved. In 1902, Maryland refinished the section from Cumberland to Frostburg with broken lime and screenings. By 1913, several stretches of the Road in Pennsylvania had been resurfaced and the state highway commissioner expected to complete the work to the West Virginia line as quickly as possible. The West Virginia section was said to be in good condition.[19]

One of the most significant improvements during these years was the rebuilding and concrete paving of a sixteen-mile section of Zanesville's infamous West Pike, mentioned earlier. The improvement of this section, from 1914 to 1916, was part of an experiment by the federal government to test a variety of road materials under different kinds of weather and soil conditions. More important, it illustrated that the federal government was once again assuming a role in building the nation's highways. The federal government contributed $120,000 toward the project, with similar amounts from the state and the counties that would enjoy the advantages of an improved road surface.[20] Several stone bridges along the West Pike were also rehabilitated at this time. Federal interest in regional highway quality increased during World War I when the National Road became a strategic route for shipping war supplies by truck. In Ohio's Guernsey County, a five-mile section of unimproved road was paved with bricks in just six weeks using prison labor.[21]

These projects proved to be the exception, however. The federal government, the most likely entity for getting the nation "out of the mud," was

GLENN A. HARPER

slow to act. Although Congress created the Office of Road Inquiry in 1893 to collect data, answer inquiries, and encourage local, county, and state participation in road-building, it was not until 1916 that the government reluctantly passed the Good Roads Act and then only after much prodding from private enterprise and lobbying interests who would benefit from the construction of good roads. The act provided $75 million to be spent during the next five years in those states that had organized "responsible highway departments." Although woefully underfunded (New York State had approved bonds for highway construction valued at $100 million), the Good Roads Act and the Highway Act (1921) significantly increased federal highway construction.[22]

Lobbying for road improvements eventually came to be known as the Good Roads Movement. Chief among lobbying interests in promoting federal involvement in highway construction was the National Highway Association. Incorporated in 1912, the association existed to "favor, foster and further the development of National Highways and good roads everywhere." The association favored a system of national highways built and maintained at federal expense as opposed to what they described as "federal aid" or "gifts of money to States and Civil Divisions" for building and maintaining state, county, and township roads referred to as "post roads, star, and rural free delivery routes." Referring to many of these as "dead-end" roads, the NHA wanted the federal government to finance the "improvement of certain continuous, through-roads extending across a state and connecting at each end with similar routes in the adjoining states." Improved roads, they believed, would bring money and prosperity to local areas.[23]

Among the proposed through roads was the National Old Trails Road, a consolidation of several highways to form a coast-to-coast route, with the National Road as the eastern link.[24] In a 1914 publication entitled *National Old Trails Road Ocean to Ocean Highway,* Charles Davis touted the National Old Trails Road as the "foremost from historic, commercial, and scenic considerations," but it was the history of the National Road itself that Davis used to help establish the need for federal highways. Profusely illustrating the text with scenes along the National Road, Davis argued that the precedence of federal highway construction and maintenance had been established 100 years earlier with the building of the National Road. He also noted that as long as the federal government owned and maintained the National Road, it had been kept in "excellent repair." As soon as the Road was turned over to the various states, however, it fell into disrepair, with the road surface and the "fine masonry bridges" disintegrating and deteriorating.

Thus, Davis contended that a large part of the money spent to build the Road had been wasted because of lack of maintenance. Davis did concede that in recent years some states had attempted to rebuild portions of the National Road with "Federal Aid" (which he referred to as "pork barrel"). But without a "systematic plan of action" and with each state attempting to build roads without any coordination with neighboring states, road-building had been retarded and chaotic.[25]

Ideas for a system of national highways had apparently come from numerous sources. Judge J. M. Lowe of Kansas City, speaking at the National Good Roads Convention at Oklahoma City in 1910, was probably the first to publicly promote the concept of highways along "Famous Old Trails." In 1911, the Missouri Old Trails Road Association took the initiative and adopted a resolution at its state meeting calling for the formation of a transcontinental highway association extending from Washington, D.C., and Baltimore to California. The highway would follow the route of the "Old Cumberland Pike," while incorporating several other "old trails," including Boone's Lick Road, Old Santa Fe Trail, and the Grand Canyon Route. About the same time, a National Old Trails Association was established "to study trails and post roads as they recorded the steady march of civilization from the East to the West." In 1912, a National Old Trails Road Convention attracted 500 delegates from nine states. All National Road states were represented.[26]

One of the main motivations for establishing the National Old Trails Road was the desire to honor the spirit and fortitude of the pioneers not once, but with a series of monuments along the road. Continuing the tradition of women playing a prominent role in the preservation movement, the Daughters of the American Revolution (DAR) appear to have been the first national organization to actively promote the commemoration and perpetuation of "Old Trails." In 1909, members of the Missouri DAR decided to memorialize the Santa Fe Trail with a system of markers. In 1911, the Missouri state regent appointed an Old Trails Commission "to establish a national memorial highway."[27] In 1912, the Great Crossing Chapter of the DAR placed a boulder at Great Crossing, Somerfield, Pennsylvania, where the National Road traversed the Youghiogheny River.[28]

Mrs. H. E. Candice Cornell Engell, writing for *Daughters of the American Revolution Magazine* two years later, promised these markers were but a beginning. "The National Old Trails Road should . . . be marked with many monuments and boulders commemorating heroes and heroic deeds, and with a multitude of sign and guide posts calling the attention of travellers to the scenic beauties in the vicinity as well as to the historic points."[29] The DAR's commemorative efforts culminated with the now famous Madonna of the Trail statues. Designed by German sculptor August Leimbach and made of cast concrete, twelve duplicate Madonnas symbolizing the sturdy, hardworking pioneer woman stand along the National Old Trails Road, including five along the National Road. Ten feet high and weighing five tons, these massive statues still present a striking image wherever one encounters them.[30]

Other monuments acknowledge lesser-known or local historic events. A small stone at the foot of the hill approaching Norwich, Ohio, identifies the spot where a stagecoach overturned, killing Chris Baldwin, librarian to the American Antiquity Society. A stone marker in Plainfield, Indiana, marks the spot where Pres. Martin Van Buren was unceremoniously dumped from his stagecoach. More recently, state historical societies have placed large cast plaques along the National Road recognizing the historic or architectural significance of numerous sites. Historic markers convey both obvious and subtle messages. They not only tell about the event, person, or place they were designed to commemorate, but also something about the values and priorities of the people responsible for their construction and those who continue to care for them. The construction of monuments and markers helps insure that the meaning of National Road history will be preserved. Such efforts, however, merely continue the tradition of memorializing historic events, while usually failing to protect the associated built environment of the National Road, which can provide the visual context for the events being memorialized.

## THE NATIONAL ROAD AS A "GOOD ROAD"

For the National Road, the most obvious result of the Good Roads Movement was the construction of US 40, which was built on or beside the original right-of-way. Capitalizing on the well-known historic significance of the earlier National Road, one postcard album referred to the new road as the "National Highway U.S. 40 Scenic and Historic Main Street of America."[31] Ironically, by the time the National Road was promoted as the "Main Street of America," it had become simply one of several national transportation

**Madonna of the Trail, near Beallsville, Pennsylvania**

The culmination of the DAR's efforts to commemorate National Road history was the creation of the now-famous Madonna of the Trail statues. These monumental statues are unique but also typical of early automobile-era attempts to memorialize National Road history rather than to preserve outright large numbers of buildings, sites, and structures.

## The Pennsylvania House, Springfield, Ohio

In 1937, the DAR acquired the historic Pennsylvania House, an old inn west of downtown Springfield, Ohio, and restored it as a museum. It is now listed on the National Register of Historic Places. These two photographs show the building as it appeared shortly before it was purchased by the Lagonda Chapter and as it appears today.

GLENN A. HARPER

arteries, taking some of the luster off the title. Numerous pike towns that owed their existence to the National Road and whose well-being rose and fell with the corresponding fortunes of the Road were now bypassed entirely. For Addison and Centerville, Pennsylvania, for Fairview, Middlebourne, and Norwich, Ohio, "Main Street of America" must have been a painful reminder of better days. While US 40's construction increased the prominence of some historic sites, it relegated others to further obscurity or contributed to their destruction. Such was the fate of one of Ohio's famous S-bridges, near Hendrysburg. The bridge was destroyed in 1933 during Road reconstruction. Despite its significance, saving the bridge was said to be too costly to justify changing the course of the highway.[32]

There were notable exceptions to the continued destruction of buildings and structures along the National Road. The local DAR chapter rescued the derelict toll house at Addison, Pennsylvania.[33] Similarly, the Lagonda Chapter acquired the Pennsylvania House, an old inn west of Springfield, Ohio, in 1937 and restored it as a museum.[34]

A few old inns also reopened or saw their business increase for the first time in decades. Instead of oases for weary stagecoach travelers, these ancient hostelries became nostalgic destinations for automobile parties, serving as newly fashionable tearooms, as small tourist hotels, and as keepers of

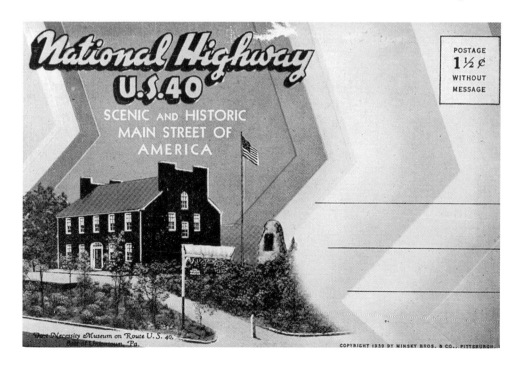

**The National Highway**

Capitalizing on the well-known historic significance of the earlier National Road, one postcard album referred to the new road as the "National Highway U.S. 40 Scenic and Historic Main Street of America."

**Early automobiles on the National Road**

The automobile's impact is apparent in this August 1914 photograph of the Youghiogheny House (previously the Endsley House) in Somerfield, Pennsylvania. Often the destination of automobile touring parties, the Youghiogheny and other old inns along the Road saw their business rival the liveliest of the early Pike days.

National Road history. The Lafayette Inn, in West Alexander, Pennsylvania, famous for its one-time encounter with the famous Frenchman, continued serving meals to hungry tourists. The new Headley Inn owners evicted the sheep and began operating a restaurant and two sleeping rooms. Business at the famous old Youghiogheny House, in Somerfield, Pennsylvania, was said to rival the busiest of the early pike days.[35]

Other historic sites also benefited from the increased traffic on US 40. Because of its proximity to the recently designated Fort Necessity National Battlefield Park, the Fazenbaker family (who were primarily responsible for the stewardship of the Fort Necessity site) sold the 1827 Mount Washington Tavern and surrounding farmland to the Commonwealth of Pennsylvania, which opened the tavern as the Fort Necessity Museum in 1932. For the next thirty years, Mrs. W. P. Martin, a local citizen, served as museum custodian and host to a growing number of visitors. Typical of 1930s house museums, the tavern contained a hodgepodge of antiques with no attempt to interpret the site authentically. Because of Mrs. Martin's meticulous maintenance of the property, however, most of the original architectural integrity of the inn was intact when the National Park Service acquired it in 1962. Today, Mount Washington Tavern is a focal point of Fort Necessity National Battlefield Park. Partially furnished as an inn and exhibit space, it is used to interpret the National Road and nineteenth-century tavern life.[36]

Not everyone was looking for the nostalgia and ambience of an aging inn. In its new life, the Road generated a remodeling and building boom of hotels, motels, motor camps, and service stations to serve the fast-paced tourist trade. Many new and remodeled facilities shrewdly attempted to exploit the growing interest in National Road history, either through name recognition—architectural style—or by exhibiting relics of the past. Highrise hotels embellished with the desired Classical Revival and Colonial Revival details sprang up in the cities and towns along the Road. Uniontown, Pennsylvania's Georgian Revival White Swan Hotel exhibited heirlooms and mementos from the hallowed inn of the same name it replaced, and published a brief Road guide for its customers. The owners of the Old Brick Tavern in Clarysville, Maryland, simply constructed a Neoclassical Revival porch complete with Doric columns and a rooftop latticework railing, vaguely reminiscent of Mount Vernon.[37] Many new facilities were designed specifically to cater to the motoring public's needs. The Leland Hotel in Richmond, Indiana, included a 200-car rooftop parking garage and gas and oil services for hotel guests.[38] Individually and collectively, automobile-era sites endowed the National Road with another layer of history. They have since gained significance in their own right and are thus worthy of preservation.

Automobile traffic on US 40 peaked about 1960 and quickly diminished with the construction of Interstate 70 during the 1960s. One notable preservation project during this period was the restoration of Searight's toll house in 1966 by the Pennsylvania Historical and Museum Commission. For the second time in a century, however, the National Road lost its designation as a focal point of the nation's transportation system and again receded into history. Renewed interest in the Road's heritage was generated by the nation's bicentennial. In 1976, the National Road was declared a National Historic Civil Engineering Landmark by the American Society of Civil Engineers.

## TRAVEL GUIDES AND THE "ROMANCE OF THE ROAD"

The *Ohio Guide,* compiled by workers of the Writer's Program of the Works Progress Administration and published in 1940, noted that travelers along US 40 would see no excitement and sense little romance. According to the *Guide,* such emotions belonged to the past and were only hinted at by the milestones, S-bridges, stone dwellings, old inns, and stagecoach taverns still standing along the route.[39] But the hint was usually enough, for travelers had long been captivated by the chronicle of American history that the Road represented. The automobile made this history more accessible to a greater number of people, but it remained for travel guides to enhance the traveler's experience. Unfortunately, exposing ever greater numbers of travelers to historic sites along the National Road seems to have had only minimal influence on the preservation of these sites.

Although numerous nineteenth-century travelers had recorded their observations and experiences, Thomas B. Searight was the first to write a detailed account of people, places, and events along the National Road. Searight was also among the last of his generation who, having seen the Road at its zenith and witnessed its decline, could speak of its history so personally and authoritatively. Written (according to Robert Bruce) for the generation that knew its human characters, his book *The Old Pike: A History of The National Road,* published in 1894, is a massive work that provides us with eyewitness accounts of Road life and brings to life the men who planned and built the road, the proprietors and their coachlines, the stage drivers and wagoners, and the taverns and tavernkeepers. It remains today an invaluable reference for the student of National Road life.[40]

But Searight's romantic account was written primarily for the armchair historian, not the curious traveler or Road explorer. It was never intended as a Road guide. Nor did Searight or Archer Hulbert's 1901 "monograph" provide maps or descriptions of topographical features necessary to the modern motoring tourist. In fairness to both authors (as Bruce acknowledged), the two publications were written before topographic maps were available and when road conditions were of less concern. Searight could hardly have predicted the need for the authoritative travel guides created by the widespread use of the automobile.

Guidebooks for cyclists first appeared in the 1880s. The Automobile Club of America issued its first guidebook in 1900 and the *Official Automobile Blue Book,* covering the eastern United States, made its first appearance in 1901. By 1909 both automobile maps and guides were common. The 1909 *Automobile Club of America Tour Book* listed twenty ACA published maps and the guides and maps of several other publishers.[41]

The first and by far the most comprehensive of the guides focusing on the National Road was written by Robert Bruce and published in 1916. Generously entitled *The National Road: Most Historic Thoroughfare in the United States, and Strategic Eastern Link in the National Old Trails Ocean-to-Ocean Highway,* Bruce's guide is significant in the preservation history of the National Road for several reasons. Published by the National Highway Association, it clearly established the National Road as a key component of the National Old Trails Road advocated by this group. In featuring the Road both as the prototype of the so-called national highway and the eastern link of the National Old Trails Road, Bruce generated a considerable amount of publicity, exposing the National Road to a whole new generation of users.[42]

Bruce's guide was the first widely published information about the National Road catering specifically to the motor tourist. He clearly emphasized tourism. Reading like a chamber of commerce brochure, Bruce's guide entices the traveler by describing the Road as "easily first among the several through highways running west from the Atlantic seaboard, and ranking with the Santa Fe and Oregon trails of the far West." He then described the Road as "a wonderfully scenic route . . . [with] a historic background beyond comparison with any of its rivals." Bruce also noted that "no other highway in this country has ever equalled the National Road in political and commercial importance, or has had so many picturesque country taverns built upon it."

To direct the motorist, Bruce provided what he called "detailed maps" (small scale) of road sections between towns and villages and large-scale maps of the towns through which the Road passed. He briefly described the natural, historic, and scenic characteristics of each mapped section. When more than one map was included on a page, he numbered them so that they could be read east to west or west to east. Bruce was apparently also the first to identify, describe, and map the location of significant historic sites along the Road, carefully noting obvious, obscure, and even vanished "old places" that "could easily be identified by the leisurely traveler."

Bruce employed what today we refer to as historic context (a body of information including theme, time, and place) to explain and describe the National Road's historic landscape. That is, he did not just describe a historic building or structure for the motorist, but he also provided a synopsis of the personalities and events that had helped create the Road's built environment. Bruce was probably also the first to describe historic sites within the context of the Road's linear geography, a key element of modern preservation planning for historic transportation corridors. Sighting the shortcomings of "formal guide-books," he argued that the "traveler has had nothing to help him identify the interesting old houses, or to connect those and various other points of interest graphically with the past."

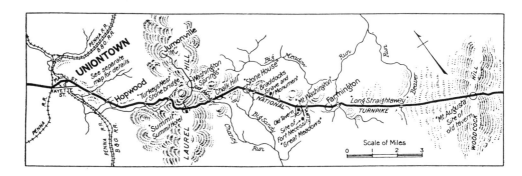

**A Robert Bruce map of the National Road at Uniontown, Pennsylvania**

National Road automobile guide author Robert Bruce was among the first to provide detailed road maps, including descriptions of natural, historic, and scenic sites, for the benefit of the automobile traveler.

Bruce's work suggests that he recognized the educational and interpretative opportunities that the National Road presented for tourists. Describing an old stone bridge east of Frederick, Maryland (known as the "bottle" bridge because of its jug-shaped stone pillar), he noted that "one must leave the car and take a careful look at the dimensions of the solid stone arches and the depth of the roadway; and to realize that it was built without aid of derricks, cranes and other facilities considered necessary for such work today."

Finally, Bruce correctly envisioned the automobile's role in the National Road's eventual resurrection. While acknowledging competition from rail transportation and conceding that business travelers, mail, and freight regularly traveled by train, he observed that "under favorable conditions a good driver can safely run an automobile between Cumberland and Wheeling in not much more time than it takes by the fast trains of the B. & O." More important, Bruce predicted the eventual rebuilding and upgrading of the National Road as part of a modern transcontinental highway system, to accommodate what he called "a new form of travel." He was convinced that it was the automobile and the consequent "demand for improved through roads" that was responsible for the National Road's current "transformation."

Bruce's travel guide has a major shortcoming. It was never completed. Bruce ended his guide at Wheeling, meaning that motorists traveling the Ohio, Indiana, and Illinois sections of the Road (fully two-thirds of the length) would not have the benefit of his knowledge and observation skills. Although he mentioned the possibility of another "series of articles" that would continue the journey west to St. Louis and possibly to western sections of the National Old Trails Road, such a guide was never written.

Nor is Bruce's guide necessarily an accurate description and interpretation of the National Road as it appeared when he made his field trip in the

GLENN A. HARPER

spring of 1915. Although he justifiably chose to describe the Road's landscape in the context of its early nineteenth-century prominence, he deliberately ignored or downplayed many of the changes and intrusions that had significantly altered that landscape by 1915. For example, he only briefly mentioned the industrialization of larger Pike towns such as Brownsville, Washington, and Wheeling, and the corresponding changes in the economic and ethnic makeup of the people living along the Road. Instead, he chose to concentrate on the idyllic rural landscapes, scenic views and vistas, and historic sites that he knew would interest tourists.

Later guides reflect the quickened pace of the automobile age and the commercial enterprises and services demanded by the motoring public. Typical of these is the 1926 issue of the *Mohawk-Hobbs Grade and Surface Guide: National Old Trails and Connections* (primarily the National Road), published by the Tourist Service Department of the Mohawk Rubber Company. Although this guide acknowledged historic sites along the route, they are identified with little more than one-line descriptions. For example, Braddock's grave is described as "interesting," and the motorist is advised to "read the tablets." Instead, the *Mohawk-Hobbs Guide* focused on practical information to aid the motorist, locating and describing hotels, garages, lunch stands, camps, and camping space. Small maps provide a general overview of each section while a larger "profile and surface" chart provides such key information as elevation and the type of road surface.[43]

Reflecting its increasing involvement in the nation's highway system, the federal government published a new round of travel guides in the 1930s and 1940s. Known as the American Guide Series, they were compiled by authors and professional writers of the Writer's Program of the Works Progress Administration in an attempt to keep men and women of this profession employed during the Great Depression. Organized according to state, each guide included essays on such themes as history, government, agriculture, and education, and provided "point-by-point" tours of state and federal highways.[44]

Although travel guides obviously helped focus the attention of a new generation of Road users on National Road heritage, they appear to have had little impact on preserving that heritage. As noted earlier, the automobile did encourage the adaptive use of a few old inns and possibly other buildings as tearooms, restaurants, or other tourist-related facilities. But for every building that was saved, numerous other National Road resources such as stone bridges and other structures and buildings were lost when US 40 was widened and upgraded or when Interstates 68 and 70 were built. In fact, changes along some sections of the contemporary National Road are so extensive they have rendered much of the information included in the various travel guides obsolete.

Nevertheless, travel guides remain important references for they describe the condition of the National Road's cultural landscape as it appeared prior to World War II, before improvements irreversibly altered much of that landscape. Bruce's work is particularly valuable for students of the nineteenth-century Road in Maryland, Pennsylvania, and West Virginia. His now-historic photographs are especially illuminating as evidence of both continuity and change along the Road. Travel guide references to still-extant historic sites will remain important sources of information for future preservation planning along the National Road.

## CARING FOR THE ROAD IN THE TWENTY-FIRST CENTURY

An examination of the historic preservation movement in America during the 1980s and 1990s reveals an increasing shift away from an emphasis on preserving individual buildings, structures, and sites, to large multiresource historic districts, and more recently to the emergence of more comprehensive preservation planning strategies among coalitions of conservationists, historic preservationists, and others who share an interest in protecting the distinctive features of our regional landscapes.

The federal government and a few states are also developing more comprehensive approaches to the preservation of large multiresource landscapes. Current preservation strategies frequently combine both historic and natural resource protection and often are part of local and regional planning processes. Because of the variety of natural and cultural resources often identified with such projects, they usually require multidisciplined evaluations and complex protection and management plans. Equally important, they demand vision, broad community support, strong local leadership and cooperation among public and private organizations and institutions and governments.

Currently there are several planning mechanisms or at least conceptual frameworks in various stages of development, one or more of which may ultimately influence National Road preservation efforts. These include National and State Scenic-Byways, National and State Trails programs, National

GLENN A. HARPER

Heritage Corridors, National Heritage Areas, and State Heritage Parks.

Although the federal and state administrative agencies may vary, these programs have several things in common: Their goals are to protect outstanding natural, cultural, scenic, and recreational resources, encourage local economic development, preserve traditional lifeways, and enhance the quality of life. Management and protection strategies generally preclude any large-scale land acquisition and instead rely on public/private partnerships and cooperative agreements. Strong local and grassroots leadership and participation at all stages of project planning and implementation is important. In fact, many trail, corridor, and scenic-byway programs are initiated at the local level. Finally, because these programs often attempt to protect resources of state or national significance, they usually require some form of state or federal authorization.[45]

The National Heritage Corridor concept, which is increasingly defined within the even broader concept of National Heritage Areas, appears to offer the most flexibility in accomplishing a comprehensive National Road preservation program. National Heritage Corridors are linear resources that typically include roads, rivers, or canals. Corridor designation is a public/private initiative that attempts to link and preserve natural, cultural, and recreational sites as a means of promoting tourism for the economic benefit of local communities. At present, the Heritage Corridor movement is centered in the Northeast and Midwest and generally focuses on early and mid-nineteenth-century transportation and industrial development, a basis for much of the historic and architectural significance of the National Road. National Heritage Corridors are designated by an act of Congress. There is, however, no umbrella legislation governing their formation and authorization and no federal staff overseeing their administration. Not surprisingly, many Heritage Corridor projects are planned and promoted at the local or grassroots level, often with the able technical assistance of the Rivers and Trails Conservation Assistance Program of the National Park Service. Three National Heritage Corridors have received federal designation.[46]

The lack of standardized criteria for designating National Heritage Corridors, Heritage Areas, and other large multiresource landscapes may soon be rectified. Because of the efforts of the National Park Service, the National Trust for Historic Preservation, the newly organized National Coalition for Heritage Areas, and numerous other organizations and individuals, legislation to establish a national system of heritage areas has been introduced in both the 103rd and 104th Congress. The most recent pending legislation calls upon Congress to establish a rational, systematic, and equitable federal designation process, including designation criteria, and to provide technical assistance funding for feasibility studies prior to designation and for management functions after designation.

Under the proposed legislation, heritage areas must originate from and be sustained by state, regional, and local efforts and will be managed at the local level even if they receive federal designation. Responding to a increasingly vocal property rights advocates minority, the legislation, if passed, does not increase the role of the federal government in land use planning issues. Nevertheless, a strong, partnership-based role for the federal government is critical if the heritage area movement is to be successful. Technical assistance and start-up funds are nearly always necessary, and federal designation is important for educational and marketing purposes. Also, because of its broad knowledge of heritage areas nationally, the federal government can serve as a clearinghouse for technical information and expertise. Finally, because many heritage areas and corridors pass through or are adjacent to federal lands, federal land management agency partnerships will always be necessary and desirable.[47]

**National Road Heritage Park study map**

Efforts to plan comprehensively for the preservation and future protection of the National Road landscape must consider the variety and linear nature of the natural, historic, and recreational resources. This map, produced for Pennsylvania's National Road Heritage Park Feasibility Study, by Mary Means & Associates, highlights natural and recreational resource boundaries and historic sites.

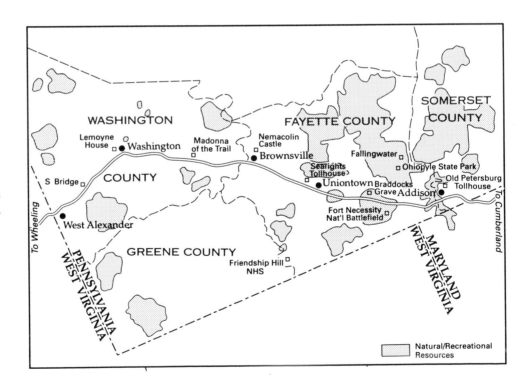

GLENN A. HARPER

The growing understanding and appreciation for regional and linear cultural landscapes has begun to influence preservation efforts along the National Road. Instead of concentrating on a single historic building or structure or even a historic district, much of this activity is now regional in scope, sometimes crossing several political jurisdictions. Representatives of governments, agencies, and private and nonprofit groups from the entire ninety-mile length of the National Road's Pennsylvania segment now sit on that state's National Road Heritage Park Steering Committee. Increasingly, Road preservation efforts include a comprehensive preservation planning process incorporating the identification and conservation of natural, historic, and cultural resources; economic development; intergovernment/interagency cooperation; recreation; education; and interpretation.

## THREATS TO NATIONAL ROAD CORRIDOR RESOURCES

For the National Road, such preservation strategies cannot come soon enough. Individual historic sites and even large sections of the corridor continue to be lost or irretrievably altered. Neglect continues to be the most prevalent rationale for preserving National Road resources, particularly along some of the Road's more remote sections. In rural eastern Ohio, numerous old sections of Road and easily accessible Pike towns, bypassed by US 40 and later Interstate 70, are filled with reminders of the National Road's heyday. While a few of these properties continue to function as homes and businesses, many others sit empty and receive little or no maintenance, a practice that eventually leads to what preservationists usually refer to as demolition by neglect. A recent trip through the quiet village of Old Washington, Ohio, revealed the remnants of several stone foundations as the only evidence of recently demolished houses. In many communities a general lack of preservation knowledge and interest, combined with long-depressed local economies, has further contributed to the decline and destruction of National Road resources. Owners also may not be aware of the historic and architectural significance of their properties, but even when conscious and interested, they often lack the financial resources to perform even basic maintenance. While nineteenth-century buildings and structures continue to be threatened, they have the advantage of sheer numbers and more readily acknowledged significance. Meanwhile, US 40–era motels, service stations, and other automobile-related resources, fewer in number to begin with, are often overlooked or dismissed as nonhistoric.

Much of the change the National Road has experienced can be attributed to the common nature of transportation corridors. Highways were built for transportation and commerce. The underlying assumption is that as transportation technology improves and commerce grows, transportation corridors will also undergo major improvements. Brian A. Butko, editorial assistant for *Pittsburgh History*, recently identified a basic paradox of historic highway preservation that might be attributed to the evolutionary nature of transportation corridors. "Preserving a roadscape actually changes its reason for being, but its temporary life actually increases the urgency to save it."[48] Goods move along highways with comparative ease and highway access encourages people to build new homes and industries at roadside. Development escalates the demand for road improvements to handle additional traffic. New shoulders and lanes are added and intersections are rebuilt. Higher traffic capacity attracts more roadside development, thus perpetuating the cycle.[49] With the increasing number of vehicles using historic highways, safety and liability issues often take precedence over the historic significance of the roadscape. The recent demolition of a massive historic redstone wall by the Pennsylvania Department of Transportation clearly illustrates the dilemma resulting from the dynamic nature of transportation corridors. Built by a local church, the wall lined both sides of the National Road on the east side of Uniontown. It served as a kind of gateway to the city and was an important contributing element to the local cultural landscape. Nevertheless, it was hammered to pieces as part of an agreement to widen and realign the Road to improve safety and traffic flow.

To some degree, the rate of major road improvements along US 40 has slowed since the construction of parallel Interstates 68 and 70—as did the building of US 40 bypasses decades earlier slow or, in some cases, even halt development along old Road sections. With the reversion of US 40 to a conveyor of local and regional traffic, future Road improvements will probably be relatively minor, including bridge rehabilitation or replacement, intersection improvements, and resurfacing. Some National Road states, however, plan major improvements that could cause irreparable damage to the historic, scenic and recreational resources along the Road's corridor.[50]

## STATE PRESERVATION EFFORTS

In spite of, and perhaps because of, losses like the redstone wall at Uniontown, Pennsylvania appears to have advanced further than any other Na-

GLENN A. HARPER

tional Road state in its efforts to comprehensively plan for the preservation and future protection of the National Road landscape. Current projects include designation of the National Road–US 40 corridor through three southwestern Pennsylvania counties as one of five Pennsylvania Heritage Park planning areas.[51] Pennsylvania's efforts to stimulate preservation along the National Road, however, predate the State Heritage Park effort. In 1986, the Bureau for Historic Preservation contracted with California University of Pennsylvania to complete a National Road Historic Resources Survey, the only such comprehensive survey completed in any of the six National Road states. Completed in 1987, the survey focuses on resources directly related to the National Road, including inns and taverns, toll houses, mile markers, hotels and motels, bridges and culverts, service stations and garages, cabin camps and eateries.[52]

Lobbying Congress for federal assistance also has proved successful in Pennsylvania, where the congressionally created Southwestern Pennsylvania Heritage Preservation Commission oversees National Park Service efforts to recognize, preserve, and protect the iron, steel, coal, and transportation-related resources of nine counties in southwestern Pennsylvania in order to revitalize this once-thriving industrial region.

At the request of the Heritage Preservation Commission, in 1992, staff from the National Park Service, Denver Service Center, formed the Western Pennsylvania Partnerships Branch to begin gathering data for a Special Resource Study of the National Road Corridor. The purpose of the study was to determine if some parts of the corridor might meet the criteria necessary for creating a new unit of the National Park System, or if they might be more appropriately managed and interpreted by state or other agencies or private organizations.

Recognizing that any future efforts to protect and enhance the National Road will require a network of cooperation between government agencies and private organizations spanning six states, the partnership began a procedure known as the "Delphi process" to obtain written commentary and feedback from knowledgeable and interested people representing agencies and organizations along the National Road. Published in 1994, the study includes the history and significance of the resources, current conditions and threats, their suitability and feasibility for inclusion in the National Park Service system, and four alternatives and management options for National Road resource protection and interpretation.[53] The Commonwealth is also seeking state early implementation funds and Intermodal Surface Transportation Efficiency Act (ISTEA) funds to protect its remaining mile markers, fabricate new markers, and repair the roofs of the two remaining toll houses.

Other states have recently initiated projects that address preservation issues along the National Road. The Maryland Historical Trust and the Maryland Department of Transportation are considering a proposal for a heritage development study and possible state designation for the National Road in Maryland. In West Virginia, the Wheeling National Heritage Area highlights the region's natural setting and numerous historic resources to interpret its role in nineteenth-century expansion. Because the greatest period of growth and national significance for Wheeling came with the building of the National Road, plans call for conserving, interpreting, promoting, and developing "Wheeling Heritage" within the context of the city's National Road heritage. As part of this effort, the West Virginia State Historic Preservation Office also completed a sixteen-mile architectural survey of the National Road corridor. Based on the results of the survey, a 2½-mile corridor historic district was listed on the National Register of Historic Places, and additional National Register listings are under consideration. Wheeling is also exploring ways to link their projects with Pennsylvania's National Road Heritage Park.[54]

West Virginia University's Institute for the History of Technology and Industrial Archaeology is busy locating and recording National Road resources. As part of its ongoing effort to study the nation's nineteenth-century internal improvements movement, the institute is currently involved in a multiyear project to document the engineering and construction of the original Cumberland-to-Wheeling Road section. The project uses historic maps, aerial photographs, and intensive onsite investigations to locate original Road alignment. A series of maps will detail surviving cultural resources. The institute is also documenting to Historic American Engineering Record (HAER) standards, the 1836 LaVale, Maryland, toll house. Other structures to be documented according to HAER standards include the Casselman bridge and the remains of a Pennsylvania S-bridge.[55]

Although Ohio's efforts to identify, document, and preserve the resources along its 220-mile National Road corridor have been sporadic at best, the Ohio Historic Preservation Office is planning to correct this deficiency partially with a comprehensive historic properties survey and inventory of existing sections of the National Road and its associated buildings, sites, structures, and objects. Funded with ISTEA funds through the Ohio Department of Transportation, the project will include a written narrative of historic context for the National Road and US 40, with particular emphasis on construction and period of significance in Ohio. Another Ohio ISTEA-funded National Road project involves the preservation and enhancement of an 1830 S-bridge in the village of New Concord, Ohio. The project includes minor stone repair and tuck-pointing, bridge surface stabilization, landscaping, and improved vehicular and pedestrian access.[56]

A unique effort to recognize and promote National Road heritage is the work of Ohio artist and educational consultant Vicki Burton. Best known for her fine line drawings of prominent National Road sites, Vicki was also instrumental in helping to design an education curriculum for grades 4 through 8, which utilizes first-person interpretation and hands-on teaching techniques. Sponsored by the Ohio Historical Society, the curriculum, entitled "Another Place Another Time," focuses on four Ohio historic sites, including the National Road. Students participating in the National Road program become a nineteenth-century road crew, surveying, map reading, and actually building a small simulated section of road with stone (macadam) and brick. Approximately twenty-five classes participate in the program annually and Burton believes it is responsible for a growing knowledge and appreciation of local history. Along with Elizabeth Reeb and Alan King of the Ohio Historical Society, Burton also served as a consulting editor for a June 1991 issue of *Cobblestone* (a history magazine for children) which featured the National Road.[57]

Preservation activity has also begun to increase along the Road's westernmost segment. Leading efforts in Indiana is the Historic Landmarks Foundation of Indiana, a strong statewide preservation organization. The foundation organized the Indiana National Road Association to identify, promote, preserve, and interpret the Road's cultural value, and to increase Road access and use by the public.

Working with the Indiana Departments of Transportation and Commerce, Division of Tourism, and the National Trust for Historic Preservation, the association has undertaken a National Road corridor management plan for the three easternmost counties through which the Road passes. The plan addresses issues relating to tourism and economic development and protection of the Road's scenic and historic resource. The association hopes to implement the plan, which will eventually cover the entire Indiana National Road corridor, through a network of committees in National Road communities across the state.

The Historic Landmarks Foundation also owns the historic Huddleston Farmhouse Inn Museum, which features permanent and rotating exhibits on house history, the National Road, and eastern Indiana architecture, and has been proposed as a National Road visitor center. In addition, the foundation administers Landmark Tours, which occasionally conducts bus tours focusing on National Road history and historic sites. Prominent among private historic preservation efforts along the Indiana portion of the National Road is the recent restoration of the grand Italianate-style Mellville-McHaffie farmhouse (recently christened Rising Hall) by Walt and June Prosser.[58] Lyle E. Kruger, chief of surveys for the Illinois Department of Transportation, has chosen to promote National Road history in mass-media fashion. Using historic surveyors' field notes and aerial photography, Kruger has prepared a video entitled, "Surveying the National Road: Then and Now."

## TOURISM AND HISTORIC PRESERVATION

Much current preservation planning is now motivated by the concept of heritage development, which recognizes that a region's history is reflected in both the natural and built environment and in the traditions and customs of its people. According to this concept, evidence of a region's history can be found in its scenic and natural areas, its historic architecture, its folkways and folklife resources, its commercial and industrial heritage, and in its recreational activities. The benefits of heritage development are often evident in growing community pride and in increased tourism and other forms of economic development. Many communities have begun to capitalize on the growing number of Americans who desire to experience authentic "history." Heritage development often focuses on tourism as a means of stimulating and strengthening local economies. Sometimes referred to as cultural or heritage tourism, it is one of the most rapidly growing segments of the tourism industry. Travel guide author Arthur Frommer notes that "every study of travel motivations has shown that an interest in the achievements of the past is among the three major reasons why people travel. The other two are rest or recreation, and the desire to view great natural sites."[59]

Tourism is not new along the National Road. As we have seen, travelers have long been aware of the Road's historic significance. The nation's bicentennial marked the beginning of the current revival of interest in the National Road. But, like the revivals earlier in the century generated by America's love for the automobile, bicentennial projects generally chose to celebrate and commemorate National Road history and did not produce any substantive strategies for maintaining and protecting the remaining sections of the old Road or related buildings, structures, and objects.

The exception has been the continued effort to focus on prominent individual sites such as Fort Necessity National Battlefield, Mount Washington Tavern, and the two remaining toll houses in Pennsylvania, and sites further west, such as the Pennsylvania House Inn in Springfield, Ohio, and the Huddleston Farmhouse Inn Museum near Cambridge City, Indiana. Owned by various public and private entities, these sites have continued the museum approach to preserving the history and significance of the National Road begun during the early years of automobile touring. Often the repository of significant artifact collections, volunteer and professional staff attempt to interpret various aspects of life along the National Road within the context of the site where the museum collection is housed.

The culmination of National Road museology can be found at the National Road–Zane Gray Museum, on US 40 near Zanesville, Ohio. Opened in 1973 and owned and operated by the Ohio Historical Society, this museum is the only institution along the National Road's entire length built to interpret the Road's history. The museum houses a diorama portraying the Road's development from its original construction to the arrival of the automobile. Exhibits illustrate how vehicle technology prompted road improvements and life-size reconstructions depict typical nineteenth-century scenes along the Road. The museum also commemorates the life and career of Zane Gray, an important literary figure linked to the National Road by circumstance and history. Gray's great-grandfather Ebenezer Zane blazed the first public road through frontier Ohio, Zane's Trace, which roughly follows the same route from Wheeling to Zanesville as the later National Road. He was also the cofounder and namesake of Zanesville. Considered father of the adult western, Zane Gray also wrote several historical novels set in the wilds of Ohio. His first novel, *Betty Zane,* is about the winning of the Ohio Valley from Native Americans and the opening of the West to white settlement. It was, of course, the Road's western section that provided major access to this region.[60]

The best examples of National Road tourism today can be found in the towns and villages along the Road. Numerous business associations, consortiums, and task forces in the six National Road states, particularly east of Ohio, are rediscovering their "Pike town" heritage. The most visible result of the growing interest in the National Road at the local level is the National Pike Festival. Billed as the world's longest festival, this annual event encourages participants to "travel the Road that Made the Nation." Celebrated from Maryland to eastern Ohio, the festival commemorates the history of the Road with a series of activities including a wagon train that travels through several National Road towns. Again, Pennsylvania took the lead in developing a festival that promotes and capitalizes on the succession of historic and cultural sites that make up the National Road corridor. Celebrated here since 1973, the festival expanded in 1989 to include the western Maryland counties of Washington, Allegheny, and Garrett, and in 1991 by Ohio County in West Virginia, and Belmont, Guernsey, and Muskingum counties in Ohio.[61]

Towns along the Road's western sections are also beginning to recognize and celebrate their National Road heritage. Vandalia, Illinois, holds a Cumberland Road Festival the first Saturday in May each year. Indiana has developed, better than any other state, the concept of the Road as a route of history for the benefit of individual tourists. A publication entitled "Eastern Indiana's Corridor of History," produced in cooperation with the Tourism Development Division of the Indiana Department of Commerce and the Eastern Regional Office of Historic Landmarks Foundation, provides in one brochure a self-guided tour of National Road towns in the eastern part of the state. Historic sites are identified and keyed to individual town maps. The towns also are identified along a simple line drawing of the Road, as are motels, restaurants, campgrounds, and interchanges that parallel Interstate 70. Photographs identify local landmarks. The most significant aspect of this handsome brochure, however, is its success in interpreting for the tourist the Road as a linear historic resource. Towns are not identified as isolated entities but are tied together by the common theme of the National Road. The "Corridor of History" brochure should serve as a prototype for similar self-guided tours of other sections of the Road.[62]

## HERITAGE TOURISM: PRESERVING OR REMAKING THE LANDSCAPE

Contributing author and geographer Peirce Lewis and others have previously written about the national penchant to view history "not as a context within which we live and from which we spring, but instead as a thing, as a commodity to be bought and sold, like a piece of real estate."[63] The selling of our heritage manifests itself in many ways, including the growing number of so-called historic villages (reconstructed and relocated historic properties), conveniently located for easy access from nearby interstates, and the evolution of historic towns and villages from traditional commercial centers to weekend tourist meccas. Even the major federal financial incentive for rehabilitating historic buildings, the investment tax credit, is limited to buildings used in a trade or business or held for income production.

"The American way of history" has not been lost on such mega-enterprises as Disneyland, which long ago recognized America's nostalgia for Main Street and designed a pseudo-historic street of shops as an intimate part of the visitor experience.[64] The McDonalds Corporation often personalizes its standardized corporate decor by incorporating some aspect of local history into the interior design of its franchises. For example, the Cambridge and Zanesville, Ohio, McDonaldses exhibit line drawings of National Road sites, and the placemats of National Road restaurants in Pennsylvania may soon include similar artwork.

The preservation movement has widely embraced economic gain as a rational for maintaining and protecting the historic built environment. Preservation pays—or so goes the argument—and, in the case of historic sites, preservation attracts tourists, which translates into jobs and economic development. It is no coincidence that tourism is generally referred to as an industry. There is nothing inherently wrong with historic sites turning a profit. In our capitalistic society, profit is still considered by many to be the major reason for the continued existence of old buildings. We simply need to recognize the long-range implications of profit-motivated preservation and the way in which it may create or modify a single historic property or an entire landscape.

Along the National Road, the effects of tourism are increasingly evident. Two examples illustrate the issues involved. Spruce Forest Artisan Village, located on US 40 one mile east of Grantsville, Maryland, straddles an orig-

**Wagon train at the National Road Festival**

The most visible result of the growing interest in the National Road as a tourist attraction is the annual National Road Festival. Billed as the world's longest festival, this event encourages participants to "travel the Road that Made the Nation." Celebrated from Maryland to eastern Ohio, the festival commemorates the Road's history with a series of activities, including a wagon train that travels through several National Road towns.

inal section of the National Road at the site of the Little Crossings Inn, Stantons Mill, and the famous National Road Casselman River single-span stone-arch bridge constructed in 1813. Unfortunately the "village," which in a recent publicity brochure asks the visitor to "step back in time," consists of a curious collection of moved and/or altered log buildings, whose siting bears little resemblance to their original location and has severely compromised the historic and architectural integrity of the original buildings at this location.[65] Peirce Lewis has argued eloquently that one of the main justifications for historic preservation is to preserve cultural memory, to maintain a sense of history. To do so we must have tangible, truthful reminders of the landscape and environment in which our ancestors lived. Is it possible to preserve a historic landscape, large enough and authentic enough to be credible? Or can we recreate such an environment? "Can we tell the truth out of context?"[66] Spruce Village may be an unqualified financial success, but its very presence blurs and misrepresents National Road history.

Centerville, Indiana, a Pike town with a unique collection of Federal-style archway row buildings, has found a way to entice travelers off nearby Interstate 70. Its Main Street storefronts are filled with antiques and on weekends Centerville is crowded with suburban shoppers. Many consider this eastern Indiana town the antique capital of the state. Few would argue that for Centerville tourism means economic prosperity. From a historic standpoint, however, tourism has modified the streetscape. Although the facades remain, the antiquing of Centerville has forever altered the historic function of the commercial business district and probably the very cultural identity of the community. In such a homogeneous boomtown atmosphere, is it possible to maintain the traditional function of the town as a conveyor of goods and services to residents and surrounding citizens, or do we simply turn it over to the tourists and express our gratitude that the historic built environment is still basically intact? Many National Road communities probably wish they had that choice to make, but everyone involved in preserving the National Road corridor will ultimately have to confront the way in which changes like those occurring in Centerville and elsewhere along the Road will influence resource protection strategies, visitor experience, and interpretive development.

## A PRESERVATION PRIMER FOR THE NATIONAL ROAD

Current preservation activities by the federal and some state governments increase the likelihood that a comprehensive preservation planning

GLENN A. HARPER

strategy for the National Road will eventually be implemented. Local communities, however, cannot afford to wait for other measures to protect their National Road resources. The Road landscape continues to be the victim of neglect, inappropriate development, and insensitive highway upgrading and expansion.

Protecting a historic transportation corridor requires the same steps necessary for the protection of individual historic sites, though the scope of documentation, the range of official designation opportunities, and protection strategies may be greater and more difficult to achieve. The process may be broken down into the following steps: (1) identification, (2) survey and analysis, (3) registration and designation, and (4) protection.

### Identification

Identification means determining the boundaries of the historic corridor or other landscape in question. Pennsylvania's *National Road: Historic Resource Survey* was confined to a 400-foot-wide corridor that included the original roadbed and the vast majority of nineteenth- and twentieth-century buildings and structures. Later realignments and the construction of US 40 may influence boundary decisions.

### Survey and Analysis

A historic properties survey is a systematic collection of information on the historical and architectural character of a community, corridor, or other cultural landscape. Historic property surveys are used to identify buildings, sites, structures, and objects worthy of preservation. They are a key step in local, regional, and state preservation planning processes. For example, Pennsylvania's survey was an important contributing document to the state's *National Road Heritage Park Feasibility Study*.[67]

There are several acceptable methodologies for surveying roadside resources. The linear survey, which involves surveying everything of historic and architectural significance between two end points of a highway or other historic transportation corridor, provides the most inclusive and comprehensive history of the route.[68]

To be most useful, a survey of the National Road should include (1) a written narrative, (2) a detailed set of historic and contemporary maps, (3) survey and inventory of individual properties, and (4) a cultural resource inventory. Understanding corridor history can aid in identifying the area to be surveyed, enable surveyors to view buildings, structures, and other landscape characteristics within broad patterns of history rather than as isolated artifacts, and can help determine survey techniques and necessary survey team disciplines. Maps can identify original roadbed and later realignments, property ownership, and original town plats. Original roadbed, Pike towns, and other building clusters, inns and taverns, stone bridges and culverts, mile markers, commemorative monuments and plaques, and hotels, motels, service stations, campgrounds, and eateries from the automobile era should be surveyed. A cultural resource inventory, including a review of letters, diaries, oral stories, ceremonies, festivals, and local arts and crafts, will supplement and enhance the findings of the landscape survey.[69]

### Registration/Designation

The historic and architectural significance of a highway or other historic transportation corridor is the basis for registering the route under appropriate federal, state, or local historical registers and/or designation of the route under federal or state historic route systems. Registration and designation may provide limited resource protection under applicable state and federal laws and are also usually prerequisites for obtaining federal and state financial and technical assistance.[70]

The best-known and most effective registration process is the National Register of Historic Places, the nation's official list of historic properties recognized by the federal government as worthy of preservation. Administered by State Historic Preservation Offices and overseen by the National Park Service, the program is part of a national policy to coordinate and support public and private efforts to identify, evaluate, and protect our cultural and natural resources.[71]

Like historic property surveys, the National Register of Historic Places is intended to encourage preservation at the local level. The listing of local commercial and residential historic districts, for example, is often the impetus for the enactment of local historic district ordinances, a type of overlay zoning. The National Register has had considerably less impact in rural areas and along historic transportation corridors and other linear resources, which often cross several legal jurisdictions and political boundaries. Nor does registration by itself guarantee protection. The Peacock Road, a remarkable eastern Ohio remnant of original National Road right-of-way listed on the National Register, receives no township maintenance and continues to deteriorate. Often people in the community where the property is located are not even aware of its National Register status. Similar to the National Register, the National Historic Landmarks program recognizes buildings, structures, sites, and objects of national significance and provides a slightly higher level of protection. Unfortunately, there appears to be little consistency in designating National Historic Landmarks along the National Road. One of three S-bridges in eastern Ohio is designated a National Historic Landmark while the other two are not even listed on the National Register of Historic Places. One might ask why the National Road itself is not a National Historic Landmark.[72]

### Protection

Unlike a building or structure where a single means of protection (an easement or local ordinance) may be sufficient, linear resources may be subject to a variety of ownership issues, resource threats, and legal jurisdictions, sometimes aggravated by regional differences and local political and social sentiments. In preparing Pennsylvania's *National Road Heritage Park Feasibility Study,* consultants confronted a century-old precedent of North-South social and political orientation and communication along the east-west route of the Road, and a regional infrastructure depleted by decades of economic decline.[73]

Historic transportation corridor protection plans may require a combination of public and private ownership and cooperative agreements, property acquisition techniques such as easements and covenants, regulatory protection through local historic district zoning, and land-owner cooperation. Few plans will include large-scale land acquisition, necessitating a partnership approach if the corridor in question is to be protected.

### A FUTURE FOR THE NATIONAL ROAD

With the passage of the Intermodal Surface Transportation Efficiency Act in 1991, a new era in transportation planning began—an era that may foster and strengthen National Road corridor protection efforts. For the first time in the nation's history, major highway funding is available for activities that enhance the environment and encourage alternative forms of transportation. These include wetland banking, wildlife habitat protection, preservation of historic sites, activities that contribute to higher air quality standards, highway beautification, and a wide range of bicycle and pedestrian projects.[74]

What does the future hold for the National Road? As we have seen, at no time since the beginning of the automobile era has the Road been the focus of so much attention from governments, organizations, and individuals. Have planning and tourism projects begun to translate into any comprehensive long-range strategy for protecting and preserving the National Road landscape? The answer is a guarded yes. Preserving the National Road for future generations, however, will require publicity, education, and coordinated resource management. The story of the National Road, "the nation's premier historic transportation corridor," must be shared. It also must be firmly fixed in the minds of those who will decide how to preserve the Road and its artifacts and those who will travel the Road and visit its many historic sites. The story can be told chronologically, thematically, and geographically, but a clear explanation and interpretation of the history and significance of the National Road is critical to continued preservation efforts.

An overall management policy for the National Road must be established. It may be necessary for the federal government (the National Park Service) to coordinate management and protection strategies. This could be achieved through one of the congressionally designated land management alternatives discussed earlier. An equally viable technique at the state level is the state heritage park program such as Pennsylvania is currently implementing. No matter what level of management coordination is chosen, however, the policy must address resource protection, education, interpretation, alternative forms of transportation, safety and liability issues, heritage tourism, and other forms of economic development. Implementing the management policy will probably require a mixture of public and private cooperative agreements. Local communities must be full partners in planning and carrying out the broad management goals if National Road preservation efforts are to have any credibility and ultimately any success.

Land-use controls will also be necessary. These may include such techniques as land trusts, scenic easements, and zoning. Mary Means, of Mary Means & Associates, the Virginia-based planning firm hired to prepare the Pennsylvania State Heritage Park feasibility studies for both the National Road and the Lincoln Highway, notes that it is very difficult to convince rural residents that they must implement zoning and other land-use controls. Landowners, some of them fiercely proud and independent, usually do not want to hear about property rights restrictions, although potential profits from tourism may encourage them to support historic transportation corridor protection.

GLENN A. HARPER

This is especially true in areas that have experienced little economic development. Means believes that "most small towns are searching for their next economic life and the economic benefits of a revitalized National Road is something that local residents can understand."[75] Success will require that everyone involved, no matter what their motivation, believe that the cultural landscape of the National Road is worth saving. They must also be convinced that in preserving the National Road they are also improving their quality of life.

George Stewart, author of *U.S. 40: Cross-Section of the United States of America,* believed the road to be "the richest historically of any of the transcontinental highways in the nation."[76] As the most significant portion of Route 40, the National Road provides Americans a rare opportunity to preserve what Tom Schlereth has called a "cross section of our culture, an outdoor museum of the ways we were and are."[77] How we preserve and protect this outdoor museum will determine in large part what future generations know about our culture and how we chose to honor its history.

# Access and Landscape

KARL RAITZ AND GRADY CLAY

IT HAS OCCURRED TO MANY EUROPEAN AND AMERICAN OBSERVERS that the differences between "here" and "there," between "town" and "country," between "city" and "suburb," are being obliterated, that "you can't tell where you are anymore," that geographic distinctions of past times are passé, that the mass production of environments under a world-wide consumer-based capitalist economy makes uniformity inevitable.

This judgment is premature. It confesses a failure in observation, and often an unwillingness to look deeper at the phenomena brought into play along the National Road and its now-multiple roadsides. What this book should make clear is that the landscapes of the National Road have revealed to careful observation a new depth to the history of North America. They remind us that great works of landscape art—that is, the landscapes we have made that can be seen in the National Road corridor—are the product of generations of skilled and aspiring specialists, as well as millions of everyday citizens' acts of necessity. This is a landscape of and by its interveners. None of it has merely "happened." Most of it reveals—and has helped shape—habits, customs, laws, and tools, some of them unfitted and some superbly designed for the tasks at hand and yet to come. All of it reflects hard work.

Played out along these roadsides are myths as well as scenarios that include national policy, Manifest Destiny, and technological imperatives. You can find here material to complement Frederick Jackson Turner's thesis that the frontier is a form-giver to the American character. You can find here evidence of the best and worst land-management tactics, from single-cropping corn to clear-cutting hardwoods; from gerrymandering to land-locking, and the log rolling and fee-splitting that occurred in the great restructuring of territory that is the unvarying result of road-building.

Beyond all this lies the great reparceling of the United States that is yet to come: the continuing migration into and out of cities, the urbanization of countryside, the impact of a thousand more miles of road and a hundred more jurisdictions upon air, waters, and lands, and all who inhabit and use them. While energy is still cheap, new inhabitants of this nation will continue to demand new roads. Every new road mile will reprovision all the forces that the National Road generated: internal migration, resettlement, new jobs, lawsuits, chicanery and all the customs that the occasions require. The notion of single-purpose roadways, which the National Road embodied, and which the interstate system expanded, has clearly proved itself inadequate for an increasingly complex future. Merely to "open up new territory" is insufficient. All roads, every piece of right-of-way must be examined in a new light to see how many functions it can perform beyond simple vehicular movement. Road construction itself needs to be so organized as to handle new demands on it: from abutters, from neighbors, as well as from other users who need a sense of beauty.

There will be increasing need for multipurpose right-of-ways, for the development of air and subterranean rights along with those of the road surface itself. There will continue to be redefinitions of the right of access to and from new roadways, whether local or national. Those common building materials of dirt, clay, and stone will become more valuable and their conservation more imperative. The impact of road-building and road use on their many environments will be even more rigorously studied and affected by law.

KARL RAITZ AND GRADY CLAY

Roadways and their adjacent lands increasingly will become transportation and distribution corridors for utilities of every sort, both above and below ground. Their design may well be expanded to provide local landing strips, hardstands for countless enterprises, or building blocks for many futures. The inevitability that development follows roads will make it imperative to incorporate better city-planning and landscape architecture practices into road construction. Even the present supremacy of state power over local road-building will be thrown into question, as large cities come to dominate state legislatures even more than in the past.

Invisible above and below the roadway lie the booming electronic pathways—some wire cable, others fiber optic. How much work now done by roads can and will be eliminated by computerized management, or done electronically with a new form of access? How many shortcuts, route consolidations, and reroutings controlled by distant and on-board computers will alter traffic flows on the highways? The National Road was the nation's first federally funded road *west*. Since its inception in 1806, it has never been a stationary highway.

APPENDIX    # Historic Archaeology and the National Road

HISTORIC ARCHAEOLOGY INTEGRATES TRADITIONAL ARCHAEOLOGICAL METHODS, such as field surveys and excavations, with documentary and archival records, resulting in a more complete and accurate history than the written record alone might provide. What kind of information does historic archaeology provide and how can it be used to document and ultimately preserve and protect the historic resources of the National Road?

The historic record has numerous accounts of famous politicians, and other national figures of their day, who traveled the National Road and spent the night at one or another inn or tavern. But what do we know about the tavern owners and their employees, the period furnishings of the inn, the utensils with which they prepared food for their guests, the glass, ceramic tableware, and other household items? What information do we have about the drovers who occupied nearby wagonstands, the local blacksmith, or the neighbors who may have supplied food to the tavern and hay to the wagonstands?[1]

Investigating the below-ground remains of a building, such as a tavern destroyed by fire decades earlier, can indicate the type and depth of the foundation and evidence of rebuilding and expansion. The interpretation of soil types (stratigraphy) around the foundation can help establish the sequence of construction. The size, configuration, and construction sequence of other missing or altered architectural features such as bay windows and porches or the location and size of outbuildings such as spring-houses and stables may also be determined through archaeological research. Privies, which were often filled with household refuse after being replaced with a new privy or later with indoor plumbing, may provide a particularly valuable cache of artifacts.[2]

Historic landscape archaeology can reveal much about the historic character of land adjacent to buildings. Gardens and other landscaping characteristics such as walls and walkways and structural and nonstructural features, including wells, trash pits, and storage pits, can also be located through archaeological research. Archaeology can even contribute anthropological data pertaining to the social status of a site's occupants, through the reconstruction of diet based on bone and botanical remains, and from artifact studies that evaluate the relative cost of ceramics and other products.[3]

Landscape archaeology may also obtain data from erosion and vegetation patterns. Techniques include the analysis of soil, pollen, and other sediments. Planting patterns can be obtained from core sampling, while surficial surveys can identify remnant vegetation and boundary demarcations. An analysis of existing vegetation or plant succession can provide further evidence of land use. Remote sensing devices can detect buried foundations, roadways, and culverts, sometimes reducing the need for excavation.[4]

The potential for historic archaeological resources, even in places that may appear to be hopelessly disturbed, should not be overlooked. These may include plowed agricultural fields as well as the more urban areas through which the National Road passes. Many towns and villages, particularly along the eastern portion of the Road, have now been occupied for well over 150 years. These communities may contain evidence of earlier life beneath their streets, the crawlspaces of standing buildings, and even paved parking lots.

As part of an ongoing study of taverns and inns along the Pennsylvania section of the National Road, the California State College Archaeological Field School excavated the Peter Colley Tavern in Briar Hill, Pennsylvania, during 1972 and 1973. The purpose of the excavation was to attempt to characterize or identify a typical set of tavern wagon activities and to determine whether the relatively affluent position of the tavern owners could be determined from domestic artifacts found at the site. Although the evidence that would have substantiated either hypothesis was inconclusive, the excavation of the Colley Tavern site did result in locating an outdoor bake-oven foundation, the foundation of a long-forgotten outbuilding, a stone-lined cistern, and eight shallow refuse pits. Inside, an original chimney was discovered between two fireplaces and it was determined, based on the absence of an internal stairway, that only the basement may have functioned as a tavern, with the Colley family occupying the second floor.[5]

Among the most important discoveries was the unearthing of an original section of roadbed, approximately ten feet in front of the Colley tavern door and twelve inches below the present ground level. While the history of the National Road has been studied extensively, much less is known about the techniques used to construct and maintain the Road. Exposing the Road at several points in front of the Peter Colley Tavern enabled project archaeologists to compare actual macadam pavement characteristics with original Road specifications.[6]

Based on the information obtained from excavations like that at the Peter Colley Tavern, it is clear that historic archaeology can not only add to our knowledge of National Road resources, but may also contribute to the interpretative potential of these sites. Further, any plan for protecting National Road resources should include historic archaeology. Both the federal and some National Road state governments require a review of highway, mining, wastewater treatment, and other projects along the National Road to determine what effects these projects will have on historic resources listed on or eligible for the National Register of Historic Places. To be most effective, however, preservationists should seek to establish state legislation and local ordinances that will protect both the below- and above-ground historic resources. Both are vital to our understanding of National Road history.

# A Chronology of Contextual Events

1690s Frontier folk follow a path blazed by Thomas Batts and Robert Fallam along the New and Kanawha Rivers across what would later be called West Virginia and trade with American Indians along the Ohio River.

1727 Palatinate German settlers move across the Blue Ridge in southeastern Pennsylvania and settle in the Great Valley.

1750 Thomas Walker crosses Virginia's Blue Ridge and finds the Cumberland Gap and the Warriors' Path that would lead settlers toward the Kentucky rivers that drained northwest into the Ohio River.

1755 English general Edward Braddock leads a small military force along a path cut by 300 axmen toward the French Fort Duquesne at the Forks of the Ohio. The path would become known as Braddock's Road.

1758 Forbes Road opened across Pennsylvania to the Forks of the Ohio River; later the site is named Pittsburgh.

1759 Bituminous coal discovered near Pittsburgh, Pennsylvania.

1763    The Treaty of Paris signed, marking an official end to the Seven Years' War in Europe and the French and Indian War in North America. The French cede their lands east of the Mississippi River, opening the Ohio River Valley to frontier settlement.

1785    A congressional ordinance reserves land north and west of the Ohio River for the federal government; the land will be surveyed into townships and sections.

1787    The Northwest Ordinance establishes political control over the territory north and west of the Ohio River and allows for the creation of new states.

1790    The first federal census of the United States.

1795    The Treaty of Greenville opens land to white settlers in south and central Ohio.

1795    Pinckney's Treaty with Spain grants Americans the rights to trade through New Orleans.

1796    Congress authorizes Ebenezer Zane to survey a "trace" from Wheeling, West Virginia, to Maysville, Kentucky.

1801    Albert Gallatin becomes President Jefferson's treasury secretary.

1803    Ohio admitted to the Union as a state.

1803    The Louisiana Purchase is secured from France.

1803–5  Lewis and Clark Expedition, from St. Louis to Astoria, Oregon.

1806    Congress approves a national road to connect the settled East to the Ohio River.

1808    Albert Gallatin's *Report on Roads and Canals* presented to the U.S. Senate.

1808    Congress approves funding for surveying the National Road.

1811    Construction on the National Road begins.

1811    The first steamboat to operate on the Ohio and Mississippi Rivers is launched at Pittsburgh.

1814    First Y-bridge built across the Licking and Muskingum Rivers at Zanesville, Ohio.

1816    Indiana admitted to the Union as a state.

1818    Illinois admitted to the Union as a state.

1818    The National Road reaches Wheeling on the Ohio River.

1821    Missouri admitted to the Union as a state.

1825    National Road construction begins on the Ohio River's west bank at St. Clairsville, Ohio.

1825    The Erie Canal opens, linking Albany, New York, on the Hudson River with Buffalo on Lake Erie.

1828–31 The National Road completed to Zanesville, Ohio. (Note: Sources vary on the exact dates of commencement and completion.)

| 1832 | During the year, more than 190,000 head of livestock pass the National Road toll house in Zanesville, Ohio; most are driven to eastern markets. |
|---|---|
| 1832 | Between 40 and 100 wagons per day move along the National Road through Richmond, Indiana. |
| 1832 | The Ohio-Erie Canal, connecting Portsmouth and Cleveland, opens. |
| 1833 | The National Road completed to Columbus, Ohio. |
| 1834 | Abraham Lincoln elected to the Illinois State Legislature. |
| 1835–41 | The National Road completed to Richmond, Indiana. (Note: Sources vary on the exact dates of commencement and completion.) |
| 1838 | The National Road completed to Springfield, Ohio. |
| 1838 | The National Road completed from Indianapolis to Terre Haute, Indiana. |
| 1839 | The National Road reaches Vandalia, Illinois. |
| 1839 | The nation's first iron bridge completed; it carried the National Road over Dunlap's Creek at Brownsville, Pennsylvania. |
| 1839 | Tolls collected on the National Road in Ohio during the year total more than $62,000. |
| 1840 | The federal census reveals that Ohio now ranks third in total population among the 31 states. |
| 1845 | The Miami and Erie Canal completed, linking Lake Erie and Cincinnati, Ohio. |
| 1845 | Steel rails for railroad tracks first manufactured in Danville, Pennsylvania. |
| 1846 | About 2,000 Mormons begin an exodus from Nauvoo, Illinois, cross the frozen Mississippi and head west, eventually finding "the place" by the Great Salt Lake in Utah. |
| 1847 | Cyrus McCormick moves from the Shenandoah Valley of Virginia to Chicago and opens a reaper manufacturing plant there. |
| 1848 | Walt Whitman travels the National Road by stagecoach from Cumberland, Maryland, to Brownsville, Pennsylvania. |
| 1849 | At Wheeling, West Virginia, a new suspension bridge opens to carry National Road traffic across the Ohio River. |
| 1851 | The Illinois Central Railroad is granted a charter. |
| 1852 | The Baltimore & Ohio Railroad reaches Wheeling, West Virginia. (At that time, West Virginia was part of Virginia.) |
| 1856 | By this date, the federal government has ceded all rights to the entire National Road to the states. |
| 1857 | The Ohio Stage Company, operating on the National Road, fails. |
| 1858 | Abraham Lincoln and Stephen A. Douglas engage in a series of debates in Illinois, including one in Alton, that center on the issue of excluding slavery from U.S. territories. |

1859    E. L. Drake brings in the first petroleum well in Pennsylvania at Titus-ville.

1867    The first practical Bessemer steel furnace in the United States begins op-eration in Steelton, Pennsylvania.

1870    John D. Rockefeller organizes the Standard Oil Company at Cleveland, Ohio.

1870    Benjamin F. Goodrich arrives in Akron, Ohio, from Melrose, New York, and begins to manufacture firehose and other rubber products.

1893    The first all-concrete road in the nation is built in Ohio.

1894    Thomas B. Searight publishes *The Old Pike: A History of the National Road*.

1898    F. A. Seiberling organizes the Goodyear Rubber Company in Akron, Ohio.

1899    J. Ward Packard manufactures the first Packard automobile in Warren, Ohio.

1900    Americans own about 8,000 registered automobiles.

1903    Orville and Wilbur Wright of Dayton, Ohio, accomplish the first pow-ered airplane flight from Kill Devil Hill at Kitty Hawk, North Carolina.

1903    An automobile is driven across the continent from San Francisco to New York City for the first time.

1905    Americans own about 78,000 registered motor vehicles.

1908    Henry Ford's first Model-T comes off the assembly line.

1910    Americans own about 458,500 registered motor vehicles.

1910    The Mack Company builds the first motorized hook-and-ladder firetruck.

1910    By the end of the year, more than 125,000 automotive inventions have been patented, including the steering wheel to replace the tiller, by Packard, in 1900.

1911    Carl Graham Fisher inaugurates the Indianapolis 500 automobile race at his brick-paved motor speedway.

1913    The Lincoln Memorial Highway Association is organized to promote construction of an east-west highway across the country. Assembled partly from existing sections of road and newly constructed roads, the Lincoln Highway eventually became US 30.

1914    Carl Eric Wickman starts a regular bus service out of a small Minnesota mining town that he expands into the Greyhound Bus system with 46,000 miles of routes by the mid-1930s.

1916    The Good Roads Act provides federal funding for improving postal roads and farm-to-market roads. The National Park Service is also established.

1919    Gen. J. J. Pershing's cross-country military convoy demonstrates the poor quality of American roads and bridges.

1920    The federal census records as many people living in cities as on farms for the first time.

| 1920 | U.S. automobile registrations reach 8.1 million for the first time. |
| 1910–20 | The population of Akron, Ohio, the rubber manufacturing center, increases from 69,000 to 209,000 during the decade. |
| 1921 | Edgar Ingram and Walter Anderson open a restaurant in Wichita, Kansas, called White Castle specializing in inexpensive, high-quality hamburgers. |
| 1923 | The state of Indiana removes more than one million advertising signs from over 4,000 miles of state roads to improve drivers' visibility. |
| 1923 | The Bronx River Parkway, the first modern parkway with all intersections directed into underpasses or overpasses, is completed in the state of New York. |
| 1924 | The average retail price of automobiles sold is $814, and about one-half of all cars and trucks sold are Fords. |
| 1924 | Americans own about 17,000,000 registered motor vehicles. |
| 1924 | The total mileage of concrete pavement in the United States exceeds 31,000 miles. |
| 1925 | The Joint Board on Interstate Highways establishes national highway sign standards. |
| 1926 | Federal law standardizes federal highway numbering and the National Road becomes US 40. |
| 1928 | The Woodbridge cloverleaf, the first highway interchange in the nation with a grade separation, is built in New Jersey at the junction of State Highways 25 and 4. |
| 1931 | The Standard Oil Company introduces a new gasoline station building, a simple glass and metal box-shaped structure. |
| 1932 | Congress imposes a one cent per gallon tax on gasoline. |
| 1935 | Howard Johnson begins to franchise roadside restaurants to local "agents," provided they build according to company specifications and sell Johnson's food and ice cream products. |
| 1936 | The State of Indiana begins a highway improvement program to widen US 40 to four lanes in high-traffic sections. |
| 1937 | The Lagonda Chapter of the Daughters of the American Revolution acquire the Pennsylvania House, an old National Road Inn at Springfield, Ohio, and restore it into a museum. |
| 1939 | The New York World's Fair includes an exhibit by General Motors called Futurama that projects an American highway system with express highways that would permit automobile speeds of 100 miles per hour. |
| 1939 | The number of gasoline stations in the United States exceeds 241,000 with total retail sales of $2.8 billion. |
| 1939 | An oil boom occurs in several southern Illinois oil fields. |
| 1939 | Maurice and Richard McDonald open a drive-in restaurant in San Bernardino, California. |

1940    American automobile registrations reach 27.4 million, of which 4.8 million are truck registrations.

1940    The Pennsylvania Turnpike, the first modern long-distance four-lane highway, is officially opened for traffic along its entire 159-mile length.

1941    Congress passes the Defense Highway Act, designating $10 million to state governments, on a matching basis, to survey and plan trunk highways.

1944    Congress authorizes the Federal Aid Highway Act, which designates $500 million per year for three years to assist in construction of rural and urban roads. The construction of Route 66, from Chicago to Los Angeles, is included in the bill.

1947    The United States has a total of 39,964 miles of multilane (three or more lanes) highways.

1948    The 1944 Federal Aid Highway Act is extended for two additional years at $450 million per year.

1953    George Stewart publishes *U.S. 40: Cross-Section of the United States of America*.

1953    H. A. Inness Brown, publisher of *Gasoline Retailer*, states that the recently completed New Jersey Turnpike is allowing about 80,000 vehicles per day to bypass established roadside businesses.

1954    Americans own about 54 million registered motor vehicles.

1955    Ray Kroc opens his first McDonald's fast-food restaurant in Des Plains, Illinois.

1956    The Federal Aid Highway Act of 1956 is approved. Section 108 of Title I is titled "National System of Interstate and Defense Highways."

1965    The Federal Highway Beautification Act is approved, thanks to the efforts of Lady Bird Johnson, wife of the president.

1991    The "National Freeway," on Interstate 68 in western Maryland and Pennsylvania, is dedicated.

1992    American automobile registrations reach 144 million.

1996    The two-volume set, *The National Road* and *A Guide to the National Road*, edited by Karl Raitz, is published.

# Notes

**Chapter 1. The Landscape of Mobility**

1. Hovenden's painting was voted "the most popular painting at the World's Columbian Exposition at Chicago" in 1893 (Carol Troyen in Stebbins et al., 1983).

2. Technically, the Road ran from Cumberland to Wheeling, but in fact was part of a more ambitious scheme to link Chesapeake Bay at Baltimore with the Mississippi River at St. Louis.

3. The dates for the age of the railroad are approximate because they differ from one part of the country to another. Railroads began to transform the industrial Northeast as early as the 1830s, while their full impact was not felt in the West and South until the 1870s. As for the ending date, the railroads were a long time dying. Although autos and trucks had begun to supplant rail traffic in the Northeast as early as the 1920s, passenger rail traffic continued at high volumes until the early 1950s. By 1970, the passenger system was in such desperate straits that the federal government took over the tattered remnants.

4. America was not the only place where railroads were the instrument of political and economic conquest. The largest and most valuable territories in the British empire were largely held in place by a web of railroads that included huge parts of India, Australia, Can-

ada, and South Africa. Equally, railroads were used as instruments of imperial aggression. Thus, when Cecil Rhodes spoke of making Africa "all red" (i.e., all British), his imperial ambitions were expressed in terms of building a "Cape-to-Cairo Railroad." In Europe, Germany's growing power rested on Bismarck's railroad system, designed to move German armies from east to west and back again with lightning speed—a feat that would make the Blitzkrieg possible long before the Nazis made that term infamous. Russia's great thrust to the east through Siberia and northern China in the 1890s and early 1900s was supported by the Trans-Siberian Railroad, finished to Vladivostok in 1904. (It is no accident that the Russo-Japanese War broke out in exactly the same year.) Indeed, the explosion of Japanese power in northern China resulted from Japan's creation of a Manchurian railroad system, partly seized from the Russians, partly built from scratch. Everywhere across the world, imperialism traveled by rail, and in plundered countries like Mexico, foreign power inevitably arrived on rails built with foreign money, bringing foreign investment, and usually followed by foreign domination. Sometimes domination was followed by political annexation, as in India. Sometimes conquest was unofficial; Mexico, putatively, was independent. But there was never any doubt: whoever owned the railroads also owned the country's economy.

5. Cronon 1991.

6. Lewis 1976, 48–49.

7. See Reps 1979, and Hudson 1985.

8. Reps 1979.

9. Strictly speaking, the western railroads were not "transcontinental," although that term was widely used. In effect, they connected the dense rail network of the humid East with the West Coast. They were not so much "transcontinental" as they were trans-arid-West. The seven lines were: the Great Northern; Northern Pacific; Milwaukee Road; Union Pacific; Atcheson, Topeka, & Santa Fe; Central Pacific; and Southern Pacific.

10. For an account of how that worked in one part of the country, see Frank Norris, *The Octopus,* a turn-of-the-century muckraking novel about the evil deeds of the Southern Pacific Railroad in California (1958).

11. There is a huge amount of literature on the history of the automobile in America. For a sweeping account of automobiles, their social and technological environment, and their impact upon American life, see Sears 1977. The book is engagingly written and gorgeously illustrated.

12. Ford was hardly alone. Indeed, some historians, especially Rae 1971, opine that Ford's main genius was self-promotion, and the ability to gather around him the men of genius whose ideas he selectively appropriated.

13. In 1920 the U.S. Census reported for the first time that more than 50 percent of the American population was urban.

14. It was not unusual for auto moguls to dabble in politics, sometimes with considerable effect. James Couzins, one of Ford's early stockholders, retired from the company as a multimillionaire and then retired to a comfortable seat in the U.S. Senate from Michigan. Henry Ford himself, after organizing his famous "Peace Ship" expedition to Europe in 1916, was so popular that without campaigning he very nearly won a Senate seat in 1918, and there was widespread talk of making him the Democratic Party's nomination for president in 1924.

15. Hokanson 1988.

16. Sears 1977, 186.

17. Several simple rules help explain most of the federal numbering. East-west roads were assigned even numbers; north-south roads were odd. Numbering began in the East and ascended westward: thus, the main road

from Maine to Florida, which passed through most of the big coastal cities, was appropriately numbered US 1, while the road from San Diego to Seattle was US 101. Also with the east-west roads, low numbers were used in the North (US 2 plays tag with the Canadian border for much of its length), high numbers in the South. Primary arterial roads were assigned numbers with one or two digits, while roads that fed into those arterials or paralleled them were given the same number plus one or more hundred. Thus US 31 runs from Mobile to Sault Ste. Marie, and is approximately paralleled by US 131. Main diagonal arterials often received memorable numbers, among them the famous US 66 from Chicago to Los Angeles, heavily used by Okies during the flight from the Dust Bowl to California in the 1930s, and the subject of numerous mournful songs. The states followed suit, although their numbering systems were far less orderly than the federal system. There are notable exceptions. California's famous Route 1 hovers spectacularly along the Pacific Coast; Route 49 is the route of the '49ers and follows the Mother Lode along the Sierra Nevada foothills.

18. The defects of traveling by rail in America, just before the arrival of the automobile, are described in a clear-eyed unromantic passage in Belasco 1979.

19. Pennsylvania's statewide speed limit at the time was 50 miles per hour. On the turnpike, the limit was an unheard-of 70. For a history of the turnpike, see Cupper 1990.

20. Rose 1990, 92.

21. No money was earmarked for maintenance, which turned out to be financially embarrassing to states that had been given Babylon but could not afford to keep it in repair.

22. Among the most scorching critics of the interstate system were Tunnard and Pushkarev 1963, who complained that the interstates, as designed, were unaesthetic, boring, and dangerous. But despite the authors' acid language, their complaints were basically cosmetic. Even more vitriolic was John Keats, in *The Insolent Chariots,* a broadside attack on automobiles, automobile culture, and the auto industry in particular (1958). But no form of criticism could cool Americans' passion for unlimited use of automobiles.

23. Federal intervention saved the railroad freight system through the creation of a nationally chartered public company called Conrail, which eventually found ways to turn a profit. A similar effort to rescue the passenger system through Amtrak met with considerably less success. By the 1980s, the American passenger rail system was a shadow of its former self, heavily subsidized, but self-supporting only in the heavily traveled corridors between Boston and Washington and between Los Angeles and San Diego.

24. The Pennsylvania Turnpike was incorporated into the interstate system and patriotically numbered I-76.

25. In fact, most civilian drivers are annoyed if they have to slow down for a military convoy on a high-speed interstate highway. No one is fooled. The interstate system is for civilians, and the military may use it if they mind their manners.

26. Except on the stretch between Cumberland and Wheeling, where I-70 jogs to the north of US 40.

27. Kennan 1993, 160–61.

28. Lewis 1983.

29. Kennan 1993, 161–64.

30. Kennan is moderate in his views compared to other writers. Keats's *The Insolent Chariots* exemplifies the genre. The book is savagely illustrated by the celebrated cartoonist Robert Osborn, and was severally reprinted and then (unusual for the time) reprinted in paperback. The tradition of deploring the automobile and its effects continues today. For a sample of a recent polemic, see Kunster 1993.

### Chapter 2. The Face of the Country

1. Morse 1789, 509.

2. Volney 1804, 24.

3. Morse and Green 1971, 142.

4. Gallatin 1808, 732.

5. Jefferson 1808, 714.

6. Dallas 1816, 301.

7. Williams, Moore, and Kerr 1806, 474, 476. Note that the spelling of "Allegheny" will vary from one source to another. Currently, if one counts county names as well as its use for rivers and mountains, "Allegheny" is spelled five different ways across the breadth of the Appalachians.

8. The topographic changes along the National Road corridor are best illustrated by a superb cross-section and a series of bird's-eye-views drawn by Erwin Raisz for George Stewart's *U.S. 40*; Stewart 1953, 66–67, 70–71, 84–85, and 112–13. Patapsco, incidentally, is an Algonquin word meaning "jutting-[ledge]-[of]-rock-at" (Stewart 1970, 361).

9. Stone 1895, 13.

10. Smith 1925, 199.

11. Williams and Moore 1808, 715.

12. Ibid., 714.

13. Braun 1967, 222, 237.

14. Knight 1826a, 29. Jonathan Knight no doubt appreciated the building stone that he found along this section although he apparently was not sufficiently taken with the land to actually move here upon completion of his surveying duties. The ruin of his fine stone house still stands near the Malden Inn along Old US 40 west of West Brownsville, Pennsylvania.

15. Ibid., 30–31.

16. Brewerton 1836, 9.

17. Division of Earth Sciences 1959.

18. Knight 1828, 9.

19. Ibid., 15.

20. Austin 1932.

21. Ibid., 10.

22. For example, Jonathan Knight observed that Richmond stood on a bluff eighty feet above the Whitewater River. Canfield 1835, 4.

23. Knight 1826b, 7; and Crawford 1820, 7.

24. Lacock, Shriver, and McRee 1821, 8–10.

25. Knight 1828, 12, 13, 15, 18.

26. Braun 1967, 189, 305–10.

27. Knight 1828, 14–15.

28. Parkinson, Wiggington, and Jenny 1991.

29. Ernst 1819, 75.

30. Fehrenbacher et al. 1984.

31. Jones 1983, 102–3.

32. Thwaites 1904, 299.

33. Conzen 1990, 373.

34. Zelinsky 1992, 126–27.

35. Hudson 1988, 403–11.

36. Ensminger 1992, 161.

37. WPA 1945, 338–39; and Schlereth 1985, 120.

38. Jordan and Kaups 1987, 62.

39. Johnson 1976, 42–46.

40. Hart 1972, 269–70.

41. Jones 1983, 124–27.

42. Hart 1991, 108–9.

43. Hart 1986, 52.

44. Ensminger 1992, 1–50.

45. Ibid., 148, 152.

46. Hart 1986, 59–68.

47. Brown 1896, 21–22.

48. Pillsbury 1970, 433–40.

49. Pillsbury 1977, 13–23.

50. Kniffen 1936, 179–93.

51. Shortridge 1989, 99–105.

### Chapter 3. The Idea of a National Road

1. Zerubavel 1992.

2. Morse 1789, 467–68.

3. Franklin 1959, 4:227; discussed by Greene 1993, 98–101.

4. Adams 1955, 6, 11.

5. Shimer 1972; Morse 1789, 51.

6. Morse 1789, 166; Brown 1943, 467; Adams 1955.

7. Morse 1789, 468.

8. Adams 1955, 11, 20.

9. Armstrong 1976, 55.

10. Rohrbough 1978, 157–61.

11. McCoy 1980, 10; Appleby 1992, 260.

12. McCoy 1980, 9.

13. Wood 1993, 46.

14. Appleby 1992, 253.

15. McCoy 1980, 121–32; see also Matthews 1991.

16. McCoy 1980, 150–58. Subsequent page numbers in text are from the same source.

17. Cayton and Onuf 1990, 5.

18. McCoy 1980, 197–98. Subsequent page numbers in text are from the same source.

19. Morse 1793, 519; Taylor 1995, 14, 27.

20. Taylor 1995.

21. Ibid.

22. Walters 1957, 76–87, 143–54.

23. Ibid., 163–69.

24. Billington 1967, 342.

25. Armstrong 1976, 2, 14–15, 61.

26. Morse 1789, 46; Morse 1793, 161.

27. Morse 1793, 525.

28. Armstrong 1976, 56.

29. Jordan 1948, 72.

30. Armstrong 1976, 60–61.

31. Stewart 1953, 90.

32. Armstrong 1976, 61.

33. Walters 1957, 182; Seely 1993, 22.

34. Armstrong 1976, 61–62; Seely 1993, 22.

35. Stewart 1953, 117.

36. Walters 1957, 182–83; Boorstin 1965, 252; Meinig 1993, 313–16; Seely 1993, 22.

37. Adams 1879; Walters 1957.

38. Cited by Seely 1993, 22.

39. McCoy 1980, 250; Seely 1993, 22.

40. Armstrong 1976, 61.

41. Ibid., 62.

42. Seely 1993, 22.

43. Armstrong 1976, 58.

44. Rohrbough 1978, 279.

45. Taylor 1951, 20–21.

46. Meinig 1993, 349.

47. Seely 1993, 22.

48. Billington 1967, 353; Seely 1993, 22–23.

49. Meinig 1993, 351.

50. Ibid., 332.

51. Boorstin 1965, 252.

52. Meinig 1993, 255.

## Chapter 4. Surveying and Building the Road

1. Jordan 1948, foreword.

2. Ierley 1990, 17.

3. U.S. Department of Transportation, Federal Highway Administration, 1976, 8.

4. Gallatin 1808.

5. *Public Statutes at Large,* 2:226.

6. From government document in Searight 1894, 22. A number of government documents cited in this chapter are reproduced in Searight, and in those cases the author has chosen to cite that work instead of the actual government document from which they originate. For convenience, the reader need only consult Searight to see the reprinted document and obtain the correct citation.

7. Jordan 1948, 78; Ierley 1990, 229.

8. Searight 1894, 26.

9. Ibid., 30.

10. Ierley 1990, 39.

11. Searight 1894, 29. Subsequent page numbers in text are from the same source.

12. From a poster advertising construction bids on eastern section of the Road in 1819. Morse and Green 1971, 66.

13. Searight 1894, 319–20.

14. Ibid.

15. Institute for the History of Technology and Industrial Archaeology 1994.

16. Ierley 1990, 49–50.

17. Searight 1894, 319–20.

18. Ibid.

19. Jordan 1948, 84.

20. Ierley 1990, 48.

21. Jordan 1948, 87–88.

22. Ierley 1990, 54–55.

23. *American State Papers* 1834, 175–77.

24. Merritt 1983, 16–14, 16–15.

25. Ierley 1990, 41.

26. U.S. House of Representatives 1828b, 2–3.

27. Searight 1894, 374.

28. Singer et al. 1958, 527–28.

29. Kirby et al. 1956, 200–204.

30. MacDonald 1928, 1190.

31. Singer et al. 1957, 534.

32. Turner and Goulden n.d., 329–30.

33. Ibid.

34. Both published works on roadbuilding; Gillespie in 1847 and Gillmore in 1876.

35. U.S. House of Representatives 1828b, 2; U.S. Department of Transportation, Federal Highway Administration 1976, 20.

36. Hulbert 1901, 36; Searight 1894, 320.

37. Searight 1894.

38. Ibid.

39. Boyd 1954, 11.

40. Searight 1894, 102.

41. Young 1904, 32–33.

42. Jordan 1948, 89.

43. Searight 1894, 102.

44. Rose 1976, 36.

45. U.S. House of Representatives 1828a, 7.

46. U.S. Senate 1834a, 81.

47. Searight 1894, 100–106, 320.

48. U.S. Senate 1828, 13.

49. U.S. Senate 1838, 271–72.

50. Searight 1894, 102–6.

51. U.S. Senate 1838, 273.

52. Ibid.

53. Searight 1894, 102–6.

54. MacDonald 1928, 1192.

55. U.S. Senate 1834b, 173.

56. U.S. House of Representatives 1836, 27.

57. Searight 1894, 298.

58. Hulbert 1901, 72.

59. Ibid.

60. U.S. Department of Transportation, Federal Highway Administration 1976, 21.

61. Ierley 1990, 63.

62. U.S. Department of Transportation, Federal Highway Administration 1976, 20–21.

63. Searight 1894, 101.

64. U.S. House of Representatives 1828b.

65. Ierley 1990, 65.

66. Ibid.

67. Searight 1894, 101–5.

68. Rose 1976, 36.

69. Ibid.

70. Mahan 1838, 109–60.

71. Searight 1894, 66.

72. U.S. Senate 1834c, 3.

73. Searight 1894, 57.

74. Association of Graduates, USMA 1990, 249.

75. Association of Graduates, USMA 1949, 11–13.

76. Searight 1894, 65.

77. Ierley 1990, 65.

78. Hulbert 1901, 42–44.

79. Ibid.

80. U.S. Senate 1834c, 5, and 1834a, 83.

81. Hulbert 1901, 43–44.

82. Kemp 1994.

83. Schodek 1987, 79.

84. Searight 1894, 104–5.

85. Hulbert 1901, 76, 77.

86. Rideing 1879, 816.

87. Rose 1976, 73; U.S. Department of Transportation, Federal Highway Administration 1976, 41, 42–43.

88. Rose 1976, 88; U.S. Department of Transportation, Federal Highway Administration 1976, 109.

89. Jordan 1948, 385.

90. Rose 1976, 87.

91. Ierley 1990, 191.

92. Jordan 1948, 386.

93. Ralph Reedy, personal interview by Daniel Reedy, Livingston, Ill., 1993.

### Chapter 5. Extending the Road West

1. Schneider 1975, 1–2; Young 1902, 17.

2. Schneider 1975, 2–3.

3. Hulbert 1904, 17–18; MacGill et al. 1917,

13–15; Waitley 1970, 125–63; Young 1902, 10–11.

4. Schneider 1975, 3.

5. Hulbert 1904, 18–25; Schneider 1975, 3–6; Young 1902, 14–15, 18–22.

6. Brown 1948, 99, 106; Hulbert 1904, 19–25; Meinig 1993, 313–16, 339–41; Taylor 1968, 18, 19.

7. Jordan 1948, 163–64.

8. Dunbar 1915, 692–700; Hulbert 1904, 18–19; MacGill et al. 1917, 121; Searight 1894, 20; Schneider 1975, 4; Young 1902, 15.

9. Hulbert 1904, 21–23; Schneider 1975, 6; Young 1902, 21.

10. *New American State Papers* 1972, 105, 106–7.

11. Schneider 1975, 6; Young 1902, 21–23.

12. *New American State Papers* 1972, 107.

13. Hulbert 1904, 21; Schneider 1975, 7.

14. *New American State Papers* 1972, 107, 118–19; Schneider 1975, 6–7.

15. Young 1902, 23.

16. *New American State Papers* 1972, 110.

17. Hulbert 1904, 71–72; Young 1902, 23–24; Brown 1948, 106.

18. Buley 1950, 1:19, 76, 2:107; Howard 1972, 210; Hulbert 1904, 193–95; Stewart 1953, 115.

19. Young 1902, 24.

20. Ibid., 27.

21. Hulbert 1904, 76–77; Stewart 1953, 114–15; Young 1902, 24.

22. *New American State Papers* 1972, 210–40; Young 1902, 25–26.

23. Hulbert 1904, 21–23; Young 1902, 21, 25–27.

24. Steele 1977, 5; WPA 1940a, 47.

25. *New American State Papers* 1972, 294–305; Hulbert 1904, 194; Young 1902, 28.

26. *New American State Papers* 1972, 389–407; Young 1902, 28–29.

27. Young 1902, 29, 30; Hardin 1967, 5; Stewart 1953, 144–45.

28. Gustorf 1962, 154; Hulbert 1904, 193–95.

29. Hardin 1967, 7; Howard 1972, 210; Steele 1977, 5; Young 1902, 28.

30. Buley 1950, 2:449; see below for a more complete discussion.

31. Larson 1987, 363–87; see below for a more complete discussion.

32. Scheiber 1962, 236.

33. Hulbert 1904, 83–84; Rohrbough 1978, 177.

34. Dunbar 1915, 694–700; MacGill et al. 1917, 121; Rohrbough 1978, 176–77; Young 1902, 15.

35. Farrell 1971, 7; Turner 1962, 164; Hulbert 1904, 74–75, 76; Hart 1972, 258–63; Hart 1974, 73–81; Rohrbough 1978, 157–81; U.S. Bureau of the Census 1960, 13.

36. Young 1902, 24; Buley 1950, 1:448.

37. Hart 1974, 73–81.

38. Using the survey dates might reveal when the promise of the Road happened, but funds to support surveys were released fairly quickly; using the date funds were appropriated to build the Road (meaning bids could be advertized for and contracts let) is another approach, but sometimes years separated appropriation and completion and often additional funds were requested because of unexpected construction cost overruns. The detailed list of appropriation legislation appearing in Hulbert 1904, 191–202, shows this sequence.

39. Dunbar 1915, 720; Hulbert 1904, 21, 23; Schneider 1975, 5; Steele 1977, 5; Stewart 1953, 116; Young 1902, 25–27, 31, 33.

40. Hardin 1967, 14, 18–19.

41. Dunbar 1915, 692. A variety of sources was used to determine the date the Road was opened to a particular point. These sources occasionally provide conflicting dates for some openings, owing perhaps to different definitions of "complete." Road opening dates and levels of completeness were determined primarily by consulting Hardin 1967, Hulbert

1904, Ierley 1990, Jordan 1948, Meinig 1993, Schneider 1975, Steele 1977, Stewart 1953, WPA 1940a, and Young 1902.

42. Young 1902, 33.

43. Hardin 1967, 15; Ierley 1990, 104.

44. Gould 1934, 82–83.

45. Hart 1972, 261; U.S. Bureau of the Census 1898, plates 3 and 4.

46. Brown 1948, 236–64; Buley 1950, 1:1–50, 2:49–50; Lawlis 1947a, 23–40; Lawlis 1947b, 125–39; Meinig 1993, 229–30; Zimmer 1982, 61–88.

47. Pence and Armstrong 1933, 21, 28, 34–35, 37, 40; Thorndale and Dollarhide 1987, 101, 102, 104, 108, 109, 111, 269, 270, 273.

48. "Reminiscences of the Taylor-Livingston Family" 1904, 501.

49. Buley 1950, 1:474–75, 478–81; Dunbar 1915, 717–40; Hulbert 1904, 119–41; Schneider 1975, 21–22; see also extensive portions of Searight 1894.

50. Buley 1950, 1:478–81; Jones 1955, 294, 168–94, 287–319; Schlereth 1985, 65.

51. Chambers 1907, 78; see also Buley 1950, 1:471–72; Dunbar 1915, 721–26.

52. Schneider 1975, 22; see also Dunbar 1915, 737–40; Searight 1894, 16.

53. Chambers 1907, 76–77.

54. Dunbar 1915, 734; Schneider 1975, 21.

55. Searight 1894, 16, 298; Hulbert 1904, 109–14.

56. Jordan 1948, 137; Zimmerman 1931, 147–48; Schneider 1975, 28.

57. WPA 1940a, 45.

58. Steele 1977, 16.

59. "Reminiscences of the Taylor-Livingston Family" 1904, 501.

60. Gould 1934, 80–84; Hardin 1967, 17; Flint 1828, 2:132, 168–69, 345.

61. Brown 1948, 184–86, 286; Hulbert 1904, 17–18; Lewis 1962, 5, 11, 12, map; Meinig 1993, 229–30, 357, 360, 403–4; Zimmer 1982, 61–88.

62. Hudson 1988, 395–413; Meinig 1993, 222–24, 229–30; Meyer 1976a, 3–13; Meyer 1976b, 151–60; Meyer 1980, 97–112; Rose 1985, 201–32; Rose 1986, 242–63; Rose 1988, 159–67; Steckel 1983, 14–36; Stewart 1953, 117; Swierenga 1989, 73–105; Wilhelm 1982.

63. U.S. Bureau of the Census 1853, xxxvi–xxxviii.

64. Rose 1988, 159–67.

65. Hudson 1988, 395–413.

66. Buley 1950, vol. 1, map between pp. 446 and 447, 449; Jordan 1948, 89; Lewis 1962, map; MacGill et al. 1917, 19–26; National Geographic Society 1988, 192–93; Wilson 1991.

67. MacGill et al. 1917, 123; Vonada 1992, 68.

68. Buley 1950, 1:449–56, 490–518; MacGill et al. 1917; Gray 1982, 113–34; Shaw 1982, 89–112; Stover 1982, 135–56; Taylor 1968; MacGill et al. 1917, 123.

69. Hall 1947, 7; Jordan 1948, 119.

70. Meinig 1993, 361; Jordan 1948, 119.

71. Suppiger 1956, 433.

72. Hulbert 1904, 76; WPA 1945, 342–43; Schlereth 1985, 62–65; Schneider 1975, 13; Steele 1977, 10, 11; Hardin 1967, 8, 9; Jordan 1948, 154.

73. Hulbert 1904, 193–95; Meinig 1993, 445; Stewart 1953, 144.

74. Steele 1977, 10, 16.

75. Chambers 1907, 72–73; Dunbar 1915, 708–12, 720; Hardin 1967, 17–22; Turner 1962, 198, 202–3; Young 1902, 78.

76. Hulbert 1904, 92–93; Schneider 1975, 15; Stewart 1953, 119; Young 1902, 85–103.

77. Buley 1950, 1:449.

78. Hulbert 1904, 85–88.

79. Meinig 1993, 342.

80. Dunbar 1915, 716; MacGill et al. 1917, 21; Chambers 1907, 72; *Dictionary of American Biography* 1964, vol. 10, pt. 2, 592–95.

81. Gray 1982, 113–34; MacGill et al. 1917, 488–502; Meinig 1993, 252; Shaw 1982,

89–112; Stewart 1953, 116, 119; Stover 1982, 135–56; Taylor 1968, 45–55, 92–94, 74–103.

82. Brown 1948, 106.

83. Ibid., 103–6, 264–66; Taylor 1968, 32–36; Young 1902, 17–18.

84. Brown 1948, 266–68; Farrell 1971, 15–22; Finn 1942, 1–40; MacGill et al. 1917, 282–90; Taylor 1968, 45–47.

85. Cottman 1907, 117–24; Hulbert 1904, 84; Taylor 1968, 47–48, 91; Howard 1972, 193–207; MacGill et al. 1917, 513–47.

86. Clanin 1982, 30–60; Larson 1987, 363–87; Nettles 1924, 332–57; Scheiber 1982, 1–27. For a more thorough discussion of these issues, see chapter 1 of this volume.

87. Schneider 1975, 5.

88. Steele 1977, 12, 13.

89. Ibid., 14; Schneider 1975, 11, 13; Jordan 1948, 127, 137; Young 1902, 34.

90. Schneider 1975, 7; Meinig 1993, 221–558.

91. MacGill et al. 1917, 18; Stewart 1953, 117.

## Chapter 6. Adapting the Road to New Transport Technology

1. Borchert 1967, 302. I would like to thank Sonya Simms for valuable research assistance and also the expert staffs of the Newberry Library, the Mercantile Library, the Ohio Historical Library, the Indiana State Library, the Hagley Museum and Library, and the Illinois State Historical Library.

2. Miller 1927, 3; Little 1987, 59; Cramer 1808, 21.

3. U.S. House 1826, 1; excerpts of the legislation appear in Hulbert 1901b, 420; Hulme 1904, 77.

4. Woods 1904, 207–21; and Miller 1927, 11–70.

5. Flint 1904, 86; Miller 1927, 12. The numbers may vary depending upon the source materials.

6. Schneider 1975, 9–10; Burns 1919, 221–22; Miller 1927, 70; Hardin 1967, 16–18.

7. Searight 1894, 57–58; State Road Commission of Maryland 1959, 23–26; Hulbert 1901b, 444–55; Burns 1919, 234–35.

8. Yoder 1969, 16, 28; Miller 1927, 12; Hulbert 1901b, 484; and Cuming 1904, 227–29.

9. Howe 1902, 1:309; Kwedar and Hawes 1981, 31–38.

10. Raitz and Jones 1988. See, for example, the illustration of Columbus, Ohio, in Howe 1902, 1:616.

11. Allen 1990, 141; Robinson 1983, 4.

12. Allen 1990, 185–90; Robinson 1983, 8–14.

13. Leavitt 1934, 21; Walsh 1978, 10.

14. Walsh 1978, 10; Leavitt 1934, 23; Scheiber 1969, 192–96.

15. Muller 1976, 182–85. An extensive discussion of Mississippi River towns is found in Mahoney 1990.

16. Hulbert 1901b, 473.

17. Sanderlin 1946, 45–60; Goodrich 1960, 79; Hungerford 1928, 1:15–31.

18. Hungerford 1928, 1:240, 297.

19. Hunter 1949, 490–93.

20. Fishlow 1965, 265; Clark 1966, 228.

21. Hungerford 1928, 2:108; Walsh 1978, 20; Cronon 1991, 81–93.

22. Muller 1976, 194; Hudson 1994.

23. Hunter 1949, 625; Ambler 1932, 284–85.

24. Taylor and Neu 1956, 33, and map inserts, 77–83; Scott and Miller 1979, 132; Hungerford 1928, 2:109–10; Monroe 1988, 272–80.

25. Williams 1989, 153–57.

26. Scheiber 1962; Muller 1976, 187.

27. Muller 1976, 194.

28. A splendid treatment of railroad landscapes is Stilgoe 1983, esp. 73–104.

29. For an excellent discussion of the process of founding railroad towns see Hudson 1985. The centralization of railroad man-

agement is recounted by Chandler 1977, esp. 81–121. Raitz and Jones 1988.

30. Searight 1894, 13.

31. Hulbert 1901b.

32. U.S. Department of Transportation 1976, 200.

33. State Road Commission of Maryland 1959, 25; Burns 1919, 234; Hulbert 1901b, 491.

34. Byrne 1893, 3–6.

35. Seely 1986, 38–39, 800–801.

36. Baker 1909; Frost 1910.

37. McShane 1979, 279–307.

38. Seely 1986, 36–37, 39, 43.

39. Paxson 1946, 245.

40. Hugill 1982; Flink 1970; U.S. Department of Transportation 1976.

41. Agg 1916; Hugill 1982, 332; U.S. Department of Transportation 1976, 95–97.

42. Quoted in Paxson 1946, 245.

43. Ibid., 246.

44. The most extensive treatment of this is Burnham 1961.

45. American Automobile Association 1922, 107–201, 291.

46. Paxson 1946, 247; Schlereth 1985, 10–12; and U.S. Department of Transportation 1976, 110.

47. Seely 1984.

48. Gubbels 1938, 20.

49. *Outdoor Indiana* (May 1935): 8.

50. *Outdoor Indiana* (June 1934): 3; Gubbels 1938, 22–23.

51. U.S. Department of Transportation 1976, 133; *Outdoor Indiana* (March 1935): 24; (August 1939): 7; (February 1939): 4; *Illinois Highways* (October 1916): 126–27; Gubbels 1938, 15.

52. Gubbels 1938, 43; Schlereth 1985, 25–28.

53. Armstrong 1976, 116–17; Paxson 1946, 253, *Outdoor Indiana* (October 1936): 20–21; (March 1937): 21–22, 30. Concrete construction technology is discussed in Copp and Zanella 1993, 192–242.

54. Bateman 1928, 56; Gubbels 1938, 50.

55. *Outdoor Indiana* (January 1937): 3, 7; Schlereth 1985, 94.

56. Belasco 1979, 129–43, 170; Jakle 1980, 41–43.

57. Guth 1926, 33–34; Mainpa 1928, 88; Vieyra 1979, 14; Jakle 1978, 521.

58. Colten and Mulville-Friel 1990, 33; Lamb 1985.

59. Flynn 1932, 6–9, 12–19; Childs 1985, 25; Hilton and Due 1960, 106–34.

60. Bugge and Snow 1959, 23–31; Cabell 1940, 61.

61. Rose 1990, 41.

62. Bugge and Snow 1959, 14, 30; Bruce and Clarkeson 1950, 197–203, 210–15; Rose 1990, 41; U.S. Department of Transportation 1976, 472–76.

63. U.S. Department of Transportation 1976, 476.

64. Garrett 1988, 200; Bruce and Clarkeson 1950, 5; Taff 1950, 3–17.

65. Garrett 1988, 199.

66. Barton and associates 1958, 28.

67. American Society of Planning Officials 1973, 30–32. The most complete analysis of this environmental problem appears in Italiano 1987.

68. Norris 1987; Jakle 1980; Levin 1961; Thiel 1965.

69. Based on field observations (1985 and 1991), and U.S. Geological Survey 1942, 1966, and 1981.

## Chapter 7. Travelers' Impressions of the National Road

1. Drake 1834, 7.

2. Gould 1934, 81.

3. Anon. 1969, 86.

4. Dixon 1849, 79.

5. Von Raumer 1845, 438; Prentice 1848, 39; Faris 1919, 114.

6. Buckingham 1842, 3:267, 294.

7. Oliver 1843, 102.

8. Woods 1822, 41; Welby 1821, 66; Wright 1819, 40.

9. Hoffman 1835, 46.

10. Gould 1934, 82.

11. Buckingham 1842, 3:261, 299; Oliver 1843, 106.

12. Ibid., 108, 197.

13. Beste 1855, 1:298, 311.

14. Ibid., 2:7; Weld 1855, 237; Douglas 1909, 507; Johnson 1908, 368.

15. Blair 1921, 346.

16. Stewart 1953, 135.

17. Gurney 1841, 34.

18. Henshaw 1830, 259.

19. Whitman 1921, 1:181.

20. Buckingham 1842, 2:266, 269.

21. Ibid., 2:256; Stuart-Woortly 1851, 88.

22. Whitman 1921, 1:183.

23. Gurney 1841, 35.

24. Weston 1836, 114.

25. Douglas 1909, 512.

26. Ilf and Petrov 1936, 64.

27. Buckingham 1842, 3:294; Oliver 1843, 107.

28. Whitman 1921, 1:185, 186.

29. Cuming 1810, 206.

30. Beste 1855, 2:68.

31. Ibid.

32. Ibid., 2:74.

33. Hulbert 1904, 187.

34. Harris 1805, 51, 53; Ogden 1823, 25.

35. Dicey 1863, 168.

36. Henshaw 1938, 263.

37. Flagg 1910, 146; Faux 1823, 107, 177; Birkbeck 1819, 63.

38. Birkbeck 1819, 66, 99.

39. Cuming 1810, 181.

40. Gould 1934, 81.

41. Melish 1818, 431.

42. Henshaw 1938, 286.

43. Buckingham 1842, 2:270, 278.

44. Steele 1841, 264; Rosenberg 1851, 212; Dicey 1863, 164.

45. Bruce 1916, 65.

46. Dicey 1863, 176.

47. Wharton 1956, 134, 136.

48. Buckingham 1842, 2:275; Gurney 1841, 30; Pulszky and Pulszky 1853, 1:286; Caswell 1839, 229.

49. Beste 1855, 1:264; Gould 1934, 81.

50. Stewart 1953, 113.

51. Rideing 1879, 812.

52. Hale 1911, 163.

53. Bruce 1916, 36.

54. Ibid., 37, 50.

55. Stewart 1953, esp. 80; Vale and Vale 1983, esp. 39.

56. Tunnard and Pushkarev 1963, 231.

57. Gordon and Gordon 1928, 42, 96.

58. Stewart 1953, 22, 28.

59. Tunnard and Pushkarev 1963, 172.

60. Flagg 1925, 27, 28.

61. Ibid., 41; Stewart 1953, 79.

**Chapter 8. The Road as a Corridor for Ideas**

1. Switzer 1993.

2. The Land Ordinance of 1785 stipulated the implementation of the federal rectangular survey (Township and Range), the establishment of land offices, and the sale of land based on minimum size and price. In 1787, Congress passed the Northwest Ordinance, which granted any new state formed from the territory equality and the establishment of government, religion, and education. The new states would enter the Union as free states.

3. Jordan 1948, 74, 169.

4. Rohrbough 1968, 271.

5. Jordan 1948, 99.

6. Rideing 1879, 816.

7. Lewis 1972, 330.

8. Ibid., 338.

9. Meinig 1979, 168.

10. Raitz and Jones 1988, 17–36.

11. Jordan 1948, 259.

12. Raitz and Jones 1988, 17–36.

13. Jordan 1948, 126–27.

14. Noble 1984, 11–14.

15. Yoder 1969, 175.

16. Ibid., 179.

17. Searight 1894, 293.

18. Jakle 1977, 4.

19. Ibid., 160.

20. Ibid., 172–74.

21. Earle 1987, 175–76.

22. In recent years several studies have appeared dealing specifically with the origin and nativity of settlers in the Midwest. A selected list includes Hudson 1986, Meyer 1976b, Rose 1985, 1986, and 1991, Wilhelm 1982.

23. Hudson 1984, 35–45.

24. Jordan 1948, 131.

25. Hulbert 1901b, 406.

26. Jordan 1948, 184.

27. Wilhelm 1982, 25.

28. Jones 1983, 61.

29. Ibid., 66.

30. Glass 1986.

31. Lewis 1983, 32–40.

32. Zelinsky 1977, 131.

33. Price 1968, 41.

34. Kniffen 1965, 555.

35. Kniffen 1936, 179–93.

36. Kniffen 1965, 561.

37. Lewis 1975a, 12.

38. Pillsbury 1977, 12–31.

39. Bastian 1977, 115–36.

40. Balloon framing made its appearance in the Chicago area in 1832. The frame consists of dimensional timbers such as two-by-fours or two-by-sixes and is nailed together. It was first described by Wheeler in 1855.

41. McAlester and McAlester 1984.

42. Ensminger 1983, 98–114.

43. Bastian 1977, 131.

44. Two American scholars, Robert Ensminger and Terry Jordan, independently, substantiated the origin of the Pennsylvania-German barn during field research in Switzerland. Their findings were subsequently published in Ensminger 1980/81, and Jordan 1980.

45. Ensminger 1992.

46. Hudson 1984. 44.

47. Wilhelm 1991, 72, 79.

48. Rose 1988, 159–67.

49. Jordan 1948, 154.

50. One of the better sources on the Underground Railroad is Blockson 1987. Another, set primarily in Ohio, is Snider 1979.

51. Hart 1986, 51.

52. Jones 1983, 89–90.

53. Noble and Korsok 1975, 46–53.

54. Jones 1983, 84.

55. Hurt 1993, 24.

56. Jones 1983, 89.

57. Hurt 1993, 25.

58. Ibid., 27, 28.

59. Schneider 1974, 126.

60. Hart 1974, 74, 78.

61. Noble 1984, 126.

62. Hart 1975, 60.

63. Price 1968, 49–51.

64. Ohman 1982, 173.

65. Bastian 1977, 121–23.

66. Montell and Morse 1976, 38.

67. There are several guides to American architecture available. A very good one is McAlester and McAlester 1988. Two others are Blumenson 1977 and Whiffen 1969.

68. The "Doctrine of First Effective Settlement" makes the point that the initial, permanent settlement group of an area will have a lasting cultural influence on all subsequent occupants no matter how different their background. The doctrine is discussed in Zelinsky 1992.

69. Kniffen 1965, 566–67.

70. A recent survey by Sculle and Price (1993) of "transverse" barns in southern Illinois suggests the term "transverse frame barn." The survey also suggests new insights about the likely development of this barn type.

71. Boller 1990.

72. Hulbert 1901b, 495.

73. Labatut and Lane 1972, 72.

74. Rideing 1879, 811.

75. Jordan 1948, 303.

76. WPA 1940a, 12.

**Chapter 9. The US 40 Roadside**

1. MacDonald 1938, 3.

2. Page 1918.

3. MacDonald 1922, 6.

4. Pennybacker and Eldridge 1912, 18.

5. *Literary Digest* 1923, 62.

6. Bird 1924, 78.

7. Bureau of Public Roads and the Ohio Department of Highways and Public Works 1927, 26.

8. In a concession to an earlier era when navigation required knowledge of important physical features—creeks, rivers, gaps, and the like—standard informational signs announced each creek crossing. This might not be useful knowledge to Oldsmobile or Packard drivers crossing on substantial concrete and steel bridges but it likely continued a tradition of marking one's route and progress by counting important natural transitions in grade, and ford or bridging points. *American City* 1925, 412–13.

9. MacDonald 1928b, 10.

10. McKay 1927, 66.

11. Bureau of Public Roads and the Department of Highways of the Commonwealth of Pennsylvania 1928, 18.

12. Warfield 1929, 605.

13. De Maeztu 1924, 583.

14. *Fortune* 1934, 54.

15. Swan 1922, 496–500; cf. Berman 1982, 158.

16. *Literary Digest* 1924, 21–22.

17. *Literary Digest* 1926a, 12–13.

18. *Literary Digest* 1924, 57–59.

19. Weinberg 1937, 99–101.

20. Pound 1938, 390–91.

21. *American City* 1926b, 664.

22. *New Republic* 1936, 34.

23. Brown 1937, 53.

24. *Fortune* 1934, 53.

25. *Fortune* 1949, 106.

26. DeVoto 1940, 557.

27. Mertz 1925, 694.

28. *Fortune* 1932, 34–35.

29. *House and Garden* 1925, 94–95.

30. The material on gas stations was drawn from Jakle 1978, 520–42. For more information on the development of the gas station, see Jakle and Sculle 1994.

31. *Literary Digest* 1926b, 68.

32. *Business Week* 1953, 62.

33. Mertz 1925, 698.

34. Hobbs 1924, 16.

35. For an extensive discussion of the evolution of the motel see Jakle 1980, 34–49.

36. DeVoto 1953, 45–48.

37. *Harper's* 1950, 100–101.

38. Durant 1950, 24.

39. Jakle 1982, 76–93.

40. Balderston 1928, 341; Lawton and Lawton 1941, 261–72.

41. Lawton and Lawton 1941, 264.

42. MacDonald 1924, 14.

43. Smith 1937, 298–300.

44. Crissey 1922, 56.

45. Browne 1924, 20–22.

46. *Business Week* 1931, 18, 20.

47. MacDonald 1932, 38.

48. Thruelsen 1941, 18–19.

49. Taylor 1948, 12.

50. Hungerford 1924, 149.

51. Public Roads Administration 1949, 16–17.

52. Coffin 1952, 56.

53. Stewart 1953, 94.

54. Baer 1922, 189–91.

**Chapter 10. The Interstate 70 Landscape**

1. Rose 1990.

2. Flink 1988.

3. Jakle 1990, 296.

4. Vance 1990, 512.

5. Eisenhower 1955.

6. Jakle 1990, 296; Rae 1965, 238; Rae 1971, 248; Flink 1988, 359–62; Rose 1990, 31; Bugge and Snow 1959, 7–9; Dicken 1986, 279–316.

7. Rose 1990, 41–54.

8. See, for example: U.S. Department of Transportation, Federal Highway Administration 1984.

9. Davies 1975, 23.

10. Rose 1990, 102.

11. Lewis 1979.

12. American Association of State Highway and Transportation Officials 1984a, 1984b.

13. Mercury Publishing 1992.

14. Johnson 1976.

15. Information on these murders comes from a series of articles written in 1991 for the *Columbus Dispatch* by staff reporter Michael Barrens.

16. Luxenberg 1985.

17. For an introduction to ideas of "spatial disciplines" and "tactics of inhabiting" see Foucault 1979; Gordon 1980; de Certeau 1984.

18. Rose 1990, 102.

19. Flink 1972, 451–73.

20. Freece and Horton 1985, 1.

21. Patton 1986, 178.

22. Briggs 1983; Lichter and Fuguitt 1980.

23. The idea of a "galactic city" comes from Lewis 1983.

24. For example, Norris 1987; Claus and Hardwick 1972; Mason and Moore 1973; Corsi 1975; Benhart and Welsh 1992.

25. USGS 1:24,000 Topographic Maps, Dunreith, Indiana, 1950, 1970, photorevised 1981; Ripple 1975.

26. Rae 1971, 190–91.

27. *Greenfield Daily Reporter* October 9, 1957, August 22, 1957, May 11, 1953, June 8, 1951; Howard et al. 1983; "Greenfield Then and Now" n.d.; Greenfield city maps 1950–91; Ripple 1975; field study.

28. USGS topographic maps: Richmond 1960, photorevised 1981; New Paris, Ohio-Indiana 1960, photorevised 1981; Palladium-Item March 22, 1959, December 3, 1982, March 26, 1991, May 20, 1963, May 11, 1965, May 11, 1966; Ripple 1975; field study.

29. Information from Edwards 1993.

30. U.S. Department of Transportation, U.S. Department of Housing and Urban Development 1980; USGS 1:125,000 topographic maps: Columbus 1912; USGS 1:24,000 topographic maps: Galloway, Ohio 1955, 1966, photorevised 1973, 1981; Southwest Columbus 1965, photorevised 1973, 1982; Pataskala, Ohio 1958, photorevised 1967, 1974, 1985; Reynoldsburg, Ohio 1955, 1964, photorevised 1973, 1985; Growth Areas in Franklin County, 1970–80.

31. See Clay 1973 for the terminology origins of "guerrilla suburbia."

32. Corsi 1975.

33. Lewis 1983, 40.

34. Bugge and Snow 1959, 3–4.

35. For an introduction to "modern" landscapes and their inherent tensions see Relph 1987.

36. Patton 1986, 12.

37. Geertz 1973.

## Chapter 11. Never a Stationary Highway

1. Foucault 1973, xx.

2. Jackson 1984, 34.

3. Jordan 1948, 226.

4. Cowley 1931, 35.

5. Hart 1992, 166–79.

6. Sack 1992, 139.

7. Zukin 1992, 222–23.

8. Williams 1974, 80–82.

9. Mackaye and Mumford 1931, 347.

10. Williams 1974, 84–85.

11. *Literary Digest* 1928, 51–52.

12. *Literary Digest* 1922, 54.

13. Millar 1932, 104.

14. Wood 1923, 267; and Reast 1923, 40–41.

15. *American City* 1931, 185.

16. Hopkins 1924, 478–81.

17. Harrison 1926, 163–65.

18. *American City* 1923, 494.

19. Schivelbusch 1988, 148.

20. Ibid., 142.

21. Reast 1923, 41.

22. *American City* 1926a, 665.

23. *Overland Monthly* 1930, 214.

24. Berman 1953, 141.

25. Relph 1987, 122–23.

26. We wish to acknowledge the ancestry of these strip diagrams to a series of sketch maps drawn by Charles William Brubaker for Clay 1972, 74–75.

27. Levin 1947, 4–5.

28. Crane 1929, 120.

29. Hoffman 1939, 32.

30. Clark 1936, 53.

31. Lewis 1926, 385.

32. Cowley 1931, 34.

33. Data supplied by William F. Edwards, Ohio Department of Transportation, Columbus, Ohio, 1993.

34. Ibid.

35. Zelinsky, 1992, 120–29.

## Chapter 12. Preserving the National Road Landscape

1. Rideing 1879, 801–6.

2. Jordan 1948, 106.

3. Hosmer 1965, 41–57.

4. Murtagh 1988, 28–31.

5. Faris 1919, 103–4; Jordan 1948, 108; Forrest 1956, 105; WPA 1940b, 596–97. The details surrounding the first and second burials of General Braddock are confusing at best. As previously noted, the original grave was never clearly marked because of the need for concealment. The date of reburial is also unclear. Faris and Jordan identify 1804 as the year in which Braddock's remains were discovered and reinterred, while the WPA guide says the general's bones were unearthed in 1812 and not reburied until 1820. Even the genus of the large tree growing over the sec-

ond grave site is in question; some sources call it Braddock's elm, others Braddock's oak. The benefactor of the 1870s landscaping is disputed as well, with Faris crediting a Pittsburgh nurseryman with the improvements instead of King.

6. WPA 1940b, 596; Forrest 1956, 107–8; Jordan 1948, 108. In 1933, historic areas administered by a variety of federal agencies (including War Department battlefields) were transferred by presidential order to the National Park Service; Murtagh 1988, 207.

7. WPA 1940b, 596; Forrest 1956, 108–9, 112.

8. Murtagh 1988, 32, 35–37.

9. For excellent discussions of the history of the historic preservation movement in the United States, see Hosmer 1965 and Murtagh 1988.

10. Bache 1910, 422–23.

11. Hulbert 1901a, 15, 122–23.

12. Hugill 1982, 327, 334; Paxson 1946, 238; Jordan 1948, 300.

13. Jordan 1948, 369, 378; Hulbert 1901a, 118; Fuller 1965, 18.

14. *State of Maryland, Geological Survey* (1899), 234–35.

15. Fuller 1965, 17–18.

16. Douglas 1909, 512; Wilson 1902, 317–20; Jordan 1948, 378, 383; Forrest 1956, 106–7; Forrest 1955, 259.

17. Bernice Lewis, Park District—Dayton and Montgomery County, interview with author, August 1993. Although no written record of the abandonment of Tadmor has been located, the Miami Conservancy Office in Dayton, Ohio, and the Dunbar Library Special Collections and Archives at Wright State University in Dayton maintain information on the relocation of a railroad and the National Road at the time the flood-control reservoir or retarding basin was constructed.

18. Forrest 1956, 134.

19. Jordan 1948, 381; *Literary Digest* 1913, 853.

20. Fuller 1965, 16.

21. A six-tenths-of-a-mile section of this road, now known as Township Road 650 or Peacock Road, was listed on the National Register of Historic Places in 1985. Part of the original 1828 right-of-way, it typifies original National Road construction characteristics of following, not avoiding, ridges, steep hills, and other topographic features generally avoided or simply eliminated with modern highway construction. For a complete description and history of Peacock Road and bibliographical references, see National Register of Historic Places, Inventory-Nomination Form, Peacock Road, Center Township Road, Ohio Historic Preservation Office, Columbus.

22. Paxson 1946, 240, 242; Hugill 1982, 342. These included bicyclists, farmers concerned about the quality of roads between farm and market, local automobile clubs, the American Automobile Association, the American Association of State Highway Officials, the American Road Builders Association, and the manufacturers of automobiles, tires and other auto-related products.

23. Davis 1914, IV, 2–4.

24. Bureau of Public Roads chief Thomas H. MacDonald named two dozen such highway schemes in his 1923 annual report; Paxson 1946, 246–47.

25. Davis 1914, 4, 6.

26. Ibid., 33–35.

27. Bartlett 1969, 693.

28. Engell 1914, 335; WPA 1940b, 595. This boulder was moved to a site adjacent to the Addison toll house about 1942, when a dam was constructed, flooding much of the river valley and submerging the stone arch bridge and the village of Somerfield.

29. Engell 1914, 335.

30. Five of the twelve statues are located along the National Road, at Washington, Pa., Wheeling, W.V., Springfield, Ohio, Richmond, Ind., and Vandalia, Ill.; Bartlett 1969, 693, 695.

31. Postcard, Minsky Bros. & Co., 1939.

32. Frary 1970, 25.

33. Forrest 1955, 259.

34. The Pennsylvania House is located less than a mile from Ohio's Madonna of the Trail, another Lagonda Chapter project; Davis 1990, 24.

35. Liebs 1985, 197–98; Faris 1919, 13, 15, 119; Schneider 1943; Photo 1710, Box 7, Forrest Family Papers, Historical Society of Western Pennsylvania, Pittsburgh.

36. Forrest 1956, 112.

37. America's lengthy love affair with its colonial heritage can probably be traced to the nostalgia for the past generated by the nation's 1876 centennial in Philadelphia. Art history professor William B. Rhoads notes, however, that much of the early twentieth–century interest in early American architecture and its various revivals resulted from the expanded travel and tourism opportunities that the automobile provided. In fact, Rhoads refers to the Colonial Revival–style rehabilitation and new construction as "roadside colonial." See Rhoads 1986.

38. Postcard, Curt Teich, mid-1920s; Hindeman 1931; Bache 1910, 422. National Register of Historic Places Registration Form, Leland Hotel.

39. *Ohio Guide* 1940, 489.

40. Searight's book was republished in 1990 by Heritage Books, Inc.

41. Ristow 1946, 399–401.

42. Discussion of Bruce's guide is from Bruce 1916, 7, 9–10, 13, 20, 23, 56, 68, 82.

43. Hobbs 1926, 1, 18.

44. *Ohio Guide* 1940, vii–viii.

45. For a brief summary and case studies of several federal and state programs currently being used to protect linear resources, see Mastran 1992.

46. The three National Heritage Corridors are the Illinois & Michigan (I&M) Canal National Heritage Corridor in Illinois (1984);

the Blackstone River Valley National Heritage Corridor in Massachusetts and Rhode Island (1986); and the Delaware and Lehigh Valley Navigational Canal National Heritage Corridor (1988).

47. National Trust for Historic Preservation 1995.

48. Butko 1993, 36.

49. *Special Resource Study* 1994, 19, 20.

50. Ibid., 19–20.

51. Thomas & Means Associates, Inc. 1991; Information Series, no. 88 (1994): 29.

52. Kuncio 1991; Grantz 1987.

53. *Special Resource Study* 1994.

54. *Wheeling Heritage* 1991; Information Series, no. 88 (1994): 46.

55. Peyton 1993.

56. Ohio Department of Transportation, Transportation Enhancement Application, Ohio Historic Preservation Office 1993; Ohio Department of Transportation, Transportation Enhancement Application, Village of New Concord, 1993.

57. Ohio Historical Society, n.d.; *Cobblestone* 1991.

58. Davis 1993, 8.

59. Frommer 1988, 10.

60. National Road/Zane Grey Museum, n.d.

61. Washington County Tourism 1993.

62. Tourism Development Division, Indiana Department of Commerce and Eastern Regional Office of Historic Landmarks Foundation, n.d.

63. Lewis 1975b, 5.

64. Lowenthal 1966, 27–32.

65. Spruce Forest Artisan Village History Walk 1991

66. Lewis 1975b, 9.

67. For additional information about historic propery surveys see Parker 1987a and b.

68. For a description of three methodologies for surveying roadside resources see Jones 1993.

69. Thomas & Means Associates, Inc. 1991, 15, appendix H; Grantz 1987.

70. *Information: Routes of History* 1985.

71. For additional information regarding National Register eligibility criteria and what National Register listing means and does not mean, see brochure entitled the "National Register of Historic Places" (n.d.), U.S. Department of the Interior, National Park Service, or contact a State Historic Preservation Office.

72. For a list of National Road properties listed on the National Register of Historic Places or designated National Historic Landmarks, contact the National Park Service, Washington D.C., or State Historic Preservation Offices in the six states through which the Road passes, or see *The National Road Special Resource Study* 1993.

73. Thomas & Means Associates, Inc. 1991, 25.

74. U.S. Department of Transportation, n.d.

75. Butko 1993, 38.

76. Stewart 1953.

77. Schlereth 1985, 144.

## Appendix: Historic Archaeology and the National Road

1. Parker 1987a.

2. Mansberger and Dyson, n.d.

3. Ibid.

4. McClelland et al., n.d., 19.

5. Michael and Carlisle 1976, 21, 25; Michael and Carlisle 1973, 37–39.

6. Michael 1975, 50.

# References

Adams, Henry. 1879. *The Life of Albert Gallatin*. New York: Lippincott.

——. 1955. *The United States in 1800*. Ithaca, N.Y.: Cornell University Press.

Agg, T. R. 1916. *The Construction of Roads and Pavements*. New York: McGraw-Hill.

Allen, Michael. 1990. *Western Rivermen, 1763–1861*. Baton Rouge: Louisiana State University Press.

Ambler, Charles H. 1932. *A History of Transportation in the Ohio Valley*. Glendale, Ohio: Arthur H. Clark.

American Association of State Highway and Transportation Officials. 1984a. *A Policy on Design Standards—Interstate System*. Washington, D.C.: American Association of State Highway and Transportation Officials.

——. 1984b. *A Policy on Geometric Design of Highways and Streets*. Washington, D.C.: American Association of State Highway and Transportation Officials.

American Automobile Association. 1922. *Highways Green Book: Third Annual Edition*. Washington, D.C.: American Automobile Association.

*American City*. 1923. "Business Men Find Street Lighting Invaluable." 29.

———. 1925. "Standard Signs Adopted for Federal Highways." 33.

———. 1926a. "The Lighting of Business Districts." 35.

———. 1926b. "Traffic Congestion, Parking Facilities, and Retail Business." 34.

———. 1931. "Brightest Streets." 44.

American Society of Planning Officials. 1973. *The Design and Location of Service Stations*. Planning Advisory, Report 293. Chicago: American Society of Planning Officials.

*American State Papers*. 1834. Volume 2. Washington, D.C.: Gales and Seaton.

Anonymous. 1969. *An Excursion through the United States and Canada during the Year 1822–23 by an English Gentleman*. New York: Negro Universities Press.

Appleby, Joyce. 1992. *Liberalism and Republicanism in the Historical Imagination*. Cambridge: Harvard University Press.

Armstrong, Ellis L., ed. 1976. *History of the Public Works in the United States, 1776–1976*. Chicago: American Public Works Association.

Association of Graduates, U.S. Military Academy. 1949. *Register of Graduates and Former Cadets, 1802–1945*. West Point, N.Y.

———. 1990. *Register of Graduates and Former Cadets, 1802–1990*. West Point, N.Y.

Austin, William Lane, U.S. Bureau of the Census. 1932. *Drainage of Agricultural Lands*. Washington, D.C.: Government Printing Office.

Bache, Rene. 1910. "Building a Thousand-mile Boulevard." *Technical World* 14.

Baer, Theo. 1922. "The Attached Garage." *House Beautiful* 52.

Baker, I. O. 1909. *A Treatise on Roads and Pavements*. New York: Wiley.

Balderston, Marion. 1928. "Our Popular Foible." *Living Age* 334.

Bartlett, Helen. 1969. "The Madonna of the Trail." *Daughters of the American Revolution Magazine* (October).

Barton, George W., and associates. 1958. *Highways and Their Meaning to Illinois Citizens*. Springfield: Illinois Department of Public Works, Division of Highways.

Bastian, Robert W. 1977. "Indiana Folk Architecture: A Lower Midwestern Index." *Pioneer America* 9.

Bateman, J. H. 1928. *Highway Engineering*. New York: Wiley.

Baudrillard, Jean. 1988. *America*. Trans. by Chris Turner. New York: Verso.

Belasco, Warren J. 1979. *Americans on the Road: From Autocamp to Motel, 1910–1945*. Cambridge: MIT Press.

Belloc, Hilaire. 1923. *The Road*. Manchester, England: Charles W. Hobson.

Benhart, John E., and William Welsh. 1992. "The Interstate Corridor of South-central Pennsylvania: Land Use in Nonmetropolitan America." *Small Town* 22, 4.

Berman, A. B. 1953. "Spectacular Fluorescents Attract Business." *American City* 68.

Berman, Marshall. 1982. *All That Is Solid Melts Into Air: The Experience of Modernity*. New York: Simon and Schuster.

Beste, J. Richard. 1855. *The Wabash: Or Adventures of an English Gentleman's Family in the Interior of America.* 2 vols. London: Hurst and Blackett.

Billington, Ray Allen. 1967. *Westward Expansion: A History of the American Frontier.* 3d ed. New York: Macmillan.

Bird, Malcolm. 1924. "On the Road." *Scientific American* 131.

Birkbeck, Morris. 1819. *Notes on a Journey in America from the Coast of Virginia to the Territory of Illinois.* 5th ed. London: James Ridgeway.

Blair, Will P. 1921. "Brick Roads." In *Highways Green Book.* Washington, D.C.: American Automobile Association.

Blockson, Charles L. 1987. *The Underground Railroad.* New York: Prentice-Hall.

Blumenson, John J.-G. 1977. *Identifying American Architecture: A Pictorial Guide to Styles and Terms, 1600–1945.* Nashville: American Association for State and Local History.

Boller, Robert. 1990. "Settlement Patterns and Building Types as a Result of Initial Occupance in South Central Ohio." Master's thesis, Ohio University, Athens, Ohio.

Boorstin, Daniel J. 1965. *The Americans: The National Experience.* New York: Random House.

Borchert, John R. 1967. "American Metropolitan Evolution." *Geographical Review* 57:302–32.

Boyd, Peter C. 1954. *History of the Town of Triadelphia on Its 125th Anniversary.* Triadelphia, W.V.

Braun, E. Lucy. 1967. *Deciduous Forests of Eastern North America* New York: Hafner Publishing.

Brewerton, Henry. 1836. *National Road West of the Ohio.* 24th Cong., 1st Sess. Executive Documents 291, Doc. 230.

Briggs, Ronald. 1983. "The Impact of the Interstate Highway System on Nonmetropolitan Development, 1950–1975." In *Beyond the urban fringe: Land use issues of nonmetropolitan America,* ed. Rutherford H. Platt and George Macinko. Minneapolis: University of Minnesota Press.

Brown, Jacob. 1896. *Brown's Miscellaneous Writings.* Cumberland, Md.: J. J. Miller.

Brown, Leon R. 1937. "Effective Control by Parking Meters." *American City* 52.

Brown, Ralph H. 1943. *Mirror for Americans: Likeness of the Eastern Seaboard, 1810.* New York: American Geographical Society. Reprinted 1968 by De Capo Press, New York.

———. 1948. *Historical Geography of the United States.* New York: Harcourt, Brace and World.

Browne, E. L. 1924. "Transportation of Hogs by Motor Truck." *Public Roads* 5.

Bruce, Arthur G., and John Clarkeson. 1950. *Highway Design and Construction.* 3d ed. Scranton: International Textbook.

Bruce, Robert. 1916. *The National Road: Most Historic Thoroughfare in the United States, and Eastern Division of the National Old Trails Ocean-to-Ocean Highway.* Washington, D.C.: National Highways Association.

Buckingham, J[ames] S[ilk]. 1842. *The Eastern and Western States of America.* 3 vols. London: Fisher, Son and Co.

Bugge, W. A., and W. Brewster Snow. 1959. "The Complete Highway." In *The Highway and the Landscape,* ed. W. Brewster Snow. New Brunswick, N.J.: Rutgers University Press.

Buley, R. Carlyle. 1950. *The Old Northwest: Pioneer Period, 1815–1840.* 2 vols. Indianapolis: Indiana Historical Society Press.

Bureau of Public Roads and the Department of Highways of the Commonwealth of Pennsylvania. 1928. "Report of a Survey of Transportation on the State Highways of Pennsylvania." Washington, D.C.: Bureau of Public Roads.

Bureau of Public Roads and the Ohio Department of Highways and Public Works. 1927. "Report of a Survey of Transportation on the State Highway System of Ohio." Washington, D.C.: USDA.

Burnham, John C. 1961. "The Gasoline Tax and the Automobile Revolution." *Mississippi Valley Historical Review* 48.

Burns, Lee. 1919. "The National Road in Indiana." *Indiana Historical Society Publications* 7.

*Business Week.* 1931. "Railroads Hard Hit as Truck Lines Expand in Middle West." April 22.

———. 1953. "What Pulls Motorists to a Favorite Service Station?" March 21.

Butko, Brian A. 1993. "Historic Highway Preservation—Not a Deadend Street." *CRM* 16.

Byrne, Austin. 1893. *A Treatise on Highway Construction.* New York: Wiley.

Cabell, H. F. 1940. "The Economic Aspects of Interregional Highways." *Roads and Streets* 83.

Canfield, A. 1835. *National Road—Springfield, Ohio, to Richmond, Indiana.* 24th Cong., 1st sess. House Documents 288, Doc. 62.

Caswell, Henry. 1839. *America and the American Church.* London: J.G. and F. Rivington.

Cayton, Andrew R. L., and Peter S. Onuf. 1990. *The Midwest and the Nation: Rethinking the History of an American Region.* Bloomington: Indiana University Press.

Chambers, Smiley N. 1907. "Internal Improvements in Indiana: No. 2—The National Road." *Indiana Magazine of History* 3.

Chandler, Alfred D. 1977. *The Visible Hand: The Managerial Revolution in American Business.* Cambridge: Harvard University Press.

Childs, William R. 1985. *Trucking and the Public Interest: The Emergence of Federal Regulation.* Knoxville: University of Tennessee Press.

Clanin, Douglas E. 1982. "Internal Improvements in National Politics, 1816–1830." In *Transportation and the Early Nation.* Indianapolis: Indiana Historical Society.

Clark, Frederick P. 1936. "Limited Motorways," or "Freeways." *American City* 51.

Clark, John G. 1966. *The Grain Trade in the Old Northwest.* Urbana: University of Illinois Press.

Claus, R. James, and Walter G. Hardwick. 1972. *The Mobile Consumer: Automobile-Oriented Retailing and Site Selection.* New York: Macmillan.

Clay, Grady. 1972. *Close-up: How to Read the American City.* Chicago: University of Chicago Press.

———. 1973. *Close-up: How to Read the American City.* New York: Praeger.

———. 1994. *Real Places: An Unconventional Guide to America's Generic Landscape.* Chicago: University of Chicago Press.

*Cobblestone.* 1991. "The National Road." June.

Coffin, Tris. 1952. "Modern Cars Ride on Ancient Roads." *Nation's Business* 40.

Colten, C. E., and Diane Mulville-Friel. 1990. *Guidelines and Methods for Conducting Property Transfer Site Histories.* Research Report 049. Champaign, Ill.: Hazardous Waste Research and Information Center.

Columbus planning maps. N.d. "Growth Areas in Franklin County, 1970–1980 / Mean Housing Values in Franklin County." Unattributed Columbus planning maps drawn from census information. Columbus, Ohio: Columbus City Library Local History Collection.

Conzen, Michael P. 1990. Afterword. In *The Making of the American Landscape,* ed. Conzen. London: Unwin Hyman.

Copp, Newton H., and Andrew W. Zanella. 1993. *Discovery, Innovation, and Risk: Case Studies in Science and Technology.* Cambridge: MIT Press.

Corsi, Thomas M. 1975. "Development at Interchanges: The Ohio Turnpike." *Traffic Quarterly* 29.

Cottman, George S. 1907. "The Internal Improvement System of Indiana." *Indiana Magazine of History* 3.

Cowley, Malcolm. 1931. "Continental Highway." *The New Republic* 66.

Cramer, Zadoc. 1808. *The Navigator.* Pittsburgh: Cramer and Spear.

Crane, Jacob L., Jr. 1929. "Various Views Expressed on By-passing of Traffic." *American City* 40.

Crawford, W. H. 1820. *Message from the president.* 16th Cong., 2d sess. House Documents 53, Doc. 82.

Crissey, Forrest. 1922. "Our New Transportation System." *Saturday Evening Post* 195.

Cronon, William. 1991. *Nature's Metropolis: Chicago and the Great West.* New York: Norton.

Cuming, F[ortescue]. 1810. *Sketches of a Tour to the Western Country.* Pittsburgh: Cramer, Spear, and Eichbaum.

———. 1904. "Cuming's Tour to the Western Country (1807–1809)." In *Early Western Travels, 1748–1846,* ed. R. G. Thwaites. Cleveland: Arthur H. Clark.

Cupper, Dan. 1990. *The Pennsylvania Turnpike: A History.* Lebanon, Pa.: Applied Arts Publishers.

Dallas, A. J. 1816. "Cumberland Road." 10th Cong., 1st sess. *American State Papers,* Vol. 21, Miscellaneous Vol. 2, Serial 038.

Daniels, Marjorie. 1993. Letter to Glenn Harper, June 2.

Davies, Richard O., ed. 1975. *The Age of Asphalt.* New York: Lippincott.

Davis, Charles H. 1914. *National Old Trails Road, Ocean to Ocean Highway.* Boston: Everett Press.

Davis, David M. 1990. *The Inn at the End of the Road: A History of the Pennsylvania House, Springfield, Ohio.* Springfield: Miller Printing.

Davis, Marsh. 1993. "Lost Cause Becomes Roadside Attraction." *Preservationist* (March/April).

de Certeau, Michel. 1984. *The Practice of Everyday Life.* Berkeley: University of California Press.

De Maeztu, Ramiro. 1924. "Automobiles and National Character." *Living Age* 322.

DeVoto, Bernard. 1940. "Road Test." *Harpers* 181.

———. 1953. "The Easy Chair-Motel Town." *Harpers* 207.

Dicey, Edward. 1863. *Six Months in the Federal States,* vol. 1. London: Alexander MacMillan.

Dicken, Peter. 1986. *Global Shift: Industrial Change in a Turbulent World.* London: Harper and Row.

*Dictionary of American Biography.* 1964. 10 vols. New York: Charles Scribner's Sons.

Division of Earth Sciences, National Research Council. 1959. "Glacial Map of the United States East of the Rocky Mountains." Scale 1:1,750,000. New York: Geological Society of America.

Dixon, James. 1849. *Methodism in America.* London: John Mason.

Douglas, Albert. 1909. "Auto Trip Over the Old National Road." *Ohio Archaeological and Historical Publications* 18.

Drake, Daniel. 1834. *Discourse on the History, Character, and Prospects of the West.* Cincinnati: Truman and Smith.

Dunbar, Seymour. 1915. *A History of Travel in America.* 4 vols. Indianapolis: Bobbs-Merrill.

Durant, John. 1950. "The Movies Take to the Pastures." *Saturday Evening Post* 223.

Earle, Carville. 1987. "Regional Development West of the Appalachians, 1850–1860." In *North America: The Historical Geography of a Changing Continent,* ed. Robert D. Mitchell and Paul A. Groves. Totowa, N.J.: Rowman and Littlefield.

Edwards, William F. 1993. "Ohio Traffic Counts: US40, I-70, and I-75, 1956 to 1993." Ohio Department of Transportation.

Eisenhower, Dwight D. 1975 (1955). Special message to the Congress regarding a national highway program. In *The Age of Asphalt,* ed. Davies.

Engell, H. E. Candace Cornell. 1914. "Romance of the Road." *Daughters of the American Revolution Magazine* 45.

Ensminger, Robert F. 1980/81. "A Search for the Origin of the Pennsylvania Barn." *Pennsylvania Folklife* 30.

———. 1983. "A Comparative Study of Pennsylvania and Wisconsin Forebay Barns." *Pennsylvania Folklife* 32.

———. 1992. *The Pennsylvania Barn, Its Origin, Evolution, and Distribution in North America*. Baltimore: Johns Hopkins University Press.

Ernst, Ferdinand. 1819. Bemerkungen auf einer Reise durch das Innere der Vereinigten Staaten von Nord-Amerika im Jahre 1819. In *Prairie State impressions of Illinois, 1673–1967, by Travelers and Other Observers*, ed. Paul M. Angle (1968). Chicago: University of Chicago Press.

Faris, John T. 1919. *Seeing Pennsylvania*. Philadelphia: Lippincott.

Farrell, Richard T. 1971. "Internal Improvement Projects in Southwestern Ohio, 1815–1834." *Ohio History* 80.

Faux, William. 1823. *Memorable Days in America*. London: W. Simpkin and R. Marshall.

Fehrenbacher, J. B., et al. 1984. General Soil Map of Illinois. In *Soils of Illinois*, Bulletin 778. Urbana: University of Illinois College of Agriculture Experiment Station in cooperation with the Soil Conservation Service and the USDA.

Finn, Chester E. 1942. "The Ohio Canals: Public Enterprise on the Frontier." *Ohio State Archeological and Historical Quarterly* 51.

Fishlow, Albert. 1965. *American Railroads and the Transformation of the Ante-bellum Economy*. Cambridge: Harvard University Press.

Flagg, Gershom. 1910. Letters, 1816–1836. In *Pioneer Letters of Gershom Flagg*, ed. Solon J. Buck. Springfield: Illinois State Historical Society.

Flagg, James M. 1925. *Boulevards All the Way*. New York: Doran.

Flink, James J. 1970. *American Adopts the Automobile, 1895–1910*. Cambridge: MIT Press.

———. 1972. "Three Stages of Automobile Consciousness." *American Quarterly* 24, 4.

———. 1988. *The Automobile Age*. Cambridge, Mass.: MIT Press.

Flint, James. 1904. "Flint's Letters from America, 1818–1820." In *Early Western Travels, 1748–1846*, ed. R. G. Thwaites. Cleveland: Clark.

Flint, Timothy. 1828. *A Condensed Geography and History of the Western States or the Mississippi Valley*. 2 vols. Cincinnati: William M. Farnsworth.

Flynn, Leo J. 1932. *Coordination of Motor Transportation*. 72d Cong., 1st sess. S. Doc. 43.

Ford, Henry II. 1975 (1966). "The Highway System: The Needs of the Cities." In *The Age of Asphalt*, ed. Richard O. Davies. New York: Lippincott.

Forrest, Earle R. 1955. "History of the National Pine in Washington County, Pa." Typescript of articles published in the *Washington Reporter* and *Washington Observer*.

———. 1956. "History of the National Pine in Fayette and Somerset Counties, Pennsylvania." Typescript of articles published in the *Washington Reporter* and *Washington Observer*.

*Fortune*. 1932. "Mr. Jenkins and Sir Henri." 6.

———. 1934. "The American Roadside." 10.

———. 1949. "Enter the Road Builders." 40.

Foucault, Michel. 1973. *The Order of Things: An Archaeology of the Human Sciences*. New York: Vintage Books.

———. 1979. *Discipline and Punish*. New York: Vintage Books.

Franklin, Benjamin. 1959 (1751). "Observations Concerning the Increase of Mankind, Peopling Countries, &tc." In *The Papers of Benjamin Franklin,* ed. Leonard W. Larabee et al. 27 vols. New Haven: Yale University Press.

Frary, I. T. 1970 (1936). *Early Homes of Ohio*. New York: Dover Publications.

Freece, John W., and Tom Horton. 1985. "Freeway Will Miss Green Ridge State Forest, State Says." *Baltimore Sun*. March 2.

Frommer, Arthur. 1988. "Viewpoint: Historic Preservation and Tourism." *Preservation Forum 2*.

Frost, Harwood. 1910. *The Art of Roadmaking*. New York: McGraw-Hill.

Fuller, Wayne E. 1965. "The Ohio Road Experiment, 1913–1916." *Ohio History* 74.

Gallatin, Albert. 1808. *Roads and Canals. American State Papers,* 10th Cong., 1st sess. Vol. 20, Miscellaneous Vol. 1, Serial 037.

Garrett, Wilbur E., ed. 1988. *Historical Atlas of the United States*. Washington, D.C.: National Geographic Society.

Geertz, Clifford. 1973. *The Interpretation of Cultures*. New York: Basic Books.

Gillespie, W. M. 1847. *Manual of the Principles and Practices of Road Making*. New York.

Gillmore, Q. A. 1876. *A Practical Treatise on Roads, Streets, and Pavements*. New York.

Glass, Joseph W. 1986. *The Pennsylvania Culture Region: A View from the Barn*. Ann Arbor, Mich.: UMI Research Press.

Glassie, Henry. 1968. *Patern in the Material Folk Culture of the Eastern United States*. Philadelphia: University of Pennsylvania Press.

Goodrich, Carter. 1960. *Government Promotion of American Canals and Railroads, 1800–1890*. New York: Columbia University Press.

Gordon, Colin, ed. 1980. *Power/Knowledge: Selected Interviews and Other Writings, 1972–1977, by Michel Foucault*. New York: Pantheon Books.

Gordon, Jan, and Cora J. Gordon. 1928. *On Wandering Wheels: Through Roadside Camps from Maine to Georgia in an Old Sedan Car*. New York: Dodd, Mead.

Gould, J. 1934. "Wanderings in the West in 1839." *Indiana Magazine of History* 30.

Grantz, Denise L. 1987. *National Road: Historic Resource Survey Final Report and Analysis*. California, Pa.: California University of Pennsylvania.

Gray, Ralph D. 1982. "The Canal Era in Indiana." In *Transportation and the Early Nation*. Indianapolis: Indiana Historical Society.

Greene, Jack P. 1993. *The Intellectual Construction of America: Exceptionalism and Identity from 1492 to 1800*. Chapel Hill: University of North Carolina Press.

"Greenfield Then and Now." N.d. Unattributed xerox. Greenfield, Ind.: Greenfield Public Library.

Gubbels, Jac L. 1938. *American Highways and Roadsides*. Boston: Houghton Mifflin.

Gurney, Joseph. 1841. *A Journey in North America, Described in Familiar Letters to Amelia Opie*. Norwich: J. Fletcher.

Gustorf, Fred. 1962. "Frontier Perils Told by an Early Illinois Visitor." *Journal of the Illinois State Historical Society* 55.

Guth, Alexander G. 1926. "The Automobile Service Station." *Architectural Forum* 45:33–56.

Hale, William B. 1911. "The Old National Road." *Century Magazine* 83.

Hall, Virginius C. 1947. "Ohio in Knee Pants." *Ohio State Archeological and Historical Quarterly* 56.

Hardin, Thomas L. 1967. "The National Road in Illinois." *Journal of the Illinois State Historical Society* 61.

*Harper's.* 1950. "After Hours." 200.

Harris, Thaddeus M. 1805. *Journal of a Tour into the Territory Northwest of the Alleghany Mountains.* Boston: Manning and Loring.

Harrison, Ward. 1926. "Relighting Indianapolis." *American City* 34.

Hart, John Fraser. 1972. "The Middle West." *Annals of the Association of American Geographers* 62.

———. 1974. "The Spread of the Frontier and the Growth of Population." *Geoscience and Man* 5.

———. 1975. *The Look of the Land.* Englewood Cliffs, N.J.: Prentice-Hall, Inc.

———. 1986. "Change in the Corn Belt." *Geographical Review* 76.

———. 1991. *The Land that Feeds Us.* New York: Norton.

———. 1992. "Nonfarm Farms." *Geographical Review* 82.

Henshaw, Hiram. 1830. "A Diary Written by Captain Hiram Henshaw." In *Chronicles of Old Berkeley,* ed. Mabel H. Gardiner and Ann H. Gardiner, 282–314. Durham, N.C.: Seeman Press.

Hilton, George W., and J. F. Due. 1960. *The Electric Interurban Railways in America.* Stanford: Stanford University Press.

Hindeman, William Blake. 1931. "The History of the National Highway Route 40" (brochure).

Hobbs, Howard F. 1924. *Hobbs Grade and Surface Guide: National Old Trails and Connections.* Akron, Ohio: Mohawk Rubber Co.

———. 1926. *Mohawk Hobbs Grade and Surface Guide: National Old Trails and Connections.* Akron, Ohio: Mohawk Rubber Co.

Hoffman, C[harles] F. 1835. *A Winter in the Far West.* London: Richard Bentley.

Hoffman, Paul. 1939. "America Goes to Town." *Saturday Evening Post* 211.

Hokanson, Drake. 1988. *The Lincoln Highway, Main Street across America.* Iowa City: University of Iowa Press.

Hopkins, M. S. 1924. "The Street-Lighting Demonstration at Columbus, Ohio." *American City* 30.

Hosmer, Charles B. 1965. *Presence of the Past.* New York: G. P. Putnam's Sons.

*House and Garden.* 1925. "Filling Stations for Town Betterment." 47.

Howard, Robert P. 1972. *Illinois: A History of the Prairie State*. Grand Rapids, Mich.: Eerdmans.

Howard, Needles, Tammen, and Bergendoff. 1983. *Revitalization Plan for Greenfield, Indiana*. Indianapolis.

Howe, Henry. 1902. *Historical Collections of Ohio*. 2 vols. Cincinnati: C. J. Krehbiel and Co.

Hudson, John C. 1984. "The Middle West as a Cultural Hybrid." *Pioneer America Society Transactions* 7.

———. 1985. *Plains Country Towns*. Minneapolis: University of Minnesota Press.

———. 1986. "Yankeeland in the Midwest." *Journal of Geography* 85.

———. 1988. "North American Origins of Middlewestern Frontier Populations." *Annals of the Association of American Geographers* 78.

Hudson, John C. 1994. *Making the Corn Belt: A Geographical History of Middle-Western Agriculture*. Bloomington: Indiana University Press.

Hugill, Peter J. 1982. "Good Roads and the Automobile in the United States, 1880–1929." *Geographical Review* 72.

Hulbert, Archer B. 1901a. *The Old National Road: A Chapter of American Expansion*. Columbus: Press of F. J. Heer.

———. 1901b. "The Old National Road—The Historic Highway of America." *Ohio Archaeological and Historical Publications* 9.

———. 1904. *The Cumberland Road: Historic Highways of America*, vol. 10. Cleveland: Arthur H. Clark.

Hulme, Thomas. 1904. "Thomas Hulme's Journal, 1818–1819." In *Early Western Travels, 1748–1846*, ed. R. G. Thwaites. Cleveland: Clark.

Hungerford, Edward. 1924. "What of the American Highway." *Saturday Evening Post* 197.

———. 1928. *The Story of the Baltimore & Ohio Railroad, 1827–1927*. 2 vols. New York: Putnam's Sons.

Hunter, Louis C. 1949. *Steamboats on the Western Rivers: An Economic and Technological History*. Cambridge: Harvard University Press.

Hurt, Douglas R. 1993. "Bettering the Beef: Felix Renick and the Ohio Company for Importing English Cattle." *Timeline* 10.

Ierley, Merritt. 1990. *Traveling the National Road: Across the Centuries on America's First Highway*. Woodstock, N.Y.: Overlook Press.

Ilf, Ilya, and Eugene Petrov. 1936. *Little Golden America*. London: George Routledge.

*Illinois Highways*. 1914–16. 1–3.

*Information: Routes of History: Recreational Use and Preservation of Historic Transportation Corridors*. 1985. Information Series No. 38. Washington D.C.: National Trust for Historic Preservation.

Institute for the History of Technology and Industrial Archaeology. 1994. HABS/HAER documentation of Casselman Bridge. Morgantown, W.V.

Italiano, M. L. 1987. *Liability for Underground Storage Tanks*. New York: Practicing Law Institute.

Jackson, J. B. 1984. *Discovering the Vernacular Landscape*. New Haven: Yale University Press.

Jakle, John A. 1977. *Images of the Ohio Valley*. New York: Oxford University Press.

——. 1978. "The American Gasoline Station, 1920–1970." *Journal of American Culture* 1.

——. 1980. "Motel by the Roadside: America's Room for the Night." *Journal of Cultural Geography* 1.

——. 1982. "Roadside Restaurants and Place-Product-Packaging." *Journal of Cultural Geography* 3.

——. 1990. "Landscapes Redesigned for the Automobile." In *The Making of the American Landscape,* ed. Michael P. Conzen. Boston: Unwin Hyman.

Jakle, John A., and Keith A. Sculle. *The Gas Station in America*. Baltimore: Johns Hopkins University Press, 1994.

Jefferson, Thomas. 1808. *American State Papers: Cumberland Road*. 10th Cong., 1st sess. Vol. 20, Miscellaneous Vol. 1, Serial 037.

Johnson, Hildegard Binder. 1976. *Order Upon the Land*. New York: Oxford University Press.

Johnson, R. H. 1908. "A Winter Tour from New York to Savannah." *Travel* 13.

Jones, Dwayne. 1993. "Developing a Survey Methodology for Roadside Resources." *CRM* 16.

Jones, Robert L. 1955. "The Beef Cattle Industry in Ohio Prior to the Civil War." *Ohio Historical Quarterly* 64.

——. 1983. *History of Agriculture in Ohio to 1880*. Kent, Ohio: Kent State University Press.

Jordan, Philip D. 1948. *The National Road*. New York: Bobbs-Merrill Co.

Jordan, Terry G. 1980. "Alpine, Alemannic, and American Log Architecture." *Annals of the Association of American Geographers* 70.

Jordan, Terry G., and Matti Kaups. 1987. "Folk Architecture in Cultural and Ecological Context." *Geographical Review* 77.

Keats, John. 1958. *The Insolent Chariots*. New York: Lippincott.

Kemp, Emory L. 1994. Cement mills along the Potomac. Monograph, West Virginia University Institute for the History of Technology and Industrial Archaeology.

Kennan, George F. 1993. *Around the Cragged Hill: A Personal and Political Philosophy*. New York: Norton.

Kirby, Richard S., Sidney Withington, Arthur B. Darling, and Frederick G. Kilgour. 1956. *Engineering in History*. New York: McGraw-Hill.

Kniffen, Fred B. 1936. "Louisiana House Types." *Annals of the Association of American Geographers* 26.

———. 1965. "Folk Housing: Key to Diffusion." *Annals of the Association of American Geographers* 55.

Knight, Jonathan. 1826a. *Memoir, Road from Wheeling to Missouri.* 19th Cong., 1st sess. House Documents 134, Doc. 51.

———. 1826b. *Road—Zanesville to Columbus.* 19th Cong., 2d sess. House Documents 149, Doc. 31.

———. 1828. *The Continuation of the Cumberland Road: Report.* 20th Cong., 1st sess. Senate Documents 165, Doc. 99.

Kuncio, Gerald M. 1991. Letter to Glenn A. Harper (August 7).

Kunster, James H. 1993. *The Geography of Nowhere: The Rise and Decline of America's Man-made Landscape.* New York: Simon & Schuster.

Kwedar, M. F., and Edward L. Hawes. 1981. *Inns and Taverns in the Midwest: Typical Functions, Forms and Layouts.* Publication Series 2, Research Report 5. Springfield: Clayville Rural Life Center and Museum.

Labatut, Jean, and Wheaton J. Lane. 1972. *Highways in Our National Life.* New York: Arno Press.

Lacock, Abner, David Shriver, and William McRee. 1821. *Presidential Message.* 16th Cong., 2d sess. House Documents 53, Doc. 82.

Lamb, R. F. 1985. "Morphology and Vitality of Business Districts in Upstate New York Villages." *Professional Geographer* 37.

Larson, John L. 1987. "'Bind the Republic Together': The National Union and the Struggle for a System of Internal Improvements." *Journal of American History* 74.

Lawlis, Chelsea L. 1947a. "The Settlement of the Whitewater Valley, 1790–1810." *Indiana Magazine of History* 43.

———. 1947b. "The Great Migration and the Whitewater Valley." *Indiana Magazine of History* 43.

Lawton, Elizabeth B., and Walter L. Lawton. 1941. "The Story of a Highway." *Nature Magazine* 34.

Leavitt, Charles T. 1934. "Transportation and the Livestock Industry of the Middle West to 1860." *Agricultural History* 8.

Leavitt, Helen. 1970. *Superhighway—Superhoax.* Garden City, N.Y.: Doubleday.

Levin, David R. 1947. *Public Control of Highway Access and Roadside Development.* Washington, D.C.: Public Roads Administration.

———. 1961. "The Highway Interchange Land-Use Problem." In *Land Use and Development at Highway interchanges: A Symposium,* 1–24. Bulletin 288. Washington, D.C.: National Research Council, Highway Research Board.

Lewis, Harold M. 1926. "Building Lines in Village Centers and Creation of By-pass Routes." *American City* 35.

Lewis, Marcus W. 1962. *The Development of Early Emigrant Trails in the United States East of the Mississippi River.* Washington, D.C.: National Genealogical Society.

Lewis, Peirce F. 1972. "Small Town in Pennsylvania." *Annals of the Association of American Geographers* 62.

———. 1975a. "Common Houses, Cultural Spoor." *Landscape* 19.

———. 1975b. "The Future of the Past: Our Clouded Vision of Historic Preservation." *Pioneer America* 7.

———. 1976. *New Orleans: The Making of an Urban Landscape*. Cambridge, Mass.: Ballinger.

———. 1979. "Axioms for Reading the Landscape." In *The interpretation of ordinary landscapes,* ed. D. W. Meinig. New York: Oxford University Press.

———. 1983. "The Galactic Metropolis." In *Beyond the urban fringe: Land use issues of nonmetropolitan America,* ed. Rutherford H. Platt and George Macinko. Minneapolis: University of Minnesota Press.

Lichter, Daniel T., and Glenn V. Fuguitt. 1980. "Response to Transportation Innovation: The Case of the Interstate Highway." *Social Forces* 59.

Liebs, Chester H. 1985. *Main Street to Miracle Mile*. Boston: Little, Brown.

*Literary Digest*. 1913. "Neglect of the Old National Road." April.

———. 1922. "Against Lighting Country Roads." 72.

———. 1923. "Four Great Highways from Sea to Sea." 77.

———. 1924. "Wanted—More Hitching-Posts for Cars." 80.

———. 1926a. "Edison Looks Down on the Sky-scraper." 91.

———. 1926b. "The Filling Station as General Store." 90.

———. 1928. "The 'Black Magic' of Night Motoring." 96.

Little, Elizabeth A. 1987. "Inland Waterways in the Northeast." *Midcontinent Journal of Archeology* 13.

Lowenthal, David. 1966. "The American Way of History." *Columbia University Forum* 9.

Luxenberg, Stan. 1985. *Roadside Empires: How the Chains Franchised America*. New York: Viking Penguin.

McAlester, Virginia, and Lee McAlester. 1984. *A Field Guide to American Houses*. New York: Knopf.

McClelland, Linda Flint, J. Timothy Keller, Genevieve P. Keller, and Robert Z. Melnick. N.d. *Guidelines for Evaluating and Documenting Rural Historic Landscapes*. National Register Bulletin 30. Washington D.C.: U.S. Department of the Interior, National Park Service Interagency Resources Division.

McCoy, Drew R. 1980. *The Elusive Republic: Political Economy in Jeffersonian America*. Chapel Hill: University of North Carolina Press.

MacDonald, Thomas H. 1922. Report of the Chief of the Bureau of Public Roads. Washington, D.C.: USDA.

———. 1924. Report of the Chief of the Bureau of Public Roads. Washington, D.C.: USDA.

———. 1928a. "The History and Development of Road Building in the United States." *Transactions of the American Society of Civil Engineers* 92, Paper No. 1685. New York: ASCE.

———. 1928b. Report of the Chief of the Bureau of Public Roads. Washington, D.C.: USDA.

———. 1932. Report of the Chief of the Bureau of Public Roads. Washington, D.C.: USDA.

———. 1938. Report of the Chief of the Bureau of Public Roads. Washington, D.C.: USDA.

MacGill, Caroline E., et al. 1917. *History of Transportation in the United States before 1860.* Washington, D.C.: Carnegie Institution.

McKay, J. Gordon. 1927. "Digest of Report of Ohio Highway Transportation Survey." *Public Roads* 8.

Mackaye, Benton, and Lewis Mumford. 1931. "Townless Highways for the Motorist." *Harpers* 163.

McShane, Clay. 1979. "Transforming the Use of Urban Space: A Look at the Revolution in Street Pavements." *Journal of Urban History* 5.

Mahan, D. H. 1838. *Elementary Course of Civil Engineering for the Use of Cadets of the United States Military Academy.* New York: Wiley & Putnam.

Mahoney, Timothy R. 1990. *River Towns in the Great West.* Cambridge: Cambridge University Press.

Mainpa, N. M. 1928. "Uniform Stations Strung along Highway Catch Tourist Business." *National Petroleum News* 20.

Mansberger, Floyd, and Carol Dyson. N.d. "Historical Archaeology Filling in the Gaps."

Mason, Joseph B., and Charles T. Moore. 1973. "Commercial Site Selection at Interstate Interchanges." *Traffic Quarterly* 27.

Mastran, Shelley S. 1992. "A Look at Greenways: A Survey of Programs and Selected Case Studies." *Historic Preservation Forum* 6.

Matthews, Jean V. 1991. *Toward a New Society: American Thought and Culture, 1800–1830.* Boston: Twayne Publishers.

Meinig, D. W. 1979. "Symbolic Landscapes: Some Idealization of American Communities." In *The Interpretation of Ordinary Landscapes,* ed. D. W. Meinig. New York: Oxford University Press.

———. 1986. *The Shaping of America: A Geographical Perspective on 500 Years of History.* Vol. 1, *Atlantic America, 1492–1800.* New Haven: Yale University Press.

———. 1993. *The Shaping of America: A Geographical Perspective on 500 Years of History.* Vol. 2, *Continental America, 1800–1867.* New Haven: Yale University Press.

Melish, John. 1818. *Travels through the United States of America.* Belfast: J. Smyth.

———. 1826. *Geographical Description of the United States.* [New ed.] New York: A. T. Goodrich.

Mercury Publishing. 1992. *Muskingum County Plat Book*. Kettering, Ohio.

Merritt, Frederick S. 1983. *Standard Handbook for Civil Engineers*. New York: McGraw-Hill.

Mertz, Charles. 1925. "The Once Open Road." *Harpers* 151.

Meyer, Douglas K. 1976a. "Illinois Culture Regions at Mid-nineteenth Century." *Bulletin of the Illinois Geographical Society* 18.

———. 1976b. "Southern Illinois Migration Fields: The Shawnee Hills in 1850." *Professional Geographer* 28.

———. 1980. "Immigrant Clusters in the Illinois Military Tract." *Pioneer America* 12.

Michael, Ronald L. 1975. "Construction of National Road Bed—Historical and Archaeological Evidence." *APT* 7.

Michael, Ronald L., and Ronald C. Carlisle. 1973. "The Peter Colley Tavern, 1801–1854." *Pennsylvania Folklife* 23 (Autumn).

———. 1976. "Peter Colley Tavern: Nineteenth Century Wagon Tavern." *Pennsylvania Archaeologist* 46 (April).

Millar, Preston S. 1932. "More Light on the Dangers of Darkness." *American City* 47.

Miller, C. 1927. "The Romance of the National Pike." *Western Pennsylvania Historical Magazine* 10.

Mitchell, Robert D., and Paul A. Groves, eds. 1987. *North America: The Historical Geography of a Changing Continent*. Totowa, N.J.: Rowman and Littlefield.

Monroe, Elizabeth B. 1988. "Spanning the Commerce Clause: The Wheeling Bridge Case, 1850–1856." *American Journal of Legal History* 32.

Montell, Lynwood W., and Michael Lynn Morse. 1976. *Kentucky Folk Architecture*. Lexington: University Press of Kentucky.

Morse, Jedidiah. 1789. *The American Geography; or a View of the Present Situation of the United States of America*. Elizabethtown, N.J.: By the author.

———. 1793. *The American Universal Geography*. Vol. 1., *American Geography*. Boston: Isaiah Thomas and Ebenezer T. Andrews.

Morse, Joseph E., and R. Duff Green. 1971. *Thomas B. Searight's "The Old Pike."* Orange, Va.: Green Tree Press.

Muller, Edward K. 1976. "Selective Urban Growth in the Middle Ohio Valley, 1800–1860." *Geographical Review* 66.

Murtagh, William J. 1988. *Keeping Time: The History and Theory of Preservation in America*. Pittstown, N.J.: Main Street Press.

National Geographic Society. 1988. *Historical Atlas of the United States*. Washington, D.C.: National Geographic Society.

The National Register of Historic Places. N.d. Washington, D.C.: U.S. Department of the Interior, National Park Service (brochure).

National Road/Zane Grey Museum. N.d. Ohio Historical Society (brochure).

National Trust for Historic Preservation. 1995. "National Heritage Areas Legislation." May.

Nettles, Curtis. 1924. "The Mississippi Valley and the Constitution." *Mississippi Valley Historical Review* 11.

*New American State Papers.* 1972. *Transportation.* Vol. 2, *General-Roads.* Wilmington, Del.: Scholarly Resources Inc.

*New Republic.* 1936. "America's New Gadget." 87.

Noble, Allen G. 1984. *Wood, Brick, and Stone: The North American Settlement Landscape.* Vol. 2, *Barns and Farm Structures.* Amherst, Mass.: University of Massachusetts Press.

Noble, Allen G., and Albert J. Korsok. 1975. *Ohio—An American Heartland.* Bulletin 65. Columbus, Ohio: Division of Geological Survey.

Norris, B. Franklin. 1958 (1901). *The Octopus* Reprint. Cambridge, Mass.: Riverside Press.

Norris, Darrell A. 1987. "Interstate Highway Exit Morphology." *Professional Geographer* 39.

Ogden, George W. 1823. *Letters from the West.* New Bedford, Mass.: Melcher and Rogers.

*The Ohio Guide.* 1940. New York: Oxford University Press.

Ohio Historical Society. N.d. "Another Place, Another Time" (brochure).

Ohman, Marian M. 1982. "Diffusion of Foursquare Courthouses to the Midwest, 1785–1885." *Geographical Review* 72.

Oliver, William. 1843. *Eight Months in Illinois.* Newcastle upon Tyne: William A. Mitchell.

*Outdoor Indiana.* 1934–49. Vols. 1–16.

*Overland Monthly.* 1930. "Architecture of the Night." 88.

Page, L. W. 1918. Report of the director of public roads. Washington D.C.: USDA.

Parker, Patricia L. 1987a. *Local Preservation: Is There Archaeology in Your Community?* Washington, D.C.: National Park Service.

———. 1987b. *Local Preservation Questions and Answers about Historic Properties Survey.* Washington D.C.: National Park Service.

Parkinson, Robert, Michael Wiggington, and Paul C. Jenny. 1991. General Soil Map, Licking County, Ohio. In *Soil Survey of Licking County, Ohio.* Washington, D.C.: USDA, Soil Conservation Service.

Patton, Phil. 1986. *Open Road: A Celebration of the American Highway.* New York: Simon and Schuster.

Paxson, Frederick L. 1946. "The Highway Movement, 1916–1935." *American Historical Review* 51.

Pence, George, and Nellie C. Armstrong. 1933. *Indiana Boundaries, Territory, State, and County.* Indianapolis: Indiana Historical Bureau.

Pennybacker, J. E., and Maurice O. Eldridge. 1912. "Mileage and Cost of Public Roads in the United States." Bulletin No. 41, Office of Public Roads. Washington, D.C.: USDA.

Peyton, Billy Joe. 1993. "Finding and Recording the National Road." *Summer Review* 3.

Pillsbury, Richard. 1970. "The Urban Street Pattern as a Culture Indicator: Pennsylvania, 1682–1815." *Annals Association of American Geographers* 70.

———. 1977. "Patterns in the Folk and Vernacular House Forms of the Pennsylvania Culture Region." *Pioneer America* 9.

Postl, Karl. [Charles Sealsfield]. 1828. *The Americans as They Are*. London: Hurst, Chance and Company.

Pound, Arthur. 1938. "No Parking." *Atlantic Monthly* 161.

Prentice, Archibald. 1848. *A Tour in the United States*. London: Charles Gilpin.

Price, Edward T. 1968. "The Central Courthouse Square in the American County Seat." *Geographical Review* 58.

Public Roads Administration. 1949. *Highway Practice in the United States of America*. Washington, D.C.: Federal Works Agency.

*Public Statutes at Large of the United States of America*. 1845–47. Vols. 2, 3, and 4. Boston: Little, Brown.

Pulszky, Ferenez A., and Theresa Pulszky. 1853. *White, Red, Black, Sketches of Society in the United States*. London: Trubner.

Rae, John B. 1965. *The American Automobile: A Brief History*. Chicago: University of Chicago Press.

———. 1971. *The Road and the Car in American Life*. Cambridge, Mass.: MIT Press.

Raitz, Karl B., and John Paul Jones III. 1988. "The City Hotel as Landscape Artifact and Community Symbol." *Journal of Cultural Geography* 9.

Reast, F. M. 1923. "Adequate Street Lighting a Municipal Necessity." *American City* 29.

Reedy, Daniel. 1993. Interview with Ralph Reedy. Livingston, Ill.

Relph, Edward. 1987. *The Modern Urban Landscape*. Baltimore: Johns Hopkins University Press.

"Reminiscences of the Taylor-Livingston Family." 1904. *Ohio Archeological and Historical Publications*. 13.

Reps, John W. 1979. *Cities of the American West: A History of Frontier Urban Planning*. Princeton: Princeton University Press.

Rhoads, William B. 1986. "Roadside Colonial: Early American Design for the Automobile Age." *Winterthur Portfolio* 21.

Rideing, William H. 1879. "The Old National Pike." *Harper's New Monthly Magazine* 59.

Ripple, David A. 1975. *History of the Interstate System of Indiana*. Vol. 3, *Route History*. Lafayette, Ind.: Purdue University Press.

Ristow, Walter W. 1946. "American Road Maps and Guides." *Scientific Monthly* 62.

Robinson, Michael C. 1983. *History of Navigation in the Ohio River Basin*. Navigation History NWS-83-5. Washington, D.C.: U.S. Army Engineer Water Resources Support Center.

Rohrbough, Malcolm J. 1968. *The Land Office Business: The Settlement and Administration of American Public Lands, 1789–1837*. New York: Oxford University Press.

———. 1978. *The Trans-Appalachian Frontier: People, Societies, and Institutions, 1775–1850.* New York: Oxford University Press.

Rose, Albert C. 1976. *Historic American Roads: From Frontier Trails to Superhighways.* New York: Crown Publishers.

Rose, Gregory S. 1985. "Hoosier Origins: The Nativity of Indiana's United States–born Population in 1850." *Indiana Magazine of History* 81.

———. 1986. "Upland Southerners: The County Origins of Southern Migrants to Indiana by 1850." *Indiana Magazine of History* 82.

———. 1988. "The National Road Border between the North and the South in the Midwest by 1870." *Geoscience and Man* 25.

———. 1991. "The Distribution of Indiana's Ethnic and Racial Minorities in 1850." *Indiana Magazine of History* 87, no. 3 (September): 224–60.

Rose, Mark H. 1990. *Interstate: Express Highway Politics, 1939–1989.* Knoxville: University of Tennessee Press.

Rosenberg, Charles G. 1851. *Jenny Lind in America.* New York: Stringer and Townsend.

Sack, Robert. 1992. *Place, Modernity, and the Consumer's World.* Baltimore: Johns Hopkins University Press.

Sanderlin, Walter S. 1946. *The Great National Project: A History of the Chesapeake and Ohio Canal.* Baltimore: Johns Hopkins Press.

Scheiber, Harry N. 1962. "Urban Rivalry and Internal Improvements in the Old Northwest, 1820–1860." *Ohio History* 71.

———. 1969. *Ohio Canal Era: A Case Study of Government and the Economy, 1820–1861.* Athens: Ohio University Press.

———. 1982. "The Transportation Revolution and American Law: Constitutionalism and Public Policy." In *Transportation and the Early Nation.* Indianapolis: Indiana Historical Society.

Schivelbusch, Wolfgang. 1988. *Disenchanted Night: The Industrialization of Light in the Nineteenth Century.* Berkeley: University of California Press.

Schlereth, Thomas J. 1985. *U.S. 40: A Roadscape of the American Experience.* Indianapolis: Indiana Historical Society.

Schneider, Norris F. 1943. "Headley Inn." *Zanesville News.* August 15.

———. 1974. "The National Road: Main Street of America." *Ohio History* 83.

———. 1975. *The National Road: Main Street of America.* Columbus: Ohio Historical Society.

Schodek, Daniel L. 1987. *Landmarks in American Civil Engineering.* Cambridge, Mass.: MIT Press.

Scott, Quinta, and H. S. Miller. 1979. *The Eads Bridge.* Columbia: University of Missouri Press.

Sculle, Keith A., and H. Wayne Price. 1993. "The Traditional Barns of Hardin

County, Illinois: A Survey and Interpretation." *Material Culture* 25, no. 1 (Spring): 1–28.

Searight, Thomas B. 1894. *The Old Pike: A History of the National Road*. Uniontown, Pa.: By the Author.

Sears, Stephen W. 1977. *The American Heritage History of the Automobile in America*. New York: American Heritage Publishing.

Seely, Bruce. 1984. "The Scientific Mystique in Engineering: Highway Research at the Bureau of Public Roads, 1918–1940." *Technology and Culture* 25.

———. 1986. "Railroads, Good Roads, and Motor Vehicles: Managing Technological Change." *Railroad History* 155.

———. 1993. "A Republic Bound Together." *Wilson Quarterly* 17.

Shaw, Ronald E. 1982. "The Canal Era in the Old Northwest." In *Transportation and the early nation*. Indianapolis: Indiana Historical Society.

Shimer, John A. 1972. *Field Guide to Landforms in the United States*. New York: Macmillan.

Shortridge, James R. 1989. *The Middle West: Its Meaning in American Culture*. Lawrence: University of Kansas Press.

Singer, Charles, E. J. Holmyard, A. R. Hall, and Trevor I. Williams. 1958. *A History of Technology*. Vol. 4, *The Industrial Revolution*. New York: Oxford University Press.

Smith, J. Russell. 1925. *North America*. New York: Harcourt, Brace.

Smith, Philip H. 1937. "Highway Freighters." *Scientific American* 156.

Snider, Wayne L. 1979. *Black Pioneers, Patriots, and Persons*. Columbus: Ohio Historical Society.

*Special Resource Study. The National Road 1994*. 1994. Delphi Mailing Number 2, National Park Service-Denver Service Center.

*Spruce Forest Artisan Village History Walk*. 1991. Brochure.

State Road Commission of Maryland. 1959. *A History of Road Building in Maryland*. Baltimore: Leeser Co.

Stebbins, Theodore E., Jr., et al., eds. 1983. *A New World: Masterpieces of American Painting, 1760–1910*. Boston: Museum of Fine Arts.

Steckel, Richard H. 1983. "The Economic Foundations of East-West Migration during the Nineteenth Century." *Explorations in Economic History* 20.

Steele, Eliza R. 1841. *A Summer Journey in the West*. New York: J. S. Taylor.

Steele, Patrick, ed. 1977. *Then and Now: The National Road and Its People*. Indianapolis: Indiana Committee for the Humanities.

Stewart, George R. 1953. *U.S. 40, Cross Section of the United States of America*. Boston: Houghton Mifflin.

———. 1970. *American Place-names*. New York: Oxford University Press.

Stilgoe, John R. 1983. *Metropolitan Corridor: Railroads and the American Scene*. New Haven: Yale University Press.

Stone, Roy. 1895. *Road Building in the United States*. Bulletin No. 17. Washington, D.C.: U.S. Department of Agriculture.

Stover, John F. 1982. "Iron Roads in the Old Northwest: The Railroad and the Growing Nation." In *Transportation and the Early Nation*. Indianapolis: Indiana Historical Society.

Stuart-Woortly, Lady Emmeline. 1851. *Travels in the United States*. New York: Harper and Brothers.

Suppiger, Joseph, ed. 1956. "Historical Notes." *Journal of the Illinois State Historical Society* 49.

Swan, Herbert S. 1922. "Our City Thoroughfares—Shall They Be Highways or Garages?" *American City* 27.

Swierenga, Robert P. 1989. "The Settlement of the Old Northwest: Ethnic Pluralism in a Featureless Plain." *Journal of the Early Republic* 9.

Switzer, John. 1993. "National Road Brought Stagecoach and Oysters." *Columbus Dispatch*, January 31.

Taff, Charles A. 1950. *Commercial Motor Transportation*. Chicago: Richard D. Irwin.

Taylor, Alan. 1995. "Land and Liberty in the Post-Revolutionary Frontier." In *Devising Liberty in the Early American Republic*, ed. David T. Konig. Palo Alto: Stanford University Press.

Taylor, Frank J. 1948. "Gearjammers' Paradise." *Saturday Evening Post* 220.

Taylor, George R. 1951. *The Transportation Revolution, 1815–1860*. New York: Harper.

———. 1968. *The Transportation Revolution, 1815–1860*. New York: Harper and Row.

Taylor, George R., and Irene Neu. 1956. *The American Railroad Network, 1861–1890*. Cambridge: Harvard University Press.

Thiel, Floyd I. 1965. "Highway Interchange Area Development." In *Indirect Effects of Highway Location and Improvements*. Highway Research Record 96. Washington, D.C.: National Research Council, Division of Engineering and Industrial Research.

Thomas & Means Associates, Inc. 1991. *National Road Heritage Park Feasibility Study*.

Thorndale, William, and William Dollarhide. 1987. *Map Guide to the U.S. Federal Censuses, 1790–1920*. Baltimore: Genealogical Publishing.

Thruelsen, Richard. 1941. "Men at Work: Road Driver." *Saturday Evening Post* 213.

Thwaites, Reuben G. 1904. *Early Western Travels, 1748–1846*. Vol. 5, *Bradbury's Travels in the Interior of America, 1809–1811*. Cleveland: Arthur H. Clark.

Tourism Development Division, Indiana Department of Commerce and Eastern Regional Office of Historic Landmarks Foundation. N.d. Eastern Indiana's corridor of history: The National Road (brochure).

Tunnard, Christopher, and Boris Pushkarev. 1963. *Man-made America: Chaos or Control?* New Haven: Yale University Press.

Turner, Frederick Jackson. 1962. *Rise of the New West, 1819–1829*. New York: Collier Books.

Turner, Roland, and Steven L. Goulden, eds. N.d. *Great Engineers and Pioneers in Tech-*

*nology.* Vol. 1, *From Antiquity through the Industrial Revolution.* New York: St. Martin's Press.

U.S. Bureau of the Census. 1853. *Seventh Census of the United States, 1850.* Washington, D.C.: Robert Armstrong, Public Printer.

———. 1898. *Statistical Atlas of the United States, Based upon the Results of the 11th Census.* Washington, D.C.: Government Printing Office.

———. 1960. *Historical Statistics of the United States, Colonial Times to 1957.* Washington, D.C.: Government Printing Office.

U.S. Department of Transportation, Federal Highway Administration. 1976. *America's Highways, 1776–1976: A History of the Federal Aid Program.* Washington, D.C.: Government Printing Office.

———. 1984. *America on the Move! The Story of the Federal-Aid Highway Program.* Washington, D.C.: Government Printing Office.

U.S. Department of Transportation, U.S. Department of Housing and Urban Development. 1980. *The Land Use and Urban Development Impacts of Beltways.* Washington, D.C.: Government Printing Office.

U.S. House, Committee on Roads and Canals. 1826. *National Road—Cumberland to Washington,* Report No. 100. 19th Cong., 1st sess. Washington, D.C.: Government Printing Office.

U.S. House of Representatives. 1828a. Documents no. 184, 20th Cong., 2d sess. H. Doc. 14.

———. 1828b. Documents no. 185, 20th Cong., 2d sess. H. Doc. 78.

———. 1836. Documents no. 302, 24th Cong., 2d sess. H. Doc. 52.

U.S. Senate. 1828. Documents no. 165, 20th Cong., 1st sess. S. Doc. 99.

———. 1834a. Documents no. 238, 23d Cong., 1st sess. S. Doc. 1.

———. 1834b. Documents no. 266, 23d Cong., 2d sess. S. Doc. 1.

———. 1834c. Documents no. 267, 23d Cong., 2d sess. S. Doc. 9.

———. 1838. Documents no. 338, 25th Cong., 3d sess. S. Doc. 1.

Vale, Thomas, and Geraldine Vale. 1983. *U.S. 40 Today: Thirty Years of Landscape Change.* Madison: University of Wisconsin Press.

Vance, James E., Jr. 1990. *Capturing the Horizon: The Historical Geography of Transportation Since the Sixteenth Century.* Baltimore: Johns Hopkins University Press.

Vieyra, D. I. 1979. *An Architectural History of America's Gas Stations.* New York: Macmillan.

Volney, Constantin F. C. 1804. *A View of the Soil and Climate of the United States of America.* Philadelphia: J. Conrad and Company.

Von Raumer, Frederick. 1845. *America and the American People.* New York: J. and H. G. Langley.

Vonada, Damaine, ed. 1992. *The Ohio Almanac, 1992–93.* Wilmington, Ohio: Orange Frazer Press.

Waitley, Douglas. 1970. *Roads of Destiny: The Trails that Shaped a Nation.* Washington, D.C.: Robert B. Luce, Inc.

Walsh, Margaret. 1978. "The Spatial Evolution of the Mid-Western Pork Industry, 1835–75." *Journal of Historical Geography* 4.

Walters, Raymond, Jr. 1957. *Albert Gallatin: Jeffersonian Financier and Diplomat.* New York: Macmillan.

Warfield, Frances. 1929. "America on Wheels." *Outlook* 152.

Washington County Tourism. 1993. "Southwestern Pennsylvania's National Pike Festival." Washington County Tourism, Washington, Pennsylvania and Laurel Highlands Tourism, Ligonier, Pa. Brochure.

Weinberg, Robert C. 1937. "For Better Places to Park." *American City* 52.

Welby, Adlard. 1821. *A Visit to North America and the English Settlements of Illinois.* London: J. Drury.

Weld, Charles. 1855. *A Vacation Tour in the United States and Canada.* London: Longmans, Green, Longmans, and Roberts.

Weston, Richard A. 1836. *A Visit to the United States and Canada in 1833.* Edinburgh: Richard Weston and Sons.

Wharton, Thomas K. 1956. "The Journal of Thomas K. Wharton." *Ohio Historical Quarterly* 65.

Wheeler, Gervase. 1855. *Homes for the People in Suburb and Country: The Villa, the Mansion, and the Cottage, Adapted to American Climate and Wants.* New York: N.p.

*Wheeling Heritage.* 1991. (September).

Whiffen, Marcus. 1969. *American Architecture Since 1780.* Cambridge, Mass.: MIT Press.

Whitman, Walt. 1921. "Excerpts from a Traveler's Note Book—Nos. 1, 2, and 3." In *The Uncollected Poetry and Prose of Walt Whitman,* Vol. 1, ed. Emory Holloway. New York: Doubleday.

———. 1932. "Excerpts from a Traveler's Note Book—Crossing the Alleghanies." In *The Uncollected Poetry and Prose of Walt Whitman,* Vol. 1, ed. Emory Holloway. New York: Peter Smith.

Wilhelm, Hubert G. H. 1982. *The Origin and Distribution of Settlement Groups: Ohio, 1850.* Athens, Ohio: Cutler Printing.

———. 1991. "Settlement and Selected Landscape Imprints in the Ohio Valley." In *Always a River, the Ohio River and the American Experience.* Bloomington: Indiana University Press.

Williams, Elie, and Thomas Moore. 1808. "Cumberland Road." 10th Cong., 1st sess. *American State Papers,* Vol. 20, Miscellaneous Vol. 1, Serial 037.

Williams, Elie, Thomas Moore, and Joseph Kerr. 1806. "Cumberland Road." 10th Cong., 1st sess. *American State Papers,* Vol. 20, Miscellaneous Vol. 1, Serial 037.

Williams, Michael. 1989. *Americans and Their Forests: A Historical Geography.* New York: Cambridge University Press.

Williams, Raymond. 1974. *Television: Technology and Cultural Form*. Hanover, N.H.: University Press of New England.

Wilson, George R. 1991. *Early Indiana Trails and Surveys*. Indianapolis: Indiana Historical Society.

Wilson, Rufus Rockwell. 1902. "The National Pike and Its Memories." *New England Magazine*.

Wood, Gordon. 1993. "Jefferson in His Time." *Wilson Quarterly* 17.

Wood, L. A. S. 1923. "Modern Street Lighting Marks Progressive Communities." *American City* 28.

Woods, John. 1822. *Two Years' Residence in the Settlement on the English Prairie in the Illinois Country*. London: Longmans, Hurst, Rees, Orme, and Brown.

——. 1904. "Woods's Two Years Residence, 1820–21." In *Early western travels, 1748–1846,* ed. R. G. Thwaites. Cleveland: Clark.

WPA (Work Projects Administration/Works Progress Administration). 1940a. *The National Road in Song and Story*. Columbus: Ohio Historical Society.

——. 1940b. *Pennsylvania: A Guide to the Keystone State*. New York: Oxford University Press.

——. 1945 (1941). *Indiana: A Guide to the Hoosier State*. New York: Oxford University Press.

Wright, John S. 1819. *Letters from the West*. Salem, N.Y.: Dodd and Stevenson.

Yoder, Paton. 1969. *Taverns and Travelers: Inns of the Early Midwest*. Bloomington: Indiana University Press.

Young, Jeremiah Simeon. 1902. *A Political and Constitutional Study of the Cumberland Road*. Chicago: University of Chicago Press.

Zelinsky, Wilbur. 1977. "The Pennsylvania Town: An Overdue Geographical Account." *Geographical Review* 67.

——. 1973; 1992. *The Cultural Geography of the United States*. Englewood Cliffs, N.J.: Prentice-Hall.

Zerubavel, Eviatar. 1992. *Terra Cognita: The Mental Discovery of America*. New Brunswick, N.J.: Rutgers University Press.

Zimmer, Donald T. 1982. "The Ohio River: Pathway to Settlement." In *Transportation and the Early Nation*. Indianapolis: Indiana Historical Society.

Zimmerman, Carrie B. 1931. "Ohio, the Gateway to the West." *Ohio Archeological and Historical Society Publications* 40.

Zukin, Sharon. 1992. "Postmodern Urban Landscapes: Mapping Culture and Power." In *Modernity and Identity,* ed. Scott Lash and Jonathan Friedman. Oxford: Blackwell.

# Contributors

GRADY CLAY has interpreted urbanization's impact in several countries and media since 1949. He was the first urban affairs editor of the *Louisville-Courier-Journal,* and (to 1984) editor of *Landscape Architecture* magazine. His books include *Close-up: How to Read the American City; Alleys: A Hidden Resource; Right Before Your Eyes;* and *Real Places: An Unconventional Guide to America's Generic Landscape* (1994). His weekly public radio essays, "Crossing the American Grain," are in their third year.

CRAIG E. COLTEN has spent more than a decade rambling across the middlewestern portion of the National Road. His dissertation at Syracuse University in 1984 concentrated on pioneer town founding along the National Road in Ohio, while more recent work for the Illinois State Museum examined the environmental impacts of industrialization near US 40's intersection with the Mississippi River. He is now senior project manager for PHR Environmental Consultants in Washington, D.C., and makes all-too-frequent treks along I-70.

GLENN A. HARPER received an M.S. degree in historic preservation and architectural history from Ball State University. He is currently the regional coordinator for the Ohio Historic Preservation Office and an adjunct faculty member in the American Culture Studies program and College of Technology at Bowling Green State University. He also teaches historic and vernacular architecture at Ball State University in the College of Architecture and Planning.

JOHN A. JAKLE's interests spread across historical, cultural, and urban social geography with focus on interpreting the American landscape as built environment. Books include *Images of the Ohio Valley, The Tourist, The Visual Elements of Landscape, Common Houses in America's Small Towns* (coauthored with Robert W. Bastian and Douglas K. Meyer), and *Derelict Landscapes*. His most recent work, coauthored with Keith Sculle, is entitled *The Gas Station in America*. John received a Ph.D. degree from Indiana University. He taught at the University of Maine and at Western Michigan University before joining the faculty at the University of Illinois at Urbana-Champaign where he is currently professor of geography.

PEIRCE LEWIS is professor of geography and member of the faculty in American Studies at the Pennsylvania State University in University Park. For more than three decades, he has been a student of American physical and human landscapes—especially the ordinary urban and rural landscapes created by ordinary Americans. His writings on these subjects have been published widely and have received awards from the Association of American Geographers and the International Geographical Union. He has been a Guggenheim Fellow, and a Fellow in the Woodrow Wilson International Center for Scholars at the Smithsonian Institution in Washington. He has served as president of the Association of American Geographers. A master teacher, he is a recipient of the Lindback Foundation Award, Penn State's highest award for distinguished teaching, among other prestigious teaching honors.

BILLY JOE PEYTON is associate director for research at the Institute for the History of Technology and Industrial Archaeology at West Virginia University. He received his M.A. in history from WVU and is currently completing his Ph.D. dissertation on "Engineering, Construction, and Industrial Archaeology of the National Road: 1811–1838." He is also the principal investigator on a joint IHTIA/National Park Service project to map the original Road alignment and document extant nineteenth-century engineering structures from Cumberland to Wheeling.

KARL RAITZ grew up on the Upper Middle West's black dirt prairie and cultivated an interest in landscapes at the University of Minnesota where he received a Ph.D. in geography. As a member of the geography and anthropology faculties, he has taught at the University of Kentucky for over two decades and finds the Bluegrass Region in this border state an ideal base from which to explore the landscapes of eastern America.

GREGORY S. ROSE is associate professor of geography at the Ohio State University, Marion Campus. He received his Ph.D. from Michigan State University. His research and publications concern the historical and cultural geography of the Old Northwest, with particular attention on the origins and distributions of frontier-era settlers.

RICHARD H. SCHEIN is a cultural geographer who has spent most of his life in close proximity to Interstates 91, 90, 81, 80, 76, and, most recently, near the intersection of I-64 and I-75. When not on the road, his research is focused upon the historical geography of the eastern United States, cities, and the American cultural landscape. He admits that he would much rather travel the National Road and US 40 than the interstate. Rich has a Ph.D. in geography from Syracuse University and teaches at the University of Kentucky.

THOMAS J. SCHLERETH is professor of American studies and professor of history at the University of Notre Dame where he teaches American cultural, intellectual, architectural and landscape history in addition to material culture studies. He serves as a contributing editor for the *Journal of American History* and a general editor for the Midwest History and Culture series published by the Indiana University Press. His most recent book is *Victorian America: Transformations in Everyday Life, 1876–1915*.

HUBERT G. H. WILHELM is a native of Germany. He participated in a rural high school student exchange to the USA in 1950–51, and immigrated to the States in 1954. He received a M.A. degree from the University of Illinois in 1960 and completed a Ph.D. program at Louisiana State University in 1963. He is the author of numerous research papers on the rural American landscape.

Cultural geographer JOSEPH S. WOOD received geography degrees from Middlebury College, the University of Vermont, and the Pennsylvania State University. He has taught at the University of Nebraska at Omaha and South China Normal University, and he is presently associate professor and chair in the department of geography and earth systems science at George Mason University in Fairfax, Virginia. His interest in the cultural landscape ranges across New England villages to northern Virginia suburbs.

# Index

Conemaugh River, 15
Conestoga wagon, 176, 283
Congress, U.S.: abandonment of National Road funding, 18, 114, 169, 173, 191; and "American System" tariffs, 117–18; approval of National Road project, 160, 171, 257–58; construction specifications for National Road, 127, 138, 195, 197; and federal land sales, 64, 107, 112, 279; funding of National Road, 61, 113–14, 127, 133, 143, 144; and historic preservation, 380, 397–98, 401; and Interstate Highway System, 36–37, 219–20; and national highway system, 31, 212–13, 289; and National Old Trails Road, 158; and Office of Road Inquiry, 209, 385; and railroad funding, 187; and repairs to National Road, 148–49, 155, 197; and river channel improvements, 201; road construction funding, 31, 36–37, 112, 212, 220, 289, 385; and route of National Road, 47, 61, 101, 114, 127, 161, 162–63, 164, 166, 168; Senate Committee on Internal Improvements, 126–27; Senate Committee on Roads and Canals, 167–68; and state control of National Road, 114, 198
Connecticut River, 12–13
Connecticut Western Reserve, 46, 71, 268, 275
Conococheague Creek, 18
Conococheague River, 291
Constitution (U.S.), 104, 105; bicentennial of, 89; and road building, 110, 118, 119, 190
Construction: contracts, 135, 137, 138, 142; costs, 60, 132, 133, 142, 144, 145, 147; industry, 322; log, 280, 281

Consumerism, 357–58
Corn Belt, 66, 68, 72, 205, 277, 356, 373
Corn production, 66, 243, 277
Corporations, 109–10
Cottage courts, 300
Cotton Belt, 374
Counties, formation of, 174, 175–76
*Country Life,* 382
Courthouses, 271, 279–80
Cowley, Malcolm, 371
Croft, Thomas, 190
Cron, F. W., 193
Cumberland, Md., 49, 114, 123, 230; eastern connection to, 113; interstate highways and, 327; and National Road route, 101, 111, 112, 130; US 40 traffic, 370
Cumberland County, Ill., 185
Cumberland Gap, 99–100
Cumberland Plateau, 99
Cumberland River, 99
Cumberland Road, 94, 112, 113
*Cumberland Road* (Dallas), 45
Cumberland Road Festival, 406
Cuming, Fortescue, 198, 240, 244
Cunningham, Ann Pamela, 378
Currier and Ives, 9
Cuyahoga River, 110

Dallas, A. J., 45, 47
Danville, Ind., 279–80
Daughters of the American Revolution (DAR), 386–87, 389
Davis, Charles, 385–86
Dayton, Ohio, 165–66, 207, 373
Delafield, Richard, 151, 152, 154
Delaware Bay, 50
Delaware River, 13, 48

Denver, Colo., 21
Department of Agriculture, 211, 212, 288
DeVoto, Bernard, 302
Dicey, Edward, 243, 246
Diesel engines, 310
Disney, Walt, 262
Disneyland, 407
Dixie Highway, 157
Dixon, James, 230
Donnelsville, Ohio, 353–54
Douglas, Albert, 157, 236, 238–39
Douglas, Stephen A., 276
Drake, Daniel, 228
Drive-ins: restaurants, 305–6; theaters, 304
Dunbar, Seymour, 177
Dunlap's Creek Bridge, 154
Duryea, Charles, 382

Eads Bridge (St. Louis), 206
Eagle Hotel (Zanesville), 201
East Cambridge, Ill., 185–86
"Eastern Indiana's Corridor of History," 406
East Germantown, Ind., 185
East St. Louis, Ill., 221, 222
Eaton, Ohio, 165–66
Edison, Thomas A., 294
Effingham, Ill., 71, 185
Egalitarianism, 229
Eisenhower, Dwight D., 320, 321–22
Ellet, Charles, 156
Engell, H. E. Candice Cornell, 386–87
Englewood, Ohio, 297
Ensminger, Robert, 274
Environmental laws, 221–22
Erie Canal, 14, 15, 78, 189, 200, 265
Etna, Ohio, 70
Europe, 96, 104; American trade with, 105; immigration from, 283; railroads in, 20; road building in, 141, 351
Evans, Evan, 135

126–27; Department of Transportation, 402; historic preservation in, 402, 406; housing architecture in, 272; operation of National Road, 198, 203, 384; road building in, 213; water transportation in, 12; westward migration from, 72, 180

Maryland Assembly, 204

Maryland Historical Trust, 402

Maryland Wildlife Federation, 331

Mason-Dixon Line, 72, 113, 119, 181

Massachusetts Route 128, 39

Maysville Turnpike, 118

Meeson, Isaac, 130

Meigs, R. J., Jr., 147

McIlville McHaffie farmhouse, 404

Melody Drive-In Theater (Springfield, Ohio), 304

Memphis, Tenn., 21

Merchants National Bank (Indianapolis), 294

Mertz, Charles, 298

"Metal" finishing, 136–37

Miami & Erie Canal, 16, 189

Miami Valley, 66, 276, 277

Middle Atlantic region, cultural influence in Middle West, 62–63, 269, 271, 274

Middlebourne, Ohio, 389

Middle Town Valley, 54

Middle West (also called "West"): agrarian republicanism and, 104–5, 106, 107, 109; agriculture in, 205, 269, 276; architecture of, 271, 274, 280, 282; canals and, 16, 19, 202; cultural influences on, 72, 181–82, 266–67, 269, 275; early roads to, 99–101, 111–12; glacial formation, 57–58; land sales in, 107, 108, 112, 116–17, 120, 278–79; National Road and, 44, 63,

72, 102–3, 109, 113, 120, 121, 169–71, 259–60, 265, 267, 283–84; Ohio River and, 264–65; railroads and, 23, 71, 205, 265; rivers, 13, 19, 45–46; settlement of, 16, 63, 71–72, 96–98, 107–8, 170–72, 265, 283; and tariffs, 119–20; Township and Range survey, 64–65, 326; trade with, 101–2, 116, 205; travelers' impressions of, 228; urbanization, 202; War of 1812 and, 117

Midland culture hearth, 62–63, 70

Midland Trail, 157

Migration, 71–72, 103, 266, 267, 416; influence of National Road and, 178, 179–81, 192; and Middle Atlantic cultural influence, 62–63, 269, 271, 274; North-South cultural boundary, 181–83; public land sales and, 242; from Southern states, 275–76. *See also* Settlement

Miles City, Mont., 22

Military Academy (US), 150–51

Military defense, 38–39, 115, 321–22

Military-industrial complex, 321

Miller, Aaron, 197

Mining industry, 53

*Mirror for Americans* (Brown), 256

Mississippi, 106, 112

Mississippi River, 13, 61, 108, 167

Mississippi Valley, 109

Missouri: legislature, 167; Old Trails Commission, 386; statehood, 112, 119

Missouri Compromise, 119

Missouri Old Trails Road Association, 386

Missouri River, 13, 19

Mr. G Drive-In (Baltimore), 305

*Mohawk-Hobbs Grade and Surface Guide,* 395

Mohawk River, 14

Mohawk Rubber Company, 395

Mohawk Trail, 180

Mohawk Valley, 99

Mollisols, 61

Monongahela River, 52, 99, 130

Monroe, James, 118, 148–49, 257

Montana, 22

Moore, Thomas, 52–53, 127, 131–32, 133

Moran, Edward, 6

Morse, Jedidiah, 96, 101–2, 108, 110–11, 114, 121

Motels, 218, 221, 301–3, 355–56, 365

"Motel towns," 302

Motor courts, 300–301

Motorcycles, 9–10

Motorists, 29, 33

Mount Prospect, Md., 251

Mount Vernon, 378

Mount Washington Tavern (Fort Necessity), 70, 390, 405

Muller, Edward, 207

Mumford, Lewis, 359

Muskingum River, 245, 266

Muskingum Valley, 268

Narrows, The, 49, 123

Nashville, Tenn., 21

*Natchez* (steamboat), 7

National Coalition for Heritage Areas, 397

National Freeway, 331

National Good Roads Convention, 386

National Heritage Areas, 396–97

National Highway Association, 385, 393

National highway system: creation of, 30–32, 44, 194,

Ohio River, 13, 275; canal connections to, 15, 16, 202; completion of National Road to, 61, 143, 187, 191–92, 197, 265; ferries across, 246; railroad bridges across, 206; road connections to, 184; and route of National Road, 53–54, 55, 130, 163; steamboat navigation, 61, 200–201, 206; trade on, 46–47, 102, 178, 195, 200–202; tributaries, 45–46; and westward migration, 62–63, 180, 183, 264; Wheeling suspension bridge, 156, 246

Ohio Route 13, 372

Ohio Route 256, 341–43

Ohio Territory, 98

Ohio University, 273

Ohio Valley, 61–62, 96, 195, 207, 264–65

Oil industry, 29, 296

Old Brick Tavern (Clarysville, Md.), 391

Old Glade Road, 62

Old Iron Bridge (Brownsville, Pa.), 154

*Old National Road* (Hulbert), 381, 392

*Old Pike: A History of the National Road* (Searight), 159, 392

Old Santa Fe Trail, 386

Old Washington, Ohio, 70, 312, 399

Oliver, William, 232, 234–35, 239

One-way streets, 314, 371–72

Ordinance of 1785. *See* Land Ordinance

Ordinance of 1787. *See* Northwest Ordinance

Orme, Robert, 125

Orndorff, Henry, 256

Otter, Thomas Proudly, 80

Outdoor Advertising Association, 306

*Outing,* 382

Oyster Line, 256

Page, L. W., 288

Panama Pacific International Exposition (1915), 364

Panic of 1819, 171

Paradise Inn Motel (Effingham, Ill.), 364

Paris, Treaty of (1783), 45

Parker, Benjamin, 177, 179

Parking, 293; bypass highways and, 370; garages, 294; meters, 295

Pasadena Freeway, 34

Patapsco Sound, 50

Patrick, W. H. N., 380

Peacock Road, 410

Penn, William, 62, 66, 269

Penn Central Railroad, 38

Pennsylvania: architecture of, 269–70, 271, 272, 273–74; canal construction, 14–15; construction of National Road in, 136; cultural influence in Middle West, 260, 261–62, 268, 269–70, 271, 273–74, 281; Department of Transportation, 400; early roads across, 99 100, 102, 126; historic preservation in, 377, 391, 399, 400–402, 406, 412; impact of National Road in, 268; legislature, 131, 380; and *National Road: Historic Resource Survey,* 409; National Road Heritage Park, 399, 409, 411; operation of National Road, 198, 384; road building in, 213; route of National Road through, 113, 162–63, 171, 258; taverns and inns, 420; toll collections, 146, 198; towns in, 261–62, 269–70; US 40 in, 290, 314, 356; westward migration from, 72, 180, 182, 267, 268, 283

Pennsylvania Canal, 16–17

Pennsylvania-German barn, 66–67, 273–74, 281

Pennsylvania Historical and Museum Commission, 391

Pennsylvania House Inn (Springfield, Ohio), 388, 389, 405

Pennsylvania Main Line Canal, 15

Pennsylvania Railroad, 20, 38, 205, 206, 207, 212, 221

Pennsylvania Road. *See* Forbes Road

Pennsylvania Route 31, 62

Pennsylvania Turnpike, 34, 219

Pennsylvania wagons, 238

Pershing, John J., 321

Peter Colley Tavern (Briar Hill, Pa.), 420–21

Petrov, Eugene, 239

Philadelphia, Pa., 125, 315; railroads, 20; street grid plan, 70, 269; water transportation and, 12, 16–17, 49, 110–11; western trade and, 116, 121, 197

Pickaway County, Ohio, 277

Pickaway Plains, 277–78

Pickerington, Ohio, 340, 341–43

Piedmont region, 50, 54, 66, 98

Pikes Peak Ocean-to-Ocean Highway, 157

Pinckney's Treaty (1795), 106, 108

Pittsburgh, Pa., 16–17, 21, 197, 264; Forbes Road to, 100, 111–12; route of National Road and, 53, 162

*Pittsburgh History,* 400

Pittsburgh Pike, 200

Plainfield, Ind., 387

Pleistocene era, 49, 57

"Podium effect," 354

Pony Express, 7

Population density, 172, 174, 175, 297

Population growth, 126, 171

Postl, Karl (Charles Sealsfield), 227
Post Office Appropriation Bill (1912), 157
Post offices, 76
Potomac River, 13; canal connections to, 15, 203; and route of National Road, 48, 51–52, 98, 110, 111, 123–24
Prairie House (Terre Haute), 240, 241
Prairie land, 65, 232
Prairie-style architecture, 71
Prentice, Archibald, 231
*Presence of the Past* (Hosmer), 376
Project Adequate Roads, 322–23
Property rights, 412
Property values. *See* Land values
Prosser, June, 404
Prosser, Walt, 404
Provincetown, Mass., 83
Pushkarev, Boris, 252
Putnam County, Ind., 58

Quakers, 63

Race riots, 276
Railroads: automobiles' displacement of, 25–26, 32, 40–41, 218–19, 220–21; canal and river transport displaced by, 18–19, 20, 23–24, 204–6; and cities, 20–21, 24, 40, 41; and cultural interchange, 269, 274–75; federal financing of, 22–23, 187; gauge integration, 206; highway grade crossings, 216–17; Interstate Highway System and, 38, 223, 334; and National Road, 156, 169–70, 187, 188, 194, 207–9, 241, 263–64, 269, 286; and nineteenth-century road system, 24, 114–15, 156, 188, 210, 265, 286; roadbed construc-

tion, 213; and towns, 21–22, 41, 71, 207–8; trucking industry and, 38, 218, 220, 223, 308, 311–12, 333–34; and westward expansion, 20–23, 170, 203–4; World War II and, 35
*Real Places* (Clay), 351
Red Brick Tavern (Lafayette, Ohio), 70, 307
Reeb, Elizabeth, 403
Reeside, James, 377
*Remarks on the Present System of Road-Making* (McAdam), 140–41
Renick, Felix, 278
Renick, George, 278
Repairs and maintenance, 149–50, 152–54, 155, 197, 198, 233
*Report on the Subject of Public Roads and Canals* (Gallatin), 115, 126
Republicanism, 103–4, 107, 109
Restaurants, 305–6
Revolutionary War, 107
"Revolution of 1800," 106
Richmond, Ind., 114, 246, 297–98, 391; completion of National Road to, 173, 179, 186; I-70 and, 336–38; railroads and, 207, 208
Richmond, Va., 21
Rideing, William Henry, 376
Rider, Arthur, 128–29, 132
Ridge and Valley, 98–99, 100, 312; geological formation, 51, 52, 60–61; National Road construction over, 55, 56; settlement of, 69
Riley, James Whitcomb, 70
Rising Hall, 404
Rivera, Diego, 82
Rivera, Geraldo, 334
Rivers, 12–13, 19, 45, 48, 49–50, 200–201, 205–6
Rivers and Trails Conservation Assistance Program, 397
*Road, The* (Belloc), 3

Roads: access to, 260, 351–52, 357, 360, 361; automobiles and, 27–30, 33, 157; canals and, 13, 18; connections to National Road, 184–85; Constitution and, 110, 118, 119, 190; construction technologies, 28, 139–41, 211–12, 213–15, 288–89, 353; and consumerism, 357–60; deficiencies of early twentieth century, 33, 35, 41, 211, 286, 289; "dominating highways," 252–53; eighteenth-century, 18, 101, 102, 124–26, 188; farmers and, 24, 28, 29, 41, 212, 286–87; federal land sales and, 112, 116–17, 160, 260; Gallatin's planned network of, 47, 93–94, 102, 112, 115, 117, 126; lobbying interests and, 28–30, 322–23, 385; "Main Street," 261–62, 269–71, 286, 292; military rationale for, 107, 115, 212, 321–22; national numbering systems, 31, 290; public financing of, 30–31, 34–35, 36–37, 115, 118, 212–13, 260, 288, 289, 322, 323–24, 385; railroads' ascendancy and deterioration of, 24, 156, 209–11, 265, 286; Township and Range survey and, 64–65; and westward expansion, 110, 117, 124, 159–60
*Robert E. Lee* (steamboat), 7
Rochester, N.Y., 16
Rockefeller, John D., 380
Roosevelt, Franklin D., 4, 34
Rose, Gregory, 276
Rose, Mark, 321
Ross County, Ohio, 278, 281
Route 40 Advocates, 331
Route numbering system, 31, 290
Rowhouses, 270, 272

Rural Free Delivery, 76
Rushville, Ind., 332

St. Clair, Arthur, 113
St. Clairsville, Ohio, 163, 171, 186, 199, 271
St. Louis, Mo., 16, 17, 21, 71, 167, 206, 279
Salisbury, Ind., 186
San Francisco, Calif., 21
Sangamon River, 61
Santa Fe Trail, 386
Santee River, 13
Savage Mountain, 49
Savannah, Ga., 21
Savannah River, 13
S-bridges, 136, 389, 403, 411
Schlereth, Tom, 413
Schools, 85
Scioto River, 217, 218, 247
Scioto Valley, 277, 278, 281
Searight, Thomas B., 134, 146, 177–78, 209
*The Old Pike: A History of the National Road,* 159, 392; toll house of, 69, 391
Sectionalism, 119–20, 190
Seeleyville, Ind., 355–56
Segal, George, 87
Service industries, 320
Settlement: canals and, 16–17; cultural influences in, 63, 260–62, 265, 266–67, 269, 279, 281, 283; eastern seaboard, 11–12, 124; National Road and, 170–72, 176, 178, 179, 183, 185, 279, 283; Township and Range survey and, 64–65; trans-Appalachian, 97–98, 99–100, 103, 107–8. *See also* Migration
Seven Ranges, 265–66
Sheeler, Charles, 81
Shelbyville, Tenn., 279
Shenandoah River, 98
Shenandoah Valley, 47–48
Shepherd, Moses, 137
Shopping centers, 361

Shriver, David L., Jr., 134–35, 138, 143
Sideling Hill, 344–45
Signs, highway, 289–90
Silver Swan Motel (Springfield, Ohio), 303
Skyscrapers, 294
Slavery, 5, 276
Smith, Adam, 110
Smith, J. Russell, 51
Smith House (Zanesville), 262
Society for the Preservation of New England Antiquities (SPNEA), 380
Society for Promoting the Improvement of Roads and Inland Navigation, 125
Socony-Vacuum gas stations, 309–10
Soils, 60–61
Somerfield, Pa., 384, 386, 390
Sons of the American Revolution, 380
South: canal system and, 16, 17; cultural influence, National Road boundary of, 72, 181–82, 183, 275–76; influence on agriculture, 276–78, 281; influence on architecture, 280, 281; influence on town layouts, 271, 279–80; opposition to National Road funding, 17–18, 189–90, 258; and sectional politics, 119–20, 190
Southern Pacific Railroad Company, 23
South Mountain, 50, 54
South Pennsylvania Railroad, 34
South Vienna, Ohio, 313
Southwestern Pennsylvania Heritage Preservation Commission, 401
Soviet Union, 35
Speed limits, 330
Spiceland, Ind., 332–33
Springfield, Ill., 165, 168, 170, 314, 372

Springfield, Ohio, 114, 173, 218, 223, 246, 297–98
Spruce Forest Artisan Village, 407–8
Stagecoaches, 177, 237–38, 239–40, 283
State Heritage Parks, 396–97
States: admittance to statehood, 97–98, 112; federal highway subsidies, 31, 37, 118, 213, 290; highway departments, 31, 213; and historic preservation, 400–404, 412; and Interstate Highway System, 37, 39; operation of National Road, 114, 149–50, 155, 187, 191, 198, 385–86; Revolutionary War debts, 107; and route of National Road, 119, 184, 189–90
States' rights, 120
Statue of Liberty, 5–6
Steamboats, 61, 200–201, 206
Steele, Eliza, 245
Steinbeck, John, 5
Steubenville, Ohio, 163, 265–66
Stewart, George R., 249, 252, 253–54
*U.S. 40: Cross-Section of the United States of America,* 236, 251, 413
Stilesville, Ind., 185
Stilgoe, John, 208
Stillwater River, 59
Stream valleys, 59
Streetcars, 248
Street grids, 22, 70, 248, 269
Streetlights, 362–63, 364
Stuart-Woortly, Lady, 238
Suburbanization, 41, 315, 331
*Superhighway—Superhoax* (Leavitt), 330
Supreme Court, 306
Surveying, 64, 128–29, 270–71
Susquehanna River, 13, 15, 48, 110–11
Sweitzer barn, 66–67, 274
Syracuse, N.Y., 14, 16

US 80, 31
US 90, 31

Vale, Geraldine, 251
Vale, Thomas, 251
Van Buren, Martin, 387
Vandalia, Ill.: completion of National Road to, 114, 147, 173; Cumberland Road Festival, 406; highway bypasses, 221; as National Road terminus, 18, 168, 188; and route of National Road, 164–65, 167, 185–86; as state capital, 164, 167, 186
Villages, 70, 315, 371; historic, 407
Virginia, 100, 159; population of, 12, 275; water transportation and, 12; westward migration from, 180, 182, 273
Virginia Military District, 275, 277, 280, 366
Volney, Constantin, 46
Von Raumer, Frederick, 231

Wabash & Erie Canal, 16, 189
Wabash River, 59, 175
Wagons: Conestoga, 176, 283; Pennsylvania, 238
War Department, 151, 380
War of 1812, 117, 133, 171
Warrior's Path, 180
Washington, D.C., 111, 315
Washington, George: Fort Necessity campaign, 111, 113, 379; memorials to, 377, 378, 379, 380; as president, 105, 109, 111; and western road improvements, 159–60, 171, 192
Washington, Pa., 114, 162–63, 286, 300, 311, 395
Washington Beltway, 39
Washington & Potomac Canal, 189
Washington's Road, 124

Water transportation, 12–13, 19–20, 200–201, 202–3, 223
Wayne County, Ind., 190
Wayne County, Mich., Highway Department, 28
*Wealth of Nations* (Smith), 110
Weld, Charles, 235–36
West. *See* Middle West
West Alexander, Pa., 384, 390
West Pike, 382, 384
West Virginia, 112, 297, 384, 402, 406; State Historic Preservation Office, 402
West Virginia University, 402
Wever, Caspar W., 139, 143
Wheat Belt, 267–68
Wheat production, 267–68, 276
Wheeling, W.V., 197, 352, 395; completion of National Road to, 114, 192; interstate highways and, 327; Ohio River suspension bridge, 156, 246; and route of National Road, 55, 163–64; travelers' impressions of, 245–46
Wheeling Creek, 55, 136
Wheeling National Heritage Area, 402
Wheeling River, 53–54, 55
*Wheeling Times and Advertiser,* 185
Whig Party, 113
Whiskey Rebellion, 108
Whitehill, Walter Muir, 376
White Mountains, 14
White River, 175
White Swan Hotel (Uniontown, Pa.), 391
Whitewater River valley, 175
Whitman, Walt, 73, 237, 238, 239–40
Wilderness Road, 99–101, 124, 180, 264, 275
Wilkins, Mike, 89
William Henry Hotel (Washington, Pa.), 300

Williams, Elie, 52–53, 127–28, 131–32
Williamsburg, Va., 21, 380
Wills Creek, 52, 111
Wills Mountain, 49, 123
Wilson, Rufus Rockwell, 383
Wolke, Jay, 88
Wood, Grant, 85, 86
Wood, Thomas Waterman, 76
Woodbridge, Ind., 241
Woods, John, 197, 233
Works Progress Administration (WPA), 34, 391, 395
World War I, 239
World War II, 35, 218, 292
Worthington, Thomas, 112
Wright, Frank Lloyd, 71
Wright, John, 233

Yancey, William L., 188
Yellowstone Trail, 157
Youghiogheny House (Somerfield, Pa.), 390
Youghiogheny River, 52, 135, 384

Zane, Ebenezer, 54, 113, 257, 405
Zane's Trace, 163, 266, 405; and route of National Road, 55, 113, 133, 165, 184, 257, 365; town backstreets on, 261; and westward migration, 175, 267
Zanesville, Ohio, 114, 257, 271, 329; construction of National Road to, 55–56, 173, 186; and historic preservation, 405, 407; state land office, 266; traffic volume at, 178, 179; travelers' impressions of, 245; water transportation and, 202; West Pike improvement, 384
Zelinsky, Wilbur, 270
Zoning restrictions, 41

## ILLUSTRATION CREDITS

PAGE

4  Courtesy Philadelphia Museum of Art: Given by Ellen Harrison McMichael in memory of C. Emory McMichael.

5  © 1994 T. H. Benton and Rita P. Benton Testamentary Trusts/VAGA, New York, NY.

6  With permission of the Museum of the City of New York.

7  Peirce Lewis.

8  Currier and Ives.

10  By permission of the Ford Motor Company.

10  Harley-Davidson.

11  International Harvester.

14  Copyright by Erwin Raisz 1957, reprinted with permission by GEOPLUS, Danvers, MA.

17  Copyright by Erwin Raisz 1957, reprinted with permission by GEOPLUS, Danvers, MA.

18  Drawing by Susan Trammell (1995).

23  From a postcard of the early 1930s.

26  Map by Peirce Lewis from Mitchell and Groves, 1987.

32  From John Sears (1977).

42  Peirce Lewis.

50–  After Erwin Raisz. In George R. Stewart. 1953.

57  *U.S. 40: Cross-Section of the United States of America.* Boston: Houghton Mifflin Company, pp. 70–71, 66–67, 84–85, 112–13. Reproduced by permission.

63  After Conzen 1990, Glassie 1968, and others.

67  After Robert F. Ensminger, *The Pennsylvania Barn* (Baltimore: Johns Hopkins University Press, 1992), 103. By permission.

95  Melish 1826.

99  Copyright by Erwin Raisz 1957, reprinted with permission by GEOPLUS, Danvers, MA.

100  After Ray Allen Billington, *Westward Expansion: A History of the American Frontier,* 3rd ed., New York: Macmillan Co., 1967, p. 248, and others.

101  Photograph courtesy of the National Archives, U.S. Bureau of Public Roads.

116  From John Austin Stevens, *Albert Gallatin* (New York: Houghton Mifflin, 1898).

120  Reproduced by permission from the collections of the Library of Congress.

136  Drawing by Susan Trammell (1995).

137  Photograph courtesy of Billy Joe Peyton, IHTIA.

138  Public Roads Administration.

143  After a drawing by John T. Hriblan, IHTIA.

148  Photograph courtesy of the Ohio Historical Society, Columbus, Ohio.

150  *Harper's New Monthly Magazine* (November 1879).

151  Bureau of Public Roads.

153  After a drawing by John T. Hriblan, IHTIA.

155  Bureau of Public Roads.

156  From an engraving completed about 1850, artist unknown. Reprinted with permission of Oglebay Institute's Mansion Museum.

158  Bureau of Public Roads.

174  U.S. Bureau of the Census. 1898; and various sources for dates of National Road "completion."

174  Thorndale and Dollarhide 1987; and various sources for dates of National Road "completion."

181  Research by the author using microfilms of the manuscript 1850 census, and Wilhelm 1982.

183  Research by the author using microfilms of the manuscript 1850 census and Wilhelm 1982.

199  Howe 1902, 1:309.

201  Howe 1902, 2:332.

207  Howe 1902, 1:321.

210  Courtesy Ohio Historical Society, Henry Howe Collection, P-15, Box 1, Folder 12, Negative 8930, Columbus, Ohio.

216  Courtesy Ohio Historical Society, National Road Collection, P-333, Box 1, Folder 1, Negative 1453, Columbus, Ohio.

217  Courtesy Ohio Historical Society, City of Columbus, Department of Public Works Collection, Negative 8935, Columbus, Ohio.

222  Courtesy Illinois State Historical Library, East St. Louis Journal Pictures, Highway Folder, Springfield, Illinois.

223  Photo courtesy of Rich Remsberg.

259  From Rideing 1879.

263  Reprinted with the permission of the Indiana State Library and Macmillan Publishing Company from *The National Road* by Philip D. Jordan. Copyright 1948 by The Bobbs-Merrill Company, renewed 1976 by Philip D. Jordan.

270  Drawing by Susan Trammell (1995) from a photograph from the Henry Douglas collection.

271  Drawing by Susan Trammell (1995).

273  Charles Walters (1994).

287  With permission of the Ohio Historical Society.

288  With permission of the Ohio Historical Society.

290  Charles Walters (1994).

291  Photograph courtesy of the Library of Congress.

293 Reproduced courtesy of Oldsmobile Division, General Motors Corporation, Lansing, Mich.
299 Charles Walters (1994).
302 Charles Walters (1994).
304 Karl Raitz (1994).
305 Charles Walters (1994).
307 Michael Putnam (1995).
310 Charles Walters (1994).
311 Charles Walters (1994).
312 Michael Putnam (1995).
313 Karl Raitz (1994).
314 Gregory Conniff (1994).
315 Gregory Conniff (1994).
318 Karl Raitz (1994).
325 Karl Raitz (1994).
329 Charles Walters (1994).
345 Photograph from a postcard in the Richard Schein collection.
355 Karl Raitz (1994).
356 Karl Raitz (1994).
364 Charles Walters (1994).
368 After drawings by Karl Raitz.
369 After drawings by Karl Raitz.
377 Photo of engraving in the *Harper's New Monthly Magazine* (November 1879) issue.
379 Michael Putnam (1995).
383 Photographs courtesy of the Ohio Historical Society, Columbus, Ohio.
387 Gregory Conniff (1994).
388 Photographs by Charles A. Thomas courtesy of the DAR, Lagonda Chapter, Springfield, Ohio.
389 From a postcard in the Glenn Harper collection.
390 Photograph courtesy of the Historical Society of Western Pennsylvania, Pittsburgh.
394 From Bruce 1916.
398 Map courtesy of Mary Means & Associates (1991).
407 Drawing by Susan Trammell (1995).